THE LIFETIME GUIDE
TO THE

Jewish Holidays

ABUNDANT WAYS TO BRING THE JOY,
MEANING AND RELEVANCE OF
CELEBRATION INTO YOUR HOME
AND HEART YEAR AFTER YEAR

LESLI KOPPELMAN ROSS

JEWISH
LEGACY
PRESS

MIAMI

Published by Jewish Legacy Press, an imprint of ICIC, Inc., 3000 Island Blvd, Suite 2606, Aventura, FL 33160, info@jewishlegacypress.com

Printed in the United States of America
Cover concept by Jordon I. Ross
Cover art by Tina Ohayon
Inside Book Formatting by Lawna Patterson Oldfield and Dawn Von Strolley Grove

Publisher's—Cataloging In Publication
(Provided by Quality Books Inc.)
Ross, Lesli Koppelman
    The lifetime guide to the Jewish holidays: abundant ways to bring the joy, meaning and relevance of celebration into your home and heart year after year / Lesli Koppelman Ross.
        p. cm.
    Includes bibliographical references and index.
    Rev. ed of: Celebrate! / written and illustrated by Lesli Koppelman Ross. Northvale, N.J. : J. Aronson, c1994.
    ISBN 0-9726449-0-3 (hardcover)
    ISBN 0-9726449-1-1 (softcover)
    1. Fasts and feasts—Judaism. 2. Judaism—Customs and practices. I. Ross, Lesli Koppelman. Celebrate! II. Title

BM690.R595 2003   296.4'3
                                                                                QB102-200921

LCCN 2002096958

Ten percent of proceeds from this book donated to charities that support Jewish education

CONTENTS

For my grandparents and parents,
who gave me the past,

For Beth, Ariel, Ezra, Matthew,
Ora, Ilana, Joey, Dara and Jonathan,
who are the future, and

For Jordon, who makes the present special.
May we have much to celebrate *ad maya v'esrim*.

$\mathcal{T}hanks$

$\mathcal{N}$ ow comes the impossible task of expressing appreciation to all the people who contributed, directly and indirectly, to this book. They have been my teachers, formal and informal, known to me and not. I thank all those who have inspired—with even a brief word— new ways of thinking that led to better understanding and unexpected insights.

Like good Jewish education and meaningful holiday celebration, I must start with family and home. I am fortunate that my paternal grandparents, Max and Madelyn Koppelman—of blessed memory, who lived the humility and *khesed* integral to the *yom tov* mindset—and my maternal grandparents, Jack and Irene Lowinger, of blessed memory—by whose gracious hospitality so many holiday celebrations in our family took place—safeguarded Jewish tradition so that I was able to experience it as a child. I daily feel their influence and embrace, and am immensely grateful.

I wish to lovingly thank my parents, Lee and Connie Koppelman, for whom being Jewish always has been a matter of pride, and who also gave me a strong connection with Israel that resulted in my lifelong love affair with that country. In their home I first learned to chant the *"Mah Nishtahna"*; arranged and lit candles in a music box menorah that played *"Maoz Tzur"*; and was costumed, in my mother's satin robe and mother-of-pearl beads, as Queen Esther.

I will always associate the beginning of my adult Jewish education with Rabbi Dr. Jay Goldburg, whose explanations at a Sukkot holiday talk made me realize that my values and ideals meshed beautifully with the Judaism from which I had drifted after college. Rabbi Dov Heller patiently guided me during the first years of my learning. Thanks also have to be extended to Rabbi Elazar Grunberger, and Mrs. Shelley List, with whom I subsequently learned, and who, along with numerous other friends in St. Louis' University City, opened their homes to me for Shabbat and *yom tov* celebrations that are among my sweetest memories.

At the top of that list are two very special people. Both contributed immeasurably to this book. HaRav Sholom Rivkin, Av Bet Din and Chief Rabbi of St. Louis, clarified matters of halakhah, identified sources, and, helped me refine my thinking for parts of the text. Rebbetzin Paula Rivkin, in reviewing the entire manuscript, offered invaluable comments and suggestions. (It should go without saying that the fault for any errors that remain in the text lies entirely with me.) Above and beyond what they have added to this work, I am grateful for the Rivkins' continual encouragement, love and support. Through their scholarship, *ahavat Yisrael,* humanitarian concerns, open-mindedness and even-handedness, they exemplify what Judaism and being Jewish are truly about. They will always be an inspiration.

I also want to thank the faculty of the Wexner Heritage Foundation with whom I was privileged to study, especially Rabbi Nathan Laufer, Rabbi David Silber, Dr. Bernard Steinberg and Rabbi Joseph Telushkin, who opened worlds of Scripture, commentary, history and Jewish value in stimulating and insightful ways. Among the many other superb educators I've had the opportunity to hear and learn with over the years and who have influenced my thinking are: Rabbi Howard Bald, Rabbi Motti Berger, Rabbi Natan T. Lopes Cardozo, Mrs. Tzipporah Heller, Rabbi Jonathan Horowitz, Avraham Infeld and Rabbi Shlomo Riskin.

Appreciation is also extended to the staff of the library at Chicago's Spertus College of Judaica, and in particular to Dan Sharon, reference librarian *extraordinaire.* His aid and expertise made my job considerably easier.

In addition, thanks go to the agents at Multimedia Product Development, Inc., Jane Jordan Browne, Danielle Egan-Miller and Scott Mendel, who worked so persistently on my behalf, and the many friends, relatives and acquaintances who were always excited and encouraging about this book, especially my sister Laurel Heard, for training her educator's eyes on the manuscript and offering valuable reactions and suggestions; Tom Silverstein, a family member and friend, who helped me through all sorts of computer problems; my brother Keith Koppelman, for his evaluations and website assistance; and my sister Claudia Koppelman, for her assistance and support.

And I am especially grateful to and for my wonderful husband Jordon, who made it possible for this book to be produced, for his unflagging support and unfailing good humor, even through missed dinners, solitary evenings, late late nights and other interruptions of marital bliss.

Special Ways FOR SPECIAL DAYS

"Nothing, in the memories of my childhood years, shines so clearly and so lovingly as this evening of the Passover. The luminous shadows of it have been cast forever across my life, and the magic does not decrease with the years. For on that evening the house was a palace, my father was a king and all of us were members of a royal family, queen and princes and princesses. Even the poorest guest that sat at table with us was an ambassador. My joy was too full to be contained; it spilled over, and poured itself through the room and over the people in it. I wanted the older people to tell me wonderful stories, and I wanted to tell others in return. I was full of the glorious exodus from the land of Egypt, and I lived, in my own way, through all the acts of that greatest of world-dramas."*

*P*erhaps you can conjure the sensations of similar scenes—the intimate glow of Khanukah candles and the aroma, rising above the crackle of oil, of latkes browning to crispness; or the pine-scented embrace of pleasantly cool autumn air, the *sukkah*, providing the perfect setting for a meal of pound cake, grape juice and a McIntosh apple so fresh it sends sweet nectar running down your chin; or the melody of laughter, bells and popping balloons dancing like colored streamers around you, costumed for Purim from Mom's closet of old clothes and a toy chest of props.

If you are fortunate enough to have such recollections, they probably provide the strongest and most positive foundations of your Jewish identity. But not having experienced the holidays with this mixture of awe and excitement, sensory stimulation and family warmth does not mean you cannot create these kinds of memories in your own home. One thing Judaism teaches is that it is *never* too late to learn and to do.

The holidays have always occupied a special place within Jewish consciousness. Initially, they helped forge the nation, establish its relationship with God and define its purpose. During the Commonwealths (1000–600 BCE and 152–60 BCE), they promoted unity and served as a reminder of communal goals.

---

*Shmarya Levin, *Childhood in Exile*, trans. by Maurice Samuel (New York: Harcourt, Brace & World, 1929), pp. 170–171.

Throughout our long exile, they provided relief from a dark existence and reinforced belief in a better future. No matter how oppressed, Jews celebrated freedom, no matter how sad, they rejoiced with abandon, no matter how dreary their present, they anticipated a glorious tomorrow.

Sadly, considering the longevity, wealth and beauty of our tradition, we live at a time when many Jewish children are growing up with little or no exposure to it at all. This is not the first time in our history that large numbers of Jews have abandoned Jewish practice, often because they no longer understood it or the depth behind it.

In previous periods, we had King Josiah, who rediscovered a discarded scroll of the Law during a renovation of the Temple, and Ezra and Nehemiah, who reintroduced the people to what they had forgotten before and during the Babylonian exile. Medieval rabbis devised engaging customs to strengthen the resolve of a persecuted people, and mystics injected spirituality into every aspect of Jewish life. Later the Khassidim emphasized joy in worship over dour intellectual pursuit. In such ways our leaders always managed to reinvigorate Jewish practice and increase commitment to Jewish ideals.

Their emphasis in doing so, like similar efforts today, often focused on family observance. They knew that the family, as the teacher of value, is the seat of Jewish identity, and the home, as the transmitter of memory, is the key to Jewish continuity. At the center of home observance have always been the holidays— with their special smells, sounds, tastes and rituals, with their rational underpinnings, historic connections and humane values. This is the stuff of both positive emotional experience and inspiring intellectual appeal that fosters lasting meaningfulness.

The problem for many of us is that we did not have much exposure to the holidays and often our Jewish education, if we had any at all, ended in childhood. That means we never progressed beyond simplistic Sunday school explanations, truncated—often fairy tale—history, or superficial glimpses of what Judaism, a religion as intricately layered and beautifully adorned as an ornamented Torah scroll—encompasses. This deficit impedes our ability to comfortably teach others about the celebrations of a way of life designed to elevate the spirit, stimulate the mind and satisfy the body. But there is no reason our Jewish education cannot begin, or continue, now.

Encompassing numerous dimensions, the holidays open the entire spectrum of Jewish life and thought to us. Through the progress of the Jewish year, we are exposed to who we are as individuals and what we are as a nation. We see what happened to us, how we are supposed to behave and the long-term reasons behind our actions. The full cycle runs the gamut of emotion and style of celebration. Within a context of recurring themes (exile and redemption, today's reality and tomorrow's perfection, creating justice and ensuring continuity), each holiday presents its own history lesson, moral message and opportunity for personal growth. In enjoyable and engaging ways, the Jewish year encases the treasured legacy that is your and your children's rightful inheritance.

This book is designed to help you use that legacy to enrich your life and your family's life today, and bequeath it to your descendants for tomorrow—as your ancestors did for you. In previous generations it was the Jewish, not the universal Gregorian, calendar that defined the passage of a Jew's life. According to it a Jew would sow and reap, rejoice and weep. Public events were set on Hebrew dates; birthdays and anniversaries remembered in reference to them ("she was born on the fifth candle of Khanukah," for example). Through the rhythm of the Jewish year, our grandparents and great-grandparents and their forebears learned to live as Jews. If you observe a year of holidays, you will also know what it means, and how to be, Jewish. So come join the celebration.

Dear Reader

his is the book on holidays I was looking for when I began, as an adult, to reconnect with my heritage—one that synthesized material I could only get from a variety of sources, went beyond the superficial to embrace the richness and depth of our tradition, and, with a full range of information on why and how to celebrate, provided a foundation for both knowledge and action.

The purpose of *The Lifetime Guide* is to help you do just that: introduce or enhance holiday tradition in your own home. While ostensibly directed at people with little in the way of previous Jewish experience, this book, because of its range of information, can be useful to a wide variety of people: the first-time celebrant and the veteran of many holidays; those who want to follow tradition to the letter as well as those who want to increase their understanding of some aspect of observance; those looking for an authentic folk custom and those needing inspiration for new ways to celebrate. Of course, trying to accommodate readers from diverse Jewish backgrounds, Jewish educational levels and philosophical orientations toward Jewish practice poses a number of inherent dilemmas.

If you are looking for a general overview of a holiday, you might think there is more here than you need to know or want to undertake. Not necessarily. This book is comprehensive so that it will remain a valuable resource in your library as your interests—and your children's ages—change. It allows you to make personal connections with the holidays from different angles and levels according to your own situation. (Religious importance not important to you? Perhaps you can more easily relate to historical development. Or are fascinated by folklore. Or have an interest in holiday cuisine.) Sections like those on halakhah may not be of any concern to you. So skip them. They are here as reference when and if you need them.

In fact, the book is arranged so that you do not have to wade through material you do not want in order to get at what you need. It can be read in portions, consulted to find answers to questions—yours and your children's—or used to guide you through steps of preparation or execution. Notations throughout refer you to other sections or chapters so that you can easily find needed background explanations that will enhance your understanding of particular points.

There was another reason for being comprehensive: Since Jewish culture is so rich, sometimes various aspects may seem to be in conflict. I wanted to avoid setting up contradictions based on omission. Having a full explanation can give you a better appreciation for why we do certain things, and insights into how they can be incorporated into your own celebrations.

On the other hand, if you come from a more observant vantage point, you might question the inclusion of theories drawn from non-religious literature of how certain thoughts or practices evolved. Raising these points—which are not new to anyone who takes a secular view of Judaism—allows for them to be lifted out of the realm of easily dismissed superstition and placed within Judaism's rational moral and spiritual framework. In the text, I have indicated views that are considered to be outside of classic Jewish thought.

The overall approach is decidedly a traditional one. (The point of this book, after all, is to support a renewal or enhancement of traditional holiday observance.) However, this does not mean "Orthodox" over Conservative, Reform or Reconstructionist practices (divisions that did not even exist for most of Jewish history and that you still will not find in most countries where there are Jewish communities today). I do indicate differences, where they occur, in the specific holiday practices of the various movements.

In past generations, choices of what and how to observe were more likely to be made from a position of awareness and understanding than is often the case today. And since most of us try to make any worthwhile decisions in life out of knowledge rather than ignorance, I wanted to present what is recognized as classic Jewish thought in all its depth and variety (which is not necessarily in conflict with liberal interpretations). How you define yourself as a Jew, what *mitzvot* you choose to follow, the holiday observances you want to keep are entirely up to you. But at least you will have exposure to the basis of all Jewish interpretation, literal or liberal.

Jewish text has never been "the last word" but the beginning of analysis and action. I hope you will use this book in the same way, as a resource and impetus.

GETTING THE MOST OUT OF THIS BOOK

Each chapter consists of two main sections. "Why We Celebrate" presents the factual basis for understanding the holiday and its development, along with its significance within Jewish life. "How We Celebrate" gives you all the practical information you need in order to follow the traditional observances connected with the holiday.

The following outlines what you will find in each subsection, and provides additional guidance to help you maximize the usefulness of this book.

WHY WE CELEBRATE

HISTORIC FOUNDATION This section explains the origin and development of the holiday. Part of the purpose is to show that the holidays, like Judaism and the Jewish people, are not monolithic or static. Rather, they are filled with diversity and dynamism. Over time they have been shaped by changing needs and circumstances, but always with faithfulness to the original spiritual values. We may continue to make the holidays relevant to our lives today—as long as we do so within the framework of the tradition. If you want to get an overview of Jewish history, you might want to read this section of each chapter.

RELIGIOUS IMPORTANCE This section shows how the holiday promotes certain principles, values and philosophies of Judaism. If you read all the "Religious Importance" sections, you will gain an understanding of what Judaism is all about. One thing you will notice is that you cannot talk about our religion without mentioning God. Belief in God is the number one commandment and number one principle of faith on which Judaism is built.

Classically, that was no problem. And for those of us who embrace God in our everyday lives—feeling comfortable acknowledging Him, talking about and to Him, consciously and actively working to obey Him—that is still no problem. But for people not used to thinking about God, or even spirituality, the whole subject may be strange and discomforting. If you have difficulty relating to it, perhaps substituting your own concepts (nature, community, goodness, conscience, social action) will help you better deal with the basic principle.

While recognizing that there are different opinions as to how to understand God, as there have been throughout our history, I have chosen to present the tradition of Jewish thought passed down for three thousand years, a tradition still widely held—despite the so-called advancements of civilization. Jewish religious beliefs reflect human nature, psychological, emotional and even scientific truths, and are as applicable today as ever.

PERSONAL MEANING Adherence to the holiday calendar has lasted over such a long period of time because our festivals reflect much more than isolated points on our national timeline. In addition to marking our progress as a people through history, and as a community through the year, with their recurrent themes and moral messages, the holidays present opportunities for personal introspection and growth. The combination of the warm familiarity of a holiday that comes year after year, and the fact that you are different each time you celebrate it, helps keep observance perennially new.

Here you will find explanations of how and why the ancient commemorations have meaning today, and questions to ask yourself and your children to highlight their significance for you and take you to new levels of understanding and commitment.

HOW WE CELEBRATE

Many people who find ritual irrelevant or bothersome simply do not understand what they are doing or what is being done around them, or why. Discomfort and reluctance connected with going into a synagogue or someone else's home when "strange things" will be happening is understandable. (The feeling is captured in an amusing song written by a newly-observant man, "I Got the I Don't Know What Page We're On in the Prayer Book Blues.")

The second part of each chapter can help remedy that. It provides the practical information you need in order to observe the holiday, and/or to understand how it is being observed by others. You may not want to do everything presented nor do you have to—but you'll have the full range of possibilities from which to choose the aspects of observance that matter to you.

RITUAL ITEMS For many of the holidays, we use special items, either in the home or synagogue, as part of celebration. (If you visit a Jewish museum, you are likely to see a collection of this Judaica, often works of great artistry and artistic creativity, from different parts of the world and different eras.) Any ceremonial supplies you need or are likely to encounter are described and explained. (You do not have to incur a great expense for them; synagogues provide many of the ritual items for their members to use during services, and those required for home use can all be made at little or no cost. Doing so with your children is a great way to teach them about holidays and get them involved in preparations.) For those who want to purchase any of the items and do not have local access through synagogue shops or Jewish book/supply stores, you'll find Internet and catalogue services listed in "More Good Information" at the end of this book.

OBSERVANCE This section details what we do on the holiday at home, in synagogue and/or in other public settings. The rituals we follow are a combination of those specifically commanded in Torah, the rites and liturgies developed by the rabbis to substitute for celebration no longer possible after we lost the Temple, and customs so widely accepted through common practice that over time they became incorporated into holiday celebration. The "whys" of observance have been included along with the "hows."

PREPARATION Like any special event in life, meaningful observance of a holiday does not just happen: there are things we do to get ready, psychologically, spiritually and physically. During the period of preparation, which might be as short as a few days or as long as forty, we have a great opportunity to build joyful anticipation and excitement for the holiday within the family.

HALAKHAH The word, which means Jewish law (halakhot, laws, in the plural), comes from the same root as the words *holeikh* (go, as in "I go down the road") and *halikhot* (ways). It is the body of statutes, ordinances, and rules that govern every aspect of the Jewish way of life—personal and civil, public and private, spiritual and ethical. We can credit adherence to it for keeping the Jews a distinct people despite our lengthy sojourn among alien nations.

The original source for halakhah is the Torah with its six hundred and thir-teen commandments (*mitzvot*) regulating the relationship between individuals and between wo/man and God. In the twelfth century, the brilliant scholar Moses ben Maimon (popularly known as Maimonides or by the acronym Rambam; 1135–1204) codified the law in his fourteen-volume *Mishneh* (Second) *Torah,* a commentary on the laws of the Bible based on Talmudic inter-pretation and his own philosophy. Three centuries later, the eminent Sephardic Rabbi Joseph Karo (1488–1575) wrote the *Shulkhan Arukh* (Set Table), the last great code of rabbinic Judaism. The latter is considered the authority on issues of halakhah, and the source for Jewish law followed today, although Maimonides, on whose work Karo based his, is also consulted.

I have included halakhah for the holidays for two reasons. One is the obvi-ous: so that readers who want to follow the Jewish calendar fully in accordance with our tradition will have the legal guidance at their fingertips. In addition, the halakhah often provides lovely insights into the Jewish value system, the evaluative process of the rabbis, the situation of Jews in different times and places and the evolution of practices connected with a holiday. This comes through in what was permitted, where exceptions to the rule were written into law, what was given precedence in situations of conflict and how interpretations of law changed over time and in the particular circumstances of a community.

In general, I have included only those halakhot most relevant in modern cir-cumstances. Suggestions of more detailed resources for less likely or highly spe-cific situations appear in "More Good Information." Laws standard for all festivals are covered in the first chapter, on Pesakh, with subsequent referrals back to them.

CUSTOMS Different communities at different times developed holiday ritu-als based on their own particular interpretations of Scripture and local circum-stances. Sometimes they resulted from a tremendous blow to a community, when an infusion of spirituality or renewed optimism was needed. At others they developed out of economic conditions, or the relationship with the non-Jewish community—from whom they sometimes borrowed practices. Often quaint, they add tremendous color to the tapestry of Jewish life and show us something of our history among the nations. You might see some of these practices in the homes of people who come from different cultural backgrounds than your own. And just as Jews took customs of local populations and, by giving them a Jewish slant, made them their own, or introduced innovative practices that enhanced a holiday's meaning for them, you can adapt any of these folk customs to add meaning, interest and fun to your family's celebration.

TRADITIONAL FOODS We eat certain foods on the holidays either because they are directly commanded (such as matzah on Pesakh); represent some aspect of the event behind the holiday (like pancakes fried in oil for Khanukah's miracle of the oil), or symbolize a value of the holiday (honey on Rosh Hashanah for a sweet year). Some of them were chosen because, while meeting a symbolic or halakhic dictate, they also happened to be within the physical reach and budget of the majority of Jews in a particular region at a given time. Cookbooks containing appropriate holiday recipes are listed in specific chapters and in "More Good Information."

SONGS TO SING Since there are songbooks, as well as numerous recordings and a growing library of music videos that are much more comprehensive than a book like this could ever be, you won't find full refrains and notation staffs for holiday songs. Instead, I have suggested songs that are traditionally sung for an occasion, or would be most appropriate. In special cases, background or explanation is also provided. You have your pick of collections of sheet music and recordings that include them. Some can be heard through Internet sites such as those listed in "More Good Information."

STORIES TO READ To help heighten awareness of and pride in the variety of written works on a holiday's themes and observances, and the caliber of writers who have produced them, this section introduces some of the classic poems, plays, stories, essays and books touching on the holidays created by literary luminaries. Annotated listings, including select current titles, follow.

OF ADDED NOTE Works of music have been created around themes related to the holidays, museums have been constructed to house exhibits related to events behind the holidays, and historic sites in Israel connected with those events have been made accessible to the public. Information about them is provided at the end of the chapters where applicable, so that you can listen to the compositions and visit the sites to further support your family's experience of a holiday.

Except in cases where a piece or genre connected with a holiday is particularly unusual or interesting, art is not listed separately. There are so many renditions of holiday themes and observance—by great masters (particularly Rembrandt, who depicted numerous holiday-related Bible scenes), early Jewish artists Moritz Oppenheim, Bernard Picard, Maurice Gottleib and Alphonse Levy (who beautifully recorded synagogue and home celebrations) and such modern Jewish artists as Marc Chagall, Shalom of Safed, Reuven Rubin, David Sharir and Jossi Stern. Seeing how artists—Jewish and non-Jewish—have been inspired by the themes of our holidays can be an added source of pride in the Jewish heritage for our young people. A librarian can direct you to books of the collected works of an artist, collections of art of the Old Testament and other volumes of works that portray the holidays.

BLESSINGS

This section presents the Hebrew text, transliteration and translation for the blessings used to usher in and observe specific aspects of the holidays. When to recite each and any special instructions governing them are more fully explained in the holiday chapters.

FOR FURTHER EXPLORATION/ MORE GOOD INFORMATION

While the classic designation for us, "people of the book," comes from our adherence to Torah, we also gained the reputation, because of our stress on education, of being voracious readers—and our library keeps growing to prove it. Materials suggested under "For Further Exploration" represent a tiny sampling of what is available (in written and other works). I chose materials that contribute special understanding and appreciation, and connect with a theme or message of the holiday in an elucidating and/or inspiring way. (Collectively the listings include books produced by all major movements in Judaism; all conform to a traditional Jewish view and are in accordance with the standards of halakhah.)

Folktales very often meet the criteria—and there are numerous and wonderful ones. However, rather than list them throughout, I have included several collections in the back-of-the-book section "More Good Information." Be sure to check it as well.

In this section you will find books within a holiday series, or those that cover numerous aspects of a holiday or many holidays together, guides to halakhah, prayer books, cookbooks and songbooks, along with Internet sites where you can find related information and materials, and Internet/mail-order sources for Judaica, books, and music and video recordings. (Please note that legends and stories appear in multiple volumes, and from time to time titles are reprinted or reissued by different publishers, so the same material will be found in books other than those presented here, or in an edition for which the bibliographic information differs. New Internet resources, like new books and recordings, are continually produced.)

Books listed can be found at public libraries, in synagogue, Jewish center or other Jewish organization libraries, through inter-library loan, real and virtual booksellers, directly from publishers, or companies specializing in out-of-print books.

Professional educators and/or publishers provided the age ranges designated for children's books. You may find that your younger children will enjoy some of the books suggested for older ones when they are read aloud. I have not included the picture and board books for very young children, simply because there is not much to recommend one over another and new versions are continually being produced. But if you have an infant or toddler, know that such resources do exist and that my failure to include them in no way reflects judgment of their value. On the contrary, the first three years are critical for Jewish, like any, education, and such books are very helpful in introducing the basic concepts of holiday observance to your children.

A NOTE ON *Sources*

In quoting from Scripture I have largely relied on two editions: *Tanakh—A New Translation of* THE HOLY SCRIPTURES *According to the Traditional Hebrew Text* (Philadelphia: The Jewish Publication Society, 1985); and Aryeh Kaplan's THE LIVING TORAH—*The Five Books of Moses and the Haftarot* (New York: Maznaim Publishing Corporation, 1981).

The first, entirely in English, has the advantage of including not only the Five Books of Moses, but the Prophets and Writings as well. Produced by a committee of scholars representing the three main branches of organized Jewish life, it uses contemporary language that makes the text accessible and alive. While the volume by the esteemed Rabbi Aryeh Kaplan contains only Torah and the sections of Prophets assigned for Sabbath and festival readings, they appear in both the original Hebrew and contemporary English. Footnotes explain phrases and terms; maps, diagrams and drawings augment the text; and a table of contents breaks down each portion into the significant subjects covered in it. (Other editions of the Hebrew Bible—there are many—contain varying levels and styles of commentary.)

Throughout the text of this book are chapter and verse references for information based on Scripture. So often we are taught "It is written." But where? For example, any of us who went to Hebrew/Sunday school learned the story about Abraham, our forefather and the first monotheist, smashing his father's idols. Have you ever tried to find in it the Bible? Don't bother; it's not there. That's because it is a rabbinic legend, a midrash, used to fill in what Torah does not explicitly say.

I have indicated when a tradition is found in Talmud or midrash, and for any from Torah—which is more easily accessible to most readers—exactly where you can locate it—in case you want to explore a source more fully. References to "our sages" or "the rabbis" generally indicate the great scholars early in the first millennium who codified and commented on our tradition.

A NOTE ON *Transliteration*

The English rendition of a Hebrew word can take a variety of forms (a good example is the candlelighting holiday Chanukah—or Channukah, Hanukkah, Khanukah. . .). The "ch" combination, used to represent the back-of-the-throat rasping sound of the Hebrew letters khaf (כ) and khet (ח) is particularly problematic, because someone unfamiliar with Hebrew who does not know the word in advance would, on seeing it spelled Cheshvan, pronounce the first syllable of the name of the month like Cheshire Cat.

Some printed materials indicate the guttural sound by using an "H" with a dot placed under it. As you may have already noticed, I have chosen instead to use a combination of letters that seems to be gaining wider usage, and approximates the sound of the Hebrew, "kh." This does have the effect of making some familiar words look odd (like Khabad, Khassid, Khayim), but gives a more accurate guide to how a word is said. (For consistency sake I use the kh combination throughout the text, even for recognized names such as those above. The only place alternate spellings appear is in bibliographic references, where names and titles are spelled in their original forms, or in names of individuals.)

There are also differences in rendering the Hebrew letters bet (ב), which has either a "b" or "v" sound depending on whether or not there is a dot in the middle of it; and the tof (ת), which in the same way has either an "s" or a "t" sound. Ashkenazi liturgical pronunciation prefers the former in both cases (Akiba, Abot, Sukkos, Shabbos), which gives a Yiddish sound to words, while the Sephardim and modern Hebrew prefer the latter (Akiva, Avot, Sukkot, Shabbat). The second is also the system I use in the text.

The introductory page for each chapter indicates the way the holiday's name is said in Hebrew, and in cases where different, how it is pronounced in Yiddish. We may think of the Yiddish as the anglicized version, too; it is the one with which many of us are more familiar because it is the version that entered common usage after Yiddish-speaking immigrants from Europe introduced it here.

I have tried to be faithful to the plural forms of words in the Hebrew (Sedarim rather than Seders, matzot instead of matzahs). All transliteration is phonetic; full pronunciation guidance (with syllable accents) is included in the glossary listings. (Foreign words and liturgical terms are italicized or not, capitalized or not, according to current dictionary standards.)

A NOTE ON *Gender Reference*

I gave a good deal of consideration to how to solve the problem of gender designation in the text. Although sometimes cumbersome, in the interests of neutrality, I have used a s/he, wo/man or his/her format. There may be instances in which I have used a masculine term because it is less awkward, encompasses both genders, or, like it or not, is still the officially recognized collective word in the English language.

Please keep in mind, however, particularly when reading about historic development, that in many instances, the masculine personal pronoun is used simply because it is accurate: traditionally there were things done only by men. This is not a value judgment; it has to do with responsibility as defined by Jewish law, and not of the superiority of one sex over the other.

References to God are masculine, because that is the classic and least awkward form, and until our language adopts some gender-neutral word, the least confusing. It should also be noted that according to Judaism, God is of no specific gender. In Hebrew, this is obvious. Some of "His" names are actually in the plural, and one, Shekhinah, the Divine Presence in the World—is in the feminine. God is neither masculine nor feminine, "He" is both—just as the original human being was created, in God's image, as a creature with masculine and feminine attributes that were later separated (with some cross-over) so that Adam could have a complementary, equal but different, partner.

Cycle of Celebration —
THE JEWISH CALENDAR

*O*ne of the most distinctive elements of Judaism—and one that has helped preserve our unique way of life—is our calendar. It is a system that recognizes God's involvement in both nature and history, yet encourages us to be masters of our own time.

When God created the celestial illuminations to separate day from night, He also intended that they "serve as signs for the set times" or festivals (*moadim* [GENESIS 1:14]). Unlike the strictly solar Gregorian calendar (based on the three hundred and sixty-five and one-quarter days it takes for the earth to circle the sun), or the strictly lunar Mohammedan calendar (based on the twenty-nine and one-half days it takes for the moon to circle the earth), the Jewish calendar relies on both the sun and the moon. The first, determining the agricultural year, grounds us in nature. The latter, waxing and waning, reflects our history and destiny of renewal after diminishment.

DIVIDING OUR TIME

After the Creation account, the next biblical reference to time comes just before the Exodus, when "this month" is designated as "the first of months of the year for you" (EXODUS 12:2). The sages identify the verse as the first commandment, directing us to be responsible for designating divisions of time and avoiding time's oppression by enjoying days of complete rest. Declaring the beginning of any month—necessary in order to determine when to celebrate the "set times" given as "the fifteenth day of the first month" or the "tenth day of the seventh month" for example—became the basis for establishing the Jewish calendar.

The importance of community in Jewish life dictated that all Jews celebrate holidays at the same time. That meant a standard start of a new month had to be known by everyone so they could count the days before a festival in unison. At the time of the First Temple, the High Priest made the determination based on the moon's first appearance in the sky.

During the era of the Second Temple, two eyewitnesses would testify before the Sanhedrin (rabbinical court) that they had seen the crescent sliver. If the witnesses arrived by late afternoon on the thirtieth day after a month began, it was declared to be Rosh (literally "head," understood as "new") Khodesh (month). If they came later, the following day was proclaimed to be the first of the new month. To let everyone else know, bonfires were set on hilltops in Jerusalem, then in the next ring of settlements and so on, until the news reached Jewish communities as far away as Babylonia.

When the Romans who later occupied the Holy Land prohibited the signal fires, and the Samaritan separatists lit their own fires on different nights to cause confusion, the court resorted to sending messenger relays. With this slower communication system, it could take several days—even weeks—before the official start of the new month was known by communities in remote areas of the land or furthest from Jerusalem (which was very far after the destruction of the Second Temple and the dispersal of Jews throughout the world).

To avoid designating the wrong day, those far-flung communities decided to observe Rosh Khodesh on the thirtieth and thirty-first days after the previous one, and, since they sometimes did not find out when the month had started until it was half over, they also began to celebrate all festivals (but not fasts) for two days. This practice became the universal custom outside the Land of Israel.

Even the relay system had to be abandoned, because under the oppression of Constantine (337–361), all religious observance was prohibited and the Jews of the Holy Land could no longer proclaim the new moon. A fixed calendar that could specify the days well in advance was needed.

One had actually been in the works, based on mathematics and astronomical study by the rabbis, since shortly after the dispersion. Finally codified by Rabbi Hillel II, it was adopted in 359 (and adjusted for close to five hundred years after that). Although a set calendar eliminated the need for a second day of Rosh Khodesh or holidays, the Jews outside the Land insisted on keeping it (a demonstration of the power of common practice in our tradition). The custom continues today except among Reform Jews and in Israel.

THE CALENDAR STRUCTURE

The Jewish calendar consists of twelve lunar months of either twenty-nine or thirty days. With the shorter ones, the day following the end of the month becomes Rosh Khodesh of the next month, and is celebrated for one day. With the longer ones, the last day of the month and the first of the next month are observed as a two-day Rosh Khodesh.

Torah refers to the months primarily by number (first month, second month, etc.). When the Jews returned to Israel from Babylonia, they introduced the names they had learned there: Nissan (corresponding to the "first month" and March-April), Iyar (April-May), Sivan (May-June), Tammuz (June-July), Av (July-August), Elul (August-September), Tishrei (September-October), Kheshvan (October-November), Kislev (November-December), Tevet (December-January), Shevat (January-February), and Adar (February-March). Kheshvan is often called Markheshvan (*mar* meaning bitter or mister, both since it is a month that contains no special occasions—therefore bitter, and because in compensation the rabbis wanted to give it an air of importance—Mr. Kheshvan.)

It is often believed that the Jewish year begins in the autumn, with Tishrei. In a way it does: that is when we celebrate what we call the Jewish New Year (Rosh Hashanah, literally "head" of the year). Even printed Jewish calendars start with Tishrei, and the count of the year changes then.

While Tishrei is the first month for religious matters (such as the beginning of our spiritual year, and of Sabbatical and Jubilee years), our festival year begins with Nissan, the month in which our redemption from slavery and our life as a holy nation began (SEE "HISTORIC FOUNDATION" IN CHAPTER ON PESAKH). In the days of the Jewish commonwealths, this was also the date for calculating the length of reign of Jewish kings. (Actually, we have four new years, the other two being Shevat, for tithing of trees [SEE CHAPER ON TU B'SHEVAT], and Elul, for tithing of cattle.)

The even-numbered months with the exception of Kheshvan have twenty-nine days each, and the odd-numbered months with the exception of Kislev have thirty days each. The two were left open to give the rabbis room to manipulate the calendar so that certain festivals would not occur on particular days of the week. For example, if Yom Kippur fell on a Friday or Sunday, complications would arise because of its juxtaposition with Shabbat. Giving extra days, when necessary, in the flexible months avoids those problems.

One other adjustment was necessary. If you add up the days in all the

months, you get a total of three hundred and fifty-four. (The lunar year technically lasts three hundred and fifty-four days, eight hours, forty-eight minutes
and thirty-six seconds.) The solar year, as we all know, lasts three hundred and
sixty-five days (plus six hours and forty-eight seconds). The discrepancy of just
under eleven days, if not somehow resolved, would result in each holiday falling
that much earlier each succeeding year. That would wreak particular havoc with
the festivals that have seasonal significance—putting the spring festival of
redemption and rebirth in the dead of winter, the fall harvest festival in the
middle of the growing season and so on.

To compensate, the rabbis inserted an additional (intercalary) thirty-day
month seven times in each nineteen-year cycle—creating leap years in the third,
sixth, eighth, eleventh, fourteenth, seventeenth and nineteenth years. Placed
between the end of one year and the beginning of the next, the extra month is
called Adar Sheni (Second Adar).

THE HOLIDAYS

The schedule of holidays we observe is a combination of the festivals
ordained in Torah, which provide opportunities for us to renew our relationship
with God; feasts and fasts added by the rabbis during and just after the Second
Temple period, which commemorate significant triumphs and defeats; and the
modern commemorative days introduced since 1949, which mark monumental
changes in the situation of the Jewish people in the world.

The "set times of the Lord, the sacred occasions which you shall celebrate
each at its appointed time" (LEVITICUS 23:4) include the three pilgrimage festivals
(Pesakh, Shavuot and Sukkot). While superficially marking a stage in the agricultural year, each is a progressive step toward true freedom and spiritual maturity. The other two "set times," Rosh Hashanah and Yom Kippur, encapsulate the
purpose of all the festivals: improving ourselves and drawing close to God.

The post-biblical holidays ordained by the sages commemorate our triumph
in exile over a threat to our physical existence (Purim), our triumph on the Land
over a threat to our spiritual existence (Khanukah) and catastrophes that threatened both (Tisha B'Av and the minor fast days related to it, Shiva Asar
B'Tammuz, Tzom Gedalia, and Asarah B'Tevet). They are paralleled by the days

most recently added to the calendar (by law in the State of Israel and acceptance by the Jewish people), Yom Hashoah (Holocaust Remembrance Day) for the destruction, and Yom Ha'atzmaut (Israel Independence Day) and Yom Yerushalayim (Jerusalem Unification Day) for the resurrection. The two other special occasions are folk festivals that add a bit of levity to the year, Tu B'Shevat and Lag B'Omer.

There is one holiday you will not find as a separate subject in this book: Shabbat (Sabbath), the weekly opportunity for spiritual renewal. It warrants a tome in itself (many have been written). You should be aware, however, that with its release from quotidian routine, the Sabbath is the model for observance of all the major festivals. And like them, it is observed (at least in part) in memory of the Exodus from Egypt, which provided the foundation for the concepts of freedom and mastery of time that pervade Judaism and the Jewish calendar.

BLESSING THE SIGNS OF OUR TIMES

Judaism is adamant against the worship of the sun and moon (and any other objects of nature or otherwise) in themselves, but as orbs created with Divine purpose for human benefit, they are objects to be appropriately appreciated.

As commanded by Torah, the new moon was to be marked with the sounding of trumpets and special sacrifices (NUMBERS 10:10). It was also an occasion for feasting, as alluded to in I Samuel's account of King Saul's days. The offerings and special blessings for the new moon were later made at the Temple.

In the centuries after the Second Temple was destroyed, the people continued to have a special meal and men in particular did not work on the day/s of the new month. Women did little housework and children were given the time off from school.

Somewhere along the line, the occasion became a special respite for women. According to midrash (rabbinic expansion on Scripture), when Aaron told the people to take earrings from their wives and children in order to make the Golden Calf (EXODUS 32:2), the women did not willfully comply. In recognition of their refusal to participate in idol worship, they were given Rosh Khodesh as a perpetual holiday, a day on which they did not have to work. In recent years, as Jewish women searched for ways to connect with our heritage, particularly through rituals of their own, they rediscovered Rosh Khodesh. In congregational settings and outside of them, women have introduced special ceremonies for the occasion.

Aside from them, the observance today primarily consists of additions to the liturgy. (Some particularly pious people also continue the custom begun by the Jewish mystics in the sixteenth century: They treat the day before Rosh Khodesh as a minor day of repentance [Yom Kippur Katan] and use it to fast and pray for forgiveness for transgressions made during the previous month.) At the morning service on the Sabbath prior to Rosh Khodesh, called Shabbat Mevarkhim ("when blessing is made"), the exact time the new month will start is announced and special prayers recited. On the day of the new moon itself, we recite *Hallel* (Psalms of Praise) during the morning service, read a special Torah portion (NUMBERS 28:9–15) detailing the sacrifices to be made for the New Moon, and add special phrases to the other daily services and the grace said after meals.

The Orthodox also follow the custom of blessing the new moon (*kiddush levanah*), normally between seventy-two hours after Rosh Khodesh and mid month, under an open sky so the moon can be clearly seen. It is customary to perform the ceremony in the company of a *minyan* at *motzei* (departure of) *Shabbat*.

While you might think we bless the sun every day, when it appears anew, the *Birkat* (Blessing) *Hakhamah* ([of] the "Warm") is actually said only when the star is in the same position, on the same day of the week and the same time of day as it was when created. Due to the discrepancy between our assignment of days and weeks in a year, and the actual time it takes for the earth to complete its circuit around the sun (which is slightly longer), the sun's position relative to our viewing perspective on earth shifts slightly each year. Twenty-eight years of accumulated discrepancies puts its back at its original starting point.

At that time, as Talmud instructs, a special benediction is made. On the Wednesday morning (the sun was created on the fourth day [GENESIS 1:14–19]) in Nissan,* between when the sun fully clears the horizon and the third hour of the day, we recite (preferably in a group of people, but alone if necessary) a blessing recognizing God's works of Creation.

---

*The rabbis disputed whether Creation occurred in Nissan or Tishrei. We celebrate the birthday of the world in Tishrei, but for purposes of the *Birkat Hakhamah,* they designated Nissan, one of the other new years.) The next blessing of the sun will take place in the year 2009.

COUNTING DAYS AND YEARS

The Jewish accounting of time defines a day from nightfall to nightfall, based on the order of Creation: "and there was evening, and there was morning, a [first, second, etc.] day" (*"vay'hi erev, vay'hi voker, yom —"* [GENESIS 1]). This means that like every day, a Jewish holiday begins on the evening (erev) prior to the day (rather than at midnight, as it does for most of the world). For example, if Nissan 15, the beginning of Passover, coincides with Thursday, April 18, all holiday observances take effect on the evening of Wednesday, April 17. Nightfall is indicated by the appearance of three stars, clearly visible to the unaided eye, in the sky. It arrives approximately fifty minutes after sunset, the time of transition between a secular day and a sacred occasion.

Tishrei marks the passing of one year into the next. Most of the world counts years from the birth of Jesus, designating those before that event as BC (before Christ) and those after as AD (Anno Domini, or year of the Lord). We count years from the date of Creation, and use the designations BCE, Before the Common Era, instead of BC, and CE, Common Era, instead of AD. The date of the Jewish year is the Common Era year plus 3760 (the date BCE traditionally cited as that of Creation). For example, 2003 is 5763 Jewish.

$\mathscr{P}$esakh—*Feast of Freedom*

(PEH'-SAKH),
NISSAN 15–22
(SPRING; LATE MARCH—MID APRIL)

Known as Passover (and for the unleavened bread—matzah—eaten during it), the oldest Jewish festival celebrates the historic delivery of Israel from a life of slavery in Egypt. The first of the three pilgrimages, it is one of the most widely celebrated of all Jewish holidays, a time of family observance, rejoicing for past salvation, and expectation of future redemption.

Origins—WHY WE CELEBRATE PESAKH

Traditions—HOW WE CELEBRATE PESAKH

Origins—

WHY WE CELEBRATE PESAKH

Where Did It Begin? Historic Foundation

THE BIBLICAL BIRTH OF A NATION

Passover originated with one of the two most significant events of Jewish history: *yetziat* (departure) *mitzrayim* (from Egypt) of the Israelites who had been in bondage there. This one occurrence defined the nation of Israel, which was born out of it.

You are probably familiar with at least some portions of the basic story of the Exodus, as this momentous development is called: The Egyptians were alarmed at the tremendous growth rate among the Israelite population in their kingdom. To eliminate the possibility that the resident foreigners would align with an enemy to attack from within, they enslaved the Israelites. The bondage—applied to building the massive cities of Pithom and Ramses from scratch mud and straw—did nothing to stem their prolific increase. So Pharaoh ordered the Egyptian midwives to kill the male newborns of the slaves. When they surreptitiously disobeyed, Pharaoh decreed that every Israelite male infant be drowned in the Nile.

Determined to save him from the fate of the other newborns, one mother placed her son in a basket prepared to float on the river. Pharaoh's daughter retrieved him and gave him the name Moses (which in Egyptian meant "drawn from [*uses*] the water [*mou*]"). Through the actions of Moses' sister Miriam, his own mother was engaged to nurse him. Only after he was old enough to have gained some exposure to his heritage (probably at age three), did Moses' mother turn him over to the princess to rear as her own. From then on, Moses grew up as a prince in Pharaoh's palace.

After killing an Egyptian taskmaster for beating an Israelite slave, the adult and innately just Moses fled to Midian, where he tended flock, married the priest Jethro's daughter Tzipporah, had two sons and in the desert experienced

3

a significant encounter with God, in the form of the Burning Bush.

At God's insistence, and with the assistance of his older brother Aaron, Moses returned to Egypt to liberate his people. He repeatedly demanded of Pharaoh "Let my people go!", kept pressure on the vain and hard-hearted tyrant through a series of heaven-sent plagues, and shepherded the finally-released slaves to a new physical, psychological and spiritual reality east of the Reed Sea. (Believed to be one of the lagoons on the shores of the Mediterranean, the body of water was erroneously identified as the Red Sea when Torah [the Five Books of Moses, also called, in Christian terms, the Old Testament] was translated into Greek in the third century BCE.)

The first fifteen chapters of Torah's book of Exodus chronicle the history from enslavement to emancipation. The account of how the Israelites came to be in Egypt to begin with is told earlier, at the end of the book of Genesis (37–50): Joseph, the son of the patriarch Jacob, was sold by his jealous brothers to a passing caravan leader, who in turn sold him as a slave to an influential aristocrat in Egypt. Imprisoned on false charges because he refused the advances of his boss' amorous wife, Joseph later garnered recognition for his ability to interpret dreams. When he understood those of Pharaoh to foretell a famine, he was elevated to a position second only to the ruler, and devised a plan to ensure the survival of the country.

After being reunited with his brothers, when they were forced to Egypt by famine in Canaan, Joseph arranged for his father's entire family of shepherds— the progenitors of the Twelve Tribes of Israel—to settle in the Egyptian region of Goshen, where they prospered (GENESIS 50:21–24).

How soon the Egyptians forgot the good Joseph had brought them. After the one-time national hero's death, a new Pharaoh "who did not know Joseph" (EXODUS 1:8) ruled. As a security measure, he imposed the bondage, an oppression that had been predicted to Joseph's great-grandfather Abraham: "Know well that your offspring shall be strangers in a land not theirs, and they shall be enslaved and oppressed four hundred years, but I will execute judgment on the nation they shall serve, and in the end they shall go free with great wealth" (GENESIS 15:13–14).

Through Moses, God made good on His promise. After the nine plagues that He unleashed on the Egyptians, He instructed the Israelites to "borrow" objects of gold and silver from their Egyptian neighbors. Probably awed, and not a little frightened by the strange goings on in their land and, Torah tells us, holding Moses in esteem (EXODUS 11:3), the Egyptians readily parted with their valuables (EXODUS 12:35).

Then, God provided detailed instructions to the Israelites for a special meal: each household was to choose an unblemished male yearling lamb, sheep or goat on the tenth of the designated month, watch over the lamb until the fourteenth, slaughter it at twilight, use hyssop (a marjoram-like herb) to smear its blood on the doorposts and lintels of their homes, and roast the entire animal over fire. Fully dressed, including sandals on their feet and staffs in their hands, they were to eat the lamb hurriedly with unleavened bread and bitter herbs, being careful to not break any of the animal's bones or keep leftovers until morning.

Along with the women and girls, only males who had been circumcised could partake of this paschal offering, and no foreigner—one who had not committed himself to the community through circumcision—could be present. While they complied, God passed through the land, killing every firstborn Egyptian, human and animal, but kept His promise to "pass over" (*pasakh*) the homes of every Israelite who had marked his dwelling with the blood of the paschal (*pesakh*) sacrifice (EXODUS 12:31).

Even before their last meal in Egypt, the Israelites were told—not once but three times (EXODUS 12:14, 17, 24)—that in commemoration, this day was to be celebrated in all ages. From the evening of the fourteenth of Nissan through the evening of the twenty-first, all leaven was to be removed from their homes and only unleavened bread was to be eaten. They were not to do any work on the sacred first and seventh days.

FIRST STEPS TO FREEDOM

During the night, as their firstborn were struck down, the Egyptians urged the Israelites to leave, taking all their flocks and belongings with them. And so, already dressed for a hasty getaway, six hundred thousand Israelite men, plus women and children (said to have totaled three million), walked out of the house of bondage.

Realizing the valuable human resource he had released, Pharaoh reneged—just as he had following every other plague, once he was out of immediate danger. He sent his chariots and soldiers after the Israelites camped near the Reed Sea, who were and immediately ready to turn tail and resubjugate themselves to Pharaoh rather than die in the wilderness. It would be one of their many expressions of loss of faith, indications that getting the people out of slavery was much easier than getting the slavery out of the people.

Using a strong east wind against the sea all night, God turned the water into dry land, through which the frightened Israelites passed to the other side. When the Egyptians pursued, the waters closed, drowning them, and reinspiring the Israelites with faith in God and their leader Moses. Then they were on their way to Mount Sinai, to receiving instructions for their mission in life (SEE CHAPTER ON SHAVUOT).

During their travels, the Israelites received the commandment to observe Pesakh (which later came to mean both the paschal sacrifice and the holiday itself) four more times: It follows several laws of social justice (EXODUS 23:14–17), when the *Khag* (feast or festival) *Hamatzot* (of unleavened bread), Torah's designation for the holiday, is included as one of the three (*Shalosh*) seasonal pilgrimage festivals (*Regalim*) to be celebrated annually. It is repeated after Moses' receipt of the second set of tablets containing the Ten Commandments (SEE CHAPTER ON YOM KIPPUR) and an admonition against idolatry (EXODUS 34:18). In the list of all sacred days and festivals, the Israelites are commanded to commemorate the Exodus with a paschal offering and other sacrifices on each of the seven days, and by eating unleavened bread during the entire period (LEVITICUS 23:5). Finally, all of the particulars of Pesakh observance and what they represent are summarized (DEUTERONOMY 16:1–8).

FOR FURTHUR EXPLORATION

FOR ALL

Exodus, chapters 1–15, in any *Khumash* (The Five Books of Moses)
> The entire story on which Passover celebration is based, including the commandments of how to observe the holiday, is told.

The Ten Commandments—The Movie
> Don't miss the classic film version of the Exodus and journey to Sinai, Cecil B. DeMille's epic starring Yul Brenner as Pharaoh, Charlton Heston as Moses, green special effects as the Angel of Death and Jello as the Parting of the Reed Sea.

FOR ADULTS

Wilson, Dorothy Clarke. *Prince of Egypt*. Philadelphia: Westminster Press, 1949.
  Whether or not you accept the author's explanations for the perceived miracles of the Exodus, she does a good job of presenting the emotion and thought behind the Jewish value system as one man, Moses, struggles to find truth. The well-written (if at times flowery) novel closely follows the biblical account and draws on midrash, historical and anthropological theory.

Zornberg, Aviva. *The Particulars of Rapture: Reflections on Exodus*. New York: Doubleday, 2001.
  Although not an easy book, this can be an exciting and enlightening one. The author, an Orthodox rabbi's daughter as well educated in literature, philosophy and psychology as in rabbinic and Khassidic commentaries, applies an innovative feminist and psychological approach wholly within our tradition of continually interpreting our texts to find their relevance.

FOR CHILDREN

Lehmann, Asher. *The Young Moses*. New York: The Judaica Press, 1987.
  For young people and based on midrash, this novel was originally published in Germany after World War I when Jews faced the kinds of dilemmas in life choices Moses did. The issues still resonate today. Ages 11–14.

Stein, Larry. *Josh Discovers Passover!* Deerfield, IL: Ruach Publishing, 2002.
  Putting on his grandfather's prayer shawl transports Josh back to Egypt, where he experiences the Exodus story with Moses. In addition to the story, each page features questions and multiple-choice answers written with humor, plus a lesson about Passover. Ages 4–9.

The Prince of Egypt (animated movie)
  The Dreamworks Pictures version of the Exodus is dramatic, moving and at times visually thrilling. Differences from the original text can easily be discussed with young viewers—especially aided by companion materials, such as those produced by San Francisco's Bureau of Jewish Education (available online at www.bjesf.org/MAIN/PRINCE/prince.html, or from the organization, 639 14th Street, San Francisco, CA 94118–3599, 415–751–6983 x 105; jfep@bjesf.org).

THE HISTORICAL EVIDENCE

By Jewish tradition, the Exodus took place on Thursday, the fifteenth of Nissan in the year 2448 after Creation (variously identified as 1313, 1308, 1306 and 1280 BCE). Working with stated time spans in the Bible books I Kings and Judges, plus excavations in Israel, archaeologists and historians generally place it at the latter date.

Although no Egyptian records corroborate the Torah's story—not unusual in a culture that erased any evidence of weakness—aspects of that country's history provide neat correspondence to it. Historians look back to Amenophis IV, also known as Iknaton (1383–1365 BCE), as a starting point. He abolished multiple idol worship in favor of monotheism of the sun. While he erroneously objectified his deity, he may have gotten the right idea through the influence of the

Israelites, one of the foreign groups allowed to sojourn in the rich grazeland of Goshen on the edge of the kingdom. According to one theory, when his short-lived religious revolution was reversed, and polytheistic nature worship reinstated, the Israelites became victims of persecution.

Ramses II (1300–1234 or 1347–1280 BCE), known for his ego, massive building program, and use of foreign slaves, gets the most votes as the Pharaoh who initially impressed the Israelites into forced labor. It ended with the Exodus under his son, Merneptah, who ruled a declining Egypt at the close of the thirteenth century BCE. (Torah specifies that two pharaohs were involved in the oppression [EXODUS 1:8–10; 2:23].)

This timing coincides with the four hundred and thirty years Israel spent in Egyptian exile (EXODUS 12:40), counted from the time the patriarch Abraham began his wandering in Egypt-dominated Canaan around the age of seventy. (Midrash resolves the discrepancy between these four hundred and thirty years and the four hundred years told to Abraham: the four centuries began with the birth of Isaac. The covenant God made with Abraham, the beginning of the Egyptian period, occurred three decades earlier. According to Jewish tradition, Israel sojourned in Egypt only two hundred and ten years, beginning when Jacob settled there. That period is said to have been equivalent to four hundred in suffering.)

The search for artifacts and documents that can verify the Bible's account continues today and archaeologists and historians still debate its veracity. Scholars (Winston Churchill among them) do not doubt that Israel was in Egypt, and many conclude, based on supportive evidence drawn from the political and social situation of the time, plus the logic of human psychology, that the Exodus story is based on fact. For one thing, they point out, no other people in the history of the world has ever conceived a national myth that gives itself such a disgraceful past. It could only be a reflection of an actual occurrence. (The fact that we emphasize our lowly status demonstrates a key tenet of our tradition: For the Jew, what is important is not what you were, but what you have become.)

While not denying that an unusual departure from Egypt took place, some secular scholars—contrary to classic Jewish tradition—claim that the Exodus account is the result of history mixed with fragments of folklore and legend influenced by other nations. They cite, for instance, a common myth of a child hidden at birth, often rescued from a watery death, who grows up to be a great leader and threat to the existing power structure. They also note that the particular rites by which Israel commemorated the event were borrowed from two distinct pre-existing seasonal festivals observed by the Israelites themselves, long before the Exodus occurred and combined with new meaning into *Khag Hapesakh/Khag Hamatzot*.

Shepherd families celebrated one at the time of the spring full moon when the flocks produced new lambs. It involved rituals similar to the paschal sacrifice designed to elicit good luck and protect the sheep and goats before the tribe left their winter quarters for spring grazing. The Israelite shepherds supposedly brought this festival with them when they settled in the rural areas of Canaan (predominantly the south).

The peasants in the land—the northern farmers—recognized the arrival of spring with a festival related to new grain. Prior to starting the barley harvest, the Jews would get rid of all their sour (fermented) dough (used instead of yeast as a leavening agent), and old bread—perhaps to protect against an unproductive year. They offered the first sheaf of the newly cut grain as a sacrifice.

Over time, say these scholars, Israel gave the rites deeper meaning based on their experiences—which included slavery and liberation from it.

POST-EXODUS PESAKH

The children of Israel were still wandering in the desert when they celebrated the first anniversary of the Exodus (NUMBERS 9:1–5). Since they had been commanded that anyone considered ritually impure could not offer a sacrifice (LEVITICUS 22:3–6), a second Passover, Pesakh Sheni, was instituted for those who on Nissan 14 had had contact with a corpse. To be held one month later (Iyar 14), in the same way as on Nissan 14, it was to be observed in the future by anyone who had been prevented from making the sacrifice in Nissan because s/he had been either ritually impure or on a journey.

This was the last Pesakh observed by the journeying Israelites until they crossed the Jordan River into Canaan at the Passover season thirty-nine years

9

later. Then, the first religious act ordained was circumcision for every male. With the exception of Caleb ben Yefunah and Joshua ben Nun (the only of the twelve spies sent to scout Canaan to have retained their faith in God [NUMBERS 14:24–30]), the circumcised men who had left Egypt had all died in the wilderness, and those born after the Exodus had not been entered into the covenant because of the rigors of desert existence.

The act of allegiance reaffirmed their part of the covenant made between Abraham, Isaac and Jacob and God, the deal God offered the Israelites in Egypt and they accepted at Sinai (SEE "RELIGIOUS IMPORTANCE" IN CHAPTER ON SHAVUOT): He would be their God and lead them to the Land of milk and honey, they would be His people, following His laws and acting as His agents for good on Earth. Once each man had become part of the people of Israel, sharing its responsibilities and destiny through this act of identification, the community was able to offer the paschal lamb (JOSHUA 5:2–10). Every year afterwards, the sacrifice would be a reminder of the nation's responsibilities under the covenantal contract.

As long as the elders who guided the people after Joshua's death remained alive, the Israelites stayed true to their Redeemer (*Go'al Yisrael*). But in the face of ignorance, lack of leadership, inaccessibility to Torah and strong pagan influences around them, the next generation, which had not personally experienced the rigors of slavery and the miracles of salvation, wandered away from their parents' traditions. Pesakh, commemoration of one of the greatest developments to have ever happened to the Jews, was probably no more than a private family affair for a small minority of pious people.

For hundreds of years the Israelites pursued an off-again, on-again relationship with their religion. They revived it under Samuel (the eleventh-century BCE prophet), abandoned it after Solomon's kingdom split into rival idolatrous Israel and Jerusalem-centered Judah (932 BCE), briefly approached it at Judean King Hezekiah's instigation (726 BCE), then largely ignored it until they were within a generation of losing the Temple (619 BCE).

At that time, in a clean-up campaign at the sanctuary, King Josiah's people found some Torah scrolls. Shocked at how much tradition had been lost, the monarch initiated a reformation, eliminating all altars outside the capital and establishing Jerusalem as the only meeting place for all pilgrimages. A public reading of Deuteronomy (the Torah book that reiterates the laws), led to immediate repentance by the people, capped by a public celebration of Passover attended by three hundred thousand people. "Since the time of the prophet Samuel, no Passover like that one had ever been kept in Israel. . ." (II CHRONICLES 35:18).

IN AND OUT OF BABYLON

The Jews exiled to Babylon after destruction of the Temple in 586 BCE (SEE CHAPTER ON TISHA B'AV) celebrated the Egyptian redemption as a model for their own hoped-for deliverance. Although in the absence of the sanctuary they could not make the paschal (or any other) sacrifice, they developed new ritual in prayer service.

Those who remained in the Diaspora (Greek for dispersion, indicating any place Jews live outside the Land of Israel and their situation away from the homeland) continued to observe the holiday long after others returned to the Land when the Temple was rebuilt (516 BCE). Jewish life in the Holy Land was revived (largely through the efforts of the scribe and leader Ezra), and though there continued to be periods of neglect and ignorance (such as the one leading up to the Maccabean Revolt in the second century BCE [SEE CHAPTER ON KHANUKAH], Passover from then on continued to be widely celebrated.

While maintaining the Bible's framework for observance, the ritual was expanded and enriched. Purposely not participating in the Pesakh sacrifice subjected the offender to the penalty of *karet* (being cut off from the community). So the Jews made tremendous effort to get to Jerusalem. Anyone within a thirty-day journey (about nine hundred miles in those days), including a woman, was obligated to make the pilgrimage. Gradually during the Second Temple period, Pesakh emerged as the greatest Jewish national holiday.

The residents of Jerusalem welcomed the population-doubling pilgrims into their homes, providing free accommodation (the city was considered the common property of all the people); the travelers customarily left the skins of the paschal lambs for their hosts in appreciation. Overflow crowds stayed in surrounding villages or camped in the fields. A carnival atmosphere pervaded, the days and nights filled with festive meals, music, Torah study and Temple pageantry that began on the morning of *Erev Pesakh* (Nissan 14).

A series of signals from the Temple, and the Mount of Olives opposite, informed the people when to stop eating leavened foods and when to destroy any leavened food left in their possession. Starting at noon, in three groups successively crowding the Temple courtyard, the Israelites brought their paschal offerings, and unlike other sacrifices, slaughtered the animals themselves with the assistance of the priests and to the accompaniment of the Levite orchestra.

As prescribed by Torah, each family unit roasted its own lamb, on a portable clay stove set up in the home courtyards. Dressed in white, groups embracing different status and economic strata joined together. With biblical references, they told the story of the night of the Exodus, based on Torah's commandment to pass it on to one's children (EXODUS 12:26–27, 13:8, 13:14, DEUTERONOMY 6:20).

BEFORE THE FALL

Two historic developments led the evolution of Pesakh observance into the form we know today: the dominion of Rome over the Land of Israel, and the emergence of rabbinic Judaism.

In the centuries following Ezra's religious revival, controversy over the approach to Torah (and probably not a little to political maneuvering) split Jewish leadership. The Sadducees believed in literally following Torah, and only what it explicitly stated. The Pharisees, heirs of Ezra and fathers of rabbinic Judaism, believed in extrapolating from Torah according to the Oral Tradition, also called Oral law (*Torah Sheh B'al Peh*), believed by them to have been given at Mount Sinai along with the Written Law (Torah, or *Torah Sheh Bikhtav*) and passed from generation to generation by word of mouth (SEE CHAPTER ON SHAVUOT). It allowed them to interpret the Torah's precepts for changing conditions in the world and the Jewish community.

A major disagreement related to Passover concerned their respective understandings of the Torah's designated timing for the counting of the Omer (a measure of grain, commonly identified as a sheaf), the agricultural element of Passover and the system for marking off the fifty days between Pesakh and its companion holiday, Shavuot. (At the start of the counting, a handful of meal ground from the grain was burned at the altar, the rest baked and eaten by the priest. A measure was sacrificed every day of the period.) Not a single Jew could eat bread made from grain of the new harvest until the Omer sacrifice had been made. (The Israelites believed it symbolized protection for the harvest from harmful conditions, particularly winds).

Although one reference makes the first day relative ("start to count when the sickle is first put to standing grain" [DEUTERONOMY 16:9]), the original instruction tells the Israelites to offer the first sheaf, which initiates the count of seven weeks, on "the day after the Sabbath" (LEVITICUS 23:15). The Sadducees insisted that Torah meant the Sabbath that fell during Pesakh, and therefore started their count on that Saturday night. The Pharisees took "Sabbath" to mean the day of rest that was the first sacred day of Passover, and therefore began their count at the start of the second day of the festival—even if it meant cutting the barley on Saturday, an act normally forbidden that day. (Talmud describes an elaborate barley-cutting ceremony the Pharisees conducted on Shabbat just to emphasize their point.)

> *What is national freedom if not a people's inner freedom to cultivate its abilities along the beaten path of its history.*
>
> AHAD HAAM

It is interesting that the Ethiopian Jews, who did not reject Oral Law as did the Sadducees but were cut off from mainstream Judaism before it was written and explained, understood that "Sabbath" to mean the day after Passover ended, since the entire festival is a period of rest. So they began their count, and celebrated Shavuot, six days later than the rest of the Jewish world.

The triumph of the Pharisees in the last century prior to the destruction of the Second Temple led to new observances and themes for the holiday. An expanded religious ceremony, which we know as the Passover Seder (meaning order, for the order of service), began to develop. Looking for symbols of freedom and luxury, the sages found them in the culture to which Israel had been exposed for about two hundred years: Roman banquets and Greek (Hellenistic) symposia: drinking wine throughout the meal (with a blessing of thanks to God), reclining on sofas, eating leisurely and discussing the topic of the evening.

During the Roman occupation, Passover's theme of redemption fanned the hopes of a messianic deliverance. Having long believed that God would again provide miracles such as those experienced at the Exodus, the Jews anticipated a new Moses who would lead them to freedom on the eve of Passover. With this expectation the Jews continued to celebrate Pesakh as a commemoration of the first redemption, and the imminent occurrence of the second. (The last supper of Jesus, which took place during the Roman rule, was the meal of the paschal sacrifice on *Erev Pesakh* 33 CE)

Outside Jerusalem, where the sacrifice could not be made (some people symbolically ate roast lamb), Passover was observed with services at the local synagogue and at home with the same family service done in the capital. It consisted of a *kiddush* (sanctification over wine); eating herbs—some spring vegetable—dipped in vinegar or red wine; three questions asked by a child about the out-of-the-ordinary rituals being performed at the table; the household head's answers to the questions personalized to the child's level of comprehension; explanations of the significance of the night of Nissan 14; a meal of the paschal lamb, matzah, bitter herbs (*maror*) and a pasty mixture of fruit, nuts and wine called *kharoset;* a cup of wine following the post-meal grace; and for those who had eaten the actual paschal lamb (in Jerusalem only), chanting of *Hallel* (Psalms of Praise, 113–118).

AFTER THE FALL

Like all other aspects of Jewish worship, the paschal sacrifice and everything connected with it had to be reevaluated once the Temple was destroyed in 70 CE (SEE CHAPTER ON TISHA B'AV). Of the biblical commandments for observance, only the prohibition of leavening remained possible. Though now truly *Khag Hamatzot,* the festival retained the name Pesakh (for the passing over), although the *pesakh* (paschal offering) could no longer be made, and became a home ceremony featuring the story of ancient slavery and salvation. That story served as a model for the fight to liberate Jerusalem from Roman occupation in the next century, and in following generations, for the struggle to maintain Jewish life.

As if to bolster their own hopes, the sages elaborated on the number of miracles God performed for the Israelites in Egypt and emphasized the moral significance of the holiday. To commemorate their importance, the paschal sacrifice and its accompaniments appeared on the Passover table in symbolic form, and the typical two cups of wine for festive meals was doubled so one would fall at each of key points in the ceremony. Detailed formalized responses to the Seder's questions began to be set down, and expressions of thanksgiving were added, along with the proclamation that every Jew, in every generation, was to feel that s/he had personally experienced the Exodus.

Rabbi Gamaliel, the first-century sage, expanded the story beyond the events of Nissan 14 to include all the wonders and miracles of the entire Exodus. He issued the famous dictum included in the written version of the Seder, that "He who does not stress these three rituals on Passover does not fulfill his obligations: pesakh, matzah and *maror*." The three questions became four and were periodically changed in order to reflect altered aspects of the ritual and remain a challenge to children. Specific political developments were reflected in additions, such as interjection of a prayer for a brighter future by Rabbi Akiva. The sage who died a martyr in the second-century Hadrianic persecutions felt that the existing prayer thanking God for the great light of freedom and redemption was incongruous with reality for the Jews living in the shadow of Rome.

Commentary, analysis and legend were added to embellish the meaning of the Passover story throughout editing of the Mishnah (the written version of the Oral Law, second century) and development of the Talmud (commentaries on the Mishnah, fifth century) with its tractate devoted to the laws and stories of Pesakh (Pesakhim, paschal lambs).

Since Pesakh Sheni (called Minor Passover in Mishnah) was instituted strictly to allow for sacrifice to be made, absence of the Temple obviated its need. For symbolic commemoration, a prayer of supplication was taken out of the daily service. The sages determined that the period of the Omer, however, seen as a link between Pesakh and Shavuot, should still be counted, even though the offerings that marked its start and end had been eliminated. It became a period of semi-mourning, when weddings, haircuts and playing of musical instruments were prohibited (except for on the new moons of Iyar and Sivan, which fall within it, and its thirty-third day [SEE CHAPTER ON LAG B'OMER]).

During the early Talmud period (second century), one new observance was added: the fast of the firstborn. The only fast limited to a segment of the community, it is attributed to Rabbi Judah Hanasi (redactor of the Mishnah),

15

who fasted on this day. Ironically, some say that although a firstborn son, he did not forsake food in commemoration of or appreciation for Israel's firstborn having been spared when the tenth plague claimed Egyptian lives. He simply had a weak constitution and wanted to save his appetite for the anticipated Seder meal! Thus can customs be born.

MIDDLE AGES TO MODERNITY

Discussions among the sages continued for centuries until the content and format of the Seder became relatively established and universally accepted. By the eleventh century, the text—a combination of biblical passages, material from midrash, and liturgical poems—was virtually the one we use today, and in the next century appeared in a separate publication called the Haggadah.

Jews in the Medieval European ghettos loved Pesakh, finding in the events of the past inspiration and eternal hope for the future. Unfortunately, the joyous anticipation generated by the approach of the holiday gave way to abject terror beginning in the latter part of the Middle Ages with the spread of malicious blood libels at Passover time because of its proximity in date to Easter. The first accusation, in Norwich, England, in 1144, maintained that the Jews had killed a Christian child in a repeat of the crucifixion of Jesus.

The ridiculous and slanderous lie, enhanced with the claim that the murdered child's blood was needed for the baking of matzah, spread throughout Europe, inciting murderous rampages against innocent Jews. Christians in Arab lands in the nineteenth century, American anti-Semites and Nazis in the twentieth kept alive the lie that resurfaced in post-Soviet Russia and in the Arab world after failure of the Oslo "peace" process.

The sad reality inspired fictional accounts, the best-known being Heinrich Heine's *The Rabbi of Bacherach,* and Bernard Malamud's *The Fixer,* based on the 1911 Jacob Beilis case in Russia, which also served as background for Sholom Aleichem's *The Bloody Hoax.* (The 1994 book *The Beilis Transcripts: The Anti-Semitic Trial That Shook the World,* edited by Ezekiel Leikin, deals with the court proceedings.) The legendary Golem, the clay automaton said to have been created by Rabbi Judah Loew of Prague (the Maharal) in the late sixteenth century, existed primarily to guard the community against attacks spurred by the false charges.

Despite the threats, the Jews never ceased observing Pesakh, believing with the indomitable faith for which we are famous (and despised) that the story needed to be told, and deriving renewed strength from it. The only major change was the addition, between the fourteenth and sixteenth centuries, of a number of songs following the service, although these were not universally adopted.

The messages of Passover continued to inspire oppressed Jews throughout the world. Based on the description of Passover in the prophetic books of the Bible to which they had access in the Christian version, the Marranos (hidden Spanish and Portuguese Jews forced to renounce Judaism during the fifteenth-century Inquisition and their descendants) continued to observe Passover. Jews in the Warsaw ghetto observed a modified Seder on *Erev Pesakh* 1943, the night of the start of the ill-fated heroic uprising. Even concentration camp inmates somehow scrounged the barest essentials and prayed for the deliverance of their people and vanquishing of their oppressors.

In the post-World War II era, the theme of freedom became linked with the fate of displaced, Soviet, Ethiopian and other endangered communities of Jews for whose liberation we prayed and worked. It is no coincidence that the most famous of the ships bringing refugees to Palestine after the War was named *Exodus '47*, and the powerful metaphor was used to name the dramatic clandestine airlift that brought close to ten thousand Ethiopian Jews to Israel in 1984–85 (Operation Moses), and the campaign to fund immigration and settlement of Jews from the former Soviet Union (Operation Exodus).

With its universal messages of freedom from oppression for all people, and its particularistic promises of protection for the people of Israel, Passover remains the most observed holiday among Diaspora Jews.

FOR FURTHER EXPLORATION

Wiesel, Elie. *The Golem: The Story of a Legend.* Trans. by Anne Borchardt. New York: Summit Books, 1983. Full of wonder and mysticism, and enhanced by softly surreal pen and ink illustrations, the account weaves the background, accomplishments and legends about the Golem into the form of a legend itself. The warm and sometimes sad tale beautifully incorporates Jewish history, thought and religion. (There are many versions of "The Golem," published separately—or as part of story collections.)

What Does It Mean? Religious Importance
THE FOUNDATION OF JUDAISM

Yetziat Mitzrayim, the singular event commemorated by Passover, is nothing less than a defining element of Jewish thought and behavior. It set in motion the pattern for Jewish history, provided the foundation for the Jewish approach to the world, and established the agenda for Jewish national life. Its theme of exile and redemption is the leitmotif of our existence, its message of the absolute right and necessity to be free our core value.

So central are the Exodus and its lessons to Judaism that references to it recur throughout our Bible's accounts of history, and its laws, prophecies and prayers. The life of a traditional Jew is suffused with it not just once a year during an extended festival, but every single day. It is because God brought us out of Egypt that we are commanded to obey Him regarding our two-way relationship, ritual observances and ethical behavior. Among Torah passages enclosed inside the tefillin put on by Jewish men each weekday morning are those pertaining to the Exodus (EXODUS 13:1–10, 11–16). Daily services include recitation of the song sung by the Israelites after crossing the Reed Sea (*Shira* [EXODUS 15:1–18]) and a prayer covering the past, and hoped-for future, redemption. And the fact that the Sabbath, the once-a-week respite from the servitude of the workweek, memorializes the Exodus (DEUTERONOMY 5:15) elucidates the meaning of Creation, which the Sabbath also commemorates (EXODUS 20:11): Both the world and the liberated Israelite nation were brought forth with specific Divine purpose.

Even the calendar design reminds us of the Exodus. Torah emphasizes that Nissan, the month of *nissim* (miracles)—and not Tishrei, when the world was created (SEE CHAPTER ON ROSH HASHANAH)—is to head the year (EXODUS 12:2). The rabbis support its position by breaking down its designation as the month of *aviv* (springtime), into *av* (father), *iv* ([of the] twelve [months], the second part being an abbreviation for twelve, its Hebrew letter yud [׳] having the numerical value of ten, and vet [ב] of two).

Just as the earth comes to life again after being constrained by the nature of winter, Israel was renewed. The original naming of months reflected the notion that being reborn with purpose is much more significant than merely coming into existence: As we count the progression of the week with reference to its

18

most important day (Sunday is the First Day [toward Shabbat], Monday is the Second Day [toward Shabbat], etc.), the Bible numbers months beginning with Nissan.

THE JEWISH NOTION OF FREEDOM

Had God simply liberated the Israelites from Egyptian oppression, the former slaves would have been a certain ethnic group lucky enough to have had a great-great-grandfather who recognized God's existence, another nation among many. Merely released from the darkness and confinement of bondage into light and lack of restraint, they could have run rampant without direction, expressing pent up frustration and lashing out at anything in their path.

On the day the Israelites were taken out of Egypt, Moses reminded them to remember it. Later, when they reached Canaan, they were to eat matzah, get rid of leaven, and tell their children, "It is because of this that God acted for me when I left Egypt" (EXODUS 13:3–8). The sages ask what "for this" means. For the fact that they cried out in anguish? For their suffering? For the pleasure of eating unleavened bread?

SERVICE TO GOD Although our God is a merciful God (EXODUS 34:6), He did not take the Israelites out from under Egyptian oppression merely to end their suffering and restore control over their lives to individual inclination. From the time God sent Moses back from Midian to confront Pharaoh, He made it clear that He wanted the Israelites to show their appreciation for His benevolence of leading them from the house of bondage to the Land of milk and honey.

The two Torah words generally used for freedom, *khofesh* and *deror,* are not applied to the Exodus. Both imply lack of restraint, complete self-determination, a misconception of freedom prevalent in an undisciplined society like America today. This is a kind of liberty that in the end can enslave you to whims and desires that have a way of leading you from what you really want. (While you are free to eat anything you would like, don't you really want to control your weight?)

The Israelites, however, were given *kherut,* freedom to live a certain kind of life, one according to God's system of discipline. It was summarized in the Ten Commandments engraved (*kharut*) on the two tablets of stone that were to be given at the conclusion of the Passover experience, at Mount Sinai (SEE CHAPTER ON SHAVUOT). The sages equate the two—liberty (*kherut*) and the engraving of the law (*kharut*): "Only he is free who occupies himself with Torah" (PIRKEI AVOT 6:2). Rabbi Levi Isaac of Berditchev saw a reflection of the reciprocal relationship between Liberator/Lawgiver and liberated/law abiders in the dual names of the holiday. Israel called it Passover, he said, in recognition of God's mercy in redeeming them. And God called it Feast of Unleavened Bread as a compliment to Israel, who would carefully follow the commandments surrounding it.

The Jewish concept of freedom means the unrestrained ability to have a relationship with God, show obedience to Him and to accept Torah, which sets the Jew on the path in life that will allow him/her to fulfill his/her role in the overall plan for the world. The only way to be free to worship God is to be free of an earthly master. There is a universe of difference between being a servant (*ehved*) of Pharaoh and a servant—like Moses—of God (*ehved l'Elohim*). Under human oppressors, those held in bondage labor for the aggrandizement of others. Under God, we can choose obligations aimed at benefit for all.

That is why Judaism abhors slavery. No Jew is to be owned, not even by another Jew. If a Hebrew had to enslave him/herself to someone else, in the case of indebtedness, for instance, it was for a limited period of time (all debts were forgiven in Sabbatical years—every seventh; all lands reverted to original owners in Jubilee years—every fiftieth, to keep a socio-economic balance in the society and prevent development of a serf or landless class). Such was the radical value transformation the Exodus accomplished: no longer were power considered good and weakness bad, but caring and pity good and humiliation, domination and repression bad. "There shall be one law for the citizen and for the slave that dwells among you" (EXODUS 12:49). (A servant had to be treated so well the rabbis observed that one who acquired a servant acquired a master for himself!)

A servant who refused liberty at the end of his term had his ear pierced, a symbol of shame that he had not heard God's declaration of independence for all children of Israel. The piercing was done against a doorpost, recalling the site the Israelites smeared with lamb's blood to indicate their readiness to abandon their life of slavery.

Since they are not free to choose their Master (God), slaves may not recite the *Shema,* the Jewish declaration of faith in One God: A person in bondage to another lord is not at liberty to accept God's sovereignty. (The Haggadah reminds us that the degradation experienced by our ancestors was not just slavery in Egypt, but the idol worship—a lack of recognition and negation of God—that preceded it.)

Prior to the Exodus, there existed a Jewish nation, a distinct ethnic group that distinguished itself, midrash tells us, by maintaining the names, dress and language of their ancestors. But they were not given Torah until they had forsaken their human masters (by preparing the paschal lambs), made a commitment to heed God's commandments (by following the instructions for Nissan 14), and been led out of Egypt (the place—physical and psychological—limiting their lives).

RESPECTING OTHERS Although we must not be slaves, we are also commanded, repeatedly, not to ever forget we were slaves. The danger of liberty is that once given control, the formerly oppressed can take advantage of their new positions to wield power over others. How often in history have liberation movements, once achieving their immediate aims (toppling the existing structure), succeeded only in establishing a new tyranny (Church Reformation, French Revolution, Bolshevik Revolution, overthrow of the Iranian Shah, the Taliban . . .)?

The Israelites were to retain the humility of their former lives (the hallmark of the authentic Jewish personality, khutzpah notwithstanding) in order to remain sensitive to the plight of others. We treat servants like guests, provide food for widows, orphans and strangers, are kind to foreigners, use honest weights and measures in our business dealings, help the poor and do not act with prejudice—particularly toward the disadvantaged—precisely because we were slaves in Egypt. In three dozen of Torah's social laws we are instructed to take certain action based on our early experiences: the hurt we suffered was to teach us to refrain from inflicting pain on others. Our entire religion, summarized by Hillel as "do not do to others that which is hateful to you" is drawn directly from our experience as slaves. (You were slaves, you didn't like the humiliation, whippings, restrictions, so don't degrade, torture or oppress others.)

Judaism's new concept of freedom and unmatched standard of social ethics was designed to create a just balance in a world that seems to thrive on injustice. If realized, this system would revolutionize the world in ways no liberation movement since the Egyptian Exodus has even approximated. Its unique legislation—which gave the world such concepts as life, liberty, the pursuit of happiness, tolerance and the six-day work week—governs virtually every aspect of a Jew's personal life and his/her relations to the world: political, legal, ethical, spiritual, environmental, economic. It makes provisions against homelessness and corruption of courts, and for monetary retribution, ensuring the dignity of every human being, inclusion within a community, rehabilitation of criminals, and separation of power in government.

They are laws meant to liberate all people from physical, spiritual, psychological, emotional and economic oppression. For only the release of all peoples from such restraints will allow God's grand scheme for the world to be fulfilled. And Jews, with our unique heritage, have a particular responsibility to safeguard the freedom of others and to work for the freedom of those enslaved.

PAST AS PROLOGUE—AND PROTOTYPE

Only from dire circumstances would the Jews have followed Moses and God. Having been removed from them served as a reminder that no matter how terrible our situation, we must not lose hope, that there is some ultimate purpose to it: You can live through anything if you know it is not forever. The Exodus demonstrates that our suffering is in fact finite, that in exile we can expect deliverance and renewal.

The message began with the design of the very first Seder, a model for perpetual hope for the future. Not a typical celebration of independence, taking place after the fact, it was held while the Israelites were still in bondage, with the expectation that something momentous was about to happen, the belief that the promise of liberation would be fulfilled. Many generations later, the exiled Jews believed that the nation would be revived, that Jerusalem would be rebuilt—because they had an established pattern for the suffering-then-salvation sequence.

"Now we are here, next year may we observe Passover in the Land of Israel, now we are still enslaved, next year may all men be free" (HAGGADAH) has rung true in every age. The belief that the words would eventually become reality has made it possible for Jews to observe Passover without becoming discouraged no matter what the horrendous situation outside their doors. It remains the inspiration for today, when, separated from the ideal we are supposed to be creating in the world, we remain in exile (*galut*). As much as it commemorates the redemption already executed, Passover celebrates the redemption expected (*Geulah*).

MESSIANIC REDEMPTION Belief that, just as God sent Moses as His servant to redeem us once, a descendant of the House of David will arise as the *moshiakh* (messiah) is a tenet of classical Judaism. It is one of Maimonides' Thirteen Articles of Faith—central beliefs to which every Jew must ascribe—that the redemption will occur: "I believe with a perfect faith in the coming of the messiah and though he may tarry, daily I wait for his coming."

By the second century BCE two concepts of a "messiah" who/which would rescue Israel and return it to former glory had developed. One focused on a human leader—the personal messiah—who would emerge from among the Jews, guide us to independence and bring the world to accept God. (The word *moshiakh* in Hebrew is derived from *mashakh*, which simply means "to anoint," as to anoint a king, who was supposed to remain faithful to the law of God). The other foresaw a series of cosmic cataclysmic events that would destroy Israel's enemies and world evil and initiate a period of peace—the messianic age—in which the world would be perfected.

Debate over the "true messiah" concept has continued through numerous crises in our history, including the emergence of false messiahs (most notably Shabbatai Zvi in the seventeenth century), and controversy in our own time over the Lubavitcher Rebbe Menachem Mendel Schneerson, some of whose followers, believing him to be *Moshiakh*, urged him to reveal himself as such, and continued to identify him as Messiah even after his death in 1994.

Kabbalists of the sixteenth and seventeenth centuries promoted the concept, later enthusiastically embraced by the Reform movement, that we ourselves, through our efforts to perfect the world (*tikkun olam*), would bring messianic redemption. The Khabad Lubavitch Khassidim, whose wide-ranging outreach programs aim at bringing as many Jews as possible back into the fold of Jewish observance, believe this will happen by following the commandments of Torah. According to the ultra-Orthodox *Neturei Karta* (Defenders of the Faith, who do not recognize the existence of the State of Israel), only an act of God will accomplish it.

By whatever means and in whatever form, belief in a redeeming force and attempts to see it realized are very much a part of our tradition. Its power remains in the fact that the arrival of the messiah has always been seen as a future occurrence, a source for hope and—as the legendary Eastern European Jew stationed outside his village to greet the messiah found—steady work. Most of all, the undying anticipation fostered the eternal optimism that eventually things can, and will, improve, for the Jewish people and the entire world.

FOR FURTHER EXPLORATION

Schneerson, Menachem M. et al. *From Exile to Redemption: Chassidic Teachings of the Lubavitcher Rebbe.* Ed. by Eli Friedman and Jill Eliyahu Hammer. Brooklyn: Kehot Publication Society, 1998.

> This anthology of classic teachings of the last Lubavitcher Rebbe and earlier leaders of the Khabad Lubavitch Khassidim provides insights into the purpose of exile, the role of the individual Jew in ending it, and signs of redemption in our generation.

What Does It Mean to Us? Personal Significance

SELF-LIBERATION

The Haggadah instructs that each of us ("In every generation. . .") is actually supposed to feel as though we had been slaves and made the transition to a new status. How can we do this—take ancient history and make it into my story and your story?

We who live in an open democratic society tend to think of ourselves as free. But are we really, just because we are not physically bound to an overlord? What do being enslaved and unencumbered by oppression really mean? And are they mutually exclusive?

In Hebrew, Egypt is called *Mitzrayim.* According to the text on Jewish mysticism, the Zohar, the name is derived from *m'tzarim,* narrow straits (*mi,* "from," *tzar,* "narrow or tight"). When God took us out of *Mitzrayim,* He extricated us from the place of constricted opportunities, tight control, narrow-mindedness where movement was severely limited.

Each of us lives in his or her own *mitzrayim*, the external or physical narrow straits of financial or health constraints or personal tragedy, perhaps; universally the psychological burdens to which we subject ourselves. Like the duality in virtually all of Pesakh's symbols (SEE "OBSERVANCE"), they work in two ways: They turn us into both slaves and oppressors, of ourselves and of others. Passover leads us to question the values and attitudes we hold—and which hold us to those roles (Do we pursue, even worship, things like money and status for their own sake, rather than for how they can make our lives and the lives of those around us, better? Do our own insecurities or overconfidence inhibit us from fully participating in life rather than getting the most out of relationships? Do our stereotyping, prejudice or exploitation oppress other people by robbing them of their dignity rather than affording them the same opportunities we want for ourselves?)

As we get rid of leaven and replace it with matzah, we are supposed to confront whatever it is that we normally allow to persist in our lives, but which should perhaps, like the leaven, be eliminated, and that which we suppress that should, like the back-to-basics unleavened bread, be admitted. (Do you work to live or live to work? Do you play for enjoyment or to avoid having to think? Are you unhappy in a situation but so entrenched in it that you have come to accept it as the norm—as *acceptable?* Does an addiction to food, alcohol, drugs, a pattern of behavior or another person interfere with leading the life you really want for yourself? Do you allow others to take advantage of your time and resources?) Lack of restraint on anything we may want to do, routinely indulging our impulsive desires, following societal fads are not freedom, but slavery. True freedom is the exercise of free will for positive, meaningful development.

Pharaoh is seen as the evil enslaver of others. But he was bound by his own ego, which led him to ruin everything he valued, along with himself. Even his officials recognized the catastrophe his attitude brought: "Let the men go," they advised. "Don't you realize that Egypt is being destroyed?" (EXODUS 10:7). His arrogance simply got in the way.

In order to take the necessary action, we need to believe that things must change for our own good. When we do, we, like Pharaoh, make vows to change. But often, once an immediate need has passed, we, like Pharaoh giving and taking away permission to leave, revert to old habits. In the long run, we only hurt ourselves. One lesson of the Omer period (SEE "OBSERVANCE") is how easy it is to slide back into familiar ways. (Look at former USSR countries that within months of gaining democratic freedoms elected ousted communist leaders to govern them. Look at the ancient Israelites who not a week out of Egypt were ready to give up liberty and go back to their miserable lives—yearning for the comfort of the familiar evil over fear of the unknown.)

Slavery does offer a certain freedom that can be attractive: the freedom from responsibility for yourself and others, the freedom from having to establish goals, figure out how to reach them or think beyond the moment. It takes strength and guts to walk out of a known situation, which for all its pain is predictable. It is human nature to want to stay put, within the stability of the status quo. The danger is that often we don't even know we are mired in a negative situation, one we don't recognize until too late.

We tell ourselves we will look for a better job, start performing community service, be much nicer to our kids, get out of an abusive relationship, go back go school, pay off our contribution pledges . . . tomorrow. Jacob did not intend to stay in Egypt more that a short time—and look what his sojourning cost. At Passover, we should at least recognize inertia for what it is and not kid ourselves into complacency about our own situation, or that of people in unfortunate circumstances who can use our help.

Passover, with its message of hope, tells us that like the Egyptian slaves, we can liberate ourselves from our oppressive straits, we can refuse to allow oppressors, internal or external, to define us: This is the mentality of the free person. Once they had tasted freedom with the paschal lamb, the Israelites gave up the comfort of the familiar, without concern for provisions, or how they would get to or exist at their destination. They left Egypt because they believed a better life awaited them elsewhere. As Rabbi Nahman of Bratslav (eighteenth-century Khassidic leader) counseled, when you are about to leave *"mitzrayim"* you should not worry about how you will manage in a new "place." Anyone who does or who stops to get everything in order for the journey will never pick him/herself up.

As we begin the Seder with a broken, incomplete piece of matzah (SEE "OBSERVANCE"), we are encouraged to take the first steps toward change even if all the pieces are not in place. We cannot wait until the time is perfect. The European Jews in the pre-War years, who were concerned about losing property, did not recognize this. The Ethiopian Jews, at the time of Operations Moses and Solomon, who did not yet have the new clothes they had dreamed of wearing for their entry into Jerusalem, did.

A midrash tells that when the Israelites stood at the Reed Sea, the Egyptians at their backs, they wailed and moaned and longed for the taskmaster's whip rather than the lash of the sea's raging waves. They hesitated. Moses prayed. And one man, Nakhshon ben Amminadab, recognizing the opportunity before them, plunged into the waters. Only then did the sea subside, allowing the Israelites to continue. Like Nakhshon

> *The home is the first line of defense.*
>
> HENRIETTA SZOLD

ben Amminadab, we have to forge ahead, with faith that we will reach the goal—and belief that even the attempt to gain freedom is worth any effort taken to end passive stagnation in slavery.

Passover also reminds us that the process does not stop if we are comfortable with our own progress or situation, with the good fortune of our families. An important aspect of this holiday is recognition of the needs of others. Just as God helped liberate us, people enslaved today need outside assistance to become free. We have been extremely successful in rescuing Soviet and Ethiopian Jews and helping numerous other communities. It is sickening to learn that, according to a United Nations Center of Human Rights report, at least half—*half!*—the world's population in the last decade of the twentieth century lived under social, cultural, economic and political oppression. And according to London-based Anti-Slavery International, at least twenty-seven million people—many of them children—exist in situations of outright bondage *today,* well into the twenty-first century. In some parts of the world the problem is actually on the rise.

Rather than allowing ourselves to become inured to the evidence of suffering daily coming into our homes via the media and charitable organization solicitations, we should use Passover to recharge our sensitivities, which, if the message of the holiday has any impact, should lead us to action.

FOSTERING A SENSE OF BELONGING

As the anniversary of the birth of the Jewish people, Passover is a perfect time to reflect on what it means to be Jewish. You might ask yourself, and your children, on a scale of one to ten, how important is being Jewish to you? Why? What do you like or not like about being Jewish? If your child, sibling or friend said s/he planned to raise children without instilling in them a Jewish identity, how would you react? Most importantly, how would you help them discover the beauty, value and imperative of perpetuating our heritage?

"In each generation" echoes a recurring refrain in Judaism: *l'dor vador,* from generation to generation, the slogan of the continuity we consider crucial. It is quite significant that we begin the annual festival cycle by passing the tradition to our children in an important family holiday that takes place at home. While we are personally experiencing the Exodus, our job is also to make our children feel that they are a part of the story, able to identify with the Exodus and with the Jewish people.

This is a difficult task, particularly for those of us who, like the generations born in Canaan, did not experience the rigors of slavery and the miracles of salvation (mirrored in our time by the Holocaust and the establishment of Israel), who abandoned (or were not exposed to) our parents' tradition and Torah, who have been diverted by omnipresent influences of the prevailing culture.

But it is not an impossible task, because Jewish identity is established within the family, where feelings of freedom/responsibility, and a sense of belonging to something greater than the individual self are fostered. With Pesakh, we don't just recall the story of what happened to other people long ago. We relive it, as though we did experience the travails of Exodus at the time, and also through our own personal struggles, through what is happening in the community and the world around us. What causes someone to feel part of the community is largely based on what happens in the home—the stories told, the songs sung, the symbols used. What could be a better opportunity to begin to shape that Jewish identity than Passover, with its drama, music and representational food?

Judaism turns those symbols into reality (the bread of affliction transformed into the bread of freedom leads to freedom itself). The process necessitates our being knowledgeable about what the symbols and the national goals are. Avraham Infeld, the Jewish-Zionist educator, makes the point beautifully. "Being

Jewish means allowing Jewish history to make a claim on your life, to turn the collective memory of the people into a personal account. There can be no future without vision. There can be no vision if we are incapable of dreaming, and one who has no memories cannot dream." (To transmit memory, some people include on their Seder tables objects that belonged to beloved relatives, and encourage connections with the past by talking about the people who owned them and their stories, which can provide ties to family and national history.)

If we teach our children so they feel that they are part of our nation, they will be able to participate in the enterprise built on the memories (Exodus) that inspire the dream (redemption) that supports the vision (universal freedom) that fosters the efforts toward making the vision reality (perfected world). We draw on the past in order to build for a better future, like the desert generation who had to give up their former way of life so their children could occupy the Land of Milk and Honey.

Traditions—

HOW WE CELEBRATE PESAKH

What Do We Use? Ritual Items

HAGGADAH

The printed version of the Seder service, the Haggadah is a collection of Bible passages, Talmudic narrative, Second Temple supplications, *piyyutim* (liturgical poems) of the Middle Ages, prayers and readings in response to persecutions of those and recent years, and folk songs. In the words of Heinrich Heine (in *The Rabbi of Bacherach*), it is "a marvelous mixture of age-old legends, miracles of the Exodus, curious discussions, prayers and festive songs."

The word *haggadah,* from the verb *l'haggid* to tell, is derived from the Torah verse commanding "and you shall tell [*l'higadeta*] it to your child on that day" (EXODUS 13:8). The choice of verb indicates that our responsibility is not merely to recite the story, but to use it to inform and instruct. Haggadah is also related to the homiletic sayings (the stories, parables, tales) from midrash—called *aggadot* (plural of *aggadah*)—used to teach Seder participants about the history of redemption.

Since the late Middle Ages, when the Haggadah first appeared as a publication separate from the common prayer book, more than thirty-five hundred versions have been created, some of them magnificently illustrated. Illuminated editions such as the Birds Head, Damstadt, Golden and Sarajevo haggadot provide a record of Jewish social life (costumes, professions) and attitudes (as in the style of representation of the Four Sons [SEE "OBSERVANCE"]), and have contributed greatly to the development of Jewish art. (Facsimile editions are sometimes available.) The text has also been illuminated by hundreds of commentaries, which since the fifteenth century have included philosophical, theological and mystical discussions of the Haggadah's contents.

In the last century alone, hundreds of editions have been produced, not only in response to particular artists' creative impulses, but also to the developing diversity among the Jewish people. Since the days of Rabbi Akiva (second century CE), the Haggadah—never meant to be stagnant—has also functioned as an instrument for addressing reality and inspiring change; contemporary versions continue the tradition of focusing on given social and political conditions in the world. Today it is possible to use a facsimile edition of one of the historic illuminated haggadot, a Haggadah representing the philosophy of a particular movement in Judaism (Orthodox, Conservative, Reform, Reconstructionist), social-political philosophy or concern (egalitarian, feminist, secular, Holocaust, contemporary war/oppression), dietary preference (vegetarian, including the wonderfully titled *Haggadah for the Liberated Lamb*), and even national culture.

They come in Hebrew only, in Hebrew and English or any other vernacular language of Jews, and Braille, sometimes with transliterations of major segments. Illustrations range from comic book to museum quality featuring the work of modern Jewish artists such as Yaakov Agam, Leonard Baskin, Ben Shahn, Shalom of Safed, and Marc Chagall. Contemporary commentators include Elie Wiesel and Rabbi Shlomo Riskin.

In any year, you'll find a number of haggadot designed for children, featuring various approaches to the text, forms of illustration—and sometimes favorite puppet or animated characters.

CHOOSING AND USING While the old wine-stained haggadot with the antique etchings and archaic language used in some families for generations may hold sentimental value, and the food company giveaways may be appealing for their price, do yourself—and everyone else at your Seder table—a favor by having at least one Haggadah that contains commentary. A good commentary not only explains how to perform a ritual and what it means, but provides insights as to the deeper significance of parts of the service, including how to apply them to your own situation and time. The purpose of the Seder is to inspire identification with the experience and its messages. It is supposed to be an enriching, exhilarating experience, which may be difficult to achieve if you have to deal with a leaden unannotated script. The Haggadah can serve as the jumping off point for topical discussion; a good one will give you a little push.

Each person at the table ideally has his or her own copy. When they are all the same, it is easier for everyone to keep his or her place (page numbers and English translations vary). With a variety of annotated editions, on the other hand, you have a wealth of resources and each participant can contribute interesting commentary from the one s/he uses.

Throughout the year, you can find a variety of haggadot via the Internet. A store that sells Jewish books and ritual items will have a wide selection of haggadot in the month prior to Passover. (Your library may also have several editions.) Probably the easiest way to find one you feel comfortable with is to review the numerous possibilities for style of translation, illustration, denominational orientation, underlying theme, and so on. (Some people compile their own haggadot from a combination of traditional and modern, religious and secular sources.)

FOR FURTHER EXPLORATION

With all the existing options, and additional haggadot being published each year, it is impossible to list even a fraction of popular and recommended choices. Here are a few. You'll find many others, especially the most recent versions, simply visiting a store or searching the Internet under haggadot. Also on the Internet: resources like the Hagadah Heritage Project (www.hagadah.com), where you can share cherished aspects of your family's Sedarim and get lots of ideas from others.

FOR ADULTS

Apisdorf, Shimon. *The Survival Kit Family Haggadah*. Baltimore: Leviathan Press, 1997.
Part of the marvelous "Survival series" that makes Judaism relevant and enjoyable, this Haggadah is designed for those who would prefer their Seder without a religious service. It's funny, informative, and full of interesting and inspiring ways to facilitate discussion. (The companion Passover Survival Kit provides more ammunition for making the Seder an unforgettable experience.)

Moss, David. *The Moss Haggadah*. Rochester, NY: Bet Alpha Editions, 1990.
A facsimile of the Haggadah created for a private commission of 1980, and based on years of research and detailed work, this magnificent modern illumination illustrates basic themes of Judaism and Jewish history in novel and emotionally and intellectually stimulating ways. Considered one of the most important and beautiful Haggadot ever created, it includes a page-by-page commentary by the artist.

Zion, Noam, and David Dishon. *Different Night: The Family Participation Haggadah*. Jerusalem: Shalom Hartman Institute, 1997.
This is a fabulously full, innovative, creative inspiring choice. It supplements the traditional text with lots of material (games, questions, readings, discussion suggestions) to make the Seder meaningful and memorable for adults and children alike. A companion leader's guide is also available.

The Jewish Braille Institute of America offers several editions of the Haggadah in Braille, large print or talking books. All are free (110 East 30 Street, New York, NY 10016; 212–889–2525, 1-800-433-1531; www.jblibrary.org).

FOR CHILDREN, FAMILIES

Oren, Rony. *The Animated Haggadah*. Secaucus, NJ: Carol Publishing Group, 1991.
Vibrant Claymation figures cleverly illustrate this children's version of the classic text. Large type, transliteration of Hebrew and the charm and humor of the illustrations are sure to grab children's attention. It includes a couple of pages of suggestions for parents and teachers to use to initiate discussion (added after the original 1985 edition), and is available in a thirty-minute videotape. All ages.

Schecter, Ellen. *The Family Haggadah*. New York: Viking Penguin Children's Books, 1999.
The simple service and significant storytelling help encourage participation by all family members.

Silverman, Shoshana. *A Family Haggadah*. Rockville, MD: Kar-Ben Copies, Inc., 1987.
To be used on its own or with a standard Haggadah, this one combines tradition and innovation to expand on the text with questions, songs, crafts and games. The companion cassette, "Songs for a Family Seder"—make it easy to use, particularly for those with little Jewish background. Volume 1 is for children under ten years of age, Volume 2 for those older.

Stein, Larry. *The Really Fun Family Haggadah*. Deerfield, IL: Ruach Publishing, 2002.
Educational and entertaining, the Haggadah includes all the steps, explanations of the traditions, amusing multiple-choice questions, and a thirty-minute version of the Seder for those who just can't sit still longer.

Wark, Mary Ann Barrows. *We Tell It To Our Children: The Story of Passover, A Haggadah for Seders with Young Children*. St. Paul, MN: Mensch Makers Press, 1988.
Using puppetry, amusing and Judaically meaningful lyrics for well-known American folk tunes, and many illustrations, this innovative and fun presentation of the Exodus story and world Jewry easily involves everyone—pre-school through adult—in the Seder. It comes in leader (with nine realistic cut-out paper puppets) and guest editions.

See also *Building a Jewish Life/Haggadah* (Grishaver) and *My Very Own Haggadah* (Groner and Wikler) in "More Good Information" at the end of this book.

MATZAH

Unleavened bread was one of the foods the Jews in Egypt were commanded to eat along with the paschal lamb (EXODUS 12:8). In commemoration of that first Seder meal, and the haste in which the Israelites left Egypt, giving them no time to allow their bread to rise, we eat matzah at the Seder (and instead of bread throughout the holiday).

It is customary to have three pieces stacked on the table. Two are traditional for Sabbath and festivals (when we usually use two khallot), as a reminder of the double portion of manna (food from heaven) the Israelites gathered before every day of rest in the desert (EXODUS 16:11–22). We need the third to break at the beginning of the service (SEE YAKHATZ UNDER "OBSERVANCE").

The number is also said to hold symbolic significance. Among other things, the three recall the three measures of fine meal from which Sarah baked cakes for her husband Abraham's three angelic visitors (GENESIS 18:6), represent the three categories of Jews—Kohein, Levi, and Yisraeli—that make up the Jewish people, or the three patriarchs, Abraham, Isaac and Jacob, by whose merit we were redeemed from Egypt and whose covenant with God we were redeemed to fulfill.

In recent years, it has become popular to add an additional sheet of matzah, representing hope for Jews still enslaved by oppression around the world.

MEANING Matzah is one of those wonderful transcendent ritual items in Judaism, a symbol embodying a duality to teach a moral lesson. At the beginning of the Seder, we break one of the cakes of matzah and call it the bread (*lekhem*) of affliction (*oni*). It is the meager sustenance of slaves, the meanest fare of the poor, the quickly produced food of those who make a hurried, under-cover-of-dark getaway. Yet later, it represents freedom, the bread we ate when we were liberated from Egyptian bondage.

In both situations, as slaves in Egypt and once we were free, we ate the same flat wafers. What was different was our own attitude when we ate: cowering, accepting our subservience, then claiming our rightful dignity as human beings equal before God. Just as we transform mentally and physically, the symbol of our status is transformed.

ACCEPTABLE FORMS For the Seder, we may use only matzah made of the pure and simple ingredients flour and water, prepared and baked in an oven of between six- and eight-hundred degrees in less than eighteen minutes. Any longer and the fermentation that causes leavening occurs. So important is it to avoid allowing the matzah to swell, each cake is perforated to let the steam escape (that's why each wafer has those rows of little holes). To teach us to remain vigilant in our responsibilities, it must be made from flour, which has the potential to become leavened if left unattended.

No egg, milk, honey, wine, fruit juice or other enhanced versions (called *matzah ashirah,* or rich) may be eaten, except by the sick or aged who cannot digest the basic recipe. Avoiding the enhanced matzah reminds us of the importance of simplicity, of returning to basics, which the plain flour and water matzah represents. (Some rabbinic authorities approve of eating *matzah ashirah* after the Sedarim.)

Until the mid-nineteenth century invention in Austria of the first matzah machine, the unleavened bread was baked by hand. The innovation sparked controversy over whether it could in fact produce matzah acceptable according to halakhah, since authorities feared that pieces of dough could get stuck in it and become leavened. Even after acceptance of the machine, matzah continued to be baked manually, often in communal ovens and bakeries set up just for the holiday. Said to represent the unity of God, the round matzot produced that way are still preferred by particularly tradition-minded Jews because of Torah's term for the matzah baked just before the Israelites left Egypt: *ugot* (round cakes [EXODUS 12:39]). Square matzot, the kind most of us use right out of the box, are perfectly acceptable.

The pious use the extra special handmade *matzah shmurah* (commonly said reversed, in Yiddish, *shmurah matzah*). Based on the commandment, "And you should keep [watch] the festival of the matzot" (EXODUS 12:17), the sages believed watching (*shimurim*) required supervising the matzah-making process from the time of reaping to ensure that no water, which initiates the leavening, comes into contact with the wheat, whole or ground, until it is mixed into dough and eighteen minutes are clocked. Made in round cakes, sometimes with unwanted ripples and burned edges, and often tasting even more like cardboard than the prepackaged variety, they are nevertheless coveted because of the attention and care that go into producing them. (Students can tour factories in communities such as Williamsburg, Brooklyn; Jewish Community Centers in other locales sometimes set up model matzah factories prior to the holiday.)

USE Embroidered, painted silk, and other special matzah covers containing three pockets, or special boxes to hold square or round matzot, can be purchased at Judaica stores or made, but are not necessary. A plate and a napkin for covering the matzot during the Seder are also acceptable.

If you have more than a few people at your Seder, you will need additional matzah to go around for the ritual foods eaten prior to the meal. It can be made directly accessible to guests, or placed near the leader, who will distribute it at the appropriate time.

K'ARAH AND ITS CONTENTS

The centerpiece of the table, the ceremonial plate, *k'arah*, contains essential ritual foods. It may be a specially designed platter with compartments, indentations, or separate dishes that fit on or into it, each identified for the item it holds. Made of wood, copper, pewter, silver, stoneware and porcelain, Seder plates of tremendous stylistic variety are available in Judaica stores (and sometimes, by manufactures such as Lenox, in department stores that sell fine china).

While our tradition encourages incorporating aesthetics into holiday observance, it is not necessary to purchase a fancy Seder plate. Children in a family, or an adult so inclined, may make one or you may arrange the foods on any plate or tray. (Many Sephardim traditionally use wicker baskets.) If you host a large Seder, you may want to have an additional *k'arah* or two so everyone will have access to it (originally, when celebrants reclined on individual sofas at individual tables, each person had his or her own), or place around the table dishes containing extra supplies of the foods that will be consumed.

Whatever *k'arah* you select, it contains the following:

KARPAS Derived from the Greek word for grass or vegetation, karpas is a vegetable or herb. Many of us were taught that karpas should be green, like nature's renewal in spring, to symbolize Israel's renewal through redemption during that season. Hence the tradition in many families of using parsley or celery. However, color is not in fact a criterion for karpas; potato was and remains the choice of Jews who originated in certain parts of Europe. Lettuce, endive, watercress, chervil, scallion, and carrots are also appropriate. As a special incentive for children, you can even use potato chips.

Near the *karpas,* though usually not on the plate itself, is a bowl of **SALT WATER**.

One often cited explanation for use of karpas is that read backwards, it forms the Hebrew word (*s*)*parak,* the term in the book of Exodus that describes the toil of the Israelites in Egypt, preceded by the letter designation for sixty. The number suggests both sixty types of physical labors the Egyptians forced on our ancestors, and the sixty myriad (six hundred thousand) slaves (or "six hundred thousand labored"). As victors of ancient battles were crowned with wreaths of laurel greens, the Seder greens represent our victory over enslavement.

There is also a simple historical explanation: Formal dinners of the Greco-Roman culture, the basis for our Seder, began with an hors d'oeuvre, customarily a vegetable, usually dipped in vinegar or wine—replaced by our salt water, which can be seen as a symbol of birth as well as of sweat and tears.

MAROR Bitter herbs (from the Hebrew *marah,* bitter), represent the nature of our lives under oppression. Grated horseradish, most commonly used among Ashkenazim, is just one of the acceptable bitter vegetables—and the *maror* of choice because there is no mistaking its message (it will instantly clear your sinuses). The sages also listed romaine lettuce, endive, chicory and escarole. They preferred, as do the Sephardim, the first, which they likened to Jewish settlement in Egypt: first sweet to the taste, only later is the bitterness realized. They also connected the word for lettuce (*khassa*) to God's having mercy (*khas*) on the Israelites and redeeming them.

KHAZERET Some people use another form of bitter herb, usually whole (pieces of horseradish root, for example) for the second time *maror* is eaten. The term relates to the Hebrew for return, in the sense of repentance (*khazarah*), and also to mercy (*khas*), signifying that when we take the initiative to turn to God (as the Israelites did in pledging their allegiance with the paschal lamb rite), He treats us mercifully.

Many Seder plates come without a separate section for *khazeret,* and it is common to use only one form of bitter herb.

KHAROSET A mixture of apples, nuts and wine, or other fruits and spices (particularly those mentioned in the Song of Songs—figs, dates, and pomegranates—because they serve as metaphors for Israel), *kharoset* stands for the mortar and clay (*khar'sit*) the Israelites had to use to make bricks and build Pharaoh's projects.

Almonds are often used in the mixture because their name in Hebrew (*shekeidim*) suggests that God was watchful (*shaked*) over Israel. Some add spices like cinnamon or ginger in pieces or strings to recall the straw the slaves had to collect to mix with the mortar. The color of the wine, added to make the mixture appropriately pasty, recalls the blood of the Israelite infants killed by Pharaoh, and of the first plague.

While symbolizing something terribly painful, this sweet, tasty concoction is one of the most popular items on the table. In many households, family members sit with spoons poised to dig into it as soon as its ritual use is complete. Associated by its dual nature with both physical oppression (clay) and sensual delight (taste, aroma), it suggests the bittersweetness of life and expresses Jewish optimism: Even the most negative condition can contain redeeming features.

Passing down the often unwritten formula for *kharoset,* individual families produce their own distinct flavors. You can find recipes in Passover and other Jewish cookbooks (SEE "TRADITIONAL FOODS").

Z'ROAH One of two symbols on the Seder plate we do not eat, the roasted shank bone representing the paschal sacrifice proclaims freedom of religion that the slaves seized when they slaughtered their lambs. It also recalls the "outstretched arm" (*z'roah netuyah*) of God that took us out of Egypt (DEUTERONOMY 26:8).

You can get the shoulder bone of any kosher animal, containing some meat, from a butcher, or, as many do, use the neck or wing of a chicken. It should be roasted dry, just as the paschal lamb was (but you do not need to do it over an open fire).

BEITZAH The egg, the other symbol we do not eat, reminds us of another part of the paschal offering, the *korban khaggigah* (festival sacrifice) required as an expression of thanksgiving at every festival. On Passover, pilgrims ate the *korban khaggigah* first, to satisfy their appetites, and finished their meals with the paschal lamb. We also put both meat and egg on the Seder plate to demonstrate our repudiation of the custom, followed by the Egyptians, of not eating any animal product because they worshipped the animals as gods. Some connect the egg with its Aramaic word, *beiyah,* meaning want or desire, implying God's desire to deliver His people.

The egg should be hardboiled, then scorched on a stove burner or under a broiler to resemble having been roasted. It remains in the shell.

ARRANGEMENT As with just about every other aspect of the Seder, there are different opinions as to how the plate should be organized, based on each authority's concept of not slighting the matzah, or any other item, by reaching over it before it has been used. Most people follow a modified version of the pattern established by the Ari (Rabbi Isaac Luria, leading kabbalist of sixteenth-century Safed).

At the center of the plate is *maror. Karpas* is below to the left, *khazeret* (if used) below it at the bottom of the plate, *kharoset* below to the right, the bone above the *maror* to the right, and the egg above to the left. We usually put the three matzot the Ari placed at the top of the plate separate from the *k'arah,* or under it, as the Vilna Gaon did: This is practically accomplished with a three-tiered combination matzah/Seder plate, with holders for the *k'arah* foods on top.

Together, the items on the *k'arah* reflect what has happened to Jews in every dispersion throughout our history. First we experience renewal and birth (*karpas*), and establish ourselves through labor (*kharoset*). Our lives become bitter (*maror*), we sweat and cry (salt water) under oppression (*khazeret*). Through sacrifice we are redeemed (*z'roah*) and we experience rebirth (*beitzah*).

KITTEL

The leader of the Passover ritual, who at his table, the substitute for the altar, acts in place of the Temple priest, traditionally wears a white robe (*kittel*) reminiscent of the vestments of the kohanim. It reminds us that the Seder is not just a family get-together, but also a sacred occasion. Lightweight, sometimes edged with gold or silver embroidery, and belted over one's slacks and shirt, the *kittel* was also worn by Israelites on festivals as an expression of joy and freedom.

In the Jewish mystical spectrum, white represents God's mercy and loving-kindness. (The special garment also recalls that the slaves preserved their Jewishness partly by keeping their traditional clothing, for which God looked kindly on them.) Carrying additional meanings when worn on Rosh Hashanah and Yom Kippur, on those days and this, as well as when donned by a father at his son's *brit milah* (covenant through circumcision) and bridegroom on his wedding day, it signifies a transition from one state of life to another.

Previously made by women for their husbands, the cotton wrap can be purchased where religious articles are sold. Today primarily more traditional Jews use them.

FOUR CUPS AND A FIFTH FOR ELIJAH

Each person at the table needs a glass (*kos*) for wine (*yayin*) or grape juice, as drinking four cups is required for every participant. Since spills are inevitable (what would Shabbat or a festival be without fresh wine stains on the tablecloth?), it is a good idea to place each wine goblet on a plate or into a shallow bowl, and/or to put an absorbent paper napkin or towel under it.

An additional wine glass, designated as Elijah's cup (*kos Eliyahu*), is placed on the table for use later in the service.

ADDITIONAL SEDER ITEMS

To fulfill the *mitzvah* to "recline" during the service as an expression of free-dom, PILLOWS are usually placed behind the leader, if not every guest. The custom developed from the origins of the Seder when festive meals were taken Greco-Roman freeman style on comfortable chaises.

Many people have SNACK ITEMS AND CANDY on hand to keep children occupied and attentive. CANDLES, long enough to burn throughout the Seder, are popular for adding a festive touch to the table. A PITCHER AND BASIN (or any pouring device and receptacle available) and towel for the handwashing rituals, and **KIPPOT** (skullcaps, or yarmulkes, in Yiddish) for all men present are also needed.

MEMORIAL CANDLE

On the evening before the *Yizkor* memorial service will be held in synagogue (the last day of pilgrimage festivals and Yom Kippur), anyone who has lost a parent customarily lights a yahrtzeit candle in memory of the deceased. Since these candles, which come in small cans or glasses, burn for twenty-five hours, they are also popular sources of fire for candlelighting and cooking done after a festival has begun (SEE "PREPARATION"). You can find them in Jewish supply stores and supermarkets that have kosher food sections.

How Do We Celebrate? Observance

Set within the home environment and focused on the family, the key to Jewish continuity, Passover serves as a model for observing a holiday and teaching the tradition. In fact, it is the most important domestic event of all Jewish festivals.

Despite the fact that it is the most labor-intensive, complicated, time-consuming and habit-altering holiday on the calendar, it has always been extremely popular. Its messages continue to resound with truth and encouragement, and it speaks even to religious skeptics on a very basic level. Those throughout the ages who had little concern for following the *mitzvot* have often celebrated Passover, in its fullness, at least for the benefit of their children. And despite the minutia of preparation, it was always celebrated with joy, fostering renewed confidence that whatever terrible situations Jews found themselves in would eventually be relieved.

The major observances of Passover are abstention from eating any foods containing leavening, and participation in the ritual meal on the first two nights of the holiday (only the first night in Israel and among Reform Jews).

USHERING IN PESAKH

Just as we do for all biblically ordained holidays, we welcome Passover by lighting festival candles (called to *bentsh* [blessing] *likht* [light] in Yiddish), bringing blessings and light, and symbolically, the illumination of Torah, into the house. As for Shabbat, the woman of the household (or the man if no woman is present) lights at least two candles (corresponding to the two Torah passages commanding us to remember and guard the Sabbath day [EXODUS 20:8, DEUTERONOMY 5:12]); many add a candle for each child in the family.

If *yom tov* (holiday) coincides with Shabbat, you must light the candles as you would for the Sabbath, eighteen minutes before sundown. (You can get a calendar that gives the proper time—which depends on your location—from a Jewish bookstore or institution such as Khabad, or check your newspaper for the time of sunset). This is because after sundown, you may no longer light a fire, and the extra minutes help prevent you from accidentally going over the time limit. If *yom tov* falls during the week, you may light after sunset *from an existing flame* (SEE "HALAKHAH"), but it is preferable to light candles at the earlier (Shabbat) time, which signals the beginning of a welcome occasion.

By our tradition, a blessing is supposed to precede the *mitzvah* it describes. However, in the case of Shabbat, once you recite the blessing, you have already introduced the Sabbath into your home, which means you can no longer light. So in this situation, we light the candles first, and then cover our eyes, so it is as though the candles have not yet been lit. Although technically this is not necessary on *yom tov,* for the sake of avoiding confusion we consistently follow the Shabbat procedure on festivals as well. (It is customary to circle our arms over the flames three times, drawing the spirit of the day of sanctity to ourselves, ending with our hands over our eyes.)

Recite both the blessing for the candles, and the *shehekhiyanu,* a blessing made the first time each year that something is experienced: a festival begins, a piece of new clothing is worn, a particular fruit is eaten and so on (FOR THE BRAKHOT, SEE "BLESSINGS" AT THE BACK OF THIS BOOK.)

Before lighting candles to usher in the second day of *yom tov,* we have to wait for the first day to be finished, so instead of lighting prior to sunset, we light after nightfall. To ignite the wicks, we use a preexisting flame—twenty-five-hour candle, oven pilot light, stove burner—which had been lit prior to the festival candles on the first evening.

(On the seventh and eighth days of Passover, which are full festival days, candles are lit as described above. However, since these are not separate holidays in their own right, and we have already said the *shehekhiyanu* for this festival, only the blessing for the candles is made. The yahrtzeit candle in memory of a departed relative should be lit before the festival lights.)

SEDER

It has been observed that no Jewish ritual is more followed and thought of more fondly than the Passover Seder. As Jewish communal surveys and numerous literary works demonstrate, reminiscences of the shimmering holiday table, the aromas of once-a-year foods, the togetherness of family and especially the familiar tunes stir something in us, bringing more people to the Seder table than to any other Jewish celebration during the year. As Heinrich Heine observed, "even those Jews who have long forsaken the faith of their fathers and pursued foreign joys and honors are moved to the depths of their hearts when the old familiar sounds of the Passover happen to strike their ears."

Such praise for Pesakh is not to deny that many people today have mixed—if not outright negative—feelings about the Seder. Many capitulate to the whines of children and other participants complaining that the wait for the meal is too long, or the process boring or without significance. We all know people who race through the first part of the Haggadah just to get to the meal, and abandon the service after they have eaten. Or treat the occasion as a springtime Thanksgiving, a family feast unencumbered by ritual. Sadly, they are missing the point—and the exhilaration that Pesakh offers, robbing themselves and their children of beautiful meaning and memories.

If done right, the Seder can captivate, excite and inspire no less than a good stage production or a fascinating seminar. The Haggadah's inclusion of prayers and passages from different times and places in our history reflects not just one event, but also a continuous cycle of exile, oppression and redemption, through today and into the future. Working from the role of the Exodus in our national life (SEE "RELIGIOUS IMPORTANCE"), it emphasizes that the event in Egypt is just a beginning, not only of our journey, but also of our discussion on Seder nights.

The Torah commands, and the Haggadah reiterates, "in every generation each Jew should regard himself as though he personally went forth from Egypt." By reliving the experience of the Israelites, we too progress from idolatry to slavery and ignorance to meaningful worship, freedom and knowledge. Recalling that it was once possible to rise above the debasement and warped values of a surrounding and suppressing society and establish a more equitable order renews our faith that it is possible to do so again. There is tremendous hope in the saga of the Exodus—and Passover can inspire us to seize it.

The key is to keep the Seder stimulating. Certain elements of the service must, according to halakhah, be covered (explanation of the paschal lamb, matzah and *maror,* Rabbi Gamaliel's dictum, plus telling the story of the Exodus and drinking four glasses of wine) When the tradition says: "Whoever expands on the story of the Exodus deserves praise"—it does not mean that we should simply read every word of the Haggadah. Only communicating Pesakh's themes in a way that moves and motivates participants fulfills the *mitzvah*. That means the Seder can and should be tailored to meet the needs of participants.

Celebrants use all sorts of devices to accomplish the purpose, with variety the rule: different haggadot for each of the two nights (or from year to year), stressing a theme (current events, Holocaust, endangered Jewish communities); using dramatic techniques (acting, mime, costumes, puppetry) and songs to present parts of the story (or its modern equivalents), scripted or ad libbed (such as the Sephardim have long employed [SEE "CUSTOMS"]); using props and special effects (the "Plagues Bag," containing items representing each of the plagues for participants to shower on the table, has become quite popular—in purchased or homemade varieties), updating the service by listing modern day plagues (diseases, famine, war, homelessness), using *"Dayeinu"* (SEE LATER IN THIS SECTION) to express appreciation for what is right in our world.

Each individual can talk about what freedom or the Passover experience means personally, or can share the oppressions from which s/he fled. Some spend each of the Sedarim with a different group of people, or in a different setting (how about an "authentic" Greco-Roman style Seder, on sofas, or reclining on pillows on your living room floor, around a low table?). Maimonides instructed that it is necessary to make changes to draw the children into the proceedings. He suggested such attention-getters as distributing snack foods, moving the table prior to the meal, and snatching pieces of matzah from each other. What about turning your tablecloth into a map of the Israelites' journey from the House of Bondage to the Land of Milk and Honey—or a game board, on which pieces representing key figures in the Exodus story can be moved as relevant questions are correctly answered and/or guests participate in the discussion?

Many of the rituals are included just to prompt questions, particularly from children, who are the focal point and honored attendees at the Seder: They are our hope for the future—as Pharaoh knew too well (EXODUS 1:22, 10:10).

At the same time, we are all, in some ways, children. The sages instructed that if no child were present to ask the "Four Questions," the wife must do it, or another man, even a scholar. If no one else is available, the service leader must ask himself. There is always something to learn, especially, for most of us today, about what it means to be children of Israel.

TO PARTICIPATE If you will not be making a Seder, and cannot attend one made by friends or relatives, contact your Jewish Federation, a local synagogue, college or university Hillel, Family and Children's Service or other communal organization and ask to be placed with a host family. Since it is a *mitzvah* to invite strangers to the festival table, people are happy to accommodate and generally sign up for the privilege of doing so. As a last resort, you may be able to join a communal Seder, which many congregations and some organizations hold on one of the nights. (These are not the same as the interfaith/interracial Sedarim offered during the intermediate days of the holiday as an expression of shared values and concern and/or opportunities to improve mutual understanding.)

TIMING Unlike other festivals, when the candlelighting and *kiddush* that initiate the holiday are done at sundown, the Seder may not begin until nightfall since that was the time the paschal lamb, matzah and *maror* had to be eaten, and when *kiddush,* over the first of the four cups of wine, must be done. The start should not be delayed longer, however, because you want the children to remain awake, there's no point in unnecessarily delaying the meal, and the last part of the dinner must be eaten prior to midnight.

BASIC STRUCTURE Fifteen steps take us through the evening's experience. Each one prepares us physically or psychologically for the next step we—as our ancestors did—take in progressing from slavery, a life lived only in the moment, to redemption, which we see clearly in the future. They relate to the fifteen "Songs of Ascent," Psalms 120–134, chanted by the Levites as they walked up the fifteen steps to the Temple and suggest that the Seder is also an ascent (aliyah), from slavery to freedom, the beginning of the forty-nine steps that will take us higher, to Mount Sinai and Torah (SEE CHAPTER ON SHAVUOT). Through it, we become a holy nation, eventually able to ascend to Jerusalem. (The same word, aliyah, also denotes immigration to Israel.)

To ensure that the components of the Seder were preserved when not every Jew possessed a Haggadah, the rabbis devised a rhymed mnemonic that some families chant at the beginning of the Seder, and then up to the appropriate part as they reach each ritual. Variations on the tune are included in songbooks for Pesakh and on recorded versions of the Haggadah (SEE "SONGS TO SING").

The text of the Haggadah and numerous commentaries fill entire books by themselves. What follows is merely an outline of the Seder ceremony and a few highlights to help you think about what the steps mean.

Kaddesh The sanctification (usually pronounced *kiddush,* from the word for holy), initiates every Sabbath and festival and is customarily recited over a brimming cup of wine, a symbol of joy. ("Wine gladdens the heart of man" [PSALMS 104:15].) It always includes the phrase *Yetziat Mitzrayim,* connecting Pesakh with all festivals of the Jewish year, as all events of Jewish history are connected with the Exodus. Giving a regular meal a spiritual dimension, on Seder nights the *kiddush* is made over the first of the four cups of wine.

Red wine, used most prevalently, was historically thought to be superior (BASED ON PROVERBS 23:31), and also recalls the blood connected with Passover (murdered newborns, first plague, doorpost markings, circumcision required to partake of the Passover meal). Jews in the Middle Ages often substituted white wine because of the blood libels (though that did not always help), and today both are used. Grape juice, for children and those who cannot tolerate wine (especially in Pesakh quantities!) is considered as wine.

After "slaving away" during the previous days and weeks to get ready for the holiday (SEE "PREPARATION"), the wine helps us make the transition from enslavement to liberty. Each cup helps take us back in time and space, facilitating our ability to relive the experience. The four cups are said to represent the four times Pharaoh's cup is mentioned in the story of Joseph's success at dream interpretation (GENESIS 40:11–14) and the four kingdoms that subjugated Israel after the Exodus (Babylon, Persia, Greece and Rome). They also reflect the four expressions God used when He promised to bring us out of Egypt: "bring you out" (*v'ho'tziti*), "deliver you" (*v'hi'tzalti*), "redeem you" (*v'ga'alti*), and "take you unto Me" (*v'lakakhti*) (EXODUS 6:6–7).

We recline when we drink, and eat (except for the *maror* [since the slavery it symbolizes conflicts with the freedom expressed by reclining]), toward the left. It was the position on the ancient sofas, so people could free the right, for most the preferred, hand, to feed themselves. (It was believed that leaning to the right could allow food to enter the windpipe and cause one to choke.)

Urkhatz We wash our hands (*u*, and, *r'khatz*, washing) by taking a cup of water in the left hand and pouring half its contents in three splashes over the right hand, then switching and pouring the remainder over the left (lefties reverse the order). You can pass a pitcher, basin and towel from person to person, have one person walk around to each guest's place, or rise from the table to use a sink.

Although we normally say a blessing when washing (since we usually wash in preparation for eating bread), we omit the *brakhah* here because it will be a while until we begin the actual meal. The action may be left over from the ancient practice of washing hands prior to eating anything moist (our next step) because the sages said that unclean hands defiled the liquid.

Today the washing serves two purposes: to prompt questions from children ("Why is someone walking around the table with a pot of water?" "Why are we washing if we're not ready to eat?" "Why don't we say a blessing?"), and to prepare us physically for the Exodus experience: we "wash our hands" of the slave mentality, the first step to independence.

Karpas The vegetable or herb is dipped into salt water, the substance both of tears and life genesis. Initially in Egypt the Israelites grew and prospered. But birth of too many led to oppression, salty sweat and tears of pain. Salt also recalls the Temple, whose loss we mourn, where sacrifices were always salted.

This is another stimulus for questions ("You call that an hors d'oeuvre?"

"Where's the rest of dinner?" "Parsley? Why are we eating this stuff that's normally just plate decoration?") and an opportunity for parents to teach children that physical desires are not always immediately met, that a physical act can be invested with spirituality when accompanied by learning and prayer.

Yakhatz The leader breaks the middle matzah in half (*khatzi*), puts the smaller portion (have you ever gotten matzah to break evenly?) back on the plate, and wraps the larger portion (suggesting that more is hidden to us than revealed) in a napkin or modern enhancement, a special bag for the afikoman (as this piece of matzah is called). This is another one of the devices promoted by Talmud to keep children awake, and prompt them to ask, once again, what is so special about this night. Among Ashkenazim, children customarily "steal" the afikoman and ransom it at the end of the meal for a reward when the leader cannot find it. (In some families the leader hides it and the child who finds it claims a reward.)

At this point, the matzah is *lekhem oni*, the inadequate fare of the poor (slaves to their status), who must suffice with less than a full portion, and often, not knowing where the next meal will come from, saving some for later. The act of breaking the cake puts us in the position of the poor, at least symbolically. Having a partial portion also suggests that life is incomplete for all of us as long as we remain in exile.

Shattering the brittle cake brings to mind the breaking of the bonds that we come, through habit and complacency, to accept, the illusion of security in which we live, financial and especially political, which makes us think that somehow we can exist with the threat of tyranny. (Kristallnakht shattered what the Jews of Germany thought was a safe life). It is taking the first step to liberation.

Signifying the hospitality we are about to extend, breaking the matzah also prepares us to break bread with those who need it.

Maggid The telling of the story of Exodus is the raison d'être of the Seder. It turns the Seder table into a Jewish environment for learning. One interesting note about it: Except for a truly incidental reference, the name of the hero of the story, affectionately known in our tradition as *Moshe Rabbenu* (Moses our Teacher), is not mentioned. The omission was purposeful, to avoid anyone thinking that Moses, rather than God, had accomplished the redemption, and to prevent the possibility of Moses being turned into an object of idol worship—

which the Exodus was meant to eliminate. (The sites of Mount Sinai and Moses' burial are unknown for the same reason.)

Opening Our Homes/Hearts ✧ The leader begins by uncovering and lifting the plate holding the "bread of affliction our ancestors ate in Egypt" (*Ha lakhma anya. . .*) and invites all who are hungry to eat with us (fulfilling physical needs), all who are needy to join us in celebrating Passover (fulfilling spiritual yearnings). We go to the trouble of re-experiencing our servitude in Egypt so that we never forget what it means to be a slave, an outcast. Reaching beyond ourselves to help others is a sign of freedom.

This part of the Seder originated in Babylonia, where hosts actually went into the streets to extend a welcome. So that everyone would understand the invitation, hosts issued it in Aramaic, the local tongue. For this reason, many people today say it in the vernacular. (Although it is unlikely we would bring someone off the street at this point in the evening, we should think of all those who are hungry, physically, emotionally and spiritually, all who are strangers, within their own families and to their own heritage, who need our support.) With the persecutions from the Middle Ages on, opening the door became too risky, and was eliminated from the beginning of the service. As a sign of hospitality, some people have recently reinstated it.

In contrast, the lines that follow, expressing hope to be in Jerusalem next year and for all to be free, were pronounced in Hebrew. This prevented the Babylonians from understanding the words and thinking that the Jews were planning to revolt.

Matzah of Hope ✧ In the past few decades, it has become customary to include special prayers and readings on behalf of Jewish communities still oppressed, most commonly the Soviet and Ethiopian Jews, often over a specially designated piece of matzah.

The arrival of large numbers of those communities in Israel has not eliminated the need for concern. Not all have reached safety, Jews in other countries (like Syria) are still endangered, and Jews everywhere live under the afflictions of poverty, sickness and spiritual malaise. As long as some are oppressed, none of us is truly free, and collectively we are prevented from enjoying universal peace. To emphasize our responsibility in bringing all Jews together, the Matzah of Hope is also identified as the Matzah of Unity. (For a special prayer on behalf of endangered Jews, check with an advocacy group, a local synagogue or Jewish Federation—or write one yourself.)

Four Questions ✥ The content of the *"Mah Nishtanah"* (why is [this night] different), as the four questions are more popularly known, present the dual themes of the evening. *Matzah* (the first question) is both the bread of slaves and of free people. *Maror* (second question) symbolizes servitude as well as an elegant privilege: the hors d'oeuvre dipped into another substance. *Karpas* (third question) represents the suffering of slavery and the rebirth of redemption, as does dipping twice (vegetable in salt water, and later bitter herbs in *kharoset*— which itself commemorates both enslavement [Joseph's brothers, after selling him, dipped his coat in lamb's blood to convince their father he had been attacked by a wild animal {GENESIS 37:31}] and liberation [the hyssop dipped in lamb's blood to mark the Jewish households {EXODUS 12:22}]).

The act of questioning reflects freedom, evidence that we are not restrained in seeking to satisfy our intellectual curiosity through probing and analysis. Questions, not answers, allow us to progress in our learning, to acquire knowledge that lifts us out of ignorance that can be as brutal an oppressor as a tyrannical taskmaster.

The four questions are not directly answered in the Seder, a suggestion that formulating the right questions, and searching for the truth in response, is an on-going process.

Avadim Hayinu (We were slaves) ✥ What we really want to know, of course, is why we celebrate Passover, which the Haggadah explains. The sages debated whether, in following the Talmudic principle that we "begin with degradation and end with glory," we start with the debasement of slavery or that of idolatry. Is physical bondage imposed from outside more shameful, or is spiritual bondage, the result of personal choices, a worse humiliation? In including both slavery and idolatry in the Seder story (the second comes a few pages later in the Haggadah), we reach back to Abraham, who started the journey to redemption by smashing his father's idols, recognizing One God, and receiving the covenant the Israelites were taken from Egypt to uphold.

Remembering our lowly origins is a means of keeping us from rising so far above afflictions we have escaped that we forget they are very real for too many people. Yet with our eye on glory at the conclusion of the story, we know it promises a happy ending, and are encouraged to keep going forward.

Five Sages ✧ A well-known passage of the Haggadah describes one Passover evening in B'nei B'rak when leading rabbis of the post-Temple era sat up all night, so engrossed in discussing the Exodus that their students had to inform them the sun was about to rise. The report raises numerous questions (among them, especially for children, "how could they have possibly spent so long at it?"). This is an example of how the night's themes have held immediacy throughout Jewish history: it is a veiled account of Passover celebrated with political purpose.

The sages of the story lived under Roman occupation—essentially in exile in their own land—at a time when Torah study had been prohibited. On that memorialized Pesakh evening, they engaged in a crisis session to plan the best course for the community: Were they to merely keep the memories alive secretly, through the darkest periods, finding ways to worship, always hoping for and expecting redemption, or were they to resist openly, fighting for political and religious independence?

One of the participants, Rabbi Akiva, supported the rebellion leader Bar Kokhba ("son of star") whose rising the students, eager for activism, announced after the all-night debate (SEE CHAPTER ON LAG B'OMER). Later, after the devastating defeat of Bar Kokhba and the end of any kind of dynamic Jewish existence in the Holy Land until the modern era, the *galut* mentality of passivity—out of which grew the image of the meek, defenseless, physically subordinate Jew—dominated until the twentieth century.

Then Zionism reignited the pacifism vs. activism debate essentially ended by the Holocaust and establishment of the modern Jewish homeland. During the latter decades of the twentieth century, similar questions were again raised by advocacy groups grappling with determining the most prudent means of obtaining freedom for Soviet and Ethiopian Jews.

The Four Sons ✧ Four times the Torah instructs that a parent teach his/her child the story of Passover (EXODUS 12:26; 13:8; 13:14; DEUTERONOMY 6:20–21), both in response to questions (three of the passages) and even when a child does not ask. The wording of each suggests a different level of personal involvement with the Exodus story and its commemoration, and reflects a different level of commitment to the Jewish people (the intellectually curious "wise" [*khakham*], who includes himself in the community and is eager for details of all the laws; the rebellious "wicked" [*rasha*], who disassociates himself from the group and is negative toward its ritual; the "simple" [*tam*] perhaps immature or naive, who has natural faith; and the unquestioning [*sheh eino yodei'ah lishol*], who needs to be treated and taught from beginning to end with sensitivity).

On one level the questions acknowledge that individuals have varying interests and capacity to understand, and that the responses they elicit should be given accordingly. Many commentators contend that the *arba'ah* (four) *banim* (sons, or children) refer not only—or not at all—to minors or aspects of them within all of us. Rather, they stand for ideological groups that threatened rabbinic Judaism in the first and second centuries, when the Haggadah was written (Hellenes, Judeo-Christians, Sadducees, Essenes), or political attitudes of Jews living under Roman rule (supporters of revolution, those who refused to join the revolt even at its crisis point, those who had been enslaved by Rome and those who had not been exposed to Judaism and did not know what the revolt was all about).

Since the Exodus, freedom has always spoken with a Hebrew accent.

HEINRICH HEINE

The most significant interpretation for our age is that ascribed to Rabbi Joseph Isaac Schneersohn (1880–1950), the Lubavitcher Rebbe, who saw in the *arba'ah banim* the four generations of the American Jewish experience, each one successively removed from European roots of Jewish observance: the religious immigrant; the rejecting second generation; the confused third generation in conflict between the tradition of his/her grandparents' home and the trouncing of *mitzvot* by his/her parents; and the alienated ignorant fourth generation, who never knew his/her great-grandfather and has no basis on which to even form a question. It is the ignorance and indifference that every generation must combat, by making Judaism and Jewish education relevant and appealing so that the next child in line is not so far from our heritage that s/he does not know that Pesakh has arrived, or what it signifies.

By now you've probably noticed that there are quite a few "fours" in this ceremony (glasses of wine, questions, ritual foods, sons). The number is used to describe a long list of things with Jewish significance (matriarchs, epochs of the universe, groupings of the tribes in the wilderness, fringes [tzitzit] on the corners of ritual garments, species used on the holiday of Sukkot and on and on). A mystical number in several religions, in Judaism it suggests stability and wholeness, as in defining a square that is the base of a house—or the "four corners of the earth" from which the Jews will be collected together at the time of redemption.

The Ten Plagues ✧ Scholars love to give natural explanations for the ten plagues (*mahkot*). They may be right—and still not negate traditional Jewish belief that the plagues were arranged "by Heaven" (the Jewish definition of miracle is a natural occurrence that comes at the opportune moment), or that they hold relevant symbolic significance. For instance, they are interpreted as measure-for-measure (*midah-k'neged-midah*) retribution for the Egyptians' own actions.

According to this explanation, blood was for the drowned infants; frogs covering everything for the taskmasters constantly on the Israelites' backs; welt-causing lice getting under the skin for the whip of overseers; beasts to mirror the Egyptians' beastly behavior; cattle disease for stealing the livestock of the Jews when they were shepherds and herdsmen; boils for making the Jews live in filthy, skin-irritating conditions; hail for the evil words rained down on the Jews; locusts to destroy grains for the straw the Jews had to collect to make bricks; darkness for the general condition slavery imposes on its victims; and death of the firstborn for torture of God's firstborn, Israel.

The plagues have also been understood as means of humiliating the Egyptians for the worthless gods they worshipped, portraying them as bloody (the Nile), obnoxious (a frog-headed creature), diseased (livestock) eclipsed (the sun) and dead (heir to the throne). Affecting the ground itself, creatures that live on it and the atmosphere, the plagues demonstrated the Israelite God's sovereignty over all the earth, nature, life and death.

The way we incorporate the ten plagues in our ceremony highlights an important Jewish value: we must never sink to the level of our oppressors. We were taken out of Egypt not just to end the brutal subjugation, but so that we would not be lost in their unjust, decadent, life-wasting culture. As we recite each of the plagues, we remove a drop of wine from our cups. Ashkenazim do so either with the pinky or index finger (symbolizing the "finger of God" Pharaoh's priests recognized as the force behind their troubles [EXODUS 8:15] or with a spoon. (Among Sephardim, as the man of the house pours wine into a bowl, the woman of the house pours water into it so the liquid resembles the lamb's blood the Israelites used to identify their homes.) Despite all the horrendous actions of our enslavers, they were still human beings. And since our salvation involved their suffering, our joy cannot be complete. For that reason we diminish the wine, symbol of gladness, to express our sorrow. (Since these drops represent plagues, it is inappropriate to lick your finger or spoon after spilling them.)

For the same reason, only the half Hallel is recited during the last six days of Passover. Midrash relates that when the Egyptians were drowning in the Reed Sea, the angels wanted to sing praises. God rebuked them. "How can you sing Hallelujah when My children are drowning?" Proverbs instructs, "If your enemy falls, do not exult. If he trips, let your heart not rejoice." (24:17). Our tradition teaches us that while we should categorically reject Egyptian practices, we are not to despise the Egyptians, who, despite later abuse, did feed and shelter us during the famine. The expression of sensitivity is a reminder that once we win freedom we are to use it appropriately, not applying our new strength to oppress others.

Dayeinu ✡ A Seder favorite, the lively song with the one-word refrain (much longer in English: "It would have been sufficient for us") is a progression of expressions of gratitude for each of fifteen stages in the redemption from Egypt. Although we needed to reach Sinai and then the Temple to achieve our spiritual potential, the song teaches us to appreciate whatever we have, however short of the goal it might be (the glass half full rather than the glass half empty approach). Each step provides a promise of something better than the current situation, a reflection of the Jew's eternal optimism. At the same time, the situation at each step is better than the previous one and an accomplishment in itself. Creating a personal *dayeinu*, or a family version as part of the Seder, can be a powerfully affirming exercise.

Hallel Following explanation of the symbolic foods (*z'roah*, matzah, *maror*), and commandment for each of us to feel as though we personally left Egypt, we chant the first part of the "Psalms of Praise." Called Egyptian *Hallel*, it consists of two psalms (113 and 114) dealing with the delivery from Egypt that were chanted by the Levites in the Temple when the paschal sacrifices were offered. They form one of the oldest portions of the Haggadah.

Rakhatz After the second cup of wine, we wash our hands, as in *urkhatz*, this time with the blessing. It is another transition point, as we are about to begin the meal. We refresh our spirits in preparation for the physical celebration of a new physical state.

Motzi/Matzah Each participant takes a piece of the top matzah and the broken middle matzah (since there is disagreement as to whether the blessing applies to the bread of affliction or the top festival bread, we take both), salts them and eats, following the *brakhah,* reclining to the left.

Maror We dip for the second time, with the bitter herbs (use a spoon if your choice is horseradish) into the *kharoset.* When the Temple stood, *maror,* representing bondage and exile, was eaten at the end of the Seder, say our rabbis, because the celebrants knew they would end up going into exile. Today, when we are in exile, we eat them first, as a prelude to the post-dinner concentration on future redemption.

Korekh The first-century sage Hillel invented the sandwich (*korekh*) of matzah and *maror* because of the Torah injunction to eat the two with the Passover lamb (EXODUS 12:8). He understood they were to be eaten together. Each person at the Seder constructs a sandwich out of two pieces of matzah and some *maror.* We do not lean while eating it since the bitter herbs signify slavery, but the sandwich actually combines that state with redemption (the matzah).

This duality prompts us to think about how the two factors coexist in our own lives and how each reminds us of the other: When we are oppressed, the taste of freedom lingers. And when we are free, we recall the pain of oppression. This awareness keeps us mindful of those who still live under it, and helps us guard our own behavior.

Shulkhan Orekh Eating a sanctified meal on our set (*orekh*) table (*shulkhan*) is part of the Jewish system of food preparation and consumption (kashrut, keeping kosher) designed to elevate every step of the process above animal need to holy service (and likewise, to elevate us above our animal nature to more spiritual consciousness). The model is particularly appropriate for this occasion: The first commandment given to and followed by the Israelites in Egypt concerned preparation of the family meal they would make at home as a sign of their commitment to serve God. It shows how we can use the opportunity of Seder to strengthen feelings of belonging to the family and family of Israel while teaching Jewish spiritual values.

Tzafun The meal is usually not completed without the hidden (*tzafun*) afikoman—which means that the child who has successfully hidden or stolen it (in a family that follows one of those customs) has a good chance of being rewarded for relinquishing it. The leader "buys" the designated piece of matzah back for money, a prepared gift, or the promise to provide the requested ransom. A stand-in for the paschal lamb (or the matzah eaten with it), which was the last item eaten in the Pesakh meal, it must be consumed prior to midnight, as the *pesakh* was. Nothing is to be eaten afterwards (some authorities say water, apple juice, seltzer, coffee and tea fall outside of "nothing"). If you do not have the afikoman, use any piece of matzah to end the meal.

Usually explained as "dessert," afikoman comes from the Greek word describing post-banquet revelries. It may have been borrowed by the Jews to identify the desserts that followed a meal. Since no sweets were eaten after the sacrifice, and secular song and dance were prohibited, afikoman came to mean the last bit of the paschal lamb, later symbolized by this last piece of matzah, which finished the meal, providing a promise of the future, leaving behind its taste of liberty.

Its hiddenness during the part of the Seder that relived a time of oppression suggests that deliverance can come at any time, when the instigator for it (like Moses, whom some say the afikoman represents) suddenly appears.

Bareikh In the blessing (*birkat,* a form of *bareikh/barukh*) for the food (*hamazon*) just eaten, we thank God for physical, emotional and spiritual gifts: sustenance, the Land He gave us on which to grow food in security, and our spiritual center there, Jerusalem. Drinking of the third cup of wine concludes the thanksgiving.

Elijah's Cup ✡ We open the door to welcome Elijah the prophet, who will announce the messiah, into our homes. A benchmark in the Seder, particularly for the children who historically were advised to watch Elijah's cup carefully to see if any wine from it disappeared, it is actually a curious part of the proceedings.

During the very first Seder that took place in Egypt, on the eve of departure, to remain safe, the Israelite slaves had to remain behind their closed doors, out of the reaches of the Angel of Death, separate from the surrounding Egyptian society. Generations later, in Jerusalem, the priests opened the Temple doors immediately after midnight, on completion of the Pesakh meal, and left them open until morning. The practice may have prompted Sephardim, such as the Djerban Jews of Tunisia, to keep their doors wide open for the entire duration of the Seder. With this custom they demonstrated their faith that the time of the Exodus is *leil* (night) *shimorim* (of guarding), when God protects the Jewish people with special watchfulness. (Traditional Jews omit as superfluous the part of the *Shema* [Hear O Israel] asking for God's protection while they sleep. Before bed on Seder nights, they recite only the prayer's first paragraph.) Our sages, no less believing, were also practical: The Maharal counseled that while it was inappropriate for the Jews to bolt their doors on the special night of Passover, in seeking protection for themselves they were not to merely rely on miracles either. It was, in fact, in response to the horrifying blood libels of Europe that the Jews began the custom of (fearfully) opening the door at this point in the Seder—to prove to Christian neighbors that they had nothing heinous to hide.

Traditionally, the opening of the door was followed by an invective against the nations ("Pour out Your wrath. . ."), clearly a reflection of the frustration felt by the Jews of the Middle Ages, who, as victims of Crusades, pogroms and countless indignities, introduced it.

While there is a logical connection between Passover, the holiday of redemption, and Elijah, the advance man of the future redeemer, until recently, the name of the prophet did not even appear in the Haggadah except in the *Birkat Hamazon,* and that is standard year-round text. The custom of including a special cup for the prophet on the Seder table arose out of disagreement as to whether a fifth expression of deliverance (EXODUS 6:8 [SEE EARLIER EXPLANATION OF KADDESH]) called for an additional cup of wine, since it referred to something that would occur later, in messianic days, and not as part of the Exodus. Elijah was identified with the end of days because God entrusted him to witness the Jews' continued observance of the *mitzvot* (like Seder and circumcision, every one of which he is said to attend). With the notion that prior to the messiah's arrival Elijah would solve all doubts and settle differences of opinion, the question of four or five cups was left to his ruling. In case it would be affirmative, the fifth cup was provided but not consumed (except by the Yemenites).

In a rich tradition of folklore, Elijah has often appeared on earth, usually in the form of a beggar, to help the sick and impoverished. So it was not unusual for people to expect him to show up on their doorstep on the event dedicated to salvation and to take a sip.

Like preparation of the paschal lamb, we open the door for Elijah (it's not as if he could not let himself in) because it is we who must act to bring about the desired goal. Some people issue the greeting *"barukh habah"* (welcome) and sing the hope that the prophet will arrive soon (*"Eliyahu Hanavi, Eliyahu Hatishbi. . ."*) usually intoned at the close of Shabbat. Based on Khassidic practice, to show their involvement in trying to facilitate redemption, some families have each person pour wine from his/her cup to fill Elijah's, or place their cups around the one for Elijah.

Remembrance for the Six Million ✧ At this point, some haggadot include a ritual to commemorate those murdered in one of the most recent oppressions (SEE CHAPTER ON YOM HASHOAH). It includes special readings, poems, diary excerpts, prayers and passages by and about victims of the ghettos and concentration camps, along with the song *"Ani Ma'amin"* (I Believe), the expression of total faith that the messiah will come.

Hallel The rest of the "Psalms of Praise" (115–118) follow the meal. Pledging service to God, thanking Him for many forms of goodness including freeing us, it concentrates on national redemption. The Great Hallel (*Hallel Hagadol*, Psalm 136), recounting the delivery from Pharaoh and other oppressors, deals with universal redemption. Its refrain *ki* (for) *l'olam* (meaning both forever and for the world) *khasdo* (both "His mercy" and "His loving-kindness")—or "For His mercy endures forever" and "For His mercy endures for the world" stresses that the goal of perfecting the world will be achieved only when all people are freed of all forms of oppression (tyranny, poverty, war, hunger, prejudice and other obstacles to reaching full potential).

Nirtzah After we count the Omer (SEE NEXT SECTION) and drink the final cup of wine, we express the desire (*rahtzah*) that our concluded Seder is acceptable (*nirtzah*), and that we will celebrate in freedom next year. We proclaim *"L'shanah haba'ah b'Yerushalayim"* (Next year in Jerusalem; when in Israel, "next year in Jerusalem rebuilt," *habnuyah*), the dream of Jews since we lost the Temple (SEE CHAPTER ON TISHA B'AV). Although we have reclaimed the capital, until conditions in the world are drastically changed, the exile continues. It is not just a geographic boundary. It is a separation in the soul, within a community, among nations. One of the dangers we face as Jews living in a fairly tolerant democratic nation is that we are so comfortable as to not even realize we are in exile. If the preparation for and enactment of the Seder has been experienced meaningfully, we emerge from it conscious of how the world needs to be dramatically improved, of the exiles in our lives that we need to reconcile in order to truly be in Jerusalem, a city whose name suggests peace (*shalom*) and completeness (*shaleim*).

Post-Seder Songs In the Middle Ages, reluctant to leave the festive table, participants added religious folk songs, number madrigals, nursery rhymes and hymns, which remain a popular part of the celebration. It is fun to sing them when enough people around the table are familiar with the words and music (SEE "SONGS TO SING").

FOR FURTHER EXPLORATION

Olitsky, Rabbi Kerry. *Preparing Your Heart for Passover: A Guide for Spiritual Readiness.* Philadelphia: The Jewish Publication Society, 2002.

> This short but information-packed book fosters the spiritual connection with Passover's rituals (even for those normally uninvolved with religious practice), and explores the personal aspects of every step in the process of preparing for and celebrating the holiday with meaning.

Steingroot, Ira. *Keeping Passover: Everything You Need to Know to Bring the Ancient Tradition to Life and Create Your Own Passover Celebration.* San Francisco: Harper San Francisco, 1995.

> The subtitle says it all. Along with insights and ideas are such practical tips as how to get your matzah balls to come out to your liking, and making chopped liver.

Studies on the Haggadah From the Teachings of Nechama Leibowitz. Edited by Yitshak Reiner and Shmuel Peerless. Jerusalem: Urim Publications, 2002.

> In this stimulating guide through the Haggadah, the editors have distilled the teachings on the Seder of Nechama Leibowitz (1905–1997), an outstanding and highly acclaimed Torah scholar and educator. More than one hundred analytical questions relating to the Exodus and its celebration (with suggested answers) are sure to provoke discussion and enliven the Seder.

COUNTING THE OMER

Toward the end of the second Seder we begin anticipating Shavuot, the next holiday and in essence the conclusion of Pesakh, by counting the days until its arrival. It is customary to stand (based on the "standing sheaves" of the Omer sacrifice [DEUTERONOMY 16:9]), we recite the blessing and say the count for the day.

On each subsequent night of *Sefirah* (the counting period), and always at night, when the Jewish day begins, we increase the count and state it in days and weeks. ("Today is the x day of the Omer, which equals x weeks and x days of the

Omer"; "*Ha yom x yamim, sheh heim x shavuah u'x yamim la'Omer.*") Some people follow the count by reciting Psalm 67, since it contains seven verses and a total of forty-nine words. Many also say the age-old *Harakhamon* prayer for the final redemption ("May the Compassionate One [*Harakhamon*] restore the Temple speedily in our days"), since its fulfillment would make it possible to reinstate the Omer observance to a biblical, not just rabbinic, commandment (SEE "BLESSINGS").

KHOL HAMOED

The intermediate (*khol*) festival days (*hamoed*), days three through six or two through six in Israel and for the Reform, have a special designation. While they are not full festivals, they are nonetheless holy relative to ordinary days. Leviticus refers to them as *mikro'ei kodesh,* days of sanctity. Even though there are no biblical prohibitions against work or travel, to distinguish the time from normal weekdays, and provide greater opportunity for Torah study, the rabbis ruled that gainful work is forbidden (you can work if material loss would occur).

We read the Torah in synagogue on each intermediate day, conduct the *Mussaf* (additional) service ordained for Shabbat and festivals, and recite the partial *Hallel* (since only part is said on the seventh day, which is a full festival, we cannot elevate a semi-festival above it).

SYNAGOGUE

The liturgy of Pesakh is basically identical to that of the other pilgrimage festivals. The *Amidah* (standing prayer that is the centerpiece of all daily services) refers to the holiday as *Khag Hamatzot*, and describes it as *Zeman Kheiruteinu,* time of our freedom.

PRAYER FOR DEW During *Mussaf* on the first day we recite a prayer for protection against weather conditions that could harm farming efforts: *Tefillat Tal.* Midrash says that Isaac gave blessings for dew and sustenance to Jacob on Passover night. In Israel the holiday marks the end of the rainy season and the beginning of a long dry summer when the land, prior to

Israel's modern irrigation achievements, was dependent on dew. Seen, just like rain, as a gift from heaven, its absence as Divine punishment, the morning moisture is requested as a blessing for life and plenty.

Wearing a *kittel* to reflect a proper solemn and supplicating mood, the cantor recites the prayer, a series of acrostic poems. The Ashkenazim say the phrase "Who causes the wind to blow and the dew to descend" on the first day of Pesakh; the Sephardim continue to say it until the fall prayer for rain is begun on Shemini Atzeret (SEE CHAPTER ON SUKKOT).

READING FROM TORAH AND PROPHETS The Scriptural selections—drawn from four of the Five Books of Moses—all deal, as you would expect, with the Exodus, laws of the festival, later celebrations of Pesakh and the sacrifices of the day. Prophetic portions read on the first two days recount Passover celebrations at the time of Joshua and under King Josiah (JOSHUA 5:2–6:1–27; II KINGS 23:1–9; 21–25), and on the last two days are a Song of Deliverance by King David—which parallels the Song of the Sea read the same day, and a messianic vision (II SAMUEL 22:1–51; ISAIAH 10:32–12:6).

INTERMEDIATE SABBATH In addition to reviewing the laws of Sabbath and Pesakh (EXODUS 33:12–34:26), on the Sabbath that falls within the festival, we read the prophetic account of the revival of dried bones and resurrection of the dead (EZEKIEL 37:1–14), a reference to the nation of Israel. Popular tradition says the renewal will occur in Nissan.

SHIR HASHIRIM Each of the Bible's five scrolls (Song of Songs, Ruth, Lamentations, Ecclesiastes, and Esther) is assigned for reading on a festival. For Passover, it is the first, Shir Hashirim. Ostensibly a richly imaged sensuous poem of love between a man and woman, it was accepted by the sages as an allegory of the love between God, the people of Israel and Torah. For this reason, Rabbi Akiva said while "all the books of the Bible are holy. . .this is the holiest." Its themes of spring ("Arise my love, my fair one, and come away. For now the winter is past, the rains are over and gone. The blossoms have appeared in the land. . ." [2:10–12]) and sexuality ("Sweetness drops from your lips, O bride; honey and milk are under your tongue; and the scent of your robe is like the scent of Lebanon" [4:11]) complement the Festival of Spring (*Khag Ha'aviv*) Pesakh is sometimes called. In addition, it contains specific references to Pharaoh and his chariots, and symbolic references to the night of watching, the Exodus, the hope and fear of redemption, four different exiles Israel is to endure, and the deliverance from each.

If Pesakh begins on Sabbath or Sunday, the Ashkenazim recite Shir Hashirim prior to the Torah reading on the first day. The Sephardim sing it before the afternoon service on the seventh or eighth day. (In some communities it is customary to also read Song of Songs at the Seder after the Haggadah has been completed.)

SEVENTH DAY Tradition holds that the parting and crossing of the Reed Sea occurred on the seventh day following the night of the Exodus. Torah does not mention the specific day or connect the day of crossing with celebration, since we do not rejoice when our enemies fall. We do express joy for our deliverance, by repeating the exultant "Song of the Sea" originated by Moses and the children of Israel after they had reached safety, and included in the morning's Torah reading (EXODUS 13:17–15:26). The congregation customarily stands and sings along, to a special tune that varies by local tradition.

Since the miracle of the Reed Sea occurred at night, some Khassidic sects conduct a special ceremony at midnight, near a sea when possible. (The beach in Tel Aviv is crowded for it.) Many pious Jews stay up most, if not all, night, aiming at improving themselves and their faith by studying excerpts from the Written (Torah) and Oral (as compiled in Mishnah) Law, and Zohar collected in a special book called *Tikkun* (improvement).

YIZKOR On the last day of Pesakh (as well as other pilgrimage festivals and Yom Kippur), a special service for the memory of deceased loved ones and the righteous precedes the additional festival service. Named for the first word of the opening prayer, *Yizkor,* meaning "May God remember," it is an ancient practice based on the Jewish belief that one's life does not end when the body dies. Instead, the eternal soul continues to exist in the influence a person has had upon others. We keep the memory of the dead alive by remembering them in these special prayers (and, according to tradition, by resolving to follow in their ways and teachings, presumably according to Torah).

Originally, *Yizkor* was recited on Yom Kippur. Later, after the first Crusades, it became customary to read the names of a community's martyred dead the week before Shavuot. Based on the idea that the living could atone for the dead by reciting the prayers—and by making a pledge to donate money to charity in memory of one's departed loved ones, it became practice to include *Yizkor* on all festivals when the Torah portion concerns our responsibilities to the poor.

Superstitious Eastern European Jews wanting to avoid the "evil eye" left the sanctuary during *Yizkor* if their parents were still alive. This practice is widely followed to this day (some prayer books even include an instruction to the point). However, it is considered a *mitzvah* for every Jew to say the prayers in remembrance of their loved ones and inspirational people other than one's parents. Anyone who has not completed a year of mourning for a parent does leave, as s/he may be overcome by sorrow and inadvertently disturb others on a day when mourning is prohibited.

HAVDALLAH Pesakh ends after nightfall, when a shortened version of *Havdallah*, the brief and beautiful ceremony to separate (*l'havdil*) sacred and holy time takes place. Unless the day coincides with Shabbat, when the full *Havdallah* (contained in a standard prayer book) done at the close of every Sabbath is made, the *motzei* (departure [of]) *Pesakh* version consists only of the blessing over wine (followed by drinking it) and the statement of separation. It is done at the close of *Ma'ariv* (evening service) in the synagogue or, at home, after three stars have appeared in the sky (SEE "BLESSINGS").

Many people immediately run out to buy bread and consume something they did not have all week—pizza, pasta, ice cream or beer.

ISRU KHAG

The day following Pesakh (and the other pilgrimage festivals) is a semi-holiday on which the spirit of the festival is retained so we can sustain it and carry it with us into the work week. Called *Isru* (from *asar*, to tie or bind), *Khag* (festival), today it is marked only by prohibition of fasting and omission of penitential prayers.

CONTINUATION OF THE OMER

In observant circles, marriages do not take place during the counting of the Omer, when traditional mourning customs are followed. Haircuts, wearing of new clothes, listening to music and attending public entertainment are also prohibited out of respect for the thousands of Rabbi Akiva's students who died in the first thirty-two days of *Sefirah*—or so the tradition holds (SEE CHAPTERS ON LAG B'OMER AND SHAVUOT).

PESAKH SHENI

Since the second Passover was instituted only to allow for sacrifice to be made (SEE EARLIER EXPLANATION), it has been marked from the time of the Temple's destruction only by the omission of prayers of supplication (*Takhanun*) from the daily services. In commemoration of its former significance, some people eat matzah on Iyar 14.

Where Do We Begin? Preparation

It seems that the laughter of Purim has hardly died down and the effects of its wine have hardly waned when we have to get ready for Pesakh. There is exactly one month between the two, time traditionally devoted to massive housecleaning, food preparation and study of the holiday laws.

No other holiday in the Jewish calendar requires more advance work than Pesakh—but please do not let that discourage you. (Are you dissuaded from making a lavish wedding, taking an exotic vacation or moving into a new house because it entails months of planning and activity?) There is something very refreshing about having to examine and alter our physical environment, about having to question and perhaps jolt a complacent frame of mind. When you are scrubbing countertops and scouring crevices, turning your house upside down and inside out, remember that making the transformation between slave and free person—which we are supposed to fully relive—does not happen overnight or without individual effort.

Despite the fact that halakhah covers every aspect of the preparation for (and observance of) Passover, probably no other situation or occasion in Jewish life is observed with such a diversity of actual practice. Many Jews today choose not to adhere to the precepts of the holiday. That's another story. The traditional range is not a matter of opting to follow particular regulations or not, but the variety of ways in which the laws are interpreted and met. As a Yiddish proverb puts it, "Every Jew has his own code of Jewish law and his own brand of madness." As no two Sedarim are conducted in exactly the same manner, no two households adhere to Pesakh kashrut in exactly the same manner, although the intent and the goal are identical.

KHAMETZ

The reason for the fastidious scouring and scrubbing is that all forms of leavening (*khametz*) must be completely removed from our homes, offices and cars. There is no stricter law with regard to Jewish dietary habits than this one— which is even more stringent than the prohibition against eating pork. (Although not encouraged, you may have pork in your possession, and even feed it to your dog, but you may do neither of those things with *khametz*.)

Khametz literally means sour, or something that has been fermented, an edible food affected by the leavening process, which causes foods to puff up or "rise." It consists of five types of cereal and grain—wheat, barley, spelt, oats, and rye— and includes any pure forms of them, food made from them that is already leavened (bread, cake) or has the potential to become leavened (flour). Grain-based alcoholic beverages (liquor and beer), vinegar (except the pure cider variety or wine vinegar made especially for Passover), processed, canned and bottled foods containing *khametz* (cornstarch and syrups, too!) are all off limits.

Two additional types of substance are affected by the laws of *khametz*: something inedible that induces fermentation, such as yeast or already fermented dough (*se'or*), and *khametz* that is unfit for human consumption (called *nuksheh*, or *nifsal me'akhilat kelev:* unfit even for a dog to eat). The first is absolutely prohibited. The second is a bit more complicated, with subcategories and differing opinions among rabbinic authorities as to what is permitted.

In general, inedible things like perfumes that contain ethyl alcohol, and the children's modeling compound Play-Doh, both pure *khametz*, must be removed. Then there are items containing the prohibited substances that you do not have to discard or sell as you do *khametz*, and some that you may actually use (for example, those toiletries containing grain alcohol in solid form—such as creams and stick deodorant, some make-up, nail polish, shoe polish, ink, paint, and air freshener). Some authorities allow year-round medications, vitamins and toothpaste; others say only those specially approved or produced for Passover may be used. It is advisable to check with a local authority regarding specific items.

Ashkenazim also eliminate use of rice, millet, peas, beans, peanuts, corn and buckwheat, which Sephardim allow. The restriction began in the Middle Ages, when these foodstuffs were ground into flour. Although they do not ferment, the products made from them resembled *khametz*, or were handled by dealers who might have inadvertently mixed leavened grain into them, so the rabbis ruled they could not be used. Collectively, they are referred to as *kitniyot* (legumes). While forbidden for eating, they may be owned, and some authorities permit use of their derivatives. (You will find approved-for-Passover brands of corn and peanut oil.)

WHAT IT MEANS Thinking about *khametz* not just as a food substance, but as a psychological and theological metaphor gives us an appreciation for why we Jews become so obsessed with totally eliminating it. The first-century Alexandrian-Jewish philosopher Philo called *khametz*, the stuff that makes baked goods expand and swell up with air, the puff of pride, self-aggrandizement. Allowed to stand around all year, *khametz* gets into nooks and crannies, becoming stale in places we do not even realize it is imbedded—in the way of routine thought patterns and behavior.

When we rout out *khametz*, we are really trying to rout out the negative, stale, deadening, enslaving elements, the egotism and subconscious habits that interfere with fully realizing our potentials. Searching every corner of our homes is a physical reflection of a deep soul search, changing our diet an external expression of an internal transformation. Like the Israelites who made a break from accepting slavery and idolatry in Egypt, we can sweep away whatever it is that binds us to meaningless efforts—whether it is outside influences or the internal compulsions that subjugate us to wasteful or harmful actions.

There is only a thin line between virtue and vice, as between polar opposites (love and hate, brilliance and imbecility, pain and pleasure)—or between the pride that gives us the impetus to accomplish good things in the world and the pride that makes us so arrogant that, like Pharaoh, we think we are God.

The same is true of the difference between *khametz,* which we must completely eliminate during Passover, and matzah, which we must eat. The extension of a line of a letter (the ה of מצה , matzah, into the ח of חמץ , *khametz* [ץ is the form of tzaddi, the letter in the middle of matzah, when it becomes the last letter of a word]), and the lapse of a second (flour of one of the five grains mixed with water and baked in 18:01 minutes instead of 18:00 minutes), is not matzah but *khametz.* If we stand back and let things develop unchecked, we have the prohibited *khametz.* If we step in to ensure that protective boundaries are not violated, we have the permitted matzah. One small stroke, one brief moment, can make all the difference in what we create around us.

HOME

For this one week, to be conscious of our change in status, we live differently than we do the rest of the year. Most noticeably, our eating habits change. In addition to food, we cannot use the appliances, utensils, dishes or work surfaces we normally do, at least without making them kosher (acceptable according to Jewish dietary, and for this week, specifically Pesakh, laws). There is no question that this is an involved process, made less burdensome when shared by family members.

Any area of your home where food has been taken—or could have been taken—must be thoroughly cleaned. This includes bathrooms (remember that some medications, cosmetics, even baby powder, as it contains cornstarch, are *khametz).* Do not overlook a playhouse, tree house, basement, attic, garage, shed, doghouse, pet cage or car.

Shelves and their contents and moldings should be dusted, floors swept and vacuumed, chair and sofa cushions lifted so any morsels that have fallen between can be removed, and even clothing pockets turned inside out. If you ever carry snacks in a handbag or tote, it should be overturned as well, along with children's schoolbags and lunchboxes. Offices, even if far from home, get the same treatment. Most people begin the process by tackling rooms where food is not usually eaten, or which can be made at least temporarily off-limits for food.

There is just one allowable exception: A non-Jewish boarder, tenant or guest who has exclusive use of a particular area on your premises does not have to clean his/her quarters (neither do you) and may bring *khametz* into it. It is not considered your property.

The *khametz* in your possession should be handled in one of several ways. You may destroy it (probably the best option for open packages). You may give it away, for instance to a non-Jewish food pantry. Or you may separate it from everything else in the house—in a room, boxes or cabinets that are locked or sealed, which will allow you to sell it to a non-Jew for the duration of the holiday (SEE "SELLING KHAMETZ"). A piece of tape is a popular "sealer" and a visual reminder not to open the storage area. (Achieve a more festive look by tying ribbon around cabinet knobs.)

KITCHEN This room obviously requires the most detailed preparation.

Shelves and Cabinets You must clean all shelves and cabinets to get rid of crumbs, spills and open containers of food containing *khametz*. If you can afford separate sets of dishes, utensils and cookware for use only during Passover, and have the luxury of sufficient space for dedicated Pesakh cabinets and drawers (which remain off-limits the rest of the year), the cleaned year-round cabinets are simply sealed.

If you do not have the space, at least some of your everyday items will have to be packed away. In that case, once the surfaces are free of *khametz,* line them with paper—any kind will do. Then you are ready to put your *Pesahdikeh* (the Yiddishized description) dishes and foods into them.

Refrigerator/Freezer It is possible to kasher appliances and utensils on the principle that they expel foodstuffs the same way they absorb them—heat for baked-on residue, boiling for boiled-in morsels, soaking for cold liquids. Since cold does not cause any absorption, washing is the only requirement. After removing *khametz* items and defrosting the freezer (if not frost free), all surfaces of both the freezer and refrigerator must be scoured, including bins and compartments. Some people line surfaces with paper, foil or heavy plastic. Unless shelves are solid, air slits need to be made to ensure circulation.

Oven An oven, when hot enough, will release the *khametz* that has become embedded in it in the process of baking, roasting and broiling of foods. Clean it thoroughly, as you normally would (with oven cleaner or on the self-cleaning cycle). The particularly punctilious go after stubborn spots with a blowtorch (small ones are available at hardware stores; make sure you know how to handle one before using it in your house, it could be dangerous). The racks must also be cleaned (soak to loosen caked-on grease, scour with steel wool or use oven cleaner—or that blowtorch).

After allowing it to go unused for twenty-four hours, with the racks inside, turn the oven to its highest setting for one hour (or use the self-cleaning cycle again). If the interior surface is metal, place a pot of steaming water inside during the process. If it is porcelain (usually painted gray or black), some authorities recommend that you use a metal insert, shaped like a box, and available in certain Jewish bookstores or by special order from a hardware store. As an alternative, some authorities recommend that surfaces be covered with aluminum foil (though no one seems to know how to make it stay in place). Others insist neither covering is necessary.

Stovetop Clean the entire surface, the burners and trays thoroughly (the coils on an electric range do not have to be washed), don't use the stove for twenty-four hours, then turn the burners to their highest setting—for fifteen minutes on a gas range, five minutes glowing red on an electric. The dishes under the burners may be covered with foil or replaced (hardware and convenience stores and some supermarkets carry them). Some people cover the entire stove surface with foil or metal sheets (purchased through a Jewish book store or hardware store). Do not, however, attempt to cover a glass ceramic stovetop or its radiant burners.

Microwave Clean the oven thoroughly, let it stand for the standard twenty-four hours, then put a dish—one that has not been used for the past twenty-four hours—filled with boiling water inside, turn on the oven until it is filled with steam (about five minutes), then wipe out the inside. When using the oven during Pesakh, put a thick piece of padding to separate the bottom of the oven from the cooking dish, and completely cover the food being heated.

Sink Scour the entire surface—basin, faucets, spout, drain, garbage disposal. For twenty-four hours, do not run or pour hot water into it. Then reclean it and pour boiling water over all surfaces. Although a metal sink is considered purged of *khametz* it is common practice to put a liner of some sort on the bottom to prevent contact between your Pesakh ware and the surface used for *khametz* all year. A porcelain or enamel sink, made kosher the same way, cannot be completely rid of *khametz* because it is porous, so a sink liner or stand to keep Pesakh ware from touching the bottom, or dishpan set into the sink, must be used.

Dishwasher Those with stainless steel interiors—and according to some authorities those with porcelain interiors as well—are made kosher through their own heating process. Run it through a cycle, remove the racks, and wash the interior completely. After twenty-four hours of non-use, run a cycle at full temperature. Some rabbis permit use of the machine and the racks if you run them through the full cleaning cycle at the highest temperature three times following the initial cleaning. Others maintain that plastic or rubber racks need to be replaced, which you can do through a manufacturer's dealer.

Countertops/Tables Clean surfaces thoroughly, then pour boiling water over them when possible (be careful with this, some materials will warp; lots of towels on the floor will speed clean-up afterward). If you do not or cannot kasher your counters this way (for example, if they are tile with grout fillings), clean thoroughly and then cover them with contact paper, foil or plastic sheeting (heavy plastic available in wide rolls from hardware stores works well). It is customary to use a tablecloth on any dining surface. (A year-round cloth that has been laundered without starch is fine.)

Small Appliances The motor bases of blenders, food processors, mixers and so on used year-round can be used for Pesakh as long as the exteriors are thoroughly cleaned and the motor housings are opened so the coils can be brushed free of food particles that have fallen inside. The blades, beaters and plastic bowls and containers have to be replaced. You can get extra sets at manufacturer service centers (although sometimes it is easier and less expensive to buy a whole new machine).

Dishes, Utensils, Pots Technically, you can kasher for Passover items of glass, metal, stone, wood and natural rubber used year round according to the same principle used for major appliances. Items not used directly on the fire, like bowls, utensils and flatware, and pots used to prepare liquid foods, as by boiling, undergo *haggalah* (immersion in boiling water). Anything that has come in direct contact with fire without the addition of liquid is heated to glowing in fire (*libun*). Surfaces on which food is prepared or eaten (like dishes and cutting boards) are purged, like sinks, by pouring boiling water over them (*irui*), and glassware—including Corning and Pyrex—used only for cold food and beverages and not for pure khametz (grain alcohol) is soaked in cold water (*m'ilui v'irui*). In each case, the items to be made kosher must first be carefully cleaned and set aside for twenty-four hours.

HOWEVER (and this is a very big "but")—most people prefer to use separate sets of kitchenware for Pesakh, even, perhaps especially, those most concerned with following halakhah—and advise others to do the same. It is simply too complex and difficult to kasher everything properly. If it is absolutely out of the question to replace your everyday kitchenware (there are many inexpensive options, including disposable foil bakeware and pots and tableware from discount stores and outlets), consult a detailed guide and find someone who has done it before—along with a rabbinic authority who can answer the questions sure to arise.

One last note on cleaning: If you decide to avoid all this by staying with a friend or relative or at a hotel in this country or abroad that is kosher for Passover, you still need to search for and sell your *khametz,* which requires cleaning it out of your home and "organizing" what remains in specific storage areas (SEE "HALAKHAH").

FOR FURTHER EXPLORATION

Greenberg, Blu. *How to Run a Traditional Jewish Household.* New York: Simon and Schuster, 1985, pp. 408–412.

> If you plan to ignore the warning and kasher your everyday utensils and so on for Passover, this is a good guide to lead you through the process. Each of the procedures is explained, and options in tools to use in accomplishing them are suggested. (Good luck.)

BEDIKAT KHAMETZ Once you have done your best to cleanse your home, collected the *khametz* items and utensils (except what you need for breakfast on the last day before Pesakh starts), it is time for the *khametz* search and destroy mission. For young children it can have the excitement of a treasure hunt, for older ones and adults, it is an opportunity for introspection.

On the evening of Nissan 14 (the night before *Erev Pesakh*), we conduct a ceremonial hunt for leaven throughout the house. It starts with recitation of a blessing, and so that it won't be said in vain—as would be the case if you were not to find any *khametz* (a likely outcome after the previous month's intense labor), it is customary to place pieces of bread in easily accessible places. Any number will do, although ten has become traditional (ten plagues; ten commandments; ten mystical characteristics of God; ten sons of Haman [SEE CHAPTER ON PURIM]). If you do not use ten, be sure to pick a number you will easily remember so you know when all the pieces have been retrieved.

For the search you need a candle, something in which to collect the crumbs (a wooden spoon is traditional, but even a piece of cardboard will do), and something to sweep the crumbs into the receptacle (a feather, or a palm leaf from the Sukkot lulav is standard). With the family assembled, the head of the house is usually the one to light the candle and say the *brakhah*.

Without speaking, begin the search. (If you speak of matters other than your immediate purpose before completing the search, you must repeat the *brakhah*.) Using the feather or other object to brush the crumbs into the receptacle avoids having direct contact with the leaven. The candle, which allows you to see into every corner, also turns the search back on yourself: "The spirit of man is the lamp of God, searching all the inward parts" (PROVERBS 20:27).

To play out the connection, some families have introduced the addition of each person writing down on a scrap of paper the personal *khametz* s/he would like to eliminate from his/her life. The folded scraps are added to the *khametz* collected in the spoon or cardboard and wrapped (put in a bag, tied up in a cloth or napkin) so that no pieces will be lost.

The expression of nullification that follows should be said in a language you understand, since it is a legal declaration (the original is in Aramaic).

The next morning, we destroy (*biur*) the *khametz* by wind (breaking it into crumbs to be scattered), water (crushing and throwing it into a body of water or a toilet), or the most common means—and the most dramatic for children—fire (burning it outside, often in a bonfire, or, if necessary, indoors in a sink). In some city neighborhoods, local fire departments arrange community *biurim*.

While your *khametz* is burning, you recite a slightly different nullification, to accommodate the *khametz* left from breakfast and added to that from the *bedikat*. The permanent riddance is a direct response to Torah's commandment to "destroy leaven from your houses" (EXODUS 12:15, 19, 13:7). The rabbis understood the purpose as eliminating idolatry from our world, based on a sequence of commandments in Torah: not to make molten gods (EXODUS 34:17), and to observe the Feast of Unleavened Bread (EXODUS 34:18). Idolatry is not limited to the worship of objects that cannot protect us, but encompasses the pursuit of values that don't do any better at providing us with real security (money, materialism, celebrity [SEE "RELIGIOUS IMPORTANCE" IN CHAPTER ON SUKKOT]).

Originally, getting rid of leaven had to be completed by the time of the paschal sacrifice, midday, from which time *khametz* could no longer be eaten. To protect anyone from accidentally going over the deadline, the rabbis determined that *khametz* could only be eaten in the first third of the day, or in its first four hours "Jewish holiday time." It is determined by dividing the day—defined as the time between sunrise and sunset—by twelve to arrive at the number of minutes in each daylight hour (not necessarily, for this purpose, sixty). It works out to something like 9:30 and 10:00 AM as the deadline for eating *khametz* and 10:30 to 11:00 AM for destroying it.

If Pesakh begins on Saturday night, the search is done on Thursday night and the burning on Friday morning (SEE "HALAKHAH" FOR DETAILS; SEE "BLESSINGS" FOR WORDING).

SELLING KHAMETZ Originally, all Jews disposed of whatever *khametz* they owned by selling it in the marketplace, and restocked after Pesakh. This later became a costly proposition for those in businesses like liquor production or baking. The sale of (*mekhirat*) *khametz* was devised to spare them tremendous financial loss. It allowed the Jews to sell the stock with the understanding that it could (and would) be bought back after the holiday. The goods were transferred to the new (temporary) owner.

In the Middle Ages an astute commentator noted that instead of schlepping the merchandise back and forth, the seller could just lease the rooms in which it was stored and provide the key—along with the legally executed contract—to the purchaser. Over time, as Jews had less contact with the outside world, it was suggested that instead of each one having to find a non-Jew with whom to do business, any number could give power of attorney to a common agent, who would arrange the sale for them.

Although called a "legal fiction," this process, which we follow today, is a totally legitimate transaction. You can arrange for your *khametz* to be sold through a rabbi (if you do not, according to Jewish law you may not derive benefit from it during Pesakh or afterwards, either). If you don't have one or don't want to call a synagogue, you can go through a local Khabad center (check a phone directory under Chabad). Arrangements can be made any time in the weeks before Pesakh up to the deadline for eating *khametz*: The sale must be completed by the time you have to have all leavening out of your possession. This involves filling out a brief form giving the rabbi power of attorney (some will take authorization over the phone) and usually a nominal fee. The rabbi-agent produces a bill of sale. The non-Jewish purchaser makes a small down payment, which is returned with interest at the close of Pesakh, when the would-be purchaser changes his mind. (Since this is a legitimate legal process, the non-Jew could decide to go through with the sale, or the agent could decide not to buy it back. There is no record of that ever having happened.) This sale covers only foodstuffs, not utensils, dishes and so on. Those you may simply keep stored.

Since you cannot use any of the *khametz* you have sold until the agent has had ample time to buy it back at the end of Pesakh, most people go out for something fresh for their first *khametz* meal after nightfall on Nissan 23.

FOOD Everything we eat during Pesakh must be entirely free of leavening. Since *khametz* shows up in foods we would not think of as leavened, and in forms we would not readily recognize (dextrose, sorbitol, decaffinated tea. . .), we buy foods that are prepared under rabbinic supervision to ensure that they adhere to halakhah and that no leaven—or hand, utensil or equipment touched by leaven—has come into contact with them.

Since food is produced today with sophisticated machinery, with little likelihood of *khametz* getting mixed in as was the case when everything was made by hand, pure items like coffee, tea, sugar, honey, fresh/dried/frozen fruits and vegetables, kosher meat/poultry/fish, raw nuts (except peanuts and sunflower seeds, which are *kitniyot*), milk, pepper, garlic powders (while some people have a custom of not using garlic—fresh or otherwise—there is no prohibition against it), many dairy products that are kosher all year, and paper, plastic and oil wraps do not require special certification.

Still, many observant Jews use only those labeled as having been manufactured under the direct supervision of rabbinic authority. (There is a wide variety of kashrut approvals, local, regional and national. You will see the names of specific rabbis with the kosher certification on the packaging, along with a variety of symbols, U inside an O, Star K, CRC, K inside a triangle. . .But a package marked "Kosher for Passover"— כשר לפסח —is not necessarily and one without a marking may be perfectly acceptable.)

If your baby is on a formula not approved for Passover use and that may contain *khametz* or *kitniyot,* check with your physician about changing it, and/or a rabbi about permission to use it. The same is true with medication. Leniency is always the rule when health is affected, so some items that contain *khametz* may be allowed.

During Pesakh you may not feed your pet *khametz*—which almost all pet foods contain. If you cannot find a variety without wheat or *kitniyot* (in the past, Fancy Feast cat food, Alpo and Mighty Dog dog foods all have been acceptable), you may have to switch to a different diet (check with your veterinarian; some people indulge their animals with table food). Otherwise, arrange to "sell" the animal to a friend or neighbor in an arrangement similar to selling your *khametz* or board it for the eight days (this includes hamsters, birds, etc.).

Once matzah is baked, it can no longer become leaven, so it is used in crushed and finely ground form to make the matzah farfel and meal we use in cooking and baking for the holiday. You may be surprised to see Pesakh recipes calling for baking soda and baking powder, which are used to make cake rise. Unlike yeasts and sour dough they are not considered leavening (any more than are all the eggs used to get fluffy Pesakh cakes). Since baking powder may contain starch (made of flour), you must use the kind made especially for Passover. However, baking soda is merely a derivative of salt (sodium bicarbonate), and therefore approved for Pesakh use. (Be careful with table salt, though—iodine and polysorbates render some brands unfit for Passover.)

There are ways to control the cost of Pesakh provisions: Pay attention to where you do not have to have a kosher for Pesakh label, or where you can buy a kosher for Pesakh product that is available all year for the all-year price. Buy meat, poultry and fish a couple weeks before the holiday (prior to price increases); you can store it in your freezer—already cleaned for Passover, with the shelves lined—wrapped and well separated from any *khametz*. You do not have to purchase staples and produce in a kosher grocery; use your regular supermarket. If you shop in advance, keep non-perishable Pesakh supplies wrapped in grocery bags in a closet or room that has been cleared of khametz.

FOR FURTHER EXPLORATION

Passover Directory. New York: Orthodox Union.

   Published annually, this extensive guide lists items from national brand and private label (local and regional) manufacturers under "OU" supervision that are kosher for Passover (11 Broadway, New York, NY 10004, 212-563-4000, 212-564-9058 fax, www.ou.org/chagim/pesach, info@ou.org).

SPECIAL PREPARATIONS On Jewish holidays considered sacred time—as the first two and last two days of Pesakh are—there are certain activities anyone who follows Jew law will set aside for the sake of maintaining the proper atmosphere of the occasion, just as s/he does on Shabbat (SEE "HALAKHAH"). Their practical implications need to be taken into account in advance.

Eruv Tavshilin On *yom tov* (holiday), we may bake and cook any food needed for that day itself, since freshly cooked food enhances the joy that is supposed to accompany the occasion. We may not, however, cook for any other day of the week. This is to give the *yom tov* the respect it deserves. But the restriction poses a problem when the day immediately precedes Shabbat (when the second or eighth day of Pesakh falls on Friday). So a construct called in Aramaic *eruv* (mixture) *tavshilin* ([of] cooked foods) was created to allow us to prepare a special portion for Sabbath on the holiday. It involves making a symbolic meal of two foods—bread (matzah in the case of Pesakh) and an egg, fish or meat—on Wednesday afternoon. Put them on a plate, raise it and recite a blessing followed by a formula in Aramaic, the vernacular of Babylon and the language of Talmud compiled there (SEE "BLESSINGS").

It is then considered as though we had already cooked for the Sabbath, and any other cooking we do later for it (on the yom tov) is incidental. The prepared food must remain in place until after Shabbat. (Many put it out of the way, on top of a refrigerator, for example, so it is not inadvertently eaten.) A legal fiction, it is a means of reconciling conflicting *mitzvot*. As all legal fictions (like selling *khametz*), it was created with the intent of sparing people from hardship, the underlying purpose of the whole Jewish way of life.

Use of Fire While you may not light a new fire (strike a match, turn on electricity) on the holiday, you may use an existing fire to light another. To light candles on the second night, or to cook, you will need to have a candle, pilot light, or stove burner already lit. Many people use a yahrtzeit candle or an eight-day festival candle (sold, like the regular memorial candles, in religious supply stores).

TZEDAKAH

We should not be so obsessed with the preparation of food that we not consider the too many people who go without it. If we fulfill all the precepts of Pesakh preparation and the Seder but fail to provide for those in need, it is as if we have negated the holiday's significance. We are supposed to think not only of the travails of the past and the glories of the future, but the deficits all around us in our own society. We invite "all who are hungry to come and eat" so that even those oppressed by poverty or solitude can at least for one evening feel that they belong to the community and celebrate and feast as equals.

In Rabbi Isaac Meir of Gur's lesson to his Khassidim, the ninth plague is presented as a message about helping others in need. During the darkness, no one saw his neighbor and no one budged for three days. Someone who ignores his neighbor's suffering deserves the punishment of darkness so that he cannot rise from his place. It is mercy and charity that bring light into the world.

When you are planning your menus and guest lists for the Sedarim, consider those in need. Many people make arrangements to host Jewish travelers, college students, military personnel stationed in the vicinity, the elderly or congregation members who are alone (done through a synagogue, Hillel chapter, Jewish Federation or other communal agency).

In addition, we contribute to a special fund (*Ma-ot*) for wheat (*Khitim*), which supplies matzah and other Passover provisions for those in need. Even if you have fulfilled all other annual commitments for *tzedakah* (commonly understood as charity, but meaning justice), you are obligated to donate over and above them to *Ma-ot Khitim*. In times past, when community elders showed up at the door, if the inhabitant of the house did not need to receive, s/he had to give: everyone, at one end or the other, was involved. To avoid embarrassing a recipient, s/he would not be directly confronted. Many believed Elijah had visited them. Today, recipients are told, "here is your Pesakh order." In some communities, the boxes are packed and hand delivered through a massive volunteer effort the week before the holiday.

Some rabbis collect money for *Ma-ot Khitim* when they make the *khametz* sale arrangements. You can also contribute directly to the local fund (check with a rabbi or synagogue office if you cannot find a listing for it). Collection starts at the beginning of Nissan.

GETTING SET FOR SEDER

It is customary to begin reviewing the Pesakh story and preparing for the Seder at least two weeks prior to the festival starting at Rosh Khodesh Nissan. This is the time to evaluate different haggadot, consult varying commentaries, and figure out how you want to convey or have participants explore the significance and personal connections with the Seder's themes. Come up with songs, games, skits, questions you can incorporate to keep participants engaged.

Involve your children in the planning. They will be more vested in the celebration—and will be great helpers in preparing dramatic approaches, props and so on and contributing valuable ideas. Especially with young children, it is important to tell the story of Moses and the Exodus in advance, several times. As anyone who has had to read the same book repeatedly, or witnessed a child playing the same videotape over and over again knows, children like to be familiar with their entertainments. Through repetition, you will also be able to teach even three- to four-year-olds the *"Mah Nishtanah"* (don't they learn the songs they repeatedly hear on videos and TV?) allowing them to have a bit of the limelight.

In addition to preparing parts of the Seder enactment, older children can be engaged in making matzah covers, Seder plates, place cards and so on, and, on the day of Pesakh, parts of the meal and the ritual foods (preparing *kharoset* is a good chore). Halakhah specifies minimum quantities for ritual foods, which observant Jews follow (DETAILED UNDER "HALAKHAH"). If you plan to adhere to them, you will want to pre-measure the portions (they can be put into sandwich bags and cupcake liners, one for each participant). Simply rule out a piece of cardboard for the area to be covered for matzah and romaine lettuce, and use a measuring cup for horseradish. (Romaine lettuce, though preferred as *maror,* poses a problem because it is very difficult to completely clean the leaves of minute bugs [which we are prohibited from eating] camouflaged in them. A solution is to put the leaves in a bowl of water with some vinegar [make sure it's kosher for Passover], which dislodges the insects—and still examine the leaves very carefully.)

Many synagogues and sometimes other Jewish communal organizations or educational outreach programs run seminars and model Sedarim to teach novices how to do the service, and provide the experienced with new ideas.

SYNAGOGUE

Each of the five Sabbaths leading up to Pesakh features a Torah and prophetic reading chosen to remind us of some aspect of or reinforce our spiritual and physical preparation for the upcoming festival: bringing payment for sacrifices to be made after Nissan 1 (Shekalim, form of currency [EXODUS 30:11–16, II KINGS 11:17–12:17]); destroying evil in the world (Zakhor, remember [DEUTERONOMY 25:17–19, I SAMUEL 15:1–34]); purifying ourselves and our homes, based on the symbolic Red Heifer purification ceremony (Parah, heifer [NUMBERS 19:1–22, EZEKIEL 36:16–38]); the month of Nissan and regulations for making the paschal sacrifice (Hakhodesh, the month [EXODUS 12:1–20, EZEKIEL 45:16–46:18]); and the future redemption that will come just as the first one did (Hagadol, the great [MALAKHAI 3:4–24]).

The last may have gotten its name (The Great Sabbath) as the others did, for a key word in the Haftarah (the prophetic portion that completes the Torah reading): "Behold I will send you Elijah the Prophet before the coming of *the great* and terrible day of the Lord." Some say it was named in commemoration of the beginning of the Egyptian redemption, which was on Saturday, Nissan 10, when the Israelites started to prepare their lambs (SEE "HISTORIC FOUNDATION") and the miracles begun when the Egyptians did not interfere.

Most think it defines length as much as spiritual height: On this day it became customary for the leading rabbi in a community to deliver a long learned discourse on the themes and laws of Passover. At a time when many people crowded into towns and cities to be with their families, it was a good opportunity to reach large numbers. The rabbis were simply following the example of Moses, who, according to midrash, spoke to Israel on the laws of Passover prior to the Exodus. (If *Erev Pesakh* falls on Shabbat, the day retains the name but the sermon is moved back to the preceding week so it will have some practical benefit.)

In addition to reminding us of the first redemption and announcing the future one, the reading from Malakhai commands the bringing of tithes, the failure of which, the sages said, causes famine. The connection with Pesakh is through its identity as the time of judgment of the world for famine-preventing crops.

In the afternoon service, the congregation customarily reads the Haggadah from *"Avadim hayinu"* through *"Dayeinu"* in commemoration of the miracles that began the Shabbat preceding deliverance, and as a preparatory review.

FAST OF THE FIRSTBORN

The sunrise to sunset *ta'anit* (fast) *bekhorim* ([of the] firstborn) is the only fast that applies to just a segment of the community: all males who are the firstborn children in their families (the oldest son, if not number one in birth order, is not obligated). The father of a child too young to fast fasts for him, and if he himself is *bekhor,* the mother fasts for the child on the day of *Erev Pesakh.* Since it is forbidden to abstain from eating on Shabbat (except for Yom Kippur), when *Erev Pesakh* falls on Saturday night, the fast takes place on Thursday.

A widely practiced custom provides an exemption. A celebratory meal called a *siyyum* (conclusion) generally accompanies completion of study of a tractate of Talmud. On the principle that fasting is prohibited on a joyous occasion, rabbis initiated the practice of studying a portion of a Talmud tractate after morning services—held particularly early—on *Erev Pesakh*. All the firstborn are invited to attend learning. The cake and schnapps served afterwards constitute a *seudat* (meal) *mitzvah* ([in honor of a] commandment, in this case studying the Torah)—a joyous celebration from which they must not abstain.

EREV PESAKH

If you want to be particularly careful in Pesakh observance, after your last *khametz* meal rinse your mouth well. (Some rabbis advise changing to a new toothbrush, but unless there are food particles in the old one, which would call for a change anyway, this is unnecessary.) Since you have gotten rid of all the *khametzdikeh* foodstuffs by mid-morning, lunch should be kosher for Pesakh— but by custom you should not have any matzah until the Seder. Pious Jews often refrain from eating matzah for two weeks to a month prior to make it particularly special at the Seder.

All work from the afternoon on (sixth hour of the "Jewish" day [SEE EXPLANATION UNDER "BEDIKAT KHAMETZ"]) should be directed solely at preparing for the holiday. (It corresponds to the time the paschal lamb was being offered in the Temple, a half-holiday on which ordinary work was prohibited.) After *Minkhah* (afternoon service), it is traditional to recite the order of the sacrifice, the words substituting for the lambs. All personal needs—haircuts, manicures, and so on—should be completed by midday. Some men go to the *mikvah* (ritual bath), and the pious like to bake their own matzah (only possible where communal kitchens are set up to accommodate them). The table should be completely set for the Seder.

What Are We Supposed to Do? Halakhah

Recounting the miracles of Nissan 14 and 15, explaining the ritual foods, eating matzah and *maror,* removing *khametz* from our possession, and abstaining from eating leavened bread are described in the previous sections on Observance and Preparation according to halakhah. What follows are regulations for festivals in general, as well as more technical aspects of Pesakh preparation and observance that reflect the legal traditions surrounding the holiday.

DAYS LIKE SABBATH

Torah commands that the first days of Pesakh, Shavuot and Sukkot, the seventh day of Pesakh and the eighth day of Sukkot, plus Rosh Hashanah are *yom tovim*, when work is prohibited (EXODUS 12:16; LEVITICUS 23:7–36); in the Diaspora, one additional day is added in each case (SEE "THE JEWISH CALENDAR"AT THE BEGINNING OF THIS BOOK).

With the exception of permission to prepare food and transfer fire, there is no difference in halakhah between these days and Shabbat. This means that the thirty-nine categories of work prohibited on Shabbat, with those exceptions, are also prohibited on a festival day. These categories, called *melakhot,* are the forms of labor that were involved in building the Tabernacle and its implements in the wilderness (EXODUS 25–40) and do not necessarily correspond to what we would normally consider labor. For instance, you may move furniture in your house, but may not even touch a pen. You may sweep the floor with a soft broom, but may not carry a handkerchief in your pocket from home to synagogue. While at first glance the system may seem illogical, what is permitted and what is prohibited neatly correspond to the whole idea of a sacred day of rest, when everything in the world is in harmony.

FESTIVAL LAWS

FOOD PREPARATION Unlike Shabbat, when each person is supposed to study Torah and feel a personal connection with God, festivals are occasions for the nation to unite. They were the times of pilgrimage to Jerusalem for communal rejoicing—which encompasses feasting together. Preparing fresh food and carrying needed items from one home to another to allow people to visit back and forth are therefore permitted.

The allowance to use fire for cooking was expanded to provide for other comforts such as illumination and warmth: If you take the flame from an existing one, you may light a fire in a fireplace. However, you may not extinguish a fire.

HONORING THE HOLIDAY Thinking about the occasion, as you do in preparing for it, brings it *kavod* (honor). Therefore, you should personally participate in preparation of needed items (fine foods, for instance), and make

81

yourself ready. You should enter a holiday well groomed and dressed in holiday clothing. It is considered a *mitzvah* to bathe in warm water, wash and, if needed, cut your hair and trim your fingernails on the eve of *yom tov*.

SIMKHAH Joy (*simkhah*) is traditionally defined differently for different people. For men, eating sumptuously is considered a fulfillment of joy. According to Maimonides, children should be given roasted grain (popcorn), nuts and sweets, and women should have new clothes and jewelry.

Pleasure Eating two meals a day, one at night and one during the day, both of which include bread (or matzah), wine (in addition to that used for *kiddush*), and meat, is the means to the *oneg* (pleasure) required on a holiday. Lighting candles, which will provide illumination and an aesthetic enhancement during the night, also brings pleasure. Even if you have limited means, you are supposed to spend whatever is necessary to create pleasure and joy.

Torah Study Since the words of Torah provide another kind of joy—that of enlightenment and knowledge, there is an obligation to study Scripture on *yom tov*.

Dual Joy Based on King Solomon's dedication of the First Temple, when he preceded the week of Sukkot with a week devoted solely to consecration of the Temple (I KINGS 8:65), we do not mix one joy with another. This affords each occasion its rightful honor. Therefore, weddings are not performed during a festival (including its intermediate days).

Feeding Others Part of experiencing joy comes from providing food and drink for others who need it—stranger, orphan, widow (SEE CHAPTER ON SUKKOT), which we are obligated to do whenever we partake in festive meals.

MOURNING So as not to interfere with rejoicing, which must be the prevalent mood of a *yom tov*, the laws of mourning are not observed. For thirty days prior to a festival, eulogies are forbidden. A holiday that arrives while you are sitting shiva (seven-day mourning period following the burial of a parent, spouse or child) suspends the remainder of the week. (If burial takes place during *khol hamoed*, shiva does not begin until the festival is concluded, and then runs its full course. The last day of the festival in the Diaspora, since it is a rabbinic addition, counts as the first day of shiva.) Public displays of grief are curtailed so that you do not dampen anyone else's spirits: the mood of the community takes precedence.

Prayers that express acceptance of God's actions in the world, even painful ones, are omitted: *Takhanun* ("supplication"), which usually follows the *Amidah; Y'hi rahtzon* (May it be the will) after the Monday and Thursday Torah readings; *Av Harakhamim* (Compassionate Father) normally recited on Sabbath morning; and *Tzedakatekha* (Your Righteousness), usually part of the Sabbath afternoon service. (In addition to the festival days themselves, these omissions apply for the entire month of Nissan. Since the majority of its days are festive, all the days in the month are considered to be. The first twelve days commemorate the original tribal gifts to the Tabernacle [NUMBERS 7:12–83], then come the eight days of Passover, and the day following it).

TEFILLIN The phylacteries put on every weekday morning by men are not worn on festivals (or Sabbath), because as a sign of the relationship between God and man (EXODUS 31:13), they would be redundant: festivals and Shabbat are also signs of the connection. There is disagreement regarding use during *khol humoed*. Those in favor advise that they be removed during *Hallel*, Torah reading and *Mussaf*, which stress the day's festive nature. (Some Ashkenazim in the Diaspora wear them; Israelis, Sephardim and Ashkenazim who follow Sephardic custom do not.)

ADDITIONAL PRAYER *Ya'aleh V'Yavo* (May There Rise and Come), requesting that God remember, bless and redeem Israel, said on all biblically-ordained holidays, is inserted into all *Amidah* prayers, and the *Birkat Hamazon*.

PROHIBITION OF KHAMETZ

Those halakhot regarding getting rid of *khametz* are derived from five passages in Torah (EXODUS 12:19, 20; 13:3, 7; DEUTERONOMY 16:3, 4). For violation of only one other positive commandment is being cut off from the community (*karet*) the punishment: circumcision. In both cases, the violator separates him/herself by refusing to demonstrate allegiance and identifying with the common destiny. Keeping *khametz* shows refusal to abandon enslavement.

Since any *khametz* owned by a Jew and not sold during Pesakh (*khametz sheh aver alav hapesakh*) may never be used by a Jew, you must be careful when purchasing *khametz* at the close of the holiday. (Many people will wait until they are certain that merchandise is new before buying it from Jewish-owned shops.)

KHAMETZ SEARCH If you do not search for *khametz* on the evening of Nissan 14, you may do it during the day, but still use a candle, not natural light, unless the sun is very strong. If you have not searched by midday, when *khametz* is prohibited, do it later—even on Pesakh itself, and dispose of it immediately. You remain obligated to perform this symbolic elimination of enslavement even after the holiday, if you fail to do it before, and to burn any leaven that had remained in the house during Passover.

If you leave home within thirty days prior to Passover and will not return until after the holiday, either appoint someone to conduct the search on your behalf, or search before you leave, without saying the blessing. You recite the nullification for the *khametz* wherever you are on the fourteenth of Nissan. If you leave home more than thirty days in advance of the holiday, check with a rabbi regarding the necessity of conducting the search.

SATURDAY NIGHT SEDER Complications in kashering the kitchen and conducting *bedikat khametz* arise when Pesakh begins as Shabbat ends. You may not burn the *khametz* or kasher the oven on Shabbat since these acts require fire, and you cannot finish the Pesakh preparation prior to Sabbath because it is customary to have two khallot with Friday dinner and the second Sabbath meal (breakfast) on Saturday, and matzah should not be used prior to the Seder.

The procedure is to conduct the search for *khametz* Thursday evening and burn it Friday morning by the time the selling of *khametz* normally takes place. (Since you may still eat *khametz* on Friday, *biur* and *mekirat* can actually be done anytime until sundown.) Except for the Sabbath khallot, all *khametz* should be out of your possession. Kasher the kitchen for Pesakh and prepare Shabbat food in Pesakh pots with Pesakh utensils. (You have to cook on Friday for the Seder meal since it immediately follows the Sabbath.) Be sure to keep the bread separate from the rest of the food, and especially from Pesakh dishes. (Disposable tableware is advisable.)

On the morning of Shabbat, eat *khametz* at the second Sabbath meal. Then dispose of remaining leaven (it may be flushed away, but cannot be burned) or cover it with a vessel until Sunday night, then burn it. The formula for nullification should be recited during the fifth hour of the day (late morning).

SEDER

All adults are obligated to eat matzah and drink four cups of wine. Redemption was achieved largely through the merits of women (the midwives who refused to kill Jewish infants, Miriam, Pharaoh's daughter, Moses' mother) and both men and women were delivered from Egypt.

WINE Unless necessary for health reasons, you are supposed to drink full-strength wine. Having the wine, considered publicizing the miracle of freedom (SEE ALSO CHAPTER ON KHANUKAH), is a requirement, even if you have to sell belongings, borrow money or take on extra work to pay for it.

A cup must contain a minimum of 3.3 fluid ounces. If Seder falls on Friday night, the first cup of the person making *kiddush* on behalf of everyone else must contain at least 4.12 fluid ounces (the minimum for Shabbat).

RITUAL FOODS Each of the items required for the Seder is supposed to be eaten in minimum quantities, based on equivalents for the bulk of an olive (which must have been huge in Talmudic days when the amounts were determined!), referred to as *k'zayit* (like an olive).

The matzah for *motzi* is figured to be a piece 7 x 6¼ inches. *Maror* in the form of grated horseradish is 1.1 fluid ounces, .7 fluid ounces for *korekh*. If you use romaine leaves, they should cover an area of 8 x 10 inches for each and if stalks, 3 x 5 inches. Matzah for *korekh* measures 7 x 4 inches, and for afikoman, 7 x 6¼ inches.

KHOL HAMOED

A number of activities prohibited on Shabbat and *yom tov* are also forbidden on *khol hamoed*. The sages said that anyone who treated the intermediate festival days lightly—by not abstaining from the prohibited labors—was basically wor-shipping idols. The whole idea is to maintain the spirit of a festival and give yourself extra time to study traditional text. Determining what is allowed or not is often conditional on specific situations. In general, there is leniency for "work" that enhances one's enjoyment of the holiday. An authority or detailed guide should be consulted for details.

FOR FURTHER EXPLORATION

There are several books on the halakhot of Pesakh, *yom tov* and *khol hamoed* (SEE "MORE GOOD INFORMA-TION"). Typing "Halachos of Pesach" in the address line for an Internet search will bring up additional sources for the information, including a set of cassette tapes from ArtScroll produced in 2002, and a guide written by Rabbi Y.D. Webster available to read at users.aol.com/rabbiyd/bedika.html.   ☙

What Other Things Do People Do? Customs

OTHER TIMES AND PLACES

UNIQUE OBSERVANCE Without benefit of Talmudic interpretation, the Ethiopian Jews derived their adherence to Torah from their own studied interpretation of its laws. They modeled their Seder not on the banquets of wealthy free people as in Palestine, but on the original Pesakh meal: They ate meat and matzah rapidly, as if ready to flee, outdoors in moonlight. The elders told the story of the Exodus, asked questions of the children and emphasized the Jews' struggles to reach the Holy Land— which they, with their two-thousand-year history in Ethiopia, and unceasing dreams of Jerusalem—identified with readily. They devoted the first day to synagogue services, and rested from work the entire week. In keeping with the Torah commandment to leave nothing overnight, they ate all food prepared as soon as it was ready.

SPRING CLEANING Throughout the Ashkenazi and Sephardic worlds, homemakers moved furniture, examined every corner, cleaned everything in every cabinet, laundered draperies and painted the walls. The Libyan Jews, who made their own whitewash by burning and then crushing the limestone from nearby mountain quarries, slept outside rather than in a room already prepared for Pesakh.

On the morning of *Erev Pesakh,* the beadle went through each Eastern European Jewish town, alerting people to burn their *khametz.* The men brought the wrapped spoons and bread morsels to the fire at the study hall near the synagogue. The Jews of China gave their *khametz* to neighborhood beggars.

FOOD PREPARATION European Jews turned raisins into wine, hops into mead, root vegetables into pickled condiments, beets into borscht (a soup) and *eingemakhts* (preserves). The Jews of India pressed dates to make a thick syrup they mixed with ground walnuts for *kharoset.* It was not unusual for one person to make *kharoset* for an entire town in Eastern Europe, which children would pick up in exchange for a few coins that were then donated for education or the needy. The local rabbi sometimes provided *matzah shmurah* for everyone, or the sexton sold it door-to-door. Rice, a Pesakh staple for Syrian Jews, had to be carefully sifted to get rid of any wheat chaff that had fallen into it. The Libyans hollowed out new millstones so they could grind Pesakh wheat for all their needs. Tying scarves around their mouths, they refrained from speaking to avoid having saliva land in the flour and causing it to ferment.

Some Moroccan families would not eat black olives for the entire month of Nissan: They believed the fruit caused forgetfulness, and during Nissan, the Jews were commanded to remember the Exodus. Calling the evening of Seder *Leil* (Night) *al-Rosh* (of the Heads), they customarily ate sheep heads in remembrance of the paschal sacrifice.

BAKING MATZAH At one time, matzah was so bread-like, there is a question in Talmud as to whether it could be thicker than four fingers. By the Middle Ages, it had been limited to the width of one finger, but still had to be baked fresh daily, or it became inedible. Gradually it evolved into the thin crisp cracker we know today, which can be made in advance for the entire eight days. (Some, like the Tunisian Jews of Djerba, still make matzah by hand that has the look and consistency of pita bread.)

Eastern European communities ran matzah bakeries for common use. Each family would provide its own flour and pay the baker to make the matzah. Since it was considered commendable for everyone to be personally involved in ensuring that the utmost diligence attended matzah production, people often made it themselves in communal facilities. (The medieval synagogue in Carpentras, France, and the Tuscan village of Pitigliano maintained underground matzah factories, for instance. Sometimes one family invited the community to use its home bakery.) Many poor Jews earned enough to pay for everything they needed to properly observe the holiday by working in the matzah factories, set up as assembly lines. (One of the arguments against acceptance of the matzah-making machine was that these people would be put out of work by it—and would not have necessary funds for the holiday.)

Water to be used for the matzah dough had to be drawn the previous night and kept cool, since warm water leads to faster fermentation. At the time of water drawing, the Libyans each broke a ceramic vessel used during the year, to signal that *khametz* would no longer be present. As the pious poured the water into a barrel, they recited the Hebrew alphabet to sanctify the water with the holy letters of Torah.

Since Torah identifies matzah with the paschal lamb, and the sacrifice was made in the Temple after the sixth hour of the day, it was thought that matzah should be baked at that time. Pious Jews often waited until then to bake at least the matzot they would use for the Sedarim.

For a time it was popular to fashion matzah into figurative shapes, or to imprint the cakes with designs. Authorities worried that in the time it took to be creative, the dough would ferment and become *khametz,* so the artistry stopped. The Jews of Cochin made quick hatch marks to identify their matzot for the three categories of Jews, two lines for Kohein, three for Levi and four for Israeli ("one" was reserved for God).

In Sephardic communities, the women made the matzah since they baked year round and could complete their task rapidly. As they worked, they sang special songs and recited special poems. Other communities forbade women to speak so their pace would not be slowed. Among the Ashkenazim, to ensure that the process proceeded with speed, both men and women participated.

FAST OF THE FIRSTBORN Some Sephardic women observed the fast of the firstborn. The Syrians, who still stringently observe it, include their women in the *siyyum* and *seudat mitzvah* following morning services. As an alternative, a community would sometimes arrange for the poor to be married on the day of *Erev Pesakh*. The firstborn were invited, since the wedding meal is a *seudat mitzvah* exempting them from the fast.

SEDER TRADITIONS Among families descended from those of Levantine lands, it is not unusual to see haggadot placed on participants' laps, a reminder of the Spanish Inquisition, when Jews had to hide the fact they were celebrating Passover.

The Table Sephardim often placed gold and silver vessels on their Seder tables to suggest the jewelry and other riches the Israelites received from the Egyptians prior to their departure (EXODUS 11:2). For the passage about the crossing of the Reed Sea and to recall the Egyptians' demise, some placed bowls containing live fish on the table.

Seder Plate In North African Jewish communities, as well as India, it is customary to pass the *k'arah* in a circular motion over the heads of everyone at the table. Encompassing all gathered in the historic experience, the gesture acknowledges that "as the world turns," first we were slaves, and then free. In Moroccan families, as the plate is placed over each person's head, the woman of the house says a blessing.

The firstborn child of some Sephardic families eats the egg from the Seder plate at the end of the meal. In other homes, the egg is offered to an unmarried girl, who hopes it will help her find a good husband.

Acting and Afikoman, at the Seder and After Many communities added dramatizations to their Exodus reenactment, usually around the image of the Jew departing Egypt and wandering in exile expecting redemption. Syrians in traditional Middle Eastern attire act out the story of the Israelites in slavery. Prior to the start of Seder in Djerba, Tunisia, young people come to pay their respects to the rabbi, some carrying sacks and staffs resting on their shoulders, hobo style. It used to be customary that when the middle matzah was broken during the service, a member of each household would be sent to neighbors to predict the messiah's arrival.

The Jews in Morocco, Caucasus and other Sephardic communities used the cloth-wrapped afikoman in variations dramatizations of the wandering Israelite. In Eastern Europe, dramatizations extended to synagogue, also, where water was sprinkled on the floor during *Shira* on the seventh day (SEE "RELIGIOUS IMPORTANCE" AND "OBSERVANCE"), and congregants dipped their toes "to experience" the sea.

From the custom in Kurdistan of binding a *ketubah* (Jewish marriage contract) to the bride's arm, the practice developed of tying the afikoman to the arm of a son the parents hoped would marry, wishing that the symbolic act would lead in the coming year to his binding a *ketubah* on his new bride's arm. In Asia, Iran, North Africa and Greece, Jews kept a piece of the afikoman in their pockets or houses for good luck during the year, sometimes making a small hole in it so it could be hung like an amulet. Keeping the remains of the afikoman in rice, flour and salt was thought by the Jews of Kurdistan to protect them against going without the staples.

The Moroccans in particular believed this matzah had the power to safeguard them during ocean travel, and would throw it into the water to calm it in a storm (based on an appropriate verse from Psalms (54:9), whose first letters in Hebrew spell the word matzah.) Some believed that if kept for seven years, it could stop floods. Others attributed to it the capacity to stop fire and, when held in hand, to protect a woman and infant during childbirth.

KHOL HAMOED As a time of general joy, when people took time off from work, the intermediate days were used in Medieval Europe for election of community leaders, selection of committee members, and completing volunteer projects put off in the day-to-day crush of responsibility. The Moroccans and Libyans made a special *seudah* featuring small dishes and little portions of food for very young children, which the youngsters themselves helped to prepare. Some Moroccans cut a child's hair for the first time at a public celebration during this period. (It was also common to do so during *khol hamoed* Sukkot, or, as is still popular in Israel, on Lag B'Omer [SEE CHAPTER ON THAT HOLIDAY]).

POST PESAKH At one time the pious customarily fasted on the Monday, Thursday and next Monday after Pesakh (and Sukkot) to atone for excesses of indulgence on the holiday. Called bet (the second Hebrew letter), hei (the fifth Hebrew letter), bet, corresponding to the second and fifth days of the week, the fasts were postponed to the following month since Nissan is devoted to celebration.

On the day after Passover, the Moroccan Jews walked outside of town and recited the blessing over trees, said once a year when new buds appear (SEE "HALAKHAH" IN CHAPTER ON TU B'SHEVAT). For the Sabbath after Pesakh, when the approaching start of the month of Iyar was announced, khallah was sometimes formed in the shape of a key. Sprinkled with sesame seeds representing the *mahn* (manna) that began to fall in Iyar, the khallah stood for the key to our livelihood, which is in God's hands.

Maimouna The Moroccan Jews are known for the exuberant festival held on the evening and day after Pesakh, and whose origins remain unclear. According to one explanation, it marks the yahrtzeit (anniversary of death) of Maimon ben Joseph, the father of the great Jewish philosopher Maimonides, a scholar in his own right who lived in Fez (Morocco), wrote on Jewish-Islamic relations and died around 1170.

Others say the originators derived *Maimouna* from the Arabic word for wealth and good fortune (literally "protected by God," *ma'amoun*). Since Pesakh initiates the beginning of the new agricultural year, its conclusion presents an opportune occasion to pray for plentiful crops, which symbolize general prosperity.

Still others connect the observance with the word *emunah* (belief), claiming it celebrates belief in Israel's redemption. Along the same lines, there is also support (said to be traced to Maimonides' explanation) for the word being an Arabic adaptation of the phrase *Ani ma'amin* (I believe), the classic expression of faith in the coming of the messiah (*ana* for *ani*, placed after the verb *ma'amin*, as is common in Arabic, yielding ma'amin ana, which became *maimouna* in the local Judeo dialect). It may have been a greeting exchanged to bolster one another's disappointment that Passover had come and gone without the long-anticipated return to Jerusalem.

Flowers, wheat stalks, and sometimes live fish in bowls (this time symbolizing birth and fertility) decorated dining tables. In another bowl golden rings hidden in flour suggested hoped-for wealth or blessings. Singing, dancing and visiting with friends accompanied a dairy meal of buttermilk, sweets and special pancakes called *muflita* served with honey. The Libyans made a khallah-like round loaf with a hard-boiled egg secured in the center with strips of dough. Single men and women received blessings that they would be married in the year ahead. Women wore their fanciest clothes, girls donned white and children dressed in costumes of the Berbers (native North Africans) and Arabs who shared their celebration and provided the flowers, milk, butter, honey, wheat and other produce to the Jews' homes.

Numerous legends about acts of salvation that occurred on this date arose, and the festival spread through North Africa and to America, where the *Maimouna* meal provides closure for Passover, and to Israel, where the community gathers in Jerusalem. The holiday traditionally continues the next day with picnics and outings at beaches, fields and cemeteries.

Pesakh Sheni Some Sephardim hold a *hillula* (celebration) at the grave of Rabbi Meir B'al Ha-Nes (Meir "Master of Miracles"). Although it is not clear which of several Rabbi Meirs involved with miracles is buried in the tomb in Tiberias—where celebrants flock for prayers of intercession, singing, dancing and feasting—Iyar 14 is the anniversary of the rabbi's death. Like that of Shimon Bar Yokhai (SEE CHAPTER ON LAG B'OMER), it is an occasion for rejoicing.

IN OUR TIME

WOMEN'S SEDARIM Since 1975, when the first feminist Seder was held in Haifa, the idea has spread to Europe and America, and been enthusiastically embraced. These special celebrations, while following much of the tradition, incorporate new rituals honoring Moses' sister, Miriam, and highlighting women's contributions to Jewish culture.

Based on the midrash that credits the merit of the prophetess for the fact that a miraculous well accompanied the Israelites in the dessert, an extra cup (along the lines of Elijah's) graces the table. Although any drinking vessel can be used, there are specially designed ones, many created by artists and incorporating symbolism related to Miriam and her life. Seder participants pour water from their glasses to fill hers, and then pass it around with a special blessing.

This type of Seder generally includes special readings and dance inspired by Miriam's joyous response to the crossing of the Reed Sea. In addition, participants often talk about a Jewish woman, one selected in advance, admired for her role in Jewish life.

FOR FURTHER EXPLORATION

Text, music, biographies of women worthy of being highlighted at the Seder and other information about the new ritual are available at www.MiriamsCup.com.

GREETING

In the days leading up to Pesakh, we wish each other *khag* (holiday) or *Pesakh kasher* (kosher) *v'samei'akh* (and joyous), or a *freilikhen un kushern Pesakh*. *Mo'adim* (festival days) *l'simkhah* (of joy) is traditional, answered by the Sephardim with *khagim uzmanim l'sassone* (holidays and special times of rejoicing). Yiddish-speaking Jews and their descendants say *gut* (good or happy) *yom tov* (holiday).

DRESS

New clothes are customary for Pesakh. (Traditionally, rabbis advised that if one could not afford an entire suit or outfit, at least shoes were to be bought.) If obtaining them is impossible, then clothing should be clean, and as good as clothes worn for Sabbath (the attire one would put on to meet and receive an honored visitor, attend a special event and so on—not the playground and health club attire often seen in synagogues in our informal society). The Seder leader traditionally wears a *kittel* (SEE "RITUAL ITEMS").

What Is There to Eat? Traditional Foods

Food, always a central aspect of Jewish celebration, is a major obsession on this holiday because of the prohibition of *khametz*. Today we can get practically any foodstuff in a kosher for Passover variety, and gourmet and healthful recipes take us far beyond the limits of hardboiled eggs and cream cheese and jelly matzah sandwiches.

How you make the Seder meal festive is largely a matter of local tradition and individual taste, so to speak. The only restriction—aside from *khametz*, of course—is against eating roasted lamb (to emphasize that we can no longer make the paschal sacrifice since we have lost the Temple). North African Jews generally eat lamb prepared some way other than roasting as the main course; Ashkenazim avoid it altogether. Some do not eat any kind of roasted meat.

Mirroring the shankbone and egg from the Seder plate (which may be eaten), Eastern European Jews often made stuffed roasted chicken necks for the meal itself, and it is a widespread, though not universal, custom to start the meal with a whole hardboiled egg in salt water. For some, it is symbolic of the loss of the

Temple. The first meal in a house of mourning is traditionally egg, its roundness representing the wholeness of life and the "wheel of fortune" through which our lives continually change. The connection was also made because the first day of Pesakh always falls on the same day of the week as Tisha B'Av, our national day of mourning for the Temple's destruction.

One other explanation connects the egg to our status in exile. While all other foods soften as they cook, the egg becomes harder, like the character of the Jew in response to oppression.

At their Seder meal, the Jews of India ate spinach baked with eggs, fried matzah with leeks and eggs, and a pudding of matzah, meat and eggs. The German Jews made a form of dumpling, called *kloesse,* a ball made of soaked matzah, fried onions and eggs, boiled, and served with meat.

Khassidim and pious Jews often refrain from eating any matzah or matzah meal that has been soaked in water, called in Yiddish *gebrokt.* Even though the rabbis ruled that once baked, matzah can no longer ferment and become *khametz*—and matzah meal and matzah farfel are forms of already baked matzah—the strict do not take any chances, foregoing such delicacies as *kneid-lakh* (matzah meal dumplings either delicate as a cloud or as unsubtle as a cannonball depending on your taste, developed through your mother's or grandmother's particular cooking style), *matzah brei* (matzah softened by brief soaking in water mixed with eggs and scrambled—with additions of cheese and vegetables or cinnamon, sugar and raisins); and matzah farfel kugels. They do allow themselves such pleasures on the eighth day, when, since it was added for the Diaspora and is not a Torah commandment, they are more lenient.

It is good news to the diet conscious that Pesakh dishes, normally heavy on the eggs and fat, can just as easily be made with a glance toward health, as reflected in some of the newer cookbooks. Even *khremslekh,* the classic Pesakh pancakes, can be made with egg whites.

FOR FURTHER EXPLORATION

Check the listings under "More Good Information," especially for international variations on *kharoset.*

FOR ADULTS

Ashkenazi-Hankin, Gail. *Passover Lite Kosher Cookbook.* Gretna, LA: Pelican Publishing Co., 1996.
> The two hundred recipes for traditional and contemporary dishes provide evidence that it is possible to emerge from this week-plus-long holiday without gaining weight. Each includes nutritional counts.

New York Times Passover Cookbook. Ed. by Linda Amstar. New York: William Morrow and Company, Inc., 1999.

> Though it includes family favorites passed down for generations, with innovative recipes from cele-brated contemporary chefs, including Wolfgang Puck and Alice Waters, this is not your mother's Passover cookbook. There are some real gems among the two hundred selections, some illustrated with four-color photos.

The Spice and Spirit of Kosher Passover Cooking. Brooklyn: Lubavitch Women's Cookbook Publications, 2002.

> Created by the Lubavitch Women's Organization and reprinted numerous times over the past decades, this book includes helpful, easily-followed information on Pesakh kashrut, the laws and customs of foods on this holiday, guides to preparation—and a collection of three hundred favorite recipes submitted by Lubavitch women.

FOR CHILDREN

Tabs, Judy and Barbara Steinberg. *Matzah Meals—A Passover Cookbook for Kids.* Rockville, MD: Kar-Ben Copies, Inc., 1985.

> In addition to more than seventy recipes tested by kids themselves—some of which involve no cook-ing and can be made by preschoolers—the book includes the Passover story and a Seder menu for young people. All ages.

Do You Hear Music? Songs to Sing

The *shtetl* (small village) of Eastern European Jews produced a number of folk songs about preparing for the holiday, with focus on the matzah baker, homemaker and the children. But the music we identify with is that of the Seder. In addition to sung passages (some of them to catchy folk tunes adapted for the Seder by the Khassidim, who raised music used in worship to new levels) spirited rendition of classic folk songs at the close of the service forms a high point in many homes.

THE SEDER SERVICE

As much as it is a story to be told, the Haggadah is a book to be sung. That is one of the reasons a Seder can be so much fun and so powerful. To be able to share in the experience, you will want to become familiar with at least some of the tunes beforehand. You can easily secure a CD or cassette tape for you and your children to listen to and copy. Every child should learn the *"Mah Nishtanah,"* which is as much a part of one's Jewish cultural heritage as "My Country 'tis of Thee" is of one's American cultural heritage.

"Ha Lakhma Anya" (This is the bread of affliction), *"Avadim Hayinu"* (We were slaves), and *"V'hi Shei Amdah"* (God's help has sustained), major parts in the

Exodus story, all have catchy upbeat tunes, as does *"Dayeinu"* a perennial favorite whose chorus can be learned on the spot. *"Shir Hama'alot"* (Song of Ascents), Psalm 126, which introduces the post-meal grace; *Birkat Hamazon* itself; *"Eliyahu Hanavi"* (Elijah the Prophet), the refrain wishing for the prophet to quickly bring the messiah); *"Ani Ma'amin"* (I believe), the affirmation included at some Sedarim in recognition of Holocaust victims), and the rousing *"L'Shana Haba'ah B'Yerushalayim"* (Next year in Jerusalem) are all standards, used on other occasions as well.

Your family might also want to learn one of the several versions of the chant of the order of service.

FOLK SONGS

Four well-known and popular folk songs appear in a majority of haggadot. *"Adir Hu"* (Mighty is He), an alphabetic acrostic sung to a melody popular for hundreds of years, repeats the hope that Zion will soon be restored and the Temple rebuilt. Another alphabetic acrostic, *"Ki Lo Na'eh"* (To Him Praise Belongs), probably from France or Germany of the Middle Ages, wraps effusive praise around phrases from various Bible books. The fun in this song is in singing each verse successively faster without tripping over your tongue.

In *"Ekhad Mi Yodei'ah?"* (Who Knows One?), the Seder host asks the children a series of questions whose answers pertain to Jewish heritage (one God, two tablets of the covenant, three patriarchs . . . eleven stars in Joseph's dream. . .up to thirteen). Non-religious number madrigals usually stopped at twelve because of widespread belief in the unluckiness of the next number. Judaism, which despite persistent folk customs frowns on superstition, holds it in esteem (the age of bar mitzvah, number of Maimonides' creeds of the faith, Attributes of God and the numerical value of the Hebrew letters in the word *ekhad* [one], which refers to the unity of God, stressed throughout the song.)

"Khad Gadya (An Only Kid) is a Jewish "House That Jack Built" or "Old Lady Who Swallowed a Fly," with each development in the story building on the previous one. Written in Aramaic, it differs from similar folktales of the Middle Ages and amusing nursery rhymes in that aside from being fun to sing, it teaches. Scores of books and articles have been written about its moral significance and historical symbolism.

The song suggests that Divine justice operates in the world, promising retribution for all oppressors. No matter how dominant over another person or group someone is, God rules over all, and will eventually even out inequities.

A number of scholars have interpreted *"Khad Gadya"* as an allegory of Israel's fate among nations. Israel (the kid) is redeemed by God from Egypt through Moses and Aaron (two *zuzim*), or in an alternate reading, by the two tablets of the commandments. Then Israel is subjected to a great empire, which is defeated by a succession of other empires until God redeems His "kid." The cat is said to represent Assyria; the dog, Babylon; the stick, Persia; the fire, Greece; the water, Rome; the ox, Muslims; the butcher, the Crusaders; the Angel of Death, the Ottomans or, according to some, European nations.

Still another analysis reads the song as a record of Israel's relationship to Torah: God "sold" us the Torah for the two words we said at Sinai, "we will do and we will listen" (SEE "RELIGIOUS IMPORTANCE" IN CHAPTER ON SHAVUOT). Once in the Holy Land, jealousy (like cats) made us neglect Torah, so hostile nations were sent against us—and so on in a series of neglects and embraces of our tradition—through David, Babylonia, return from exile, Hellenism, the Maccabees, and Rome, which caused the current exile, in which we hope for the messiah.

German Jews in the eighteenth century turned the song into a game for children with each scene acted out. You can enhance a simple singing by assigning each of the roles in the song to one of your Seder guests, and having them make the appropriate sound of the animal or object as it is mentioned.

FOR FURTHER EXPLORATION

You can learn how to conduct the Seder—or merely participate in its musical parts—from instructional recordings, or by listening to a compact disc or audiotape featuring Passover music. (Numerous versions are available.) It is also possible to hear the music via the Internet (typing "Passover Seder Music" in the address box will yield choices like Passover on the Net [www.holidays.net/passover]. Tara Publications (SEE "MORE GOOD INFORMATION") produces quite a few songbooks, cassettes, CDs and videos.   ☞✥

What Tales Are Told? Stories to be Read

Descriptions of Passover celebrations have enlivened numerous literary works, and the themes of the holiday have been used as the backdrop for others, going back to at least the second century, with the play *The Exodus from Egypt* written by the Jewish dramatist Ezekiel of Alexandria.

At the beginning of *Peony,* Pearl S. Buck describes a Seder in Kaifeng, China, in the mid-1800s. Samuel Yosef Agnon's *The Bridal Canopy* weaves Passover through the narration, and Sholom Aleichem effectively uses the commemoration of the ancient liberation movement as the "bookends" for his novel about the stirrings of revolution and Jewish nationalism in early twentieth-century Russia (*Into the Storm*). Both Leon Uris and Elie Wiesel used Pesakh messages and metaphors in their respective novels, *Exodus* and *The Fifth Son,* and several writers have fictionalized the life of Moses.

Among other Jewish philosophers and writers who used the holiday as the subject of essays and poems are Franz Rosensweig, Heinrich Heine, Ahad Ha-Am, Berl Katzenelson, Theodor Herzl, Abraham Ben Meir Ibn Ezra, Israel Zangwill, Solomon Ibn Gabirol, Judah Halevi and Hayim Nahman Bialik.

FOR FURTHER EXPLORATION

FOLKTALES

Schram, Peninnah. *Tales of Elijah the Prophet.* Northvale, NJ: Jason Aronson Inc., 1991.
> In the thirty-seven folk stories in this wonderful collection, Elijah appears in a variety of guises to work his miracles and bolster faith. Although the prophet is most closely associated with Passover, this book is a treasure for the entire year.

Don't forget to check "More Good Information" for legend, folktale and story sources.

FOR CHILDREN

Bat-Ami, Miriam. *Dear Elijah.* Philadelphia: Jewish Publication Society, 1997.
> Starting a month before Pesakh, a twelve-year-old religious girl whose father awaits heart surgery writes letters to the prophet, via her diary. Amid lots of details of the coming holiday and through it, she confides her fears and struggles with her beliefs. Ages 10–14.

Cohen, Barbara. *The Carp in the Bathtub.* Rockville, MD: Kar-Ben Copies, Inc., 1987.
> A Passover classic, this is the heartwarming story of how two children try to save the fish they have befriended from being made into their mother's holiday gefilte fish. Ages 7–9.

Feder, Harriet K. *Not Yet, Elijah!* Rockville, MD: Kar-Ben Copies, Inc., 1989.
> The young narrator of the rhymed story keeps Elijah, waiting at the door and impatient to come in, at bay through all parts of the service. This is a cute presentation of the order of Seder. Ages 6–10.

Lepon, Shoshana. *The Ten Plagues of Egypt.* New York: The Judaica Press, 1988.
> Humorous rhymes and funny, engaging, brightly colored illustrations illuminate the story, based on information from midrash. Ages 4 and up.

Miller, Deborah Uchill. *Only Nine Chairs—A Tall Tale for Passover.* Rockville, MD: Kar-Ben Copies, Inc., 1982.
> An adorable rhymed story of a family with nineteen guests for Pesakh and only nine chairs presents the Seder as great fun. Ages 5–9.

Parpar Nechmad/Lovely Butterfly—Passover
Puppets, games, animation, stories and holiday songs are used in this award-winning Israeli series to present holidays and their traditions. Although done in Hebrew, the tape is geared for those with very little understanding of the language. Ages 2–6.

Passover at Bubbe's
Puppets star in this highly lauded enactment of the history of Passover, narrated by Bubbe (grandma).

Shalom Sesame: Jerusalem Jones and the Lost Afikoman
Sarah Jessica Parker stars with the Sesame Street characters in a special Passover program of the Israeli "Sesame Street" set in Israel. The thirty-minute tape is in English and introduces elementary Hebrew words. Ages 2–12.

GAMES

In addition to holiday match and card games, board games such as *Exodus: The Game of Passover, Let My People Go,* and *Passover Slides and Ladders* take players through the Exodus experience and from beginning to end of the Seder (available through Holigames, 888-612-0699, 520-327-5355 fax, www.holigames.com, holigames@holigames.com; Judaica for Kids, 3044 Old Denton Road, Suite 111, PMB 199, Carrollton, TX 75007, 214-850-6267, 972-236-3142 fax, judaicaforkids.com, buyer@judaicaforkids.com; The Learning Planet, PO Box 17333, West Palm Beach, FL 33416, 561-686-9456, 561-686-2415 fax, www.learningplanet.com, info@learningplanet.com).

Of Added Note

ART

Michelangelo's sculpted Moses (at the church of San Pietro in Vincoli in Rome) is famous for the horns growing out of the prophet's head, the result of mistranslation of the word *keren,* meaning ray (or horn) of light shining from the prophet's face following his encounter with God (EXODUS 34:29).

MUSIC

In the nineteenth century, Gioacchino Rossini created the opera *Mose in Egitto* (Moses in Egypt), and in this century, Arnold Schoenberg wrote (but never finished) *Moses and Aaron,* using solo and choral speaking and singing voices to present his interpretation of the Bible story as a conflict between two great personalities. Darius Milhaud's orchestral ballet suite, *Opus Americanum No. 2—Moses,* traverses a variety of moods reflecting periods and events in the leader's life. George Frideric Handel and Max Ettinger both composed oratorios, *Israel* in *Egypt* and *The Song of Moses*. The fanciful Andrew Lloyd Weber rock opera, *Joseph and the Amazing Technicolor Dreamcoat,* in a variety of musical styles presents the prelude to the Exodus.

Moses' experience also inspired the great black spiritual *Let My People Go,* which not only held tremendous significance for the American slaves and civil rights movement, but also was often heard at rallies on behalf of Soviet Jewry.

Yom Hashoah—
Holocaust Remembrance Day

(YOME' HA SHOW' AH)
NISSAN 27
(SPRING; MID APRIL—EARLY MAY)

This modern day of recognition was established to allow us to collectively mourn the thousands of Jewish communities, millions of Jewish men, women and children, and infinite unrealized potential destroyed in the greatest atrocity ever perpetrated against our (or any other) people. As a response enveloped by intense emotion and deep questioning, its observance will undoubtedly remain fluid until the perspective of time helps us adequately define its format and place it within the pattern of Jewish commemoration.

Origins—WHY WE CELEBRATE YOM HASHOAH

Traditions—HOW WE CELEBRATE YOM HASHOAH

Origins—
WHY WE CELEBRATE YOM HASHOAH

How Did It Begin? Historic Background

THE CATASTROPHE

On April 12, 1951, the Knesset (Parliament) of Israel declared Nissan 27 the day of commemoration for the most devastating oppression we have suffered in our long history: the attempt by the Nazis (National Socialist Party of Germany) and their collaborators to make the world *Judenrein*—to completely annihilate the Jewish people from the face of the earth. Their efforts resulted in the destruction of more than one-third of the world's pre-war Jewish population by particularly sadistic means.

Almost five million men and women, and more than one million children were slaughtered, worked, starved or tortured to death in what came to be called, in the decade after the fact, the Holocaust. The word is derived from the Greek *holo* (whole) *kaustos* (burnt), a thorough destruction, especially by fire. *Holokaustos* is the translation of the name of the Temple animal sacrifice that ascended (*olah*) in its entirety to heaven, as it was burnt whole. Use of the term in connection with the deaths of the six million Jews, the majority of whose bodies were burned in the crematoria of Auschwitz, Treblinka, Majdenek, Birkenau, Bergen-Belsen, Chelmo and other extermination camps, suggests that they are to be regarded as sacrifices to God. The modern Hebrew word for the Holocaust, Shoah, means devastation or ruin.

It began with the Nazis' ascent to power and the naming of Adolf Hitler as chancellor of Germany in 1933. Almost immediately, he instituted restrictions on Jews, stripping them of civil rights (barring them from public places and all aspects of public life), property (confiscating their homes and businesses) and their very status as human beings: The Nuremberg Racial Purity Laws of 1935 limited German national life to members of the Aryan "master race," effectively classifying Jews as subhuman inferiors and setting the foundation for the heinous treatment of them.

November 9, 1938, signaled the beginning of the government-sanctioned genocide (a word coined in response to the Nazis' program) of German—and later Eastern European and French—Jewry. On that date, which came to be known as Kristallnakht (Crystal Night), mobs rampaged through Germany and Austria smashing the windows of Jewish-owned businesses and synagogues and torching the buildings. The Jews themselves were fined one billion marks for the damages, and forced to their hands and knees—the old and crippled included—to scrub the streets strewn with shattered glass and charred debris.

To make them easy targets, the Germans required the Jews to sew yellow six-pointed stars onto their clothing (a revival of a Medieval practice of using clothes to distinguish and sometimes humiliate the Jews). Persecution escalated to forced labor, ghettoization, wanton torture and murder, concentration camp internment and implementation of "The Final Solution to the Jewish problem," systematic mass murder—by gunning victims into pits dug to hold tens of thousands, and later, in the gas chambers of the death camps.

THE COMMEMORATION

Choosing the date for memorializing unprecedented persecution was somewhat complicated. First of all, unlike other commemorations on our calendar, this one could not be linked to a specific event or biblical designation. Hashoah continued, agonizingly, every day, every season, every year, actively, for twelve years. With countless acts of inhuman brutality against innocents, tremendous numbers slaughtered, thousands of sites of horror, how could one date be chosen to sum up the wrenching memory of it?

There was also the question of whether, despite its magnitude, the Holocaust was "just" one of the many persecutions, expulsions and slaughters that have punctuated our history (in which case commemoration could be incorporated into existing national mourning days), or whether it had been a unique occurrence that did not fit neatly into the recurring pattern of promise, persecution and protection in which and by which we had survived two thousand years (a case that demanded a date dedicated solely to the memory of its victims).

Initially, the Chief Rabbinate of Israel placed the Shoah within the context of

Jewish history and the set holiday calendar. For *Yom Kaddish Klali* (general day of saying the memorial prayer for the dead), the rabbis chose Asarah B'Tevet (the tenth day of the tenth month), an ancient, and in practice minor, fast day marking the start of the Babylonian siege of Jerusalem that led to the destruction of the first Temple (SEE CHAPTER ON TISHA B'AV).

Since so many people did not know the exact date of death for relatives killed in the Holocaust (*kaddish* is normally said on the anniversary of death), and so many people had died without leaving survivors to say the special prayer for them, the rabbinate declared that the date would serve for Holocaust remembrance in general. There was just one problem: no popular support for appending a memorial drawn on fresh, deep, widespread pain to an unfelt, almost forgotten ancient loss.

Many thought that if Holocaust commemoration were to be entwined with a day of mourning already observed, it would be more appropriately tied to Tisha B'Av, a day recalled for a number of the worst calamities to strike us. Even that could not be reconciled. The ancient tragedies already marked by the day were well scarred over by the centuries intervening since their occurrence. The Holocaust was an oozing, gaping wound. In addition, for many people, it could not be viewed as part of the pattern of Jewish life—not just in terms of calendar placement, but in terms of basic assumptions about our role, relationship with God and progression through history.

The survivors who had participated in the resistance movement wanted any Holocaust commemoration to highlight the heroic activities of the Jews who had met the Germans with armed strength. For them, only one date held meaning: April 19, 1943, when they actively began to defy the Nazis' efforts to liquidate the Warsaw ghetto. Weakened by hunger and disease, fighting with the disadvantage of few people and fewer weapons, receiving no support from the non-Jewish partisans, their uprising amazingly managed to hold back the enemy for more than three weeks. Recognizing that they could not ultimately win, they were determined not to quietly accept an imposed death, but to go down having taken their fates into their own hands.

On the Jewish calendar, April 19, 1943, fell on Nissan 15—the first day of Passover. (The Nazis often chose days significant to the Jews for special suffering, part of the attempt to further demoralize their victims.) While the coincidence of the feast of freedom and a modern struggle for liberation from an evil oppressor offered poetic inspiration, the Orthodox found the choice of Nissan 15 for Holocaust remembrance unacceptable: they would not allow the grief of Yom Hashoah to overwhelm the joy of our central holiday.

There was one other consideration: a strong desire to place Holocaust remembrance sometime prior and proximate to Yom Ha'atzmaut (Israel Independence Day). Even though the establishment of the State of Israel was in no way viewed as compensation for the Third Reich's crimes, or a result of them, it is a powerful rejoinder. One day we grieve for tremendous soul-crushing losses. Shortly after, we celebrate the triumph of Jewish survival, an important psychological and physical affirmation.

Although displeased, because it still violated the traditional prohibition of mourning during the festive month of Nissan, the rabbis accepted Nissan 27, four days following Passover and one week before Israel Independence Day, as *Yom Hashoah u'Mered Hageta'ot* (. . . and Ghetto Revolt Remembrance Day).

Very soon after establishing the date, all forms of heroism, not just armed resistance, were recognized and honored by Yom Hashoah. Contrary to a widespread but erroneous attitude, the Jews of Europe did not go meekly to their deaths, like lambs to the slaughter. Despite every means imaginable to degrade and dehumanize them, break their bodies and their spirits, rob them of their souls and turn them into slaves and worse—into objects (their hair into mattress stuffing, skin into lampshades, tooth fillings into jewelry), they persisted in surviving as human beings and as Jews.

In the face of inhumanity, great numbers of them continued to assert their humanity: they sang, they danced, they maintained underground social services—they even retained their sense of humor. Though illegal and punishable by death, in the ghettos they taught their children to read, continued yeshivah education, held prayer *minyanim* (groups of ten, the minimum number of men required for public service), consecrated marriages under the *khuppah* (wedding canopy), and brought their infant sons into the covenant through circumcision. They recorded what was happening to them, confident someone would one day read the accounts and ultimately discover meaning in their suffering.

In the camps, too, there were those who managed to retain faith, observe holidays, and express little kindnesses. Even as they walked naked to their deaths, they maintained a spiritual strength and dignity that countered the efforts of their tormentors to reduce them to nothingness.

In recognition of all these acts of defiance, the memorial day became known as *Yom Hashoah v'Hagevurah* (. . . and Heroism), popularly referred to as Yom Hashoah. Responsibility for creating greater awareness of the day among Israelis was mandated, by 1953 law, to Yad Vashem (Hand—or monument—and a Name, the Israeli Holocaust memorial museum, archive and educational center whose title comes from Isaiah "I will give them, in My house and within My walls, a monument and a name better than sons or daughters. I will give them an everlasting name which shall not perish" [56:5].).

The day was largely ignored by the Israelis, ambivalent about focusing on the pain, embarrassed by what

It is not within our ability to understand or explain the tranquil well-being of the wicked or the afflictions of the righteous.

PIRKEI AVOT 4:19

they often thought had been meek submission to the Nazis, reluctant to promote any contradiction to the image of the new Jew, the strong sabra (native Israeli, named for the fruit of a cactus plant that has a tough exterior but is sweet inside). Public commemoration increased after Knesset passage of the 1959 Holocaust and Heroism Remembrance Day Law, which calls for public tribute to the victims of the Nazi war against the Jews. (A 1961 amendment requires that places of entertainment in Israel be closed on the eve of Yom Hashoah.)

Acceptance of the commemoration was substantially helped by the 1960 abduction to Israel of Adolf Eichmann, chief implementer of "The Final Solution," from hiding in Argentina. Yet it was not until after the exhilarating victory of the 1967 Six-Day War, seen as a balance to the emotional and psychological losses of the Holocaust, and the humbling close call of the 1973 Yom Kippur War, that the country was able to embrace its survivors, seriously study the Holocaust, and openly commemorate those lost in it.

Although established as a secular day (by the government of Israel) rather than a sacred day (which only the rabbinic establishment can do), as a memorial to Jewish dead, it is considered a holy occasion, and is widely marked by services and ceremonies in Israel and throughout the Diaspora.

President Carter's Commission on the Holocaust, established in 1979 to recommend an American policy for commemoration, organized the first American national ceremony in Washington, DC. Congressional law passed in 1980 mandates an annual national memorial, and the encouragement and sponsorship of similar observations throughout the country. Synagogues, Jewish communal organizations, and city and state governments sponsor a variety of public commemorative programs, supported by Jewish and non-Jewish organizations, individuals and government leaders.

FOR FURTHER EXPLORATION

Blatter, Janet and Sybil Milton. *Spiritual Resistance—Art From Concentration Camps, 1940–1945.* New York: Rutledge Press, 1981.
> Landscapes, portraits and scenes of life in the camps—as wells as ghettos, transit camps, prisons and among the partisans—are evocative of the pain, and the spirit, of the Holocaust's victims. Essays provide background, and biographies of the artists are included.

Dawidowicz, Lucy. *The War Against the Jews 1933–1945.* New York: Bantam Books, 1986.
> Considered a definitive work on the subject, in three parts it covers—from a physical and moral viewpoint—how the German National Socialists were able to murder six million Jews, how the Jews responded to the brutality against them, and how the devastation affected Jewish life in Europe.

Harrel, Isser. *The House on Garibaldi Street: The First Full Account of the Capture of Adolf Eichmann.* London: Frank Cass & Co., 1997.
> Written by the former head of Israel's secret service, who was in charge of the operation, this novel-like account details the capture and abduction of Adolf Eichmann. (The book was the basis of a movie starring Chaim Topol.)

The Holocaust Chronicle—A History in Words and Pictures. Ed. by John L. Roth et al. New York: Publications International, 2000.
> With a chapter for each year from 1933 through 1946, a prologue explaining ancient roots of the Holocaust and epilogue detailing its aftermath, plus eighteen hundred images (photographs, illustrations, maps, posters) with explanatory text, this encyclopedic volume is a good source and starting point for exploration of the subject. A companion website, www.holocaustchronicle.org, provides the full text of the print version, selected images, and links to related websites.

Lipman, Steve. *Laughter in Hell: The Use of Humor During the Holocaust.* Northvale, NJ: Jason Aronson, Inc., 1993.
> This collection of jokes and other applications of humor in the ghettos and camps demonstrates how Jews used this special form of resistance, expressing the expectation that good would eventually triumph.

What Does It Mean? Religious Importance

Religion attempts to make sense of the world around us, finding order and meaning in what often seems chaotic and meaningless. Nothing has shaken the foundation of our religion like the chaotic and senseless Shoah. Its devastation was so widespread, its perpetration of evil so extensive, it raised searing theological questions about God and His role in the world; about good, evil and justice; about the value of life and death; about Jewish destiny. How and why could the Holocaust have happened? Did it fit within the pattern of Jewish history, or was it a unique occurrence that would end it? Could it be read as a fulfillment of an ancient Torah prophecy or did it threaten the integrity of the entire Torah system? Could the Jewish people respond to it as we have to previous drastic turning points in our history, or would it totally turn us away from the heritage and its burdens?

BROKEN PROMISES

Until the Holocaust, the traditional view of God and His connection with Israel had remained intact: God was our Provider and Protector. Even though bad things would happen to His people—which we saw as the justified result of our failure to honor Him and the way of life He presented to us (SEE CHAPTER ON TISHA B'AV), periods of oppression would always be followed by salvation. Jews continued to believe that eventually the persecution-ending, exile-gathering, peace-bringing redemption would occur. As the Passover Haggadah expresses it, "in every generation enemies rise up seeking to destroy us, but God delivers us from their hands."

This expectation carried the Jews through the failed Bar Kokhba revolt (SEE CHAPTER ON LAG B'OMER), the Crusades, repeated humiliations and expulsions, pogroms and myriad persecutions, even the Spanish Inquisition. But it was shaken (and for some completely shattered) by the success of the Nazis in decimating European Jewry. The destruction—not only of a numbing number of Jews, but of a disproportionate percentage of scholars and rabbis, along with the major centers of Jewish culture and learning—challenged the long-held belief that God intervenes in the world to balance injustice by punishing evil and rewarding good.

Was God dead? Was He just indifferent—or worse, a sadist? If He could not be counted on to live up to His reputation for mercy and intervene, what good was He? And if He did not intervene, by what reasoning did He merit our allegiance? Judaism teaches that maintaining Jewish continuity will bring blessings to one's descendants. But the descendants of identified Jews (anyone with one Jewish grandparent) were the ones who fell into Hitler's trap, the observant along with the secular, the pious along with the *apikores* (apostate). For those left to sort out the implications of the devastation, nothing could possibly justify what was seen as God's brutal and wholesale betrayal of the Jewish people.

This tremendous upset called into question whether the covenant (SEE CHAPTER ON SHAVUOT)—what was supposed to be an eternal contract between God and Israel—had expired. Without it, there was no sense of order in the universe, no purpose in life, no hope for a better future, no meaning in past or present suffering, no need for Jews or Jewish life. Of course, this was exactly the conclusion desired by the Nazis, who had to eliminate belief in absolute Divine power (which was, according to God's plan, eventually supposed to be universally recognized so that everyone would accept, and benefit by, His standards) and any reference to it in order to wield their own absolute power.

This was also exactly the response of many victims, for whom the covenant had been rendered null and void. They could not believe that God and the Holocaust's degree of evil could co-exist. Or they could not recognize a God who would allow such evil to operate. They had no faith that such crimes would never again occur, and, feeling no hope in life, and expecting no meaning in death, saw no reason to perpetuate Judaism. To spare their descendants the horrors they had endured, they abandoned their heritage, sometimes converting and raising their children as non-Jews.

FULFILLED PROPHECIES

The ultra-Orthodox asserted that rather than destroying it, the Holocaust actually reaffirmed the covenant. For them the devastation in Europe clearly fit the covenant's projected pattern of Jewish history, and was a typical case of God punishing Israel for its sins—in this case, assimilation and Zionism.

Suggesting that more than one million innocent children were brutally sacrificed—either because German Jews wanted to be acceptable to their non-Jewish neighbors, or because European Jews realized that modernity's superficial tolerance of differences between supposedly equal human beings ultimately provided no protection for them—is an abhorrent explanation widely rejected (and another justification for many to deny God a place in their lives).

Despite the discomfort this view generates, however, our tradition does place responsibility for our situations in the world on our shoulders. At the end of his life, when the children of Israel were finally about to cross into the Promised Land, Moses prophetically warned them of what they would bring on themselves if they did not keep the conditions of the covenant: loss of their homeland, degradation, incredible suffering, dispersal to other nations, captivity, disease, idolatry, insecurity, despair, suspense and terror (DEUTERONOMY 28:15–68; 32:5). In their distress, they would finally seek God and return to Him, and then they would receive the blessings the covenant promises (DEUTERONOMY 30:1–10).

As a people, we have experienced other traumatic turning points in our history. They required evaluation and reaffirmation of the Jewish agenda, and revolutionary thinking and constructs to allow Judaism and the Jewish people to go forward. After the shocking destruction of the Temple and upheaval of an entire way of life, the rabbis created new forms of worship, ritual and structure for the Jewish community. After the Spanish Inquisition, the kabbalists (Jewish mystics) invested existing Jewish practice and new ritual with spiritual and mystical significance and taught that every act could contribute to healing the world.

As notes Rabbi Irving Greenberg, the popular Orthodox theologian (who has contributed greatly to the examination of Judaism in the shadow of the Holocaust), we were prepared to make and accept such changes because at each stage of our development as a people, we had moved further away from the manifest God—from direct revelation at Sinai to prophetic voice to rabbinic authority—and become more reliant on our own initiation of action. At each stage, God's presence became less obvious, but it was always believed that He was with His people, wherever they were.

The best example of this is the story of Esther, the quintessential account of the Jewish exile in a non-Jewish land. God did not appear and is not mentioned, but it is understood that He acted behind the scenes, able to exert His influence once the Jews themselves had accepted responsibility for their situation and took steps to effect its outcome (SEE CHAPTER ON PURIM). As we went out into the world, we were supposed to assume more of the burden of the Israel-God partnership that had been established to improve it.

Acceptance of our role in countering evil does not necessarily mitigate the view that the covenant was broken. The fact that God had told us to expect the treatment the Jews actually suffered was no excuse. Whether out of sadism, indifference, shame, sorrow, or the mistaken belief that humans would rise to the potential of our responsibility, in letting His people so severely suffer, He was seen to have cancelled the contract.

RENEWING THE CONTRACT

In the end, walking away from God and Judaism only leaves a void. What system of belief compares? (Hermann Broder, the central character of Isaac Bashevis Singer's post-war novel, *Enemies: A Love Story*, finds all socio-political alternatives bankrupt.) No model of social justice or rationale for long-standing hope has been devised to supplant the Jewish view of the world and Jewish destiny.

The United States Army chaplain who was to conduct Shavuot services following the liberation of Buchenwald wondered whether it might not be too soon to test the religious sentiments of the survivors. But thousands came to demonstrate their allegiance to God, Torah and Judaism. The Jews freed from Nazi oppression rededicated themselves to the same laws of God their ancestors, the Israelites freed from Egyptian enslavement, accepted in the desert. This was typical of the overwhelming reply to the Holocaust: a reconnection with Jewish tradition in some way, a rebellion against Hitler's attempt to destroy Jewish lives and values by asserting them, a challenge to his plan to eliminate witness to evil by more forcefully refusing to forfeit the role of the world's conscience. Confronted with the power of evil on earth, we have chosen to renew our job of fighting against it. The Holocaust proved that our mission is far from finished, and if we do not fulfill it, it is unlikely the world will adopt it. Against unrelenting efforts to destroy us, we Jews have responded by embracing life, giving birth, rebuilding, and providing support for fellow Jews and Jewish causes in unprecedented volume.

At the beginning of Creation, the vessels meant to hold Divine light proved too weak and shattered. So another means of sending spirituality into the world was devised. The first set of tablets of the Ten Commandments, the tangible contract between God and His people, were smashed and had to be replaced. The post-Holocaust world—a world in which we know the possibilities of evil—demands no less an opportunity for repair. The covenant, along with the Jewish people, tradition and memory—even if torn up or torn from us—like the dream it represents, was not fully destroyed. Without satisfactorily being able to answer the questions thrust on us by the Holocaust, we have, as Rabbi Greenberg explains, volunteered to pick up the crumpled, sullied agreement, proclaiming our intention to move ahead under its terms, waving it in God's face, challenging Him to meet our commitment by fulfilling His promises. Rabbi Shlomo Riskin, another popular Orthodox theologian, asserts that as we have suffered the curses, we will continue trying to mend the world, and we expect to enjoy the blessings. In the end, the response of the Jewish people to the Holocaust has been to reaffirm our expectation of fulfillment of the Exodus message that delivery follows devastation, and to decide to heed the biblical command (DEUTERONOMY 30:15–19) to "choose life and good" so that the Jews and our descendants will live.

FOR FURTHER EXPLORATION

Eliach, Yaffa. *Hassidic Tales of the Holocaust.* New York: Vintage Books, 1988.
> The stories, written during and after the Holocaust by Khassidim, and often recording actual occurrences, demonstrate tremendous faith and the spiritual strength that guarantees ultimate Jewish survival.

Holocaust: Religious and Philosophical Implications. Ed. by John Roth and Michael Berenbaum. New York: Paragon House, 1989.
> An anthology, this book was compiled to make a variety of written works often used by Holocaust scholars more widely accessible. In one place are essays by such leading Holocaust thinkers and writers as Primo Levi, Raul Hilberg, Yehuda Bauer, Elie Wiesel, Emil Fackenheim, Eliezer Berkovits, and Irving Greenberg.

Job, in the Writings (*Ketuvim*) section of the Jewish Bible.
> The classic account of suffering, Job deals with the question of why evil exists in the world. The book has been a source of solace for many Holocaust survivors and others who have experienced personal tragedy.

What Does It Mean to Us? Personal Significance

Emil Fackenheim, a leading post-war Jewish philosopher, put forth a six hundred and fourteenth commandment regarding our lives after the Holocaust: It is forbidden to grant Hitler posthumous victories. We are not to give up on God, we are not to relinquish the idea that the world will become the place we historically dreamed it would, we are not to turn our backs on Judaism, Jewish history or the Jewish people, we are not to forget the martyrs of the Shoah.

His commandment has its critics. But it echoes the essence of the six hundred and thirteen commandments in Torah that regulate every aspect of our existence: live ("choose life"). Traditionally we have done so by remembering—who we are, where we came from, what we have to contribute, who came before us—and rebuilding—our confidence, our culture, our connections to past and future.

We always talk about remembering in conjunction with the Holocaust. Remember the six million. The world must remember so that a holocaust can never again happen. Remember those who perished in order to honor them and give their deaths meaning.

It is memory that has allowed us to last through thousands of years of history. Our religion and our people are founded on the collective memory of revelation at Sinai (SEE CHAPTER ON SHAVUOT). Scripture, throughout, commands us to remember: remember the Sabbath day (EXODUS 20:8), observe the Sabbath as a reminder of the Creation (EXODUS 20:11) and of the Exodus (DEUTERONOMY 5:15); remember—continually—the Exodus (SEE CHAPTER ON PESAKH), remember what the evil Amalek did (SEE CHAPTER ON PURIM).

All those memories define us and help us stay focused on the goal of our national mission. As the Baal Shem Tov (the founder of the Khassidic movement) taught, "Forgetfulness leads to exile while remembrance is the secret of redemption," words which appropriately guard the exit from the history museum at Yad Vashem in Jerusalem. The wall above the eternal flame in the Hall of Remembrance of the United States Holocaust Memorial Museum in Washington, DC, also invokes memory. "Only guard yourself and guard your soul carefully, lest you forget the things your eyes saw and lest these things depart your heart all the days of your life. And you shall make them known to your children and to your children's children" (DEUTERONOMY 4:9).

The biblical citation etched into that wall, while an apt admonition in the face of Auschwitz, is out of context. What the original usage enjoins us never to forget is the experience at Mount Sinai and the laws given to us there, the positive context for purposeful living (SEE CHAPTER ON SHAVUOT).

What we have to keep in mind in recalling the Holocaust is that memory must function, as it does in the Bible, as a positive force. It should not be used to inflict guilt and exact vengeance, and certainly not (as unfortunately occurs) as the defining element of Jewish life. We cannot raise our children to be healthy, constructive Jews by cowering them with expectations that the anti-Semitic world will force Jewish identification on them. Being Jewish mainly because the Holocaust happened or anti-Semitism continues is not sufficient reason to hang on to a culture.

> *To be detested by the whole race of man one must carry within him something truly great.*
>
> BERNARD LAZARE

It was not because rabid anti-Semitism surrounded them that the Jews who maintained their heritage for thousands of years did so. (Until Hitler's demonic program, they always had the option to abandon Judaism for another belief system.) They did so because their way of life had value.

While you are teaching your children about this painful period, remember to teach them that: Don't talk only about the destruction, but about what was destroyed, the rich culture, the intellectual accomplishments, the colorful tradition that was Eastern European Jewish life. Our heritage, our unique value system, our contributions to the world are what we must remember along with our troubled history. These are the memories that will prompt us to effectively engage in the revitalization of Jewish life.

The question each of us must ask is "how will I participate in Jewish renewal?" It may be through your children: raising them to be informed identified Jews. (One suggested response to the tremendous loss of Jewish life is that each family have one more child than it had planned, to replenish the population, and its potential progeny, cut down by Hitler.) Strengthening the community by supporting—with money and volunteer efforts—the institutions devoted to promoting Jewish life (physical, spiritual, emotional and intellectual) is a widespread response. Helping ensure that Israel continues to grow and progress so there will always be a safe haven for Jews is of utmost importance.

If you are creative, produce art, literature, music, dance, or film on Jewish themes. Whether or not you are, read Jewish books, visit Jewish museums, attend Jewish programs, subscribe to Jewish periodicals. And, above all, learn.

Learning has always been a cornerstone of Jewish continuity and renewal. In biblical days, the Israelites emerged from periods of idolatry, devastation and exile by returning to Torah—reading it, trying to understand and live by it. From the ashes of the respected European yeshivot destroyed in the 1940s have arisen new Jewish academies and other educational programs in Israel and in America (many of them supported by funds from Jews who are not themselves particularly tradition-minded, or Jewishly well educated). Day school, supplemental, family and adult educational programs are continually being expanded. Make sure your children have access to formal Jewish education, a good Jewish youth group or summer camp, and take advantage of learning opportunities yourself (don't overlook the possibility of organizing or attending a study group in someone's home).

All of these acts, while honoring the memory of the generations that preceded us, will create positive new memories and strong new Jewish realities for the generations that follow.

FOR FURTHER EXPLORATION

The memoirs by Bella Chagall, autobiographical stories of Sholom Aleichem and accounts of Israel Zangwill paint vivid word pictures of Eastern European Jewish life. They can be useful for family learning and discussion, especially when supported by photographic essays.

Dobroszycki, Lucjan and Barbara Kershenblatt-Gimblett. *Image Before My Eyes: A Photographic History of Jewish Life in Poland Before the Holocaust.* New York: Schocken Books, 1995.
  The three hundred photos that provide a pictorial account of all aspects of Jewish life of Poland, one of largest communities prior to the War, is supplemented by explanatory commentary.

Vishniac, Roman. *A Vanished World.* Farrar, Straus & Giroux, 1986.
  This incredible collection of photographs, a small sampling of the sixteen thousand taken by the photographer with a hidden camera between 1934 and 1939, records the life of Eastern European Jewry as it was being decimated.

Each year the US Holocaust Memorial Museum produces a number of pieces useful in learning and teaching about the Holocaust: selective annotated bibliographies and videographies, guidelines for teaching the subject in a sensitive and productive manner, ideas for commemorative events, on-line activities for students and teacher workshops and the Educators Resource Packet (Education Department, 100 Rauol Wallenberg Place SW, Washington, DC 20024-2150, 202-488-0400, 202-314-7819 for Educators Resource Packet, www.ushmm.org)

Traditions—

HOW WE CELEBRATE YOM HASHOAH

What Do We Use? Ritual Items

Due to the nature of this commemoration and the fact that observance is still in formation, there are no needed ritual items per se; however, two practices gaining adherence make use of easily accessible symbols.

MEMORIAL CANDLES

Usually lit on the anniversary of death for parents (and by some people for grandparents), and on the evening prior to the *Yizkor* memorial service held on the last day of pilgrimage festivals and on Yom Kippur, these candles last a full day. The regular white ones are readily available in Jewish supply stores and supermarkets that have kosher sections. Yellow ones, produced especially for Yom Hashoah, can be ordered. If you are going to light the candles, you will need six of them.

FOR FURTHER EXPLORATION

The Federation of Jewish Men's Clubs distributes yellow memorial candles every year in time for Yom Hashoah. They come in cases of forty-eight that can be divided for distribution among family or group members (475 Riverside Drive, Suite 450, New York, NY 10115, 800-488-4210, 212-749-8100, 212-316-4271 fax, International@FJMC.org). The organization's website features information and ideas related to implementation of the Yom Hashoah Yellow Candle Program™ (www.fjmc.org; pull down the menu under the bar labeled Jewish, click on Yom Hashoah).

YELLOW TULIPS

Flowers symbolize the rebirth that comes in spring—and for Yom Hashoah represent the renewal of the Jewish people. The color of choice comes from the yellow of the six-pointed ("Jewish") stars the Nazis forced the Jews to wear on their clothing. In addition to being a spring bloom likely to mature in time for Yom Hashoah, the tulip is the national flower of Holland, one of the few countries (along with Denmark, Sweden and Bulgaria) that refused to turn its Jews over to the Nazis and actively tried to ensure their safety.

You can purchase the flowers from a florist, or plant bulbs in the fall so they will blossom in time for the occasion. Six are sometimes displayed, like the candles, one for each million Jews murdered by the Nazis.

How Do We Celebrate? Observance

Until the Holocaust, the "newest" important commemoration on the Jewish calendar was Tisha B'Av, and that is almost two thousand years old. Even the minor holiday Tu B'Shevat, as a festive day, has half a millennium of observance behind it. Many of the rituals and customs we follow in celebrating our holidays evolved over time, developing and taking hold not just because they may have been commanded, but also because they represented something meaningful. It may be generations before the commemoration of Yom Hashoah takes its "final" shape. In the meantime, certain formats are emerging for public and private ceremonies, and practices drawn from Judaism's existing trove of mourning, remembrance and affirmation rituals are being tentatively applied for the day.

In the United States, Yom Hashoah is often observed on the Sunday closest to Nissan 27, although commemorations may be scheduled on the weekday evening of the day, or close to April 19. While they generally take place in a communal setting, there is growing encouragement of home recognition of the day as well.

IN THE SYNAGOGUE

Many congregations create their own services, built around Psalms (traditionally recited in memory of the dead); selections from Lamentations, the sacred book read on Tisha B'Av, and literature written by victims of the Holocaust. (*Gates of Prayer*, the Reform movement's daily and festival prayer book, includes selections to be read on the occasion. The Mourners' *Kaddish* and

Eil Molei Rakhamim (Exalted, Compassionate God), part of the traditional service for mourning the dead and the prayer recited at graveside, are frequently used. These services often add remembrances of the Righteous Gentiles (*Khasidei Umot Ha'olam*), those non-Jews who risked their own lives to protect Jews during the Nazis' reign of terror.

It is also common to incorporate periods of silence (an observance repeatedly suggested as the most appropriate response, an opportunity to meditate on the troubling questions raised by the Holocaust). Some congregations sit in darkness. Lighting candles is becoming more and more prevalent, to recall the dead and introduce light and all it signifies: obscuring of the kind of ignorance that makes genocide possible, life, Torah learning, God's spirit. Typically, six memorial candles are lit, to represent the six million martyrs. In some places, a seventh candle honors the non-Jewish victims or the Righteous Gentiles.

Congregations have also used the drama *Nightwords: A Liturgy on the Holocaust* by David Roskies. Created in 1971, it works as a communal seder for Yom Hashoah evening. Congregants read the powerful script, taking the parts assigned to them as they arrive, remove their shoes, and situate themselves on the floor in the posture of mourners. Another option is reading of the scroll created by Elie Wiesel and Albert Friedlander, modeled after the five biblical *megillot* (Song of Songs, Ruth, Lamentations, Ecclesiastes and Esther), each of which is assigned for reading on a specific holiday.

FOR FURTHER EXPLORATION

Roskies, David. *Nightwords: A Liturgy on the Holocaust.* New York: CLAL, 1999
   Weaving modern Yiddish, Hebrew and English poetry with biblical excerpts, philosophical passages, Holocaust accounts, traditional prayer and raw facts, the service's thirty-six roles represent the three dozen righteous individuals believed in Jewish tradition to exist at any moment and on whose merit the world continues. (The audiocassette recording, which includes commentary, is sold through CLAL, 440 Park Avenue South, New York, NY 10016-8012, 212-779-3300, 212-779-1009 fax, www.clal.org. You can download the printed text from the CLAL website: On the home page, click on "online magazine," then scroll down to the bottom of the page and click on "CLAL Holy Days Archive," which takes you to a list of the holidays, including "Yom Hashoah II–Nightwords).

Wiesel, Elie, and Albert H. Friedlander. *The Six Days of Destruction—Meditations Toward Hope.* New York: Paulist Press, 1988.
   This new "scroll" uses the Genesis story of Creation, with an account focused on an individual for each day, to give a history of the Holocaust. A service for Jewish communities and one for interreligious groups follow.

PUBLIC EVENTS

A ceremony attended by the President of the United States, members of Congress and other government officials is held in Washington, DC, annually. The program generally includes remarks by dignitaries, lighting of memorial candles, prayers for the dead, US Army Band renditions of *"Ani Ma'amin,"* the "Partisan's Hymn" and other relevant songs. (Between 1986 and 1995, the Eisenhower Liberation Medal was awarded to a member of the United States Armed Forces involved in the liberation of the camps, or his/her survivor.)

In communities throughout the country, programs take a variety of forms: survivors speaking about their harrowing experiences; discussions with the children of survivors; accounts of the war; readings of diaries, memoirs, memorial books and literature of the Holocaust; performances incorporating first-hand accounts, history and music. Singing the "Partisans' Hymn" (during which survivors traditionally stand), and *"Ani Ma'amin"* is often included at these public assemblies.

In some locations, popularly college campuses, night or twenty-four-hour vigils are held. They may start with a film or lecture on the richness of the world that was destroyed. Presentations on life in the ghettos and camps, examples of the culture of those environments, discussions with survivors, and a memorial prayer or service might follow. Vigils often feature the continual reading aloud of names of victims, sometimes over the background recitation of psalms. Since 1988, B'nai B'rith has sponsored "Unto Every Person There is a Name" on the steps of the United States Capitol and in numerous sites throughout America. The ceremony, designed each year by an international committee, features the reading of names from a list provided annually by Yad Vashem to coordinate with the chosen theme (child victims, for example).

In New York, the annual Warsaw Ghetto Uprising Memorial takes place on April 19 or the nearest Sunday. It features speeches by survivors and public figures and ceremonies similar to those for Yom Hashoah.

FOR FURTHER EXPLORATION

If an organization with which you are affiliated wants to include a reading of victims' names as part of a commemorative event, the list can be procured through B'nai B'rith (823 United Nations Plaza, New York, NY 10017, 212-490-3290, cji@bnaibrith.org; reference "Unto Every Person There Is A Name"). ༺☼༻

IN ISRAEL

Yom Hashoah in the Jewish homeland is a national memorial day. On the eve of the commemoration, when a special ceremony takes place at Yad Vashem, all theaters and places of amusement are closed. During the day, banks, schools and most businesses do not open. At 11:00 AM a siren blast brings the entire country to a halt. Media broadcasts are interrupted, cars come to a standstill and drivers get out of them to stand at attention for two minutes of silence. Throughout the day and all around the country, numerous memorial observances take place.

IN THE HOME

For Yom Hashoah no "official" private ritual exists—any more than an "official" synagogue or community ritual exists. However, as Jews throughout the world continue to grapple with the meaning and implications of the Holocaust, and try to find the most appropriate means of remembering it and properly honoring its victims, some are introducing family commemorations. There is a particular need for them as most public ceremonies are geared for adults only, and as with all Jewish holidays, it is imperative that we teach our children the significance of this one. As for other holidays, we need to introduce particular activities, rituals, and music.

In time, there may be a standardized haggadah for Yom Hashoah. At present, the two most prevalent means of observing the occasion in the home are lighting six yahrtzeit (memorial) candles (yellow, if possible) and displaying yellow tulips.

An attempt was made early on to create a special menorah for Yom Hashoah, and one may yet be realized (in ceremonies at which a seventh candle is lit, a menorah is sometimes used). For now, a line, circle or star of individual memorial candles can be arranged on a table or windowsill. Some people place six tulips on the table with the candles, or in their windows to be seen by those outside. Others plant them, so they will bloom in front of their homes in time for Nissan 27. (It has been suggested that yellow tulips adorn the outside of every synagogue and Jewish institution.)

Having your children help with the planting and tending of the flowers is one way to involve them with a commemoration that is inherently difficult to present to young people. A ceremony of arranging the flowers and lighting the candles is followed in many homes by the singing of *"Ani Ma'amin,"* an affirmation of faith in the future.

Considering the suffering endured by millions of people, it is appropriate for any meals eaten on Yom Hashoah to be sparse and simple, with no sweets or embellishments (SEE "TRADITIONAL FOODS"). Many advocate a fast. In conjunction with abstention from normal entertainments (music, television), dinnertime and the rest of the evening could be devoted to discussions (stimulated by a book the family has read or a movie the family has watched), reading selections of Holocaust literature or looking at books of poems and drawings by children who died in the camps. Talking about family members who suffered and/or died in the Holocaust, and applying conditions and lessons of the Holocaust to current situations in the world are also appropriate.

Children should be encouraged to share what they have learned in school (the Holocaust is taught in Jewish schools, and, at least in states in which Holocaust education is mandatory, public schools as well)—including songs of the Holocaust. Their questions should be welcomed.

FOR FURTHER EXPLORATION

Haggadah for the Yom haShoah Seder. Ed. by Avi Weiss. New York: Amcha and Jonas Publishing, 2000.
Just as the Passover Seder is meant to help each of us, in every generation, feel as though we, too, were slaves in Egypt, this haggadah aims at helping us feel that we lived through the Holocaust. Readings, songs, reflections from survivors and rituals (like removing shoes, watches and jewelry, burning pages printed with the Hebrew alphabet, having children and parents stand in separate areas, eating potato peels) are designed to convey some sense of what the victims endured.

TZEDAKAH

The significance of *tzedakah* in Judaism comes home in a story told about the Italian Jewish community. Even in the closing days of World War II, when the Nazis were losing and knew it, they would not divert attention or resources from killing as many Jews as possible. The only exception was when they could ransom their victims in order to build the private coffers they would need to protect themselves from the Allies.

The Nazis bargained that they would not deport the Jews remaining in Rome if the community handed over fifty bullion of gold. After years of war, the Roman Jews could collect only twenty-five bullion. They appealed to the Vatican, not to give them the difference, but to only lend it to them. The Vatican refused. For lack of money to buy their lives, the Jews were marched to their deaths.

Twenty-eight years later, the Roman Jews who had rebuilt the community were praying in synagogue when they learned that the Yom Kippur War had begun. They stopped their service, closed the doors, and voted to immediately send the equivalent of fifty bullion of gold to Israel.

Saving Jewish lives—and Jewish life—is what *tzedakah* is all about. As a contribution to bringing justice to the world by righting imbalances, each gift is an expression of belief that life on earth can be better, that the world *can* be perfected. The Jews made this assertion after the war, raising an unprecedented amount of money to help the displaced and to support efforts for the establishment of a Jewish homeland. (The best-known Jewish American umbrella fundraising effort, United Jewish Appeal [now known as United Jewish Communities], resulted from the American Jewish community's response to the outbreak of hostility against the German and Austrian Jews on Kristallnakht.)

Traditionally, Jews also make contributions to charitable causes in memory of the deceased. On this occasion of remembering the vast number of people who were murdered, it is entirely appropriate to donate money either to those institutions dedicated to honoring Holocaust victims (such as Yad Vashem in Jerusalem, the US Holocaust Memorial Museum in Washington, DC, the Simon Wiesenthal Center in Los Angeles, or a Holocaust museum, memorial or center in your vicinity), or to those Jewish schools, synagogues, institutions and organizations devoted to Jewish survival and continuity. A gift in a multiple of khai (Hebrew for life, with a value of eighteen: ח, khet, is eight, י, yud, ten), always significant in Judaism, has particular symbolic strength here.

Where Do We Begin? Preparation

If you want to have tulips bloom in front of your home in time for Yom Hashoah, you need to plant them in the fall. Otherwise, you can order the flowers from a florist. Yellow memorial candles must be ordered several months in advance (SEE "RITUAL ITEMS").

To be ready to have a more extensive commemoration at home, during the week or two prior to Holocaust Remembrance Day, choose books or a movie to review with your family, or jot down questions to initiate discussion on the subject of the Holocaust, anti-Semitism, hatred, heroism, humanity, the richness of European Jewish life before the war, and so on. If you have photographs, letters and memorabilia of family members who were victims of or affected by the Holocaust, don't forget to locate and organize them for display or use.

What Are We Supposed to Do? Halakhah

Neither a biblically nor rabbinically ordained holiday, Yom Hashoah has no religious sanction, and therefore there is no halakhah connected with it. However, most authorities would agree that, consistent with our history and religious tradition, it is a *mitzvah* to remember. Just as every Jew in every generation recalls the slavery of Egypt and the salvation of Exodus, every Jew—survivor, child of survivor, generations that come many years after those who experienced the devastation—must remember what we, and the rest of the world, experienced.

The purpose of the memory should not be to exact revenge on the children of the perpetrators, or, as is usually claimed, so that it will not happen again. (Genocide has happened again, and is happening again. It is questionable whether our memory, our chastisements of the world can change what seems to be inevitable human nature.) We remember in order to honor the dead and give some meaning to their lives. And we remember, too, as a warning to ourselves, of the limits of assimilation, the dangers of complacency, the conquering will to live and our on-going role in the world.

In time, as our commemorations become more established, certain practices (like fasts from food or speaking—*tzom shtikah*, a Medieval kabbalistic practice) and rituals may take on the force of halakhah, when they are adapted by the majority of the community, and practiced as custom over a long period of time. (It is said that such observances can be just as important, and binding, as a commandment of God: *"minhag Yisrael Torah hi."*)

What Other Things Do People Do? Customs

DRESS

This is another area in which there are no set guidelines, although over time, some of the practices initiated by select families or groups could become standard. In some congregations, it is customary for people to adopt the mourning custom of not wearing leather shoes, either donning cloth or rubber foot covering, or removing their shoes outside the sanctuary. Although it may seem offensive to some people, participants at some commemorations, or throughout the day of Yom Hashoah, wear yellow armbands or yellow stars that have been sewn onto their coats or jackets. Shoddy clothing, clothing torn as a symbol of mourning, or a black ribbon that has been torn, for the same reason, have all been suggested as appropriate.

What is There to Eat? Traditional Foods

Home observance of Yom Hashoah is not widespread enough for customary practices regarding meals on this day to have developed. The majority of people probably do nothing out of the ordinary at all. However, those who want to create a meaningful impact in their families often model dinner on a typical concentration camp meal—stale almost rotten bread, potato peels, extremely diluted soup. The contrast of such a meal with what one normally eats could actually be more significant than a fast.

Do You Hear Music? Songs to Sing

Music, which we so often use to express joy and exultation, is an effective reflection of the whole range of human emotion. In the ghettos, concentration and death camps, it mirrored the situation around the condemned Jews—sadness and grief—but also their inner strengths: defiance and hope. As Shoshana Kalisch, a survivor of Auschwitz and compiler of a sampling of the songs of her environment, points out, singing in the face of Nazi atrocities was a unique form of resistance, a means of helping the victims retain their belief that life did have meaning, and encouraging others whose spirits flagged.

Two songs emerged as anthems of the victims of the Shoah. *"Ani Ma'amin"* (I Believe) portrays the Jews' unshakable allegiance to their tradition. Even as they were marched into the gas chambers, they sang the affirmation based on the Thirteen Articles of Faith by Maimonides (the twelfth-century Jewish philosopher and scholar): "I believe with a perfect faith in the coming of the messiah. I believe, and although he may tarry, in spite of it all I believe." Though their own salvation was lost, they had no doubts as to the outcome for their people.

"Zog Nit Keyn Mol" (Never Say [you're going your last way]) had immediate impact. When twenty-year old Hirsch Glick, a poet and partisan living in the Vilna ghetto, heard the news of the Warsaw ghetto uprising, he immediately wrote words to a well-known Russian melody by Soviet composer Dimitri Porkass. The song spread throughout the ghetto, to others, and to the camps. A testament to the Jews' defiance and their undying faith, it became the hymn of the Jewish resistance fighters and internationally recognized as a song of courage.

FOR FURTHER EXPLORATION

Kalisch, Shoshana, with Barbara Meister. *Yes, We Sang! Songs of the Ghettos and Concentration Camps.* New York: Harper & Row Publishers, Inc., 1985.

> Compiled by a survivor of Auschwitz who lost most of her family, the collection of twenty-five songs (with piano accompaniment, transliterated Yiddish and English translation) expresses the strength and grief of the Jews' lives. Each song is enhanced by introductory narrative about the circumstances of its origins, and the lives of its composers or performers, often entwined with the author's experiences. ☞☆

What Tales Are Told? Stories to Read

Thousands and thousands of volumes of non-fiction and fiction have been written on the Holocaust, filling shelves after shelves of library space. There are vast amounts of material available for every age group, and more is produced each year. Poets, novelists, historians, theologians, philosophers, and ordinary people who lived through extraordinary circumstances have examined and/or reported on the Holocaust from a myriad of angles.

Names like Anne Frank, Elie Wiesel, and Primo Levi are immediately recognized, and their books are well worth reading. But there are scores of others. A number of good resources can guide you to the memoirs (of children and adults), community memorial books, diaries, biographies, novels, histories, photo essays, collections of artwork and analyses most appropriate for the ages of your children and most interesting for you.

FOR FURTHER EXPLORATION

FOR ADULTS

Frank, Anne. *The Diary of Anne Frank: The Definitive Edition*. Ed. by Otto Frank and Miriam Pressler. New York: Doubleday, 1995.

> The original diary that Anne Frank herself edited and rewrote, a version edited by her father, and comparison to the first published Dutch edition with notes about omitted details are supplemented with information about the Frank family's life before and during the war, their betrayal, Mr. Frank's life after the war, and a report on the diary's authenticity. (In 1987, Miep Gies, who helped hide the family, published her memoirs about the war years, *Anne Frank Remembered* [New York: Simon and Schuster, 1987], and several other books based on the life of the young diarist have since appeared.

Spiegelman, Art. *Maus: A Survivor's Tale*. New York: Pantheon Books, 1993.

> In this highly acclaimed two-volume work, the cartoonist son of a survivor tells of his father's Holocaust experiences, and his own coming to terms with his father and his life, in the form of a comic strip, with the Jews portrayed as mice and the Germans as cats. It is incredibly honest and moving.

Wiesel, Elie. *Night*. New York: Bantam Books, 1982.

> The memoir originally published decades ago—one of the first written by a survivor about his life during the Holocaust and one of the best ever written—is based on Wiesel's experiences at Auschwitz, and is appropriate reading for anyone over the age of thirteen. (Wiesel's novels and reminiscences *Accident, Dawn, Gates of the Forest, Legends of Our Time, One Generation After* and *The Town Beyond the Wall,* and his play *Zalman, or the Madness of God* all deal with Holocaust themes.)

FOR YOUNG ADULTS

Frank, Anne. *The Diary of a Young Girl*. Upper Saddle River, NJ: Prentice Hall, 1993.

> The classic account (first published in 1947) was written by a teenage Dutch girl who hid in a secret attic with her parents, sister and four other people until they were betrayed to the Nazis. Ages 14 and up.

Roseman, Kenneth. *Escape from the Holocaust*. New York: UAHC Press, 1998.

> Presenting several options for each of various situations set during the Holocaust, the interactive book allows readers to determine what they would do and see the ramifications of their decisions. It is surprisingly—and perhaps too—benign, presenting myriad opportunities for escape—and needs to be supplemented. Ages 9–12.

Salvaged Pages: Young Writers' Diaries of the Holocaust. Ed. By Alexandra Zapruder. New Haven: Yale University Press, 2002.

> Anne Frank was not the only adolescent Holocaust victim to record her observations and feelings. This anthology presents fifteen memoirs from Europe recorded on scrounged paper and in the margins of books. The editor provides information on what happened to the diarists.

FOR CHILDREN

Adler, David A. *The Number on My Grandfather's Arm.* New York: UAHC Press, 1987.
A young girl learns about the Holocaust when she notices her grandfather's odd tattoo. This is a sensitive introduction of the subject for young readers. Ages 6–8.

Ginsburg, Marvell. *The Tattooed Torah.* New York: UAHC Press, 1983.
Based on the true story of the discovery and restoration of the Brno (Slovakia) Torah, the book describes the dark days of World War II, and the rebirth of Judaism in the children of the congregation that became the Torah's new home. Ages 6–10.

Klein, Gerda Weissman. *Promise of a New Spring.* Chappaqua, NY: Rossel Books, 1982.
Starting with a simple and brief history of the rise of the Nazis and the concentration camps, this picture book uses the metaphor of a forest that must put down new roots and regenerate itself after its natural order has been destroyed by fire. Ages 6–10.

Wild, Margaret, and Julie Vivas. *Let the Celebrations Begin!* New York: Orchard Books, 1991.
When they know their camp is about to be liberated, the women scurry to create toys out of scraps of cloth for a party they plan to give the children. Based on a recollection, it is an upbeat story for young people, but may bring tears to the eyes of adults reading it to them. Ages 4–8.

FILMS

As with written works, there is no dearth of movies dealing with the Holocaust as a broad subject, and as it affected families and individuals, in documentaries, fiction and dramatized versions of true stories. Many of the commercial films are available for rent. Public and Jewish libraries, Jewish resource centers and Holocaust centers often have titles in their collections.

The 1972 blockbuster *Cabaret* chillingly portrays life in Berlin in the early years of the Nazi regime. *Night and Fog* (1955), the classic graphic film by French director Alain Resnais, reveals concentration camp life. *Shoah,* Claude Lanzmann's two-part nine and a half-hour epic documentary was greeted as a landmark achievement when released in 1985.

A number of wonderful theatrical run movies, some adapted from novels, some based on true stories, depict the fates of individuals and families: *The Diary of Anne Frank* (1959), *Shop on Main Street* (1965), *Garden of the Finzi-Contini* (1971), *The Sorrow and the Pity* (1972), *Lacombe, Lucien* (1973), *Les Violins du Bal* (1974), *Voyage of the Damned* (1976), *Julia* (1977), *Au Revoir Les Enfants* (1987), *Triumph of the Spirit* (1989), *Enemies: A Love Story* (1989), *Europa, Europa* (1992), and the brilliant *Schindler's List* (1993). While it stirred controversy for its use of humor in creating a quasi-fantasy about life in a camp, Roberto Begnini's La Vita e` Bella/Life is Beautiful (1998) is a wonderful, heart-rending achievement.

Both *Judgment at Nuremberg* (1961) and *Man in the Glass Booth* (1975) are effective Hollywood versions of Nazi war crimes trials (the first based on the actual proceedings against Nazi officials, the second a fictional account of the Eichmann trial).

Other notable films include *The Nasty Girl* (1990), *Le Chambon: Weapons of the Spirit* (1988), *The Long Way Home* (1997), *Into the Arms of Strangers—Stories of the Kindertransport* (2000; the last two documentary Academy Award® winners), *The Grey Zone* (2002), based on the true story of the *Sonderkommando* units (Jews in death camps used by the Nazis to assist in the extermination process) and *The Pianist* (2002).

Recent television dramatizations (watch for reruns or rentals) include *Haven* (2000), about the only group of Jewish refugees admitted into the US during the war; *Conspiracy* (2001), the chilling recreation of the Wansee Conference at which Nazi leaders settled on the Final Solution; and *Anne Frank* (2001), encompassing her pre-war life and last days in the camp.

Of Added Note

MUSIC

A number of books to come out of the Holocaust, as well as traditional text dealing with the subject of faith, have been used as the basis for musical creations. Several cantatas and a one-act opera are based on *The Diary of Anne Frank*. Samuel Adler composed a musico-drama (with libretto by Albert Friedlander) borrowing the theme of the near-sacrifice by Abraham of his son Isaac (SEE TORAH SELECTION UNDER "OBSERVANCE" IN CHAPTER ON ROSH HASHANAH): *The Binding: Modern Akeida*. In Elie Wiesel's cantata *Ani Ma'amin,* with music by Darius Milhaud, the patriarchs are asked to intervene to save the children of the Holocaust. Several adaptations, including a choreography, have been made of *I Never Saw Another Butterfly*. Dmitri Shostakovitch set Yevgeny Yevtushenko's "Babi Yar" to music in his *13th Symphony,* for orchestra, voice and choir, and Arnold Schoenberg incorporated the *Shema* into his *Survivor from Warsaw* for male speaker, chorus and orchestra.

MUSEUMS AND RESOURCE CENTERS

There are more than one hundred Holocaust museums, memorials and resource centers in the United States alone. The most well-known are the **BEIT HASHOAH/MUSEUM OF TOLERANCE** of the Simon Wiesenthal Center in Los Angeles; the much heralded **UNITED STATES HOLOCAUST MEMORIAL MUSEUM** in Washington, DC, which opened on the Mall in the heart of the capital in April of 1993; and **MUSEUM OF JEWISH HERIATAGE—A LIVING MEMORIAL TO THE HOLOCAUST**, in lower Manhattan's Battery Park City since 1997. Many others have useful resources, including exhibits and educational materials, to help us remember what happened, and teach our children. A listing can be obtained from the United States Holocaust Memorial Museum.

In Israel, in addition to **YAD VASHEM**, a must on the itinerary of every visitor to the state, and mandatory for official state visits, there is another museum devoted to Holocaust memory: **BEIT LAHAMEI HAGETTAOT** (The Ghetto Fighters' Museum), at the kibbutz of the same name founded by the surviving partisans (north of the city of Acre).

The sites of several of the concentration camps—where there are memorials, museums and in some cases actual camp structures—can be visited: in Poland, **AUSCHWITZ, CHELMO, MAJDENEK,** and **TREBLINKA**; in Germany, **BERGEN-BELSEN, BUCHENWALD,** and **DACHAU**; in Austria, **MAULTHAUSEN**; in the Czech Republic, **THERESIENSTADT**; and in the Netherlands, **WESTERBORK**. **THE JEWISH MUSEUM BERLIN**, devoted to two millennia of German-Jewish history, is particularly notable for its fractured architecture, reflecting what happened to the community.

Yom Ha'atzmaut—
Israel Independence Day

(YOME' HAHTZ'MAH OOT')
IYAR 5
(SPRING; LATE APRIL—EARLY MAY)

The first holiday added to our calendar in close to two thousand years, Yom Ha'atzmaut marks the return to our homeland promised by Scripture. A day of thanksgiving and joy, it is celebrated with a festival religious service and secular frivolity.

Origins—WHY WE CELEBRATE YOM HA'ATZMAUT

Traditions—HOW WE CELEBRATE YOM HA'ATZMAUT

Origins—

WHY WE CELEBRATE YOM HA'ATZMAUT

Where Did It Begin? Historic Foundation

At 4:00 PM on the fifth of Iyar 5708 (1948), the fiery Zionist leader David Ben-Gurion, surrounded by members of the Provisional Council of State on the bunker-like ground floor of the Tel Aviv Art Museum, issued a proclamation to the world: "We, members of the people's council, representatives of the Jewish community of Eretz Yisrael and of the Zionist movement . . . by virtue of our natural and historic right and on the strength of the resolution of the United Nations General Assembly hereby declare the establishment of a Jewish state in Eretz Yisrael, to be known as the State of Israel" (DECLARATION OF INDEPENDENCE OF THE STATE OF ISRAEL).

With that announcement, the two thousand years of waiting to be restored to our homeland—two thousand years of longing, wandering and suffering—ended.

THE ZIONIST DREAM

From the moment God instructed Abraham to leave his father's home and go to the Land He would show him (GENESIS 12:1), Eretz Yisrael became the focal point in Jewish life. It was part of an inseparable triumvirate with the Jewish People and Jewish God, its character a reflection of our people's soul, its condition a reflection of our behavior. Torah, Prophets and Writings continually talk about the Land and our relationship to it—the destination, the home, the place from which we were exiled or the place to which we would return.

The sages considered the commandment to inhabit the Land of Israel equal in importance to all the precepts of Torah combined. Since God gave the Land to us, our connection to it is sacred. Maimonides instructed that we are supposed to live there even if it means leaving a more comfortable abode elsewhere,

133

and the thirteenth-century sage Nakhmanides said that we are to fight to rid it of foreign dominion, and not allow it to become desolate. Having this involvement with the Land was seen as being such an essential part of a complete Jewish life, a spouse whose partner refused to accompany him or her to Eretz Yisrael was granted a divorce.

The yearning for it expressed after the first (Babylonian) expulsion became the theme psalm after the seemingly "permanent" second (Roman) one: "If I forget thee, O Jerusalem, Let my right hand forget her cunning. Let my tongue cleave to the roof of my mouth, if I remember thee not; If I set not Jerusalem above my chiefest joy" (PSALMS 137:5–6).

No celebration was completely happy (a glass broken at a wedding being a reminder of the Temple's destruction), no persecution completely hopeless ("Next year in Jerusalem" proclaimed at Pesakh and Yom Kippur being a wish and expectation). Facing Jerusalem during prayer and conjuring return in the three daily services by asking God to rebuild Jerusalem speedily in our days kept the pain of the loss fresh, the desire for restoration strong. Many Jews obtained vials of Palestine soil, which was sprinkled into their coffins when they died so that they could, in a sense, return to the Holy Land.

Pious Jews did travel to Palestine, particularly toward the end of their lives, and money collected in the Diaspora helped support the small impoverished remnant that lived there throughout the exile. Yet despite the intense emotion and faith surrounding the reestablishment of Jewish government and life in Zion (a traditional synonym for Israel and Jerusalem), the Jewish people did not act to make it happen. The lesson they had derived from the disastrous Bar Kokhba revolt (SEE CHAPTER ON LAG B'OMER) was that they should not take matters into their own hands, but wait for Divine Deliverance. That attitude lasted until the late nineteenth century.

The anti-Jewish laws of 1881 and resulting pogroms in Russia, and the Dreyfus Affair of 1894 in France (in which a French Army captain was unjustly accused of treason just because he was Jewish) finally convinced many Jews that the end to anti-Semitic persecution, and acceptance into their respective national societies, which they had hoped would result from the Enlightenment (with its "Rights of Man," religious tolerance and opportunities for secular education), would never come to be.

One of those Jews was Theodor Herzl, a Viennese playwright, novelist and journalist, who had previously advocated that the Jews convert en masse in order to avert anti-Semitism. Hearing the mobs cry for the death of his people at Dreyfus' degradation ceremony (which he covered along with the treason trial for Vienna's *Neue Freie Presse*) convinced him otherwise. Herzl realized that as long as a wrong was committed by—or merely attributed to—any Jew, all Jews were suspect. The only solution was not assimilation, but nationalism.

The essay he penned in response to what he witnessed in France, *Der Judenstaadt* (The Jewish State), promoted the idea of establishing a Jewish home-land in what had been the Jews' historic Middle Eastern home. Though others (Moses Hess in *Rome and Jerusalem* and Leo Pinsker in *Auto-Emancipation*) had suggested the notion before him, Herzl was the first to establish a political movement based on it and a course of action to accomplish it.

When his meetings with wealthy influential Jews and heads of state (first of Turkey, which at the time ruled Palestine [as the Land of Israel had been renamed by the Romans after their ancient conquest of it], then of Germany and England in the hope they could influence the sultan) failed to bring results, he gathered Jewish leaders from throughout the world at the First Zionist Congress in Basel, Switzerland, in 1897. Coalescing support with the rallying call "If you will it, it is not legend," Herzl called subsequent congresses that attracted increasing numbers of delegates. From them came the World Zionist Organization (an umbrella structure focused on the establishment of a Jewish home) and the Jewish National Fund (which raised money to purchase land in Palestine so Jews could settle there).

RESETTLEMENT OF THE LAND

Although not free of Turkish harassment, the Jews were permitted by the sultan to live in Palestine and found their villages, farms and institutions. Between 1882 and 1903, twenty-five thousand pioneers (*khalutzim*) from Russia, Poland and Romania were part of Aliyah Aleph, the first mass immigration of Jews to the Holy Land since the return from Babylonian exile.

135

After Herzl's untimely death in 1904 at age forty-four (due to heart disease), and throughout World War I, his successors continued negotiating for a Jewish home. As post-war rule of Palestine was about to pass from Constantinople to London, England's Foreign Minister, Lord Arthur Balfour, influenced by his long association with Zionist leader Chaim Weizmann, sent to the Jewish philanthropist Lord Rothschild a letter that became famous as the Balfour Declaration. The critical sentence stated: "His Majesty's Government view with favor the establishment in Palestine of a national home for the Jewish people."

The Jews rejoiced. The Arabs protested—but their worldwide efforts were not sufficient to prevent the League of Nations from awarding the Mandate for Establishment of a Jewish Homeland in the Territory to Britain in 1922. The *yishuv* (Jewish community in Palestine, literally "settlement") prepared by developing a labor movement, self-defense force and structure for future self-governance. The Arabs prepared by stepping up hostilities against them. Under pressure from the Arabs, the British began to waffle on the Balfour Declaration. They claimed (fallaciously) that its intent was ambiguous.

Jewish immigration to Palestine was curtailed—most severely by issuance in 1939 of the infamous White Paper (referred to by the Jews as Black Paper). It presented a gutless and hollow interpretation of Lord Balfour's letter, and caused countless tragedies by refusing entry to Europe's unwanted Jews.

The *yishuv* fought against the British (while at the same time fighting *with* them against the Nazis) with Aliyah Bet—an illegal immigration that smuggled one hundred and twenty-five thousand Jews into the country. In addition, acts of sabotage and aggression were carried out by the country's underground self-defense forces: Haganah (Defense), which became the core of the new state's army, and the more militant Irgun Tzvai Leumi (National Military Organization) and Lekhi (Freedom Fighters for Israel), known by its detractors as the Stern Gang after its founder, poet Abraham Stern.

ESTABLISHMENT OF THE STATE

After the First Zionist Congress, Theodor Herzl had written in his diary that there would be a Jewish state, "in five years, perhaps, and certainly in fifty." Fifty years later, on November 29, 1947, members of the United Nations, no doubt chastened by the world events of the previous decade, voted to partition Palestine into two tiny states, one for the Jews and one for the Arabs. The plan created a checkerboard of the mandate territory that left the Jews vulnerable. Still they immediately accepted. The Arabs would not.

The British, doing little to discourage or avoid Arab hostility against the Jews, as quietly as possible waited out their last months in the Middle East. On the morning of May 14, 1948, they lowered their flags, took their belongings and, as the joke about British departures goes, left without saying good-bye. (The other part of the joke is that Jews say good-bye without leaving.)

The Declaration of Independence of the state proclaimed that day, which granted freedom, justice and peace to everyone, guaranteed freedom of religion, and safeguarded the holy places of all faiths, also extended a hand "to all neighboring states and their peoples in an offer of peace and good neighborliness." It appealed to them "to establish bonds of cooperation and mutual help with the sovereign Jewish people settled in its own land." The State of Israel was prepared, the Declaration continued, "to do its share in common effort for the advancement of the entire Middle East."

The response took less than twenty-four hours: Egypt, Lebanon, Syria, Jordan and Iraq, plus troops from Saudi Arabia, simultaneously invaded the tiny nascent refuge for the people no other nation in the world wanted. They outnumbered and outgunned the Israelis. An international arms blockade on the region further handicapped the fledgling nation.

Anyone available—recently arrived refugees, schoolchildren, women—was enlisted. Jews in other countries clandestinely collected and smuggled armaments, raised money, and lobbied decision makers. Many others volunteered their services directly to the new State, World War II veterans often joining in combat. Lack of training and poor organization hampered the Israelis and caused unnecessary casualties. Yet just three years after the Holocaust, with the enemy screaming for their extermination, the Israelis had one advantage. While the Arabs' objective was to kill them, their objective was most basic: survival.

The War of Independence lasted until early 1949. When fighting stopped, the Israelis had been able to push the Arabs out of the new sections of Jerusalem they had invaded, but lost to Jordanian control the beloved Old City with its historic religious monuments. Elsewhere, Israel had been more successful, extending her borders from the precarious partition plan to embrace the Negev in the south and the Galilee in the north. The gains came at a heavy price: six thousand people, almost one percent of the population (comparable to a loss for the United States of two million), died in the hostilities.

First Egypt, then the other countries contiguous with Israel agreed to a cease-fire. Iraq refused to negotiate an armistice altogether. (Egypt signed a peace treaty in 1979 and Jordan in 1994, after three more major armed confrontations. The other original aggressors remained in a state of war with Israel.) But Israel, an independent homeland for the Jews, had come into existence.

CELEBRATING INDEPENDENCE

Clearly this development in Jewish history called for commemoration, and in 1949, Israeli law established Iyar 5 as a national holiday, Yom Ha'atzmaut (Independence Day). Less clear was just how the day would best be observed. Was the proper mood joy for the victory, or sorrow for the fallen? Was the achievement to be credited to the efforts and sacrifices of those who struggled and died to create the state, from the early pioneers to the war heroes? Or was the establishment of the modern state of Israel part of a biblical fulfillment, and therefore loaded with messianic implications?

The underlying conflict between the secular and religious philosophies necessitated compromise even in the wording of the Declaration of Independence. For the secularists, mention of God would have attributed the establishment of the State to Divine deliverance—which they were not prepared to do. For the religious, leaving out mention of God would have arrogantly credited only human efforts. Everyone was comfortable with the concluding phrase, "With trust in the Rock of Israel, we sign our own hands as witnesses. . . ." Since Hebrew has no capital letters, Rock [or rock] would be read either as meant by the psalmist ["Rock and Redeemer"], or as the "strength" of Israel.

The chief rabbinate was reluctant to assume the authority necessary to declare a holy day after a lapse of two thousand years. Yet the rabbis unequivocally saw the achievement of independence and victory over destruction as a miracle: the beginning of our long-awaited redemption, which we were obligated to commemorate with a feast day. Like a traditional Jewish festival of thanksgiving, it was to be celebrated in synagogue, with special additions to the liturgy and festive attire, and at home with a festive meal and singing. Daily and business pursuits were to be suspended.

Secular authorities stressed aspects of family celebration, suggesting a home observance similar to a Passover Seder. For that purpose, the Israel Defense Forces issued an Independence Night Haggadah containing a service that includes drinking three cups of wine (for the State, armed forces and Jewish people) and provides a selection of readings and prayers.

Memorials to those who had died trying to bring the state into being were a large part of Yom Ha'atzmaut observance—such a large part they threatened to obliterate the joy. For that reason the two aspects of independence observance were separated, with Iyar 4 designated as Yom Hazikkaron, Israel's Memorial Day (SEE "PREPARATION"). Then the mood of Yom Ha'atzmaut became exuberant, and the most popular celebrations moved from the synagogue and home out into the streets.

Until after the country's twentieth anniversary, a major feature of the day was the massive military parade, meant as much to intimidate hostile neighbors as to bolster pride and self-confidence at home. Displays of nationalistic decorations, parades, parties, fireworks, folk dancing, torchlight processions and long-distance relay runs became standard. Over the years, other events, like the International Bible Contest for Jewish youth, special sports competitions, art exhibits, cultural performances and the Hebrew Song Festival have been added to the day's festivities.

The number of Yom Ha'atzmaut observances outside Israel continues to grow. Some congregations in the Diaspora have adopted new liturgies for the day, and cities with substantial Jewish communities annually organize programs to demonstrate solidarity with the Jewish homeland. Celebratory observance is standard in Jewish day schools.

FOR FURTHER EXPLORATION

For both adults and children, there are a number of biographies and autobiographies or memoirs of people who were instrumental in Israel's independence and early leadership—among them Weizmann, Ben-Gurion, Dayan, Meir, and of course Herzl. Any of them will add to your understanding of Israel's birth and development.

For Adults

Collins, Larry, and Dominique Lapierre. *O Jerusalem!* New York: Touchstone Books, 1988.
 Detailed, exciting and poetic, this epic account of Israel's struggle for independence starts from the events leading up to it and continues through the cease-fire. It is a classic—and also available as a set of audiocassettes (Blackstone Audio Books, 1997).

Herzl, Theodor. *The Jewish State.* Trans. by Sylvie D'Avigdor. Mineola, NY: Dover Publications, 1989.
 Starting with an analysis of the problem of anti-Semitism, Herzl's essay provides a detailed practical plan—from liquidating assets in the Diaspora to town planning in the Holy Land—for turning the idea into Israel. (The full text can be read at several Internet sites.)

The Zionist Idea: A Historical Analysis and Reader. Ed. by Arthur Hertzberg. Philadelphia: The Jewish Publication Society, 1997.
 Through the writings of great Jewish thinkers and poets, the development of the ideology that resulted in the state of Israel is traced. The selections show the internal intellectual and moral forces operating in Jewish life from the mid-1800s until the mid-1900s, and which were as responsible as the external forces (like anti-Semitism) in the establishment of Israel.

For Children

Burstein, Chaya M. *What's An Israel?* Rockville, MD: Kar-Ben copies, Inc., 1983.
 This is a wonderful introduction for the young child to the country, its cities, countryside and major attractions. A few simple Hebrew words are introduced and there are short lists of basic facts, and games, puzzles, mazes and pictures to color. Ages 2–4.

Roseman, Kenneth. *Jeremiah's Promise: An Adventure in Modern Israel.* New York: UAHC Press, 2002.
 Part of the "Do-It-Yourself Jewish Adventure Series," in which the choice the reader makes at each plot turn determines outcome, this one begins in Poland in the spring of 1945 with the decision to go to Palestine. As the new country is formed, the adventure wends through cities, kibbutzim, army service, and other places and aspects of Israel's early days. Ages 10–13. ⊙✡

What Does It Mean? Religious Importance

For two thousand years, Jews had dreamed about, yearned for, imagined and idealized Israel. "Next year in Jerusalem" was not the rote phrase so many of us absently say, but a living hope. The planned return to Israel was not a macho nationalistic drive to regain territory stolen from its rightful owners. It was a prerequisite for being able to accomplish our mission, an essential piece of a whole Jewish life, a sacred obligation.

The establishment of the State of Israel looked like the day of redemption we had been waiting for. It seemed to fit the pattern of deliverance the ancient Jews experienced and the prophets promised to their children. The chief rabbinate was encouraged, but cautious (hence, *"the beginning* of the flowering of our redemption" in the Prayer for the Welfare of the State of Israel recited in synagogue on Sabbath and festival days). Never before had a people been dispersed, remained distinct, and returned thousands of years later to reclaim and rule a piece of property from which they had been forcibly expelled. Never before had such near total devastation been followed almost immediately by the community's resurrection. There were signs of Ezekiel's dry bones (37:1–14) all over it.

Still, some questioned whether it could just be an anomalous blip in history. After all, the Maccabees (SEE CHAPTER ON KHANUKAH), seen as saviors in their day, had been successful—but only briefly. Bar Kokhba (SEE CHAPTER ON LAG B'OMER), considered to be the Messiah, had recaptured Jersualem—for an even briefer period of time. Would the new Israelis eventually follow in their footsteps?

The circumstances surrounding the establishment of Israel suggested something different. It occurred during an opportune moment before the Iron Curtain firmly descended (and US-USSR cooperation, needed for establishment of the state, dissipated), anti-Semitism rose, post-Holocaust sympathy waned or the British changed their departure timetable. (And was it just coincidence that the rabbis considered six hundred thousand people to be critical for a Jewish population base [the size of a crowd of Jews for which Talmud instructs a special blessing be made]—and that at the time of Israel's independence, there were just slightly more than that number of Jews in the Land?) Within months, days—even hours—the windows of opportunity could have closed. Recognizing that fact, although he risked Arab attack, Ben-Gurion made the now-or-possibly-never decision.

According to a story current in Israel prior to the Six-Day War, when a rabbi was asked about that impending crisis, he replied it would be resolved either the natural way or by miracle. The natural way, he explained, would be to settle it by miracle. And it would be a miracle to settle it in a natural way (recorded in Emanuel Feldman's *The 28th of Iyar*).

Nakhmanides believed the redemption would come in a natural course of events, with the consent of nations, and would begin with just a partial ingathering of the exiles. As it did. Considering what had happened in prior decades, and what was going on in the world, wouldn't we say that what he defined as a course of events was a miracle? Earlier sages had observed that those who benefit from Divine delivery do not recognize what they have experienced as such. (The Tourism Ministry did not encounter criticism when, in the 1980s, it touted Israel as "The Miracle on the Mediterranean.")

Even if secularists would not call it that, achieving statehood was still a phenomenal change in the status of the Jewish people, and every bit the chance for a cultural and spiritual, as well as political resurgence the prophecies promised, an opportunity to build the foundation for the just society Torah envisions and prescribes. We were back in control in our homeland, the only place on earth where all *mitzvot* apply and where all can be performed (DEUTERONOMY 11:31–32), and therefore, where our full potential, in every aspect of life, can be achieved.

What Does It Mean to Us? Personal Significance

Since the Jewish homeland is no longer the abstract dream it was to our grandparents and their grandparents, but a real place of tremendous possibilities, we are theoretically closer to fulfilling the biblical prophecies regarding ingathering and perfection of the world. This raises a logical question for a Jew: Should I live in the Jewish state?

Dreaming that the Jews would come home, Ben-Gurion found it incongruent, because of Israel's historic significance and the Jews' suffering-filled history, that they did not readily accept the invitation. (The 1950 Law of Return, the first piece of legislation passed by the Knesset, grants any Jew the right to immigrate to Israel and become a citizen immediately. An American may retain dual citizenship, as long s/he does not volunteer to serve in the Israeli defense forces; draftees do not lose American citizenship.)

The displaced refugees of the Second World War, Jews endangered by overt persecution, and religiously inclined Jews readily responded. But despite the pressures individual Israelis have been known to place on their cousins in the Diaspora, despite the acrimonious barbs on the subject tossed in the Israel-Diaspora relations debates, most Jews living comfortably in Western societies remain unlikely to pack up and move east. (An old joke defines a Zionist as someone all in favor of a child making aliyah to Israel—someone else's child.)

It may even seem odd that, being patriotic citizens of one country, we should feel so attached to another that we celebrate its independence as though it were our own. But in numerous ways, it is. For millennia, for the vast majority of our people, Eretz Yisrael was the center of the Jewish universe. Through history,

142

prayers, songs, customs, stories and celebrations, it remained a part of every Jew. Today, official tour guides advise Jewish visitors, "Enjoy everything you see here. It's yours."

The heroic birth of modern Israel restored to Jews throughout the world a sense of pride in our heritage, and its continued existence gives us a feeling of security. No matter how safe we think we are, it provides a psychological crutch: If something disastrous were to occur, we know there is one place on earth that will welcome us. (The argument is often made for continued residence in the Diaspora based on the observation that never before in history have Jews reached the status we have in a democratic country that guarantees our rights. We have to remember that two hundred years is a short experiment in terms of world history. The Jews of Spain during the two-hundred-year run of their Golden Age, and the Jews of cultured civilized Germany in which they could so readily assimilate, failed to foresee the horrors that later befell them.)

Many of the Jews who died in the Holocaust were rejected at the border of country after country. Ships carrying refugees (like the *St. Louis,* which was returned from US shores) were sunk rather than being allowed to discharge their condemned cargo in any of numerous nations. They and countless others could have been saved had an Israel, with open arms for all Jews regardless of age, health, profession or skin color, existed then. Look what its existence has meant to Soviet and Ethiopian Jews. Consider the option it offers Jews endangered by physical threat or economic crisis anywhere—such as Europeans subject to renewed expression of vicious anti-Semitism rampant during the Palestinians' second intifada, or Argentines whose financial stability evaporated around the same time, early in the twenty-first century.

If our history in the world has reinforced anything (aside from anti-Semitism's senseless persistence), it is that we Jews, like it or not, are inextricably bound to each other. We may not want to live in Israel, but we may some day have to. We ourselves may not have to live in Israel, but other Jews who dwell in societies not as free as ours, and whose welfare we, as our brothers' and sisters' keepers, are responsible for, may need to find safe haven there. Therefore, it is up to every one of us to make sure that Israel remains viable, so that when and if we, or our children, or our cousins, need it, it is there.

But we should not look at Israel as just a safety net. No other place has the history or spiritual significance for us that Israel does. Soon it will be the largest Jewish community in the world, and already boasts some of the best minds and most advanced technologies. With tremendous potential in all fields of endeavor, it will continue to develop as the dynamic center of Jewish culture and achievement.

The question for each of us is how can we best maintain a connection with Israel and contribute to its strength and survival. You can find as many ways as you have interests and opportunities to pursue them. Use Yom Ha'atzmaut to explore possibilities, to review materials you have collected about programs, organizations and so on, or to gather information.

Become knowledgeable about Israel by attending lectures or taking classes, subscribing to Israeli periodicals, reading books about Israel and/or by Israeli authors. Familiarize yourself with Israeli culture: attend performances given by Israeli artists—musicians, dancers, and actors. Listen to tapes of Israeli music in your home or vehicle, participate in Israeli folk dance classes, view exhibitions of Israeli art. Support Israel's economic independence by investing in Israeli business or industry, contributing to organizations here or in Israel that support human services and economic development and by buying Israeli products. When Israel is threatened by terrorists and hostile neighbors, urge our elected officials to continue their support of the country. Write letters of appreciation when they do. Counter propaganda spread about Israel in conversations, classes or the media by speaking out and writing letters providing the truth. Encourage friends, family members and colleagues to also advocate on behalf of Israel. (Imperative during times of crisis, such actions are no less important during periods of calm.)

Develop relationships with the people of Israel: learn Hebrew, not only so you can communicate with them, but to be better able to understand how they think. Be a Volunteer for Israel (spending several weeks providing needed human resources to free the overtaxed Israeli reservists to work at their regular jobs). Buy a second home there.

Get your kids involved in Zionist youth groups and camps. Make sure they learn Hebrew, too. Encourage them to have Israeli pen pals with whom to practice the language and learn about the country, and arrange exchange visits. Send them on an Israel summer program or take a family mission. Arrange for your child to have his/her bar/bat mitzvah in Israel, or to "twin" with an Ethiopian Israeli child of bar/bat mitzvah age (arranged through the North American Conference on Ethiopian Jewry, headquartered in New York and Jerusalem).

Get involved with a Zionist organization yourself (find one through the umbrella World Zionist Organization) or support organizations for Israeli institutions (American/Canadian Friends of . . . pick an Israeli college, museum, sports organization, cultural institution, hospital).

From the beginning of our history, Jews outside the Land of Israel have had a lot to do with what happened or could happen within it—from Abraham to Joseph to Moses to the prophets to the sages of the Talmud in Babylon to the leaders in the Diaspora who kept the Zionist idea alive. Like each of them, each of us has an incredible opportunity to contribute to the realization of an ancient dream and a modern necessity.

FOR FURTHER EXPLORATION

FOR ADULTS

Gems in Israel (www.GemsinIsrael.com)
>   The website spotlights Israel's lesser known places and people in monthly features. Among its travel resources are talking maps providing correct place name pronunciation.

Sofer, Barbara. *Kids Love Israel/Israel Loves Kids: A Travel Guide for Families.* Rockville, MD: Kar-Ben Copies, 1996
>   Valuable for both the visitor and resident in Israel, the well-organized guidebook presents more than two hundred sites in major cities and less known locations. With an emphasis on young travelers, it suggests lots of activity-oriented places and interactions with diverse people.

FOR CHILDREN

Burstein, Chaya M. *Kids Catalog of Israel.* Philadelphia: The Jewish Publication Society, 1998.
>   With this terrific comprehensive guide, your kids will learn what Israeli children say, how they celebrate holidays, what they eat, dance and play, what American and Israeli youth have in common and how they differ. Aspects of Israel's history, places to see and so on are included. Ages 8 and up.

Shalom Sesame: The Land of Israel; Tel Aviv; Kibbutz; The People of Israel
>   The well known Muppets and group of celebrity friends (led by Itzhak Perlman) star in these programs, covering their visit to Israel. Each mixes animation, song, comedy and learning in thirty minutes to introduce the cities, countryside and population. Each show is available individually, or in a set along with one on Jerusalem. In English, they feature some elementary Hebrew. Ages 2–12.

ORGANIZATIONS

A number of organizations provide opportunities for active connection with Israel and Israelis. Among them are **AMERICAN-ISRAEL CHAMBER OF COMMERCE**, to assist those doing business in Israel (www.amisbusiness.com); **AMERICAN-ISRAEL FRIENDSHIP LEAGUE**, for cultural and scientific exchange (New York, San Francisco, Tucson, Denver and www.aifl.org); **ISRAEL ALIYAH CENTER**, to aid people considering living in Israel, short or long term (at Jewish Federations, Community Centers, or Israeli consulates and www.aliyah.org); **ISRAEL INFORMATION CENTER**, for publications on a wide range of topics (available through Israel's embassies and consulates and www.israel.org/mfa/go.asp?MFA HOIOWO); **UNITED JEWISH COMMUNITIES** (also known as Jewish Federation or Jewish United Fund), **AMERICAN JEWISH CONGRESS** and **HADASSAH** (for travel programs to Israel (local offices throughout the country and www.uja.org; www.hadassah.org; www.ajcongress.org).

For additional information on Israel, contact the Consulate General in Atlanta, Boston, Chicago, Houston, Los Angeles, Miami, New York, Philadelphia, San Francisco, Montreal or Toronto or the Embassy of Israel in Washington or Ottawa.   ✡

Traditions—
HOW WE CELEBRATE YOM HA'ATZMAUT
How Do We Celebrate? Observance

The number of Israel Independence Day celebrations held on (or, outside Israel, near) Iyar 5 has continued to increase since the start of the Third Jewish Commonwealth. For Jews throughout the world, it is a time of great festivity and gratitude, with commemorations religious and secular.

SYNAGOGUE

While not widely adopted in the Diaspora, special liturgies are fairly common in Israel, where government leaders regularly attend the festive prayer services. The one for evening designed by Israel's Chief Rabbinate in 1949 begins with psalms of thanksgiving (107, 97, 98) and ends with a single blast of a shofar and a prayer that as we have witnessed the beginning of redemption, we will also merit hearing the shofar announcing the messiah.

Their morning service includes the introductory psalms customarily recited on Shabbat and festivals, *Hallel,* also recited on festivals but here without the introductory blessings, and, again without the preceding blessings, the prophetic portion (ISAIAH 10:32–11:12). A preview of the messianic era, it contains the familiar line "The wolf shall dwell with the lamb, the lion lie down with the kid" (11:6).

The choice of this particular reading suggests the Rabbinate's belief that Israel independence is in fact on a redemption par with the Exodus, since the same Haftarah is read in the Diaspora on the last day of Passover. Still, many rabbis were and are reluctant to put the two in the same category. That is why they omit the blessings: It is fine, and appropriate, to express gratitude to God for this incredible shift in our national fortune—so we say *Hallel*. But if this is not *the* historic redemption we have been waiting for, the introductory blessing—which states that our recitation is a commandment of God—along with God's name, would be said in vain. The same reasoning holds for the Haftarah.

Not everyone has agreed with the rabbis' reticence. Some feel that the official service comes up short in reflecting the magnitude of the unique occurrence it celebrates, one that fits the pattern of exile and

> *Empires and dynasties flourish and pass away; the proud metropolis becomes a solitude, the conquering kingdom even a desert, but Israel still remains.*
>
> BENJAMIN DISRAELI

redemption recurrent throughout Jewish history. So organizations and congregations on their own say the blessings prior to *Hallel* and the Haftarah. They include the *shehekhiyanu*, in thanks for being brought to this point, which is fully accepted as appropriate for anyone who regards Israel's independence as an occasion of real joy. During the *Amidah*, they recite *Al Hanissim* (For the Miracles), just as we do on Khanukah and Purim.

Some also read sections of the Torah describing what would happen when the Israelites entered the Land, (DEUTERONOMY 7:1–8:18) or about being returned to the Land after exile and misfortune (DEUTERONOMY 30:1–10). The Prayer for the Welfare of the State of Israel, one in memory of those fallen, prayers for Jerusalem and a Zion Lover's Prayer have also been added to services, along with the song expressing belief in the coming of the messiah, *"Ani Ma'amin"* (SEE "SONGS TO SING" IN CHAPTER ON YOM HASHOAH). Many of these changes were incorporated into the *makhzor* (festival prayer book) developed by *Hakibbutz Hadati* (the religious kibbutz movement). A Sephardic prayer book issued in 1991 and endorsed by Jerusalem's Chief Rabbi Shalom Mashash contains material for study, drawn from traditional sources addressing redemption of the Land. Rabbi Mashash himself composed a liturgical poem recited after the

Independence Day evening service *Amidah* in several Jerusalem and Haifa synagogues.

Communities around the world have added their own touches. An announcement of the number of years since the establishment of the state prior to sounding the shofar at the *Ma'ariv* service is modeled on the Yemenite Tisha B'Av custom of proclaiming the number of years since the destruction of the Temple. Some communities chant *Ma'ariv* to the *yom tov nusakh* (holiday melody). Some Moroccan and other congregations use a *Tikkun L'Yom Ha'atzmaut,* an anthology of readings and prayers (parts of *Kabbalat Shabbat, Shema, L'shana haba'ah b'Yerushalayim, Shir Hama'alot*—perhaps sung to the tune of Israel's national anthem—and *Ani Ma'amin*) for *Ma'ariv* and *Shakharit.* Some add Psalm 27 ("The Lord is my light and my help").

The Conservative movement prayer book includes a customized version of *Al Hanissim* along with suggested readings related to Israel. The Reform movement prayer book features a service written especially for Independence Day.

HOME

For many families, Yom Ha'atzmaut is an occasion for a special meal together. *Seder HaAvodah le-Yom haAtzmaut,* a prayer service developed by the Italian Synagogue in Jerusalem in the mid-1950s, also suggests rituals for a festive meal: having wine over which to recite the *borei pri hagafen* blessing; a new fruit over which to recite *shehekhiyanu* (SEE "OBSERVANCE" IN CHAPTER ON PESAKH); and three matzot and a loaf of leavened bread, in remembrance of the thanksgiving offering in the Temple, which consisted of both forms of bread. (The bread is broken over the matzah, and small amounts of each are eaten.)

Even without doing a seder people often want to add something, like singing at the table—as they would on the Sabbath or festivals. (Candlelighting and *kiddush* are not as yet accepted practices for this occasion.)

Listening to tapes of Israeli music, reading stories about Israel, watching one of the increasing number of videos that have something to do with Israel are good family activities. It is appropriate to use Israeli flags, pictures of Israel, souvenirs of trips to the country, or products made there as decorations in honor of the holiday.

TZEDAKAH

In the years when Herzl's goal was still a dream, metal "blue boxes" were common in Jewish homes. Distributed by the Jewish National Fund (*Keren Kayemet L'Yisrael*), they instructed the holders to contribute regularly (by dropping coins inside) to "Redeem the Land of Israel." The money collected from these *pushkehs* did indeed buy tracts of land so the Jews would legally own them

Today the Jewish National Fund (JNF) remains dedicated to the physical land and its resources in order to maintain quality of life for the people inhabiting it. With the priorities of afforestation and land reclamation, its projects include water and soil conservation, care of natural woodlands, maintenance of parks and recreation sites and road building. It has been an important source of jobs for immigrants who were part of the great influx in the late 1980s and early 1990s. You can still have a "blue box" in your home (so that family members can add their contributions just before Shabbat or holiday candlelighting). Many people make outright gifts directly to JNF or buy trees in honor of special occasions (SEE CHAPTER ON TU B'SHEVAT).

Any organization that contributes to the security or development of Israel, or works toward improving Israel-Diaspora relations, is an appropriate object for Yom Ha'atzmaut donations. You might consider, for example, Israel Bonds (which supports the economic infrastructure of the country), Friends of the Israel Defense Forces (which provides special services for Israeli soldiers), Melitz Centers for Jewish-Zionist Education (which brings Israeli and American Jews together) and Hadassah, the Zionist Women's Organization (which maintains Hadassah Hospital and scores of programs in Israel).

PUBLIC FESTIVITIES

ISRAEL Streets and buildings are brightly decorated with flags and lights. A siren blast signals the start of Yom Ha'atzmaut at nightfall when the speaker of the Knesset, surrounded by dignitaries, lights a torch at the grave of the father of modern Zionism, Theodor Herzl. Twelve others—one for each of Israel's tribes—are lit by individuals chosen as representatives of areas of achievement in the nation's history, culture and struggle for survival. Salvos numbering the

149

years of independence make up the concluding gun salute. Surrounded by giddy abandon, public and private parties, outdoor bands and orchestras, fireworks, and dancing in the streets last well into the night.

Parades (minus the military component since 1968) wind through cities the next day. The President of Israel hosts a reception for the diplomatic corps and soldiers who have had distinguished careers, and an open house for everyone else. At a special ceremony at Hebrew University in Jerusalem, the Minister of Education and Culture awards the prestigious Israel Prizes for outstanding accomplishment in literature, art and science. The International Bible Competition for Youth and the Hebrew Song Festival finals also take place. Picnicking and hiking short distances somewhere in Israel not previously walked are popular activities.

DIASPORA Cities with active Jewish communities devote the day (or one close to it) to public demonstration of solidarity with and support for Israel. Synagogues, Hebrew schools, Jewish community centers and Zionist organizations produce a variety of programs.

For many years, a performance troupe from Israel toured the States in the weeks around Yom Ha'atzmaut for special "Salute to Israel" programs. For decades, New York has hosted the Israel Day Parade. Other cities have also organized parades when funding was available, or presented Israel-oriented fairs, songfests, concerts, and Walks with Israel (in which participants are sponsored with pledges of money for the country). It is common to display the Israeli flag and wear its colors, blue and white (from the traditional prayer shawl: white for mercy, blue—originally derived from a specific marine creature—representing the sea reflecting the color of the sky, suggesting the Heavens, God's throne, and His presence).

Jewish periodicals usually publicize events in the weeks prior to Independence Day. You should also be able to get information about them from your local Jewish Federation or Jewish Community Center.

FOR FURTHER EXPLORATION

Program Guide for Yom Ha'atzmaut and Yom Yerushalayim
    Every year, the American Zionist Movement publishes the guide to provide background information and ideas for home, school and community celebrations. (Available from the AZM offices in New York, Chicago and Los Angeles.)

Where Do We Begin? Preparation

A day of intense mourning precedes the exhilaration of Yom Ha'atzmaut in Israel. Set aside to honor all those who died defending the country—in formation and as a state, Yom Hazikkaron (Martyr and Heroes' Memorial Day) is like no Memorial Day most Americans have ever witnessed or experienced. Flags are lowered to half-mast, memorial candles lit in homes, schools and synagogues. At mid morning, the wail of a siren focuses all attention on those whose lives made everything surrounding the mourners possible. For two minutes, the entire country stops: Cars halt. People come to their feet. Even young children know how and why to stand serenely, sorrowfully.

Religious services include Psalm 9 (about God striking down Israel's enemies), *Yizkor* (the memorial service also conducted on the last day of each pilgrimage festival and Yom Kippur), the army's version of *El Molei Rakhamim* (the prayer said at graveside), and Psalm 144 ("Blessed is the Lord, my Rock, Who trains my hands for battle . . . save me from the hands of foreigners").

Most impressive, though, are the crowds solemnly winding to Mount Herzl and other military cemeteries. Throughout the day people stream, like converging tributaries, old and young, sabras and immigrants, men and women from all parts of society. There is no one in Israel who has remained untouched; in the decades of fighting, everyone has lost someone dear. They place the flowers universally brought, and linger over the graves, too many testifying to the youth of war victims. Outside the burial grounds, you cannot go anywhere without encountering wreath-adorned roadside monuments where former servicemen and soldiers stand guard and more ceremonies and services take place.

As the first stars appear, the siren calls everyone to attention again, initiating the most incredible transformation. It is as though a switch were suddenly thrown: The entire nation in the merest instant brushes away its tears, casts off its somber air, and literally begins dancing in the streets. A carnival atmosphere erupts. Having paid respects to those who sacrificed themselves for independence, it is time to celebrate what they helped create. In traditional Jewish manner, the survivors move forward, exuberantly, to embrace life.

Outside of Israel, some congregations hold memorial services for Yom Hazikkaron. It has been suggested they become more widespread, and that other prayers and readings be recited, such as Israel's Declaration of Independence, poems by fallen *Tzahal* (Israeli Army) soldiers, and David's lament over the battle deaths of Saul and Jonathan, "How mighty are the fallen!" (II SAMUEL 1:19–27).

Any other advance activity will depend on how you and your community observe Yom Ha'atzmaut. You may need to purchase tickets for a performance event, register and secure sponsors for a Walk With Israel, pull pictures and items purchased in Israel out of storage to use as decorations, or prepare food for a special Independence Day picnic or more formal meal.

FOR FURTHER EXPLORATION

The Orthodox Union website maintains a special section for Israel's Memorial Day (www.ou.org/yerushalayim/yomhazikaron/). There, and at the American Zionist Movement website, you will find suggestions for commemorative ceremonies (www.azm.org).

What Are We Supposed to Do? Halakhah

MOURNING

The mourning customs followed for festival days (SEE CHAPTER ON PESAKH) are in effect. However, there is no interruption of the restrictions of the Omer period in which Yom Ha'atzmaut falls (SEE CHAPTER ON LAG B'OMER).

COINCIDENCE WITH SHABBAT

So that the Sabbath will not be desecrated by celebratory activities, and so that celebration will not be cut short by the preparation for and arrival of Shabbat, if Iyar 5 falls on Friday or Saturday, Yom Ha'atzmaut celebrations are held on the previous Thursday.

What Other Things Do People Do? Customs

GREETING

People wish each other *khag samei'akh* (happy festival). The formal greeting among very religious people is *moadim l'simkhah* (have a happy festival), to which the response is *le geulah shleimah* (toward a complete redemption).

What Is There to Eat? Traditional Foods

People often try to eat "Israeli foods" on this national holiday (although the dishes identified with the country—falafel, tahina, hummus, baba gannouj, pita, etc.—are actually all part of the cuisine of the entire region adopted by the Jews who settled there). Items associated with milk and honey or the seven species for which Israel is blessed (wheat, barley, grapes, pomegranate, olive, fig and date [DEUTERONOMY 8:7]) are also popular.

Do You Hear Music? Songs to Sing

The most significant song associated with Israel Independence Day is, of course, the country's national anthem, *"Hatikvah"* (The Hope), the theme song of the Zionist movement and the settlers on the pre-state Land. Naphtali Herz Imber, who wrote the words in 1878, read his poem to the farmers in the early settlement Rishon Lezion (which means First to Zion) when visiting the village in 1882. His audience loved it. One member, Samuel Cohen, composed the melody based on a folk tune from his native Moldavia (apparently the same folk tune used by Bedrich Smetana for "The Moldave").

The song captures our undying hope of return to Zion: "As long as a Jew's heart beats within his breast, and he faces forward to the east with his eye on Zion, our ancient hope continues, the hope of two thousand years, to be a free people in our own land, in The Land of Zion and Jerusalem."

The lively *"Im tirtzu, ein zo aggadah,"* Herzl's urging to the Jews to make Israel a reality ("If you will it, it is no legend") is appropriate, as are songs that joyfully express Israel's survival, such as *"Am Yisrael Khai"* (The People of Israel Live) and *"David Melekh Yisrael"* (David King of Israel Lives). *"Haveinu Shalom Aleikhem"* (We Bring You Greetings of Peace), reflecting our hopes of final redemption, is also the message we tried to introduce in the region. Scores of folk songs, many from the pioneering days of the *yishuv,* extol the Land and describe living and working on it, and deal with the army and fighting (including the moving *"B'Arvot Hanegev"* (In the Wilderness of The Negev [a soldier has fallen]).

What Tales Are Told? Stories to Read

For background to the saga that led to the establishment of Israel, there is probably no better an initial source than the Bible. Deuteronomy, in addition to providing a preview of exile and return, outlines how the Jews are to live on the land. Amos and Micah (in the Prophets section) also stress proper behavior. Prophets Jeremiah and Ezekiel foresee the return of Israel to her homeland. Judah Halevi, Hayim Nahman Bialik and Rachel were among poets who expressed great love for it.

A number of books, particularly for young people, demonstrate the ingathering with stories of children from different parts of the world who have made aliyah and established new lives in Israel.

FOR FURTHER EXPLORATION

FOR ADULTS

Michener, James. *The Source*. New York: Fawcett Books, 1992.
> It's worth struggling past the first chapters of this novel about the development of the Land and people of Israel through history, told in parallel stories about members of a modern archaeological team working on the dig of an ancient settlement, and of the people whose world the dig uncovers.

Uris, Leon. *Exodus*. New York: Random House, 2000.
> Taking off from the actual ship Exodus, which unsuccessfully tried to reach Palestine with its Jewish war refugees, Uris gives a fictionalized account of the establishment of the State of Israel. A bestseller originally published in the 1950s, the book generated tremendous pro-Israel support in America and reawakened Jewish sentiment among the Soviet Jews who circulated underground copies after 1967. The movie made from the novel is worth seeing, but the book provides much more background to Israel's independence, including the Holocaust.

—————. *The Haj*. Garden City, NY: Doubleday & Company, Inc., 1984.
> Experts on Arab culture say this novel accurately portrays the mentality and history of the Arabs with whom Israel must establish peace—and insights into why so many attempts to do so since the beginning of the State have failed. Through the relationship of two families, one Jewish, the other Arab, Uris presents Israel's establishment and growth from the point of view of the Arabs who lived in the territory before mandate days.

FOR CHILDREN

Carmi, Giora. *And Shira Imagined*. Philadelphia: The Jewish Publication Society, 1988.
> At each site in Israel Shira and her parents visit, they see what is there now. When her parents explain what it was like before, Shira "imagines" a brightly colorful scene that incorporates objects familiar to her. The picture book is meant to be a first look at Israel for young children. Ages 4–8.

Levitin, Sonia. *The Return*. New York: Fawcett Books, 1988.
> The National Jewish Book Award winner tells the exciting story of an Ethiopian girl who flees Ethiopia to make a new life in Israel, as her people had dreamed about for two thousand years. Age 12 and up. (*Falasha No More* by Arlene Kushner, *My Name is Rachamim* by Jonathan P. Kendall, and

Alina: A Russian Girl Comes to Israel by Mina Meir tell of other journeys to the homeland and struggles to feel at home there for the seven- to eleven-year old audience. Ruth Gruber's exciting and poignant *Rescue* tells the story of Ethiopian Jewry's homecoming.) ☞✡

Of Added Note

SITES IN ISRAEL

It is possible to trace the birth of the State of Israel through visits to a number of museums in the country. **HERZL MUSEUM** (Jerusalem) documents the life of the founder of the Zionist movement with a significant collection of personal memorabilia and reconstruction of his Vienna study using its original furnishings. Several recreations or restorations provide a sense of what life was like for the early pioneers in Palestine. A member of the family who lived there prior to evacuation in the War of Independence has recreated the atmosphere of a nineteenth-century home, the **OLD YISHUV COURT MUSEUM** (Jerusalem, Jewish Quarter). **TEL HAI MUSEUM** (Kibbutz Tel Hai, in the Galilee) is a reconstruction of the settlement begun in 1907 and evacuated under Arab attack in 1920. **MUSEUM FOR THE HISTORY OF GEDERA AND THE BILUIM** (Gedera, east of Ashdod off the Southern Mediterranean coast), **MUSEUM OF THE HISTORY OF TEL AVIV-YAFO** (Tel Aviv), and **RISHON LEZION HISTORY MUSEUM** (Rishon Lezion) record the early days of these communities.

The history of various defense organizations and clandestine activities is well documented at **BEIT HAGANAH** (Tel Aviv); **GOLANI BRIGADE MUSEUM** (Golani Junction in the Galilee); **MUSEUM OF CLANDESTINE IMMIGRATION** (Port of Haifa), which includes one of the illegal ships, the *"Af-al-pi-khen"* or "In Spite Of;" **BEIT HASHOMER** (Kibbutz Giladi, in the Galilee), about "The Watchman" protective force that played a large role in development of modern Jewish settlements in the area; and **MUSEUM OF HEROISM** (Acre), housed in the prison where members of the Jewish underground were held and executed in the last years of the British mandate.

Memorials to those fallen in Israel's wars are housed at **BEIT GIDI** (Tel Aviv), documenting the battle for Jaffa in 1948; **YAD LEBANIM** (Petakh Tikvah), in honor of those who fell in that settlement in 1948; and **EIN DOR MUSEUM OF**

155

ARCHAEOLOGY (Kibbutz Ein Dor, in the Galilee), which honors members of the kibbutz lost in all of Israel's wars.

You can visit the restored **INDEPENDENCE HALL** (Tel Aviv), where Ben-Gurion proclaimed the State of Israel. Exhibits trace the development of the state's two symbols, the menorah and Star of David, and the period between the UN Partition and Israel Declaration of Independence. The **WEIZMANN MUSEUM/WEIZMANN HOUSE** (Rehovot) document the life of Israel's first president, Chaim Weizmann. **BEN-GURION'S HOUSE** (Tel Aviv) and the **BEN-GURION HOUSE AND GRAVESITE** (Kibbutz Sde Boker, in the Negev) are also open to the public.

For additional information, contact an Israel Government Tourist Office in Chicago, Dallas, Los Angeles, New York or Toronto.

Lag B'Omer—
Folk Festival in Memory of Scholars

(LAHG' BUH OH'MAIR)
IYAR 18
(SPRING; EARLY–LATE MAY)

A minor holiday, Thirty-third Day of the Omer (as its name literally means) developed a following among ordinary people and was added to the calendar as a noted but non-sacred day. Supported by a series of legends around second-century sages, it is observed as a spring outing especially popular among school children and the Sephardim.

Origins—WHY WE CELEBRATE LAG B'OMER

Traditions—HOW WE CELEBRATE LAG B'OMER

Origins—

WHY WE CELEBRATE LAG B'OMER

Where Did It Begin? Historic Foundation

Lag B'Omer is one holiday whose origins we may never know for certain. Like many Jewish festivals, it might have roots in the cycle of planting and harvest, but the two most popular explanations concern great men in our history, both of whom lived under the oppressive Roman occupation that followed the destruction of the Second Temple (SEE CHAPTER ON TISHA B'AV).

AKIVA AND THE "STAR'S" LIGHT

Rabbi Akiva was a great second-century Jewish scholar and leader. Although the Romans had prohibited the practice of Judaism and the teaching of Torah, he continued to transmit the tradition to students who were attracted to his yeshivah (academy of Jewish learning). Although extremely talented, they failed to treat each other with respect. For this behavior, our sages claimed, a terrible plague claimed the lives of twenty-four thousand of them.

According to our tradition, we mourn during the Omer period (SEE "HISTORIC FOUNDATION" IN CHAPTER ON PESAKH) because of the deaths, but interrupt our grief to mark the end of the plague. Lag B'Omer (the Hebrew letter lamed [ל] has the numerical equivalent of thirty and gimmel [ג] of three) may be the day the dying actually ended, a day marking a suspension in the deaths (most communities resume the mourning practices of the Omer on the thirty-fourth day), or a day chosen to represent the day on which no more students lost their lives.

It is commonly believed that "plague" was a euphemism. The burdens of spiritual oppression, land confiscation and heavy monetary tributes under which the Jews subjugated to Rome lived were capped when the conquering rulers decided to erect a temple to their god Jupiter in Jerusalem (which they had renamed Aelia Capitolina). Unwilling to stand for that outrage, the Jews rebelled.

Shimon Bar Kosiva distinguished himself in leading a small army against the occupying troops. Said to have been strong enough to uproot a tree with his bare hands while riding a horse, he emerged as a new Judah Maccabee, whose guerrilla attacks had been so successful against the Greeks three centuries earlier (SEE CHAPTER ON KHANUKAH). Thoroughly impressed with him, Rabbi Akiva changed Bar Kosiva's name (which meant "son of deceiver") to Bar (son of) Kokhba (star), a shining light who would guide the Jews to renewed independence, based on Numbers 24:17: "A star shall go forth from Jacob, and a staff shall rise from Israel, crushing all of Moab's princes, and dominating all of Seth's descendants." Believing him to be the Messiah, Akiva encouraged his students to join Bar Kokhba's efforts against the Romans. When they prepared to join the revolt, they dressed as hunters so they could carry bows and arrows to the woods without arousing suspicion.

Bar Kokhba was successful—for a while. He recaptured and for three years held Jerusalem, until Emperor Hadrian heard about the rebel victories and reinforced his troops in the territory. In the ensuing put down of the revolt, the Romans killed tens of thousands of Jews, including, in 132 CE, the supposed Messiah and his men. According to the third-century Roman historian Dio Cassius, in addition to the close to six hundred thousand Jews slaughtered, countless others died of sickness and fire, and fifty fortresses and almost one thousand of the most important settlements were destroyed. After the devastating defeat of the last Jewish stronghold, Betar (southwest of Jerusalem) in 135, the rulers prohibited Jews from being within sighting distance of Jerusalem (except on the day of mourning for its destruction, Tisha B'Av), and Jewish life in Palestina (the name Rome gave the area) effectively ended until the modern era.

Although parts of the Talmud were written as the events unfolded, the commentary barely discusses the Bar Kokhba revolt, a statement of the rabbis' attitude toward the entire episode. Believing that it would ultimately be a futile cause of tremendous bloodshed (which it was), many of them opposed the rebellion. They feared it would turn Bar Kokhba—whom they thought arrogant—and Akiva's followers into martyrs and inspire similar useless efforts in the future. That is why the cause of the students' deaths was veiled as disease, rather than reported as war.

During the Gaonic period (the time of the great Torah scholars between the sixth and eleventh centuries) the rabbis could more objectively assess the historic occurrences. They recognized the end of the "plague" as the date Bar

Kokhba and company had recaptured Jerusalem, and made it an official semi-holiday. This fits with the idea that Lag B'Omer marked a "suspension" of dying—because the war continued after this temporary victory.

Recognition was not afforded Bar Kokhba himself until Jewish nationalism developed at the end of the nineteenth century. However, that did not stop the process of turning him into a folk hero by the Jews who, enduring generations of persecution and dreaming of a return to their homeland, used the legend to prop up their hopes. In Eastern Europe and later in America, it became customary for Jewish school students to go to parks or woods on Lag B'Omer, for picnics, recounting stories about the heroes of the holiday, and playing with bows and arrows in commemoration of the fighting against the Romans.

FOR FURTHER EXPLORATION

FOR ADULTS

Finkelstein, Louis. *Akiba—Scholar, Saint and Martyr.* Northvale, NJ: Jason Aronson Inc., 1990.
> This is a readable, comprehensive look at the life, political leadership, ethical thinking, religious contributions and martyrdom of one of our greatest sages.

Yadin, Yigal. *Bar Kokhba: The Rediscovery of the Legendary Hero of the Last Jewish Revolt Against Imperial Rome.* New York: Random House, 1971.
> Written by the professor of archaeology who led the excavations, this fascinating account follows the discoveries—including fifteen dispatches written or dictated by the military commander himself that brought Bar Kokhba from the realm of legend to real life, and reconstructs life and developments at his time.

FOR CHILDREN AND YOUNG ADULTS

Whitman, Amram. *Bar Kokhba.* New York: Bloch Publishing Company, Inc., 1985.
> In this novel for young adults, the excitement, dangers and hopes experienced by the Jews during their doomed fight for freedom come alive in action and dialogue. Ages 12–15.

BAR YOKHAI AND THE LIGHT OF TORAH

One of Akiva's greatest students was Rabbi Shimon Bar Yokhai. Like his teacher, Bar Yokhai openly defied the decree against the study and teaching of Torah. Sentenced to die after Bar Kokhba's death in battle and the fatal torture of Akiva (which we recall in memorials to the Ten Martyrs on Tisha B'Av and Yom Kippur), he went into hiding with his son Eleazar. For thirteen years, accompanied only by Torah and other sacred writings, they lived in a cave, sustained by a carob tree that grew at its entrance and a spring just outside it. According to one story, students visited them one day each year—said to have been Lag B'Omer—for the purpose of learning and/or bringing them food. They—like the students in the Bar Kokhba account—carried bows and arrows and disguised themselves as hunters. Father and son emerged only after Hadrian's death, and were recognized as great sages.

Before he died—on the thirty-third day of the Omer—Bar Yokhai revealed to his disciples the sacred wisdom he had discovered through his years of intense Torah study. Tradition says that the day was filled with endless joy and with great light, and that the sun did not set until he had completed telling his students all he wanted to relate. He words were recorded in what was to become the basic text of kabbala (Jewish mysticism), the Zohar ("splendid, brilliant light"). The book first appeared in the thirteenth century, brought to light by Moses ben Shemtov de Leon. Even though generally believed to be a product of the Middle Ages, it was attributed to the insights and teachings of Bar Yokhai.

Bar Yokhai's last request was that his death and its anniversary be observed by celebration, rather than the mourning and fasting that normally accompany the loss of a great scholar. He was happy that his life's work had been finished. Anticipating a mystical marriage of his soul with God, he rejoiced as a bridegroom does on his wedding day and wanted everyone to share his joy. Upon his death, the story goes, a rainbow appeared in the sky for the first time since his birth. The symbol that God would not destroy the earth as He had with the flood of Noah's time (GENESIS 6:13–9:17), the rainbow, had been replaced by the righteous sage himself as God's commitment to sustain the world.

It was not until the Middle Ages that the connection between the joyous yahrtzeit (death anniversary) of the father of Jewish mysticism and the thirty-third day of the Omer was made. Rabbi Khayim Vital and the sixteenth-century kabbalists of Safed (a town in Israel's northern Galilee region, near Lake Kinneret and Tiberias) started the custom of gathering the night before Lag B'Omer in nearby Meron, the mountaintop site of the supposed tombs of Yokhai and his son, and singing and dancing around bonfires until dawn.

The celebration spread throughout the Sephardic world, and was termed *hillula* (Aramaic for festival or celebration). Used especially to denote a wedding celebration, the word was later applied to the yahrtzeit of famous rabbis and scholars (whose souls wed with God), occasions often accompanied by pilgrimage and rejoicing. Children often played with bows and arrows, here said to symbolize the rainbow (in Hebrew the archer's bow and the multi-colored arc are both *keshet*) that appeared when the rabbi died.

THE AGRICULTURAL CONNECTION

The time of year in which Lag B'Omer falls—late spring—is a nerve-wracking one for farmers. Between the barley and wheat crops, they worry about how weather, insects or plant disease could affect their food supplies and livelihoods. The fear that the earth would not resume producing sustenance was universal in primitive societies, and certainly not a time the farmers wanted to or could be merry and frivolous.

The farmers' concerns mirror those experienced by the post-Exodus Israelites in the desert just after their liberation, which occurred at this time of year. Having exhausted their provisions from Egypt, they complained about their situation and expressed the wish to return to the house of bondage, where at least they had their fill of bread (EXODUS 16:3). The next day, God told Moses that they would receive manna (bread from heaven) in another day, on Iyar 18—which is Lag B'Omer. According to some authorities, this is the reason we celebrate the date.

Once the Temple was destroyed, the Jews could no longer bring the barley offerings that marked each day of the Omer period that began during Pesakh, or the wheat bread that ended it on Shavuot. They became especially sad at the lack of the particular sacrifice through which they believed they could ensure a good outcome for the produce, and remained in mourning for the Temple. The restrictions of the period may have been institutionalized reflections of these feelings, with the thirty-third day a brief built-in relief.

Secular scholars and historians have pointed out the ancient Roman belief that souls came back to earth at this time of year to haunt the living, and would only be appeased by funerals. Mid spring, a nonproductive period between growing seasons, was viewed as an inauspicious time for human production, too. Therefore, for thirty-two days (basically coincident with the month of May) no weddings took place (Roman folk sayings about unlucky May marriages were later echoed in England, France and Germany), and on the thirty-third day, a festival was held. The time frame served the Jews. The pagan prohibitions, like other non-Jewish customs that have crept into Judaism throughout our history, could have been adapted because they fit our own needs.

Others have drawn parallels with the Medieval European May Day celebrations, when children customarily shot bows and arrows in the woods (originally to chase demons who could spoil vegetation), and bonfires were lit to frighten the demons and witches so they could not harm livestock. Evil spirits were thought to be particularly prevalent on May 1, which was preceded by Walpurgis Night (Witches' Sabbath). The German peasants went into the woods to shoot at them, and in England archery contests were held—perhaps the genesis of the Robin Hood legend. The Jews may have picked up the custom as being reminiscent of shooting at our own "demons," the oppressors who occupied our land and threatened our way of life.

What Does It Mean? Religious Importance

Although Lag B'Omer—by any definition—is not a sacred occasion, both versions of the reason we celebrate it underline a main principle of Jewish life. The importance of Torah, of maintaining it, studying it, and ensuring continuity through teaching it, were the motivating factors in the lives of both men.

While endangering themselves in the process, these rabbis resisted the Romans to uphold the values of Judaism, spreading their learning and love of Torah, promoting it as the only worthwhile way of life. A midrash relates that when Pappus ben Judah came upon Akiva holding a public lesson, in clear defiance of the Roman decree, he wondered if the sage were not afraid of the government. Akiva responded with a parable: A fox walking by a river asked the fish, swimming rapidly in every direction, why they were fleeing. To avoid the nets and traps set by men, they replied. So the fox invited them to escape to dry land. But the fish retorted, "If we are afraid in a place where we can stay alive, how much more fearful we would be where we are certain to die!"

As afraid as the Jews were to study Torah in defiance of Rome, they believed they had much more to lose by trying to live without it. They recognized that

Torah, which provided an unparalleled moral structure and guided them to personal and communal fulfillment, was their "sole means of survival and long life" (DEUTERONOMY 30:20).

The deaths of Akiva's students, the failure of the Bar Kokhba revolt, the destruction of Betar and the execution of Akiva severely darkened the Jewish world. However, as a result of the Roman oppression, Shimon Bar Yokhai shined the brilliant light (Zohar) on our understanding of the universe. The process of learning, illuminating the world and inspiring others is what Torah, and Judaism, are all about.

What Does It Mean to Us? Personal Significance

Until he was forty years old, the poor shepherd Akiva ben Joseph could not even read and had no interest in education. He fell in love with Rachel, the daughter of his rich boss, who also loved him, but said she would marry him only if he became a Torah scholar. At his age, he thought it an impossible task. But one day, while watching the sheep, he noticed that the continual passage of water on a stone had created a groove in it. He realized that if steady drops of water could wear down rock, certainly he could learn by continually applying himself. He went on to become one of the greatest Torah scholars to have ever lived (and Rachel's husband). Once he himself was learned, he taught others.

By his example, we learn that it is never too late to begin to learn about our heritage. Little by little we can make accomplishments. It is unlikely they would be of the magnitude of Akiva's (unless, like him, we were to dedicate ourselves solely to learning—which he did for twenty-four years) but certainly worthwhile. Akiva's life also demonstrates that it is not enough to have knowledge; you must share it with others, as he did, despite the hardships involved.

We learn about the necessity to balance learning with other aspects of life from Shimon Bar Yokhai. After he spent twelve years in his cave, the legend goes, the prophet Elijah appeared to tell him that the Roman Emperor Hadrian, who had sentenced him to death, had himself died. The first thing Bar Yokhai and his son saw upon emerging were farmers busy plowing and seeding their fields. It seemed to them a waste of time that should have been devoted to

Torah. The anger reflected in Bar Yokhai's eyes burned the fields and trees. A heavenly voice challenged him. "Would you destroy My world?!" and ordered the two back to the cave for an additional year.

They learned, through more Torah study, that the greatest holiness is in the physical world, that we are supposed to use the material to become spiritual and serve God. When Bar Yokhai finally emerged from hiding, he applied himself to healing the world.

Together, these two great men, Akiva and Bar Yokhai, demonstrate the important messages of our heritage: learn, teach and do. Even if you have spent little or no time in your life reading about or attending a program or class about some aspect of Judaism, there is no reason you cannot do so now. Once you have increased your knowledge, share it with your spouse, child, sibling, parent, friend, or neighbor. You will also be able to apply what you have learned to help make the world a better place.

One of the keys to doing so, as we learned at Passover, is to treat all other people with respect. It is a courtesy we often disregard within our own community. Even though each one of Rabbi Akiva's students was reputed to be special in a unique way, each one recognized only his own style of serving God, discounting his fellow students. With all their learning they ignored a fundamental principle of Judaism, love of a fellow Jew (*Ahavat Yisrael*).

Attributing their deaths to this transgression is supposed to teach us the importance of embracing all members of the community and accepting diversity within the whole. Yokhai's forced return to the cave to refine his perspective teaches that not everyone has to be involved in the same pursuits: It is enough if the intentions and goals match.

Consider what you are doing, or failing to do, to promote *Klal Yisrael,* the unity of the Jewish people. Do you belittle Jews who have chosen to be either more or less observant/traditional than you? Do you say disparaging things about a particular group of Jews based on their dress, behavior, or lifestyle? Do you let opportunities to challenge the negative comments of others pass? The judgments that accompany perceived differences are often a result of ignorance, theirs and yours. The entire community can be richer and stronger if we drop our prejudices (it is said that the worst anti-Semites are Jews) and speak with and try to learn from each other, the scholar from the farmer, the farmer from the scholar, the *streimel*-wearer from the *kippah*-shunner and vice versa. The more you know, the better prepared you will be to determine what form your service to God could take.

Traditions—
HOW WE CELEBRATE LAG B'OMER

How Do We Celebrate? Observance

Though both call it Scholars or Students Day, Ashkenazim and Sephardim have developed two different styles of and reasons for celebrating the folk festival.

ASHKENAZIM AND AKIVA

In America (as Eastern Europe before) Lag B'Omer is primarily an occasion for Jewish school students. Based on the stories of Akiva and the Bar Kokhba revolt, they have traditionally been taken on field trips—generally to forests, woods and parks—for archery (reminiscent of the scholar-soldiers and their bows and arrows), hikes, picnics and sporting events. In Israel, children go on *tiyulim* (outings). On hilltops and empty lots throughout the country, they make bonfires, sing and dance around them, and roast potatoes.

SEPHARDIM AND RASHBI

HILLULA Hundreds of thousands of Khassidim and others attuned to kabbala, Sephardim from throughout Israel and nearby countries, and anyone else who likes a good party, stream to Mount Meron in northen Israel for the *hillula* of Rabbi Shimon Bar Yokhai (referred to by his acronym Rashbi—RAbbi SHimon Bar Yokhai). Since 1833, a procession has started at the Beit Abu synagogue in the nearby city of Safed, known for its connections to mysticism. Participants carry an ancient Torah scroll (greeted by flowers and rose water thrown from overhead balconies) to the outskirts of the city. From there, the celebrants (who used to walk the distance) are transported by vehicle to the tomb at the top of the mountain, where a huge bonfire is lit at midnight.

The entire route and every available spot up and down the slopes host pilgrims, their cars, campers and tents (some quite elaborate, looking more like tavernas than temporary sleeping quarters, with their lanterns, music systems and full cooking facilities). Fires dot the entire site. Oriental music and the smoky scent of lambs roasting on hundreds of individual spits pervade the air.

What is the Zohar? The Holy One took a gem from His crown and dropped it on the earth. The gem split and scattered into millions of brilliant gleams . . . which came to satisfy all the famished who thirst for light, and to quicken and warm all that had been killed by the cold of science and the darkness of ignorance, by the blindness of nature and the cruelty of men.

HILLEL ZEITLIN

In contemporary times, the *hillula* has taken on more and more of a carnival atmosphere, with hawkers selling all sorts of flea market merchandise and representatives of every yeshivah and Jewish institution offering *brakhot* for a price. The closer to the graves, the more dense the crowds jostling to get to the burial places to plea for cures for illness, pain and infertility. Those praying for miracles light candles in the indentations in the stone walls. Many people leave candy or personal items at the tomb.

Since ancient days it has been customary to throw silk scarves and other clothing into the fire (called *hadlakot,* or ignitings) despite rabbis' protests against the wastefulness. Over the years those running the observances have attempted to persuade would-be burners to sell the garments and distribute the proceeds to the poor in honor of Bar Yokhai.

Some say the bonfires reflect the ancient communications system between settlements (at their recapture of Jerusalem Bar Kokhba and his men lit signal fires that were relayed by successive groups of villages throughout the country). A strong connection also exists between fire and Shimon Bar Yohkai himself.

Proverbs likens the soul to a candle (20:27). In the Zohar, attributed to Bar

Yokhai, the comparison is explained: If you watch a flame, you will see that it moves back and forth, and stretches itself, continually reaching higher, like the soul striving for spiritual fulfillment. (This explains why a religious Jew "shuckles" back and forth when he prays: He is imitating the movement of fire, helping his soul become elevated.) It is said that the soul of a *tzaddik* (a righteous person), like a huge flame, rises to the highest level after he dies.

The day after the procession and bonfires, celebration continues on Meron. In the parks of nearby Safed, family clans gather for picnics featuring lively music, dancing, and a profusion of food.

HAIRCUT From ancient days it has been customary to wait until a Jewish boy turns three before giving him his first haircut. That age marks the time he is ready to learn. Along with getting his hair cut, in such a way that leaves the *peiyot* (the hair on the sides of the head forbidden to be completely removed [LEVITICUS 19:27]), he receives his first *kippah* and tzitzit, and is introduced to Torah study with candy and honey so that he associates it with sweetness.

The Ari (Rabbi Isaac Ben Solomon Luria), most revered of the sixteenth-century Jewish mystics, began the tradition of giving boys the first haircut—called *khalakah* in Hebrew, *upsherenish* in Yiddish—at Meron. The ceremony may have become associated with Lag B'Omer simply because haircuts are not allowed during the Omer period and relaxation of that restriction on this one day provided the opportunity to celebrate the "coming of age" of little boys who had turned three after the beginning of Passover. Believing that they will secure health, happiness and long life for the child, Khassidim and Sephardim in particular bring their three-year-old sons to Bar Yokhai's place of burial on that day. Parents want to have a rabbi or dignitary participate as friends and family members each take a snip of the long locks, often throwing them into the bonfire. It is common for a joyous party to be held afterwards.

What Are We Supposed to Do? Halakhah

RELIEF FROM RESTRICTIONS

On only thirty-two of the forty-nine days between Pesakh and Shavuot are the prohibitions of mourning ordained for *Sefirah* permitted. On the seven days of Pesakh, two days of Rosh Khodesh Iyar, one day of Rosh Khodesh Sivan, plus seven Shabbatim—all of them festivals—mourning ceases. The Gemarah (commentary on the written version of the Oral Law) states that Akiva's students died only on the non-festival days—those thirty-two—and that is why the mourning practices are imposed then and the thirty-third day represents a day of relief.

However, there are differences of opinion as to whether the prohibitions are supposed to last thirty-two days (the entire Omer period of non-exempted days), until the thirty-third day (symbolic of the period of dying), or from after the thirty-third day. The most common observance is to suspend the Omer restrictions on the thirty-third day, and then resume them on the thirty-fourth, until Shavuot. If you are unsure about the custom in your place of residence, consult a local rabbinic authority.

MARRIAGE

A wedding, permitted on Lag B'Omer, is to be held during the day. While it should not begin the night before (mourning is supposed to continue into at least part of the thirty-third day), the marriage feast may extend into the evening and night of the thirty-fourth day.

HAIRCUTS

If Lag B'Omer falls on Sunday, it is permissible (and customary) to have a haircut—not allowed since before Pesakh—on Friday, in honor of Shabbat.

What Other Things Do People Do? Customs

OTHER TIMES AND PLACES

CANDLES AND CONTRIBUTIONS In Judeo-Spanish, Syrian and Sephardic communities, it was customary on Lag B'Omer to light candles and raise communal funds. Moroccan Jews accompanied sale of tapers in memory of Rabbi Shimon Bar Yokhai and *tzaddikim* buried in their country by study of

Zohar and singing. They called the occasion *Leilui* (Night) *Nishmat* (of the Souls) *Hatzaddikim* (of the Righteous).

TUNISIAN HILLULA Nowhere were such proceedings more elaborate than Tunisia, where the Jews of Djerba have long hosted a two-day *hillula*. Before the majority of North African Jewry left their native countries after the 1967 Six-Day War, tens of thousands traveled to the small traditional Jewish village of Hara Seghira on the island off the southern coast of Tunisia. (The celebration still draws a respectable gathering, mostly from Tunisia, but also from France, Israel and Morocco.)

Pilgrims bring to life the usually quiet hostel built for the occasion opposite the historic El Ghriba Synagogue (target of a 2002 terrorist attack). Many of the women, dressed in white and adorned with traditional jeweled wedding head-pieces, bracelets and anklets, situate themselves on the balcony running around the entire courtyard filled with men, women and children. Amidst music, singing and drinking, honors are auctioned for the privilege of placing layers of colored veils on a huge traveling menorah, shaped like a wedding cake equipped with places for hundreds of candles around its multiple brass tiers. After substantial fundraising, a joyous procession of the pilgrims, local people and musicians lead the menorah through the community.

Later in the synagogue, pilgrims buy candles to place in the menorah, on available spots in the sanctuary, or, particularly for women seeking special bless-ings, in the small crawl-space grotto under the Ark. It is believed that if a woman who wants to find a marriage partner or conceive a child places a raw egg in the space, lets it cook overnight in the heat of all the candles around it, and eats it the next day, her prayers will be answered.

What Is There to Eat? Traditional Foods

The only food regularly associated with Lag B'Omer is the hardboiled egg. This may be connected with the mourning of the previous days (as eggs, symbolizing the wholeness of life, are the customary first food in a house of mourning), but likely was because they were easy for children to take on their Lag B'Omer picnics.

What Tales Are Told? Stories to Read

Aside from the folktales, legends and stories such as those contained in the collections listed in "More Good Information," there is little available specifically for Lag B'Omer.

Of Added Note

IN ISRAEL

The military dispatches from Bar Kokhba discovered among the Dead Sea documents are displayed at the **SHRINE OF THE BOOK**, part of the Israel Museum in Jerusalem. Some of the thousands of Bar Kokhba coins (inscribed "Year One of the Redemption of Israel," "Year Two of the Freedom of Israel" and "Freedom of Jerusalem") are also on display at the **ISRAEL MUSEUM**. To protect themselves and their rich olive oil business from the Romans, the Jews during the second century moved underground into an incredible labyrinth of caves in the limestone area south of Jerusalem. Discovered and excavated in the 1970s and 1980s, the caves, administered by the neighboring moshav (communal farm) **AMATZIA**, are open to the public. The ingenuity of the builders, who created secret entries through cisterns, false alleys and small windows to trick and trap intruders, and floors to preserve leaks of valuable olive oil, make it a fascinating place to visit.

Yom Yerushalayim—
Jerusalem Reunification Day

(YOME' YEH ROO' SHAH LIE' YIM)
IYAR 28
(SPRING)

The last holiday added to the Jewish calendar, "Jerusalem Day" celebrates the reestablishment of Israeli control over our entire eternal capital and spiritual center following the recapture of the longed-for Old City in 1967. Observance is continually expanding outside Israel because of the significance of the sacred city in Jewish history and continuity.

Origins—WHY WE CELEBRATE YOM YERUSHALAYIM

Traditions—HOW WE CELEBRATE YOM YERUSHALAYIM

Origins—

WHY WE CELEBRATE YOM YERUSHALAYIM

Where Did It Begin? Historic Foundation

JERUSALEM LOST AND FOUND

According to the United Nations Partition Plan for Palestine, Jerusalem—the city considered holy by the world's three major monotheistic religions, and the scene of battle for control since David led the Israelites to it two hundred years after the initial conquest of the Land—was to have been internationalized. During the War of Independence (SEE CHAPTER ON YOM HA'ATZMAUT), the Arabs surrounded it, leaving those within the ancient capital without electricity, enough food, water or ammunition—an eerie reenactment of the sieges in 586 BCE and 70 CE (SEE CHAPTER ON TISHA B'AV).

When the War ended, the cease-fire line ran right through Jerusalem, with the Jews on the wrong side of it. The Old City, the part with historic and emotional significance for us, ended up under Jordanian control. Despite the terms of the armistice that guaranteed access to the historic district, not a single Jew was allowed to go to Judaism's holiest remaining site, the Western Wall (*Kotel Ha Ma'aravi*).

According to Jewish tradition, the Wall—not part of the Temple itself, but the last standing section of the great retaining and defense structure for the Temple Mount built by Herod—was where God's presence on earth, the Shekhinah, moved when Her ("God's Spirit" is feminine) previous abode in the Temple's Holy of Holies was destroyed. For that reason it was the holy spot in Israel Jews most wanted to visit for there, they believed, they stood in God's presence.

So from the time of the destruction of Jerusalem in the year 70, pious Jews undertook often treacherous journeys to find their way to the Wall, where their heartfelt supplications were accompanied by such expressions of emotion that non-Jews named the location the Wailing Wall. Being blocked from it after the War of Independence, when we were so close, was frustrating and painful.

Having never signed a peace treaty with Israel following their defeat in 1949, the neighboring Arab nations remained in a state of war. Terrorist and sniper attacks across the borders were common. Agricultural settlements in the country's north were often shelled by artillery. All Israeli homes had to be equipped with bomb shelters in which many children of the post-independence generation spent their nights.

Two days after Yom Ha'atzmaut in 1967, Gamal Abdul Nasser, President of Egypt, began amassing troops in the Sinai Peninsula and insisted that the United Nations remove its peacekeeping forces from the region. The next week, he closed the Straits of Tiran, strangling Israel's Red Sea supply route. Israel called up just about every able-bodied man between the ages of eighteen and fifty-five, secular and religious, student and employee, professional and laborer.

> *In the din and tumult of the age . . . the still small voice of Jerusalem remains our only music.*
>
> ISRAEL ZANGWILL

Pressure on Israel mounted toward an unbearable level. Arab rhetoric, the inaction of world powers, the overwhelming weight of nations supporting her foes, the extent of the enemies' forces training their weapons on every border created a feeling of isolation within Israel, the fear there and among Jews worldwide that the nation, just a quarter century after Auschwitz, faced imminent annihilation.

On June 5, Israel did what was necessary for survival: The country preemptively attacked, beginning what became the Six-Day War. In its first strikes, Israel destroyed the grounded Egyptian air force and hundreds of tanks, along with the majority of Syria's planes. Two days later, on June 7, 1967—Iyar 28, 5727—stunned, ecstatic, and awed Israeli soldiers stood before the Kotel, praying, singing, weeping. The chief chaplain intoned the memorial prayer for those lost in the battle. The shofar cried out again and again, obliterating gunshots from the nearby streets as the area was secured. The blue and white flag was hoisted, *Hallel* chanted. Those back at command headquarters heard the incredible announcement: "All of Jerusalem is in our hands!"

The war continued for only four more days. A month earlier, Israel had desperately wanted to avoid it, had feared for its very existence, was suffering economically with the call up of virtually all of its men of working age. Now, in addition to Jerusalem, Israel held territory captured on all three fronts, from all three aggressors: the Sinai Peninsula and Gaza (Egypt), the Golan Heights (Syria) and Judea and Samaria (Jordan's "West Bank").

To an even greater degree than after independence was won, Israel, and being Jewish, were seen in a different light. American Jews who previously had had no particular interest in Israel felt vicarious pleasure in its fortunes. Israel's triumph, won by strong, directed, brave men and women clearly in control of their own fates, led to a surge of Jewish identity, a feeling of pride in being Jewish, and an awakening of Jewish nationalistic feelings. In the Soviet Union, news of Israel's spectacular and unexpected victory spurred the refusenik movement (Jews who applied for permission to emigrate from their country to Israel but were "refused" by their government, fired from jobs and often harassed and/or imprisoned).

CEMENTING AND CELEBRATING UNIFICATION

Despite claims on Jerusalem by other religious groups, for whom it also holds significance, only for Jews was it ever a national capital or the focus of a people's literary, religious, spiritual and historic experience. Both the secularists and the religious were anxious to establish immutable sovereignty over the entire city, the rightful seat of government and the religious center for world Jewry. Within a few years, both groups lent widespread support for making Iyar 28 Yom Yerushalayim (Jerusalem Unification Day). Their two approaches led to a mixture of secular and religious celebrations that take place predominantly in Israel but are increasing in number in the Diaspora as well.

In 1992, in honor of the twenty-fifth anniversary of reunification, the office of the Israeli Prime Minister initiated a program to foster commitment to Jerusalem as the eternal capital of the Jewish people and the political center of the Jewish state. The office distributed copies of the "Jerusalem Covenant" (printed in Hebrew, English, French, Spanish, German and Russian versions) to Jewish communities throughout the world. Each was to organize a signing ceremony involving local leaders, organization members, dignitaries and other supporters, and then display the covenant as testimony to local identification with the Holy City. Guest books were placed near the signed Covenant to allow other supporters to add their names through 1996, the trimillennium of King David's conquest of the city, and a year of activities in honor of that anniversary.

FOR FURTHER EXPLORATION

Narkiss, General Uzi. *The Liberation of Jerusalem—The Battle of 1967*. London: Vallentine, Mitchell, 1983.
    Commander of the central front and one of the first officers to break into the Old City, the author gives a day-by-day, moment-by-moment account of the turning point in Jewish history, replete with the emotions and concerns prior to battle.

Oren, Michael B. *Six Days of War—June 1967 and the Making of the Modern Middle East*. New York: Oxford University Press, 2002.
    The most comprehensive account of the war to date draws on top-secret and rare documents and exclusive interviews to present a dramatic examination, from numerous perspectives, of the developments and personalities of this critical time in Middle Eastern and world history.   ☺✡

What Does It Mean? Religious Importance

A highly unusual spiritual atmosphere pervaded Israel in the weeks leading up to the war and the months following it—even among those who normally scoffed at anything vaguely religious. Perhaps it was the need, in the face of seemingly insurmountable odds, to have faith in something beyond themselves, or the tremendous desire to believe the promises for a better future, that they *would* be delivered by a merciful God, a conviction that had repeatedly sustained the Jews in previous precarious situations. For the first time in generations, there was widespread feeling—documented in newspaper articles, diaries and books about the war—that God was playing an active role in the events around them.

People increased their *tzedakah* contributions, spent more time at Jewish learning, were more careful to perform *mitzvot* and treated others with more courtesy than normal. They prayed more fervently, confident that with their efforts, God would not allow another two and a half million Jews to be murdered. Normally non-religious Jews easily mentioned God in conversation. Many people saw whatever was happening—the anxiety, the economic burden, the war no Israeli wanted—as part of His master plan. Spiritual leaders adeptly recognized the contemporary signs of ancient prophecies and reassuringly related current events to traditional text.

Reports of battle experiences considered supernatural filtered back from the fronts. Even tough military veterans sensed something extraordinary underway. After the capture of Jerusalem, and certainly by the seventh day, Israelis usually loathe to acknowledge, never mind credit, God, believed a miracle had indeed occurred. After so many years, and so much devastation, perhaps God *was* again looking toward His people. Even those hardened to spiritual expression were swept up in the talk and thought prevalent in the country that perhaps the messianic days long ago promised were at last on their way. (With the overwhelmingly secular nature of Israel's population, however, the Israelis credited themselves—their strength, their intelligence, their superior army—for the triumph and any movement toward redemption. That attitude created a feeling of invincibility. Unfortunately, it caused people, even within the government and military, to misread and ignore signs of trouble leading up to the disastrous Yom Kippur War six years later.)

If the circumstances surrounding the War of Independence had created a window of opportunity through which Israel was renewed, the Six-Day War threw open a window of opportunity through which the world could be redeemed. With Jerusalem in our possession, all the concrete prerequisites for accomplishing our mission were in place. It remained for the Israelis and the Jews of the world to take advantage of the situation to achieve Judaism's long-standing goals and bring the world closer to perfection by establishing a just society. The advent of Yom Yerushalayim carried the potential to be a far-reaching turning point in Jewish and world history.

FOR FURTHER EXPLORATION

Feldman, Emanuel. *The 28th of Iyar.* New York: Bloch Publishing Company, 1968.
  An American rabbi on sabbatical in Israel decided to stay as tensions mounted. With humor and pathos, his account captures the mood of the country and relays the increased spirituality at a time that the hand of God was clearly felt.   ☺☆

What Does It Mean To Us? Personal Significance

Jerusalem has always existed on two levels: the physical and the ideal. The physical was the political and religious center of the country, the seat of government and the focus for pilgrimage and prayer. The ideal was the spiritual symbol of the nation, the vision of prophets and dream of exiles, the image in the minds and feeling in the hearts of generations of Jews who never saw the place, but knew it by the essence its name embodies: peace (*Yerushalayim—shalayim, shalom*).

The Six-Day War gave us back the physical Jerusalem. Israel is committed to retaining it—undivided—as the State's capital, despite the fact that practically the entire rest of the world refuses to recognize it as such—only Costa Rica and El Salvador have established their embassies there—and the Arabs insist its status be negotiated.

When you have an opportunity to express support for the city to remain the capital of Israel and the Jewish nation, in letters to government leaders, or special ceremonies, take advantage of them. You can also contribute to the stability, growth and beauty of the city through organizations devoted to improving the quality of life there (such as Teddy Kollek's Jerusalem Foundation and various support organizations for the city's cultural and social service institutions).

Those who want to abolish Tisha B'Av claim that the State of Israel is the Third Temple, and therefore we no longer need to mourn over the destruction of Jerusalem and exile. Again, never just a geographic destination under our administration, the Jerusalem we longed for was to be a place of harmony within the nation and between nations.

Though the mood of Yom Yerushalayim is decidedly different from that of Tisha B'Av, our thoughts on both days are similar. Mourning for the loss of Jerusalem and the battle to reclaim it will not be finished until we have achieved peace—not just the political variety, but the overriding harmony the prophets described. That is the more difficult task. How do we create the Jerusalem of ancient visions? Since it is a reflection on the civic level of the situation between individuals, we can start in our own hearts, in our own lives, in our own interactions with other people. Brotherhood requires mutual respect and tolerance, the acceptance of others who have different opinions and philosophies. We must be able to stand together with other Jews, accepting diversity within unity, before we can expect to stand shoulder to shoulder with the other nations. And that is something we can each strive to improve on a daily basis.

Traditions—

HOW WE CELEBRATE YOM YERUSHALAYIM

How Do We Celebrate? Observance

As you would expect, most recognition is given to Jerusalem Unification Day in Israel—although it is just as appropriate to celebrate it in the Diaspora, for the same reasons we celebrate Israel Independence Day. Special ceremonies and other programs outside of Israel—including some citywide commemorations such as services and musical presentations—are growing in number.

In Israel, and Diaspora congregations that choose to observe the occasion, daily services include *Hallel* and Psalm 107 (praising God for His steadfast love). Outside of synagogue, films about Jerusalem, concerts of songs devoted to the city, and prayers for its continued unity are all parts of observance. Israelis often take daylong hikes around the Old City Walls, and there have been mass rallies in Jerusalem, attended by representatives of Jewish communities throughout the world.

Do You Hear Music? Songs to Sing

The Six-Day War—and particularly the capture of Jerusalem—is so closely identified with one song it is as though it had been written specifically for it. At the Hebrew Song Festival on Yom Ha'atzmaut just before the fighting began, Naomi Shemer presented her *"Yerushalayim Shel Zahav"* (Jerusalem of Gold), which she had written the previous month. Its haunting melody and sad words mourned the desolation of Jerusalem bereft of Jews. Shemer was in the desert entertaining the troops when she learned that the Old City was in Israel's hands. Immediately she changed the images of abandonment and decay in the last stanza to reflect the new situation of people and sounds once again enlivening the city. The song caught on like wildfire and remains a favorite in the Israeli music repertoire.

What Tales Are Told? Stories to Read

Histories of the city of Jerusalem (starting with II Samuel 5, about David's conquest of it) and personal accounts abound. Legends (SEE "MORE GOOD INFORMATION") and novels that use Jerusalem as a setting provide some of the most interesting reading.

FOR FURTHER EXPLORATION

FOR ADULTS

Millgram, Abraham E. *Jerusalem Curiosities*. Philadelphia: The Jewish Publication Society, 1990.
Enlightening stories of oddities and peculiarities of Jerusalem and life in that city help convey its unique role in world history.

Vilnay, Zev. *Legends of Jerusalem*. Philadelphia: The Jewish Publication Society, 1995.
Stories, folklore, accounts of historic and spiritual occurrences said to have happened in Jerusalem or to people and things associated with it and the Temple are collected in this compendium of material about the holy city and its mystique.

FOR ALL

Children of the World Paint Jerusalem. New York: Bantam Books, 1978.
As part of the tenth anniversary celebration of the reunification of Jerusalem, the city's mayor, Teddy Kollek, invited the children of the world to paint their impressions of and feelings for the Holy City. One hundred and ten of the one hundred and fifty thousand entries were chosen for this moving book that reflects the cultures in which the young artists live, and the hopes and dreams universal among children.

Of Added Note

IN ISRAEL

It has long been a tradition to insert written petitions (in Yiddish called *kvitlakh*) in the spaces between the stones of the Kotel. If you could not go to the Wall yourself, you sent a supplication with someone else, or paid a company to deliver your prayer. Now Aish HaTorah, a Jerusalem-based yeshivah, makes it possible to do so on line. A message typed into the box on its website is printed in Jerusalem and placed in the wall by a yeshivah student. Aish HaTorah keeps a camera focused on the Wall, and through the website transmits a photograph taken every minute (www.aish.com; for images or to send a message to the Wall; click on "Wall Camera").

Two museums in Jerusalem help tell the story of the battles for the city. **THE TOURJEMAN POST** distributes a brochure giving the background from 1917, while the building and its exhibits concentrate on the period of the great divide, between 1948 and 1967. At **AMMUNITION HILL**, which had to be conquered before the Israelis could enter the Old City, a reconstruction of the battle condition memorializes those who died there. Changing exhibitions sometimes feature the moving letters and pictures of the soldiers who participated in the crucial battle.

Despite the practical problem of having two Moslem mosques on its site, there are those who believe the erection of the Third Temple is imminent—and they want to be ready to reinstate biblical Temple service as soon as it occurs. Rabbis, goldsmiths, silversmiths, weavers and other artisans working under the auspices of The Temple Institute have been engaged since 1987 in creating authentic Temple utensils based on information provided by the Bible, Talmud and archaeological research. The magnificent finished items—priestly vestments, Levite musical instruments, gold and silver vessels—are displayed and explained at **THE TREASURES OF THE TEMPLE** exhibit in the Old City's Jewish Quarter.

The **TOWER OF DAVID MUSEUM OF THE HISTORY OF JERUSALEM** presents four thousand years of the city's history in intricate models and dioramas of exacting and historically accurate detail. The Citadel, where the museum is located, is at the Old City's Jaffa Gate. Nearby is an entry point for the under three-mile **RAMPARTS WALK**, which features observation points along the top of the city walls.

The conquests of the Six-Day War provided access for archaeologists to key sites for excavation, and incredible finds have been unearthed, including parts of David's City and passageways to the Temple Mount, which are open to the public. ((Until final resolution of the long hoped-for peace in Israel, it is advisable to check with local authorities for guidance on travel within the country and the advisability of visiting any particular sites.) More information on these attractions and related tours in Israel is available through Israel Government Tourist Offices in Chicago, Dallas, Los Angeles, New York and Toronto and through www.goisrael.com.

Shavuot—
Anniversary of the Giving of the Torah

The second pilgrimage holiday began as an agricultural festival marking the transition between the barley harvest and the start of the wheat-ripening season. Later the sages identified it as the anniversary of the Revelation at Sinai of the Law that transformed Israel from a liberated people to a truly free people. Its message and the event it commemorates make it one of the most significant religious occasions of the year.

Origins—WHY WE CELEBRATE SHAVUOT

Traditions—HOW WE CELEBRATE SHAVUOT

Origins—

WHY WE CELEBRATE SHAVUOT

Where Did It Begin? Historic Foundation

A DIRECT MESSAGE FROM GOD

In the third month after the Israelites left Egypt, they reached a place in the wilderness called Mount Sinai. There, after being announced by thunder and lightening and the blast of a shofar (ram's horn), enshrouded by a cloud enveloping the mountain, God told the nation what He wanted from them. For the only time in human history, God did not limit revealing Himself to one visionary who would report to others what He had said. Every Israelite at the foot of the peak experienced the phenomenal Revelation.

"I am the Lord your God, Who brought you out of the land of Egypt, out of the house of bondage," He began in the first of the *Aşarei* (Ten) *Hadiberot* (Sayings; commonly called Commandments), which established the foundation for proper behavior between humans and God and between one person and another. "You shall have no other gods. . . .You shall not take the Name of the Lord in vain. . . . Remember the Sabbath day to keep it holy. Honor your father and your mother. . . . You shall not murder. You shall not commit adultery. You shall not steal. You shall not bear false witness. . . . You shall not covet. . . ." (EXODUS 20:2–14; DEUTERONOMY 5:6–18).

Even though they had been prepared for three days (during which time they pledged to do whatever God asked of them [EXODUS 19:8]), the actual occurrence was so overwhelming, the people were afraid they would not come out of it alive. (A midrash depicts God holding Sinai over Israel's head, threatening to turn the mountain into their grave if they refused to obey, an illusion to the coercion they felt. After all, what choice could they have while standing in the presence of their Judge, Jury, King and Redeemer? The rabbis explain it was not until Purim , when God was completely hidden from them, that the Jews could accept the covenant in faith, rather than out of fear.) Insisting that Moses assume his

187

usual role as intermediary, the Israelites were given the remainder of God's instructions, the complete Torah, through the prophet.

Despite their trepidations, this unparalleled event made every one of the Israelites direct witnesses to God's existence and the extent of His involvement in the world. From that moment, every single Jew—not just the priest, not just the prophet or even just those physically present at the historic moment—was empowered to serve God. Every Jew who would ever live is said to have been at Sinai (including converts) and each had a role to play in making God's plan for a perfect world a reality. The authority of Torah in Jewish life—as a God-given set of laws and regulations—and the authority of the learned of each generation to interpret it—not to change it by addition or subtraction (DEUTERONOMY 4:2, 13:1) but to appropriately apply it to changing situations on earth—were established.

Following the Revelation, Moses ascended Mount Sinai, where he was given the two stone Tablets (*Lukhot*) of the Covenant (*Habrit*) on which God had engraved the Ten Commandments. Everything else God told him he recorded in a scroll—the Torah, which he gave to the priests and elders before his death (DEUTERONOMY 31:9).

Chapters 19 and 20 of the Bible book Exodus describe the incredible encounter. If the Exodus created a unique physical nation, by giving people who had individually endured the same miserable fate as slaves a common, and community-forging, redemption, the Revelation at Sinai created the unique spiritual nation by giving the people a common, and unique, mission that held great consequences not only for Israel, but for the world they were charged to influence.

As significant as this formative event was, you would think that, like for the Exodus, Torah would go to lengths to mark the date and describe a commemorative ritual. But it does neither. In fact, until the first century of the Common Era, *Matan* (the giving [of]) *Torah* was not celebrated as a holiday at all, and Shavuot, with which it became associated, was strictly an agricultural festival.

A HARVEST HOLIDAY

Among the laws given to the Israelites at Sinai were those pertaining to the holidays they were to observe once they reached and successfully cultivated the Land that had been promised to them.

One of those special occasions was Shavuot, the second pilgrimage initially identified as *Khag Hakatsir* (Feast of Reaping [EXODUS 23:16]) and later as *Khag Hashavuot* (Feast of Weeks [EXODUS 34:22, NUMBERS 28:26, DEUTERONOMY 16:10, II CHRONICLES 8:13]).

When the first fruits (*bikkurim*) of the field (referring to wheat) were ready to be harvested, the Israelites were to bring an offering of new grain in the form of two loaves of leavened bread made from choice flour (LEVITICUS 23:17-22). On this sacred occasion, a law for all times and places, they were also to cease their normal work.

There was one little technical problem in keeping the holiday. Unlike every other Jewish festival, for *Khag Hakatsir*/Shavuot, or *Yom Habikkurim,* as it was also known (NUMBERS 28:26), Torah specifies no fixed date. It simply says to count seven complete weeks from the day the first sheaf of barley is waved (the beginning of the Omer [SEE "HISTORIC FOUNDATION" IN CHAPTER ON PESAKH]) and celebrate this new festival on the fiftieth day (LEVITICUS 23:15).

The first sheaf was to be offered "after the Sabbath" connected with Passover (LEVITICUS 23:11). (Identification of what "after the Sabbath" meant was a point of contention between two philosophical branches within Judaism, the Sadduccean and the Pharissean.) Later, start of the seven-week count is even less precise: "when the sickle is first put to the standing grain" (DEUTERONOMY 16:9). Since the start of the harvest depends on when the barley ripens, the indefinite timing makes sense. However, it was not left at that.

The Pharisees' conviction that counting the omer began the day after the paschal sacrifice (SEE CHAPTER ON PESAKH) set Shavuot, occurring fifty days later, on Sivan 6. That celebration at the end of the period—the weeks—of barley harvesting was festive because it also coincided with the start of the wheat and fruit harvests. Between the two grains and the produce of trees and vines, the farmers could determine how well fed and prosperous they would be for the year.

All seven kinds of food plants for which Torah praises the Land—barley, wheat, grapes, figs, pomegranates, olives and dates (DEUTERONOMY 8:8) were covered in the commandment to take "some of every first fruit of the soil which you harvest from the Land that the Lord your God is giving you" and offer it to Him (EXODUS 23:19, 34:26; DEUTERONOMY 26:2-11). This produce, which did not ripen all at once, or at the same time as the first wheat, could be offered anytime beginning at Shavuot and through the fall festival Sukkot.

IN TEMPLE TIMES

All of the festivals ordained in Torah required burnt offerings (in this case one bull, two rams and seven sheep [LEVITICUS 23:18–20]). But unlike on other holy days, when the offering was made in addition to specific rituals that defined the occasions, sacrifice was Shavuot's exclusive observance.

The wheat was the gift of the entire community. The two loaves (*shtei halekhem*) brought in thanksgiving for the wheat harvest were used in the ritual of waving—like the barley sheaves on Pesakh for the first grain harvest and the four plant species on Sukkot for the completion of the agricultural year—before being eaten by the priests. First fruits of trees, on the other hand, were required of every Jewish household. Each farming family brought what it felt compelled to offer for this "freewill contribution," based on how blessed with good crops it had been (DEUTERONOMY 16:10).

Initially, the Israelites made their sacrifices at local sanctuaries. But a religious reformation instituted around 619 BCE to unite the nation and spiritually reinvigorate the Jews abolished the provincial altars and designated Solomon's Temple as the only site for all pilgrimages and sacrifices. From then on, the people had to journey to Jerusalem to express their recognition that God was part owner of the Land, and that whatever grew there was a result of the partnership between Him (providing the land, sufficient rain, favorable conditions) and humans (plowing, planting, tending, reaping).

The peasants prepared by going to their fields, orchards and vineyards to discover the first ripe stalk or cluster or fig, date, pomegranate or olive. Tying each *bikkur* they identified with a piece of grass or thread, they declared it a first fruit. At the time for the journey to Jerusalem, they added the designated pieces to their choicest produce piled in baskets—gold and silver ones among the wealthy, wicker ones from the peasants—adorned with greens and flowers. (The people coming from long distances brought dried figs and raisins so their offerings would not spoil.) The pilgrims gathered in the nearest town, then proceeded to a district center, and from there to the capital, adding people to the procession at every stage.

An ox whose horns had been gilded, wearing a wreath of olive leaves, led the way as a flute player accompanied happy, singing Israelites to the Temple mount. Every individual—including the King of Israel himself—carried a gift basket on his shoulder, entered the Temple courtyard, and recited the declaration drawn from Torah (DEUTERONOMY 26:5–10) connecting him to the past, all the way back to Abraham ("the wandering Aramean") and the future (the expected outcome of the harvest, which the *bikkurim* suggested). In fulfillment of the accompanying commandment to rejoice with the Levite and stranger (DEUTERONOMY 26:11) the city was the site of great celebration after the ceremony (TALMUD, BIKKURIM 3:1–8).

Due to its occurrence in the midst of the summer gathering, its short duration, and the staggering of formal *bikkurim* presentations among different regions to allow for various ripening dates, the Shavuot pilgrimage did not attract the attendance enjoyed by the other two of the *Shalosh Regalim,* Pesakh and Sukkot. The fact that it was for farmers only and involved only those who made the trip to the Temple further limited attention to it.

Through the first century, unlike the other holy days that were by then recognized for their historic significance, Shavuot seems to have remained strictly an agricultural festival. Both Philo, the Alexandrian Jewish philosopher, and Flavius Josephus, the Roman Jewish historian, who recorded details of contemporary Jewish life, failed to mention any other aspect of the holiday

FOR FURTHER EXPLORATION

See *Shavuot Holiday Anthology* listed in "More Good Information" for tales about the pilgrimage based on sense-arousing Talmudic descriptions.

POST-TEMPLE TRANSFORMATION

Without rationale or ritual outside of *bikkurim,* Shavuot would have disappeared completely after the destruction of the Temple if a spiritual dimension had not been added. Particularly in the wake of the Bar Kokhba debacle (SEE CHAPTER ON LAG B'OMER), when the Jews' faith that they would be redeemed flagged, the rabbis recognized that they had to renew the people's hope. That meant forging connections between current and future situations with formative events in Israel's history.

As they did for every other observance, the rabbis gave Shavuot a place along the Jewish continuum by attaching it to the people, rather than to their homeland. The notion of the human-Divine cooperation needed for a successful harvest was broadened to encompass the God-Israel partnership necessary for all earthly endeavors. The logical choice for a related occurrence in Israel's history was the Divine Revelation at Mount Sinai, when God presented Himself and His plan for life on earth to Israel.

The groundwork for linking Revelation with Shavuot had been established during the last centuries of the Temple's existence, when the Pharisees were engaged in a philosophical-theological struggle with the Sadducees over the essence and direction of the religion. For the Sadducees, aristocrats connected with the Temple priests, it rested in the system of sacrificial rites and was based on literal reading of Torah's word. The Pharisees, who tended to come from among the people, believed that there was more to God's

The Jew was not commanded to believe, but to search after the knowledge of God.

MOSES HESS

teaching, that prayer and study were no lesser means to do God's will than sacrifice, and that Torah was meant to be interpreted on different levels.

Getting close to God, the Pharisees felt, was not just a matter of bringing Him gifts, but trying to understand Him the way one would try to understand any partner: by learning what and how He thought and felt—which is all presented in Torah. That text defined the terms of His on-going relationship with Israel and the world, a relationship that began with the courtship of the Exodus and led to marriage at Mount Sinai. It was the marriage contract by which God and Israel agreed to serve each other. By this reasoning, the date of the wedding of God and Israel was a most important one.

However, nowhere did Scripture specify when that momentous occasion occurred. Torah merely says that the Israelites arrived at Sinai *"bayom hazeh,"* on this day (EXODUS 19:1). That was purposeful, said the rabbis, to teach us that Israel's getting the Torah is a perpetual, on-going process that transcends time, place and ritual. It is given to every generation in every locale. Each time it is understood a little deeper through study, each time a commandment is followed, the Torah is transmitted and received.

Still, in order to recast Shavuot as *Zeman Matan Torateinu* (the season of the giving of our Torah), the rabbis had to find compelling evidence of the coincidence of dates in the text itself. The legacy of the Pharisees, who identified the first day of the Omer as Nissan 16, served them well. Through a process of inter-pretation of the time markers in Exodus 19, and comparison of certain phrases in that text with similar ones in other parts of the Bible, they determined that the revelation had taken place on Sivan 6—fifty days after Passover, fifty days after the first count of the Omer, the same day as Shavuot.

Further evidence rested in the root of the word Shavuot. The singular of weeks, *shavuah*, comes from the word *sheva*, seven. A holy number, seven sig-nifies perfection, the highest level of attainment in the material sphere after which we are beyond the limits of earthly time. Seven days rounded out cre-ation and form a week, seven years make a sabbatical cycle (LEVITICUS 25:2–4, DEUTERONOMY 15:1), seven times seven years comprise the jubilee cycle (LEVITICUS 25:8), which begins in the seventh month, the month of our highest spiritual attainment (the month of Rosh Hashanah, Yom Kippur and Sukkot). And Shavuot arrives at the end of a period of seven times seven weeks. From the same root comes the word *shevuah*, means taking a vow. (The Talmud tractate named Shevuot is not about this holiday, but about oaths.) At Sinai, God and Israel exchanged their vows.

Despite some dissenting opinions, the majority of rabbis accepted the date. Now the period of counting the omer took on new meaning as the spiritual link between Exodus and Revelation, with Shavuot providing a finale to Pesakh. Consequently, the rabbis referred to it in Talmud as the day of *atzeret* for Passover, the same term used to describe the last day of Sukkot. For that holiday it indicated the conclusion of the ingathering, the pulling together of all achievements. Here it is the conclusion of the process of liberation, the attainment of true freedom.

As Torah study grew in importance in Jewish life, celebrating the text also became more important. Two sages in the third century (Elazar and Joseph) stressed the requirement of feasting and rejoicing on the anniversary of its having been given.

MIDDLE AND MODERN AGES

In the weeks before Shavuot in 1096 the Crusades began, claiming hundreds of Jewish lives in the Rhine valley. To honor the dead without interfering with the joy associated with the holiday, a communal prayer for those martyred in that barbaric outbreak of anti-Semitism was introduced for the Sabbath prior to Shavuot. The timing was considered doubly significant, as the day fell during the Omer period commemorating a massacre of an earlier persecution, that of Akiva's students by the Romans (SEE CHAPTER ON LAG B'OMER). Along with *Av Harakhamim* (Father of Compassion), the first form of the memorial prayer, the list of the rampage's victims was read.

Since more people attended synagogue on Shavuot than the Shabbat prior to it, the memorial service was moved to the holiday itself, and expanded to encompass the one done on Yom Kippur since Talmudic days, which honored all dead, not only martyrs, but also pious Jews and deceased loved ones. (In time, it was added to the liturgies of the last days of the other pilgrim festivals as well.)

When Simkhat Torah developed several centuries later (SEE CHAPTER ON SUKKOT), the intense expression of joy for Torah shifted to that occasion. It was not that the people of the time felt that the beginning of our covenantal life had lost any significance, but they recognized that, as in a good marriage, depth of understanding and appreciation for one's partner grow over time. The love and attachment at a twenty-fifth or fiftieth wedding anniversary is more substantial, and more substantiated, than at the wedding. So too, there is more reason for joyous celebration after the Torah has been examined, studied and lived with than when it has merely been presented.

For the Kabbalists, in particular, though, Shavuot remained an opportunity to express intense devotion to Torah. A midrash says that even though the Israelites knew God was going to give them an incredible gift on the afternoon of Sivan 6, at noon they were still asleep. Moses had to go to their shelters (according to one version), or thunder and lightening had to be used (according to another) to rouse them. So in the sixteenth century, the Jewish mystics— who believed that every action of every individual affects the state of the world—developed an all-night vigil to compensate for the Israelites' sleepy affront to God. A compilation of selections from Torah, Talmud and Zohar, called *Tikkun* (improvement, or remedy) *Leil* ([for the] night [of]) *Shavuot,* was published for use on the holiday (although the learned often chose their own texts). Dark-to-dawn study on the first night of the holiday became customary.

Early in the nineteenth century, the German reform movement, which had eliminated bar mitzvah as the "coming of age" ceremony for its thirteen-year-old boys, instituted a new initiation into Jewish responsibility for its boys and girls: confirmation. Designed as the culmination of a course of study for teens, it originally took place on the Sabbath during Pesakh, Sukkot or Khanukah. Within a few years, it was moved to the holiday appropriate for expressing commitment to Jewish ideals and Jewish life, the commemoration of voluntary acceptance of God's law. Adopted by the Conservative movement and even some Orthodox congregations after being introduced in America in 1846, confirmation grew in popularity, becoming a widespread feature on the first night or first morning of Shavuot.

In Israel the pioneers of the early twentieth century who reclaimed the Land re-focused on the agricultural aspects of the holiday. In modern *bikkurim* festivals, children dressed in white, wearing floral wreaths and carrying baskets of produce from their local villages and kibbutzim (communal farms), joined parades and processions to ceremoniously present their first fruits amid great pageantry. Poems, singing, dancing, artwork, and performances accompanied the donations, which were sold to benefit the Jewish National Fund.

Shavuot continues to be observed this way in Israel, and throughout the Jewish world, with synagogue service.

What Does It Mean? Religious Importance

Jewish belief and behavior rest on the historic occurrence of the Divine Revelation, the cornerstone of Judaism, and on the body of knowledge revealed at it.

HEARING THE VOICE OF GOD

As religions go, Judaism is not very dogmatic—except on two points: belief in one God, and belief that Torah, Judaism's sourcebook, is the word of God spoken directly by Him to the entire nation of Israel.

While there had been differences of opinion as to what form God's communication took, and how the Israelites perceived His contact with them (they heard everything, they heard only the first two commandments and the rest through Moses, they heard only an unintelligible sound interpreted for them by Moses, Moses heard every word spoken by God in a language he could comprehend, Moses intuited the entire code), the fact that He revealed Himself, critical to Jewish thought, remained unchallenged until the late 1700s.

Then the Enlightenment, with its emphasis on the rights of each individual to follow his or her conscience, and the sublimation of faith to scientific evidence, led to differences in approach to the account of Revelation. There were those who maintained that Torah was absolutely true, a record of the word of God. There were those who insisted it was absolutely not the word of God, but the work of humans. And there were those less rigid on either view, seeing it as a divinely inspired human product representing a joint effort of God and His children.

Some of those who continued to believe that God had spoken to the Israelites distinguished between the ethical and ritual laws He had given them. Recognizing the purpose of the former, they retained them, but deemed the latter obsolete and expendable. Jews who rejected the notion of Divine Revelation still saw great value in Torah (whose Sinai story they said expresses the Israelites' understanding of something extraordinary that had happened to them in the desert): It reflects what we recognize to be true of human nature and psychology, and provides a common moral system that guides our actions in the world. For these people, it is holy not because it was given by a supernatural being, but because human beings invest it with religious meaning and purpose.

The faithful whose world view was not shaken by the Enlightenment continued to accept Torah as a complete, integrated system whose *mitzvot,* whether ethical or ritual, all have purpose within the whole, even if humans cannot discern their meaning. According to traditional Jewish thought, Jewish law, being God-given, is eternal and universal, its authority absolute. We can explain the *mitzvot* (as we can Revelation) according to any system of philosophy we like, but they remain true and binding. We do them not because we understand why, but simply because they are commanded.

If you reject this notion and believe that God did not give the Torah, Judaism is reduced to a cult whose laws, while they might reflect some Divine thought, are manmade, and therefore subjective, subject to shifting standards as societal mores change. If they are alterable over time, the laws can be transformed beyond recognition or altogether abolished—along with the system, the people, and the promise they define.

That is why the law was revealed publicly to everyone—not, as is usually the case with religious illumination, to one individual in a secluded setting. As God told Moses, He wanted the people to hear for themselves, so they would ever after trust in Moses to be conveying His concerns (EXODUS 19:9). Hearing with their own ears and seeing with their own eyes, they would have no reason to doubt, and they would be able to give an eyewitness account to their children, who would pass the national history to their children (just as we pass on the experience and lessons of the American Revolution, the signing of the Declaration of Independence, the Civil War, the Holocaust—and will do the same for September 11—and those experiences and lessons become part of the consciousness of those who were not physically present at the world-changing occurrences but were no less affected by them).

> *There is something higher than modernity. And that is eternity.*
> SOLOMON SCHECTER

Whichever explanation you accept, the revealed word of Torah stands as our national myth—which is not in any way to suggest it is not true. A myth is a story based on a community's actual experiences (real historic events) designed to make sense of the world, create identity and generate loyalty. Subjective (as is all reality), it answers existential questions and defines the community's outlook on life. To the extent that on-going experience supports it, it remains the explanation of how and why a nation came to be and what its role is, and continues to be transmitted to successive generations.

Our shared tradition and common reference point in the search for meaning in life has withstood the rise and fall of philosophies, cultures and governments for more than three thousand years. And it continues to work on some level whether you take the national myth literally or less so.

This was demonstrated beautifully during a nasty debate in Israel's Knesset, as related to and by the educator Avraham Infeld. The Orthodox wing was characteristically chastising Shulamit Aloni, the education minister controversial for her liberal religious stance. "How dare you say such things to me!" she admonished them. "How can you use such terms? After all, aren't we all brothers and sisters? Didn't we all stand together at Sinai—even if it never happened?"

The message that we are supposed to embrace on some level—at least as an element of our national culture—is the one the Israelites were reminded of in Deuteronomy's recap of their history and laws: "Has any nation ever heard God speaking out of fire, as you have and still survived? Has God ever done miracles, bringing one nation out of another nation with such tremendous miracles, signs, wonders, war, a mighty hand and outstretched arm and terrifying phenomena, as God did for you in Egypt before your very eyes? You are the ones who have been shown so that you will know that God is the Supreme Being and there is none besides Him" (DEUTERONOMY 4:33–35).

Based on this shared history, we are supposed to attest to other nations about God's involvement and standards in the world—and more. In addition to making Israel a by-standing witness, through the covenant we became a full-fledged partner with God, the messenger through which God's plan would become known and the activist through which it would be implemented.

THE CHOSEN PEOPLE

When the Israelites arrived at Sinai, God promised, "If you will obey me faithfully and keep My covenant, you shall be My treasured possession among all the peoples. . . . you shall be to Me a kingdom of priests and a holy nation" (EXODUS 19:5–6).

Note the condition expressed in the quote: "*If* you will obey Me faithfully. . . you will be. . . ." God was not conferring on the Jewish people a special status, but establishing the means by which the people could elevate itself into being a holy kingdom of priests. God did not single out the Jewish people because of any inherent virtue (our stiff-necked nature and continual backsliding into idolatry and other abominations are painstakingly recorded) or for privileged treatment (as our history painfully demonstrates). All we possess over and above our non-Jewish neighbors is the obligation to fulfill Torah, simply because we made the commitment to do so—we *chose* to do so.

Perhaps no other label has caused as much problem for Jews, or been as misunderstood, as "chosen people" (a term, by the way, that does not appear anywhere in Scripture; it is based on a Talmudic interpretation of Torah's "treasured"

[SEE ABOVE]). According to midrash, any nation could have taken the role: God asked the children of Esau "Will you accept My Torah?" They asked what was written in it. "You shall not murder." Esau's descendants would not give up their heritage of living by the sword. So God offered Torah to the children of Amnon and Moab. They also wanted a preview, and were told the Torah says you shall not commit adultery. But adultery was a national pastime they refused to abandon, so they would not accept it. The children of Ishmael also had their chance, but could not limit their economic status by abiding the commandment "You shall not steal." When God finally gave Israel the option, they all said, as one, as recorded in Torah (EXODUS 19:8, 24:3), *"na'aseh v'nishma,"* we will do and we will hear.

The Israelites leaped before they looked, promising to obey before they fully heard what would be required of them. God had demonstrated His caring, through all He had done for the patriarchs and matriarchs, and all He had done for the former slaves; He had "proven Himself" through all the history that preceded Sinai, so He deserved their allegiance. They opted to accept the Torah, the covenant for an eternal partnership through which they would help God complete Creation by perfecting the world. Had they not, tradition says, the earth would have returned to chaos, metaphorically if not physically, for what would the world be without moral law?

Chosenness refers only to this relationship with God, not to Israel compared with other nations. What Israel was chosen—and chose—to be is an example of how human beings should act toward each other. What they chose to take on was the responsibility, as teachers and priests, of being held to a stricter standard of judgment as they demonstrated universal truths that are available to anyone—regardless of race, nationality or birthright.

Torah was given in the desert, a no man's land, at Mount Sinai, whose location is not known, so that no nation, even the "chosen people," could ever claim it as its alone. Although it obligates no one but the Jews to its laws, according to Talmudic tradition, Torah was proclaimed simultaneously in seventy different languages so that every nation on earth would understand that it could also accept its laws. Israel is merely Torah's caretaker.

TORAH

In their directness and simplicity, the Ten Commandments proclaimed by God from Mount Sinai touch minds and hearts with such truth that no concepts have had more influence on religious thought or had more moral impact on humanity. The ancient world had never heard anything like them; the world since has not devised a better code of behavior.

Within the Decalogue are actually two sets of laws, one reflecting the human-God relationship, the other the relationship among people; one pertaining to the human being as an individual, the other as a member of society. Read as pairs across the tablets (One and Six, Two and Seven, etc.), they mirror and illuminate each other.

Since murder takes the life of a human being created, with the help of God, to be like God, it diminishes God's image. Adultery, allowing lust to become a driving force, is tantamount to worshipping another god. In stealing (which in particular applies to kidnapping), you deal falsely with another person, equivalent to using God's name inappropriately. Desecrating the Sabbath, which is supposed to be kept as testimony to God's power over nature (Creation) and history (Exodus), gives false witness to God's role in the world. And coveting, particularly the main object of the commandment, another's wife (EXODUS 20:14, DEUTERONOMY 5:18), leads to the break up of family, the sabotaging of a child's respect and honor due his or her parents.

Revelation at Sinai continued beyond the tenth commandment, encompassing an additional six hundred and three ethical and ritual laws, a total of six hundred and thirteen *mitzvot* (commandments, and not, as the word is sometimes understood, "good deeds"). The two hundred and forty-eight positive ones were said to correspond to what the rabbis believed to be the number of bones in the body, and the three hundred and sixty-five negative were said to correspond to the days of the year. Together they suggest that we devote every part of our bodies, every day of our lives, to following God's word.

These comprise the Torah, the essence of our unique faith and lifestyle, the historical gene, as Rabbi Shlomo Riskin so beautifully describes it, which unites all generations, our national treasure, "the precious vessel of God with which the world was created" (PIRKEI AVOT).

The word Torah is derived from the root meaning to teach (*horah;* teacher is *moreh,* or *morah* in the feminine, and teaching, *hora-ah*). It is said that everything in the world can be found in the Torah by delving into its layers of meaning. It teaches us all we need to know in order to live in this world: public, private, material, spiritual, business, pleasure, personal, interpersonal. In its Five Books of Moses (Genesis, Exodus, Leviticus, Numbers, Deuteronomy), or, known in Hebrew for the significant word in the first phrase of each book, Bereshit (in the beginning), Shemot (the names), Vayikra (and [God] called), Bemidbar (in the desert), and Devarim (the words) are history, ethics, prophecy, and psychology. The printed form (as opposed to the carefully hand-written parchment scroll) is called *Khumash,* from the Hebrew word for five (*khameish*). (The Hebrew Bible also contains *Neviim* [Prophets], the accounts of the visionaries, spiritual leaders and kings of Israel, and *Ketuvim* [Writings], additional texts attributed to prophets, kings David and Solomon, and select sages. Together, all three sections are known by the acronym *Tanakh*—Torah, Neviim, Ketuvim.)

Our tradition maintains that at the same time Moses received the written document (*Torah Shehbiktav*), he was given a corollary elucidation on it, the Oral Law (*Torah Sheh B'al Peh*). Without it, it would be impossible to comprehend what Torah means by many of its laws. Our understanding of how Sabbath is to be kept and remembered, what exactly tefillin are, and how kashrut is to be observed, for example, comes from these explanations of how to derive deeper and varied meanings from the text. (If you look at a Torah scroll, you will see that unlike the *Khumash,* it does not have any dots and dashes, used in other texts to indicate the vowel sounds. [All letters in the Hebrew alphabet are consonants.] While tradition maintains that Moses was taught the correct pronunciation for the superficial meaning, the absence of vowels is one way of allowing for various readings and interpretations.)

Moses did not write down these instructions, but taught them to Joshua, who passed them to the Judges, who transmitted them to the Elders, who continued the chain of memorizing them by heart and teaching by word of mouth to the Prophets, the Men of the Great Assembly and the great sages. It was officially recorded as the Mishnah (around 200 CE) when the rabbis feared that because of mounting persecution against the Jews, it would be lost to future generations if not preserved in written form.

Later sages added their commentaries on the Mishnah, which became the Gemarah. Together, Mishnah and Gemarah form the Talmud (from the Hebrew word for study, *lamad;* student is *talmid*), the combined heritage of rabbinic thought reflecting the way the unchanging law was interpreted with relevance to meet the needs of the Jews at any time in history.

FOR FURTHER EXPLORATION

FOR ADULTS

Aseres Hadibros/The Ten Commandments. Ed. by Rabbi Nosson Scherman and Rabbi Meir Zlotowitz. Brooklyn: Mesorah Publications, Ltd., 1986.
> Part of the acclaimed ArtScroll series, this slim volume provides detailed explanations of the most famous laws in the world.

Kaplan, Rabbi Aryeh. "The Commandments." In *Handbook of Jewish Thought.* New York: Mazmaim Publishing Corporation, 1979, pp. 59–81.
> The chapter is a great introduction not of specific commandments, but commandments in general: how they were given, their nature, why we observe them and other basic facts. All are given in brief, simple numbered points. (This book as a whole is one of the best available introductions to classic Judaism.)

FOR CHILDREN

Cowan, Paul. *A Torah is Written.* Philadelphia: Jewish Publication Society, 1986.
> Explaining Torah, its use and importance, the photo-illustrated text describes the work of one particular scribe in Brooklyn in creating a Torah scroll. The book follows every step of the process from the making of the parchment. Ages 7–11.

Topek, Susan Remick. *Ten Good Rules.* Rockville, MD: Kar-Ben Copies, Inc., 1991.
> Appealing illustrations accompany presentation of the Ten Commandments in language geared for young children. (For that reason, some of the commandments have been rewritten from negative to positive format.) Ages 3–6.

What Does It Mean to Us? Personal Significance

CONNECTING WITH TORAH

Unlike the other festivals, this one is not a recollection whose purpose is to get us to pretend to experience the event it commemorates. We do not reenact revelation, we *enact* it, and we continue to do so the day after Shavuot and the next day and throughout the year. There is no specific date, no identified place, no unique ritual associated with *Matan Torah* because the Law is given to each of us in our time, wherever we are, with our own means of finding its relevance for us as individuals.

Unless we receive Torah, by using it in our daily lives, its giving is meaningless. Our sages tell us that the world rests on three things: Torah (study), *avodah* (Divine worship) and *gemilut khassadim* (acts of loving-kindness). The second two emanate from the first. It is not enough to simply learn what is in the sacred text, Torah study being one of the six hundred and thirteen *mitzvot* (DEUTERONOMY 6:7). We must serve its Author by applying it to our actions in the world. It was not enough for the king of Israel to write one *Sefer* (book [of]) *Torah* to be deposited in the royal treasury, a symbol of its worth and that it, and not precious stones and metals, is Israel's wealth. He was enjoined to write a second one, to accompany him wherever he went and whatever he did, so that he would live by it. "Great is the study of Torah," say our sages, "for it leads to proper action" (TALMUD, KIDDUSHIN 40b).

Tradition claims that an angel comes to every one of us when we are in the womb and teaches us the entire Torah. Then, just before birth, the angel touches us between the nose and mouth (creating the phyltrum, that distinct impression), to make us forget it all. But that first instruction (like the mother's voice that is immediately recognized by the newborn who has heard it for nine months, or music that resonates with familiarity for a child who heard it in utero) makes us receptive to it later. A sweet *bubbemeiser* (grandmother's story). But it makes the point that studying Torah is like a return, a rediscovery of something we already know, a way of saying that it is inherent knowledge, ringing true because it is such a basic part of each one of us.

The key is to find a way you can relate to it. There are said to be seventy facets to Torah, different ways (like the seventy languages in which the Ten Commandments were proclaimed) in which it can be understood, based on one's particular needs and abilities. They fall into four distinct levels commonly associated with Torah learning: *pshat,* the literal meaning; *remez,* the suggested interpretation; *derush,* the moral lesson; and *sod,* the mystical significance. Just as the manna given in the desert was said to have tasted like whatever food the Israelites desired, our spiritual sustenance can satisfy individual yearnings for truth and meaning.

The idea of taking on hundreds of *mitzvot* may seem overwhelming—

although you might be amazed at how many you follow in the course of just being a decent human being. (Actually, only three hundred and sixty-nine are in practical force today, and just two hundred and seventy apply to everyone, since many deal with Temple sacrifice and others are in effect only in Israel.) While it would be ideal to accept the whole package, and Judaism strives toward perfection, it does not expect it. Our greatest leaders and heroes are shown to us with all their flaws. Read carefully about Moses [EXODUS], who dealt directly with God. He did not behave properly enough to merit being allowed to reach the Promised Land. Or read the stories about King David [I SAMUEL 16–31; II SAMUEL; I KINGS 1–2]. For all his greatness and accomplishments, he was hardly a paragon of virtue.

Instead, Judaism is concerned with your intent and the direction in which you are moving. Every single *mitzvah* you do is judged as meritorious and not discounted by any *mitzvah* you fail to fulfill. Just as one step in the wrong direction makes it that much easier for you to make another mistake, doing one *mitzvah* can lead you to do another, so each has tremendous value in and of itself.

You can start simply with the Ten Commandments. On the broad level, most of us would say that we do a pretty good job of adhering to them. However, like everything else in Torah, they have deeper and subtler meanings than what a surface reading reveals. Encapsulated admonitions of what the Torah teaches us to do and not do, they also guide the mindset and demonstration of good character.

It is unlikely that you have taken a knife, gun or other lethal instrument to a fellow human being. But do you do anything that could hurt someone's reputation or publicly embarrass him/her? Both are forms of murder, for they diminish a person. Avoiding such actions recognizes the greatness of the human race, the potential of each individual. Idolatry is not restricted to genuflecting before useless figures of stone or metal, but encompasses counting on material possessions or transient power for protection. To eschew idolatry means turning away from worthless pursuits.

Perhaps you would never have an extramarital affair. But are there other ways you disrespect a spouse or threaten the foundations of your marriage? Are you satisfied with what you have, or content to work to gain what you want—or are you so obsessed with having someone else's wealth, power, position or possessions that your life is affected? What is good for one person may not in fact be good for another, so we are instructed to not look at what others possess, but to focus on and be appreciative of our own blessings. The prohibition against adultery—and immorality in general—reminds us of the necessity for self-control and warns us not to chase what is ultimately destructive.

Do you give your parents the honor and respect they deserve just because they brought you into the world and nurtured you? Part of the commandment to study Torah is to give it to the next generation. What kind of example are you providing to your children (whom you want to "honor *their* mother and father" and be able to teach their children to "honor their grandmother and grandfather")? The simple expression of gratitude goes a long way in fulfilling this *mitzvah*.

> *When law came into the world, freedom came into the world.*
> TALMUD

How do you relate to God? Have you made any attempt to discover the meaning and purpose of His laws, to evaluate their value or uncover their relevancy for your life—or do you reject them in ignorance and/or because you expect them to be inconvenient? Recognizing God (the first commandment) means recognizing the potential toward which every human being must strive, and acknowledging the source for everything that exists in the world. The Sabbath, which we are to remember, is an opportunity to experience a bit of the potential for life on earth, a time of harmony. It is also a time for thanksgiving to God, for everything created for and provided to us. The Israelites were gently chastised in advance for any excuses they might find for not developing a relationship with Torah. "Surely this instruction which I enjoin upon you this day is not too baffling for you. Nor is it beyond reach. . . . No, the thing is very close to you, in your mouth and in your heart, to observe it" (DEUTERONOMY 30:11–14).

Remember that part of the responsibility is to teach Torah to your children. Several versions of the Ten Commandments present the concepts on their level. You can ask your children to think of situations in their own lives that illustrate each of them. Expose them to Bible characters and stories, which have also been adapted for use with children as young as toddlers, and have them retell the stories in their own words. It can inspire a lifelong process, like all learning. Shavuot was the beginning of a great adventure for the Israelites. It can be no less an adventure for you—and your family.

FOR FURTHER EXPLORATION

FOR ADULTS

Leibowitz, Yeshayahu. *Accepting the Yoke of Heaven: Commentary on the Weekly Torah Portion.* Trans. by Shmuel Himelstein. Jerusalem: Urim Publications, 2002.
>The author, the late acclaimed Jewish scholar and philosopher known to stir controversy, is sure to provoke thought in this stimulating and elucidating collection of brief commentaries, each on some aspect of the weekly Torah reading.

Discovery Seminars
Aish HaTorah College of Jewish studies runs a program designed to increase pride in being Jewish and interest in Torah study and Jewish life. The centerpiece is an elaborate series of sessions, using a modern national survival model, proving the Revelation at Sinai based on scientific and mathematical evidence that appeals to modern, skeptical minds. It is a fascinating and thought-provoking presentation done periodically at sites around the country, either as a weekend retreat or a one-day experience (Discovery, 888-88-DISCOVERY, 718-376-2775, 718-376-2702 fax; or Discovery.USA@aish.com; seminar dates and information on the website, www.Discovery.USA.com).

FOR CHILDREN

Berman, Melanie, and Joel Lurie Grishaver. *My Weekly Sidra.* Los Angeles: Torah Aura Productions, 1988.
>The basic message of each of the fifty-four weekly portions is presented in simple language and plenty of learning activities help children understand and talk about the concepts. This is a great addition to a home library. Ages 6–8.

Eisenberg, Ann. *Bible Heroes I Can Be.* Rockville, MD: Kar-Ben Copies, Inc., 1990.
>This charming picture book takes one character trait or activity of each of the major Bible characters and with a few simples words and beautiful illustrations shows how the child is naturally like them. A good way to begin to build identification. Ages 2–5.

See also resources to help in talking with children about God listed under "Preparation" in the chapter on Rosh Hashanah.

UNITY

The rabbis explain that one of the prerequisites for the giving of Torah was that the nation of Israel be united. Rashi noted that when the people of Israel "encamped" in the wilderness (EXODUS 19:2), the verb used is in the plural. When later in the same verse they "encamped" before Mount Sinai, the verb is in the singular, indicating that they had come to be of one mind, one purpose, one heart. And when they responded to Moses' initial communication from God, and subsequent instructions, "all the people answered as one, saying "All that the Lord has spoken we will do!" (EXODUS 19:8, 24:3).

Unity means that we value and respect each other as individuals with something to contribute. It is a major principle of our religion, the foundation for strength and continuity. At the Revelation the entire community heard and together accepted one set of laws. Since the community is made up of individuals, each of us is obligated to share the message given at Sinai, and with the world. So it is the responsibility of each individual Jew to fulfill its precepts, and not to expect that someone else is doing the job for him or her.

A pair of wonderful folktales delivers the same message. A couple so poor they did not have enough money to properly celebrate Passover agreed that every week each of them would put a coin from his and her meager earnings through the slot of a special box, and leave it there. Not one week passes before the husband thinks, "There is no need for me to put my hard-earned money into savings as long as my wife is adding hers," and so he spends whatever he has in hand. And the wife thinks, "Why should I contribute the few pennies I have left over from running the household as long as my husband is filling the kitty?" Come next Passover, there is no money for provisions.

With similar thoughts, the residents of Khelm, known for their "cleverness" but not their intelligence, try to ensure a stock of wine for their next Purim fest. They decide that every week each man will bring a small part of his Shabbat wine—which he would never miss—to the synagogue and pour it into a communal barrel. One Khelmite thinks, "With everyone else contributing their wine, if I put in water instead, no one will notice." Unfortunately, he is not an original thinker. When the barrel is opened for Purim, the Khelmites have only what they had deposited all year: pure water.

When each person thinks someone else is doing the job, we can collectively end up with nothing. As the saying goes, a chain is only as strong as its weakest link. Torah is the connection that has kept the chain of Jewish continuity intact. The secret of our survival is continually listening to God's voice and being awake enough to take advantage of opportunities to carry out His strategies, to safeguard our heritage to be able to pass it along to the next generation. You would not lose sight of the family jewels; neither should you misplace the national treasure.

Traditions—

HOW WE CELEBRATE SHAVUOT

What Do We Use? Ritual Items

Since there are no unique rituals associated with Shavuot, almost nothing special is needed in order to observe the holiday. However, in addition to the first item below, you might encounter the others listed, which are used for two widely practiced customs.

MEMORIAL CANDLE

On the evening prior to the *Yizkor* service, held on the second day of Shavuot—it is customary for anyone who has lost a parent to light a yahrtzeit candle at home. (Some people also light for grandparents.) You can purchase the candles at a Jewish supply store or a supermarket that has a kosher food section. Housed in a small can or juice glass, it burns for twenty-five hours. Many people use the candle as a source of fire so they can light candles or the stove on the second day of the *yom tov*.

TIKKUN LEIL SHAVUOT

To support the one major activity connected with Shavuot—Torah study—special anthologies originally drawn from traditional text by the kabbalists have been compiled. They contain brief sections of every Torah *Sidra* (weekly portion) and the first and last sentences of each tractate (major division) of the Mishnah, and may include excerpts of Zohar (the central work of Jewish mysticism), a few sentences from each book of Prophets, accounts of the most significant sections of *Tanakh,* and Maimonides' list of the six hundred and thirteen *mitzvot*. The *Tikkun Leil Shavuot,* as it is called, is often all Hebrew but does come in English/Hebrew versions. Available in some Jewish bookstores, copies may be provided by your synagogue. (While the *Tikkun* is used in traditional circles, often synagogues and communal organizations design their own programs of study for the night of Shavuot that do not rely on that particular compilation of texts.)

DECORATIVE GREENS

Synagogues and homes are traditionally adorned with fresh greens and flowers in honor of the holiday that occurs in the full bloom of spring. Small trees, leafy or flowering plants, boughs, and floral arrangements are placed around the sanctuary and near the ark, as well as around the house and on the dining table.

Favorite flowers for the occasion are lilies—standing in for the lily of the valley to which Israel is compared in the Song of Songs (2:1–2), and roses, because of a playful reinterpretation of a verse from the Book of Esther (8:14): "the decree (*dat*) was proclaimed in Shushan" becomes "the law (*dat*) was given with a rose (*shoshan*)." Often lilies and roses have been placed directly on the *Sifrei* (plural of *sefer*) *Torah*, individually, in wreaths or garlands.

As an agricultural holiday, Shavuot has always been linked to plant life. In particular, the baskets used to transport first fruits to the Temple were adorned with flowers and leaves. According to another explanation for the decorative scheme, the greens recall Sinai itself. The fact that the Israelites were warned not to allow their livestock to graze near the mountain (EXODUS 19:12–13) indicates a grassy oasis rested at its base. The greens serve as vibrant reminders that Torah is "a tree of life to those who hold fast to it" (PROVERBS 3:18). Even though the reasoning conflicts with the foundation for the holiday of Tu B'Shevat, some rabbis claimed that we use branches because Shavuot is the day of judgment for fruit trees.

Rabbi Elijah, Gaon (meaning "excellency" or "genius") of Vilna, Lithuania, the leading sage of his era (1720–1797), tried to have the custom discontinued when similar practices became widespread among Christian churches for Whitsun, the day Jesus' disciples are said to have been divinely inspired (the Christian version of Pentecost, Greek for fiftieth, and the archaic term for Shavuot). Most communities ignored him (although in some, the development of special paper cuts, particularly those featuring floral motifs, may have been a direct response to his ruling [SEE "CUSTOMS"]).

How Do We Celebrate? Observance

A Jewish folk saying identifies Shavuot as the best of all Jewish holidays, because we can eat whatever we want (unlike Pesakh with its restrictions against leaven), wherever we want (unlike Sukkot, when we must have our meals in the *sukkah*), and whenever we want (unlike Rosh Hashanah, when we have to wait through long services, or Yom Kippur, when we may not eat at all). In addition, it provides us with an opportunity to reaffirm our connection with the very foundations of our faith: it is the anniversary of our eternal commitment to God. Just as a spouse does not blithely skip over a wedding anniversary, Jews cannot ignore this day.

WHEN WE OBSERVE

Orthodox and Conservative Jews celebrate Shavuot for two days, the Reform and Israelis for one. Technically, this is one time that the second day for the Diaspora (SEE "THE JEWISH CALENDAR" EARLIER IN THIS BOOK) is totally unnecessary. Since the holiday arrives fifty days after the beginning of Passover, there was never any doubt as to its date. But so as not to set one biblically ordained holy day apart from another, the Diaspora communities added the second day of Shavuot for the sake of consistency.

USHERING IN THE HOLIDAY

Like for all festivals, we begin Shavuot by blessing the festival candles at home (SEE "OBSERVANCE" IN CHAPTER ON PESAKH). The one difference here is in timing: while on Shabbat we light prior to sunset, and on a festival that does not coincide with Shabbat we may light at sunset or later (as long as we use a pre-existing flame, such as a candle or pilot light), on Shavuot we *must* wait until nightfall (unless, of course, the holiday coincides with Shabbat). This is because we are commanded to count forty-nine full days for the Omer, and the count is made only after a day is complete. So we wait until three stars appear (the traditional indication of nightfall, and the start of a new day). In addition to the

210

brakhah for kindling, we recite *shehekhiyanu* for the arrival of the occasion (FOR PROCEDURE SEE CHAPTER ON PESAKH, FOR WORDING SEE "BLESSINGS").

Since the second day is regarded as a duplicate of the first, both blessings are repeated at the start of the festival's second day, again after nightfall. (If you are lighting a memorial candle, do so before you light the festival candles.)

The festival meal, as usual, begins with the *kiddush* (full text of the festival *kiddush* can be found in a comprehensive prayer book), which must also be done after nightfall. *Shehekhiyanu* follows it, again on both nights, as long as the person who makes *kiddush* is someone other than the one who lit candles (only one *shehekhiyanu* per person).

The *motzi* for bread is said over two loaves, which are standard for every Shabbat and festival (SEE MATZAH UNDER "RITUAL ITEMS" IN CHAPTER ON PESAKH) and have added meaning and sometimes distinctive shapes for Shavuot (SEE "TRADITIONAL FOODS"). Traditional Jews precede it with the blessing for handwashing (always done prior to a meal that begins with bread [SEE "BLESSINGS"]).

STUDY

Following the holiday meal, many people proceed to synagogue for *Ma'ariv*, followed by an all-night (or into-the-night—many only last until 12:00 AM) Torah study session based on the kabbalists' practice. We remain awake to show that, unlike the situation of our heavy-lidded ancestors at Sinai, now there would be no need to bring us to our senses; we are ready to receive Torah. The *tikkun* (which refers both to the study session and the text used for it) was the only observance developed specifically for Shavuot. (Although *tikkunim* were later introduced for Pesakh and Hoshanah Rabbah, this is the one most widely observed.)

In addition to wanting to compensate for the Israelites, the mystics had the idea that at midnight, the heavens open and favorably receive the thoughts, study and prayers of those who remain awake on the anniversary of the Revelation. (Some promoted the legend that, as on Hoshanah Rabbah [SEE CHAPTER ON SUKKOT], wishes are fulfilled at that moment. The Moroccan Jews believed staying up all night guaranteed life for the next year.) They likened the time spent in study to the hours of preparation prior to a wedding, with the chapter headings in the anthology used for study said to represent the jewels used to adorn a bride prior to her marriage, and the *tikkun* process like the *bedecken* ceremony (when the groom verifies the identity of his bride and places the veil over her face) that precedes the wedding.

Through the ages scholars have followed the *Tikkun,* but among the learned who knew how to study traditional text, it was also common to devote the time to Talmud. Today, the *tikkun* might consist of a series of seminars on a variety of topics, based on ancient or modern texts, Jewish history or current events. In Israel, the Western Wall is a popular site for it. In the United States, in addition to communal settings, a *tikkun* may take place at home, especially for children, with whom age-appropriate books and Bible stories can be the basis for activities and discussion. (A group of adults might get together to study in someone's home, too—and could continue to meet after Shavuot for regularly scheduled learning—though you might not want to stay with the late hour.) Refreshments like cheesecake and coffee are usually served. Breakfast might follow a sunrise *Shakharit* service for those who have participated in an all-night communal study group.

LITURGY

With a few additions, the prayer services for Shavuot coincide with those for the other festivals. (The regular daily and Sabbath *siddur* is used in many synagogues, since it contains the basic changes in prayers. A special festival prayer book, a *makhzor* specifically for Shavuot, contains more of the *piyyutim* associated with the occasion, which embellish the story of Revelation.) The *Amidah* refers to the occasion as *Zeman Matan Torateinu,* the Season of the Giving of our Torah. Full *Hallel* (Psalms 113–118) is recited following the *Shakharit Amidah,* and the priestly blessing, if any kohanim are present in the congregation, is done during *Mussaf.*

AKDAMUT On the first day of Shavuot, the reader and congregation responsively recite a special hymn, each taking two verses, after the Torah scroll has been opened and the first person called to it. An introduction (*akdamut*) in Aramaic to the Ten Commandments, it is an exaltation of God, His wonders in the world, Torah and the reward waiting at the end of days for those who devote themselves to it.

The first forty-four verses are a double acrostic of the Hebrew/Aramaic alphabet (first two verses start with aleph, next two with bet, etc.). The initial letters of the last forty-six verses spell the author's name and a blessing: "Meir, the son of Rabbi Yitzkhak, may he grow in Torah and good deeds, Amen. Be strong and of good courage." The syllable *ta* at the end of each line, representing the last and first letters of the Hebrew alphabet, signifies the endless cycle of Torah study.

Tradition holds that Rabbi Meir, the eleventh-century cantor of Worms, Germany, wrote the hymn of praise to God, Israel and Torah in response to being forced to publicly debate the precepts of Judaism as opposed to those of Christianity. While celebrating the Jewish people's resolve to retain Torah despite oppression, he chose to write his hymn in Aramaic so only Jews would have access to its meaning. Meir especially wanted to strengthen the people's faith during the Crusades, the first of which claimed his wife and son.

Instead of *Akdamut*, the Sephardim and Yemenite Jews read one of several versions of a *ketubah* (marriage contract) between Israel and God modeled on the traditional format for a Jewish bride and groom. It generally includes prophetic verses alluding to the covenant between God and Israel (JEREMIAH 31:31, HOSEA 2:21–22), substitutes the gifts between God and Israel (Torah, tefillin, tallit, Sabbath and festivals and their observance) for what a bride and groom normally promise each other, and lists God and Moses or Heaven and Earth as witnesses. It is invariably dated 6 Sivan 2448 (the year Revelation occurred, counting from Creation at year 0).

YATSIV PITGAM In Ashkenazi congregations on the second day of Shavuot, the beautiful chant of another *piyyut* uncharacteristically interrupts the Haftarah (prophetic reading), after the first verse. Literally "Irrefutable Decree," the poem known as "The Myriad Angels' Songs" is also an acrostic that reveals the author's name (Jacob ben Meir Levi—Rabbenu Tam [Our Perfect Master] of Troyes, the illustrious grandson of the great Torah commentator Rashi). In beautiful pastoral imagery it expresses awe at Revelation and the power of God, and seeks protection and blessings for His people. In addition to mentioning the giving of the Law, the poem may have been included in Shavuot's liturgy because Rabbenu Tam was almost killed by Crusaders on the second day of the festival.

AZHAROT A special group of *piyyutim* summarize the six hundred and thirteen commandments in rhymed form. Called *azharot* (warnings) because the numerical value of that word is six hundred thirteen, they were composed by Solomon ibn Gabirol, the celebrated poet of the Jewish Golden Age of Spain (900–1100). Sephardic and Oriental congregations that include the poem in their *Mussaf* or *Minkhah* services concentrate on the two hundred and forty-eight positive commandments on the first day, and the three hundred and sixty-five negative commandments on the second.

READINGS FROM TORAH AND PROPHETS

The selections from Torah and Prophets encompass both the agricultural and historical aspects of Shavuot. On the first day, we read the account of the three-day preparation immediately prior to the Revelation at Sinai and the giving of the Ten Commandments to the entire nation (EXODUS 19–20).

The Decalogue is read on two other occasions during the year: on the Sabbath whose reading is the portion Yitro (EXODUS 18:1–20:23), in which they appear, and the Sabbath of Va-Etkhanan (DEUTERONOMY 3:23–7:11), when they are reiterated. It is customary to stand for all three (except in some Sephardic communities)—as though we are again *ma'amad* (standing [at]) *Har* (Mount) *Sinai*, ready to accept the laws. For this holiday, a different cantillation makes the reading more dramatic.

Controversies surrounded both the special reading of the Ten Commandments and the custom of standing for it. In Temple days, the priests recited the Decalogue daily. When first-century sects and Christianity began to challenge Judaism and assert that since the ten represented the whole of the religion the other six hundred and three could be abandoned, the rabbis eliminated highlighting the few so the people would not think they could ignore the total.

Maimonides was among those who later prohibited standing while they were read, claiming the attention made those ten select aspects of the law seem superior to the others, which gave the wrong impression. Those who understood the gesture as one of welcome to God's presence—and present to Israel—overruled him.

The concluding verses of the Torah reading on both days cover the special sacrifices required for Shavuot (NUMBERS 28:26–31).

Like each person at Sinai, the prophet Ezekiel had his own vision of God, which is relayed in the Haftarah (1:1–28, 3:12) meant to parallel the experience of the Revelation. The fantastic image of the radiant and mobile God came to him at the beginning of the Babylonian exile eleven years before the destruction of Solomon's Temple. It suggests that God had left the Temple and was present with His people outside the Land.

The Torah reading on the second day (DEUTERONOMY 15:19–16:17, BEGINNING 14:22 IF IT COINCIDES WITH SABBATH) describes the requirements of the pilgrimage festivals and their connections with the harvest and animal sacrifices. The second day's Haftarah (HABBAKUK 2:20–3:19) is a prayer uttered by the prophet during the Assyrian exile (after 722 BCE) expressing the expectation that God will again deliver His people.

THE BOOK OF RUTH

Of the five scrolls in the Writings section of the Hebrew Bible the one assigned to Shavuot is Ruth. It tells the story of a Moabite princess who, after the death of her Jewish husband, brother-in-law and father-in-law, pledges her allegiance to her Jewish mother-in-law, adopts Judaism, and, because of her virtue, merits becoming the matriarch of the Davidic-messianic line. Its few short pages contain one of the most moving and well-known verses of Scripture: "For wherever you go, I will go; wherever you lodge, I will lodge; your people will be my people and your God my God" (1:16).

The sages explain that Ruth was written to teach us that those who act kindly to others will be well rewarded. The main figures in the story (Ruth, who did not want her widowed, childless mother-in-law to have to return to Bethlehem stripped of all honor with which she had left; Naomi, the loving mother-in-law who embraced her Moabite daughter-in-law and guided her into a suitable redeeming marriage; and Boaz, the Judge and kinsman who provided the poor stranger Ruth with all the sustenance she and Naomi needed, and accepted his responsibility to marry her), are exemplars of *gemillut khassadim,* one of the pillars of the world. Learning from Torah so we can follow similarly righteous ways is one of the messages of Shavuot.

It is also generally believed that the Book of Ruth was chosen for this holiday because it takes place against the backdrop of the barley and wheat harvests in Judah (2:23), tying in with the agricultural nature of the festival. Especially significant is its illustration of the laws of *pe'ah* (leaving the corners of a field unharvested) and *leket* (leaving behind individual stalks that fall from reaped bundles), for the needy to also reap and which are commanded immediately following the instructions to observe the festival of Shavuot (LEVITICUS 23:22).

How much better to acquire wisdom than gold; to acquire understanding is preferable to silver.
PROVERBS 16:16

As we learn in the last paragraph, the title character is the great-grandmother of King David, who dedicated his life to serving God and Torah, and, by tradition was born and died on the anniversary of the day it was revealed. His descendant, the Messiah, will bring about redemption, the goal of Revelation.

Most appealingly, this is a story about the voluntary embrace of Torah and Judaism, a model of what being Jewish means: accepting the destiny of the Jewish people, living among Jews, being part of the community and serving One God. Ruth's declaration to Naomi ("For wherever you go. . .") encompasses the elements necessary for self-transformation: change of lifestyle, nationality, belief and theology. It defines not only the requirements of becoming a Jew, but the essence of being a Jew: struggling to change while continually striving to improve.

Maimonides pointed out that prior to the giving of the Torah, all human beings on earth were bound to the seven Noahide Laws (dating from the righteous gentile Noah, whose family was the only one of his generation to survive the great flood [GENESIS 6:13–8:14], and delineated in Talmud). Adherence to them constitutes morality in non-Jewish society (do not deny God, do not blaspheme God, do not murder, do not engage in adultery and other sexual abominations, do not steal, do not eat the limb torn from a living animal, and establish courts to enforce the other laws). From the moment of Mount Sinai, the Jews committed to accept the additional six hundred and six that make up our body of commandments. That count is the numerical value (according to gematria) of the name of the Moabitess Ruth: (reish [ר] equals two hundred, vov [ו] six, tof [ת] four hundred), who did the same.

In traditional congregations, the book is read, either from a scroll or a printed *Khumash,* on the second day prior to the other Scriptural readings. Reform congregations often read it at confirmation services. Khassidim read it as part of the *Tikkun* rather than at services, or each member of the congregation reads it individually (on Sivan 6 in Israel, on the second day in the Diaspora) prior to the Torah reading. Some Sephardim read it before *Minkhah,* often completing chapters one and two on the first day, and three and four on the second.

YIZKOR

Following the *Shakharit* Torah reading on the second day of Shavuot, the service in memory of deceased martyrs, *tzaddikim* and loved ones takes place, as it does on the last days of all the major holidays. (The Reform generally do not include this service on Shavuot, and in Israel it is held on the morning of the previous day.) Some have the custom of leaving the sanctuary during *Yizkor* if their parents are still living, based on an old superstition, but it is considered more appropriate to remain with the congregation and pray on behalf of the people Israel has lost, and your own relatives (SEE "OBSERVANCE" IN CHAPTER ON PESAKH, AND "HISTORIC FOUNDATION" EARLIER IN THIS ONE).

CONFIRMATION

While its future is in question, the "graduation" ceremony for Jewish teens between fifteen and seventeen years of age who have completed some kind of education program established by their synagogues remains a feature in many congregations on the first evening or first morning of Shavuot. Recognition of the confirmands is worked into the holiday service.

CONCLUSION

As on all festivals, the end of sacred time is marked by the brief ceremony *Havdallah,* done in the synagogue after *Ma'ariv,* or at home after nightfall. If the end of the festival coincides with the close of Shabbat, we recite the full complement of blessings (contained in a prayer book). On a weeknight, only those over wine and separation are made (SEE "OBSERVANCE" IN CHAPTER ON YOM KIPPUR FOR EXPLANATION AND "BLESSINGS" FOR WORDING).

ISRU KHAG

Like the days following the other pilgrimage festivals, the one after Shavuot is a semi-holiday designated to help us hold onto the spirit of the holy day just a bit longer. According to Talmud, whoever observes an *issur* (continuation) for the festival by eating and drinking (which substitutes in post-Temple life for the sacrifices) is considered to have "built the altar and offered up a sacrifice on it" based on Psalms 118:27: "Bind the festival [offering] with cords onto the horns of the altar."

In the case of Shavuot, *Isru Khag* served a practical purpose during Temple days (SEE "HALAKHAH"). In our time, while the mourning laws of festival days hold (SEE "HALAKHAH" IN CHAPTER ON PESAKH), for all intents and purposes, Isru Khag goes virtually unnoticed.

Where Do We Begin? Preparation

SPIRITUAL

For the Israelites, Shavuot was the culmination of the process of transcending innate, animal nature to liberate the human being. As we learn at Pesakh, the release from physical bondage alone is not freedom. True freedom is knowing what you want to do—what you truly want being what is good for both the body and soul—and having the discipline to achieve it—which means being able to control the natural desire for immediate gratification that can sidetrack you.

The period that connects the two levels of freedom, *Sefirat Haomer* (SEE CHAP-TER ON PESAKH), began with the cutting of the first sheaf of barley that ripened. Barley is animal fodder. An animal is a being whose consciousness consists of the immediate situation. Having no vision of what is beyond the self is the least Jewish of attitudes. As we count the days representing the duration of the barley harvest, we rise toward the start of what was the wheat harvest. Wheat is human food, a symbol of *khokhma*, intelligence (based on the rabbis' dictum that a child does not utter its first word until it has tasted bread).

The offering brought to the Temple at the start of the Omer consisted of meal ground from the barley grain, a raw material representing the first step in the production of leavened bread—which was the offering at the end of the Omer, on Shavuot. The form of the sacrifice delivers a clear message: without Torah, which gives us the insights to recognize what we want, and the moral standards and social ethics to guide us to accomplishing our goals, we are like animals that respond to instinct. Raw barley needs to give way to the refined wheat, the grain to meal to bread. Raw natural intelligence needs to be refined to become the wisdom through which potential can be reached. Once our always-present animal selves are under control, we are ready to learn how to get the most out of life.

That is why counting the Omer continued even after the development of a standard calendar eliminated its initial necessity: to let the majority of people—farmers occupied with field work—know exactly when to make pilgrimage to Jerusalem. It remained an opportunity to help us move out of enslaving patterns of thought and behavior.

For the ancient Israelites, each day was a step away from the defilement of Egypt and a step toward spiritual purity. Like the Israelites who began to get ready for their encounter at Mount Sinai immediately after as they crossed the Reed Sea, we use the seven weeks beginning on Passover to similarly prepare ourselves for the arrival of Shavuot. During this time, we are supposed to evaluate our behavior and work to improve ourselves, particularly by being more faithful to God and dedicated to His ways, humble, and unified with all other Jews.

The sages devised a construct to help us follow in the Israelites' footsteps. It is based on seven Divine qualities in the kabbalistic design of the universe,

219

which were represented by the illustrious leaders of Israel—in one variation: love (Abraham), respect (Isaac), compassion (Jacob), efficiency (Moses), beauty (Aaron), loyalty (Joseph) and leadership (David). These virtues, in their extreme, become vices (lust, fear, indulgence, obsessiveness, vanity, submissiveness and stubbornness), which we must strive to avoid. So the sages dedicated each week of the Omer to one of the characteristics, and each day of the week to one of them. The unique combination on each of the forty-nine days (love-love, love-respect, love-compassion . . . respect-love, respect-leadership and so on) helps us gain insight into our own behavior in relation to the values and to focus our efforts on self-improvement, to make each day of counting count. (CLAL, The National Jewish Center for Learning and Leadership, suggests that individuals and families use the Omer count to write a *mitzvah* each day, and that they include those you keep, those you aspire to keep, those in the positive formulation ["I must . . ."], those in the negative formulation ["I must not. . ."], those reflecting your own successes and failures, and those reflecting the accomplishments and needs of your community. Piling up all the slips of paper on which the mitzvot are recorded into a "Mountain of Commitments" forms an effective centerpiece for Shavuot meals. [SEE MORE ON CLAL IN "MORE GOOD INFORMATION" AT THE END OF THIS BOOK.])

Torah study in general is customary and appropriate, with some people reading portions from every book of the Bible, and review of the Ten Commandments common. Many read Pirkei Avot (Ethics of the Fathers), a particularly accessible section of Talmud. Study culminates in the *Tikkun Leil Shavuot* meant to make up for omissions or deficiencies in our devotion to Torah during the preceding year. It helps us to be particularly receptive to the body of law we will be given the next morning.

FOR FURTHER EXPLORATION

Pirkei Avos—*Ethics of the Fathers*. Ed. by Rabbi Nosson Scherman and Rabbi Meir Zlotowitz. Brooklyn: Mesorah Publications, Ltd., 1989.

This translation of the Talmud tractate (literally Chapters of the Fathers) full of pithy sayings and concise lessons is supplemented by commentary drawn from classic rabbinic sources. One of each of its six chapters is traditionally read on the Sabbaths between Pesakh and Shavuot. (There are a number of editions of Pirkei Avot, including the respected three-volume edition Ethics from Sinai with commentary by Irving Bunim [Feldheim Publishers]. Some *makhzorim* for Shavuot also contain Pirkei Avot and ArtScroll has a version for young people as part of its Youth Series [Mesorah Publications]).

48 Ways to Wisdom
  This set of individual audiotapes was produced from lectures given at Aish HaTorah, a yeshivah in Jerusalem for Jews with little religious background. Each thirty- to forty-two-minute tape deals, from a Jewish perspective, with some aspect of everyday emotions and concerns about personal matters and interpersonal relationships. Almost all provide concrete suggestions of simple things to do to help better your thinking and behavior (available through Aish HaTorah educational centers in Boston, Cleveland, Detroit, Lakewood [NJ], Las Vegas, Los Angeles, New York, Palm Beach, Philadelphia, St. Louis, Seattle, South Florida (Hollywood), Washington, Toronto, Winnipeg, London and Jerusalem, or through www.aish.com.)

PERSONAL

All of the semi-mourning restrictions imposed for the Omer period are suspended as of Rosh Khodesh Sivan. The day of the new moon itself is a semi-holiday when mourning is not permitted. The three (*shalosh*) days (*yomei*) of setting bounds (*hagbalah*) immediately preceding Shavuot—when the Israelites had to refrain from climbing Mount Sinai and be particularly pure in their physical actions—are also considered festival days since they anticipate the Revelation. The day in between, Sivan 2, called *Yom Hameyahut* (Privileged or Choice day) borrows the status of the surrounding occasions. (Talmud gives it further distinction by identifying it as the day God told the Israelites they would be a kingdom of priests and a holy nation [EXODUS 19:6].)

For that reason, during these few days, it is customary to get a haircut and buy new clothes, activities prohibited earlier in *Sefirah*. In traditional circles, men go to the *mikvah* prior to the start of the holiday. Some also go on the morning of Shavuot in remembrance of Israel's purification prior to receiving the Torah.

TZEDAKAH

One of the ways of improving our spiritual standing is by helping others. As with all occasions in Jewish life, it is appropriate to make donations to Jewish causes. Those that perpetuate Jewish learning (Jewish schools, yeshivot, scholarship funds and Jewish camp programs) are particularly suitable at this time. Some people set aside amounts every night of the Omer corresponding to the count of the day (in pennies, dimes, dollars, etc.).

HOME

To adorn your home in the traditional manner, you will want to buy—or cut from your garden—flowers and greens to be arranged in vases or strewn on the dining table and other surfaces. People also display leafy and/or flowering houseplants.

You and your children may want to try your hands at the folk art decoration customary in Eastern Europe in the 1800s: paper cuts (SEE "CUSTOMS"). They are made by folding a square or circular piece of paper in quarters, sixths or eighths, cutting shapes along the folds, then opening up the paper to reveal a symmetric design. For Shavuot, floral patterns are most common, and the finished paper cuts are hung in windows so sunlight passing through them will cast their shapes in shadow.

If you want to cook and light candles on the holiday in accordance with Jewish law, you will need to use a preexisting flame, from a long-lasting candle or stove pilot light, for example (SEE CHAPTER ON PESAKH REGARDING THESE PREPARATIONS, AS WELL AS ARRANGEMENTS WHEN THE HOLIDAY FALLS IMMEDIATELY PRIOR TO SHABBAT).

FOR FURTHER EXPLORATION

Goldenberg, Amy. *Papercutting: Reviving a Jewish Folk Art.* Northvale, NJ: Jason Aronson, 1994.
This book teaches the development of the art form, and how to do it.

What Are We Supposed to Do? Halakhah

With the exception of specific sacrifices and the order of the prayer service, very little attention is given to Shavuot in the literature of halakhah. As a festival and a pilgrimage holiday, it shares the halakhot of other such holy days (SEE CHAPTER ON PESAKH).

COUNTING THE OMER

If you forget to count in the evening (SEE "OBSERVANCE" IN CHAPTER ON PESAKH), make the count the next day, but without the blessing. If you totally skip one count, you may start again whenever you remember to do so, but you may no longer say the blessing for the remainder of *Sefirah*. This is because the *brakhah* is based on the command to count every single day. (Omer scrolls are often used in synagogues, where the count is made at the conclusion of the evening service. Devices like calendars that allow you to flip one page for each date [easily made from a notebook] or charts with boxes to check off can be helpful reminders to count.)

TIKKUN

If you stay up all night for study, the rituals and prayers you would normally do and say in the morning are omitted since they were performed the previous day, and are not said anew if sleep has not intervened.

JOY

Torah commands us one time to rejoice on Shavuot (DEUTERONOMY 16:11), since part of the harvest is complete. However, since we have not yet seen all the fruits of our labors, our full expression of joy is reserved (SEE CHAPTER ON SUKKOT). We rejoice by eating festival meals accompanied by wine, and sharing our good fortune with those in need.

ISRU KHAG

While it is customary not to fast or deliver a eulogy on the day after any festival, for Shavuot those prohibitions are law. This is because of the double duty this day had to serve as a practical addition to the holiday itself. Sacrifices could not be made on behalf of individuals (as opposed to those for the nation) on *yom tov* itself because there was simply not enough time to do them all on one day, or, when Shavuot coincided with Shabbat, because the labor involved was prohibited. On the other pilgrimage festivals, these problems were solved by having *khol hamoed,* the intermediate days, when the sacrifices could be made. Without that time, Shavuot had to extend into *Isru Khag* for the same purpose.

What Other Things Do People Do? Customs

OTHER TIMES AND PLACES

OMER PERIOD Some people had the custom of studying the Talmud tractate Shevuot. With forty-nine pages and sharing the name of the holiday the counting period prepares us to observe, it was considered appropriate.

Women traditionally did not work after sunset during *Sefirah*. Although their laborious preparation for the previous festival, Pesakh, would have been enough to excuse them, the custom is said to be in recognition of the women who buried Akiva's students at night (SEE CHAPTER ON LAG B'OMER). With so many deaths, the entire community's life would have been disrupted by daytime funerals, as work stops for the funerals of Torah students and teachers.

GREENS Despite the admonition of the Vilna Gaon , using plants and flowers to decorate homes and synagogues for Shavuot became fairly widespread, particularly in Europe. The floor of a house might be scattered with fresh grass, or a synagogue floor with spices and roses, based on midrashim. One claims the Israelites had to be revived after fainting out of fear when they heard God's voice, the other that the fragrance of spices filled the world with pronouncement of each commandment. Because of the use of flowers to decorate the *Sifrei Torah*, in Italy the holiday was called Feast of Roses, and in Persia, Feast of Flowers.

PAPER CUTS Although the craft in general was widespread, its application for this holiday was limited geographically to Galicia, Bukovina, and adjoining areas of Poland and Russia, especially Lithuania and the Ukraine (possibly because of the Vilna Gaon). In the nineteenth and early twentieth centuries, *kheder* and yeshivah students and older men with time on their hands created the intricate lacy patterns, called *Shavuoslekh* (little Shavuot) or *roiselekh* (little roses) for their characteristic shape and design. (The works of the Jewish artists Maurice Gottleib and Mordecai Antokolski are said to have attracted the attention of non-Jewish patrons who later helped the artists enter art academies.) Based on words of the *Akdamut* hymn, legend that Mount Sinai burst into flower at the giving of the Torah, the classic image of Torah as the Tree of Life, and the Song of Songs' image of Israel as a rose, floral motifs were prevalent, though many incorporated text and classic Jewish symbols.

ENACTMENTS On the morning of the first day, the devout went to the *mikvah* so they would be prepared to greet the Torah, like a bridegroom ready to meet his bride at the marriage ceremony. North African communities dressed their *Sifrei Torah* in white, like brides, and held symbolic wedding processions after morning services. These were sometimes followed by mock battles representing the war against evil of messianic times (suggested by *Akdamut*).

PILGRIMAGE As the anniversary of King David's death, Shavuot became the time for Khassidim and Oriental Jews to visit the traditional site of his tomb on Mount Zion in Jerusalem. Some congregations lit yahrtzeit candles on the second day in his honor.

Hundreds of candles illuminated the synagogues of Kurdistan, where each individual lit on behalf of deceased relatives and brought fruit to the synagogue to bless in their memory. The Kurdistani Jews also made pilgrimage to the shrines of holy men buried in their country. Singing, dancing and special refreshments accompanied the processions. The biggest was for the prophet Nakhum, buried near a hill called Mount Sinai, which the men climbed to recite the Ten Commandments at its summit. On *Isru Khag*, crowds walked past the tomb, gave charity, and received from the *gabbai* (sexton) fruit and sweets that had rested on the grave throughout the night. Sometimes an individual who had read the Ten Commandments hosted a banquet, or members of a congregation visited the honoree for merriment and refreshment.

Calling the holiday the Feast of Visitation, Babylonian Jews traditionally paid their respects at the gravesites of noted ancestors. The Moroccans joyfully danced to their cemeteries on *Isru Khag Shavuot* to bury damaged and unused text and Scripture in the *genizah* (the storage place for such materials, which may not be discarded or destroyed). Coinciding with the date of burial of the Jews slaughtered at Betar (SEE CHAPTER ON LAG B'OMER), the occasion was marked by singing and musical accompaniment to properly commemorate those whose bravery brought honor to the Torah.

In Eastern Europe, the Khassidim made a different kind of pilgrimage, traveling great distances to be able to spend the festival with their learned and esteemed rebbes.

START OF SCHOOL During the Middle Ages, it became customary to introduce children, around the age of five, to Hebrew and Torah study on the morning of Shavuot. Letters of the alphabet and verses of Scripture would be written on a tablet enhanced with dabs of honey or bits of candy, which the children were invited to eat. They would then associate Torah and learning with sweetness, based on Psalms (119:103): "How pleasing is your world to my palate, sweeter than honey." A honey cake or egg on which verses had been written might then be given to the child.

DOUSING The comparison of Torah with water ("Your springs [teachings] will gush forth in streams in the public squares" [PROVERBS 5:16]) led to customs among the North African Jews that seem uncharacteristically rambunctious for the mood of the day. Men battled each other with goatskins of water, each trying to pour more on the next. Sometimes the person who had recited the last verse of *Azharot* was treated to a cold shower. Women more delicately sprinkled each other. These activities are also said to reflect appreciation for the role of water in two incidents in Israel's life. After his birth on Adar 7, according to rabbinic tradition, Moses' mother hid him for three months, until Sivan 6, Shavuot, then placed the infant in a basket in the Nile River, which protected him. When so overwhelmed by Revelation that the souls of the Israelites departed, God sent a heavy dew to revive His people. Throwing water imitates and expresses gratitude for the resuscitation.

In Babylon and Persia, instead of water, the Jews threw apples from the synagogue roofs, because the Israelites' response to Torah ("we will do and we will hear") was compared to the apple tree, whose fruit develops before its leaves. Among some Judeo-Spanish, it was customary to conduct *hakafot* (circuits) in the sanctuary with the Torah and then throw candies at those called to read it when the scrolls were lifted, as on Simkhat Torah (SEE CHAPTER ON SUKKOT).

GREETING

The standard *khag sameiakh* (Hebrew) or *gut yom tov* (Yiddish), "happy holiday," is exchanged on Shavuot.

DRESS

Clean Shabbat clothes are appropriate for the festival.

What Is There to Eat? Traditional Foods

CHEESE

While everyone agrees that the food of choice for Shavuot is cheese (most typically blintzes, crepe-like pancakes filled with farmers cheese, or a Sephardic equivalent such as burekas, cheese-filled dough pockets), there are differences of opinion (some quite charming) as to why it is a custom.

One derives the selection directly from Scripture, saying we eat dairy to symbolize the "Land flowing with milk and honey" (EXODUS 3:8) promised to the Israelites, or that "milk and honey are under your tongue" (SONG OF SONGS 4:11). These passages, along with "The precepts of the Lord are . . . sweeter than honey" (PSALMS 19:9–11) would also indicate we should eat honey, which is customary in some communities.

A sage discovered that the initials of the four Hebrew words in Numbers 28:26 that describe the sacrificial meal offering on Shavuot spell *mei khalav* (from milk), suggesting that dairy food is the acceptable dinner for the festival. At Sinai, the Israelites were considered to be as innocent as newborns, whose food is milk.

Those of kabbalistic bent equate the numerical value of the word *khalav*, forty (khet [ח] equals eight, lamed [ל] equals thirty, vet [ב] two) with the number of days Moses spent on Mount Sinai receiving the Ten Commandments and the rest of the teachings (EXODUS 24:18). Others look to the mountain itself, which is termed in Psalms mount of *gavnunim* (68:16), many peaks. They connect that description with the Hebrew word *g'vinah,* meaning cheese.

Scholars who trace all Jewish customs and rituals to practices common among various ethnic groups claim that spring harvest festivals characteristically featured dairy dishes, perhaps because cheese was produced at that season.

Support for the custom also arose out of the spiritual development of the Israelites in the wake of Sinai. After the Torah was given, they were obligated to follow its laws, including those governing dietary practice. As they returned to the camp from Revelation, they could not eat the previously cooked meat, which had not been prepared according to the laws of kashrut. Since butchering and cooking fresh meat would take too long for the tired, hungry Israelites, they took the dairy food that was more readily available. Symbolizing modesty, the dairy was seen as appropriate for the occasion of receiving the Torah, which should always be approached with humility.

Some Jewish communities adopted the custom of eating a meat dish following the traditional dairy meal (after waiting the thirty minutes prescribed according to the laws of kashrut, except in places where the rabbis waived the normal waiting period). The two foods represent the two loaves brought on the festival, and we are actually supposed to eat meat as a contribution to our joy on a festival day. However, this can cause practical problems, not only in terms of the time lapse, but because milk and meat dishes and utensils cannot be mixed. So it is more common to have a completely dairy meal on the first evening of Shavuot and then to have meat the next day.

Along with blintzes and burekas, cheesecake is a widely popular Shavuot item. Some eat kreplakh, three-cornered dumplings that are often meat-, but can be cheese-filled or even vegetable-filled. They are supposed to remind us of the Torah, which is comprised of three sections (Torah, *Neviim,* and *Ketuvim*) given to Israel, comprised of three categories of Jews (Kohanim, Leviim, and Yisraelim), through Moses, the third child of Amran (after Aaron and Miriam), following three days of preparation (EXODUS 19:11) in the third month of the year (EXODUS 19:1).

KHALLAH

As for most holidays, special designs were devised for the normally braided bread. A ladder with seven rungs represents the seven spheres God traversed to descend to Mount Sinai. Long loaves of the bread, to which Torah is likened (JOB 11:9) stands for the length and breadth of the Law, and square loaves, with their four corners, represent the four layers of meaning inherent in text (SEE "PERSONAL SIGNIFICANCE"). Round loaves in tiers were called *Siete Cielos* (seven heavens) in oriental countries, in others they represented the mountain and were known as Sinai Cake. Large loaves or cakes with raisins and/or almonds were also called Sinai (or, in local terms, *pashtudan* or *fladen*). The traditional two loaves, common for Shabbat and all festivals, have added meaning here for the two loaves of the wave offering brought to the Temple. They are sometimes baked connected side by side to resemble the tablets, or the zodiac sign for the month of Sivan, Gemini (twins).

Among North African Jews, it is customary to eat matzah left from Passover in bowls of milk and honey, a reminder that Shavuot is the finale of Pesakh.

Do You Hear Music? Songs to Sing

Like virtually every other aspect of Shavuot, the songs connected with it are largely part of the synagogue liturgy. A number of folk songs and Khassidic melodies, built around short phrases, extol Torah and God, Who gave it to us. Among them are *"Torah Tzivah Lanu"* (The Torah is our Inheritance), *"Barukh Eloheinu"* (Blessed is our God [Who Gave Us the Torah of Truth]), *"Yisrael V'Oraita"* (The People of Israel and the Light of Torah), *"Yamahh Moshe"* (Moshe Joyfully [Welcomes the Gift of Torah]), *"Yismekhu Adirim"* (Rejoice in the Great Gift), and *"Ki Mitzion"* (For Out of Zion).

Two popular folk songs learned by every Hebrew school student, youth group member and Jewish camper exuberantly proclaim Israel and God's existence and our belief in redemption. Each consists of only one sentence: *"Am Yisrael khai, od Avinu khai"* (The people of Israel lives, Our Father still lives), and *"David Melekh Yisrael, khai v'kayam"* (David, King of Israel lives and endures [suggesting the messiah]). The Hebrew folk song *"Eretz Zavat Khalav (khalav u'd'vash)"* (Land of Milk and Honey) and the Yiddish standard *"Oif'n Pripetchik"* (By the hearth [the rabbi teaches little children the aleph bet]) also fit the occasion.

What Tales Are Told? Stories to Read

Surprisingly, for a holiday of Shavuot's significance, little has been written specifically around its history and themes. Neither Sholom Aleichem (except to use gathering greens as a backdrop) nor Bella Chagall, who both lovingly recorded Eastern European holiday observance, treated this one, and aside from books on the Ten Commandments (SEE SUGGESTED READING UNDER "RELIGIOUS SIGNIFICANCE"), there is little available for children. However, since the subject of

Shavuot is Torah, any material drawn from our rich tradition based on Scripture is appropriate. Treasuries of folktales, such as those listed in "More Good Information," provide a wealth of choices, as do Bible stories adapted for children. You may also want to check the Internet, or with a librarian or Jewish book store for suggestions of titles that deal with various aspects of Jewish life.

FOR FURTHER EXPLORATION

GAMES

The board game *Torah Slides and Ladders,* modeled on the classic *Chutes and Ladders,* explores the Jewish way of life. Available through The Learning Planet, PO Box 17233, West Palm Beach, FL 33416, 561-686-9456, 561-686-2415 fax, info@learningplanet.com, www.learningplanet.com.) ✡

Tisha-B'Av —
National Day of Mourning

(TEESH'AH BUH-AHV'; YIDDISH: TISH' UH BUHV')

AV 9

(SUMMER; LATE JULY—MID AUGUST)

The commemoration of the destruction of the first and second Temples is also the anniversary of a number of other catastrophes in our history. As the embodiment of national disaster, it is a time for grief and remorse, yet also of renewed hope for redemption. We observe it by refraining from any pleasure-producing activities.

Origins—

WHY WE CELEBRATE TISHA B'AV

Where Did It Begin? Historic Foundation

LOSS OF FIRST TEMPLE

For all the blessings heaped on the Land of Israel (DEUTERONOMY 7:12–14, 8:7–9), its location linking continents has always been a dubious advantage: wonderful for commerce, but an open invitation to conquest. Just after 600 BCE, the Babylonians won the contest for control against Assyria (which had previously conquered the northern Kingdom of Israel and expelled its Ten Tribes). Influential Judeans (residents of the southern Kingdom of Judah, part of the territory captured) were exiled to Babylon. Under Judah's last king, Zedekiah—whom the Babylonians had installed to be a puppet—those allowed to remain retaliated with a revolt for independence.

On the tenth of Tevet, 587 BCE, King Nebukhadnezzar moved his army against the capital. On the ninth of Tammuz, six months later, the Babylonians breached the walls of the city weakened by famine and disease. One month later (given in different sources as Av 7 [II KINGS 25:8] and Av 10 [JEREMIAH 52:15], and designated in Talmud as Av 9), the chief of Nebukhadnezzar's guards, Nebuzaradan, set the Temple and every significant building in Jerusalem afire.

The loss was devastating. Picture the city in which you live as the World Trade Center site on September 11, 2001—and it having been under prolonged attack. Imagine it depleted of food and water, ablaze in every direction, littered with the rubble of crushed fortifications and houses and the victims of starvation, disease, armed combat, smoke inhalation and flame. The Temple treasures and vessels were carried off to Babylon, and thousands of Jews forced to march there in chains.

The Bible books II Kings (24–25) and Jeremiah recount this period of history from the admonitions that preceded destruction through the end of the Jewish community on the Land. The Judeans who had abandoned God for idols and idle pursuits were repeatedly warned that if they did not act justly, as they had been commanded, an enemy from the north would turn their home to desolation and ruin.

Events occurred as predicted. For the next seventy years, as Jeremiah instructed, the exiles were to build a new community in Babylon, where they would prosper. Those who had not been marched to the conquering kingdom were supposed to stay on the Land, and live quietly under Babylonian rule (JEREMIAH 40:9).

To govern the remnant—the poorest of the Jews—Nebukhadnezzar appointed Gedalia, a noble who had served as a minister under Zedekiah. Although warned that his life was in danger, Gedalia refused to take protective or preemptive measures. When a member of Judah's own royal house murdered him and his Babylonian advisors on Rosh Hashanah, the Jewish leaders were afraid Babylon would see the attack as open rebellion and respond with bloody retribution.

They refused to heed Jeremiah's assurances that they would be safe and blessed in the Land, but doomed if they returned to Egypt, as they planned: it would mock everything God had tried to do for them since bringing them out of slavery (JEREMIAH 42). Under the direction of Yokhanan ben Kareah, they did flee to Egypt (a doubly bad move, since Nebukhadnezzar later invaded). Effectively, that ended Jewish presence in Israel, and any hope of securing the foundation for restoration of the Jewish commonwealth.

No matter how comfortable their lives in Babylon might have become, the exiled Jews remained distraught, refusing to sing ("How can we sing a song of the Lord on alien soil?" [PSALMS 137:4]), determined to constantly recall Jerusalem ("If I forget you, O Jerusalem, let my right hand wither. . ." [PSALMS 137:5], and adopting the ancient expression of grief and remorse: fasting (ZEKHARIAH 8:19).

The three days that marked successive stages in the loss of Jerusalem—the tenth of Tevet for the beginning of the siege; the ninth of Tammuz for the break in the walls; and the third of Tishrei (postponed since fasting is prohibited on Rosh Hashanah, Tishrei 1 and 2) for the true beginning of exile following Gedalia's murder—were marked by sunrise to sunset fasts. Av 9, commemorating the actual *khurban* (destruction) of the Temple, became a full-day fast. (The date may have been a compromise choice to accommodate the discrepancy, between II Kings and Jeremiah, in designation of the date of the Temple's demolition. Historians note that Av 9 was a pre-existing fast day in Babylonia, where the commemoration began, and may have been conveniently adopted by the exiles for their own purposes.)

A SECOND CHANCE, A SECOND KHURBAN

As Jeremiah promised, after seven decades the Jews were allowed to return to Jerusalem, where the Temple was rebuilt—not as lavishly as Solomon's version, but a national sanctuary none the less. The prophetic book Zekhariah records that in the fourth year of Persian King Darius' reign (518 BCE), while the Temple was under reconstruction, a delegation from the Diaspora went to ask the priests and prophets in Jerusalem whether they should continue to observe the four fast days

After pointing out that denying themselves sustenance was not a ritual done for God's sake, but a reminder to act justly and with compassion for others, Zekhariah predicted that "the fast of the fourth month [Tammuz 9], the fast of the fifth month [Av 9], the fast of the seventh month [Tzom Gedalia, Tishrei 3] and the fast of the tenth month [Tevet 10] shall become occasions for joy and gladness, happy festivals for the House of Judah" (8:19). That seemed to indicate that they could be suspended (as some scholars say they were). But the prophet added a key proviso: "you must love honesty and integrity," suggesting that the end of exile was more than a physical matter. Redemptive rejoicing required a certain moral precondition.

Rav Papa, the fourth-century sage, claims that the fasts were converted to holidays and celebrated that way throughout the second Temple era, 516 BCE–70 CE. The Jerusalem Talmud notes that they remained optional days of mourning observed as fasts by the pious: Although the Jews had returned to the Land, they did not necessarily enjoy self-rule, and although they once again had a Temple, it was a poor replacement for the one they had lost.

After approximately six hundred years of residence on the Land, there was a reprisal of the events of 586, almost to the day. This time the devastation was orchestrated by the Romans, who had been there for one hundred and eighty years, after having been invited to intercede in a battle within the House of Hasmoneans (SEE CHAPTER ON KHANUKAH). After four years of armed combat, the Romans succeeded in breaking through Jerusalem's walls, on Tammuz 17, 70. Once again the inhabitants were trapped, reduced to a starving, disease-ridden community imperiled by their own factions of zealous terrorists warring with each other over the best approach to take against the enemy. None worked. On the ninth of Av, the Romans set the Temple and much of the city ablaze. The fires burned through the night and well into the next day.

> *When they have become a legend, and Rome a fable that old men will tell of in the city's gate, the tellers will be Jews and their speech Hebrew.*
> CHARLES REZNIKOFF

Titus, the conquering general, carted home the vessels, golden menorah, and ark depicted on the Arch of Titus celebrating his triumph. (The Arch still stands in the archaeological garden of the Roman Forum near the Colosseum in the capital of Italy. Jews traditionally did not walk under it; today, due to concerns for preservation, no one may). Again those captured were taken away in chains, and those left behind continued to resist.

Years before the siege of Jerusalem began, a small group had found refuge on Masada, an anvil-shaped plateau near the Dead Sea that one hundred years earlier had been fortified by the paranoid Herod, King of Judea (as the kingdom of Judah was called beginning in the Hellenistic period, fourth and third centuries BCE). Fighters who had escaped the destruction of the capital joined them there. For two years, the community of nine hundred and sixty men, women and children held out against the Romans intent on eradicating every last Jewish stronghold. When the defenders realized they would not prevail once their attackers completed an assault ramp and wheeled their battering ram to the top, the Jews decided to kill themselves rather than be taken. They left their stores of food and water so the Romans would know they had chosen to die in freedom rather than become enslaved, the antithesis of Jewish life. (Although the dramatic episode has become controversial for glorifying suicide, Masada served as the symbol of the Jewish and Israeli fighting spirit, the site of inductions for select units of the Israeli Defense Forces, and the basis of the slogan for independence, "Masada shall not fall again!")

From outside Israel and within, the Jews continued their armed struggle against Rome, first in Alexandria (117), then Betar (135), where they were decisively defeated—both times on the ninth of Av (SEE CHAPTER ON LAG B'OMER). To emphasize their complete victory, the Romans plowed over Jerusalem, changed its name to Aelia Capitolina and rebuilt it with pagan Temples and heathen gods. They changed the name of Eretz Yisrael to Palestina.

DEALING WITH DESOLATION

As devastating as the first destruction was, the second was a much more decisive blow. Many of the surviving Jews were carted off as slaves. A bloody slaughter severely crushed the remnant, and anyone left was forbidden to come within viewing distance of what had been Jerusalem (except on Av 9, when they could mourn at the ruins). No prophet wandered in their midst promising a speedy restoration. The ascetic practices adopted by a large number of Jews reflected the dimensions of their sense of loss.

Rabbi Joshua tried to convince them of the futility of such actions: According to their reasoning for forfeiting meat and wine, which had been offered on the altar that no longer existed, they would also have had to give up bread, in remembrance of the meal offering, and fruit, since first fruits could no longer be sacrificed, and water, because of the elimination of the water ceremony on Sukkot. And, as another sage pointed out, since Roman law prohibited the study of Torah and the following of its precepts—including circumcision and redemption of firstborn sons—the Jews might also think it proper to forego marriage and having children.

Instead, the rabbis sought to incorporate appropriate expressions of loss while affirming the traditional Jewish faith that out of tragedy comes possibility, out of exile comes redemption. They established a pattern of mourning balanced between two attitudes: Anyone who did not grieve over the destruction of Jerusalem would not live to rejoice over her renewal, and, while not grieving at all was impossible because of the degree of devastation, to mourn too greatly was beyond human endurance.

Almost immediately, they restored Tisha B'Av as a national day of mourning, marked by a full twenty-five-hour fast and the personal abstentions associated with the expression of grief for loss of a loved one. Again discrepancy appeared over the actual date of the defeat, with the historian Josephus claiming the tenth, the Talmud citing the ninth. Rabbi Yokhanan ben Zakkai, a leading sage of the time, said if it had been up to him, he would have chosen the tenth since the greater part of the destruction occurred then, but the rabbis chose to mark the beginning of the end, which coincided with the ancient observance of destruction, and with the fall of Betar and the leveling of Jerusalem. By the end of the first century observance had become mandatory.

After Betar and the barbaric persecutions by Emperor Hadrian, which included the martyrdom of ten of our greatest sages, the other fast days observed after the first destruction were reinstated (with the fast of Tammuz 9 moved to Tammuz 17, the date related to the greater loss). The fasts conveniently provided needed outlets for a people anxious to express its grief. (This welcome embrace of self-denial may be difficult for us, in our age of self-indulgence, to understand, but when Judah Hanasi [third-century compiler of the Mishnah], in a conciliatory mood toward Rome wanted to abolish the fast of Tisha B'Av, the people would not accept the relief.)

The rabbis ordained that every year on Tisha B'Av the Jews were to read Eikhah (Lamentations). The scroll attributed to Jeremiah gives a graphic and heart-rending eyewitness account of the destruction of the First Temple that resonates with parallels for the second. (Using the ancient text, like reviving the ancient date, was also politically expedient. With its description of events that had occurred six hundred years earlier, it avoided offending the new Roman rulers.)

The whole tenor of Judaism, until then a religion marked by joyful celebration and aesthetic worship, became more doleful. The rabbis decreed that reminders of the incompleteness of existence outside of Eretz Yisrael, and the diminishment of joy in the absence of the Temple, be incorporated into everyday life. For weekday meals with guests, one place at the table was to be left unset, and one or two dishes were to be omitted from the menu for any banquet. Women were not to wear all their jewelry at once, and an area approximately twenty-inches square in a new home was to be left unpainted or unplastered and designated in memory of the Temple. At a marriage, the groom was to put ashes on his forehead where the tefillin normally sits, and would break a glass at the conclusion of the ceremony. Instrumental accompaniment and music, aside from sung hymns and songs of praise to God, which had contributed to the beauty of Temple service, were removed from worship.

Instead of eliminating consumption of meat and wine from all meals as a constant reminder that the animal sacrifices and wine libations were no longer possible (a restriction the community would be unable to keep in the long run), the rabbis included a recounting of the Temple sacrifices in the daily liturgy. Special prayers were to be said and one's clothing torn on viewing any cities in Judea that had been destroyed, even after they were rebuilt, because they remained under foreign rule.

Those who saw the Temple site from the vantage of the desert would rend their clothes, and then tear them further on seeing Jerusalem, the way they would on learning of a loved one's death. Anyone viewing the Western Wall was to recite: "Her gates have sunk into the ground. He has smashed her bars to bits" (LAMENTATIONS 2:9). Prayers beseeching God to rebuild Jerusalem were added to the daily liturgy, and exclamations of desire to return to that city were added to the prayers of holidays most closely associated with redemption, Yom Kippur (personal), Pesakh (national) and Sukkot (universal). Wherever a Jew went, whatever a Jew did, s/he was reminded of Israel's ultimate goal.

The idea behind all these institutions was to allow the people to vent their grief and yet be able to maintain some sort of normal life. To that end, the ruling that emerged from the Gemarah discussion between Rabbis Meir, Judah and Simeon ben Gamaliel regarding whether mourning for the Temple should last the entire month of Av, only the first nine days, or just the week of the ninth supported the most lenient choice.

A DAY FOR ALL MISFORTUNE

The magnitude of the destruction that occurred not once, but twice on the same date, and the fact that some of the worst disasters to befall the Jews afterwards also occurred on Av 9, marked that day as the symbol of national catastrophe. The rabbis claimed that when the Israelites wandered in the desert, the date had already been designated to embody all Jewish misfortune.

As a prelude to having the Israelites possess the Land He had promised them, God told Moses to send representatives of the Twelve Tribes to scout Canaan and report back to the people. After forty days of spying, on the ninth of Av, ten of the twelve gave the impression that the Israelites could not prevail against the inhabitants, robbing the people of belief in their own capabilities. Rather than heeding the assurances of Joshua and Caleb, who encouraged self-confidence, or having faith in God, Who promised to protect them in their conquests, the people began to weep and complain about having been taken out of Egypt.

Disgusted with their causeless crying, Talmud explains, God essentially said, "You want to cry? I'll give you something to cry about. This will be a day of mourning for you forever." The generation of slaves was condemned to wander one year for every day the spies had spent in Canaan, and to die without entering the Land. (According to legend, each year on the eve of Tisha B'Av, a certain number of Israelites dug their own graves and were told to sleep in them, a sleep from which they never awoke.)

This incident set the pattern of rejection of God and the Land of Israel, which repeatedly brought ruin upon the Israelites. The pattern repeated in the two ensuing exiles: Because they turned to idolatry—a blatant rejection of God and His values—and engaged in adultery and murder (reasons given for loss of the first Temple), the Jews were sent away to Babylon. Then, when they rejected God through the senseless hatred (*sinas khinam*) said to have caused the second destruction, they again were told, in essence, that they did not deserve to live on a land that was supposed to be a setting of peace.

The rabbis likewise gave Tammuz 17 ancient historic significance, as the day Moses broke the first Tablets of the Covenant because the Israelites, impatient and uncertain about his return from Mount Sinai, could not refrain from making the Golden Calf (EXODUS 32:1–5; SEE CHAPTER ON YOM KIPPUR). Just forty days after Revelation, the people acted as though God were not among them. Centuries later, it was the stones of the walls protecting Jerusalem that were smashed as the enemy approached. By acting against each other, not respecting their fellow Jews as equal human beings, the people again behaved as though they were not living with God. Other catastrophic events that occurred on the same date include cessation of the daily sacrifice (through which the people drew close to God) for lack of the necessary animals, burning of a Torah scroll in the Temple (a reminder of the destroyed Ten Commandments, which represented all of Torah), and placement of an idol in the Temple sanctuary by someone named Apostumus (an act tantamount to erection of the Golden Calf).

DAY OF REPEATED INFAMY

Contrary to what we would expect, the further away in time the Jews got from the initial cause of their grief, the more stringent their mourning practices became. During the Gaonic period (sixth to eleventh centuries), it became customary to read other grief-inducing texts in addition to Lamentations, such as Job and the passages describing destruction in Jeremiah. Meat and wine were banned during the nine days before Tisha B'Av (eleventh century), then made an optional abstention for the entire three weeks beginning Tammuz 17 (thirteenth century), a restriction some pious Jews had already taken on themselves, particularly in Eretz Yisrael. Eating new fruits during the three weeks was banned, and by the sixteenth century, marriages were prohibited during this period. It had already become customary to not don tefillin (considered orna ments and therefore signs of joy inappropriate on a day of mourning) until the afternoon of Tisha B'Av.

The need for more expressions of grief resulted, no doubt, from the series of massacres and expulsions that all occurred on the ninth of Av. The Jews of York, England, were slaughtered in 1190, and in 1290, King Edward decreed that all Jews be expelled from the country. The Jews of France were imprisoned on Av 9, 1305, and informed they had to leave that country within a month. In 1492, Spain expelled its Jews, and in 1555 Rome forced its Jews into a ghetto. In 1571, the Jews were ghettoized in Florence, in 1630 expelled from Mantua, and in 1670, from Vienna. A two-week pogrom erupted against the Jews of Padua in 1684 because they observed Tisha B'Av rather than a Christian festival.

Medieval Jewish liturgical poets created numerous elegies (*kinot*) about the tragedies that befell our people, and these were added to the liturgy for the day of Tisha B'Av. Not only the pious observed the commemoration. Even those who may not have accepted the idea, promoted earlier by the prophets and then by the rabbis, that Jewish suffering resulted from Jewish sinning, regarded the three weeks leading to the major fast as an opportunity to repent, ever hopeful that their actions would hasten redemption.

Tisha B'Av devastation continued into the modern age, with the beginning of Russia's Av 9 mobilization for World War I leading a year later to the expulsion of all Jews from the border provinces. Arab attacks against Jews over access to the Western Wall erupted on Tisha B'Av 1929, and deportations from the Warsaw Ghetto to Treblinka began on this day in 1942. (Due to its character and history, Tisha B'Av was seriously considered as the day of commemoration for the Holocaust, an idea ultimately rejected because of strong sentiment that this unique catastrophe in our history needed to have its own memorial [SEE CHAPTER ON YOM HASHOAH]).

Most modern Jews find it difficult to relate to the ancient tragedy—partially because we do have our own, far more gruesome destruction to contend with, with its own day of mourning. Few Jews retain the desire to return to the rituals of Temple life, and the fact that we have also regained our sovereignty lessens, for many, the commemoration's import. The Reform movement, having seen the dispersal of Jews throughout the world as a new opportunity to fulfill our mission to humanity, long ago ceased to regard the Temple's destruction as a tragedy (although in the late twentieth century the movement gave Tisha B'Av modern significance).

Jewish camps take advantage of Tisha B'Av, the only summer holiday, for special programs. Also, observance of Tisha B'Av has increased in recent years, probably a result of the *ba'al teshuvah* (masters of return) movement, the tens of thousands of Jews who are rediscovering their heritage. They and other observant Jews recognize that as long as the quality of life promised in the vision for restoration has not been achieved, there is reason to grieve. The relevance of Tisha B'Av became all too obvious as we were jolted to the reality that our homeland could again be lost: Despite unwavering confidence among Israel's leaders and most Jews worldwide in Israel's ultimate survival and continued strength, thoughts of the possibility of another destruction were not uncommon as the Palestinians' second intifada [begun in September, 2000], with its frequent and horrendous homicide bombings, continued to rage against Israel in 2002, and virulent anti-Semitism rose to the surface in country after country around the world.

FOR FURTHER EXPLORATION

FOR ADULTS

Josephus, Flavius. *The Jewish War.* New York: Penguin Books, 1984.
This is the classic account of the war between Rome and the Jews, written by the historian who had been a leader of the Jewish revolt, was captured by the Romans, and became a Roman citizen and friend to Vespasian and Titus. Though some of his details are suspect, much of our information about this period in history is based on his writings.

Yadin, Yigal. *Masada: Herod's Fortress and the Zealot's Last Stand.* London: Weidenfeld and Nicolson, 1966.
The site of one of the most dramatic events in our history was proven to be more than legend when the excavations undertaken by volunteers from throughout the world, under the direction of Yadin between 1963 and 1965, uncovered exciting and significant evidence confirming Josephus' description of what had occurred there (based on the testimony of two Masada residents who hid instead of committing suicide with their compatriots). This is the story of the dramatic archaeological dig, its findings, and the history they brought to life.

FOR TEENS

Roseman, Kenneth. *The Tenth of Av.* New York: UAHC Press, 1998.
This engaging book puts the reader in first-century Jerusalem, in the midst of the burning city. At the end of each of its vivid pages, it presents the choices the Jews at the time, in the situation described, had to make. In the course of opting to fight or flee, follow Judaism or Christianity, become a teacher or merchant, live in Palestine or the Diaspora, the reader—who chooses his/her own path through the book—learns about history, Jewish values, historic figures and what it takes for Jewish survival. While this Do-It-Yourself Jewish Adventure is directed to young teens, even adults will find it appealing and extremely informative. (Another book in this series, *The Cardinal's Snuffbox*, similarly treats another Ninth of Av catastrophe, the Spanish Inquisition.)

What Does It Mean? Religious Importance

In the context of Jewish destiny, Tisha B'Av marked more than the destruction of a city, the scourging of a countryside, a political development. The entire Jewish way of life—which since the Exodus had been focused on the Land—and the entire Jewish way of worship—which since the desert Tabernacle had been focused on God's earthly abode—were no longer possible. Along with the base of the Temple, the foundations of a belief system and a relationship had been shaken. In addition to everything material and spiritual, the possibility and opportunities for great achievement inherent in the Jewish people living on the Land had vanished.

The ancient Jews, whose world was totally brought down around them, faced the same kinds of agonizing questions of faith and continuity Holocaust survivors in our own time have had to ponder. What did the destruction say about

243

the covenant and the God-Israel connection? Was Judaism supposed to continue? Could it? If so, what would it look like in the absence of the Temple, in exile from the Land, in the face of such complete devastation?

EXILE AS PUNISHMENT

Throughout our history, whatever happened to us was seen as a reflection of our nation's relationship with God. When He was pleased with us, we prospered and won in battle; when He was not, we experienced hard times and lost. Everything we had been taught and had witnessed during the desert wanderings—the extended length of which itself was a result of Divine displeasure—reinforced the connection. We were promised blessings for living in a way that would accomplish our mission, and warned of curses that would befall us if we did not follow the commandments issued for our own and the world's good.

So when they were led off in captivity to Babylon, the Jews only had to read Torah—which clearly stated that the Land would spit them out for immoral behavior—to realize that they were being punished for sinning against God. The prophets (Isaiah, Hosea, Habakkuk, Zephaniah, Jeremiah) for generations had warned them of the coming punishment. When it finally arrived, it was so severe it made the people question whether their violations of the terms of the covenant had caused God to revoke it.

Like the earlier prophets, those who experienced the loss of Jerusalem reassured the survivors that even though God had punished them out of the anger they provoked, His undying love would allow Him to forgive them. Jeremiah explained that God's presence was universal, that He would not abandon them, but had gone into exile, too, and would restore them to their homeland.

The second destruction created an even greater crisis of faith. Particularly with no prophetic guidance (not that the people had listened to it anyway), there was confusion over the proper response, both during the war and after it. Were they to stay and fight, flee to another stronghold and try to outlast the enemy, escape from the besieged city and secretly teach their culture and religion, or adopt different religious practices altogether—either within the context of Judaism or outside it?

Many of the Jews who returned to Israel after the Babylonian exile, facing harsh conditions and lasting foreign subjugation, could no longer believe that loyalty to God would make any difference in their lives (MALAKHAI 3:13–14). Likewise, many of those quashed by Rome also despaired. Some came to believe that Christianity, which had developed as a sect within Judaism in the last decades of the Temple's existence, was not, after all, a renewal of the connection between God and Israel. They began to see it as a new covenant to replace the one obliterated by the destruction of the Temple. Christian Jews broke away and began evolving into an entirely separate religious community, taking along with them Jews whose faith had been shattered with Jerusalem's walls.

Others, led by the great sages, continued to see Israel's fortunes and misfortunes within the established pattern of Exodus (redemption) and exile, of rewarding compliance and punishing sin, of Israel having the free will to act, and God having the power to intervene to steer the nation back on the course of its moral mission. A critical part of the pattern is its intrinsic hope. The prophets who made the most gruesomely dire predictions always had visions of ultimate salvation. The worst sinner could repent. Between the cracks, one could again sow seeds, from the rubble rebuild. If Judaism were to continue, however, it needed a new structure not reliant on particular places or physical structures.

FROM SACRIFICE TO STUDY

Trapped in the besieged Jerusalem, Rabbi Yokhanan ben Zakkai realized that people reduced to sustaining themselves on tea made from straw, as were the defenders of Jerusalem, would not be able to withstand Rome's onslaught. And he knew that the "independence or nothing" attitude adopted by the Jewish zealots in control, who refused to allow any living person to leave, was a policy of suicide that would put an end to Israel's true mission.

So Ben Zakkai and his disciples staged his death so that he could be carried out of the city in a coffin and meet with Vespasian. All he asked of the Roman commander was permission to establish an academy of Jewish learning at Yavneh (a town in the Galilee). His request was granted. Ben Zakkai realized that making the Jews as knowledgeable as possible about their culture and religion would preserve in another form the rituals no longer possible to perform. It would allow everyone, not just the priests, to participate in Jewish life.

Following the lead of their predecessors, the Pharisees (SEE "HISTORIC FOUNDA-TION" IN CHAPTER ON PESAKH), the rabbis promoted the idea that getting close to God did not require burning an animal carcass, but could be accomplished by expressing Jewish values in every aspect of one's life. Holiness was no longer housed just in an external place, but was an internalized characteristic of each person. Words (recounting Temple service, praising God, said in honesty to other people) and actions (routine behavior performed in spiritual awareness, interpersonal dealings carried out according to Jewish law, deeds of loving-kindness) could define Jewish life. Jeremiah had spoken of this "new covenant": "I will put my Teaching into their innermost being and inscribe it upon their hearts" (31:33). Torah study, through which anyone could learn how to live by the system of Jewish values, was elevated to such a high level in Jewish observance the sages said it equaled all other commandments.

The means may have changed, but the message remained unaltered: the goal of Jewish existence was still a redemption bringing universal peace. To under-score it, the rabbis said that the day of the destruction of the Temple is the day of birth of the messiah.

The Talmud relates that Rabbis Gamaliel, Eleazar ben Azariah, Joshua and Akiva went to Jerusalem together. When they reached the Temple Mount, a jackal emerged from the remains of the Holy of Holies. Recalling that any common person who went near the spot would be put to death (NUMBERS 1:51), and seeing it turned into the haunt of fearless animals, three of the sages began to weep. Akiva laughed. He remembered the prophecy "and I call reliable witnesses, Uriah the Priest and Zekhariah the son of Berekhiah" (ISAIAH 8:2). In the First Temple days of Uriah, Micah wrote: "because of you, Zion shall be plowed as a field, Jerusalem shall become heaps of ruins and the Temple Mount a shrine in the woods" (3:12). Zekhariah, who lived at the time of the Second Temple, wrote: "There shall yet be old men and women in the squares of Jerusalem" (8:4). Seeing that Uriah's prophecy had come to pass, Akiva explained, made him certain Zekhariah's would also come to be.

The sustaining lesson we learned through catastrophe was that in the aftermath of tragedy—an unavoidable part of an imperfect life—we move forward, perhaps in a different manner, but guided by the same values toward an unchanging goal. In the new revised system, anyone and everyone—each a component of the holy nation—could contribute to bringing it about.

FOR FURTHER EXPLORATION

Selections from the prophets Jeremiah, Isaiah (verses 40–66) and Ezekiel (in any Jewish Bible) beautifully convey the fall of Jerusalem, the consolation and exile of the people, and the vision of their resurgence (Ezekiel's valley of the dry bones) and return to the Land.   ☺☆

What Does It Mean to Us? Personal Significance

Have you ever been in a relationship that ended? Or watched a great chance come and go? Or made a choice you later wished you could reverse? How many times in your life have you said, "I should have" or "if only . . ." It is difficult enough to let go of something you have in hand. But often a large part of the pain comes from the sense of loss over what you *could* have had.

We would not engage in "what ifs" if we were happy with a current situation. Displeasure with it and sadness for squandered potential or lost opportunity can be incapacitating. It is extremely difficult to stride ahead while continually looking behind. The rabbis of the post-destruction decades recognized this. So they concentrated the period and practices of mourning to free the people, in order that they would be able to move forward with their lives. Focusing your mourning on identifying what is wrong, and figuring out how to make it right, can make the experience cathartic and constructive.

That is exactly the purpose of a fast day: to give us a chance to momentarily retreat from the imperfect present, the imperfect world, to step back and indulge in dissatisfaction with it—and then step forward and take action that will lead to positive change. Tisha B'Av allows us to experience loss for what was and what might have been, individually and collectively. If used well, it can help us create what can be, personally and communally.

There may be any kind of past loss or regret in your life whose hold you need to relinquish. But what is it Jewishly that you miss? If it's the smell of chicken soup on Friday night, the sales techniques of Maxwell Street, the colors and characters of the Lower East Side or Bubbe and Zaide's Yiddish-accented speech, you simply have a case of nostalgia, the source of melancholy reminiscence, perhaps, but not a reason to cry. As the once-popular poster of an oversized bagel suggested, there's more to two thousand years of Jewish civilization than this.

A concern for Tisha B'Av—which came about because the possibility of living a full Jewish way of life ended—should be the kinds of *meaningful* connections to the Jewish past, and future, you are missing. Lacking the knowledge to make time-honored traditions relevant and to infuse your everyday life with Jewish value, being culturally illiterate when it comes to Judaism (can you explain Sukkot, identify Abraham and name the Twelve Tribes of Israel with the same ease you explain Thanksgiving, identify George Washington and name the original thirteen American colonies?)—these are things to mourn. Having not had a Jewish summer camp experience, first-hand exposure to Israel, or a really good Hebrew school teacher are legitimate disadvantages to regret, and worthwhile aspects of Jewish life to consider on Tisha B'Av.

But once the day of mourning for what might have been ends, we stop "crying over spilled milk"—and go out to fill the bottle. There's still time for you, who can increase your knowledge, and your children, who can be given the opportunities you missed.

In the collective arena, most of us find it difficult to identify with the moaning and weeping the Jews of past centuries went through on this holiday. Unlike them, we have Israel and strength as equal citizens of other countries. While some religious leaders believed the reunification of Jerusalem in 1967's Six-Day War obviated the need to observe the mourning customs of Av 9, most recognize that we still lack much of what our predecessors mourned on this day: We have not eliminated anti-Semitic persecution from the world or established peace over Jerusalem or Israel, let alone the universal peace that guarantees a life of dignity, self-sufficiency and mutual respect to all; we have not effected a spiritual reconciliation to accompany our renewed sovereignty over the Land—nor have we been able to achieve unity—regardless of UJA slogans ("One People")—which the Temple, as a national symbol and gathering place, promoted.

These deficits provide national goals to ponder during our day of withdrawal and introspection, and they have local communal implications. Among the conditions the rabbis cited as having brought down the Temple (there were many: prevalence of murder and incest, desecration of the Sabbath, neglecting to educate the children, acting as though those most ignorant of the law were the equals of those most knowledgeable, standing idly by the perpetration of evil, scholars being despised by the people. . .), senseless hatred is said to have been caused by "the root of all evil." Even the position of spiritual leadership, *Kohein Gadol,* went to the highest bidder. In our communities and institutions today, is the situation much different than it was at the end of the Second Temple? Who gets the greatest honors in the synagogue, the top positions on organization boards? Should you be pressing in your community to add requirements for scholarship and character so that along

> *The gossiper stands in Syria and kills in Rome.*
> JERUSALEM TALMUD PEAH 1.1

with the necessary financial leadership you have the intellectual, spiritual and moral leadership models and direction critical for long-term success?

The rabbis also blamed the destruction on *lashon harah* (evil talk)—gossip, rumor, innuendo—even saying nice things that could prompt someone to respond with a negative comment. Trying to eliminate such conversation is undoubtedly even a much more difficult task than trying to change our communal culture. Let's face it. How many of us can resist listening to or passing along a juicy tidbit?

The problem—which the rabbis considered one of the most serious offenses because of the destructive power of words—goes deeper. Even if a comment is not made initially with malicious intent, it can wind up causing serious irreparable damage. The remarks of individuals can have national repercussions. For instance, consider how (and where and with whom) you or the people around you express discontent with Israel. Is it done in constructive ways and without providing ammunition to our enemies? Does the criticism come out of sincere concern for the future of the country and its people, or because as a Jew you feel embarrassed by Israel's actions? The problem is especially critical when Israel is under attack, physically, economically, diplomatically.

Words—whose power we should think about on Tisha B'Av—can be tools as well as weapons, can build up as well as tear down. Think of ways you can be constructive. Soothe ruffled feathers. Take advantage of opportunities to counsel cooperation and mutual respect in communal settings, stressing common ground and common goals rather than differences.

Rabbi Levi Yitzhkak of Berditchev, the Khassidic master, said that we cannot expect to achieve the "rebuilt Jerusalem" of our collective dream until we eliminate from among ourselves the destructive forces that devastated Jerusalem. All of them (idolatry, adultery, murder, hatred) represented turnings away from the Jewish way of life, as does ignorance, one of the most destructive forces we face in today's Jewish communal crisis.

The Chinese character for crisis consists of two symbols: one for danger, the other for opportunity. The combination sums up the history and meaning of Tisha B'Av. In past generations, emphasis was on the former, because the Jews continued to live in the wake of loss and the threat of persecution. So Tisha B'Av they grieve over the destruction and passively hope for the redemption. Never before in history, because of the political and cultural environments in which they lived, could the Jews act on the opportunity. We—in response to the different threat we face—can. While we still grieve for the loss of wasted possibilities and recognize the danger of not taking bold, positive steps, we do have the chance to bring redemption closer. It's an opportunity we don't want to miss.

Traditions—
HOW WE CELEBRATE TISHA B'AV

What Do We Use? Ritual Items

KINOT

Instead of the regular *siddur,* we use a special prayer book for the holiday, *Kinot* (Elegies), which contains the prayer services (*Ma'ariv, Shakharit,* and *Minkhah*), the text of Lamentations, a selection of additional elegies, and the Scriptural readings for the day. Synagogue or service organizers usually provide copies.

How Do We Celebrate? Observance

In the antithesis of the slogan for Adar (SEE CHAPTER ON PURIM), the rabbis observed: "When Av comes in, all merriment must go out." The restrictions established for Tisha B'Av and the weeks leading up to it are intended to eliminate anything that would detract from mourning or lead to levity. We limit everyday comforts. We read elegies lamenting the tremendous loss and suffering of our people. Everything is meant to help us relive the devastation of Jerusalem, experience the grief of exile. (As an incentive, the rabbis cautioned that only those who mourn the destruction of the Temple would merit the privilege of seeing it rebuilt, based on Isaiah: "Rejoice with Jerusalem and be glad for her all you who love her! Join in her jubilation all you who mourned over her" [66:10].).

USHERING IN THE HOLIDAY

In reenacting the response to the destruction of Jerusalem and other tragedies of Jewish history, every Jew becomes a mourner. That is why many of the things we do to observe the day are borrowed from the customs and rituals we follow to express grief when we lose members of our immediate families. We restrict our physical comfort and express humility by not wearing leather shoes. Likewise, the clothes we put on should be simple, used, and not fresh from the laundry or dry cleaner. For the same reasons we sit on low stools, or directly on the floor. We do not eat or drink. When we go to sleep this night, we change our habits in a way that will lessen comfort—like using fewer pillows than normal (the pious used to replace theirs with stones), taking the mattress off the box spring, or using a sleeping bag on the floor. We refrain from sexual relations.

From before sundown, when all restrictions of the holiday take effect, idle chitchat and frivolous behavior are shunned. We forego the usual ways of welcoming a holiday both because of its nature and when it starts. Our last meal prior to the fast must be completed before sundown, and since at least the beginning of Av, we have not consumed wine. So there is no *kiddush*. We do not light candles, which are elements of joy. In fact, it is customary to reduce illumination as much as possible, to acknowledge the dark days of our suffering.

THE FAST

The rabbis said that anyone who eats or drinks on Tisha B'Av, except those exempt for health reasons, would not see the joy of Jerusalem. In addition to being an ancient means of expressing remorse and sorrow, on Tisha B'Av fasting also reflects the famine, repeatedly referred to in Lamentations, which wracked the defenders of Jerusalem. (Among the most horrendous details of the siege are those pertaining to the mothers who, in the throes of starvation, cooked and ate their own children [LAMENTATIONS 2:20, 4:10].)

The *seudah* (meal) *mafseket* (interrupting), or the meal that comes between normal eating and the abstention from food, is supposed to be a sparse, lonely affair. Limited to one dish and foods traditional in a house of mourning, one customarily eats it while sitting on the floor or low stool. Since, according to Jewish law, when three people eat in each other's company they recite the *Birkat Hamazon* together (known as *zumin,* invitation, as the leader invites the others to say grace with him), several observant people eating in the same room position themselves as though each is eating alone.

SYNAGOGUE

According to tradition, communal discord brought down the Jewish sanctuary and the Jewish commonwealth. The sins cited in the fall of the First Temple were acts between individuals that caused rifts in the whole society: adultery, murder, and idolatry, which meant that people were choosing their own gods, relinquishing their common goals and values to follow different masters. The senseless hatred blamed for the second destruction made enemies among people who should have viewed each other as brothers and sisters, fracturing what might have been a united front against a common enemy. Joining with other members of the community in prayer, a major part of observance for the ninth of Av, could be seen as compensation for this fatal fragmentation.

EVENING It is customary to go to the synagogue for *Ma'ariv* services at nightfall. You will notice that the sanctuary is only faintly lit, and the *parokhet* (ark curtain) has either been removed or replaced with a black cloth. The Torah scrolls and bimah (reading desk) may also be draped in black. Without greeting each other (another custom of mourning), members of the congregation quietly find places on the floor or on chairs or benches that have been turned on their sides. Often they remove their shoes.

Following *Ma'ariv,* read in a slow, mournful voice, Eikhah (Oh how [lonely sits the city]), known in English as Lamentations and sometimes in rabbinic literature as Kinot, is chanted in its own sad melody. (The tradition that senseless hatred caused the destruction of the second Temple is derived from the initial letters of this first phrase of the book—*Eikhah yashav badah ha'ir,* which spell *eybah,* hatred.) Traditionally ascribed to the prophet Jeremiah (but more recently said to have been composed by various poets), it is the eyewitness account of a survivor (or survivors), a suite of five elegies whose suggestive imagery was thought by the sages to be as descriptive of the Roman destruction as it had been of the Babylonian.

Since the rabbis looked forward to the time that the days of mourning for the Temple's destruction would be converted to days of rejoicing for its renewal, they did not want Eikhah to take permanent form. For that reason, we do not read it from a parchment scroll (as, for example, we do for Esther on Purim), but from a printed book.

If you do not understand Hebrew, read the English translation. Its evocative language has the power to transport you to ancient Jerusalem, to make you sense what it was like to see your entire universe collapsing around you, to make you feel the pain of a parent unable to feed a child, the disgrace of a once self-sufficient citizen reduced to groveling in the streets. (The description of Jerusalem of 586 BCE, which reads like a description of Jerusalem of 70 CE, in large part also reads like an account of Warsaw of 1943.)

The motif in Judaism of life over death, renewal after devastation, hope after destruction appears strongly in the mid-section of Lamentations ("The kindness of the Lord has not ended. . . . The Lord does not reject forever, but first afflicts, then pardons. . . . Let us search and examine our ways and turn back to the Lord. . . . [3:22, 31, 40]). In keeping with this philosophy, it is customary not to end the reading of any book of the Bible, or any portion of a book, on a negative note. For that reason, after the book finishes in distress ("For truly, You have rejected us, bitterly raged against us"), the entire congregation repeats the next to the last verse of

Eikhah, *"Hashiveinu"* ("Take us back, O Lord. . .renew our days as of old!").

Most of the *kinot* chanted after Eikhah were composed during the difficult times of the Crusades and Spanish Inquisition. Describing the transgressions of the Jews and their love for Israel, the most popular ones were written by Elazar Hakallir (the eighth-century liturgical poet), Judah Halevi (1085–1145), the Spanish philosopher also considered to be the greatest post-biblical poet) and Solomon ibn Gabirol (another product of the Golden Age of Spain, 1021–1058). Embodying a timeless quality that has given them lasting impact in the liturgy, they express the prayers and dreams of a persecuted people who look to God for hope. Often in acrostic or altered acrostic form, they frequently draw on imagery from Talmud and midrash.

Most liturgies begin with a *kinah* of Hakallir, and end with a series known as Zionides, which extol the glory of Zion. In a favored one, written by Halevi, the poet expands on Jeremiah's vision of the weeping woman identified as the matri-arch Rachel (JEREMIAH 31:15). He imagines himself walking on Jerusalem's holy ground and encountering Mother Zion, who asks about the welfare of her chil-dren throughout the world. Other *kinot* recited were written in response to tragedies in Jewish history. One commemorates the public burning of the Torah in Paris, another the massacres of German Jews during the first Crusade, another the slaughter of the Jews of York, and a recent one the annihilation of European Jewry in the Holocaust.

In the full *kaddish* (the prayer said in honor of the dead, but which praises God for the living) at the end of the service we delete the line *titkabeil* ("May the prayers and supplications of the entire Family of Israel be accepted"). It would contradict what we have just said in Eikhah, "You have screened yourself off with a cloud that no prayer may pass through" (3:44). Congregations sometimes design special programs to give the Tisha B'Av experience current relevance, adding readings, stories or discussions to the evening service and Lamentations.

MORNING Like mourners prior to a funeral, men generally do not put on their tallesim or tefillin, signs of joy. (Religious men who normally wear a *tallit katan,* also called *arba kanfote,* the fringed undergarment, do so even on Tisha B'Av. Some, like the Syrian Jews, put on their prayer shawls and phylacteries at home, but remove them before going to synagogue; those who do wear them for the *Shakharit* service remove them before the reading of Eikhah and/or *Kinot*.) Lights are not used in the sanctuary.

On fast days, the central *Amidah* prayer usually contains an addition, *Nakhem* (Comfort), which requests consolation for the mourners of Jerusalem and the experience of exile. Since during the early part of the day, which corresponds to the time prior to a funeral, mourners are not open to being consoled, this prayer is omitted until the afternoon service. By then, grief is considered to have somewhat abated.

We do say the fast-day prayer *Aneinu* (answer us), which looks for response to our fast of distress; we omit other prayers normally part of daily service that express sentiments or thoughts in contrast to the subdued and dejected feeling of the day. These include the Psalm of the Day, Hymns of Unity, Hymn of Glory, and the Priestly Blessing, usually said by the *khazzan* at the end of the *Amidah*. (It requests the granting of peace, like the traditional Jewish greeting, and greetings are not exchanged on Tisha B'Av.)

Normally mourners do not attend synagogue services during the week immediately following a burial (shiva), but since everyone is a mourner on the ninth of Av, anyone grieving for the loss of a family member may attend, and may even be called to the Torah.

In keeping with the hushed aura of mourning, the Sephardim do not announce the aliyot, but quietly tell the men to be called for the three Torah reading sections in advance, and they just go up in turn. (The Sephardim also omit the joyous raising of the Torah prior to reading, as is their normal custom.) In some congregations, it is the practice to say *Barukh dayan emet* (Blessed is the true Judge), the phrase said on hearing of a death, when called for an aliyah. The *yad* (literally hand, the pointer used to note the place for reading the Torah) may be substituted with a simple instrument, such as a reed.

The Torah reading (DEUTERONOMY 4:25–40), warns that the Israelites would be banished from the Land if they followed other gods, and reminds that they would be blessed and live well on the Land if they followed the commandments. We are supposed to learn that any transgression, regardless of its severity, will be forgiven if we sincerely repent. Between aliyot, we make a *mishabeirakh* ("Who blesses") only for someone who is sick. (Normally, the special petition during this part of the service is made for all sorts of personal requests.)

The prophetic portion (JEREMIAH 8:13–9:23), describes God's grief at the transgressions of His people and His plan to make Jerusalem and Judah desolate, and to exile the Jews in punishment. Except for the last two verses, which refer to God's kindness (suggesting again that repentance will result in renewal), the Haftarah is chanted to the same melody as Lamentations.

After the Torah has been returned to the Ark, we again sit on the floor for *kinot.* (Some congregations begin by repeating Eikhah.) We are not supposed to talk or leave the synagogue at this time. The central elegy of the morning is *Artzei Halebanon* (Cedars of Lebanon), a painful record of the martyrdom of the ten rabbinic teachers who were brutally murdered during the Hadrianic persecutions for thwarting Roman law prohibiting Torah education. Including Akiva, Gamaliel and Yishmael ben Elisha, these sages are the subjects of a well-known *piyyut,* which we recite during the *Mussaf* service on Yom Kippur. In Sephardic congregations, members take turns reading the Bible book of Job, the classic tale of human suffering.

AFTERNOON The *Minkhah* service includes the parts deleted from *Shakharit.* Interestingly, we do not recite the prayers normally omitted on festivals for the reason that they would hamper the feeling of joy (SEE "HALAKHAH" IN CHAPTER ON PESAKH). This is consistent with the optimism built into Tisha B'Av— "the birthday of the messiah." From midday on, the mood somewhat lightens. While we continue to recall misfortune, our focus shifts to the hope of redemption embodied in every episode of suffering. (That is why restrictions on work and household activity are also lifted at this time.) The men may now put on their tallesim and the congregation resumes sitting on regular seats.

The Scriptural readings underscore the positive message, relating Moses' success in convincing God not to destroy Israel after the Golden Calf abomination but to uphold His promise to the patriarchs to bring them to the Land (EXODUS 32:11–14), and about the second set of Tablets, the attributes of God and the covenant with His people, standard readings for all fast days (EXODUS 34:1–10), known as Vayekhal, for the first word ("And [Moses] began" [to plead]). The prophetic portion (ISAIAH 55:6–56:8), also read on public fast days, is a consolation to the anguished exiles in Babylon, reminding them of God's mercy and promising the restoration of the Land and the people to it.

Now the *Amidah* can include *Nakhem*. In Israel, two revised versions—one issued by the chief rabbinate and one by the religious kibbutz movement—reflect the reunification of Jerusalem. In the *kaddish, titkabeil* is reinstated.

STUDY

On the festivals, we engage in Torah study because it is one of the forms of joy that heightens our experience of the holiday. In keeping with avoidance of pleasurable activities, on Tisha B'Av we abstain from "the precepts of the Lord [which] gladden the heart" (PSALMS 19:9). Only those parts of *Tanakh* and Talmud that deal with destruction, catastrophe and mourning are permitted. A standard text, of course, is the book of Job. Also allowed are the warnings and descriptions about the impending punishment of the world in Jeremiah, Midrash Eikhah (rabbinical stories and commentaries on Lamentations and the second destruction), the scroll of Eikhah with commentaries, tractate Mo-ed Katan on the laws of mourning and excommunication, the account of the destruction in tractate Gittin, and the last chapter of Taanit in the Jerusalem Talmud, which details the destruction of the Temple.

We are forbidden from engaging in analysis of text, since such stimulation of the mind is also pleasurable. We may not even answer a question of Jewish law, unless it involves a sick person or immediate need. Any learning done with children is to be based on the same sorts of subjects appropriate for adult study.

CONCLUSION OF TISHA B'AV

While the blessing for the new moon (*kiddush levanah* [SEE "THE JEWISH CALEN-DAR"]) may be recited prior to Tisha B'Av, because it should be done in a joyous mood it is common to wait until after *Ma'ariv* at the conclusion of the mourning period.

Then, the preferable procedure is to wash one's hands, break the fast with some food other than meat, and beverage other than wine, change into regular shoes, and go outside in the company of ten men. If doing all the preparatory steps would mean a *minyan* would not be available, they can be omitted. It is a lovely way to end the day, and the three weeks, since the blessing that praises God for creating the heavens likens the moon that renews itself to the Jewish people who will be renewed.

Although the fast ends at nightfall, we do not drink wine, eat meat or hold any kind of celebration until noon on Av 10, since the Temple burned all through the night of the ninth and into most of the next day. (The pious used to maintain the fast until midday on Av 10.) The other restrictions of the mourning period should also be continued until midday on the tenth.

SHABBAT AND TISHA B'AV

When the ninth of Av falls on the Sabbath, observance of the day of mourning is postponed until the tenth. (We are prohibited from expressing grief, or from fasting, on the Sabbath, a day of peace and joy. The fast of Yom Kippur, whose nature is entirely different, is the only exception). *Havdallah,* the ceremony that separates sacred and profane time, is postponed until the close of the fast day. The blessings over light (created at the end of the first day of rest) and spices (used to strengthen us at the departure of a soul-filling day of rest) are omitted since they only relate to Sabbath. The *Havdallah* blessing over wine is recited along with *hamavdil* (the passage dealing with separation [SEE "BLESSINGS"]).

CONTINUED CONSOLATION

PROPHETIC VOICE The upswing of hope begun on the afternoon of Tisha B'Av continues on the Sabbath following it. Called Shabbat Nakhamu (Console) after the first line of the day's prophetic reading (*"Nakhamu, nakhamu ami,* Console console my people . . ."* [ISAIAH 40:1–26]), it is also the first of seven haftarot of consolation, all drawn from the book of Isaiah, that deliver a message of comfort in the seven weeks following Tisha B'Av and lead us to the period of repentance and Rosh Hashanah (49:14–51:3; 54:11–55:5; 51:12–52:12; 54:1–10; 60:1–22; 61:10–63:9).

TU B'AV Six days after Tisha B'Av, the fifteenth (tu; טו, with the Hebrew letter tet [ט], nine, and vov [ו], six) of the month used to be a minor festival. Talmud remarks that there were no days as festive in Israel as those of Yom Kippur and Av 15, when the girls dressed in white and danced in the vineyards to attract husbands (SEE "HISTORIC FOUNDATION" IN CHAPTER ON YOM KIPPUR).

Several legends and several theories attempt to explain the fifteenth of Av's origins. Midrash relates it to the way the ninth of Av became designated as a day of disaster. It says that in the last year the Israelites spent in the desert, the elders who dug their graves and slept in them on the ninth of Av did not die. Thinking they had miscalculated the date, they returned to the graves the next night, and the next, until, by the fifteenth, they realized they were being spared and would be allowed to enter the Land: the sin of the spies had been forgiven.

Another explanation is more closely tied to the way the day was observed. It identifies the date as the end of the prohibition against an Israelite woman marrying a man from another tribe if she had inherited land from her father (NUMBERS 27:4–8). The prohibition had been in effect until the conquest of Canaan was completed and Israel became secure enough to not worry about transfer of property between tribes. It may also have been the end of the ban against intermarrying with the tribe of Benjamin, punished because of their depravity that led to the rape and murder of the wife of a Levite (JUDGES 19–20). The next chapter of Judges describes how the Benjaminites, once accepted back into the community of Israel, took wives from among the girls dancing in the vineyards during a festival at Shiloh. Both explanations, like the wedding motif of Yom Kippur, suggest the reunion of Israel and God, marking the end of a period of estrangement.

After the fall of Betar, the Romans inflicted additional punishment for the Jews' revolt by prohibiting them from burying their dead. Three years later, a new emperor overturned the cruel decree. Permission to bury the remains— given on the fifteenth of Av—was so significant a special blessing of thanks (*ha tov u'hameitiv,* Who is good and does good) was added as the fourth *brakhah* of the *Birkat Hamazon.*

In Temple days, Av 15 marked the last time firewood could be brought to the sanctuary for the sacrifices (after that the waning sun was not strong enough to dry the wood) and was observed with festive dancing and the lighting of torches and bonfires.

259

While some kibbutzim tried to revive the celebration with music, poetry, dancing and love songs, most vestiges of it are seen in traditional Jewish circles where penitential prayers are omitted during daily services. The bride and groom married on Av 15 do not fast, as is customary prior to a wedding; yeshivah classes are suspended after morning services, and teachers provide refreshments for the students.

Where Do We Begin? Preparation

A three-week period of grieving precedes Tisha B'Av. Known as *bein hametzarim* (between the straits, or between the fences), from Eikhah—"All her pursuers over-took her in the narrow places" (1:3)—the sages identify it as a general period of affliction for Israel. (They relate *metzarim* to the word *tzara*, affliction, which you might recognize in its Yiddish form, *tzuris*.) It corresponds to the twenty-one days from the breaching of the outer wall of Jerusalem to the day the city fell.

We relive the mounting despair of the besieged Jerusalemites, and the suffering of Jews throughout history, who experienced catastrophe after massacre after slaughter at this time of year, by adopting progressively more intense mourning practices. Some begin on Tammuz 17 and last for the full Three Weeks, others are adopted from Rosh Khodesh Av for the Nine Days. The most restrictive apply during the week in which Tisha B'Av occurs.

THE THREE WEEKS

Our period of mourning begins with one of the three minor fasts related to the loss of Jerusalem, Shiva Asar (17) B'Tammuz. It lasts from dawn until nightfall. (The two other minor fasts of destruction, Tzom [fast {of}] Gedalia on Tishrei 3, when the last Jews fled Judah, and Asarah B' (tenth of) Tevet, when Nebukhadnezzar first attacked Jerusalem, are observed the same way.)

As of Tammuz 17, no weddings are held, there is no attendance of musical performances or playing instruments, dancing, pleasure trips, getting a haircut or purchasing or using new items—clothing, luxuries, fruits—that would require the *shehekhiyanu* blessing. Since it thanks God for "bringing us to this season" and "this season" is one of catastrophe, saying it is obviously inappropriate.

With the amalgamation of misfortune accrued to these days throughout our history, the three weeks became known as a time when the Jews seemed to court trouble. (Even back in Yokhanan ben Zakkai's time it was thought of this way. The sage urged teachers to avoid corporeal punishment for fear of serious consequences.) As a result, the rabbis advised that all situations of danger be avoided. We are not supposed to swim in deep water, ride in a boat as unstable as a canoe, undergo minor or cosmetic surgery, or go to court in a lawsuit with a non-Jew.

The pious set aside time each day to reflect on the loss of the Temples.

THE NINE DAYS

In the last few centuries, activity has become more restricted than in prior times. During this period, we are not supposed to bathe, even in cold water. That means no baths, showers, swimming, wading, floating or soaking in a pool, river or other body of water. This is the area that most offends modern sensibilities, especially since the nine days fall during the hottest time of the year. There are exceptions, in honor of Sabbath, for health reasons and in cases of laborers who get dirty on the job, but otherwise, we are limited to cold sponge baths, without soap and shampoo. (The Sephardim follow these restrictions only during the week of Tisha B'Av.)

Although some people have historically taken on restrictions regarding meat and wine consumption from Tammuz 17, the general custom is to give them up at the beginning of the month of Av. Ritual slaughterers since the days of Maimonides (eleventh century) have put away their knives as of Rosh Khodesh, retrieving them only to prepare meat for the sick, Sabbath or a *seudat mitzvah* (meal connected with a commandment, such as a *brit,* bar mitzvah, pidyon haben or *siyyum* following a course of study). It is a widespread custom not to eat food that has been cooked with meat, even if the meat itself is not consumed.

Since restrictions on washing and laundering clothes begin as of Rosh Khodesh Av, any garment you or your family need to wear must be readied in advance. Many people put on new or freshly laundered clothes briefly before Rosh Khodesh, which allows them to wear those items during the nine days.

SHABBAT KHAZON

The Sabbath immediately preceding Av 9 is known as the Sabbath of Vision (*khazon*) for the prophetic reading (ISAIAH 1:1–27). After recounting heinous transgressions, it offers the hope of reconciliation, which will come when the people "cease to do evil, learn to do good." Shabbat Khazon and Shabbat Nakhamu, which provides words of consolation a week later, embrace Tisha B'Av from opposite sides, cushioning the blow of the day of destruction, allowing the mourners to go into it knowing there is salvation and emerging from it again reassured that redemption will come. The entire portion may be chanted to the melody of Eikhah; more appropriately, only the verses of admonition are rendered in that subdued chant.

TISHA B'AV ON SHABBAT

When the ninth of Av falls on Saturday or Sunday, which means that the fast and its restrictions are observed on Sunday, and you attend the evening service, you need to have a pair of non-leather shoes available at the synagogue to change into at the transition between Sabbath and the day of mourning.

What Are We Supposed to Do? Halakhah

All the laws connected with Tisha B'Av and the weeks leading up to it are designed, like the customs of the period, to decrease joy and avoid frivolity, and, like preparations, they increase in intensity.

FAST OF TAMMUZ 17

The abstention from food lasts only from seventy-two minutes before dawn (*amud hashakhar*, the rise of morning) until fifty minutes after sunset (nightfall), and does not apply to pregnant women or nursing mothers (unless they feel they will not be hurt by it), a woman who has given birth within thirty days, or someone sick, even if not in mortal danger. People who do need to eat during the day should take only what is necessary for well-being, and avoid eating luxurious items or excessively. The same ruling applies to minors who understand the meaning of the fast. Males of thirteen years and females of twelve years and older are required to fast.

While other personal comforts and pleasures are permitted, abstaining from taking a hot bath or shower, unless the fast coincides with *Erev Shabbat*, is advised. Having a haircut or shaving is prohibited. (They are permitted on the fast days of Tevet 10 and Gedalia, which otherwise share the same halakhot as Tammuz 17.) One who is not fasting should not be called to the Torah (read if at least six people in the *minyan* are fasting) or lead the prayer service.

CELEBRATION

If no other date is feasible, a wedding may be held on the eve of Tammuz 17, but not after that during the three weeks. If *Shevah Brakhot* (seven blessings, the meals marked by recitation of the benedictions traditionally held on the seven evenings following a wedding) fall during the three weeks, it is permissible to dance and sing as long as musical instruments are not played. At other meals during this period, singing without instrumental accompaniment is allowed as long as it does not lead to a joyous or raucous mood. Since grief should not be observed on Shabbat, normal Sabbath singing takes place.

Once Rosh Khodesh Av begins, all rejoicing is forbidden. If an occasion for celebration occurs on or after Rosh Khodesh Av (such as a *brit milah*), the expression of joy (for example, in the amount and style of refreshments served) should be reduced from what it would normally be. Giving gifts is inappropriate. (Consult an authority about procedures when the *brit* coincides with Tisha B'Av itself.)

MUSIC

During the three weeks, you may not attend concerts, opera, musical theater and so on. Programs such as sporting events at which music is incidental to the main activity are permitted until Rosh Khodesh Av. If you are a music teacher, professional musician or music student, you may play your instrument.

PLEASURE AND COMFORT

Certain aspects of house building, repairing, decorating and landscaping that are considered sources of pleasure are restricted during the Nine Days. If you are concerned about these matters, consult a detailed guide or local rabbinic authority.

NEW AND LAUNDERED CLOTHING AND NEEDLEWORK

Except for undergarments and children's clothing and preparation for Shabbat or a *brit,* you are not supposed to wash or clean linens or clothing, or use new or clean linen or clothes during the Nine Days. (You may purchase shoes needed for the ninth of Av.) If you must prepare garments for a trip or wedding, consult a rabbinic authority about how arrangements may be made.

SHEHEKHIYANU

Except for on Shabbat, or an opportunity for a *mitzvah,* such as *brit* or pidyon haben, all situations that call for saying *shehekhiyanu* are to be avoided during the Three Weeks. (If Tisha B'Av falls on the Sabbath, even though the restrictions of the holiday will not be observed until Sunday, the blessing may not be recited.) If a new fruit will not be available after the ninth of Av but will last until Shabbat, it should be eaten on the Sabbath, when the blessing may be made. It is permissible to purchase and wear new tefillin (but not a new tallit, since it is a garment) during the Three Weeks; a new *tallit katan* may be bought and used until Rosh Khodesh Av. Other clothing and luxury items may not be purchased or used.

MEAT AND WINE

During the Nine Days, meat or chicken (which is categorized as meat), wine, and brandy (which contains wine), all sources of joy, are prohibited—except for Rosh Khodesh and Shabbat, or a *seudat mitzvah.* The restrictions include any food made from meat, like soup, even if meat does not remain in it, and foods and beverages in which wine or grapes are used. Children over the age of six are also bound by the restrictions.

To avoid drinking the cup of wine normally taken at the end of the post-meal grace, or post-Sabbath *Havdallah,* give it to a child. If no children are present, the person who performs *Havdallah* may drink the wine at the ceremony's conclusion but one doing the *birkat* eliminates the wine.

HAIRCUTS

Beginning Tammuz 17, you should not get a haircut, except on Thursday in order to honor the Sabbath. If you have been in mourning for thirty days that end after Tammuz 17, you may get your haircut then. If being ungroomed would result in loss of a job or ridicule, you may get a haircut and shave, and a woman is permitted to shave her legs. A child's hair may not be cut during the week in which Tisha B'Av occurs.

WASHING

During the Nine Days, you are limited to washing one part of your body at a time. Soap or shampoo may be used only if you cannot otherwise remove dirt. A laborer who normally gets dirty in the course of doing a job may wash as usual to get clean. During a heat wave, you are permitted to take a cold shower, and when necessary for medical reasons, you may bathe or shower in hot water. A woman preparing for ritual immersion may wash with hot water.

If you customarily immerse in a *mikvah* on Friday in honor of Shabbat you may continue to do so during the Nine Days. When Rosh Khodesh Av falls on *Erev Shabbat,* you may bathe or shower as you normally would for the Sabbath. Otherwise, on *Erev Shabbat* during the Nine Days, it is permissible to wash your hands, feet, face and hair with hot water, and, if you bathe or shower every *Erev Shabbat,* you may do so before midday, but use soap or shampoo only if it is impossible to get clean without it.

Swimming is prohibited for boys thirteen years of age and older, and girls twelve years of age and older. Younger children may take cold showers or swim and those under six years of age may wash as usual.

On Tisha B'Av itself, except for hygienic reasons, it is forbidden to even place a finger in water—hot or cold—except to remove dirt from your hands. When rinsing your hands after using the bathroom, you should wash only up to the finger joints. While they are damp, you may pass your fingers over your eyes. (If you normally have to wash your eyes to cleanse them, particularly on rising in the morning, you may do so.) If you perspire heavily, you are allowed to use deodorant, but no other cosmetics, beauty aids, lotions or fragrances.

You may wash an infant and put oil on its body, as you normally would. If you have to wash food in order to prepare it for the post-fast meal, it is permissible—since it is unavoidable—to get your hands wet.

FAST OF AV 9

Everyone of religious majority (age thirteen for a male, twelve for a female) is required to observe the fast that begins, along with the other restrictions of the day, at sunset. This includes pregnant women and nursing mothers. You may not even rinse your mouth in the morning and until the fast ends. Someone who is ill, even if life is not threatened, may eat, but only as much as is necessary. The food should be as bland as possible. You may not prepare the meal to be eaten after the fast before midday.

LEATHER SHOES

If the only leather on your shoes consists of decorative strips, you may wear them, but not if the shoes are covered with leather or if they have leather soles.

WORK

While the work prohibitions of *yom tov* and Shabbat (SEE "HALAKHAH" IN CHAPTER ON PESAKH) are not in effect, it is traditional to refrain from a normal work schedule unless doing so would result in loss. (Akiva said that anyone who worked on Tisha B'Av would not see any benefit from it.) Writing, business pursuits and housework are not to take place before midday. A non-Jew may work for you earlier in the day, but should do so in a secluded area.

What Other Things Do People Do? Customs

OTHER TIMES AND PLACES

PRECAUTIONS The Libyan Jews so believed that the Three Weeks augured danger, they would not allow any children born at that time to be seen outside during daylight hours.

EXPRESSING GRIEF From biblical times, the pious put ashes on their heads—in the spot where the tefillin usually goes—as a sign of mourning. Some congregations would put the Torah on the floor and sprinkle it with ashes while reciting verses like "The crown has fallen from our head. Woe to us that we have sinned" (LAMENTATIONS 5:16).

In Yemenite synagogues, just before the chanting of Eikhah, a community leader proclaimed the number of years since the destruction of the second Temple, and announced that redemption had not yet arrived. The observation that anyone who did not witness the building of the Temple was regarded as having experienced its destruction in his own lifetime encouraged grief. In Algeria, the shofar was blown, as it was in ancient fast-day ceremonies at the time of the Temple, when the priests sounded horns and declared the fast in times of distress, and a procession of wailing mourners in sackcloth prostrated themselves in front of the altar.

After the morning service, it was common practice to visit a cemetery to pray at the graves of close relatives, martyrs and the righteous for speedy restoration of Zion. It was preferable to go alone to avoid frivolous conversation and actions. In some European communities, the children staged mock funerals and created symbolic graves.

EXPRESSING JOY The tradition that the messiah will be born on Tisha B'Av led to special preparations as the day's mood changed. In Libya, while the congregation was engaged in chanting *kinot,* the young boys would ride around the fields on donkeys, hopeful of meeting up with the messiah, who, according to folklore, would arrive as a poor man riding on a donkey. The women of Jerusalem whitewashed their walls and scrubbed their floors in anticipation of his impending arrival, and in other communities it was customary to sweep out the house on the afternoon of Av 9. For the same reason, many women put on jewelry or perfume in the afternoon of the fast day.

Joy returned to small Jewish communities throughout Eastern Europe on Shabbat Nakhamu. After the hiatus for celebrations, a spate of weddings took place, often beginning on Friday night and continuing, as was typical in past generations, for several days.

ISRAEL On *Erev Tisha B'Av* restaurants and places of entertainment are closed and broadcast music programs are replaced with suitable talks and the chanting of Eikhah. The Western Wall is a popular place for Tisha B'Av prayers. During the day, people also walk along the Old City walls (when the security situation allows), visit archaeological dig sites that have uncovered approaches to the Temple Mount, or visit Yad Vashem, the memorial to victims of the Holocaust.

A MONTH BY ANOTHER NAME It is widespread practice to call the month in which the day of mourning for the Temples occurs Av through the ninth, and afterwards to call it Menakhem (consolation) Av, to indicate hope for comfort and renewal.

GREETING

The custom of not exchanging greetings on Tisha B'Av is taken directly from the shiva period following a burial, when mourners and those who come to comfort them do not greet each other. (In fact, it is common practice for a visitor not to say anything to a mourner, but to wait for the mourner to speak first.) This is particularly understandable since the traditional Jewish greeting was *shalom aleikhem* (peace to you), rejoined with *aleikhem shalom* (to you peace)— structured so it began and ended with the word of utmost goodwill and blessing. One is hardly at peace at a time of mourning, especially mourning over the devastation of war.

If someone greets you, you should not ignore it, but respond in a subdued way so as not to cause embarrassment. After midday, when other restrictions imposed to foster grief are lifted, it is appropriate to exchange good wishes.

DRESS

The restriction against wearing leather shoes begins at twilight. In former times, people often went barefoot; now when people go without shoes, it is usually in synagogue only.

A common sign of mourning used to be the donning of sackcloth and ashes. While that does not seem to have ever been the custom for Tisha B'Av, we do indicate a time of distress, disarray and struggle by avoiding freshly cleaned and pressed clothes, and anything particularly fine, even if old. Jewelry is inappropriate.

What Is There to Eat? Traditional Foods

Cutting back on gustatory enjoyment customarily begins with the meal prior to the one that brings in the fast. While you do not want to deplete your strength, the rule is to stick with bland basics and eat as few tasty dishes as possible (traditionally that meant no salads, pickles, condiments, etc.)

The *seudah mafseket* is supposed to be limited to one dish (this includes two or more foods cooked together, such as a casserole). An egg or lentils are preferred. Both are served for the initial repast in a house of mourning because, without openings, they are like mourners who in their grief hold to themselves. Being round, they also suggest the complete cycle of life. In some circles, it was standard to sprinkle ashes on the egg or to eat a piece of bread dipped in ashes with it, based on Lamentations: "He has broken my teeth on gravel, has ground me into the dust (3:16)." The pious often limited themselves to bread, salt and water.

It is also permissible to bring in the fast with a meal of a few kinds of fruit or raw vegetables (although many refrain from a salad per se). Coffee and tea are fine, but it is customary to take less of any beverage accompanying the meal

269

than you normally would. Meat and chicken are forbidden for this meal and we are discouraged from eating fish.

What Tales Are Told? Stories to Read

Most of what is available for Tisha B'Av is folktale based on Talmudic sources about various aspects of the ninth of Av and the ancient catastrophes of the day. For all of us, and particularly children, it is important, as it is for commemoration of modern devastation (Yom Hashoah) to convey the greatness of what was, why Jerusalem and Judaism were and are worth fighting for, rather than simply focusing on destruction itself. There are numerous histories of Jerusalem and the First and Second Temple periods, as well as a myriad of stories about Temple days and the sages, available in numerous collections (SEE "MORE GOOD INFORMATION").

FOR FURTHER EXPLORATION

Roskies, David G. *The Literature of Destruction: Jewish Responses to Catastrophe*. Philadelphia: The Jewish Publication Society, 1988.

> The one hundred powerful selections spanning two thousand years of history show how Jews have placed violence against them in the continuum of Jewish experience defined by the God-Israel relationship and the sin-punishment-renewal cycle. Margin notes explain terms, and provide sources and historic references.

Vilnay, Zev. *Legends of Jerusalem*. Philadelphia: The Jewish Publication Society, 1995.

> Stories, folklore, accounts of historic and spiritual occurrences said to have happened in Jerusalem or to people and things associated with it and the Temple are collected in this compendium of material about the holy city. It provides a view of its history and the mystique surrounding it.

Of Added Note

MUSIC

While making or enjoying music is one of the prohibitions of the Tisha B'Av season, at some other time you might want to listen to Leonard Bernstein's symphony *Jeremiah*. It includes a vocal rendition in Hebrew of Lamentations.

IN ISRAEL

The excavations around the Temple Mount and in and around the Old City of Jerusalem made possible by the reunification of the city in 1967 have uncovered remains from the periods of both Temples. They are generally open to the public, but since some are located in Arab sectors of the city, be sure to check with local authorities before venturing out to see them to be sure it is safe to do so. You will want to check with the tourist office anyway, to find out about walking tours of First Temple and Second Temple Jerusalem, which are offered periodically.

Within the Jewish Quarter of the Old City, **THE BURNT HOUSE** provides tragic evidence of the last days of Jerusalem in 70 CE. As fascinating as the restoration of the home of the priestly Kathros family mentioned in the Talmud, and the artifacts that give us a glimpse of their lives, the most exciting part is the unrestored room of charred beams, broken pottery and ashes, which, with other finds, confirms Josephus' accounts of the conquest by Rome.

Other views of aristocratic life in old Jerusalem can be seen at the **SIEBENBERG HOUSE**, the result of an extraordinary private excavation commissioned by Theo Siebenberg under his own house when he became convinced that the site had to have been prime real estate during Second Temple days; and the **WOHL ARCHAE-OLOGICAL MUSEUM/HERODIAN QUARTER**, the remains of six mansions dating from 37 BCE to 70 CE and the luxurious household items discovered in them.

The **MUSEUM OF THE HISTORY OF THE CITY OF JERUSALEM, RAMPARTS WALK** and **TREASURES OF THE TEMPLE** (SEE DESCRIPTIONS AT END OF CHAPTER ON YOM YERUSHALAYIM) should also be investigated.

South, near the Dead Sea, it is possible to visit **MASADA**. The most spectacular and exhilarating (not to mention exhausting) approach is up the "snake path" on the east side, which you must begin before sun-up, after which it gets too hot on the strenuous forty-five-minute climb. Your reward will be a magnificent sunrise over rosy Jordanian hills as you reach the top. You may choose the somewhat easier and less heart-pounding Roman ramp on the west, or easier still, the base-to-summit cable car. The site contains Herod's palace, with frescoed walls and mosaic baths, the synagogue, *mikvah,* cisterns and storehouses.

Rosh Hashanah—
Spiritual New Year

(ROESH HAH-SHAH-NAH'; YIDDISH: RUSH' UH-SHUN'UH)
TISHREI 1 AND 2
(LATE SUMMER—EARLY FALL; SEPTEMBER)

The Jewish year reaches its spiritual heights during the intense ten-day period begun with Rosh Hashanah, when the entire world and every person are judged for the way life is being lived. It is a serious yet joyous opportunity for assessing one's existence and for reordering priorities. Taking note of our place as Jews within all of humanity, and including prayers for the welfare of every nation, it is also the most universal of Jewish holidays.

Origins—WHY WE CELEBRATE ROSH HASHANAH

Traditions—HOW WE CELEBRATE ROSH HASHANAH

Origins—
WHY WE CELEBRATE ROSH HASHANAH

Where Did It Begin? Historic Foundation

THE BIBLICAL BASIS

It is a credit to the genius of our sages that Rosh Hashanah occupies such an important place in the Jewish calendar today. The holiday we know is a far cry from the way the New Year originated. It wasn't even called by the same name. (The one time the words "Rosh Hashanah" appear in *Tanakh* [EZEKIEL 40:1] they refer to Yom Kippur.) Torah calls the first day of the seventh month *Yom Zikhron Teruah* (a memorial of sounding [the ram's horn]) and *Yom Teruah* (a day of sounding). A day of complete rest, it is to be a sacred occasion when the shofar is blown and sacrifices are made to God (LEVITICUS 23:25, NUMBERS 29:1–6).

Prior to the Babylonian exile (sixth century BCE), most Jews probably didn't even recognize the first of Tishrei. Ignorance of the Bible was common, idolatry rampant, and the opportunity to witness the sacrificial rites and hear the shofar blasts mandated for the festival limited to those who gathered at the Temple in Jerusalem. The blowing of the shofar, the one act that clearly distinguished Tishrei 1 from other festivals, wouldn't even have been enough to impress the Israelites, who heard the horn sounded at every new month and a variety of other occasions as well (SEE "OBSERVANCE"). Their attention was likely focused on the pilgrimage festival Sukkot, which occurred two weeks later.

THE POST-EXILIC "NEW YEAR"

After King Cyrus began permitting the Jews to return to Judah in the century or so after the destruction of the Temple, he dispatched Ezra to govern Jewish affairs in the Land. On Tishrei 1, 450 BCE (give or take a few decades), the scribe and Torah scholar assembled his people in Jerusalem. He confronted a community unaware of the significance of the day, ignorant of the precious heritage that had been passed down for one thousand years before them, and weakened by extensive assimilation (as evidenced by the large number of intermarriages Ezra had just dissolved).

With the Levites (the Israelite tribe that comprised the priesthood) serving as translators and interpreters, from dawn until noon Ezra read to the people from the Books of Moses. The congregation wept when they realized how much they had lost by ignoring Torah. Instructing them not to mourn, Ezra and the Levites reassured them: "Go, eat choice foods and drink sweet drinks and send portions to whomever has nothing prepared, for the day is holy to our Lord. Do not be sad for your rejoicing in the Lord is the source of your strength" (NEHEMIAH 8:1–13).

In essence, Ezra effected a rapprochement between the people of Israel and the God they had abandoned, and defined Rosh Hashanah for them. It was a time to acknowledge God as their true ruler and to begin the return to Torah. This was not a day to lament over what they had forgotten or what they had done wrong in the past, but to rejoice that they could begin to recapture their collective memory and work toward being better in the future.

IN TIMES OF TEMPLE II AND TALMUD

During the Second Temple period, when synagogues were built outside of Israel's capital, people who did not go to Jerusalem could hear the shofar sounded. Then, following the destruction of the Temple (70 CE), the whole format of worship had to be reinvented (SEE CHAPTER ON TISHA B'AV). Over a period of centuries, the sages designed a system to replace the sacrificial rite. To prayers formerly uttered by the High Priest in the Temple, they added new ones, and Jewish history amplified the day's themes.

It was natural for a people subjected to a succession of mortal rulers, and the inconsistencies such sovereignty entails, to deal with the issue of kingship and the question of who truly reigned over them. The answer, of course, was God. By the time the Mishnah recorded common Jewish practices (200 CE), the rabbis had asserted that the first of Tishrei was the day the Jews reaffirmed their loyalty to God as the Supreme King, not only over them but also over the entire world.

As the King of the World, God was also seen as its Chief Judge, and

Tishrei 1 the day of passing judgment. Perhaps influenced by Babylonian and Hellenistic myths and symbols, the sages developed a rich imagery based around the metaphor of a trial during which each living being on earth is evaluated.

In this construct, the Jews, because of their particular responsibilities, go to court, where every petitioner prays for a year of blessings. One's good deeds and repentance serve as Advocates, while the Adversary, personified in Jewish lore as Satan, takes the role of Prosecuting Attorney or Accusing Angel, arguing against the merit of the individual and the Jewish people as a whole. (The Jewish Satan [in Hebrew sah'-tahn] embodies something altogether different from the Christian concept of the red-cloaked, short-horned Devil incarnate. It represents the evil inclination [*yetzer harah* in traditional Jewish thought] latent in every human being, counterbalanced by the good inclination [*yetzer hatov*].)

The scales of the zodiac sign corresponding to Tishrei symbolize the scales that weigh how much one's *yetzer hatov* has been able to subdue the *yetzer harah*. The side to which they tip determines whether s/he is to be written in the Book of Life, Book of Death, or Book of Limbo, the three volumes opened in heaven at the start of Rosh Hashanah for recording the names of the righteous, the wicked, and those who fall between and must wait until the Day of Atonement ten days later for their final sentences.

COMMEMORATING WORLD EVENTS

The people became uncomfortable with the fact that unlike other holidays, Rosh Hashanah, because it focused on the individual and his/her relationship with self, others and God, held no connection with any historic occurrence or with the cycle of nature and the seasons. So the rabbis determined that the day does in fact mark noteworthy anniversaries, each of them a type of new beginning. On this day (as recorded in Talmud), for example, the patriarchs Abraham, Isaac and Jacob were born and died, Abraham prepared to sacrifice his son Isaac, the matriarchs Sarah and Rachel and the prophetess Hannah were remembered by God and subsequently able to conceive, and Moses declared the emancipation of the Israelites from Egyptian bondage.

Above all other historic starts cited for Rosh Hashanah stood the beginning of beginnings: the Creation of the world. The timing of Rosh Hashanah on the first day of the seventh month echoes the original seventh day, and the seventh day of every week, a break from encounter with the physical world, a time of rest and renewal. (Seven—a number "beloved above" according to the sages—signifies completion in earthly terms and is recurrent in Jewish law, observance and history.)

In Talmudic calculations, it was actually on Elul 25 that God began His magnificent endeavor—and what occurred on Tishrei 1 was the end point of His effort: the creation of humankind. This tradition clearly tells us that the real beginning of the world is humanity, in its physical and qualitative senses.

FROM THEN TO NOW

By the time of the Talmud's completion around the year 500, the holiday's observance as we know it was well established. While it refers to the New Year throughout, Talmud devotes a special tractate, Rosh Hashanah, to the festival's laws. In these commentaries Tishrei 1 took on the name Rosh Hashanah (literally Head of the Year). Other designations highlighted various aspects of its nature: *Yom Hadin* (Day of Judgment), *Yom Harat Olam* (Birthday of the World) and *Yom Hakeseh* (Day of Concealment, alluding to the position of the new moon on the first of Tishrei, the Torah's limited indication of the nature of Rosh Hashanah, and the unknown aspect of our sentences).

Aside from laws pertaining to shofar and service, the rabbis ordained—and accordingly set the calendar—that Rosh Hashanah would never fall on a Sunday, Wednesday or Friday. This brilliant provision precluded the companion holiday Yom Kippur from ever coming immediately before or following a Sabbath (which would mean two consecutive days when, according to halakhah, it would be forbidden to cook or bury the dead).

During the Middle Ages, liturgical poets added their literary interpretations of the motifs of the holiday, and common folk instituted a ceremony symbolizing the discarding of one's sins. Otherwise, the observances, mood, intention and prayer themes of Rosh Hashanah have basically remained constant.

What Does It Mean? Religious Importance

In addition to the fact that Rosh Hashanah is essentially a religious occasion, its meaning and observance embrace defining principles of Judaism.

THE NATURE OF GOD

Four times a day and, if possible, at their deaths, pious Jews declare the creed of Judaism: "Hear O Israel, the Lord our God, the Lord is One" (*Shema Yisrael, Adonai Eloheinu, Adonai Ekhad*) referred to as the *Shema* (DEUTERONOMY 6:4). It asserts the Jew's acknowledgement that there is only one God in the universe, that all life stems from Him on an on-going basis, that His rule is supreme. From the beginning of Creation, His role included judging His world, seeing it as "good," "very good," or "not good" (GENESIS 1,2).

On their first day of existence, the first human beings did the one thing God had specifically instructed them not to do: eat from the Tree of Knowledge of Good and Evil (GENESIS 2:15–16, 3:1–7). For their violation, God judged Adam and Eve, and instead of immediately implementing the death penalty He had promised as punishment for disobeying Him, God tempered his harsh sentence with mercy and gave them another chance.

This was to serve as the model for all future generations: As Talmud explains, on the anniversary of the first "trial" in the world, Adam's descendants would also stand trial, they would repent, and God would remove Himself from the Throne of Judgment and sit on the Throne of Mercy in order to pardon them.

When Ezra comforted the wayward decimated Jewish community of Jerusalem, telling the people to rejoice, he conveyed the message that God would accept their return to Him, that He listened to their prayers and would meet their change of attitude, heart and behavior with forgiveness. God was no enforcer of pre-determined fate, but, as a lawgiver and embodiment of goodness (acting justly and mercifully) and sustainer of life (creating the world initially and continually), He was a loving parent and the exemplar of what human beings could hope to achieve in character and conduct. Holding close to us this one God who allows us to learn from our mistakes makes Judaism a religion of tremendous optimism and hope.

THE NATURE OF MAN

The human being was a unique culmination of God's creative activities, a combination of the purely spiritual (God Himself) and the purely physical (the world He made): clay from the earth, breath from God, form and content, substance and sum, body and soul. And as such, s/he existed as a bridge between the two worlds, the conduit for bringing heaven to earth.

God did not create humankind in "His image" to have a physical likeness of Himself. (In fact, Judaism ascribes anthropomorphic features to God only to make His actions comprehensible to us. In Judaism, God has no such form or characteristics.) "The image" refers to God's moral essence, as reflected in the way He instructs human beings to behave toward one another and in relation to Him.

That man can repent and be forgiven means each of us, while independent to choose which options to pursue, is morally responsible for the choices we make and held accountable for them. Given free will by a God, Who as much as he wanted obedient servants did not want unthinking slaves, we have the capacity to mold our own lives. What we make of them depends on how we manage the constant struggle between the two conflicting aspects in our makeup: the *yetzer hatov,* the tendency toward saintliness, and the *yetzer harah,* the pull toward savagery. Our duty is to subdue the latter and strengthen the former in order to act morally for personal and common good.

The laws provided to us in Torah guide us to act properly. When we don't follow them, and do wrong, we must take the consequences. Yet even if we are judged on Rosh Hashanah as undeserving of life (which means we're on the wrong course for our own good), we have the chance during the intervening seven days—in which time a whole world was created!—to recreate, or if you prefer redirect, our own lives.

COMMUNAL RESPONSIBILITY

In addition to being held accountable for our actions, each individual is also responsible for the situation of the community and of the entire world. According to Maimonides, we are supposed to imagine that the scales determining our futures are even, each one of us and the world as a whole half meritorious, half guilty. One wrong act could tilt the balance toward the negative side, threatening our destruction. Conversely, one good act counts toward the collective merit and brings us closer to salvation.

You don't have to believe in the notion of heavenly weights and measures to understand the underlying concept: Each one of us contributes to the state of the world, in however large or small a way. Our words and actions have ramifications that go beyond us as individuals. They affect our families, our neighborhoods, our communities, our country, our globe. The famous Talmud example instructs that when several people are sailing in a boat, no one has a right to bore a hole under his or her own seat. Human purpose in the world involves everyone in trying to keep the vessel buoyant and sailing smoothly.

REPENTANCE

Judaism didn't need modern psychology to affirm that the discomfort we experience when we do something wrong—embarrassment, guilt, depression, anxiety—are destructive forces and therefore counter to life. (Wrong doing is a form of death. How often do these feelings eat away at us inside? Don't we say, "I could have died!" or "I felt like dying!"?)

Judaism is all about life, that we should live, that we should live in a way that allows us to experience the greatest peace with ourselves, others, the world around us and with God, the giver and sustainer of life. So there has to be a way to make up for our transgressions and eliminate their destructive results, which separate us from life. In fact, Talmud asserts that a mechanism for making up for wrongs preceded creation of the universe itself, because without it, the world could not possibly last.

This system, which tells us not to dwell on the wrongs and hurts, not to wallow in eternal guilt, and helps us move ahead in a positive way, is called *teshuvah*. It means turning away from (wrongdoing) and returning (to good, to God, to the commandments). It means that our errors need not be permanent blots on our records, that all is not lost just because we strayed—even great distances. Until the last moment of life, we have the opporturnity to admit failure and improve.

This is a tremendously reassuring attitude. It means we get a second chance, provided our repentance is sincere and purposeful. As Talmud emphasizes: "Just as when a garment becomes soiled it can be made white again, so can Israel return to God after they have sinned, by doing penance" (EXODUS RABBAH 23:10). "The Holy One, blessed be He, said to Israel . . . present to Me an opening of repentance no bigger than the eye of a needle, and I will widen it into openings through which wagons and carriages can pass" (SONG OF SONGS RABBAH 5:2). Once we initiate the process, with the faintest thought, we are on the way to relief.

Teshuvah allows us to express the negative thoughts and feelings about inappropriate actions we often repress, to purge ourselves of them, and wipe the slate clean, reestablishing our fundamental relationships, not the least of which is the internal balance within the self. Much more than a single act of asking forgiveness and forgetting, it is a process which, because it takes time, leads to self transformation by helping us deal with the past, make the most of the present, and prepare for the future.

During the ten days between Rosh Hashanah and Yom Kippur, we use the word *khet* to connote wrongdoing. Although generally translated as "sin," implying some mortal flaw or heinous crime, it comes from an archery term that means missing the mark, suggesting failure to meet potential, or a lost opportunity to act properly. Maimonides taught that *teshuvah* is not just for violations of *mitzvot*, transgressions of Jewish law and major offenses. Wrong thoughts, attitudes and dispositions also require *teshuvah* for they, too, affect our level of morality, which continually needs review and improvement.

The first step is to recognize what we did wrong, realize that it is a waste of life and potential, and express *regret* about it. This gets us past the tendency to sublimate, rationalize or deny it. We admit it to ourselves, to God, and, if the offense involved others, we confess to any wronged party. The second step entails *rejecting* the offensive behavior—we stop doing the wrong thing. Of course it's easier said than done. (It might be helpful to try listing what we think is gained by doing this thing, what is lost by doing it, what we fear we might lose by abandoning the behavior, and what we stand to gain through change.) Then *we resolve* never to fall back into it, in effect changing a habit, a pattern, perhaps a way of life. The measure of effectiveness of our progress toward transformation cannot be made until we are faced with an opportunity to engage in the same behavior for which we have repented, and we successfully *restrain* ourselves.

Tanakh contains numerous references to *teshuvah,* including the commandment to do it, both as it involves other people (NUMBERS 5:5–7) and God (DEUTERONOMY 30:1–6). A rich heritage of *aggadah* on the theme indicates its importance in the Jewish way of life. Despite all the Jewish mother jokes and tales of woe, guilt is not one of our values, for with it you convince yourself you cannot change. That means you stagnate. On the contrary, through repentance, a uniquely Jewish concept, you can continually grow.

Our sages actually placed those who do *teshuvah* on a higher plane than those who have never erred: "And let not the man who is doing *teshuvah* imagine that he is kept far from the rung of the righteous, because of the iniquities and sins he has sinned. It is not so; rather he is as beloved and desirable to the Creator, as though he had never sinned. Yes—even more—his reward is great, for having tasted sin, he has forsaken it and conquered his impulse" (TALMUD, BERAKHOT 34b).

It is considered an act of merit to help one repent, and forbidden to remind one who has done *teshuvah* of his/her sins. S/he is, after all, a new person.

What Does It Mean for Us? Personal Significance

Since this holiday is all about the moral and spiritual quality of each individual life, the significance the holiday can have for you lies entirely in what you, as an individual, make of it. In just about every aspect of Rosh Hashanah's observance you can find something to relate to your situation. So in addition to the specific points below, you'll find insights throughout the rest of this chapter.

The first human being, whose formation we celebrate on Rosh Hashanah, was the pinnacle of a process, each step of which built on the previous as part of Divine purpose. Inherent in Creation was the fact that the world, as good as it was (and "God . . . found it very good" [GENESIS 1:31]), was unfinished, and that humans would work in partnership with God to perfect it (*tikkun olam* [SEE CHAPTERS ON SHAVUOT AND TU B'SHEVAT]): Creation continues throughout time.

Just as the world evolves, developing from what previously existed, so does each life. Despite the sages' designations, rather than being a holiday of Jewish history, Rosh Hashanah is a holiday of personal history: It presents us with the opportunity to review where we have been and to renew ourselves in positive ways. As the world and all its possibilities are reborn in each person, each person can be reborn to grow closer toward his or her potential.

As part of the process, we confront our own morality every day. On Rosh Hashanah, we also confront our own mortality. Standing before God to take credit or censure for our actions brings us face-to-face with death (we are, after all, on trial, the outcome of which will determine whether we are written into the Book of Life or its opposite). The Creation epic teaches us that the universe is not random, but was created with Divine purpose giving significance and dignity to every life. So as we confront death, Rosh Hashanah makes us focus on the meaning of our individual lives.

At annual review time on your job, before giving you his or her analysis and determining whether you qualify for a raise, a good superior will ask you to evaluate yourself against your job description and any stated goals established for the year. At the new year, you are up for a raise, too, a raise in your spiritual status. The evaluation used to measure worthiness is called *kheshbone hanefesh,* an accounting of the soul.

You ask yourself: What am I doing with my life? Is it worthwhile? Where is it taking me? Is this where I want to go? Am I moving toward fulfillment of the dreams I have had for myself? What have I accomplished in the past year? What did I set out to do that I failed to accomplish? What are the ramifications of my successes and failures—to others and to me—in my overall plans? What do I need to change to reach my goals, my potential? What am I doing to contribute to the balance of scales in my life, in my family's life, in my community, in the world? How do I interact with the people around me—family members, friends, co-workers, strangers? What negative aspects of my personality do I need to deal with? How can I change them? What am I doing wrong? What can I do better? How can I be closer to the Divine ideals of how I should behave in relation to God and others?

The way you answer these questions and the ways you resolve to improve yourself can have tremendous impact. Humankind was initially created as a single being to teach us that one sole individual has the capacity to fulfill Creation. This means that every single person possesses the potential for the same, and is therefore of infinite value. (How do you measure a wasted life?) This places on every one of us the responsibility to work toward the highest level of fulfillment.

By making choices leading in that direction, choices that will keep us healthy mentally, physically and spiritually, we write ourselves into the Book of Life. "Life" and its negation are not here merely biological terms. The Torah defines life as the path it has outlined, through a series of psychologically sound, logical, humane and commonsensical laws that guide how we are to take care of ourselves, treat others and appreciate God. Death equals deviation from the commandments, because transgression of the laws carries consequences. (If we are to learn from Adam's mistake, when we don't obey, we make life more difficult for ourselves.)

Before you can find God you must lose yourself.

BAAL SHEM TOV

Study after study has shown that people suffer when they feel their lives have no overriding direction or purpose. As Maimonides admonished (in words as applicable today as they were in the twelfth century): "Awake you sleepers from your sleep, and you slumberers, arise from your slumber—examine your deeds, repent and remember your Creator. Those of you who forget the truth in the vanities of the times and dwell all year in vanity and emptiness, look into your souls, improve your ways and actions, let each of you forsake his evil path and his thoughts which are not good" (HILKHOT TESHUVAH, 3).

Such soul-searching can be a difficult and painful process, particularly for anyone who determines that major changes are warranted. Everything doesn't have to happen at once. What matters is the direction you are going. To keep things manageable, you might want to determine a priority or choose the most doable items on your accounting.

To take a practical approach, as you go through *kheshbone hanefesh* and *teshuvah,* choose something in each of three areas to concentrate on during this holiday, and resolve to improve in the coming year: in yourself, in your relationships with others, and in relation to God (or, if you prefer, the community). You can use the process and goals to help your children do the same. The idea is not to do things better in a short period of time, for a short period of time, but to raise yourself to a new level of performance and spirituality and work toward maintaining the higher standards throughout the year.

Traditions—

HOW WE CELEBRATE ROSH HASHANAH

What Do We Use? Ritual Items

SHOFAR

The only Rosh Hashanah ceremony from biblical time still practiced involves the shofar, an ancient musical instrument. It is usually made out of a ram's horn, to recall the animal sacrificed in place of Isaac (SEE 'READINGS FROM TORAH AND PROPHETS' UNDER "OBSERVANCE").

The Talmudic law dictating each step in the detailed process of converting a horn into a ritual instrument allowed for differences between communities. Ashkenazi shofarim tend to be straighter (though still curved, symbolizing that we must bend our will before God) than the often long, ornately curled ones of the Sephardim, so they could be easily concealed from anti-Semitic neighbors. Since one person in the synagogue blows the shofar for all to hear, it is not necessary to have your own—although many families do. The shofar can be blown at home, or another setting (such as a hospital) for anyone unable to attend communal services.

MAKHZOR

Instead of the *siddur,* which contains the order of services for weekdays and Sabbaths, on Rosh Hashanah (and other festivals) we use a special prayer book called a *makhzor* ("cycle," for the pattern of holidays that brings us back to where we begin). Most synagogues provide *makhzorim* for worshippers; depending on the version yours uses, you might want to have your own that contains commentary, allows you to read Hebrew and English line for line, or otherwise facilitates your following and understanding the service.

286

FOR FURTHER EXPLORATION

FOR CHILDREN

Abrams, Judith Z. *Rosh Hashanah, A Family Service.* Rockville, MD: Kar-Ben Copies, Inc., 1990.
Designed for use with young children, the simple service helps explain the concepts of Rosh Hashanah—*tefillah* (prayer), *teshuvah* (repentance) and *tzedakah* (what the author calls sharing)—with a section on each. For the Torah reading, the book age-appropriately uses the Creation story (rather than stories of Isaac's birth and near sacrifice). A couple of simple songs, and suggested activities for home and school are included. A companion cassette tape is available. Ages 4–8.

Orkand, Robert, and Joyce Orkand and Howard I. Bogot. *Gates of Awe, Holy Day Prayers for Young Children.* New York: Central Conference of American Rabbis, 1991.
Though produced by the Reform movement, this introduction to prayer for the Days of Awe may be useful for anyone. Explaining that prayer helps us think about God, it contains simple blessings that introduce God and identifies key items and personalities with brief stories showing their importance. Beautiful watercolor illustrations enhance the text. Ages 2–6.

KITTEL

Religious men wear the *kittel,* a lightweight belted white robe, over their street clothes. (On Rosh Hashanah the *khazzan* and prayer leader generally wear them; on Yom Kippur many of the men attending a traditional synagogue will.) It symbolizes the attire of the angels, to whose spiritual level we aspire, and brings to mind the simple white shroud in which Jews are buried, prompting thoughts of mortality and feelings of humility. A *kittel* can be purchased at a store that sells Jewish supplies.

How Do We Celebrate? Observance

TEN DAYS OF REPENTANCE

Rosh Hashanah begins a solemn, but decidedly not sad, period, ending with Yom Kippur, during which we focus on our behavior and how we can improve. The rabbis connected the two holidays that in Torah's terms seemed to have no direct relationship. By creating the thematic unity of the trial (Rosh Hashanah) and sentencing (Yom Kippur) linked by a period of appeal, they imbued the two holidays and intervening week with a single and sustained meaning and mood.

Popularly called the High Holy Days, which has a too-Christian ring to it, the period is better described by its activity, *Aseret Yamei Teshuvah* (Ten Days of Repentance) or its aura, *Yamim Nora'im* (Days of Awe), both of which capture the seriousness, spirituality, soul-searching and supplication that are part of this season. They begin with our attempts to elevate ourselves toward heaven, and judge ourselves against its standards.

Remembering that when Adam disobeyed God he faced the death penalty, we ask ourselves what we face, what we deserve—good or bad. Those are *awesome* thoughts that engender feelings powerful enough to affect Jews who have little or nothing to do with Judaism the rest of the year. These days and their agenda speak to real human needs, to intensely personal pains and fears (the discomfort of error, the burden of guilt for wrong-doing, the anguish of unknown consequences), and to cherished hopes and dreams (the warmth of improvement, the joy of achievement, the anticipation of reward).

PROPER MOOD

Just as God's harsh judgment is tempered with mercy, the seriousness in our task should be tempered with joy. We are confidant God will forgive us for our shortcomings and give us the chance to do better. This approach expresses our belief in the process of *teshuvah,* our implicit trust in God's goodness, and our understanding of the nature of God. This is a spiritual joy, not the frivolity and abandon of a secular new year. It is the true joy of peace of mind, of a soul at rest.

USHERING IN ROSH HASHANAH

Like Shabbat and other festivals, Rosh Hashanah begins with candlelighting (preferably done by the women of the household, but by men if no woman is present), with the appropriate blessings (on lighting, and *shehekhiyanu*). Some people bless their children, as they do on *Erev Shabbat,* using the standard form or a personalized version.

Following evening services in the synagogue (similar to those of a regular evening except perhaps for the melodies used), we enjoy a festive meal at home. As any festival meal, it is preceded by *kiddush, shehekhiyanu* (if someone other than the person who lights the candles makes *kiddush*), the blessing over hand-washing and *motzi* over bread. (You'll find the full festival *kiddush* in a *makhzor*.) Instead of dipping the bread into salt (as we normally do, since it represents the sacrifices sprinkled with salt on the Temple altar [represented today by our dining tables]; salt also reminds us of the tears shed by Jews throughout history), we dip into honey.

We follow with a piece of apple dipped in honey, symbolizing a sweet year, eaten after we recite the blessing for tree fruits (SEE "BLESSINGS").

SYNAGOGUE SIGHTS AND SERVICE

The focal point for the celebration of this holy day remains the house of worship.

OUT OF THE ORDINARY As soon as you walk into the sanctuary you will notice that things are different from the rest of the year. To reflect joy and purity, white ark curtains, Torah scroll sheaths, and bimah (reading desk) cloth replace the traditionally blue or maroon ones used the rest of the year. In an Orthodox *shul*, during the repetition of the *Amidah,* you might see the *khazzan,* sometimes accompanied by members of the congregation, not only "bend the knee and bow" but completely prostrate himself in remembrance and reenactment of the Temple service. (We don't normally bow down because this act was part of Temple service we refrain from doing out of respect for our destroyed spiritual center. [FOR FURTHER EXPLANATION SEE "OBSERVANCE" IN THE NEXT CHAPTER.])

Sometimes traditional Jews gesture wildly and shout their prayers as if they will reach heaven faster and better convey the worthiness of the petitioner. (The Baal Shem Tov, founder of the Khassidic movement, likened such actions to those of drowning men thrashing about to pull themselves out of overwhelming waters, and instructed that we therefore should not make fun of these people.) Often the worshippers stand with their heads slightly bent in contrition.

In a Sephardic synagogue, three *khazzanim* (or a *khazzan* and two *seganim,* or associates) stand at the bimah. Based on the description of Moses with his arms supported by Aaron and Hur as he presided over the battle of the Israelites against Amalek (EXODUS 17:12), the extreme manifestation of the *yetzer harah* (SEE

CHAPTER ON PURIM), the three men pray to God that the congregation will triumph over its adversaries and adversity. Sometimes silent partners, the *seganim* often trade off leading the service with the *khazzan* and each other.

In the Judeo-Spanish rite, prayers are recited in Hebrew and Ladino. Some Conservative and Reform congregations have choirs and instrumental accompaniment.

A LOGISTICAL NOTE Unfortunately, the reality of Jewish religious life in America is that large numbers of people who normally do not set foot in a synagogue want to attend some portion of services on Rosh Hashanah and Yom Kippur. Synagogues are built to accommodate their members, with a little room for growth, but generally cannot handle the kinds of crowds that appear two or three days a year. Whether the services remain in their normal setting, or shift to a nearby school, theater or other larger facility, it has become necessary for tickets to be sold for them. If you are not a member of a synagogue who receives tickets for the cost of annual dues, call in advance to order them. Special arrangements are usually made for students or those in unfortunate circumstances, so that no one is turned away for lack of funds. In fact, no synagogue will turn you away if you do not have a ticket, although you might have to stand in the back for lack of a seat, at least during the most popular parts of the services. In some locales, a communal organization or a consortium of synagogues make free or low-cost services available for unaffiliated Jews. (To find out about options, as well as to obtain a list of synagogues, call your local Jewish Federation or rabbinical council, check the Yellow Pages, or look in a local Jewish newspaper for listings. Many congregations advertise in the weeks prior to the holidays.)

DECIPHERING THE PRAYER BOOK Most of us are not adept at following a sport, playing a musical instrument or speaking a foreign tongue the first time we try. Each activity has its own structure and language whose particularities need to be learned before we are fully able to participate. You shouldn't expect a prayer service to be different. While one of Rosh Hashanah's powerful images is of three heavenly books (to record the righteous, the wicked and those in between) being opened, you're far from alone if for you the guidebook that takes us through the festival remains closed.

Even with modernizations, alterations and inclusion of more English in many versions, large numbers of Jews unfamiliar with the *makhzor* often feel uncomfortable with the services and unmoved by the experience of what they think is fulfillment of a religious obligation. The Baal Shem Tov said that someone who prayed, even if he did not know the meaning of his prayers, would still be blessed, because his worship would reach heaven. Others say that it is not the form of worship (incomprehensible prayers) but the sincerity that matters, as movingly illustrated in the stories of the poor, uneducated or mute men who could express their prayers only by reciting the alef-bet (Hebrew alphabet), speaking in the vernacular, or blowing through a flute.

These are nice and acceptable options, but not totally satisfying if you want to be comfortable and able to participate with the community—we do pray together in synagogue rather than at home alone—and be affected by the services on a personal level.

The *makhzor* for Rosh Hashanah admittedly is ancient. A type of anthology, it summarizes Jewish thought on God and man through selections from Torah and Talmud, prayers from Temple and Talmudic days, and liturgical poems of the Middle Ages. But it is not archaic. Its central elements have remained constant for the past fifteen hundred years, and across more than fifty different rites, because they resonate with truth and relevance that transcend individuals and the times and places in which we live.

Some *makhzorim* contain detailed commentaries that help us better understand what the services mean. In addition, books that follow the order of the services provide information about the development of various elements, why they have been included, and how they are significant. These and books of writings related to the High Holidays and their themes are invaluable aids, especially when taken to synagogue and used as companions to the *makhzor*.

FOR FURTHER EXPLORATION

Apisdorf, Shimon. *Rosh Hashanah-Yom Kippur Survival Kit*. Columbus, OH: Leviathan Press, 1997.
   Get this book. If all you do is read the introduction you will benefit. But do yourself a favor and don't stop there. This easy-to-read *makhzor* companion, full of wisdom and humor includes plenty of ways to make the most important days of the Jewish year meaningful.

Beginning Anew: A Woman's Companion to the High Holy Days. Ed. By Gail Twersky Reimer and Judith A. Kates. New York: Touchstone Books, 1997.
   Anyone—not just a woman—who wants greater understanding and a more meaningful experience of the holidays will find insights in this anthology. Written by lauded authors, scholars and educators, the selections reveal the psychological wisdom in Jewish tradition and holiday text.

Days of Awe: A Treasury of Traditions, Legends and Commentary on Rosh Hashanah, Yom Kippur and the Days Between. Ed. By Samuel Joseph Agnon. New York: Schocken Books, 1995.

> The 1966 literature Nobel Prize winner studied thousands of texts and excerpted from three hundred sources of Hebrew literature, ancient and modern, sacred and secular, to compile this condensation of our tradition on this period of the year. First published in 1948, it has long been considered the classic companion to the High Holidays prayer book.

Rosenbaum, Samuel. *Mahzor 101: A Guide to the Prayer Book for the High Holy Days.* New York: Cantors Assembly, 1998.

> Aimed at helping the reader make an inner preparation for the holidays to attain an emotional connection with the services, this guide focuses on basic questions of God, prayer and doubt, on what the *makhzor's* words mean to us now, and on inspiring us to experience the occasions more fully.

Sorscher, Moshe. *The Companion Guide to the Rosh Hashanah Prayer Service.* New York: The Judaica Press, 1995.

> This reader-friendly beginner's guide provides explanations of significant parts of the service, select transliterations, and page references to several of the most widely used *makhzorim*. Parables and essays help add meaning. (The book also exists in a version for Yom Kippur.)   ☺🕎

UNDERSTANDING PRAYER We cannot avoid the fact that the way we observe this festival is by praying, a major obstacle for many of us; even those who are "religious" often find prayer difficult. But it doesn't have to be.

First of all, what is prayer? We think of it as petitioning God—"remember us, bless us, grant us, give us"—for whatever we desire. This is not the Jewish concept. The Hebrew "to pray," the reflexive verb *hitpalail,* implies reflection and self-examination. When we pray, the idea is not to influence God to give us what we want, but to concentrate on what *we* need to do to achieve what we want, to get from where we are to what we can, and should, be. Through our prayers, we speak to God privately based on the belief that He welcomes our communication, hears and acts on our pleas. Yet the process is not Other-, outer-directed—our offer of praise and supplication is not for God's benefit; it is self-, inner-directed, for ours.

For "prayer," Rabbinic Hebrew uses the term *avodah,* generally translated as service (as in the service performed in the Temple, the rituals of devotion and sacrifice led by the priests), and in modern Hebrew as work, reinforcing the notion that prayer involves active effort by the one who prays. We should be asking not for the ultimate goal we desire, but the personal qualities—strength, patience, discipline—we require to reach the goal. Each of us must be concerned not so much with "does God hear my prayers, will He answer my prayers?" but with "am I listening to myself, is what I want a worthwhile desire?"

And, more importantly, "what will I do to achieve what I want for myself, my family, my community, the world?" Praying for an end to hunger, for world peace, for more resources for better education is meaningless if we do nothing to contribute to those ends.

Aside from simple expressions of such desires, most of us would find it extremely difficult to adequately formulate our "prayers." That is why we have a *makhzor*: The words of supplications were set down because most people, throughout our history, have been incapable of articulating the thoughts and feelings so eloquently communicated in the predetermined formats. They also express the ideal situation, the goal toward which we strive. They serve as the established standards without which we could not meaningfully judge ourselves.

Stripped of accolades and what sometimes come across in translation as stilted phrases, they tell us about the nature of the universe and our place within it. If we focus on what we are really praying/saying, we'll think about how we fit in. While we are expressing universal hopes, we'll be evaluating personal situations. If we comprehend this, the day is not just a recitation of praises or repetitions of requests for peace and the well-being of all mankind, for forgiveness and salvation for Jews and the Jewish people. It becomes a reflection on what each of our lives is and can be about.

FOLLOWING THE SERVICES Rosh Hashanah, like every other day, has three basic services: *Ma'ariv* (evening, after sundown, when the Jewish day begins), *Shakharit* (morning) and *Minkhah* (afternoon), plus, like Shabbat and all festivals, the *Mussaf* (additional service) following *Shakharit,* corresponding to the special Temple sacrifice commanded in the Torah for those days (NUMBERS 29:1–6).

The motif of life—of God as Creator of life; on our striving to live better lives as individuals, a people and part of the human race; on our hopes of being granted long and positive life—runs through the entire liturgy. The major themes of the day—which are fundamental tenets of Judaism—are most prominently presented during the *Amidah,* particularly of *Mussaf.* At first glance the themes might seem remote. But they can be cast in contemporary personal terms.

In *Malkhuyot* (from the Hebrew *melekh,* king), we acknowledge that God is the King of all Kings, that His rule extends over all nations. While thinking about what having an absolute authority in the universe means, and what our loyalty to Him entails, we should consider what forces in actuality rule our lives (pursuits, objects, emotional crutches, other people?), and whether they deserve the kind of influence we give them.

Zikhronot (from the Hebrew *zikhron,* memory) reminds us that God remembers all our deeds, not only the bad, for which we repent, but the positive, by which we merit forgiveness. The *zikhronot* section acknowledges that God plays a role in the world, punishing the wicked and rewarding the good. The history in which He participates is also the history that irrevocably connects us to Him and to the Jewish people. We might consider during these prayers what in our memories hinders us from moving forward—old hurts, grudges, guilt over mistakes—and what can work to our advantage—gratitude for past material and emotional support, relationships, accomplishments of which to be proud. It also presents an appropriate time to renew our connection with the Jewish community, whose history and destiny we share.

Shofarot (from the Hebrew *shofar,* ram's horn) recalls the revelation of God at Mount Sinai, when the ritual instrument was sounded, and evokes the future revelation of God at the time of redemption, which will also be announced by shofar blasts. Both times the shofar makes the clarion call to establish justice on earth. This section provides the opportunity to evaluate our own behavior against the moral standards, and recognize any obstacles we present to creating the ideal.

The ten proof texts each section contains (three from Torah, three from *Neviim* [Prophets], three from post-biblical writings, and a summary passage from Torah) ascertain the absolute veracity of the themes, emphasized, lest there be any doubt, by the sounding of the shofar at each section's conclusion. Highlighting God's universal role as well as His special relationship with the people of Israel, these passages give significance to our finite lives, occurring for a brief moment in the eternity stretching from before the creation of the world millennia in the past to beyond its redemption sometime in the future: We are part of the tradition of the progression of people helping to move the world forward.

LITURGICAL POEMS Much of the services' lyricism comes from the *piyyutim,* a distinct feature of festival liturgies. Composed throughout the Jewish world over a period of one thousand years, the liturgical poems use the illusions of Talmudic and midrashic sources to assert passionate commitment to Torah, Israel, and God, and express desperate longing for redemption. The *piyyutim* may have originated during periods of persecution, when Jews were prohibited from studying Torah, teaching the commentaries on the law, or reciting certain prayers. These poems would have been temporary replacements, combinations of instruction and worship, to allow unbroken transmission of Judaism, whose widespread use led to later sanction. (Then again, they may simply have been the products of creative individuals eager to express themselves liturgically.)

The best-known and most stirring *piyyut* comes during the *khazzan's* repetition of the *Mussaf Amidah.* While some dispute the authenticity of the story behind its composition, no one denies the power of the words or melody of *Unetanneh Tokef* (Let Us Now Relate the Power [of this day's holiness]).

According to the legend behind the poem (included in full in some *makhzorim*), in the tenth century, Rabbi Amnon of Mainz faced pressure from the Bishop to convert to Christianity. In distress after giving the impression he would consider it, the rabbi failed to reappear before the church leader. The cleric retaliated by having the rabbi's hands and feet amputated.

The poem is Amnon's unswerving affirmation of God's greatness and justice, which he uttered in front of the *Aron Kodesh* just before his death on Rosh Hashanah. The powerful evocation of God's judgment of the world, containing the poignant image of sheep passing before Him, was inserted into the liturgies of all Jewish communities for the first day of Rosh Hashanah, and for Yom Kippur. (Overtaken by the graphic picture of the fearful and solemn judgment day, worshippers in Eastern Europe would cover their heads with their *talleisim* and cry out the words of the poem amidst tears and sobs.)

OTHER PRAYERS Just before *Mussaf* the *khazzan* intones a special prayer, *Hineni* (Here I Am [impoverished]). With deep feeling, he beseeches God's acceptance of his prayers on behalf of the congregation, although he himself is unworthy. Chanted slowly and soulfully, it is moving in its humility.

Some congregations recite a prayer for the State of Israel during their services.

READINGS FROM TORAH AND PROPHETS

THE PORTIONS On the first day we read about the birth of the patriarch Isaac (by tradition, on Rosh Hashanah) and his growth to manhood; the banishment of Hagar (the concubine of Abraham, the first patriarch and monotheist) and Ishmael (the son of Abraham and Hagar, born when Abraham's pious wife Sarah was unable to conceive); and Abraham's treaty with Abimelekh (the king of the region of Gerar who acknowledged God's relationship with Abraham [GENESIS 21]).

The *maftir* (last Torah verses read), done from a second scroll, recounts the prescribed sacrificial offering for Rosh Hashanah (NUMBERS 29:1–6). In the Haftarah (I SAMUEL 1–2:10), Hannah pleads for a son, whom she promises would be dedicated to the service of God. (Her whispered prayers are the basis for the nine blessings of the *Amidah,* and the fact that we recite them quietly to ourselves during the "silent" version. The son she eventually bore became the prophet Samuel, the religious voice during the reign of the first King of Israel, Saul.)

On the second day, we read one of the most affecting Bible stories, the near sacrifice of Isaac (referred to as the *Akeidah,* from the Hebrew "to bind") by Abraham, his father, based on the commandment of God (GENESIS 22). After the same *maftir* as day one, the Haftarah we read gives Jeremiah's account (31:2–20) of Israel's future redemption. It includes a passage about the refusal of Rachel to be consoled for the exile of her children. (Rachel was the beloved wife of the patriarch Jacob, son of Isaac, who gave birth after years of barrenness to the two favorite sons of Jacob; they and the ten sons Jacob fathered with other women were the progenitors of the Twelve Tribes of Israel.)

THE MEANING Although we do not read the Creation account, as might be expected on the birthday of the world, themes of birth and motherhood are well represented in these readings. Sarah, Rachel and Hannah repeatedly beseeched God to end their barrenness. By tradition, on Rosh Hashanah God "remembered" these pious women, and allowed them to bear children. This illustrates a major motif of Rosh Hashanah, that God remembers humankind and notices and acts on our prayers.

The incident of Hagar and Ishmael in the wilderness—on one level also about motherhood—tells us something about how judgment takes place. A midrash relates that the angels demanded to know why Ishmael (banished at the insistence of Sarah for his bad influence on her son Isaac), whose descendants, the Moslem nation, would cause so much harm to Israel, should not have been left to die. God justified the salvation of Ishmael because of "where he is" (GENESIS 21:17): Based on his actions at that moment, he did not deserve to die. Similarly, on Rosh Hashanah, we are judged by our state on that day. Even if we sinned all year, if we sincerely regret our actions, we are judged by the reform, not the former transgressions.

The *Akeidah,* often seen as proof of Judaism's abhorrence of the heathen practice of child sacrifice to deities, is generally understood as the supreme test of religious conviction, the classic example of Jewish faithfulness to God. With his request, God basically asked Abraham what he was willing to give up in order to follow His word. Though distressed at the prospect of sacrificing his son— the one for whom he had waited many years, and through whom God had promised to fulfill His pledge of making Abraham the father of a great nation— Abraham believed in his values and trusted that God would only command him to do something that was ultimately for his, and collective, good.

The powerful story begs us to ask ourselves what we are willing to give up for the preservation of our values, our tradition, in essence, our futures. How do the values we hold dear conflict with other demands on our lives? What do we hold onto, what do we sacrifice, and what do our choices say about who and what we are? Just as Abraham answered, "Here I am" (*hineni*) when God called him to the test, we need to step forward and be prepared to act to preserve what really matters.

The rabbis teach us that the willingness of Abraham and Isaac (said to be thirty-seven years old at the time of his near demise and just as ready as his father to trust in God's plan), also serves as vicarious atonement, a credit to be used by succeeding generations. And more, it has served as a message of hope to those throughout the centuries who gave up much to remain Jewish, believing that in the end they, like the patriarchs, would be blessed because they remained true to something greater than themselves. (For this reason, the story is recited during every morning service throughout the year.) Similarly, their test is supposed to provide comfort to all Jews on Rosh Hashanah as we face our own trials.

FOR FURTHER EXPLORATION

FOR CHILDREN

Cohen, Barbara. *The Binding of Isaac.* New York: Lothrop, Lee & Shepard Company, 1978.
Isaac tells his grandchildren the story of how he was nearly sacrificed, handling their questions (and ours) in a warm and reassuring way. The beautiful paintings illustrating the text evoke the mood and mystery of the story. Ages 7–12.

SHOFAR

Following the Torah reading, we finally hear the greatly anticipated initial blasts of the shofar. The congregation stands as the *makrei* (reader) calls out the notes (except in Sephardic synagogues), and the *ba'al tekiah* (master of the blast, or trained shofar blower) produces the specified sounds, alternately wailing and willful, supplicating and demanding. In accordance with Talmudic rules, the blasts consist of a combination of *tekiah* (a long, straight blast, nine beats long, typically used to herald good news), *teruah* (an alarm sound, nine staccato blasts, like a sobbing or bleating), and *shevarim* (an alternate form of the Torah's *teruah,* consisting of three broken blasts, each three beats long, reminiscent of wailing).

Customarily, one hundred blasts are sounded on each day of Rosh Hashanah: thirty blasts during the shofar service between *Shakharit* and *Mussaf,* ten at the conclusion of each major section of the *Mussaf Amidah* during the *khazzan's* repetition, and forty following the full *kaddish* at the end of the *Mussaf* service. The last is a *tekiah gedolah* (big *tekiah*), a single, extended blast that, held strongly for what can seem much longer than human lung capacity would allow, often draws murmurs of approval from an appreciative congregation, as though the longer the blast the more readily accepted their prayers will be.

The count of one hundred is based in midrash. It says that the mother of the brutal Canaanite conqueror Sisera whimpered one hundred and one times in anguish over the son she presumed had been killed in battle against Deborah the Prophetess (JUDGES 4). Despite her anxiety and grief, she took solace from friends' assurances that he was detained merely in collecting spoils (JUDGES 5:28–30). Each blast of the shofar nullifies each cry of the cruel woman for her barbaric son. But in recognition of a mother's pain, we leave one of her anguished moans uncountered.

The Sephardim add a *tekiah* at the end of the service, just before *Aleinu*, so that they sound one hundred and one blasts. That is the numerical value of the name of Michael, the angelic protector of Israel (DANIEL 12:1). The extra blast is to summon him to do battle on our behalf.

If Rosh Hashanah falls on Shabbat, the shofar is not blown (SEE "HALAKHAH").

THE SHOFAR IN HISTORY The ceremonial horn holds numerous associations for Israel. Whether in celebration or warning, the shofar called the community together. It signaled Temple sacrifice and proclaimed the time of the new moon, fast and feast days, the start and end of the Sabbatical (every seven years) and Jubilee (every fiftieth year). Shofar blasts announced the coronation of kings (which we allude to in *malkhuyot*), preceded the giving of the Torah (EXODUS 19:19), when we chose God at Sinai (and which we recall on Rosh Hashanah with *zikhronot*), and will broadcast the coming of the Messiah (ZEKHARIAH 9:14) and the ingathering of the exiles to Israel (ISAIAH 27:13) for final judgment and redemption (which we pray, during *shofarot*, will arrive speedily).

In war, the shofar also called advance and retreat (as when blasts helped bring down the walls of Jericho [JOSHUA 6:20]). In fact, the shofar is not sounded until after the Torah reading because of its role in battle. During Roman rule of Palestine, the conquering army took a shofar blast emanating from a synagogue as a call to arms, and rushed in to massacre the innocent worshippers. By moving the shofar service to midday, the Jews proved to the Romans that they were assembled to pray, not plan insurrection. Also, by noon, the spies planted in synagogues when shofar blowing was prohibited had left, allowing the Jews to fulfill the *mitzvah*. The timing continued, for the sake of custom, even after the prohibition was rescinded.

WHAT SHOFAR SIGNALS FOR US In the soul-wrenching emotion-laden sounds summoning primal hopes and fears, we hear the echo of those turning points in our collective history, along with the encouragement to turn around our personal lives. Derived from the same root as the word improve (*shipair*) and related to the word for beauty or goodliness (*sheper*), the shofar summons us to make ourselves better. As Maimonides expressed it, the sound of the shofar is a great wake up alarm (SEE "PERSONAL SIGNIFICANCE").

When Moses went up Mount Sinai to receive the second set of tablets of the Ten Commandments, shofar blasts reminded the people to not return to the idolatrous practices that had resulted in the first tablets being broken (SEE NEXT CHAPTER). The blasts remind us, also, how easy it is to forget commitments made in the intensity of a spiritual or near-death experience and fall back into the bad habits we promised to abandon. As we pray to God to end disharmony between the forces of nature and the factions of nations, to make peace and restore the Temple, the sound of the shofar reminds us to retreat in our battles with others and with nature and advance in our war against the negative aspects of ourselves. At the same time, as it did in ancient days, the shofar calls us to unite as a community to work with mutual respect and purpose.

TASHLIKH

On the first day of Rosh Hashanah, before sunset (between the *Minkhah* and *Ma'ariv* services), Jews traditionally stream to a body of running water, preferably one containing fish, and symbolically cast off (*tasklikh*) our sins. The ceremony includes reading the source passage for the practice, the last verses from the prophet Micah (7:19): "He will take us back in love; He will cover up our iniquities. You will cast all their sins into the depths of the sea." Selections from Psalms, particularly 118 and 130, plus supplications and a kabbalistic prayer hoping God will treat Israel with mercy, are parts of *Tashlikh* in various communities.

The custom developed around the thirteenth century and became widespread despite objections of rabbis who feared superstitious people would believe *Tashlikh*, rather than the concerted effort of *teshuvah*, had the power to change their lives. Religious leaders opposed in particular the practice of tossing bread crumbs, representing sins, to the water, and discouraged even the act of shaking one's garments to loosen any "evil" clinging to them.

Superstitious rites most likely did influence the ceremony. Primitive people believed that the best way to win favor from evil spirits living in waterways was to give them gifts. Some peoples, including the Babylonian Jews, sent "sin-filled" containers out into the water. (The Talmud describes the practice of growing beans or peas for two or three weeks prior to the New Year in a woven basket for each child in a family. In an early variation of the Yom Kippur *kapparot* ritual [SEE "PREPARATION" IN NEXT CHAPTER], it was swung around the head seven times as a substitute for the person and then flung into the water.) Kurdistani Jews threw themselves into the water and swam around to be cleansed of their sins.

To change the practice from superstition to symbolism, the rabbis gave it ethical meaning. Through midrash, they connected the water with the *Akeidah*. When Abraham was on his way to sacrifice Isaac, they said, Satan (which could be understood as the voice inside Abraham telling him to disobey God and not kill his beloved son) tried to stop him. When Abraham refused to heed his voice, Satan became a raging river blocking Abraham's way. Abraham kept going forward. When the water reached his neck and he called out for God's help, the waters immediately subsided.

The purpose of man's life is not happiness, but worthiness.

FELIX ADLER

Water was also seen as symbolic of the Creation of the world—and all life. Kings of Israel were crowned near springs, suggesting continuity, like the King of Kings' unending sovereignty. Since the prophets Ezekiel and Daniel each received revelation near a body of water, it was seen as a place to find God's presence. As the element of purification, it also represents the opportunity for us to cleanse the body and soul and take a new course in our lives. (Later rabbis continued to protest against the ritual, on grounds that it encouraged new sins by creating a social situation where people could gossip and men and women mingle, as Isaac Bashevis Singer's story *"Tashlikh"* illustrates.)

Although the rabbis preferred that *Tasklikh* be done at water containing fish (man cannot escape God's judgment any more than fish can escape being caught in a net; we are just as likely to be ensnared and trapped at any moment as is a fish [ECCLESIASTES 9:12]), since this is, after all, a symbolic ceremony, any body of water will do—even a running hose or faucet.

If the first day of Rosh Hashanah falls on Shabbat, the Ashkenazim do *Tashlikh* the second day (so as not to carry prayer books to the water, which would violate Sabbath laws). Sephardim perform the ritual even on the Sabbath.

301

The ceremony can take place anytime during the holiday season through Hoshanah Rabbah at the end of Sukkot.

SECOND DAY

Rosh Hashanah is the only holiday whose second day is celebrated in Israel as well as in the Diaspora. Technically, the need for the second day was eliminated, as it was for all other holidays, when the calendar was established (SEE "THE JEWISH CALENDAR"). Prior to that time, Rosh Hashanah posed a particular problem, because unlike every other holiday, it falls on the first day of the month. If the witnesses to sighting of the new moon (which determined the beginning of the month) failed to testify or did not show up until late in the afternoon of the thirtieth day of Elul, it would have been too late for the people to observe what should have been a sacred day.

So our sages created "one long day" composed of the last day of the sixth month (Elul) and the first day of the seventh month (Tishrei), and called it *yom arikhata* (lengthy day). Although we go through all the ceremonies of two distinct days, the purpose of the construct was to impress upon the people that the entire time period is sacred. For that reason, observance for both days was retained as the worldwide standard (except much later in some Reform congregations, which observe only one day of Rosh Hashanah).

On the evening of the second day, candles are lit at home. So that the *shehekhiyanu* can again be recited, it is customary for the person doing the *brakhot* to have on a new piece of clothing or to place on the table a fruit not yet eaten that year to become the object of the blessing. Since you are not supposed to make a new fire (SEE "HALAKHAH" IN CHAPTER ON PESAKH) observant Jews take their flame from a candle already burning, or a stove pilot light (FOR EXPLANATION, SEE "PREPARATION"; FOR BRAKHOT SEE "BLESSINGS").

Except for a difference in *piyyutim,* smaller number of hymns and the Torah readings described above, services on the second day are essentially like those of the first.

CONCLUSION

We mark the end of the sacred day and passage into regular time with the brief ceremony used on all festivals, *Havdallah.* Unlike Shabbat, for Rosh Hashanah only the blessings over wine and separation are made (SEE "BLESSINGS").

Where Do We Begin? Preparation

SPIRITUAL READINESS

When we have a major event in our lives—a wedding or bar mitzvah, a business presentation or sports competition—we don't just wake up the morning of the anticipated occasion and do whatever is required. We spend weeks, maybe months or longer making sure all the details are arranged, that we are physically and psychologically primed. Our sages realized that preparing for the most important occasions in our spiritual year demand no less.

Originally, the annual focus on repentance was limited to the one-day observance we know as Yom Kippur. But those sages knew that if atonement were going to have any real impact on getting us to redirect our lives, it had to be more than a one-shot symbolic ceremony. So they extended the period of self-examination and self-correction to a full thirty days prior to Rosh Hashanah, the entire month of Elul—comparable to the grace period the court granted a debtor in which to pay off creditors.

Although *teshuvah* is acceptable any time, it was believed that God is particularly favorable to mankind during Elul and the first ten days of Tishrei. This forty-day period corresponds to the one Moses spent on Mount Sinai receiving the second set of tablets of the Ten Commandments. During his absence, the Israelites camped at the base of the mountain and repented for having turned away from God to worship the Golden Calf (EXODUS 32), which had resulted in the destruction of the original tablets (SEE NEXT CHAPTER). We use the time ending with Yom Kippur to give up our own false gods (greed, jealousy, gluttony, money, fame—whatever our particular harmful indulgences) and reaffirm our commitment to the one God. (Not coincidentally, forty is the number symbolic of life transition, appearing repeatedly in Jewish Scripture and tradition to illustrate turning points, like the length of the flood, Moses' sojourns on the mountain, the years of Israelite wandering in the desert, the age at which a man is considered old- and well-educated enough to delve into Jewish mysticism.)

Since repentance, prayer and charity are considered merits to counterbalance our "missed marks," with the potential to reverse what would have been a negative outcome for us, the month of Elul is the time to intensify efforts in all three areas. We go through the process of *teshuvah,* rise early for special penitential prayers, and give donations. (Today mail and phone requests from scores of Jewish organizations largely replace the solicitations in prior ages made by beggars and organization and institution representatives who appeared on private doorsteps, at synagogues and in cemeteries.)

PRAYER

Special services, *Selikhot* (forgiveness), begin at midnight on the Saturday prior to Rosh Hashanah (if the holiday falls earlier than Wednesday, *Selikhot* begin the Saturday night of the preceding week). This is to provide at least four days in which to recite the penitential prayer service, based on the desire among pious Jews to fast during the entire Ten Days of Repentance: Since the time span includes four days during which fasting is prohibited (the two of Rosh Hashanah, the Sabbath between Rosh Hashanah and Yom Kippur, and the day before Yom Kippur), the four days prior to Rosh Hashanah compensate.

Four days also defined the period in which animals to be sacrificed were examined for blemishes. As we are preparing for self-sacrifice, in a sense, we should have at least four days to examine ourselves for, and try to correct, spiritual imperfections.

The beginning of the week was chosen as the start of *Selikhot* because historically the Jews, by and large Sabbath observant, were filled with the spirit of the just-ended day of rest and therefore in the proper frame of mind to begin praying for forgiveness. According to tradition, midnight is the hour of Divine good will, when the heavens are most open to prayer. On every other day of the week before Rosh Hashanah, *Selikhot* take place before dawn. The Talmud also calls this a time of favor and compassion when the spirit of God hovers over the earth.

Today, most Jews who attend *Selikhot* go to the midnight service, generally preceded by a coffee and cake reception. Some liberal congregations use the occasion to have people come together and through prayer, song and apology work out any differences they have had during the year.

While the special *Selikhot* prayer books vary from community to community (the Sephardim, who recite *Selikhot* during the entire month of Elul, use the same contents every day, the Ashkenazim change daily), they share the themes of professing human guilt and acknowledging God's grace, asking for God's mercy and blessing, and reminding God of the hardships of exile and His positive responses to the Jewish people's cries for help in the past. (The synagogue usually provides the books. A version for children, *Selichot: A Family Service* by Judith Z. Abrams, is published by Kar-Ben Copies.)

In addition to a number of psalms and *piyyutim* on the same subjects, a key ingredient of the services is recitation of the Thirteen Divine Attributes of Mercy. They were revealed to Moses when he asked to know God in order to be assured of His favor (EXODUS 33:12–34:7). The Talmud says that when Moses implored God to forgive Israel for its lapse into idolatry, God replied that whenever in the future the Jewish people would be threatened with calamity or discipline, they would be able to arouse God's mercy by reciting these Attributes with sincere devotion (SEE "OBSERVANCE" IN CHAPTER ON YOM KIPPUR).

PERSONAL

CEMETERY VISITS Even non-observant Jews often show their respect to the deceased by visiting the graves of parents, grandparents and other loved ones during the week before Rosh Hashanah. The Ashkenazim have followed this custom since the Middle Ages, when *Erev Rosh Hashanah* trips to the tombs of the pious and scholarly began. Many still believe that the departed, especially the righteous, even if not related, can be beseeched to pray on your behalf.

In Israel, particularly under the cultural influence of Sephardim who hold great stock in the power of such prayer, this custom has turned into a tour business, with several companies busing believers from a wide range of backgrounds to the gravesites of matriarchs, patriarchs and other particularly pious Jews. Visitors touch the tombs, throw candy or leave other foods, and pray, often amid tears, to find a life partner, conceive, have a loved one healed, enjoy health and prosperity. Giving *tzedakah,* if not directly to any poor people present, is also customary, as for any cemetery visit. The traditional Prayer for the Departed (*El Molei Rakhamim,* God Full of Mercy) recited at the gravesite is found in a standard *siddur* and is provided by funeral homes.

It is common practice to place a few pebbles or small stones on the headstone, based on an old folk custom indicating that someone has been to visit the burial site as an expression of respect for the deceased. The gesture may date back as far as biblical days, when piles of rocks typically designated graves. Vandals often dispersed them, so mourners added stones to make sure the graves remained marked.

ANNULMENT OF VOWS Following *Selikhot* on the morning before Rosh Hashanah, religious Jews gather in the synagogue for the *hatarat nedarim* ceremony. Taking turns, each declares, according to a Talmudic formula (included in traditional *makhzorim*), before the symbolic court of three others that he be absolved from vows, made consciously or unintentionally, which he failed to complete. The absolution covers only vows of a personal or religious nature, not any involving promises to another person. (Throughout most of Jewish history, making vows based on planned piety or in thanks for the expected granting of a request to God were common. Since they were generally couched in Divine terms, they could not just be ignored when unfulfilled.)

The fact that any unfulfilled oaths or vows have to be excused emphasizes the sanctity of one's word, not only in the form of vows (which, once made, are considered to carry the force of a positive Torah commandment), but in anything we say. It makes us more aware of the words we use and how we use them.

TICKETS If you do not belong to a synagogue and plan to attend services, be sure to arrange for tickets in advance.

THE BODY It is traditional on *Erev Rosh Hashanah,* prior to donning Sabbath clothes, to bathe and have a hair cut. These acts are symbols not only of purity and cleanliness, but also of belief in God's mercy. In former times, they ran against the custom of going to a court trial unshorn and dressed in black. Religious men still go to the *mikvah* (ritual bath) in preparation for the holiday.

HOME

PARCHMENTS Those concerned about the kashrut of their mezzuzah scrolls and tefillin check both to make sure that the writing has not faded and that the letters on the parchment's surface have not chipped. If so, the scrolls need to be replaced.

TZEDAKAH Before candles are lit, many families deposit money in a special box (provided by an organization, purchased at a Judaica store, or made from a can or jar). The money put aside on the holidays (and Friday night, when it is also customary to add to the *tzedakah* box before lighting candles) is later donated to a Jewish cause.

CHILDREN Without any of the external attractions other holidays offer, it can be difficult for children to relate to this inner-focused one, and they need help in understanding what it means. The kinds of questions you pose for yourself can be presented on their level.

Ask them what they remember from the previous year and talk about how the family will celebrate the holiday. Ask them what they think they did well last year and what they were unhappy about in their behavior or performance. Perhaps they can think of ways they helped or hurt you, or a sibling, or a friend. Guide them in talking through their feelings about what they did—good and bad—and how they can get rid of any bad feelings and have more good ones. Help them set goals for the year.

This may be a time their questions about God arise—or a time for you to introduce the subject. Prayer books for children and the sources listed below may be helpful.

For very young children, you might want to focus on the theme of the birthday of the world, and on that wonderful musical instrument, the shofar—what it is, the role it has played in our history, how it is made. If you do not have a shofar at home, try to get access to one through a friend, synagogue or store that carries Jewish supplies so they can handle it, hear it, maybe even blow it. You can also talk about the special foods we eat (SEE "TRADITIONAL FOODS").

FOR FURTHER EXPLORATION

FOR ADULTS

Gordis, Daniel. *Becoming a Jewish Parent.* New York: Harmony Books, 1999, pp. 59–74.
    The chapter "Making Space for God, or How We Steal Wonder from Our Kids," contains some wonderful observations and valuable guidance on how to understand what children want and need when

they ask about God, about how to deal with our own doubts without quashing their beliefs, and how to raise children who comfortably include God in their lives.

Wolpe, David J. *Teaching Your Children About God.* New York: Harper Perennial, 1995.
With anecdotes, humor and suggested discussion questions, Rabbi Wolpe provides a guide to helping adults reconnect with spirituality and create an atmosphere in which children, from preschoolers to early teens, can openly explore the idea of God.

FOR CHILDREN

Sasso, Sandy Eisenberg. *God's Paintbrush.* Woodstock, VT: Jewish Lights Books, 1992.
This, warm, embracing book helps children understand God through vignettes of everyday kids' activities, feelings and thoughts. Ages 4–8. (Also available: God's Paintbrush Teachers' Guide and God's Paintbrush Celebration Kit, a non-sectarian program of crafts, games and other activities designed to spur thinking about God in children ages 4–10.)

See also *Building a Jewish Life—Rosh Hashanah/Yom Kippur* (Grishaver), and *My Very Own Rosh Hashanah, Yom Kippur* (Saypol and Wikler) in "More Good Information." ❧✡

FOOD AND FIRE If you want to use fire—for cooking, to light candles, etc.—on the second day in accordance with halakhah, you need to leave a source, such as a stove pilot light or a twenty-five hour candle, burning from before the start of the first day, and take any flame needed from that. If Rosh Hashanah falls immediately before the Sabbath and you are concerned about following Jewish law, on Wednesday you need to make an *eruv tavshilin* so you will be able to cook in preparation for Shabbat (SEE "HALAKHAH" IN CHAPTER ON PESAKH AND "BLESSINGS" AT BACK OF THE BOOK).

What Are We Supposed to Do? Halakhah

FESTIVAL LAWS

The Sabbath-like restrictions that apply to all *yom tovim,* the laws covering the preparation of food, eating a formal meal and feeding the stranger and the needy, the wearing of clean clothes and rejoicing in the occasion, apply equally to Rosh Hashanah (SEE "HALAKHAH" IN CHAPTER ON PESAKH).

TESHUVAH

Doing teshuvah is one of the six hundred and thirteen *mitzvot* commanded in the Torah (DEUTERONOMY 30:2,10). Fulfilling it requires Moses Maimonides' three steps: regretting the sinful past behavior, restraining yourself from doing the behavior again, and resolving never to do it in the future.

PRAYER

The laws covering changes in wording and inclusion or exclusion of particular parts of the regular liturgy all relate to the special nature of the Ten Days and the Divine judgment that takes place during them.

WORD CHANGES "The Holy God (*ha El hakadosh*) and "King Who loves righteousness and justice" (*Melekh o'heiv tzedakah u'mishpaht*) become "The Holy King" (*Melekh Hakadosh*) and "The King of Judgment" (*Hamelekh Hamishpaht*). The *kaddish* following Selikhot contains the sentence usually said only after the *Amidah*, "May the prayers and petitions. . .be accepted" (*titkubuil izlotehone u'vautehone*). *Le eilah* (to the heavens) is added to every *kaddish* to emphasize that God rules from His heavenly throne. (Using the normal wording instead of "Holy King" necessitates repetition of the prayer; forgetting to say "King of Judgment" does not because the usual wording also conveys the notion of sovereignty.)

When Rosh Hashanah falls on Shabbat, the words of certain *piyyutim* that are not said on the second day are changed from "a day of shofar blowing (*yom teruah*) to "a day of remembering the blowing of the shofar" (*yom zikhron teruah*).

AVINU MALKEINU We recite Our Father, our King after the *khazzan's* repetition of the *Shakharit* and *Minkhah Amidah,* except on Shabbat. This is because it was first intoned at a public fast, and no fast can be ordered to fall on a Sabbath. (Yom Kippur, ordained by Torah, falls outside this law.) Some say we omit *Avinu Malkeinu* on Shabbat because on that day we don't ask for our needs to be met.

The Talmud relates that Rabbi Eliezer recited twenty-four benedictions so God would bring rain, all to no avail. So Rabbi Akiva stepped forward and called out "Our Father, our King! You are our Father. Our Father, our King! We have no King but You. Our Father our King! We have sinned before You. Our Father, our King! Have mercy upon us. Our Father, our King! Deal kindly with us for the sake of Your name." His prayers were answered immediately. Because of their relevance in theme, and the outcome they produced, we repeat the series of requests for material and spiritual blessings throughout the Ten Days.

HALLEL Although Rosh Hashanah qualifies as a festival, the hymns of praise normally included on such days are not said. Complete joy must accompany their recitation, and although we are not to be sad on Rosh Hashanah, the fear of judgment modifies our mood enough that we cannot say *Hallel* in the proper frame of mind: "How can Israel sing hymns of praise when the King is seated on His throne in judgment and human lives hang in the balance?" (TALMUD, ROSH HASHANAH 32).

Some authorities permit the pious to shed tears during prayer to awaken God's mercy.

ZEKHIRUS — RITUAL PURITY

Special care is to be taken during this period of judgment not to violate prohibitions in relationships with other people and with God. In actions and spiritual piety (such as eating kosher foods), vigilance is required, and we are supposed to study Torah and Talmud.

SHOFAR

The Talmud covers all aspects of the shofar ritual, the central part of the Rosh Hashanah service—from the proper fashioning of one to who must sound and hear it, to how the shofar blowing takes place.

OBLIGATION The commandment specifies that one is to hear rather than blow the shofar. It applies to every man and woman, with the exception of those who are mentally incompetent or hearing impaired. Although minor children are exempt, parents should introduce their children to the sounding of the shofar from the age of three. Since the *mitzvah* falls on each individual, a congregational setting is not required, but enhances the proclamation of God's kingship and rule. Arrangements should be made to have the shofar blown for anyone who cannot attend synagogue for the communal sounding.

BLASTS The ritual requires nine blasts of the shofar consisting of three the Torah calls *teruah* (which may or may not be what we call *teruah*), each preceded and followed by an extended blast called *tekiah*. Halakhah resolves the Gemarah's disagreement as to whether all nine are Scriptural (from Torah) or scribal (from the sages) in origin (BASED ON LEVITICUS 25:9, 23:24 AND NUMBERS 29:1). It specifies one straight blast, one broken and one straight, in sets of three, with the broken blasts to be collectively the same length as the single straight one.

To unify the varying forms of the broken blast developed in different communities, and avoid dissention among the Jews following the destruction of the Temple, Rabbi Abbahu of Caesaria ruled that both versions be incorporated into the service. The order was established as three groups of *tekiah, shevarim* (three broken)-*teruah* (nine staccato), *tekiah;* three groups of *tekiah, shevarim, tekiah,* and three groups of *tekiah, teruah, tekiah,* thirty blasts per set.

Since blowing the shofar is an exercise of skill rather than performance of work prohibited on Sabbath, there is nothing about it inherently in violation of the day of rest. However, except for a short period when the sages convened in Yavneh after the destruction of the Second Temple, blowing the shofar on the Sabbath outside the Temple has been prohibited. This is to preclude someone from carrying a shofar in an area of public domain—such as between home and shul, to a hospital to sound it for a sick person, or to an expert to ascertain whether or not it is kosher. (Carrying in the public domain is prohibited on Shabbat).

ACCEPTABLE HORNS AND PROCEDURE Defined as a hollow horn into which a bony projection intrudes, a shofar can be fashioned from the horn of any kosher animal except that of an ox or cow. Gemara stipulates that since those horns are composed of many layers, they appear to be several shofarot inside each other, while a shofar must be singular. Horns of the cow and ox are also to be avoided because they recall the sin of the Golden Calf.

Detailed instructions tell how a shofar is to be made, with no holes or cracks (although what kind of crack renders a horn unfit is a matter for an expert to determine); with a curve to represent our humility before God; and no augmentation that would create a separation between the *ba'al tekiah*'s mouth and the shofar. Since the purpose of the shofar blasts is to summon God's mercy on those before Him, the *ba'al tekiah* is expected to be pious as well as capable of sounding strong, clear, blasts of proper length.

Prior to sounding the shofar, the congregation recites Psalm 47 seven times, per the kabbalists of Safed. God's name appears in the psalm seven times, representing the seven *sefirot* or levels of heaven He created. Keeping the shofar covered until it is used, the *ba'al tekiah* recites the blessing for shofar blowing and the *shehekhiyanu.*

JOY

We should leave the synagogue following Rosh Hashanah services in an upbeat confident mood. Without being gluttonous, we are to eat as well as our means allow, study Torah at the table, and, unless a nap is absolutely required to counter a headache that would interfere with attending *Minkhah* services, return to synagogue to recite psalms with the congregation.

SHEHEKHIYANU

The concept of Rosh Hashanah as one long day raised questions about the propriety of reciting the *shehekhiyanu* following the blessings for *kiddush* and candlelighting on the second night, and sounding the shofar on the second day. Since both days have the same sanctity and the blessing has already been recited on the first day, there is no need to repeat it on the second. But it is a *mitzvah* to say blessings. Therefore, when candles are lit the second night, and *kiddush* is recited, a new fruit (one not yet eaten this year) placed on the table, or a new garment worn by the person making the *brakhah* serves as the object of the blessing. However, absence of either or both does not preclude saying it. (An individual may only say *shehekhiyanu* once, so if the same person does candlelighting and *kiddush,* it is not repeated.) The shofar blower also tries to wear a new garment for the second day (except when the first day falls on Shabbat, in which case the *shehekhiyanu* has not yet been said since the shofar has not yet been sounded).

What Other Things Do People Do? Customs

OTHER TIMES AND PLACES

STUDY Throughout much of our history, the forty-day period between Elul 1 and Tishrei 10 has been a time to pray more fervently, study more diligently, recite psalms more regularly and follow *the mitzvot* more carefully. From the days of the Babylonian captivity, Jews would take time off from work to participate in Bible study groups and examine their lives. (Later, the Moroccan Jews chose a night during Elul or the Ten Days to entirely devote to learning principles from the Mishnah, laws from Maimonides' writings and Psalms. Forsaking sleep and talk, they allowed themselves only tea and coffee while they studied.) As a way of purifying the soul, many made it a habit to conduct no secular conversations during the forty days.

From mid Elul until after Sukkot, Eastern European children had only half days of school, but didn't really get to enjoy the time between the summer and fall semesters as vacation. They, too, used the time for study and self-examination.

PRAYER The ancient Jews introduced two customs for the month of Elul followed to this day: sounding the shofar every morning after *Shakharit* (except Shabbat, when it was considered a disturbance of the universe, and the last day of the month, to create a separation between the shofar blowing done throughout Elul, only a custom, and that done on Rosh Hashanah, a commandment), and reading Psalm 27 at every service until the last day of Sukkot. A plea to God to help us when we are surrounded by enemies (including the internal ones that lead us astray), it also expresses longing to dwell in the House of the Lord. (Ashkenazim say it after *Shakharit* and *Ma'ariv*, Sephardim after *Shakharit* and *Minkhah*). Per midrash, verses of this psalm refer to the holidays of the season: "The Lord is my light [Rosh Hashanah] and my help [Yom Kippur], whom should I fear? . . .He will shelter me in His pavilion [Sukkot]."

To rouse the Jews in Eastern European and Middle Eastern villages for the early *Selikhot* services, the *shammash* (beadle) would knock on windows or doors, sometimes with a special hammer, occasionally one carved in the shape of a shofar. The children in Yemen were so eager to join the adults, each tied one end of a string to his toe and hung the other end out the window so the beadle could pull on it as he passed.

SYMBOLS AND SUPERSTITIONS When Medieval-era women visited the cemetery during Elul, they would stride around the perimeter, unrolling a spool of cotton string onto the ground. They gave the rewound twine to a candlemaker to use as wicks for candles, preferably out of white wax, and long enough to burn twenty-four hours. The women then donated the candles to the synagogue for use on Yom Kippur. (In Germany, the women made the candles themselves on Tishrei 8, the day before *Erev Yom Kippur,* and the anniversary of the dedication of the First Temple. Prayers and supplications recited over every wick asked dead relatives, particularly pious women, to intercede for those still alive.)

A variety of customs—further indicating how superstitious our predecessors were—developed from the belief in Satan as our adversary (SEE "HISTORIC FOUN-DATION"). The new moon of Tishrei was not blessed so the "evil" one would not realize Rosh Hashanah had arrived. (It is customary not to bless the new moon until after the close of Yom Kippur.) The shofar was sounded throughout Elul in part to confuse his being able to keep track of the day. (If he did not realize it was Rosh Hashanah, the reasoning went, he could not present his accusations before God.) After Psalm 47, six verses were added to form an acrostic spelling *kra* (destroy) *Satan.*

In recognition of the different type of joy expressed during the Ten Days of Repentance, weddings do not take place then. Those (including the Afghanis) who thought that being happy on the night of Rosh Hashanah assures one of happiness all year, created the proper atmosphere at home after synagogue. There is a similar belief, expressed in the Jerusalem Talmud, "if one sleeps at the year's beginning, his good fortune likewise sleeps." Therefore, it is customary not to sleep during the day or be idle, which is tantamount to dozing. Study of Scripture commonly filled the time between services. A number of Sephardic Jewish communities try to read through the Book of Tehillim twice during Rosh Hashanah since the total number of its psalms (one hundred and fifty) times two equals the numerical value of the Hebrew word *kaper,* pardon.

CHARITY Jews have long gathered at the Western Wall in Jerusalem the day before Rosh Hashanah to pray and distribute *tzedakah* among the poor. The

Afghanis made their donations in the form of meat, from the sheep they slaughtered after they annulled their vows.

FASTING It was commonplace for pious Eastern European and Judeo-Spanish Jews to fast part of the day on *Erev Rosh Hashanah*. They refrained from eating between their pre-dawn pre-synagogue tea and crackers and noon. The fast indicated their willingness to place service to God above physical aspects of life and made them "advance men" in gaining God's favor, based on a parable from midrash. Often the fast was not broken until the men had purified themselves in a *mikvah,* as was customary before festivals and specifically ordained for before Rosh Hashanah and Yom Kippur. In some places, the Jews bathed in a cold stream, immersing three times in the presence of witnesses to complete the ritual process.

GREETING FRIENDS AND RELATIVES Following services on Rosh Hashanah morning, the men and children in Turkish Jewish communities went visiting while the women stayed home to receive guests. On traditional silver trays, they served white or light-colored sweets to symbolize happiness in the coming year. When the guests could eat no more, but did not want to insult their hostesses, the men wrapped the extra goodies in their white handkerchiefs, carried especially for the purpose of transporting the sweets home.

From the very beginning of Elul, sidewalk vendors set up their tables throughout cities in Israel to offer a wide array of New Year cards. A national holiday in Israel, Rosh Hashanah is a time of exchanging gifts, particularly baskets of fruit and candy, among friends and business associates (much as American companies do during the end of the secular year holidays). Bonuses and gift certificates send Israelis flooding to the stores.

GREETING

We traditionally wish each other *leshanah tovah tikateivu v'tikhateimu* (may you be inscribed and sealed [in the Book of Life] for a good year), often shortened to *leshanah tovah* (for a good year). Variations include *leshanah tovah u'mehtukah* (for a good and sweet year) and *tikatev lekhayim tovim u'leshalom* (may you be written for a good life and peace).

Since the Talmud states that the righteous are inscribed for good within the first three hours of the new year (unlike the rest of us, who must wait for our final decrees until the end of Yom Kippur), after *Erev Rosh Hashanah* you should not greet a friend with the wish that s/he be "written" because it implies you don't consider that person to be among the most righteous. The proper form between the two holidays is therefore *leshanah tovah tikhateimu* (may you be sealed for a good year).

You are also likely to hear *gut yom tov* (happy holiday) or *gut yohr* (good year) among those of Yiddish-speaking Eastern European backgrounds. Among Sephardim, *tizkeh leshanim* (may you merit long life) invites the response *tizkeh vetikhyeh veta'arikh yomim* (may you merit, may you live and may you have length of days).

The custom of sending New Year's cards containing one of these or related greetings developed from the instruction of the Maharil (Rabbi Jacob Molin). In the late fourteenth or early fifteenth century, he wrote that from the beginning of Elul, any personal letter should mention that the writer is praying on behalf of his friends, that they may be inscribed and sealed for a good year. It became common in the Diaspora to send such messages, and by the late nineteenth century in Eastern Europe, the New Year greeting card industry had begun.

DRESS

Clean Sabbath clothes are appropriate for synagogue. Since Talmudic times, it has been popular to wear white on Rosh Hashanah, the color of both joy and purity, based on a verse from the prophet Isaiah: "Though your sins be scarlet, they shall become white as the snow" (1:18). Pious men—and today usually at least the rabbi and *khazzan* of the synagogue—wear *kittelim* (SEE "RITUAL ITEMS").

It is a widespread custom to wear new clothes, so that, as they say in Bulgaria, the whole year will be new. (The Moroccans do not wear new clothes since they could make one haughty.) When putting on new clothing for the first time, it is appropriate to say a blessing (unless the new item is leather, like shoes, because its fashioning resulted in the loss of life for an animal). It is followed by the *shehekhiyanu*, recited for any new item or event each year (SEE "BLESSINGS").

What Is There to Eat? Traditional Foods

At no other time in the year is the idea that symbolic acts produce positive outcomes so effusively expressed than at Rosh Hashanah. Throughout the Jewish world, customs regarding the eating of certain foods for their sympathetic qualities developed.

No Rosh Hashanah meal would be complete without apples and honey. In addition to their representation of a year of positive blessings (sweetness), the apple, according to mysticism, represents the Shekhinah (the feminine spirit of God), which is now judging each person. The honey symbolizes the sweetness with which we hope the judgment will be made. Many people keep honey on their dining tables through the end of Sukkot, and serve apples for dipping into it during the entire festival season.

We also eat foods that are round (indicating the continuation of life and the endless nature of God's sovereignty), and which grow in abundance (representing prosperity and fertility). The Talmud suggests pumpkin, fenugreek, leek, beet, and dates. All sorts of sweet cakes, particularly honey cake and teiglakh (a mound of small balls of fried dough mixed with dried fruits and honey), were developed.

Khallot are altered from the normal long braided loaves used on Shabbat and other festivals. Round ones, often studded with raisins for extra sweetness, are customary. Some bake the breads decorated with, or in the form of, ladders (according to a midrash describing the ladders God makes in heaven on Rosh Hashanah on which some people will be raised and some lowered), crowns (representing God's reign as King of the Universe), or birds (showing God's mercy, based on Isaiah: "Even as the birds that fly, so will the Lord of Hosts protect Jerusalem" [31:5]). European Jews typically eat carrot tzimmes, a mix of carrots and honey that may also include some combination of white and sweet potatoes, dried fruit, meat and wine. The Yiddish word for carrot, *mehren,* means to increase, as we hope our merits will. Also, sliced into rounds, the carrots resemble coins in color and shape, and therefore suggest prosperity.

We avoid sour and bitter foods, along with nuts. In addition to being irritating to the throat and therefore a potential interference with prayer, according to *gematria* the numerical value of the Hebrew word nut, *egoz,* equals that of the word for sin, *khet.*

According to Ezra's admonition (NEHEMIAH 8:10) we are supposed to enjoy a substantial meal after Rosh Hashanah services. In most families, it takes place both evenings of *Erev Rosh Hashanah,* and/or midday after the synagogue break between *Mussaf* and *Minkhah* on both days. On the second night, we try to have a new fruit of the season so we can justly say the *shehekhiyanu.*

Always good at throwing a party, the Sephardim developed a special seder done on the first, sometimes also the second, evening of Rosh Hashanah. In addition to the above traditional *brakhot* and foods, they eat a series of items that are symbolic of or whose names contain allusions to some desired protection or blessing. Prior to partaking of each, they recite a *yehi rahtzon* (may it be [God's] will) that often makes a play on words between the Aramaic name given in Talmud for a food, and the Hebrew word that resembles it in sound.

Typical items include the head of a sheep (symbolizing the planned sacrifice of Isaac), or the head of a fish, to ask that we be like the head and not the tail; beet greens or Swiss chard (*selek*), that all our enemies may go away (*yistalku*); carrot (*gezer*), that the harsh sentence (*gezar din*) to be imposed on us will be torn up; pomegranates, that we may be as full of good deeds as the pomegranate is of seeds or that we may have as much prosperity; leek (*karti*), that our enemies may be cut off (*sheyikaretu*); chick peas (*kara*), cold (*kar*) on the inside, symbolizing the "cooling down" of God's stern judgment.

Some Ashkenazi *makhzorim* contain a number of *yehi rahtzons,* as do some Sephardic cookbooks. You can even make up your own in English (beet is obvious; carrot, garrote, perhaps; pepper and lettuce suggest several possibilities.)

Since along with being instructed to feast we are taught to "send portions unto him for whom nothing is prepared (NEHEMIAH 8:10), it is customary to invite the needy for Rosh Hashanah—symbolically today by providing money through appropriate organizations. It can also be accomplished by inviting someone who does not have any place to go for the holiday meals to join you.

Do You Hear Music? Songs to Sing

Like almost everything else connected with this holiday, the music centers on what goes on in the synagogue: there are no folk songs or traditional melodies except those attached to the liturgy. Some date back to the Spanish Inquisition, when many Jews publicly renounced Judaism, but privately and secretly retained their traditions. Certain melodies served as signals and passwords so that secret worshippers could avoid detection.

This music, as much of the rest of the *nusakh* (musical rendition) for the Rosh Hashanah services, is different than that normally used during the year. Even the *trop* (cantillation) for the Torah readings changes. There are recordings of them, and you may feel more comfortable in synagogue if you familiarize yourself with the sound of the liturgy beforehand. You can even learn some key tunes so that, even if you cannot sing the words, you could at least hum along during the service.

Some highlights of the service whose tunes you might want to learn in advance are: The Thirteen Attributes, *"Avinu Malkeinu"* (BOTH DISCUSSED EARLIER), *"B'Rosh Hashanah"* (On Rosh Hashanah, acknowledgement that we are judged) *"V'Kol Ma'aminim"* (And all Believe, an expression of our faith in God's character and His role in the world), and *"B'Sefer Hakhayim"* (In the Book of Life, a request that we be written in it).

FOR FURTHER EXPLORATION

Pasternak, Velvel. *High Holiday and Sukkot Melodies.* Tara Publications.
   The major tunes of the services of the fall season, with words transliterated into English, are included in the booklet and companion tape, which can be purchased as a set or individually (800-827-2400; 410-654-0880 fax, www.jewishmusic.com).   ☙✡

What Tales are Told? Stories to Read

Folktales for the holiday convey a sense of the role spirituality played in the lives of Jews of previous centuries, and the sense of wonder with which they approached this season. From the stories and reminiscences of writers like Isaac Bashevis Singer, Isaac Loeb Peretz and Bella Chagall, we can get a feeling for how our grandparents or great-grandparents in Eastern Europe celebrated. Among newer books are several that effectively present the past or provide meaningful contexts for today's observance.

FOR FURTHER EXPLORATION

FOR ALL

At the well-organized and sharply designed website www.jewishnewyear.com, a project of Khabad Lubavitch, you'll find all kinds of information for adults and children pertaining to the beginning-of-the year holidays, from the month-long lead-in to Rosh Hashanah through Simkhat Torah: study options, recipes, stories, activities for children and so on.

Waskow, Arthur, David Waskow and Shoshana Waskow. *Before There Was a Before*. Brooklyn: Lambda Publishers, 1997.
> By a father and his two grown children, this beautifully written book tells the Creation story with love, gentleness, and humor. Evoking the earth's smells, sounds, colors and sensations, it expresses the interrelatedness of all life. The refreshing look at an old story is great for parents and children to read together.

FOR CHILDREN

Baude, Pierre-Marie, *The Book of Creation*. Saxonville, MA: Picture Book Studio, 1991.
> A shepherd father agrees to tell how the world and its components came into being only after his son has been sensitive to everything around him. The poetic quality of the lengthy text conjures the image of the elder storyteller passing cultural secrets to the next generation. It incorporates the joy of Creation, appreciation for everything on earth and a message about living in peace. The award-winning illustration recalls Japanese painting and Southwest Indian prints. Ages 12 and up.

Kimmel, Eric A. *Days of Awe: Stories for Rosh Hashanah and Yom Kippur*. New York: Viking, 1991.
> The three incredibly moving stories in this book show us the key concepts of the holidays in simple every day life. Adapted from traditional sources and conveying the awe and beauty of the season, one story deals with each of the themes of charity, prayer and repentance. Ages 8–12.

Yom Kippur—
Day of Atonement

(YOME' KEY-POOR'; YIDDISH: YOME KIP'-PER)
TISHREI 10
(FALL; LATE SEPTEMBER—MID OCTOBER)

On the holiest day of the entire year, we sublimate physical needs to spiritual pursuits so that the entire nation of Israel can reconcile itself with one another, with God, and to its role in the world. The end point of the process of self-examination and repentance begun forty days earlier, and the resolution of the judgment period begun on Rosh Hashanah, it is designed to leave us purified, ready to face life with renewed vigor and purpose.

Origins—WHY WE CELEBRATE YOM KIPPUR

Traditions—HOW WE CELEBRATE YOM KIPPUR

Origins—

WHY WE CELEBRATE YOM KIPPUR

Where Did It Begin? Historic Foundation

A BIBLICAL COMMANDMENT

Yom Kippur began shortly after completion of the portable Tabernacle (house of worship) in the Sinai (EXODUS 35–40). As recorded in Torah, God gave Moses explicit instructions for this "Sabbath of Sabbaths" (*Shabbat Shabbaton*). Named *Yom Hakippurim* (later shortened in the vernacular to the singular, Yom Kippur), Day of Atonements, it calls for complete rest, prohibition of work, self-denial (or "affliction of your souls"), and specified sacrifices (LEVITICUS 16, 23:26–32, NUMBERS 29:7–11).

The purpose of the holiday and its activity was "to make atonement for the Israelites for all their sins once a year" (LEVITICUS 16:34) so that they would be "clean before the Lord" (LEVITICUS 16:30). In order to accomplish it, Aaron (and each descendant who would succeed him as *Kohein Gadol,* or High Priest) performed an intricate ritual.

Through immersion, vestment changes and the blood of the sacrificed bull, ram and a goat chosen "for God," the *Kohein Gadol* purged himself, his household, the Israelite community, the Shrine (curtained-off part of the Tabernacle that contained the Tablets of the Ten Commandments and over which God's spirit hovered in a cloud), the Tent of Meeting (the wandering Jews' sanctuary), and the sacrificial altar of all transgressions committed by the entire nation.

He then put his hand on a second goat and confessed the sins of the Israelites, essentially laying their wrongdoings on the head of the innocent animal. By sending this goat (whose purpose had been designated at the same time the other was chosen for dedication to God) out into the wilderness "for Azazel," the priest symbolically rid the community of its mistakes.

Those who rationalize biblical narrative based on the beliefs and practices of primitive peoples define the unexplained Azazel as a demonic force dwelling in the desert. (The rabbis themselves suggest it was a kind of bribe to the Adversary (SEE "HISTORIC FOUNDATION" IN CHAPTER ON ROSH HASHANAH) so he wouldn't make new accusations against Israel. Breaking the name into *az* (strong or rough), and *ayil* (ledge or buttress), could indicate the inaccessible rocks or cliffs where the animal would die. The Septuagint's translation yields *ez,* goat, and *azal,* Aramaic for go or went, which is related to the Hebrew *lazel,* meaning to remove.

Whatever the specific definition, the original scapegoat was understood as something other than what the word has come to mean. It was not unjustly blamed for causing the problems of the community and subsequently punished. It was merely a vehicle for transporting the misdeeds and consequences as far away as possible. The society could only benefit by the banishment of the animal after its members had owned up to the wrongful behavior for which they themselves were guilty.

THE FIRST YOM KIPPUR According to tradition, the conceptual model for the annual observance occurred earlier, when Moses returned from his third trip up Mount Sinai with the second set of tablets bearing the Ten Commandments. He had broken the originals upon discovering that during his absence the people had created an idol, the Golden Calf (EXODUS 32:19). He returned up the mountain to try to convince God not to completely destroy the ungrateful wayward lot of Israelites who, within a few months after being redeemed from slavery (SEE CHAPTER ON PESAKH), after the unique experience of receiving direct communication from Him at Sinai (SEE CHAPTER ON SHAVUOT), betrayed their saving God for a lump of precious metal.

Having secured another chance for the Israelites, Moses returned to the camp. Then, on the first of Elul, he again ascended, this time for the replacement tablets (DEUTERONOMY 10:10). While he was gone, the community fasted daily from sunrise to sunset, until the day of their leader's anticipated return—the tenth of Tishrei. Then they fasted from sunset to sunset. Moses found them remorseful, and announced that God accepted their repentance and commanded that the date remain the Day of Atonement throughout all generations.

AFTER THE COMMANDMENT Despite the fact that observing the tenth of Tishrei in the prescribed manner is "a law for all time" (LEVITICUS 16:29), like Rosh

Hashanah it may have been widely ignored during the First Commonwealth, a period of religious ignorance and laxity. The Talmud indicates it was totally suspended during the dedication of Solomon's Temple (I KINGS 8), which began two days before the holiday and seems to have continued with food, drink and festivities non-stop through Sukkot.

POST-BABYLONIA

In the Talmud, Rabbi Simeon ben Gamaliel makes a statement curious for what was supposed to be a solemn day on which the nation reconciled itself with God: "There were no happier days in Israel than the fifteenth of Av [SEE CHAPTER ON TISHA B'AV] and Yom Kippur." That's because for a time, the Day of Atonement had a split personality with dual purposes.

In the afternoon following the prescribed ritual, young girls dressed in white danced in the vineyards to catch the attention of eligible men. The poor wore borrowed clothes to eliminate apparent differences between the modestly situated and the aristocrat, and each maiden would encourage potential husbands to choose for her particular assets (the beautiful chiding them not to consider family position, the homely reminding them of the supremacy of inner beauty). Rabbi Gamaliel's comment referred to the many good marriages that resulted from the festival.

The overriding need to focus all attention on internal, spiritual concerns later determined a uniform character for the day. In the few hundred years following the Jews' return from their first exile, the holiday evolved into the holiest occasion of the year. Except for symbolic substitutions for previously performed ritual, it has changed little since.

Jewish writings tell us a great deal about the day's observance during the Second Temple period. Seven of the eight of Talmud tractate Yoma's chapters detail the High Priest's Temple service. Apocryphal books Ecclesiasticus and Jubilees (written in the second century BCE), document fragments from the Qumram Caves near the Dead Sea (the end of the Second Commonwealth), and the works of Philo of Alexandria, the Jewish philosopher who lived in the years surrounding the beginning of the Common Era, support and supplement what our sages recorded.

In addition to providing specifics about the preparation and performance of the Priest's duties based on Leviticus 16, the records tell us that the tenth of Tishrei—often referred to as "The Fast," "The Great Fast" (*Tzoma Rabbah*) or "Great Day" (*Yoma Rabbah*) in Talmud, and also as "Holy Day" (*Yom Hakodesh*)—was scrupulously observed not only by the pious or religious fanatics, but also by those who never acted religiously in other aspects of their lives or other days of the year (as is the case in our, and probably all, times). Those who did not go to Jerusalem spent the entire day in their local synagogues, abstaining from food and drink. Without the High Priest as intermediary, they actively confessed and prayed on their own behalf.

For the thousands who did celebrate in Jerusalem, entering the Temple in the extended procession behind the High Priest, participating in the prayers and witnessing the rituals, the atmosphere vibrated with the intensity of the drama and mystery of being close to God. Warned by Torah that he would not leave the Shrine alive unless he performed the Yom Kippur service properly (LEVITICUS 16:2–3), the High Priest spent the week prior to the holiday living on the Temple grounds in concentrated preparation, attended by the sages who helped him cleanse himself, review the law, procedure and Scripture, and guard against any last minute impurities that would render him unfit for service.

Unlike other days of the year, on this one the *Kohein Gadol* was required to officiate. And only on this, the holiest day of the year, could the holiest representative of the holist nation enter the holiest spot on earth: the High Priest, and only he, stepped into the Holy of Holies (the permanent version of the Tabernacle's Shrine), the innermost chamber of the Temple, considered God's earthly dwelling place. It was a privilege fraught with anxiety, for one impure thought by the Priest in such close proximity to the Ruler of the Universe would have resulted in his death. A personal tragedy, it also would affect the Israelites he represented in atoning for sin.

To be shielded from the full glory of God, the priest created a screen of smoke, as he had in the Shrine. Three times during the day he entered and emerged. And ten times he said the word not uttered at any other time or place: the ineffable name of God (*Shem Hameforash*), giving full body to the Tetragrammaton we recognize as the Hebrew letters yud, hei, vov, hei (YHVH), and say as *Adonai* (or religious Jews as Hashem, The Name). This was the name by which God identified Himself to Moses at the Burning Bush (EXO-DUS 3:14), a composite version of the verb "to be" (*l'hiyot*), defying tense and thereby suggesting timelessness and on-going creation. The pronunciation was so guarded only a high priest could learn it from his predecessor; we no longer know it. Overcome with feelings of humility and awe, at hearing the first syllable, every individual in the Temple congregation prostrated him/herself on the ground.

A designee led the goat chosen by lot for Azazel, his horns tied with a piece of wool dyed red, into the wilderness. Ten way stations intervened between the Temple and the cliff twelve miles distant, from which the goat was pushed to its death.

As the trip progressed, the High Priest chanted the portions of Torah dealing with Yom Kippur. By a system of signal flags the animal's escort relayed the message back to the Temple that the sins of Israel had been successfully disposed and, as the red wool had turned white (ISAIAH 1:18), the people had been absolved of their transgressions. With this reassuring news, and the emergence of the *Kohein Gadol* unharmed from God's chamber, the community rejoiced in the feast prepared by the Priest.

POST-TEMPLE

While gazing at the ruins of the Temple following the Roman siege (70 CE), Rabbi Joshua remarked, "Woe to us that the place where Jews were forgiven for their sins is destroyed." His teacher, the scholar and leader Rabbi Yokhanan ben Zakkai, replied, "We have another medium just as good for the forgiveness of sin. It is: Do good to mankind. For it is written, 'I desire mercy, not sacrifice' [HOSEA 6:6]" (AVOT DE RABBI NATAN 4).

The fact that we don't always "do good" to each other dictated the need for a day of atoning in the first place. With the destruction of the Temple, the means of achieving its purpose simply shifted from an external physical ritual—sacrifice, expulsion of the Azazel goat—to an internal psychological process—*teshuvah* and prayer.

In fact, the rabbis had worked hard to get the people to recognize that the rites and prayers of Yom Kippur were not magical formulas that alone would absolve the nation and the individuals in it of sin. This message was easier to convey once personal examination and catharsis replaced the collective purge represented by the Priest's confessions and the scapegoat.

From this more mature view, we can better understand that the goats functioned as an external representation of an internal dilemma. The animals were identical: same size, same sex, same color, same level of ritual purity. By lot, each having an equal chance, one was picked to die after serving God, the other to be relegated to death in the wilderness. Each person faces the same choices that determine the path of his/her life: to cast his/her lot with God, directing him/herself to achieving a high moral and spiritual level, or turning away from society to wander in a moral wasteland, which will lead to certain ruin. The word Azazel then suggests one who is lost or disappears (*azel*) to the force (or strength, *az*) of sin.

THROUGH THE AGES

Because of its deep psychological import, the Temple rite, in the form of being recalled, remained essential on Yom Kippur. Services changed only with poetic embellishment of descriptions drawn from Talmud, *piyyutim* of the Middle Ages, and the addition of a controversial introductory service, *Kol Nidrei,* on *Erev Yom Kippur.*

As it did in ancient times, Yom Kippur continued to pull people, if only temporarily, back to their religion. Even those holding no other connection with Judaism or the Jewish community during the rest of the year have always been drawn to the synagogue for at least part of the day, and take upon themselves the time-honored major form of affliction, fasting.

Throughout history, Jews risked their lives to participate in the communal cleansing, even in the direst circumstances. They gathered secretly in secluded cellars during the Spanish Inquisition. In makeshift corners in the Warsaw ghetto, in a worksite forest or field or behind a barracks in a concentration camp, the Jews could not let the day pass without honoring it with their prayer, and, even though already starving, forsaking food that could have meant their lives. (Yom Kippur was one of the days the Nazis would add to the Jews' torment by providing them with better food than usual.) The Jews in Mandate Palestine risked punishment by the British when they insisted on blowing the shofar at the Western Wall, and in the Soviet Union, long before the refuseniks had international support, Jews who had ostensibly forsaken their religion would often chance going to synagogue on this occasion.

The story of Franz Rosenzweig (1886–1929), philosopher and founder of the Frankfurt Lehrhaus, a Jewish free university for adult education, wonderfully illustrates the tremendous power of the day. Raised in an assimilated Jewish home where he had received little exposure to the meaning, significance and joy of his own religion, Rosenzweig planned to convert to Christianity. He decided to prepare himself to do so as a Jew, rather than a pagan, by attending Yom Kippur services. In a small Orthodox shul in Berlin, he was surprised to encounter a vitality and modern relevance to Judaism, and felt the closeness of God. Realizing that Judaism provided what he thought he could only find in the Church, and then some, he changed his plans and became a tremendous influence on Jewish life, even after his death.

With its potential for emotional and psychological impact —deeply experienced by our forebears and not at all lessened by the absence of the Holy of Holies or Azazel, it is no wonder Yom Kippur retains such a hold on Jews generally disengaged from their religious heritage. Even members of secular kibbutzim, who for years ignored the holiday, by the late twentieth century had returned to some form of observance. Perhaps fear motivates such people. Or reluctance to discard a last vestige of their tradition. Or recognition that there just could be something in it for them.

It is because of the almost universal observance of Yom Kippur that the Arabs made a serious tactical error when they decided to attack Israel on the holiday in 1973. Since virtually every Jewish Israeli was in synagogue or at home, mobilization of the Israel Defense Forces was much faster and easier than it would have been on a workday, when logistical chaos could have engulfed the country.

FOR FURTHER EXPLORATION

Exodus 32–34, Leviticus 16 and Deuteronomy 9:10–12, in any *Khumash*, detail the background to the first Yom Kippur, the requirements for its observance, and the High Priest's Temple service.

What Does It Mean? Religious Importance

You cannot fully understand the last of the Ten Days of Repentance without knowing something about the first, so you will find it helpful to refer to the previous chapter. The Jewish New Year it explains begins the intense process leading to a key pursuit of Judaism: atonement.

Read that as the quest for at-one-ment. It is striving to balance our souls and our selves (our true needs and potential versus our diverting desires and actuality). It is the attempt to counter our personal inclinations with concern for common good. And it is the reconciliation of humans as wasters of opportunity with God as Creator of an infinite number of chances to do the right thing. Stemming from a concept of the world in which humankind and the rest of the universe exist in harmony, Yom Kippur provides the opportunity for us to correct any disparities that result in disunity.

THE HUMAN–GOD PARTNERSHIP IN PROGRESS

God created human beings to work *with Him* in like-minded, shared-value partnership to perpetuate and perfect the world. Unfortunately, partnerships do not always run smoothly. A spouse has an extramarital affair. A business colleague neglects to fulfill a job's responsibilities. A party to a contract does not deliver promised goods. These failures get in the way of successfully meeting the objectives of the partnership agreement. They also create barriers between the people involved, impeding what could be mutually supportive and satisfying relationships.

We, the Jewish people connected throughout all time and place, accepted the contract for the endeavor called Judaism when we agreed to abide by the Torah offered to us at Mount Sinai (SEE CHAPTER ON SHAVUOT). Referring to the image in our tradition of Israel as the bride of God, some view it as a marriage contract. (This view gives new meaning to the custom of maidens dancing in the vineyards to attract husbands. Instead of being seen as taking advantage of an opportune holy occasion for betrothal, or a remnant of a primitive pre-harvest fertility rite, it becomes a reenactment in human terms of the first Yom Kippur, when Israel renewed her vows to God, fully embracing Him and His commandments.)

That contract, which we call a covenant, specifies that God will be our God, bringing blessings, protecting us, being accessible to us, and we will be His people, carrying His standards of morality to the world by exemplifying how people are supposed to treat each other. A condition of our acting as God's representatives on earth is that we be holy, dedicated to aspiring toward the best that we and the world can be.

When we idle after idols—money, recognition, immediate gratification, when we fail to act properly toward our fellow human beings, when we forsake quality by taking the easy path, we create negative ramifications on several levels. The direct results of our behavior cause objects, relationships, even people, to be broken. They prevent the world from moving forward toward completion. This means we can no longer live up to our side of the covenant. And this creates distance between us and our fundamental partner in the endeavor of life.

Just as the Torah teaches us how to right the wrongs we do to other people, it teaches us how to "make up" with God. Atonement, and the self-examination and confession that precede it, are the means to remove the obstacles to continuing our partnership and enjoying a mutually fulfilling relationship. Through the annual re-purification we once again become holy, which means we meet the precondition of our on-going covenant and are in the position to carry out our function according to it.

THE WHOLENESS OF HOLINESS

Being a holy nation—not set apart by God, but by our behavior—means being able to control our physical desires. The laws particular to Judaism, those that go beyond the ethical standards that apply to all humans equally, are designed to elevate us above our animal drives: kashrut (eating), *brit milah* (sex), tefillin and mezzuzah (thoughtless instinct), Shabbat (work). They exist to help us master the desires which, when indulged, lead us away from health and healthy relationships and distract us from concentrating our energies on meaningful pursuits.

Our tradition asserts that every single Jew, even one who ignores the laws, or is ignorant of them, has the potential for holiness. According to a kabbalistic version of the Creation story, before the light God made to dispel the darkness,

He created an illumination so powerful it would have allowed mankind to see from one end of the earth to the other. But the vessel into which God directed the light proved too weak to contain it and exploded into myriad glimmering shards. One of these bits of Divine light entered every Jewish soul, and therefore rests inside every Jew.

Referred to in Yiddish as *pinteleh yid,* this little spark can be understood as the inextinguishable Jewish essence, the potential for holiness each Jew possesses (and perhaps that inexplicable something that draws even the Jew most sepa-rated from the community to the synagogue on Yom Kippur). All the attention of introspection during this holiday season can fan the spark into a flame, making the God within us

Not trade but traits lead to riches or poverty.
KIDDUSHIN 4:14

recognizable. It happens as we clear away the impurities of wrongdoing.

The term usually used for this process of atonement, *kapparah,* and *kippur* share a root meaning "to cleanse thoroughly, to scour, to erase." It conveys the idea that wrongdoing is a stain to be thoroughly removed. Basic Jewish precept asserts that wrongdoing *can* be totally eliminated, that human beings, regardless of what evil we do, can regain our initial purity. Of the world's major religions, only Judaism sets aside a specific day for the completion of the process. At its close, we can stand again as the first human beings did immediately after Creation, unobstructed by prior transgressions or guilt, with the entire world of possibilities available to us.

This doesn't happen because God reaches into our depths with a scouring pad to rub out the blotches on our souls. It happens because we redirect our inner drives to meet our true, purposeful goals. While God grants us atonement by mercifully accepting our repentance and believing our sincere resolutions to do better, the purification we experience comes from our own efforts.

No matter how great they are, we will not attain God's level of holiness; we're not expected to because we are only human. Even Moses, who was closer to God than any other prophet, standing before Him and speaking directly with Him, was never allowed to see His face (EXODUS 33:20). (He also didn't arrive at his destination, but could only gaze at the Promised Land from a distance [DEUTERONOMY 32:48–52].) And the High Priests, from Aaron on, the only men allowed to enter the chamber in which God's presence rested, could not face God, but separated themselves from Him by creating a veil of incense smoke.

There will always be something, like the smoke, or the curtain at the entrance to the Holy of Holies, between us and the ideal level of holiness. But the value is not in the end point (ultimately death), but in the way we transform ourselves along the way. Life is a process, sometimes viewed in Judaism as a ladder on which we go up and down. We are supposed to push ourselves to climb up the ladder. What we learn on the journey, about ourselves, life and God, leads us to contribute to creating the conditions for the arrival of the messiah, an eternal process of improvement.

What Does It Mean to Us? Personal Significance

A well-known Talmud passage records the visit of a non-Jew to Hillel. The non-Jew promises to convert if the great sage can teach him the Torah while he stands on one foot. Hillel replies, "Do not do to others that which is hateful to you" (which we know, reworded, as The Golden Rule). "The rest is commentary. Now go and study." The ethical guideline is the essence of Judaism. Reflecting on how well we follow it is the essence of Yom Kippur.

Like Rosh Hashanah, Yom Kippur is very much about you. As you read through this chapter, you will see how every aspect of its observance relates to you as a unique individual who has a particular role in life, and you as a singular component of the Jewish people that has a particular mission in the world.

Ten days ago, you assessed your life, where it is going and whether its purpose is worthwhile. Today you concentrate on how well you measure up to standards of behavior for human beings, on who you are as a person, because the individual qualities that define you—honest or deceptive, sweet or bitter, scornful or supportive, debased or holy—ultimately determine the path you take and its endpoint.

One of our sages instructed his students to repent for all their wrong choices the day before death. When they pointed out that they wouldn't know when that would occur, he replied, "Then surely you must repent today in case you die tomorrow." If we heeded Rabbi Eleazar's teaching, we would constantly be aware of what we are doing with our lives, continually make adjustments to be sure we stay on track, regularly avoid putting off for another time the things likely to go unfinished if we do not do them today. Since we fail to follow Eleazar, we need at least one day a year to express remorse for our mistakes and our intentions to do better.

The confession we make on this holiday is identical to the one we are supposed to recite just before we die. But Yom Kippur provides us with more than a trial run. Facing imminent death, we can admit our wrongdoings and express regret for them, but we don't have the chance to actually change our behavior. On the Day of Atonement, that possibility still exists. On our deathbeds, if we do not like the answers to the questions "Has my life been worthwhile? Did I accomplish what I wanted to achieve? Did I achieve something meaningful? Was I a good person?" there's nothing we can do to change them. But if we don't like our answers on the tenth of Tishrei, we can take action on the eleventh.

On Rosh Hashanah we identified things in ourselves and in our relationships with others that we want to improve in the coming year. That provides us with goals. Now we need specific tasks that will allow us to meet them. The sixty-seven categories of behavior for which we ask forgiveness during the confession (SEE "OBSERVANCE") provide a convenient list from which each of us can pick items appropriate to our situation and agenda. Focus on the ones you fail to do to help yourself and others, or the things you are guilty of doing that create hindrances. Recognize how they limit the way you conduct your every day life. They define your character. (You can also do the opposite: focus on the *positive* things you do and think about how you can engage in more of them.)

For each of the improvements you want to make, concentrate on two or three concrete actions you can take, beginning immediately, which will contribute to the overall goal. For instance, if you have a negative outlook, you might decide that at the beginning and/or end of each day, you will list three things for which you can be thankful. If you are prone to gossip, you might limit phone conversations with a regular chat partner. If you are impolite to service personnel, you might make efforts to smile at or greet them, and remember to say "thank you."

Behaving more morally, more humanely—what in Yiddish might be called in *menschlikeit* manner—is what will make you feel closer to God (on Rosh Hashanah you also chose something to improve in relation to Him). That is the key to achieving the "spirituality" of this day—which is supposed to be the climax of the year, a religious phenomenon par excellence. Although we spend it in prayer, pouring our hearts out to God, believing that He cares enough to listen and that He will act on our pleas, we are supposed to recognize that it is merely a means to better ourselves and the world.

Our tradition includes moving tales of rabbis who leave *Selikhot,* or fail to appear for *Kol Nidrei,* because they are busy rocking a crying baby whose mother is not home or returning a stray cow to a non-Jewish neighbor. Although they are late in getting to the house of worship, with these and other *mitzvot* to aid the aged and poor, the rabbis of these stories are engaged in truly spiritual endeavors.

The challenge is to continue to be directed by concern for others once the holiday ends, to avoid relapsing back into habitual patterns of thought and action. Next Yom Kippur we will confess again, in all sixty-seven categories, with the rest of the nation. But if we have made the day meaningful for ourselves this year, we will be able to choose different areas in which to live more spiritually.

Traditions—

HOW WE CELEBRATE YOM KIPPUR

What Do We Use? Ritual Items

With one addition (SEE BELOW), the objects needed to fulfill the religious requirements of the holiday are the same ones used for Rosh Hashanah: shofar, *makhzor,* and *kittel.*

FOR FURTHER EXPLORATION

FOR ADULTS
See the previous chapter for books that supplement the prayer book.

FOR CHILDREN
Abrams, Judith Z. *Yom Kippur, A Family Service.* Rockville, MD: Kar-Ben Copies, Inc., 1990.
Designed for use with young children, the simple service explains prayer, repentance and charity and how to have a relationship with God. A companion tape is available. Ages 4–8. ✡

MEMORIAL CANDLE

Anyone who has lost a parent (some do it for grandparents) customarily lights a candle in memory of the deceased just before sundown on the eve of Yom Kippur (since *Yizkor* will be recited the next day). Available at grocery stores that have kosher food sections, or Jewish supply stores, the candles housed in small glasses or cans burn for twenty-five hours.

How Do We Celebrate? Observance

Since it is dedicated to spiritual pursuits, you may anticipate Yom Kippur as unnatural and uncomfortable, particularly if it is the only spiritual thing you do all year. But like every other aspect of Judaism, the acts we perform on this holiday have rich psychological underpinnings. Once you understand them, you will recognize that they are merely tools for our own growth.

All activity is centered in the synagogue, where services last virtually all day, usually with a short break of between forty-five minutes and an hour and a half depending on the speed and style of the *khazzan*. But no one takes attendance, so if this is beyond your endurance, stay only part of the day. Some participation is better than none, and you can acclimate yourself to spending hours in synagogue gradually. (Young people learn to fast this way, every year putting off eating for a longer length of time.)

If you prepare yourself by knowing what to expect and learning what the service means, you'll find that the day can have the kind of emotional and spiritual impact it did for our grandparents and great-grandparents, and continues to have for committed Jews throughout the world. The kinds of companion books mentioned in the chapter on Rosh Hashanah and below are highly recommended as aids.

PRIMING THE SOUL

In its instructions for observing the tenth of Tishrei (LEVITICUS 16:29,31; 23:27–32; NUMBERS 29:7–11), Torah specifies that we are to "afflict our souls." After searching Scripture and Mishnah in order to determine what affliction means, the rabbis identified five activities from which we abstain on the most solemn, but (despite the posture of many Jews, particularly of Eastern European background) not mournful, day of the year. The purpose is not to punish ourselves, but to gain control over our bodies and their potentially harmful appetites that can become ends in themselves: Rambam describes the prohibitions of Yom Kippur as "resting," as if not doing them were relief from ordeals. While not engaging in our normal daily concerns and pleasures, we become more conscious of how our physical urges so often lead us into trouble.

In Talmud's terms, for a brief time we elevate ourselves to the status of angels, who have no corporeal needs and whose sole role in the universe is to serve God. (The rabbis also explain that the things we abstain from are all those that make the soul comfortable in the body. Engaging in activities that make it uncomfortable make it more likely to rise up a bit from the body, taking us to a higher spiritual plane).

FASTING Derived directly from the Torah, abstaining from eating and drinking from before sundown until after the following sunset is probably the greatest test of self control during this holiday. How are we supposed to accept the promulgated notion that fasting frees us to worship when pangs in an empty belly and distaste in a parched mouth create strong distractions to concentration on lofty spiritual thoughts?

The abstention in and of itself cannot create a sense of spirituality. The idea is to be able to refrain from giving in to our impulses. We prove to ourselves that we can control our bodies in the extreme; under normal circumstances we should certainly be able to prevent our desires from leading to damaging excesses. Physically allowing the body to rid itself of the toxins our eating produces mirrors our efforts on this day to purge ourselves of the impurities of unhealthy thoughts and deeds.

Of course, in the extreme, the restriction of food and water results in death. On Yom Kippur, this concept has significance in two ways. First, as on Rosh Hashanah, the act of standing to be judged in a sense entails facing death, for we are waiting to see what the verdict in our trial will be, whether or not we will be written in the "Book of Life." By denying material sustenance to ourselves, we symbolically engage in self-sacrifice, a recognition of the fact that we deserve to be punished. That innocent animals lost their lives for human wrongdoing should have made people aware of their actions. Today it's not animals, but what, we should ask ourselves, is being sacrificed when we err?

Experiencing hunger that we know is temporary should also instigate us to do something for those who suffer from lack of food. This is the real purpose of the fast, as Isaiah explains in the day's prophetic reading. A problem since biblical times, it has not abated yet, with recurring wars, famines and other natural disasters leaving millions to die of starvation. When we resume feeding our bodies, we are revived, and as people who have experienced near death attest, feel as though we are starting over. When we do so, it should be with our priorities in order and a sense of renewed ability to properly direct our energies.

Since Torah stipulates that the fast begin on the ninth day, but we are to deny ourselves only on the tenth, it is understood that the fast begins before sundown and concludes the next day at nightfall.

To revive themselves during the long hours without food, worshippers sometimes sniff smelling salts (in former times, tobacco or snuff), spices, sprays of mint, flowers or a clove-filled etrog (citron) prepared after the previous Sukkot. Among the religious, spices are used this way just to give them the opportunity to say a *brakhah*. (The rabbis instructed that one hundred benedictions be said daily, which is more difficult on Yom Kippur than normally because of its restrictions. If you smell spices, the proper *brakhah* should be made (SEE "BLESSINGS").

MARITAL RELATIONS The normal and healthy drive, encouraged on Shabbat because it is an act seen to involve God and assist Him in on-going creation, is prohibited on Yom Kippur. Again, it is an appetite whose satisfaction can lead one into sin.

WASHING Cleansing oneself for pleasure or comfort is prohibited. Observant Jews do not shower, bathe, or wash their hands or faces, unless they are muddied. The focus of this day is on internal, rather than external cleanliness. We are not to think we are rid of soil just because we have applied soap and water to our skin.

ANOINTING The application of oil to the body was once done regularly, particularly after bathing, as part of the cleansing process. Today, anointing generally refers to the use of face and hand creams, which are not to be applied on Yom Kippur except for medicinal purposes. As for the prohibition against washing, thoughts should be directed to what needs to be cleaned out from the inside.

CHOICE OF SHOES You may notice a lot of people wearing sneakers—particularly the basic canvas and rubber models—to synagogue. It is not for comfort, although they certainly provide it with all the standing we do during the services. Wearing shoes (sandals in biblical days) of leather was forbidden in holy places, as we learned from Moses' experience before the Burning Bush (EXODUS 3:5), where he removed his sandals. The Kohanim removed their shoes when giving the Priestly Benediction in the Temple (as the Kohanim do today when they stand before the Ark in front of the congregation for the *Dukhan* service during which they make the blessing). Since the day of Yom Kippur entails a reliving of the Temple experience, we forego our leather shoes as well.

On the physical level, leather shoes protect the feet, providing comfort, while shoes of other materials, or going barefoot, do not. On the Day of Atonement, we forego bodily pleasure. Because of how they feel, and also their expense, even in biblical times leather shoes were considered a luxury (SONG OF SONGS 7:2), and thought to contribute to the wearer's feeling of pride and haughtiness. Since Yom Kippur and the entire Ten Days of Repentance are designed to produce feelings of humility, wearing leather shoes would interfere with one's proper frame of mind. (Despite the admonitions of over-zealous rabbis, the prohibition is specifically for leather shoes—whether the top or the sole is of leather—and not any other items made from the skins of animals.)

USHERING IN YOM KIPPUR

Although certain rituals completed prior to sundown on *Erev Yom Kippur* are not parts of the holiday itself, they are considered essential elements in its observance.

PRE-FAST MEAL Timed to end well before sundown, both so that the fast begins on Tishrei 9, as ordained, and so that you can arrive in synagogue in time for the initial services, eating the *seudah hamafseket* is considered as much a *mitzvah* as fasting the next day (SEE "TRADITIONAL FOODS"). Since the holiday has not yet begun, you do not recite the *kiddush* over wine, but it is appropriate to do a *motzi* (as religious Jews do at any meal) after the ritual handwashing (SEE "BLESSINGS").

As on Rosh Hashanah, we dip the bread into honey. *Shir Hama'alot* (Psalm 126), which expresses the desire to return to Zion, precedes the *Birkat Hamazon* as it does on Shabbat and festivals. Following the meal, it is traditional to put a clean white cloth on the table in honor of the festival. Books of Jewish significance are often placed on it to represent that prayer and Torah will suffice as sustenance on this day.

CANDLES Based on Proverbs and Prophets, candles are often used to illuminate the house: "For the commandment is a lamp [candle], and the teaching is light" (PROVERBS 6:23) recalls the Ten Commandments, the synopsis of the Torah that Moses brought to Israel on Yom Kippur. A midrash compares man's soul to a lighted candle and Isaiah's admonition to "honor the Lord with light" (58:13) refers to this holiday, when, since we cannot honor the day with feast, we do so by kindling many lights and wearing festive clothing. There should be at least one candle that will burn a full day, to provide a source for *Havdallah* at the close of the holiday.

It is also customary to light a memorial candle for deceased parents prior to kindling the *yom tov* candles with a blessing unique in that the name of the holiday replaces the standard *"yom tov."* *Shehekhiyanu* follows it (SEE "BLESSINGS").

BLESSING CHILDREN Many parents bless their children before going to synagogue. Just prior to their deaths, at the peak of their holiness, the patriarchs blessed theirs, and Moses blessed the children of Israel. On *Erev Yom Kippur,* we are, in a symbolic way, about to purify ourselves and experience death, so we offer similar blessings, expressing the hope that our children not sin, study Torah, love God and be granted long fulfilling lives. Longer than the normal Shabbat *brakhot,* they form a beautiful expression of anything a parent could wish for a child. (The text can be found at the front of a standard *makhzor*).

SYNAGOGUE

We observe Yom Kippur, unlike any other holiday on the calendar, exclusively in the synagogue. The day has the largest number of prayer services of any day of the year, five—*Ma'ariv* (evening, on *Erev Yom Kippur,* preceded before sundown by *Kol Nidrei*), and *Shakharit* (morning), *Mussaf* (additional), *Minkhah* (afternoon) and *Neilah* (closing) on the day of the tenth. (If you attend services in a traditional synagogue, you may see people standing not only for the parts of the service that require the congregation to rise, but also for the entire proceedings. They do so by custom originally based on a midrash claiming that when the Adversary (SEE "HISTORIC FOUNDATION" IN CHAPTER ON ROSH HASHANAH) beholds all of Israel upright before God, he will be forced to liken the Jews to angels who stand before God free of sin.)

With its sheer almost unbroken devotion to prayer, Yom Kippur may seem, for those unused to attending services, even more daunting than Rosh Hashanah. To get something out of the experience, read or reread the section on prayer in the previous chapter and obtain a book that will guide you through the *makhzor.* It will make an incredible difference in your appreciation and observance of the holiday.

FOR FURTHER EXPLORATION

Sorscher, Moshe. *The Companion Guide to the Yom Kippur Prayer Service.* New York. Judaica Press, 1995. This beginner's guide uses parables, essays, selected transliterations and explanations of significant prayers to add meaning to the Yom Kippur synagogue experience. Page references to several of the most popular *makhzorim* are provided.

LITURGY Expanding on the themes of the Rosh Hashanah services, the notions of sin as alienation from God, reconciliation as a human need, atonement as a possibility through inner change, and individual accountability for the status of the world pervade the prayers. A phrase from Ecclesiastes expresses the universal need to go through the process: "There is not a righteous man upon earth who does good and does not sin" (7:20). In his Yom Kippur confession, the High Priest used three different words for sin, which the Talmud explains express progressive stages in our gradual movement away from God: *khet,* an unwitting offense (and the word graciously used in our confessions), *avon,* an act of insolence, and *pesha,* an overt act of rebellion. On Yom Kippur, we take the steps that will lead us back in the other direction.

CONFESSION The central aspect of the liturgy is the confession of sin,

Viddui (literally "declaration"). The same as the prayer said prior to death (and by a groom, who is forgiven for his sins and considered a new man when he weds), it deals with moral transgressions between one person and another.

It consists of two parts, the *Viddui Ze'ira,* minor declaration, beginning *Ashamnu* (We have become guilty), and made up of a one-word transgression for each letter of the alphabet, a total of twenty-three; and *Viddui Rabbah* (major declaration), beginning *Al khet* (For the sin . . .), consisting of two more specific expressions of wrongdoing for every letter of the alphabet, a total of forty-four. (The Sephardim reduce the catalogue to a few lines.)

Together they cover a range of human behavior of an ethical nature (entrapping a neighbor, running to do evil, haughty eyes, hard-heartedness, immorality, scorning, being obstinate, giving evil counsel, and so on). Ten times during the course of Yom Kippur we recite *Viddui.* (This coincides with the ten times the High Priest pronounced the name of God, and recalls the Ten Commandments Israel accepted on Yom Kippur, the tenth day of the seventh month and the last of the Ten Days of Repentance.)

We say the *Ashamnu* both to ourselves and aloud as a congregation, the *al khets* to ourselves, with the exception of the refrain. It divides the list into four sections and is sung together three times: "For all these, O God of forgiveness, forgive us, pardon us, atone for us" (*V'al kulam, Elohei selikhot, s'lakh lanu, m'khal lanyu, kaper lanu*). It is customary to stand with your head bowed and to hit your breast (lightly thump your right fist over your heart) as you mention each *khet,* since the heart is viewed as the seat and source of sin. It is natural to feel a pang as you come to a *khet* that applies to your own behavior (the rabbis said you should experience such feeling). If you committed a wrong somehow omitted from the list, you are supposed to add it to your private declaration.

The fourth- or fifth-century originators of the recitation chose the alphabet acrostic format to emphasize that each sin, represented by a letter, destroys the world, which according to midrash God created using the letters of the Torah. (The Hebrew alphabet is believed to be a complex and mystical system whose letter forms and names contain intricacies that hint at the secrets of the world and give the words they comprise levels of meaning.) By essentially going through God's building blocks as we admit our shortcomings and ask for His forgiveness, we remind Him how He felt when He gave us the Torah at Mount Sinai: like a groom for a bride on their wedding day. It is a way to encourage His mercy.

Aside from the whole experience of prayer itself, a lot of us have difficulty with this formula for communal confession. Most of us are good, decent people, trying hard to live our lives properly, with concern for others. We may resent having to admit to something we may have successfully resisted, never contemplated—maybe never even knew existed. We may believe that with all our upright living and social awareness, we have nothing to confess, or at least nothing on a scale of sixty-seven categories.

One of the first things you notice in this long list of transgressions you've hardly enjoyed is that they all are in the plural: *we* have betrayed, *we* have robbed, for the sin that *we* sinned before You. . . . Everyone confesses to every sin. This is to emphasize that each of us is part of and responsible for the whole community of Israel. It makes us recognize that as individuals, we are inseparable parts of the Jewish people. Our status as a nation, the extent to which together we are living up to our mission, affects all of us and vice versa. If a fellow Jew sins, it is as if you yourself sinned. Like it or not, we *are* our brothers' and sisters' keepers. By confessing together, we share the burden of our shortcomings, and express our responsibility for each other.

Part of the strength in Judaism comes from the concept that every Jew, dead and alive, from Mount Sinai until the present moment, appears before God as one entity. Each of us is as much an integral part of the collective Israel as one of our hands or legs or eyes is to our individual bodies. The interrelatedness is so deep, our tradition holds that every Jewish soul that would ever be on earth, whether embodied at the time or not, was actually present at Sinai. We *were* the desert-bound ex-slaves who accepted responsibility for fulfillment of the covenant onto ourselves—all Jews, forever. And it is because we are intimately connected through time and space that Judaism places such emphasis on the collective.

Through this relationship, one Jew can, and is obligated to, act on behalf of others. As personal as *teshuvah* (repentance [SEE CHAPTER ON ROSH HASHANAH]) and atonement are, Yom Kippur worship is not something to be done in solitude any more than you pray only for your own needs. A successful final outcome for the Jewish people depends on our common efforts as individuals.

The Talmud says: "If an individual repents, God forgives him and the entire world" (YOMA 86b). We have the models of Moses and the *Kohein Gadol* to show us that one person can bring atonement for the nation. For this reason, we recall the matriarchs, patriarchs and other righteous members of our community throughout our history, so we will be judged based on their merits. At the same time, each of us is to be the one person becoming more holy for everyone's benefit, and not count on someone else to carry us along with his or her efforts.

As a community, we have surely run the gamut of offenses during the previous year. Within the litany of communal wrongs, each of us can apply the appropriate ones to ourselves. But the *makhzor's* convenient itemization serves us well in another way. It reminds us of errors in judgment, missed chances to do good, certain infractions that we might have forgotten; it identifies wrongdoings we might not think of as *khets*. (Do you know that gossip is against Jewish law—even spreading positive information about another person? What about showing contempt for parents or teachers? Or foolish speech?) As broad headings, each item mentioned can start us thinking about subcategories that ring bells for us.

DIVINE ATTRIBUTES OF MERCY When Moses asked God to reveal Himself so that the prophet would be better able to represent Him to the Israelites, God arranged for Moses to stand in a mountain cleft and see Him from behind. As God passed by, He indicated His nature: "Lord [merciful before one has sinned], Lord [merciful to the repentant sinner], All Powerful, Compassionate, Gracious, Slow to Anger, Abundant in Kindness and Truth, Preserver of Kindness for thousands of generations, Forgiver of Iniquity, willful sin and error, and Who Cleanses" (EXODUS 34:6–7; TALMUD, ROSH HASHANAH 17b). A total of twelve times during Yom Kippur we chant after the cantor *"Adonai, Adonai, El rakhum v'khanun, erekh appayim, verav khesed v'emet, notzer khesed la'alafim, noseh avon vahpeshah v'khahta'ah v'nakkeh."*

According to midrash, God instructed Moses to tell the Israelites that whenever they needed God's mercy, they could appeal for it by reciting these Thirteen Attributes of Mercy. On the one day a year devoted to winning God's favor, we intone the description that, as much as it summons God's forgiveness, reassures us that it will be given. It is no wonder we repeat it, with increasing fervor, seven times alone during the last service of the day.

REPEATED REFRAINS A number of other prayers embodying key themes of the Yom Kippur process recur throughout the liturgy. They express recognition of our place relative to the King of the Universe and our deepest hopes to be granted a favorable life. They all have catchy, easily learned tunes that invite participation.

KOL NIDREI With its beautiful haunting melody; the crescendo increasing with each of its three consecutive renditions taking it through sadness, warmth, beseeching and ultimately confidence; the two Torah scrolls previously paraded around the sanctuary held by synagogue leaders flanking the *khazzan;* and the full attention of the congregation (often a larger crowd than at any other point in the Yom Kippur service, with the possible exception of *Yizkor* or *Neilah*), the chant that ushers in Yom Kippur seems the essence of spirituality. For many people, it is a defining point of the holiday

Actually just an introduction to Yom Kippur's first service, *Ma'ariv*, expressed before the sunset signaling the start of *yom tov*, *Kol Nidrei* is not even a prayer. Meaning "all vows," it is a legal formulation relinquishing individuals from the responsibility to fulfill certain promises.

Of uncertain origin, it may have begun during a time when Jews were forced to convert to Islam or Christianity, and did so only outwardly, to save themselves. (Romantic legend has it that the plaintive tune we find so soul wrenching, as though a musical rendition of our bitter history, was composed by secret Jews during the Spanish Inquisition.)

Recited since before the ninth century, it likely had less dramatic origins than the remorse of crypto-Jews. Torah considers a vow sacred. One is not to be made casually, and once expressed, must be fulfilled (NUMBERS 30:3, DEUTERONOMY 23:22–24). The Talmud provides a loophole of sorts by stating that anyone who won't be fulfilling an oath—and this is only an oath of a personal, usually religious nature that does not involve another individual—should declare so at the beginning of the year. (Although *hatarat nedarim* still takes place before Rosh Hashanah, as it did in Talmudic times, during the Medieval period Yom Kippur was chosen as the occasion for the communal declaration since more people attended synagogue then.)

Centuries-long controversy arose between proponents of the annulment, and opponents who objected to the whole idea of granting a blanket release from promises that by their nature had the force of law. They argued, with justification, that it undermined the value of one's word. Many rabbis still forbade it after a descendant of Rashi, the great eleventh-century Torah commentator, changed the language so that the declaration is in advance for vows that will be made in the coming year, rather than after the fact for vows that had been made since the last Yom Kippur. Nevertheless, since people continued to make unfulfillable vows, the custom remained.

Anti-Semites, dismissing the fact that *Kol Nidrei* does nothing to free one of responsibilities to others, seized on it as proof of a Jew's untrustworthiness. After repeated complaints to Russian authorities in Kurland in the mid-1800s, a special introduction had to be written into the prayer books stating that the declaration applied only to vows exclusively involving the person who made them, and only applied to that person's relationship with God. At the same time, *Kol Nidrei's* melody so enticed Christians that it was once routine for them to visit synagogues on *Erev Yom Kippur* so they could hear it. (The composers Beethoven and Bruch both used it in their works.)

If you have done your fellow man a little wrong, let it be a great wrong in your eyes and rectify it. If you have done him much good, let it be little in your eyes. If he has done you a little good, let it be great in your eyes. If he has done you a great wrong, let it be little in your eyes.

RABBI NATHAN

Between 1844 and 1961, when it reinstated the declaration, the Reform movement abolished *Kol Nidrei* (often using Psalm 130, as the Jews of Palestine had before the existence of *Kol Nidrei,* to open their service). The Reconstructionists tried to eliminate the nullification as well, but ended up introducing a new form written by the movement's founder, Mordecai Kaplan.

Except for the Italian rite, which uses a Hebrew version, *Kol Nidrei* remains in Aramaic, the vernacular at the time it was written. The Italian Jews and Sephardim retain the original language of retroactive release, while the Ashkenazim take the proactive approach.

Since it is prohibited, in accordance with Talmud, to ask for release from vows on Sabbath or a festival unless the vows directly concern those days, *Kol Nidrei* must be recited prior to the start of Yom Kippur. Because of this timing, the men wear their talleisim, which are usually not put on for evening services. (The *mitzvah* concerning the wearing of ritual fringes specifies that they be seen

[NUMBERS 15:39], interpreted to mean during daylight. If one arrives late and puts on the tallit after sunset, the usual *brakhah* is omitted.) The sight of the men in their prayer shawls, a sea of white gently swaying to the bittersweet chant, adds to the aura of the occasion.

The men standing next to the *khazzan* make up the symbolic court needed for annulment of vows, and represent Aaron and Hur, who stood on either side of Moses, supporting his arms in the battle against Amalek (EXODUS 17:12). Each repetition of the declaration, said three times like any court's proclamation, expresses greater comfort in standing before the Judge. The first is almost suppressed, a whisper of awe at being in the King's palace, especially to make a request. The last shows confidence and relief at recognizing that the Ruler is a merciful father figure.

While it is as easy to dismiss the meaning of *Kol Nidrei* as it seems to excuse any ill-conceived vows we might make in the next twelve months, we should look beyond its dull legalese. We all know how difficult it is to live up to promises— especially the ones we make to ourselves. (How many New Year's resolutions have you broken? How many times have you relapsed into smoking, overeating, etc.?). Once we are away from the intensity of the situation that fostered the promise, it is easy to give in to the habitual behavior we vowed we would break. It takes a tremendous amount of will power and self-discipline to follow through on our good intentions. When we succeed, we are living up to our word. During this declaration, we should think about what our word really means, not only to ourselves, but also to anyone who trusts us based on what we say.

FOR FURTHER EXPLORATION

Gershon, Stuart Weinberg. *Kol Nidrei: Its Origin, Development & Significance.* Northvale, NJ: Jason Aronson, 1994.

> The analysis of the renunciation that ushers in the Day of Repentance and its purpose provides insights into its spiritual and legal significance, and several versions of the music to which it is chanted. ☺☆

FASTING WITH SINNERS Just before the cantor begins *Kol Nidrei,* he recites (three times, as it is another legal statement) a declaration permitting the congregation to pray with transgressors. Instituted to allow those who had been banned from the community (and those who had removed themselves from it by pretending to convert to another religion) to take part in the rites of repentance, it was based on the Talmud's assertion that a public fast is not a fast unless all Jews, including sinners, participate. (It points out that just as the Torah includes the malodorous spice *khelbanah* among the essential ingredients of the incense offering [EXODUS 30:34], transgressors are accepted as part of the Jewish people.) However, if we remember the passage from Ecclesiastes, that there is not a person on earth, no matter how righteous, who has not sinned, we realize that all of us gathered in the synagogue have transgressed, and should feel compassion and closeness in our shared experience of the day. Just as we wish others to forgive us, we should be moved to forgive others. Even those who show up only once a year, even those who have been away from Judaism a long time, are still considered part of the community. And while the community welcomes them back with open arms, they have the perfect opportunity to express the desire to be included.

UNINTERRUPTED SERVICE According to a tradition that the Yom Kippur evening service that follows *Kol Nidrei* never ends, some worshippers spend the night in the synagogue. They might sleep there, and usually study Talmud tractates Yoma and Keritot or read Psalms. Kabbalists believe that since "the gates of understanding" are open, it is a good night to study the secrets of the Torah (Jewish mysticism).

To be sure that people would not weaken themselves so much that they would be unable to participate in the next day's services, rabbis often suggested to congregants that they would do better to rest during the night. Some Reconstructionist congregations close their evening services with personal meditation that allows worshippers to leave whenever they are satisfied with their thoughts on forgiveness, so that the service never officially concludes.

SHAKHARIT The morning Torah reading (LEVITICUS 16) details the unique service performed by the High Priest on Yom Kippur. It begins with a reference to the tragic death of Aaron's sons, who were consumed by the "strange fire" (LEVITICUS 10:1–2) they produced in defiance of God's specific directions. (The Sephardim introduce the reading with a special *piyyut*, a dirge in memory of the sons, designed to produce tears based on the rabbinic teaching that one who cries on Yom Kippur for the passing of Aaron's sons will not lose a child.)

The passage serves to warn us not to take any transgression, however seemingly minor, lightly, and that not even the highly placed are immune to the dangers of sin or punishment for it. Judaism teaches that the standard by which one is judged becomes more stringent as one's status or knowledge increases. Aaron himself, brother of Moses, leader in Moses' absence, the High Priest who made peace in the community and brought many people close to Torah, could not save his own children.

In fact, he was responsible for their deaths: "The sin of the father is visited upon his sons" when a parent sets a bad example followed by his offspring. Though not punished immediately for it, Aaron sinned by allowing the Israelites to make the Golden Calf; he was the one who wrongfully used fire to mold the idol. The death of his sons by flame, for their illicit fire, was his punishment as much as theirs.

The detailed description of the sacrifices of the day is capped by the *maftir* commanding us to fast and reviewing the order of sacrifices (NUMBERS 29:7–11).

The Haftarah (ISAIAH 57:14–58:14), tells us what the meaning and endeavor of this day are supposed to be. The prophet criticizes those who think that going through the motions of self-affliction as purely physical acts will lead to atonement. The ultimate purpose of a fast day, he admonishes, is not to show God or others how pious we are by standing all day, fasting, beating our chests and calling out His name. External acts are good only to the extent that they lead us to more moral behavior: freeing the oppressed, feeding the hungry, and taking other justice-oriented action.

YIZKOR The memorial service for souls of the departed follows *Shakharit* (SEE CHAPTER ON PESAKH FOR FULL EXPLANATION). A custom since Talmudic times, it may have been introduced at the Yom Kippur service in recognition of Aaron's sons, and was later given added meaning because of historic developments (SEE CHAPTER ON SHAVUOT) and added to the services on the other festivals. Reflecting on human mortality is especially appropriate on this day, as it generates feelings of humility. Although some whose parents are still alive have the superstition of leaving the sanctuary, it is considered a *mitzvah* for everyone to participate in the service. However, anyone who has not completed a year of mourning for a parent does leave, as s/he could be overcome with sorrow and inadvertently disturb others on a day when mourning is prohibited.

Since giving charity is an integral part of the remembrance, most synagogues conduct their annual appeals for funds just before the service begins. Sephardim conduct their version of *Yizkor* before *Ma'ariv* the previous evening, the time when some congregations hold their appeals. Conservative congregations add introductory readings and verses from Psalms, and the Reform, who shorten the traditional text and add Psalm 23 and poems from the Middle Ages, hold *Yizkor* just before *Neilah*.

The service begins between 11:00 AM and noon in most synagogues. Those who exited the sanctuary return for the closing prayer, *Av Harakhamim* (Father of compassion) for all the Jews martyred for their faithfulness. Many congregations follow with special prayers for Holocaust victims and soldiers who have died defending the State of Israel.

MUSSAF The focal point of the early afternoon service is a review, in all its detail, of the *Avodah* (service) performed by the *Kohein Gadol,* the ceremony of sacrifice, scapegoat and seclusion in the Holy of Holies (SEE "HISTORIC FOUNDATION"). The rendition we read is a poetically enhanced version of the text from the Talmud.

You may get an inkling of the emotional pitch this service generated in past generations if you go to a traditional synagogue. There, at the part of the ceremony in which the High Priest mentioned the *Shem Hameforash,* the entire congregation, not just the khazzan, will often kneel on the floor, then prostrate themselves, their heads nearly touching the ground (or, in crowded synagogue rows, they will touch their knees and foreheads to the ground) as those who attended the Temple service did, calling out "Blessed be His glorious sovereign Name for ever and ever" (*Barukh Shem kavod malkhuto l'olam voed*).

This phrase, part of daily prayer, is normally said in an undertone. Forbidden at one time by rulers who considered it subversive, the Jews acquiesced—except on Yom Kippur, when they insisted on shouting it, as had their forebears at the Temple. Except for the Reform, who say it aloud year-round to demonstrate their freedom in our society, the practice is continued by tradition, based on two midrashim.

When Jacob was about to die, says one, he called his sons to his bedside so he could reveal to them all that would happen until the end of time. When the Divine spirit departed from him, thwarting his plan, the dying patriarch wondered if perhaps some taint in his family had caused the situation. His sons replied, "Hear O Israel [Jacob, their father], the Lord our God, the Lord is one [the text of the *Shema* (DEUTERONOMY 6:4)]. Our faith in God is complete, in our hearts, just as in yours, there is only one God." To which Jacob replied "*Barukh Shem. . . .*" The rabbis who could not agree as to whether these words should be incorporated into the *Shema,* since they are not directly quoted in the Torah, compromised by adding them in undertone.

The other tale relates that Moses heard the angels reciting the verse when he went up Mount Sinai, and taught it to the Israelites. But since he felt humans did not have a right to the property of higher beings, he instructed that it be said quietly. On Yom Kippur, when we elevate ourselves to the level of angels, it is permissible for us to use it openly.

The prostration occurs four times, at each retelling of the High Priest's confession, when he pronounced God's name, and at *Mussaf Aleinu,* which also recalls the Yom Kippur *Avodah.* Outside of traditional synagogues, only the *khazzan* prostrates himself, or the congregation bows, as do the Sephardim.

The Reform movement eliminates the description of the sacrifices, limiting its *Avodah* to the confession, minus the prostration. Prayers stressing Israel's moral responsibility are added. The Conservative keep most of the traditional *Avodah,* which they recite in the vernacular rather than in Hebrew, and include new prayers relevant to contemporary life.

Although it is easy in our ecologically minded, animal rightist environment to understand the Reform movement's rejection of the whole idea of symbolic sacrifice, if we know a little Hebrew, we can at least gain an appreciation for how the ancient Jews derived spiritual benefit from a practice we generally find primitive and abhorrent.

The word for sacrifice, *korban,* comes from the verb "to sacrifice," *hekriv,* which means to draw close. "Near," or "close by"—and a "relative"—is *karov,* relationship is *kirvah.* Sacrifice then was a way to get closer to God. Its value was not in being a gift to Him, but in changing the feelings of the giver. When we "make a sacrifice," don't we do so in order to be nearer reaching a goal, or in order to help another person—which makes us feel closer to that person? That's the feeling the ancient Israelites had toward God, and the feeling we, through our form of service—prayer—can hope to achieve.

The Ten Martyrs Shortly after the *Avodah,* we read an incredibly moving poem depicting the gruesome deaths of famous Talmudic sages brutally killed by the Romans during Hadrian's reign. Not historically accurate (all ten men did not die at the same time), it was written after the Crusades to put the martyrdom of Jews into the perspective of our people's history of being sacrificed for our beliefs. Evoked on Yom Kippur so that the sacrifices of the martyrs may bring forgiveness for their descendants (that connection through time and space notion), it is often followed by prayers and readings on—sometimes by—victims of the Holocaust. (We recite a different version of the martyrdom of the sages on Tisha B'Av.)

MINKHAH Unlike other festivals, the afternoon service includes a Torah reading (like the afternoon service on Shabbat), and a Haftarah.

Illicit Liaisons The Torah portion (LEVITICUS 18), details forbidden sexual relations. A "hint" to God, according to midrash, that just as He commanded us not to uncover our bodies for immoral purposes, He should not expose our sins, it may have been chosen as a further reminder of the kinds of base behavior that result from the weaknesses we try to overcome on the Day of Atonement. Since this was a time for young men to choose brides, the laws on liaisons were an appropriate way to instruct young people. Later it was considered a warning against temptation, as the women customarily attended synagogue in elegant attire. (Some congregations follow the minority choice in the Talmud and instead read the next chapter of Leviticus, which deals with holy behavior and social justice.)

Jonah For the prophetic portion, we read the children's favorite, the book of Jonah. It tells the story of the reluctant prophet who spent time in the belly of a "great fish." Rather than go warn a Gentile city that it would be destroyed if its inhabitants did not repent, as God sent him to do, Jonah tried to sail to a faraway destination. He couldn't bear the thought that the non-Jews would better heed God's word than would his own intractable people.

He did not recognize that as a Jew, his role entailed being a universal voice, spreading God's word to all nations. In the end, Jonah learned what we learn from his story: God cares about all living things. While Jonah believes in strict justice—he just wants God to destroy the place and be done with it—God judges with compassion and prefers that the Ninevites repent rather than that He destroy them. And when the Ninevites' repentance is accepted, it is not because they have performed rituals, but because they changed their behavior. We're supposed to recognize that if these people could repent, anyone can.

The other message is that it is impossible to evade God's presence or a destiny of service to Him. Although Jonah tried to disappear from his appointed path, God never lost track of his whereabouts. Like it or not, Jonah could not escape from his destiny any more than the Jewish people can escape from ours, our obligation to the people of all nations, to the world, to serving God. (When Jonah is asked by his shipmates "What is your occupation and from where do you come?" he replies, "I am a Hebrew. And I fear God." That identification defined him, and his place in the world. All else was secondary.)

NEILAH As the sun's rays begin to retreat to the treetops, we begin the last service of the day, *Neilah*, or *Neilat ha-Shearim* (closing of the gates). Originally referring to the shutting of the Temple gates at sunset, the image of the heavenly gates, which had stood open all this time to receive our supplications, slowly coming together to block accessibility to forgiveness, adds great poignancy to these last moments of appeal. The Ark is representationally kept open, and all those physically able stand for the duration of the service.

Suddenly, it can seem as though the day has ended all too fast, and we can be overtaken by a sense of urgency in getting in all our pleas for God's favor. However, since we believe, because of God's nature, that our outcome will be good, the service is chanted in a confident, happy melody. We make our last confessions, but the focus of our prayers shifts to acknowledgement of God's grace. Requests that we be sealed in the Book of Life replace all previous requests to write us in it.

As *Neilah* ends, the congregation joins the *khazzan* in the final declaration of faith: The *Shema* is chanted just once (repetition might be misconstrued as implying there is more than one God). We repeat the rejoinder phrase, *"Barukh Shem kavod . . ."* three times, emphasizing God's rule in the past, present and future. And seven times we recite *"Adonai, Hu HaElohim"* (The Lord, only He is

God [I KINGS 18:39]), escorting the Holy Presence back through the seven heavens (which God revealed to Israel at Mount Sinai to prove that there was no other God but Himself). In loud voice, the congregation is proclaiming its loyalty to God, and affirming that He and He alone is the force behind nature and history.

One blast of the shofar concludes the service. It recalls the proclamation of the Jubilee (*Yovel*), which was announced by shofar on Yom Kippur every fiftieth year (LEVITICUS 25:8–10). When we lost track of the start of the cycle, it became custom to blow the shofar annually in commemoration. But the symbol of the Jubilee holds for every year, for it emphasizes freedom from past burdens and the opportunity for everyone to start over again (LEVITICUS 25:10–17).

It is greeted with a rousing round of *"L'shanah haba'ah b'Yerushalayim,"* next year in Jerusalem, the goal of Jews throughout our historical and spiritual wanderings.

At this point, everyone wants to rush from synagogue to break the fast. But the regular evening service (*Ma'ariv*), *Havdallah,* and the blessing of the new moon, which had been put off until now, must still be completed. Altogether, they add about fifteen minutes to the time in synagogue. As great rabbis have pointed out, the way you take leave of someone is as important as the way you greet that person. Think about the awe and anticipation you felt just twenty-five hours ago. Think about everything you have meditated on during the day, all you tried to accomplish. Think about in Whose presence you stood all these hours, what you requested and what you promised. And think about others in the congregation, who want to finish the worship. In this context, you will probably be reluctant to disrespectfully race out of the sanctuary.

HAVDALLAH The close of Yom Kippur coincident with the close of Shabbat requires the full Shabbat *Havdallah*. On a weeknight, we do a shortened version of the ceremony of separation between holy and ordinary time. We omit the benediction over spices. (According to tradition, on the Sabbath each Jew receives an extra soul, *neshama yethera,* which leaves at the end of the day. The spices are to revive us from this loss.) We do say the blessing over fire usually not included in *Havdallah* after a *yom tov*—as long as the flame used to kindle the *Havdallah* candle has been burning all day (SEE "BLESSINGS").

NEW MOON In a totally happy mood impossible until this point in Tishrei because of the impending judgment that had been ahead of us, we may now properly bless the moon (*kiddush lavana*). Some congregations go outside to do so (SEE "THE JEWISH CALENDAR").

MITZVOT

In the tradition that completion of one mitzvah leads to performing another ("They go from strength to strength" [PSALMS 84:8]), and since Yom Kippur is supposed to awaken us to more devoted living, pious Jews often precede or interrupt the breaking of their fast by erecting at least the first posts of their *sukkot*. It expresses readiness for the next holiday, to emerge from the internal focus and take positive action in the outside world (SEE NEXT CHAPTER).

Where Do We Begin? Preparation

As one of our scholars of old pointed out, if you faced sentencing from the king of your country, all your attention and efforts would be directed toward defending yourself. Consumed with worry about the outcome, and knowing that you had to do everything possible to influence it, you would take a leave of absence from your job and refuse to be distracted by other matters.

Obviously, he was making a point about being in anticipation of facing your life-or-death verdict from God. It behooved everyone, he suggested, to cut back on normal activities in order to spend time alone, devoted to self-examination, focusing psychological and emotional energy and physical activity on the purpose of the holidays.

SPIRITUAL READINESS

The day of sentencing is the last of the forty-day period that begins on the first of Elul. Since all the preparation for Rosh Hashanah, and the New Year itself, is preparation for Yom Kippur, it will be helpful for you to review the section on preparation in the previous chapter. The mood, special prayers, extreme care in carrying out *mitzvot* and caution in not transgressing them continue during the intervening days of repentance as we focus more keenly on the specific improvements we can make. And of course, you cannot be ready to engage in the significance of Yom Kippur if you have not done *teshuvah* (SEE CHAPTER ON ROSH HASHANAH).

A time of mending existing relationships, it is considered unsuitable for starting new ones, so weddings and lawsuits are avoided during the ten days.

TZEDAKAH

Since charity (along with prayer and repentance) can "avert the evil decree," or influence the balance in your favor, the period prior to the Day of Atonement is particularly auspicious for donating to worthy causes. Synagogues usually have *tzedakah* boxes to accept contributions; today you are likely to be solicited by mail or phone by any number of deserving and needy social service organizations in the Jewish community. This is a good time to pay any outstanding pledges made in the past year.

TZOM GEDALIAH

The third of Tishrei (or the fourth, if the third is a Sabbath) marks the murder on the New Year of the last Jewish governor of Israel after the destruction of the First Temple. (The sun-up to sundown fast is postponed since Rosh Hashanah is a festival, when fasting is prohibited.) One of the four days of mourning connected with loss of Jewish sovereignty in the Land of Israel, it falls at this point coincidentally, but conveniently shares in its liturgy and readings from *Tanakh* the messages of this holiday season: sin, repentance and forgiveness (SEE CHAPTER ON TISHA B'AV FOR FULL EXPLANATION).

SHABBAT SHUVAH

The Sabbath between Rosh Hashanah and Yom Kippur is named Sabbath of Penitence after the prophetic reading for the day (HOSEA 14). Its first words, *"Shuvah Yisrael"* exhort Israel to "Return . . . unto the Lord your God." Before it was standard for rabbis in Eastern Europe to deliver a *d'rash* (sermon) at every Sabbath morning service, it was customary to do so on this day. Lengthy and impassioned talks on the related topic of *teshuvah* were supposed to be given in a spirit of encouragement, without attacking or disparaging the congregation. While there's no guarantee of the tone of a sermon today, you can be sure the topic will be the same.

RECONCILIATION

Since admitting wrongdoing and asking forgiveness before God cannot atone for any transgressions you have made in relation to another person, it is essential to ask forgiveness of anyone you may have hurt during the previous year. As with our confessions in synagogue, we don't always realize that we have done something wrong, and may not recognize that a word or an act has in fact hurt another person. Often this is the case with people who are closest to us— spouses, children, parents, siblings, friends. Therefore, in addition to making amends with anyone who was harmed in a specific way you are aware of, it is customary to apologize to those nearest and dearest by saying "please forgive me for anything I might have done in the past year to cause you any pain." It can be uncomfortable at first, especially if you don't normally express those kinds of sentiments, but it can make you feel incredibly close to those whose pardon you seek. (This is a model of how you can feel when you ask God to pardon you.)

When someone asks you for forgiveness, you are supposed to grant it.

KAPPAROT

Though largely abandoned today, this atonement ritual introduced in the seventh century can still be witnessed in religious enclaves like Williamsburg in Brooklyn and Mea Shearim, Israel, and in many Sephardic neighborhoods. It is one of the strangest ceremonies you will ever see in Judaism, one that smacks so much of superstition and pagan rite that it has generated much opposition, and been eliminated among most Orthodox as well as Conservative and Reform communities.

For the authentic ritual, a male takes a rooster and a female a hen. After tying its legs together, the person doing the procedure for himself or on behalf of others swings the chicken over his/her head while reciting: "this is my (our) exchange, this is my (our) substitute. This rooster (chicken) will go to its death while I (we) will enter and proceed to a good long life and to peace." The fowl is then killed and given to charity, or eaten in the pre-fast meal and its value donated to charity. Leaving its innards for other birds to feed on is considered a *mitzvah*.

The ceremony, which a parent can do for a child or one member of the family for others, can take place anytime from two days before Yom Kippur until the morning of Yom Kippur Eve, but the preferred time is just after dawn on the latter.

In former times, Palestinian Arabs sold so many white fowl to the Jews who performed the ritual they called the day the Festival of Chickens. That bird may have been chosen simply because it was the most readily available domestic animal. (Since the ceremony entails sacrifice, in the absence of the Temple any creature that had been suitable for the altar is forbidden.) Fish were sometimes used, but in some cultures, chickens carried additional significance: The Persians believed the rooster possessed magical powers to eliminate evil spirits (it drove them away with its daybreak crowing). The word for the bird in Hebrew, *gever,* also means man, giving the substitution added meat. (In modern Hebrew, *gever* is Mr., *giveret,* Mrs.)

Often today money is used in place of the chicken and then donated.

REMISSION OF VOWS

Those who did not annul their vows the day before Rosh Hashanah often do so on the afternoon prior to Yom Kippur, even though the communal annulment will take place with *Kol Nidrei*. The remission covers only vows of a personal nature that affect the person him/herself.

PERSONAL

CEMETERY VISITS Although it is customary to visit the graves of one's deceased relatives during Elul, some people go to the graves of pious individuals just before Yom Kippur starts.

STIMULANT WITHDRAWAL It is a good idea to begin to cut down on consumption of chocolate and caffeinated drinks like coffee, tea and cola at least a week prior to Tishrei 10. The headaches some people experience on Yom Kippur result from caffeine withdrawal, and can be avoided if you wean yourself from the stimulant gradually.

MITZVOT Prior to the holiday, it is appropriate to pay all outstanding debts. In accordance with performing extra *mitzvot* to appear more meritorious on Yom Kippur, in the week before the holiday, many people purchase the etrog and lulav they will need for Sukkot, the next holiday.

BODY Before *Minkhah,* which is held early on Yom Kippur to give people ample time for the pre-fast meal, religious men immerse in the *mikvah* for the sake of purity.

TICKETS If you are not a member of a synagogue, and plan to attend services, be sure to arrange for tickets in advance (SEE PREVIOUS CHAPTER).

What Are We Supposed to Do? Halakhah

REST ON THE SABBATH OF SABBATHS

All thirty-nine categories of labor prohibited on Shabbat are also forbidden on the Day of Atonement. That means that the restrictions on carrying outside and food preparation lifted for other *yom tovim* are still in effect on Yom Kippur. The laws that apply to other festivals—rejoicing, caring for the stranger and needy, wearing clean clothing—all apply (SEE "HALAKHAH" IN CHAPTER ON PESAKH). According to the principle that we are supposed to add from the profane to the sacred, all forbidden acts are to be stopped shortly before twilight and are prohibited until after nightfall.

The day is additionally sanctified through the five "afflictions" or self-denials we follow.

FASTING

We abstain from satisfying our hunger and thirst based on two Torah commandments: "You shall afflict your souls" (LEVITICUS 16:29) and "For any soul which is not afflicted on that day will be cut off" (LEVITICUS 23:29). The rabbis ascertained the connection between affliction and fasting based on additional verses in the Bible (LEVITICUS 23:30 AND DEUTERONOMY 8:3).

Females over the age of twelve and males over the age of thirteen are to abstain from taking any food or beverage. Children under the age of nine are not allowed to fast, and from nine until the age of religiously-recognized maturity should gradually learn to go without eating or drinking (usually by postponing breakfast for longer and longer periods of time).

If a doctor asserts that fasting could endanger your health, you need not fast. (There is a famous story about a rabbi who insisted that his entire congregation eat on Yom Kippur during a cholera epidemic so that the worshippers would not lose strength and succumb to the disease.) If any number of doctors states that fasting would not be harmful, and one doctor disagrees, or you yourself feel you must eat, you eat.

A pregnant woman likewise determines if she must have food. During childbirth or within three days of giving birth, a woman does not fast. If she feels it is necessary, she can eat within three to seven days after giving birth.

If you need to break the fast, you should try to do so by taking very small quantities, smaller than the size of a date, pausing between each piece, so that within nine minutes you will not have eaten more than the volume equivalent of three eggs. Where life and health are concerned, whatever is needed for one's welfare is to be given, as necessary.

OTHER SELF-DENIAL

While Torah does not specifically mandate the four additional forms of "affliction" (*inui*) practiced on Yom Kippur, the sages derived them from Torah's idea of a day of complete rest.

WASHING Prohibited for pleasure, cleansing yourself for purposes of hygiene is permitted. If your hands or feet are mud-soiled, if you have to wipe a film out of your eyes upon rising in the morning or if you are sick, you are allowed to wash. A bride within thirty days of marriage may wash her face. (In former times, the king was also permitted to wash his face.)

ANOINTING The application of oil or cream is permissible only for medicinal purposes.

MARITAL RELATIONS A husband and wife must refrain from intimacy during the Day of Atonement.

WEARING OF LEATHER SHOES After childbirth, a woman may put on leather shoes. Otherwise, shoes must be of another material, such as canvas, rubber, plastic or wood.

RITUAL PURITY

The laws that apply for Rosh Hashanah continue through the end of the period of atonement.

PRAYERS

Early-morning *Selikhot* services begun in the week prior to Rosh Hashanah continue through Yom Kippur, as do the alterations in wording of prayers made for Rosh Hashanah. When Yom Kippur falls on Shabbat, the Ashkenazim recite *Avinu Malkeinu* only at the *Neilah* service. Otherwise, it is recited after each Day of Atonement service except *Minkhah*.

Viddui, the declaration of sins, is said three times a day between Rosh Hashanah and Yom Kippur, during *Selikhot* recited before the morning service, *Minkhah* and *Ma'ariv*. (The Lubavitch Khassidim say it once in *Selikhot*, once during *Shakharit* and once during *Minkhah*.) The number of repetitions corresponds to the Torah verse "forgiving iniquity, and transgression and sin" (EXODUS 34:7). It also represents the three people who must serve as witnesses to the annulment of vows. (On the day of *Erev Yom Kippur,* it is said only once, at *Minkhah*.)

The *mitzvah* of confessing on *Erev Yom Kippur* takes place at nightfall. However, to ensure that you will enter the holiday in a state of repentance, you should confess before the pre-fast meal, in case the food and drink confuse you so that you can't say it; and you should confess after the meal in case you transgressed in any way during it; and you should also confess at the evening service, in case any wrongs were committed in the intervening time.

CONCILIATION

Since Yom Kippur cannot atone for transgressions between one person and another, everybody should make amends directly with the people involved by *Erev Yom Kippur.* If an injured party refuses to forgive, according to Jewish practice, the offender must apologize in front of three witnesses. If forgiveness is still refused, the offender is considered to be absolved (except if the injured is a teacher, in which case forgiveness cannot be requested too many times), and the person who refuses to grant the pardon after being asked three times is considered to be in the wrong.

Even if an injured party has died before you could seek a pardon, you must seek his/her absolution, by confessing at his grave in front of ten witnesses.

TESHUVAH

As Yom Kippur is the climax of the period of repentance and forgiveness for individuals and the community of Israel, everyone is obligated to do teshuvah and confess on the Day of Atonement.

What Other Things Do People Do? Customs

OTHER TIMES AND PLACES

SPIRITUAL PREPARATION Particularly conscientious prayer leaders used to go into seclusion for seven days after Rosh Hashanah, in order to improve their behavior and study the order of the service. In solitude, concentrating on holiness, they modeled their preparation on that of the High Priest in Temple days. Extremely pious Bulgarian Jewish merchants sometimes gave their shop keys to non-Jews so that on Yom Kippur, they would be totally free of any everyday material concerns.

PAYING DEBTS In Libya, after morning services on *Erev Yom Kippur,* a community meal served rich and poor together. This was the time for people to pay all pledges made in synagogue during the previous year. Trustees sat in the courtyard at foliage-decorated tables as people passed by and made their donations to welfare institutions, for the *khazzan* and *shammash* of the synagogue. During the afternoon before the start of the holiday Eastern European Jews made similar collections. On tables at synagogue entrances, various organizations or funds set out plates or *pushkehs* (collection boxes) marked "clothing the naked," "feeding the hungry," "*Talmud Torah*" (Jewish education), "Return to the Land of Israel" and so on. (Some also included plates for "call to the Torah" and a precursor to our High Holy Day tickets, "seat in the synagogue.")

SELF-PUNISHMENT Rarely seen today, from the time of Rashi (eleventh century) through the first decades of the twentieth century, older and pious Jews submitted themselves to symbolic lashings (*malkot*). A common form of punishment at one time (even prescribed in the Torah for various offenses), on *Erev Yom Kippur* the practice was purely symbolic. The flogger, in Eastern Europe a poor man of a town, spread hay on the floor. Wearing their overcoats, the penitents would stretch out face down, and say their *Ashamnu* confessions while the flogger delivered light, token blows using a leather strap and three times recited Psalm 78:38, beginning "For He is merciful and forgives iniquity." Each repetition of the verse consists of thirteen words, for a total of thirty-nine, the number of lashes formerly given to sentenced criminals. (In one of the Torah's instructions regarding flogging, it specifies that forty may be administered [DEUTERONOMY 25:3]. But it was felt that if a person received the full count prior to Yom Kippur, he might think he had eliminated all his wrongdoing, so the sages took away one lash to remind him he still had to improve.)

LIGHT During the Middle Ages, synagogues were ablaze with candles, in lamps, boxes families had filled with sand to hold them, and candelabras. Singing Psalm 97:11, "Light is sown for the righteous and gladness for the upright in heart," accompanied the kindling.

The candles were often prepared on Tishrei 8, the anniversary of the beginning of the dedication of Solomon's Temple, using wicks from cotton thread paced out in the cemetery (SEE "CUSTOMS" IN PREVIOUS CHAPTER). Each family had two candles that burned all day, one for the living, usually left at home, and one for the dead. Sometimes both were taken to synagogue, one for themselves, one for the deceased relatives, or one for body, one for soul.

DRESS In Spanish-Portuguese synagogues in America, known for their upper-class decorum, the men carrying Torah scrolls during *Kol Nidrei* dressed in formal evening clothes, including high silk hats (the attire also worn in British synagogues). They followed the opening service with special prayers for the government, congregation, the two Torah carriers, the congregations that established America's first synagogues, Jerusalem, those held in captivity, those traveling, the sick, and, uniquely, for women for the work they had done in preparing the white clothes for the *Sifrei Torah*, *Aron Kodesh* and bimah.

Drawing on the comparison between Yom Kippur and a wedding day, the Libyans had their young boys dress in their best clothes and sing wedding songs in the synagogue courtyard.

SYNAGOGUE During the *Mussaf* prostrations, paper or cloth, such as a tallit, kept the worshipper's body from coming into direct contact with the floor. (Until the fourteenth century, Frankfurt's Jews scattered grass on the floor.) The custom developed when synagogue pavements were often stone, which other peoples worshipped, so outside the Temple, Jews had to take precautions not to appear to be bowing to an idol (LEVITICUS 26:1).

When Libyans perform the priestly blessing, each head of a family extends his tallit over the heads of his children, including married sons, who place their hands on the heads of their sons as the blessing is said.

The Syrians allow anyone who so desires to come forward between *Minkhah* and the closing service to kiss the *Sifrei Torah* and ask forgiveness for any negligence that he might have engaged in relative to the sacred scrolls.

THE BREAK FAST Sephardim sometimes break their fast with a light dairy meal, then put in the first nail of the *sukkah*, and follow by eating a heavy meat and vegetable soup. Afterwards, it is customary to visit one's grandfather to receive a blessing for the new year.

Several Sephardic communities (Libya, Morocco, Bombay Bene Israel), observed the day following Yom Kippur as *Yom Simkhat Kohein,* a day of rejoicing for the High Priest. Like the High Priest of Temple days, the Kohanim would celebrate with feasting, visits to friends and family, giving donations to the poor, and foregoing all work.

Eager to avoid slipping back into lax ways, people sometimes try to arise earlier than usual for morning prayers, which often start fifteen minutes prior to the regularly scheduled time.

GREETING

Prior to the start of Yom Kippur, we wish each other *gemar khatima tova* (may the final decree be good) and *tzom kal* (an easy fast). At the end of the day it is appropriate to say *gut yom tov* or *khag sameiakh* (happy holiday). Sephardim wish each other *tizkeh leshanim* (may you merit long life), to which one responds *tizkeh vetikhyeh veta'arikh yomim* (may you merit, live and have length of days).

DRESS

Sabbath clothes are appropriate for attending synagogue. Even more so than on Rosh Hashanah, it is customary to wear new clothes, especially white ones. Particularly in a traditional *shul,* you are likely to see many women in white apparel and a number of men other than the prayer leaders each wearing a *kittel.* (You will also see many men in suits and women in garments of any color.)

Although silver ornamentation on a *kittel* is acceptable since it is likened to white, gold is not, as it recalls the Golden Calf. (In eighteenth-century Eastern Europe, men replaced the rope ties of their robes with belts on silver buckles carrying a prayer, based on Leviticus 16:30, about being cleansed of sin.) For this reason (and humility), women are supposed to refrain from wearing gold and flashy jewelry in general.

Since leather shoes are forbidden people generally wear canvas beach shoes, sneakers (watch out for running and sports shoes popular today, as most are leather), even house slippers. People attending Conservative and Reform synagogues are generally less strict in observance of this prohibition than those in more traditional synagogues.

What Is There to Eat? Traditional Foods

Although we do not eat on Yom Kippur itself, several traditions apply for the pre- and post-fast meals.

PRE-FAST

Even though there is no commandment to eat on the day prior to Yom Kippur (it is implied in conjunction with the one to fast [LEVITICUS 23:32]), the sages asserted that anyone who does is considered by Torah to have fasted on both that day and the holiday itself. It wasn't just to give us the energy to make it through the next day's fast, but to show us that we serve God both by abstinence, and by enjoyment of physical pleasures done in the proper spirit. Our dining before Yom Kippur demonstrates that we rejoice in our anticipated reunion with God. The self-denial we will shortly experience is merely a means to an end, not an end in itself and not a Jewish value. A Jewish life is not about other worldly spirituality, but spiritual existence very much grounded in the physical world. For this meal, khallot are often baked in the shape of wings, for the angels the Jews resemble on Yom Kippur (ISAIAH 6:2), or ladders, on which we climb to higher spiritual levels. After the *motzi* (SEE "OBSERVANCE"), it is dipped in honey.

You want to guard against eating anything that will cause thirst, and most people like to eat lightly to ready their bodies to experience food deprivation. A customary meal begins with chicken soup (formerly made of the rooster or hen used for the *kapparot* ceremony), often with kreplakh. These meat-filled dough pouches traditional also for Purim and Hoshanah Rabbah symbolize stern judgment (the meat) enveloped in mercy (the soft, flexible dough). Poultry, traditionally boiled (it may be from the soup pot) is the typical entree (although beef is acceptable). Bland is the rule, as salt, pepper and spices will create the desire for water. We avoid intoxicating drinks that could affect one's prayer, and we stay away from food (like chocolate) and beverages containing caffeine so that we will not suffer the ill effects of deprivation. Light, sweet vegetables and desserts such as those typical for Rosh Hashanah are also served.

BREAK FAST

A midrash relates that after the fast, a heavenly voice calls out "Go and eat your bread joyfully, drink your wine in good spirit, for the Lord has accepted your efforts" (ECCLESIASTES 9:7). Based on this, and the custom of the High Priest to make a feast upon his successful completion of the Yom Kippur service, the night following the Day of Atonement is considered a minor festival when it is appropriate to eat and drink. The synagogue usually provides juice and cookies or some plain cake—and then friends and families often join together for a break fast meal. Although in some places it has been the custom to eat a full dinner, it is more common today to eat a brunch-like dairy repast.

Do You Hear Music? Songs to Sing

As is true of Rosh Hashanah, the music for this holiday is concentrated in the liturgy, some of it quite moving. Aside from the *Viddui*, a number of *piyyutim* and the entire *Avodah* (reenactment of Temple service) distinguish the Yom Kippur service musically from that of the New Year. You will be able to pick up some of the melodies just by hearing them repeatedly in the synagogue, but as with Rosh Hashanah, you may feel more comfortable and be better able to participate if you become familiar with them in advance.

In addition to the prayers listed for Rosh Hashanah, requests that we be remembered, written and sealed in the Book of Life punctuate the service in the refrains "*Zakhreinu l'khayim*" (Remember us for Life) and "*Ukh'tov l'khayim tovim*" (And inscribe for a good life). Also key is the proclamation "*U'teshuvah, u'tefillah, u'tzedakah ma'avirin et roah hag'zeirah*" (But repentance, prayer and charity remove the evil of the decree), recognition that by our own actions we can put ourselves in a favorable position.

Other tunes to learn are those for "*Ashamnu*" (We have become guilty, the short confession), "*Anu Amekha*" (We are Your people), a summation of the entire Yom Kippur process, based on verses from the Bible, phrases of endearment expressing the intimate connection between Israel and God, and recognition of our failings; "*Shema Koleinu*" (Hear our voice), a prayer that we have the will to return to God; "*V'al Kulam*" (and for all), the *Viddui* refrain asking God to forgive us for all our transgressions; *"Ya'aleh Takhanumeinu"* (May our entreaty rise), a prayer that our prayers go to heaven at nightfall and arrive before God's throne at dawn so that our salvation and reconciliation will come at dusk; *"Salakhti"* (Forgiven), the verdict we hope to get from God; *"Ki Ninneh Ka-Homer"* (Like clay in the hand of the potter), showing our submission to God; and *"L'shanah Haba'ah B'Yerushalayim"* (Next year in Jerusalem), the age-old wish of Jews in exile.

Among the Sephardim, *"El Nora Eilah"* (God that does wondrously), chanted just before Neilah, is a popular tune whose liveliness indicates the confidence of worshippers at that point in the day.

FOR FURTHER EXPLORATION

FOR ADULTS

You can find some wonderful recordings of the Yom Kippur liturgy, including *"Kol Nidrei,"* performed by noted cantors. Check sources included in "More Useful Information."

FOR CHILDREN

High Holidays and Sukkot Melodies. Cedarhurst, NY: Board of Jewish Education of Greater New York and Tara Publications.

> The tunes for the major parts of the services are included in the booklet (with words transliterated into English), and on a companion tape.

What Tales Are Told? Stories to Read

Major Jewish writers from the Middle Ages to modern times have created wonderfully inspirational and philosophical writings about Yom Kippur.

Poet Judah Halevi's *The Kuzari* (A Book of Argument in Defense of a Despised Religion), philosopher Moses Maimonides' *Moreh Nevukim* (Guide for the Perplexed), Talmudist Jonah ben Abraham Gerondi's *Shaare Teshuvah* (Gates of Repentance), and scholar Abraham ben Hiyya's *Hegon Hanefesh* (Meditation of the Soul) treat aspects of the Day of Atonement, and have influenced philosophical and ethical literature since the medieval period.

Tremendous insight into the significance of the Days of Awe is provided in the many tales told of and by the Khassidic rabbis. Like the movement's founder, Rabbi Israel Baal Shem Tov (1700–1760), who saw only goodness in people, and the compassionate Rabbi Levi Isaac of Berditchev (1740–1809), they not only submissively prayed to God, but also *demanded* that He remit their sins. Their teachings demonstrate the kind of dynamic interaction with God, rather than a once-a-year formal or detached relationship, we can aspire to on Yom Kippur.

In more recent years, Israel Zangwill and Solomon Ibn Gabirol composed poems. Sholom Aleichem, Martin Buber, Isaac Loeb Peretz, Elie Weisel, and Samuel J. Agnon are among the writers who reflect some aspect of the holiday in their stories.

FOR FURTHER EXPLORATION

FOLKTALES AND STORIES

Refer to holiday anthologies and story collections in "More Good Information." They contain many selections for Yom Kippur.

FOR CHILDREN

Cohen, Barbara. *First Fast*. New York: UAHC Press, 1998.
> A wager between a younger and older boy before Yom Kippur teaches them about honor, honesty and integrity as a difficult choice must be made. Ages 5–9.

————. *Yussel's Prayer: A Yom Kippur Story*. New York: William Morrow, 1993
> This is a retelling of the classic story of the uneducated boy who with his simple and novel way of praying to God wins acceptance of the prayers of the insincere congregation. Ages 5–9.

Kimmel, Eric A. *Days of Awe: Stories for Rosh Hashanah and Yom Kippur*. New York: Puffin, 1996.
> The three incredibly moving stories in this book show us the key concept of the holiday season in simple every day life. Adapted from traditional sources and conveying the awe and beauty of the times, one story deals with each of the themes of charity, prayer and repentance. Ages 8–12.

Sukkot—
The Ultimate Harvest

(SOO–KOTE'; YIDDISH: SOOK'-US)
TISHREI 15-22
(FALL; LATE SEPTEMBER–MID OCTOBER)

HOSHANAH RABBAH—DAY OF THE WILLOWS
(HOE-SHAH-NAH' RAH-BAH'; YIDDISH: HOE-SHAH'-NUH RAH'-BUH)
TISHREI 21

SHEMINI ATZERET—EIGHTH DAY OF ASSEMBLY
(SHMIN'-EE AHT-TZEHR'RETTE; YIDDISH: SHMIN'-EE AHT-SER'RESS)
TISHREI 22

SIMKHAT TORAH—REJOICING IN THE TORAH
(SIM-KHAT' TOE-RAH'; YIDDISH: SIM'-KHUS TOE'RUH)
TISHREI 23

The longest, last and for a long time the greatest of the festivals specified by Torah, the third of the three pilgrimages has both seasonal and historic significance. "The Feast of Booths" begins and ends with the fulfillment of God's promises to bring us to a bountiful Land after years of wandering, and to return us to it after years of exile. As a celebration of the rewards of individual and national efforts for material and spiritual achievement, it is considered the most joyous time of the year.

Origins—WHY WE CELEBRATE SUKKOT

Traditions—HOW WE CELEBRATE SUKKOT

Origins—

WHY WE CELEBRATE SUKKOT

Where Did It Begin? Historic Foundation

A TORAH LAW

When the Israelites were still wandering in the Sinai, they were given holidays for the future. Among them was a fall festival, one of the three pilgrimages (*shalosh regalim* [SEE ALSO CHAPTERS ON PESAKH AND SHAVUOT]), to be celebrated after the Israelites had settled and successfully cultivated the Land. Entries in four successive books of Torah gradually reveal the nature and significance of the occasion.

Khag Ha Asif (Festival of Ingathering) was to take place once the produce of the vineyards and product of the threshing rooms had been collected (EXODUS 23:14–17; 34:22). Beginning on the fifteenth of the seventh month, this *Khag Adonai* (Festival of God) would last seven days, the first of them a sacred observance when no work was to be done. At that time, the Israelites were to take the "product of *hadar* trees, branches of palm trees, boughs of leafy trees and willows of the brook" (later called the four species) and somehow rejoice with them before God.

Then another dimension was added as a "law for all time": For the duration of the festival the Israelites were to live in booths (*sukkot*) "so that future generations will know that I made the Israelite people live in *sukkot* when I brought them out of the land of Egypt, I the Lord your God" (LEVITICUS 23:39–43).

Rabbi Akiva explained *sukkot* literally as physical structures that protected the Israelites from the sun. Many dispute his opinion, saying if anything, the wandering Jews would have used tents, not open-roofed sheds, the materials for which would not have been available in the desert. Secular historians claim that the booths originated later, adapted for ritual either from autumn pagan ceremonies, or from the shelters constructed in the fields by farmers harvesting their crops. Rabbi Eleazar provided the widely accepted interpretation: The booths were the Clouds of Glory that surrounded the Israelites on their journey, providing protection and guidance. In other words, they formed a spiritual construct.

Another sacred occasion was to follow the week, a day called Shemini (eighth) Atzeret (solemn assembly [LEVITICUS 23:3]). Not completely understood, *atzeret* (also used to designate the last day of Passover [DEUTERONOMY 16:8]) comes from the root for "restrain" and literally means to tarry or hold back. A midrash explains that as the children of Israel are about to take leave of God after having rejoiced with Him for a week, God, like the parent of a child about to end a cherished visit, says "It is difficult to have you leave me. Stay another day." As one greater in number than the perfect seven, the next day of the holiday (the eighth, beyond the period needed to create the world), represents a day after time—eternity—suggesting the longed-for messianic age.

Each of the eight days had its own complement of sacrifices—beginning with thirteen and decreasing by one each day through seven (a total of seventy). One sacrifice was made on the eighth day (NUMBERS 29:12–28).

In Deuteronomy's reiteration of festivals, this one is called Sukkot to stress its connection with our history. We are enjoined not just to celebrate the "Festival for God" for His agricultural and other blessings, but to rejoice along with our entire families, our servants, the Levite (priest), the stranger, fatherless and widow in the community (16:13–15). The passage that follows this instruction, commanding the appointment of judges and delivery of justice, emphasizes the relationship between Israel's ethical behavior and prosperity in the Land: "Justice, justice you shall pursue, that you may thrive and occupy the Land that the Lord your God is giving you" (DEUTERONOMY 16:20).

The connection with judgment also rests in the placement of Sukkot not only at the end of the annual festival cycle that starts with Pesakh, but at the resolution of the assessment defined by the Days of Awe. According to midrash, the protective clouds provided shortly after the Exodus disappeared when the Golden Calf emerged. Following the repentance and forgiveness of the first Yom Kippur, when the people began constructing the Tabernacle that was to be God's temporary dwelling place in the desert—indicating that they wanted Him to live with them—the clouds returned to provide temporary shelter for the Israelites in the desert—indicating God's renewed embrace of them.

IN THE LAND AND OFF IT

The specifics of the Jewish harvest festival were designed to protect the Israelites from the pagan influences they would encounter once they entered Canaan. While heathens worshipped nature itself, the Jews were to worship the Creator and Renewer of nature. While the pagans celebrated with excess and debauchery, the Israelite pilgrims were to focus on the moral significance of the festivities.

The purpose of rejoicing was not sensual abandon, but to honor and thank God for His blessings, spread good fortune and act with sensitivity. (The oddly-placed admonition following the commandments of Sukkot to "not seethe a kid in its mother's milk" [EXODUS 23:19, 34:26]—fundamental in our system of kashrut—was included here, as Maimonides points out, to eliminate the "revolting custom" of serving such dishes at pagan harvest festivals—revolting because they mixed death, the slaughter of an animal, with new life, the sustaining milk.)

On the other hand, properly directed joy was not to be hampered at this culmination of the spiritual (repentance and renewal), agricultural (harvest) and historic (successful settlement of Israel) growth. Three times the Torah commands us to experience elation in connection with the holiday: "You shall rejoice before the Lord your God seven days" (LEVITICUS 23:40); "You shall rejoice in your festival" (DEUTERONOMY 16:14); and "You shall have nothing but joy" (DEUTERONOMY 16:15).

Although Torah gave it the same status as the other pilgrimages, Sukkot became the predominant agricultural celebration. Reference to *Heh Khag*—The Festival—only meant Sukkot, and the biblical books covering the period of Israel's independent kingdom mention this holiday more than any others. Having finished their work for the year, the peasant pilgrims did not have to rush home to tend crops and with peace of mind *could* tarry in Jerusalem. Consequently, the festival became known as *Zeman Simkhahteinu*, the Season of Our Rejoicing.

Even before construction of a Temple in Jerusalem (the designated site of festivals before God), the Israelites made pilgrimages to sanctuaries in other locales, such as Shiloh (JUDGES 21:19–21, I SAMUEL 1:3). When Solomon completed his Temple (955 BCE) the very first observance held there was celebration of Sukkot, with which the dedication coincided. The focal point for pilgrimage shifted to the capital and within a few centuries, provincial altars were abolished.

Getting everyone away from local pagan harvest rites to a common Israelite celebration gave the religious leaders at least a fighting chance to appropriately direct the level of joy, although being in the holiest place in the kingdom still provided no guarantee. Two hundred years after Solomon's reign, the prophets Isaiah, Amos and Hosea observed that the overzealous pilgrims marching in sacred procession, singing hymns and playing musical instruments in praise of God often overindulged, creating the atmosphere of a bacchanalia. The prophets' protests about the drunkenness and disorderly behavior did not stop the Jews. Exile did.

During their sojourn in Babylon (beginning in the sixth century BCE), Sukkot was suspended. It was, after all, a holiday tied to the Israelites' territorial sovereignty and the Land's agricultural abundance. Without them, there was not much reason to celebrate.

When the displaced returned to the Land in the next century, they enthusiastically embraced the Torah commandments about Sukkot Ezra read to them on Rosh Hashanah. The newly-motivated Israelites ran out to get olive, pine, myrtle, palm and other leafy branches for construction of their temporary shelters, which they set in every available space, public and private. Nehemiah observed that "the whole community that returned from captivity made and dwelled in booths" (8:17), which they had not done since the days of Joshua, the first generation to inhabit the Land. (He may have been referring to the extent of celebration or use of certain materials rather than the ritual of booths itself.)

Even though the Jews were back on their own ground, the rabbis recognized the need to refocus this land-oriented festival. As with other annual events, Sukkot was separated from its physical aspects of agriculture, nature, and the seasons. Instead, the religious leaders stressed its religious, moral and nationalistic content.

Torah had provided a means for spiritual rejuvenation of the landed Jewish nation, at least once every seven years (DEUTERONOMY 31:10–13). On the second day of Sukkot at the end of each sabbatical year, all the people were to gather for a public reading of Deuteronomy, the Torah book that reviews the laws of Israel. The priests blew trumpets throughout Jerusalem to summon all, including women and particularly children, who would be influenced for the rest of their lives by what they heard. Surrounded by the populace, the king sat on a large wooden platform erected in the Temple's Women's Court and read aloud. In reviewing their responsibilities and duties, this ceremony, called *Hockheil* (gathering) was a source of inspiration for the assembled.

SECOND TEMPLE

After the connection to the Land had been minimized and Pesakh overtook Sukkot as the greatest Jewish holiday, Sukkot retained its joyousness and appeal. As described in Flavius Josephus' *Jewish Antiquities* (which includes reports of Sukkot celebrations in particular years) and Talmud (which in addition to references scattered throughout has a tractate, Sukkah, devoted to the holiday), pilgrims came from throughout the Land of Israel and every Jewish community in the world. Gathering in regional centers for the arduous trip, they then set out in colorful caravans of chariot, donkey, camel, boat (as far as the Mediterranean shore), and most often on foot (as the great Rabbi Hillel is said to have done, in his case from Babylon, a journey of two weeks). Although the commandment obligates only men, entire peasant households traveled.

Once in Jerusalem, festive in garlands of olive, palm and willow branches, fragrant with fruits and flowers, they participated in prayers, hymns and singing, and watched religious processions in the Temple. The four species (definitively identified through Oral Tradition as palm, willow and myrtle bound together into a lulav, plus an etrog [citron]) had become part of ritual: Each day of Sukkot, holding them in hand, the priests marched around the altar that had been adorned with freshly cut willow branches. As they circled, they recited a psalm asking God to "please save us" (*Hoshiah na*).

SIMKHAT BEIT HASHOAVAH At this most joyous season of the year, with all the electric anticipation along the caravan trails, the stirring ceremonies, and the lively singing and feasting, the epitome of celebration took place surrounding a water ritual: the Rejoicing (*Simkhat*) at the Place of (*Beit*) the Water Drawing (*Hashoavah*).

Every day of the year, after the priests burned the sacrifice, they poured an offering of wine on the altar. During Sukkot, a water libation (*nisukh hamayim*) also took place. Some have suggested it was a folk rite, an inducement for rain made by pouring out water at the season's onset, transformed by the rabbis into a symbolic Temple ritual.

Each morning of Sukkot, the priests went to the pool of Siloah (Silwan) near Jerusalem to fill a golden flask. Shofar blasts greeted their arrival back at the Temple's Water Gate. They then ascended and poured the water so that it flowed over the altar simultaneously with wine from another bowl. One year, the high priest Alexander Jannaeus (103–76 BCE) showed contempt for the rite by spilling the water at his feet. In response to the transgression, the worshippers threw their citrons at him.

The pelted priest had demonstrated his alliance with the Sadducees—who literally followed Torah, and only what Torah explicitly stated. (Explained as an oral instruction given to Moses at Sinai, this water rite is not mentioned in The Five Books.) The deliriously happy celebration connected with the water drawing developed when the Pharisees (who believed in the Oral Tradition and interpretation of Torah and gave us the rabbinic Judaism we know today) triumphed over them in the first century.

Based on Isaiah's promise "With joy shall you draw water out of the wells of salvation" (12:3), rejoicing began at the end of the first day, and took place every night except Shabbat. Talmud recorded that "one who had never witnessed the Rejoicing at the Place of the Water Drawing had never seen true joy in his life." (Although the celebration was for the *libation* that would be made the next morning, it was named for the preparation for the ritual—the water *drawing*—which the rabbis said showed that getting ready was sometimes of greater merit than the *mitzvah* itself because of its positive affect on the person doing it.)

Talmud describes the festivities in detail, from the lighting of immense candelabrum set in the Temple courtyard (each holding gallons of oil and fit with wicks made from priests' worn-out vestments), which generated such intense light they illuminated every courtyard in the city. A Levite orchestra of flutes, trumpets, harps and cymbals accompanied torchlight processions, and the men who had earned the capacity for real spiritual joy through their purity, character, and scholarship danced ecstatically to the hand-clapping, foot-stomping and hymn-singing crowds.

We do not imagine our distinguished sages as acrobats and tumblers, but they were often as agile physically as mentally: Rabbi Simon ben Gamaliel juggled eight lighted torches and raised himself into a handstand on two fingers, a gymnastic feat no one else could master. Others juggled eight knives, or eight glasses of wine or eight eggs before leaders and dignitaries.

At dawn, as the rejoicing wound down, the priests enacted what some have identified as the transformation of another folk rite, this one meant to rekindle a diminishing sun approaching the autumnal equinox. With trumpet blasts, the Kohanim descended the steps to the Women's Court, marched to the Eastern Gate, turned their faces west to the Temple and proclaimed, "Our fathers who were in this place stood with their backs to the Temple and their faces eastward and worshipped the sun, but our eyes are unto the Lord" (BASED ON EZEKIEL 8:16).

SEVENTH DAY During the Temple service at the end of Sukkot week, the priests' procession circled the willow adorned altar seven times instead of once. Each time they recited a refrain of *Hoshiah na*. At the conclusion of the seventh circle, they struck the willows—the branches of trees associated with life-giving water since they thrive near rivers and brooks—on the ground around the altar, an unexplained custom, possibly another rain rite.

The sacrifices made throughout the week, a total of seventy, were understood to represent the seventy nations that then existed in the world. Their well-being, like Israel's, depended on whether or not they would receive the rain needed for food supplies. Blessings like rain were understood as rewards for proper behavior (DEUTERONOMY 11:13–15). (In his vision of messianic times, Zekhariah presents lack of rain as punishment for the nations that fail to make pilgrimage to Jerusalem on Sukkot to worship God, which would show that they accept His sovereignty [14:16]. This prophecy, and those of Isaiah and Micah calling on all nations to show their acceptance of God's sovereignty by going to His Temple—combined with the connection between Sukkot and fulfillment, the ultimate being messianic redemption—encouraged many proselytes to join the pilgrims in Jerusalem.)

The final day of the festival, when the last sacrifices were offered on behalf of the other nations, therefore took on the identity as the occasion when the earth is judged regarding replenishment of water—and consequently, when mankind's fate, collectively and individually, was sealed. (Rabbininic literature identifies this *Yom Darvata*, Day of the Willow, as *Yom Hakhitum*, Day of Sealing, an extension of Yom Kippur.) Striking the willows then had the added connotation of casting away of sin, or symbolizing the thrashings one would receive in punishment for sin.

SHEMINI ATZERET The one set of sacrifices made on the closing day of the festival season was for Israel, which all week had placed concern for others above self-interest.

A prayer for rain was included in the day's supplications, and at the evening services, the people viewed the direction in which smoke from the sacrificial fire wafted as an omen. If it blew north, the poor would gratefully anticipate a good year, because it indicated a wet season, when crops would be plentiful. The rich heralded a southward blowing, indicating a dry year and higher prices for limited supplies. West portended famine, and east was read as good for all.

POST-TEMPLE

Sukkot changed little after the destruction of the Second Temple, and, despite our extended exile, remained the most joyous of Torah festivals. People continued to build booths. In remembrance of the Temple, during the first century Rabbi Yokhanan ben Zakkai instructed that ceremonies using the four species be performed every day of the week except Shabbat, even though Torah commanded them only for the first. (It says to take the four on the first day, and rejoice with them before God—which meant only in the Temple—on all seven [LEVITICUS 23:40].)

Though it sounds extreme, midrash includes the lulav and etrog along with circumcision, study of Torah and eating matzah as a religious obligation for which we are to be prepared to struggle and die. An Aramaic letter on papyrus, sent before Sukkot 134 CE by the Jewish military commander (and found among the Dead Sea documents) attests to the great effort of Bar Kokhba and his soldiers (SEE CHAPTER ON LAG B'OMER) to obtain sets of the four species during the Hadrianic persecutions of Jews remaining in Palestine. (Throughout modern Israel's history, even in the midst of military campaigns, the Israel Defense Forces has also provided for soldiers to fulfill their religious duty.)

As symbols of a revived Jewish state, the lulav and etrog were depicted on coins of the Bar Kokhba period (as they had been on the first coins minted by a

Jewish nation, under Simon the Hasmonean [SEE CHAPTER ON KHANUKAH]). For centuries they were popular decorations, engraved on ritual items and patterned into floor mosaics in ancient synagogues, among them the fifth-century Mount Carmel and sixth-century Beit Alfa.

The willow ceremonies were temporarily discontinued, then established for one day, in post-Talmudic terms called Hoshanah Rabbah (the many *hoshanahs*—a contraction of *hoshiah na*—or "The Great Salvation"). With prayer the accepted replacement for sacrifice, and the Scripture-reading table (bimah), like the dining table at home (both sanctified by words of Torah) recognized as the stand-in for the Temple altar, the processions and beating of the willows eventually resumed. During the Middle Ages, customs of Yom Kippur such as dressing the Torah scrolls in white vestments and the cantor's wearing of a *kittel* were adopted for Hoshanah Rabbah, this final day of judgment.

For the second day of Shemini Atzeret observed in the Diaspora (SEE "THE JEW-ISH CALENDAR"), something new developed. Until sometime between the ninth and twelfth centuries (depending on whose history you accept), different parts of the Jewish world followed different cycles of reading the Torah. Then the triennial system ending before Pesakh used in Eretz Yisrael was dropped in favor of Babylon's annual cycle, with the last portion of Deuteronomy assigned as the portion for the second day of Shemini Atzeret.

In connection with the reading, it became customary to remove the *Sifrei Torah* from the Ark and circle around the bimah, a ceremony for which hundreds of prayers were composed—also called *hoshanahs* for the last word of each. Named Simkhat Torah, Rejoicing in the Torah, the occasion was soon accompanied by vivacious dancing and hymn singing in synagogue, and lavish festival meals at home.

Persecutions of the fourteenth century, when expulsions, blood libels and crusades were directed against Jews who refused to forsake the text, provided the impetus for the exuberant show of support of and adherence to Torah. With symbols and activities of marriage, such as a service suggesting the wedding of Israel to the law, the celebrations demonstrated that the Jews' devotion remained unflagging and their feeling insuppressible. (The British diarist Samuel Pepys noted, in rather disdainful terms, the carryings on in a London synagogue in 1663, in disbelief that he was watching a "decent" religious community. The congregation later regulated itself to display greater decorum.)

Soon it became customary to immediately turn to the beginning of the Torah and start the reading cycle again, expressing the desire to continually study the sacred guidebook. Due to its nature, the new holiday superceded the biblically ordained and much more subdued Shemini Atzeret.

Despite loss of the original agricultural significance of Sukkot, the erection of booths brought a bit of nature to the gray ghetto and urban conditions of the Jews in past centuries. In deteriorating Diaspora situations, Sukkot increasingly was associated with exile and wandering: The Jews were again like the homeless former slaves in the wilderness, dreaming of entering the Promised Land. (Willow in particular became entwined with the despair of exile that resulted from sin, based on our first experience of it (SEE CHAPTER ON TISHA B'AV) and as immortalized in Psalms (137:1–4): "By the rivers of Babylon, there we sat, sat and wept, as we thought of Zion. There on the willows we hung up our harps."

The erection of booths sometimes caused problems for the Jews, as exemplified by the incident in a Galician town in the nineteenth century. An official ordered the *sukkot*—which he presumed had been built without government approval—torn down. The mayor, a friend of the Jews and knowledgeable about their customs, gave them ten days to do so. (The incident served as the basis of a folktale.)

MODERN TIMES

The custom of building *sukkot* in Jerusalem for pilgrims from surrounding countries, which had ended centuries before Jewish nationalist stirrings, was reestablished in the early 1900s with the emergence of political Zionism. Pilgrims from within Eretz Yisrael began making the trek to pray on the Mount of Olives opposite the Temple site, around which they walked seven times on Hoshanah Rabbah.

The settlers emphasized the renewal of Jewish life through restoration of the Land. Etrogim became one of the earliest crops, the beginnings of Israel's once dominant citrus industry. When Jerusalem was divided during the War of Independence (1948), the devout moved their prayer to Mount Zion.

American Reform Jews reintroduced the holiday's harvest nature in the 1930s, with a reenactment of the pilgrimage: groups of children carrying various fruits and vegetables singing hymns while marching around a model *sukkah* erected in the synagogue and liberally decorated with fruits and flowers.

In the Warsaw ghetto, Holocaust labor camps, and Stalinist Soviet Union, Jews continued to celebrate Sukkot. It gave them hope for a positive end point to their own journeys in exile.

Outside of Orthodox circles, Simkhat Torah somehow became categorized in the American community as a holiday for children. Conversely, in the 1950s, seemingly out of nowhere, Jews—not just the old, but young adults—defying official religious repression, began to gather at synagogues in Moscow and Leningrad on Simkhat Torah. They sang Hebrew songs and danced "Israeli" dances. Of all the holidays to pick for a reconnection with Judaism and the Jewish people, they wisely chose the joyous communal embrace of the heart of our heritage. Their courageous stance encouraged more to join them in following years, and spurred Simkhat Torah rallies in America, protesting Soviet treatment of Jews, which contributed to the eventual easing of emigration.

Largely based on the return of Jews from what was the Soviet Union to Israel, Evangelical Christians believe the messiah is on his way. Expecting the arrival during Sukkot, thousands of them gather in the Holy Land each year for the Feast of Tabernacles Conference, organized by the International Christian Assembly. Since 1980, these supporters of the State of Israel have joined tens of thousands of Israelis in their annual Sukkot processions through Jerusalem.

What Does It Mean? Religious Importance

In not commemorating a specific event in our past, but representing particular conditions that were more than one-time occurrences, Sukkot established models for periods that would recur throughout our history. Like the matzah of Pesakh that symbolizes the situation both before and after the Exodus (the bread of slavery and of salvation), this holiday's central image, the *sukkah,* also embodies duality, standing for both homelessness and settlement, wealth within poverty and the reverse.

THE REAL SOURCE OF SECURITY

While the Israelites were wandering the desert with nothing—not even the ability to provide for their own basic needs—they had to recognize and rely on God as the means of their survival. He provided manna for food (EXODUS 16:4–16), clouds for shelter and guidance (EXODUS 33:14–17, NUMBERS 9:15–23), water to drink (EXODUS 15:22–25, 17:5–7, NUMBERS 20:7–12), and conditions to prevent their clothing from deterioration (DEUTERONOMY 29:4). His *sukkot*—protection—inspired in them the faith that they would reach the designated Land, as promised.

Once they arrived, they planted and harvested foodstuffs, built houses, dug wells and wove and sewed garments. But they were not to suddenly feel that they were self-sufficient. All they created and enjoyed, while developed through their own efforts, were no less provided by God than the desert sustenance had been. Though much more obvious in times of want, the booths they lived in for a week each year were reminders of how they began and that regardless of their state—in need or in success—whatever they had came from the Supreme Provider and Protector. As Torah warned when this was readily recognized, "When you later have prosperity, be careful that you not say to yourself, 'It was my own strength and personal power that brought me all this.' You must remember that it is God your Lord Who gives you the power to become prosperous" (DEUTERONOMY 8:17–18).

It was an important lesson: Generations after the Israelites settled the Land, their "permanent" homes were destroyed because they failed to keep the conditions of the covenant (SEE CHAPTER ON TISHA B'AV) and they again became homeless wanderers. The shelter they "owned," wherever in the world they went, was the *feeling* of protection, a belief in God's guardianship that provided a sense of security much stronger and much more durable than any tangible structure. This security sustained their belief, through generations of uprooting and millennia of wandering, that they would eventually be brought home again.

Likewise, living in a *sukkah* today teaches us that the firmest foundation is not cinderblock or stone but faith in God. Did a wall ever stop a Crusader or Cossack? Is sitting shut up in a house, insulated from problems around you—like the Jews of South Africa, behind barbed-wire-topped walls guarded by killer dogs—real security? In one instant, fire, flood, earthquake or hurricane can destroy what we think of as shelter. Despite barred windows, deadbolted doors

sage Shammai instructed.) Expressing resentment or impa-
hand someone *tzedakah* or provide a helping hand detracts
we are extending ourselves. Smiling at someone can make
ours.

observed that approaching life this way can alleviate the pain of
ving that things are for the best and will work out in the end
at deal of anxiety and contributes to peace of mind. The opti
so beautifully expressed by the Jews in Auschwitz who went
deaths, is the mark of a faithful Jew who trusts in the protection
ds comfort in the shade of His *sukkah*, reassurance in the shadow
, hope in the glory of His sheltering cloud.

FOR FURTHER EXPLORATION

. *A Practical Guide to the Mitzvah of Bitochon.* Staten Island: Kolel Yeshiva of Staten

us skeptics, this booklet explains the principle of absolute trust in God, how it leads to
of mind, how it operates in relation to major practical concerns in our lives and why we
n developing it.

Does It Mean to Us? Personal Significance

days ago, on the most solemn day of the year, we learned in the face
at what really matters is living purposefully in a way that will bring
o God—to the realization of the highest moral standards. From the
ng of the synagogue, we now move outside to do something con-
the world. First we build leaf-topped booths that provide a different
d psychological environment than our regular homes do.
of shutting us off from the difficulties and unpleasantness beyond our
raps us in sensitivity to the blessings we enjoy and the plight of others.
holidays and Sabbath create Jewish *time,* with this uniquely Jewish
we literally construct Jewish *space* around us and our families. It is a
al environment between the religious intensity of Yom Kippur and the
preoccupation of normal daily life, where we can begin applying the
f the Day of Atonement.

and alarm systems, intruders can enter our homes and take all our valuables—
and our lives. At best, the roofs over our heads and walls around us are temporary physical safeguards.

When we realize how transient material possessions, how fragile life situations can be, we gain a profound appreciation for whatever we have received
and how much we owe for those blessings. Being thankful actually defines
Jewishness, as reflected in our name. We are known as *Yehudim* (Jews) after the
fourth son of Jacob and Leah, whom she named *Yehudah* (Judah), in thanks to
God (*hodiyah*) (GENESIS 29:35).

A Jew, with blessings for every aspect of life, is someone constantly aware of
God's role and grateful for what He provides, and, whether viewing it as good
or bad, believing it is ultimately for the best. In the *sukkah*, sitting under its airy
branches of *s'khakh* (its covering), we look (*sahkah*) up and out, "seeing" God's
provision for us, a model for our own responsibilities in the world.

SHARING THE BOUNTY

The purpose of our receiving gifts from God is to make it possible for us to
follow His example and provide help for others. When we move out of our
secluded homes into the thin-walled, open-doored *sukkah,* there is less of a barrier between ourselves and those around us. This tenuous box open to the elements causes us to become somewhat like the poor who endure physical
hardships throughout the year.

Philo, the first-century Alexandrian Jewish philosopher (and Maimonides
after him), noted its moral imperative. For him, the timing of the holiday at the
autumnal equinox (the point where the sun crosses the equator from the
northern to southern hemispheres and day and night are of equal length) suggests balance and the opposites that maintain it. When we enjoy good fortune,
status, camaraderie, achievement or peace, we should remember the unfortunate, common, lonely, struggling and war-torn.

That is why providing for the needy is an essential component of celebrating
this festival, why, at every step of our journey through the Jewish year, we are
reminded that we began in bondage. For the poor invited into the *sukkah,* who,
like the ex-slaves, can become prosperous and esteemed, the experience fosters

hope. For those of means, who, like so many people of wealth and influence, can fall from power and possession, it is meant to humble. Sitting in the *sukkah* stresses that all of us are equal before God, Who in the end produces the justice we fail to enact on earth.

OUR ROLE THROUGH OUR HISTORY

The fulfillment of Sukkot marks not just our first-time arrival in The Promised Land, and it is not just the annual harvest of what has been sown in the fields. It is also to be the absolute culmination of the progression that began with the Exodus, the achievement of our mission.

We use the same word to describe both the agricultural aspects of the festival and the messianic age: ingathering—of crops, of the Jewish exiles from all parts of the earth. In other words, when we have accomplished our mission, we will not only reap grapes and grains, fruits and vegetables from the seeds sown and cultivated, but the freedom, mutual respect, well-being and peace that proliferate when moral standards are upheld.

It is no coincidence that the commandments of Sukkot follow the Torah's enumeration of laws of social justice (EXODUS 23:6) and are followed by a reminder to provide justice (DEUTERONOMY 16:13–14). We were led to the Land so we could implement these values—welcoming strangers in our midst, leaving gleanings of the field for the hungry, caring for the widow and orphan, rehabilitating criminals and educating indentured servants. Our Torah-based society would be a paragon for the human community on earth. When it has been accomplished, as Zekhariah tells us, all the nations of the world will gather in Jerusalem together to praise the just God of this just nation.

According to legend, at that time God will construct a *sukkah* out of the skin of the Leviathan, a mythical sea animal of immense proportions said by the Talmud to have been created on the fifth day of the world for just this purpose. Representing a protective mantle of peace and harmony to shelter all, it is the image and hope with which we leave the *sukkah* each year (SEE "OBSERVANCE"), a reminder of the goal to be kept in view as we go back to our everyday lives in the world.

APPROAC

The building blocks to redem
ness to others by sharing what
what Torah means by "rejoicing."
standard of our potential. That is
of our wealth (our crops, our m
approach reaching the goal of Go
(*simkhah*).

We learn from this festival that jo
est capabilities, is a fundamental a
simkhah at occasions throughout the y
ering. Regardless of the amount we h
could not afford livestock to sacrifice
for the altar. And not only in times of a
ful. As Elie Wiesel observed, the Jew
Simkhat Torah, study pages of Talmud fr
and sing Sabbath songs as they were bei

That is appropriate behavior for a Jew.
about the future, and no matter what the
the promise of redemption: "I believe wit
messiah, and though he may tarry, daily I v
THIRTEEN PRINCIPLES OF FAITH).

We credit this attitude, along with the te
Jewish people. The rabbis said that in the wor
the joy we felt in performing *mitzvot*, rather th
commandments. In other words, indication of
tant than going through the motions. Khassidi
ences to joy in service to God. In fact, the movem
in Jewish worship, which its founders saw as hav

The cheerful, positive attitude with which w
in our interpersonal relations as well. Common
that people respond better to a happy face than a
ing, the whole world smiles with you . . ." "Rec

countenance," th
tience when we
from the fact th
his/her day—an
We have also
difficulties. Beli
eliminates a gre
mistic outlook,
singing to their
of God, who fir
of His presence

Goldberger, Mosh
Island, 1982.
Not for religi
complete peac
should work

Wha

Just five
of death th
us closest
closed sett
structive i
physical a
Instea
walls, it w
While all
structure
transitio
material
lessons

The mystics regarded the *sukkah* as the perfect synthesis of physical and spiritual: in order to fulfill the *mitzvah* of dwelling in it, you must enter the *sukkah* with your entire being, body and soul. Inside, you carry on mundane day-to-day functions enveloped in its inherent spirituality. While you sit in the *sukkah*, with its references to a time of universal peace, you are reminded of how much better the world can be. At the end of the week, when you find yourself still sitting in a "temporary" home (since from Judaism's point of view, until we perfect the world, we remain in exile), you are prompted to question how you can help hasten redemption, our universal and eternal goal.

It is impossible to live in our world without being reminded everyday that people are starving and lack shelter. The problem is that we can easily become insensitive. We are bombarded with unceasing news about the famine stricken, war-torn, ethnically persecuted, disaster struck. We literally come face-to-face with the unemployed, unhoused, unwashed and unfed on our streets. When we are working so hard to provide decent lives for our own families, it is understandable that many of us just want to shut out all that need and deprivation, often rationalizing that the suffering people cause their own misfortune.

In former times, in Jewish communities all over the world, there were always poor people who depended on the generosity of others for survival. If a person did not need to request communal assistance, s/he was required to contribute to providing it. Sukkot is a great time to discuss what your family can do to guard yourselves against becoming hardened to less fortunate people and their legitimate needs, and to decide on ways you can help them so that the sensitivity you feel during the holiday lasts beyond it.

Many people contribute to relief organizations and urge their legislators to take appropriate action to ease conditions for people suffering in all parts of the world. You can also take a more direct approach. If you are uncomfortable dispensing money to the beggars on the spot, you can distribute bags of food, contribute to or work in a food kitchen, help establish/promote/gain offerings for a job bank, or venture out on especially cold nights to distribute blankets or warm unused clothing from the recesses of your closets to people living on the streets. You might look to the seven illustrious men of Israel you invite to join you in the *sukkah* (SEE "OBSERVANCE") for inspiration. Each one embodies a particular quality, mirroring a facet of the character of God that needs to pervade the world.

While you are in the position of being able to assist others, you might also consider whether or not you stop often enough to be grateful for all that you have. When you recite *brakhot* are they just foreign words said by rote? Are they formulas you include only on holidays? To maintain conscious appreciation for whatever you enjoy, you might introduce a daily or weekly prayer into your family life. Many people thank God for all the good things of the previous week on Shabbat, when they light candles or bless their children. Getting children to enumerate—at candlelighting or before bed—the people and things they are glad to have in their lives is a good way to foster the awareness in them. (Observant Jews accomplish the lasting recognition by saying blessings for virtually every aspect of their existence and activity.)

Most people worry about their own financial needs and their neighbor's soul. Better that they should worry about their neighbor's financial needs and their own souls.

RABBI ISRAEL SALANTER

If we exit the festival with this increased sensitivity, we will be doing our part to bring redemption. Many communities announce the end of Simkhat Torah with the proclamation "And Jacob went on his way" (leaving the household of his deceitful father-in-law Laban [GENESIS 32:2]). It is a reminder that as we depart from our festivities and return to regular existence, we do so as Jews, like Jacob, with our own ways, ways based on awareness of God and a mission much greater than our individual selves that should influence everything we do, say and think.

The Jewish way is of course laid out in the Torah, a book unfortunately, like Jewish education and Simkhat Torah celebration, too often relegated to children. Certainly it is for children—and for adolescents, young adults, and older adults. The sages say there are seventy different levels to it, so that it not only has ageless application, but also can be understood from a broad range of perspectives, intellectual capacities and interests. Each person can understand it in his or her own way. That is why we read it again and again, as we would see a well-crafted drama, or listen to a magnificent symphony, or look at an intricate painting repeatedly, discovering new elements, nuances and meaning with each encounter.

For young children, Bible stories are colorful tales about relevant people with whom they can identify, if properly exposed to them, as readily as they do with any cartoon, television and other popular culture characters. (When he was four years old the grandson of an acquaintance thought Moses was a contemporary and questioned his grandfather about the leader as though the two were fast friends.) For teenagers, biblical personages and situations are no less real, expressing a full range of human emotion and quality, and offering the moral values young people need but are too often denied in today's system of value neutral formal education.

For adults, Torah—full of pathos, psychology, drama, love, comedy, conflict and philosophy—contains all the elements considered essential for blockbuster novels today, and in the context of a good read provides universally applicable guidance for how to get the most out of life. "Study the Torah again and again for everything is contained in it," counsel our rabbis (PIRKEI AVOT 5:25). "Constantly examine it, grow old and gray over it; and swerve not from it, for there is nothing more excellent than it."

In blessings traditionally given to children, particularly at the *brit* and baby naming, we pray that they will perform good deeds, come to the *khuppah* (wedding canopy), and grow in study of Torah. This is a very telling wish for a child. Unlike the Romans who wanted muscular, rugged soldiers, and the Greeks who wanted athletes—or American Jews who may wish for doctors and lawyers—historically Jews above all wanted children who would maintain their bond to Judaism through Torah, to understand its messages and exemplify its ethics. For this would mean that they could, through their own behavior, go out, as we do from the *sukkah*, live meaningful worthwhile lives, and change the world.

Like the children commanded to attend the *Hockheil* reading of Deuteronomy, what your children learn of Torah in their youngest years will affect them the rest of their lives—in terms of knowledge, values, feelings of connectedness to Judaism and the Jewish people. The example they see in your own involvement with Torah learning can easily convey the message that this is a book to carry through—and to carry you through—life. You have a built-in opportunity to begin learning together now at the start of the Torah-reading cycle.

FOR FURTHER EXPLORATION

Refer to the materials listed in the chapter on Shavuot.

Traditions—

HOW WE CELEBRATE SUKKOT

What Do We Use? Ritual Items

SUKKAH

The *sukkah* is the temporary dwelling, referred to as "booth" or archaically as tabernacle (from *taberna,* hut, which is why you may hear the holiday referred to as the Feast of Tabernacles), in which we are supposed to eat our meals and sleep during the week of the harvest festival.

Although regulations define the minimum size, maximum height and acceptable dimensions for its walls (SEE "HALAKHAH"), the element that makes a *sukkah* more than an agricultural shed is its "roof": a canopy made from stalks or branches arranged to provide more shade than sunlight and allow you to see the stars through it. In other words, it is something that originally grew from the earth through which we can look up and see heaven. In fact, the word *sukkah* is derived from the word for the roof—*s'khakh,* meaning covering—indicating the essence and most important element of the structure. It is a reminder that during the Israelites' forty years of wandering, God "covered" all their needs.

Since we are supposed to live in the *sukkah* according to our normal standards (as "dwell" in the commandment "and you shall dwell in booths" [LEVITICUS 23:42] indicates), we should surround ourselves with the finest accoutrements of our permanent homes—furnishings, linens, tableware. However, most people today do not transfer their favorite couches or their dining room sets into the *sukkah.* Folding tables and chairs are common.

It is a *mitzvah* for every Jew to participate in building and decorating a *sukkah.* (A *sukkah* decorating party, for the immediate family or an extended group including friends, is a great way to get into the spirit of the holiday.) If you have absolutely no space in which to construct one (don't overlook a balcony, rooftop, spot of common ground in front of an apartment building; there's a famous story of Rabbi Akiva building one on a ship's deck despite the accurate chidings of a colleague that it would blow away), try to assist in building a synagogue or community *sukkah,* or help a friend. (Some families, unable to do any of these, at least build a model that becomes part of their table decorations.)

You can use just about any materials to make the walls: cinder blocks, scrap lumber, old doors, bamboo shades, canvas or nylon sheeting attached to a frame of wood or metal piping with nails or grommets and rope.

Beams can be placed across the top to support the *s'khakh.* In Israel, authorities trim the palm trees in time for the holiday and leave the branches in piles on the streets for people to take home. In America, parks departments often oblige with the by-product of fall pruning. If you cannot obtain leafy branches, bamboo, straw, reeds, thin boards and so on may be used.

Our enjoyment of the *mitzvah* is enhanced when we consider its aesthetics, so it is appropriate to make the sukkah as beautiful as possible. Gourds, fruits, birds made from hollowed eggshells, cranberry garlands, popcorn strands and paper chains, pictures and wall tapestries, along with representations of the seven species that grow in Israel (wheat, barley, grape, fig, date, pomegranate, olive), are all traditional. Some people use cards they have received for the New Year, and previous years' etrogim, either dried or clove-studded. Spotlights, strings of small bulbs, hanging lanterns and other fixtures or candles are used to provide illumination.

Jewish bookstores and sometimes synagogues sell pre-fab *sukkot.* Manufacturers and suppliers often advertise them in Jewish publications around the holiday season.

Despite the regulations regarding erecting a "kosher *sukkah,*" a Khassidic tale teaches us about the importance of following the intent of the law over the letter of it, and encourages even the novice to erect a *sukkah.* A humble man, who had spent more than he could afford to get the choicest materials for his *sukkah,* invited Rabbi Nakhman of Bratslav to visit. The rabbi accepted, and went with a disciple. As soon as they entered, the student whispered to the Rabbi that the structure did not conform to all the laws. After they had left, the Rabbi chastised the disciple. "This Jew went to such trouble to make the booth, and you raise questions about its validity because of legal technicalities?!"

FOUR SPECIES

We take up the lulav and etrog to fulfill the commandment regarding the *arba'ah* (four) *minim* (species). The long elegant lulav consists of one palm branch (lulav, the largest element of the bundle and therefore the name of the whole assembly) embraced by a holder with a pocket on the left containing two willow branches (*aravot*) and one on the right containing three myrtle branches (*hadasim*).

Usually at least one ring holds the leaves together, and traditionally three of them up the length of the lulav above the holder, said to represent the patriarchs Abraham, Isaac and Jacob (or, continuing a theme of the Days of Awe, the wicked, the righteous and those in between). The holder, often woven, can be made only of palm leaves because the three plant types may not be separated by any foreign material, which would also disrupt the proper number of species.

Some rabbinic interpretation was necessary to identify two of the four flora not specified in Torah (LEVITICUS 23:40). The "product of *hadar* trees" they said had to be the etrog (citron), because no other tree has bark, leaves and fruit that are equally fragrant and flavorful, exemplifying beauty (*hadar*). Since Torah uses the singular for "fruit" we use one etrog. "Boughs of leafy trees" were recognized as myrtle. Since Torah uses three words to describe this species (*anaf* [branch], *eitz* [tree], and *avot* [thicket]), we use three *hadasim*. The plural designation for "willows of the brook" suggested two *aravot*.

MEANING Exactly why these particular plants were chosen, and how they are to be arranged and used may remain one of Torah's mysteries. That has not stopped rabbis from offering numerous explanations. On the superficial level, the etrog and components of the lulav together represent the entire plant kingdom and emphasize Sukkot's agricultural nature as well as, by their shapes, masculine and feminine forces. Life on earth could not be sustained without them and the four basic elements they also suggest: air (the palm standing upright), fire (the yellow citron), earth (the low-growing myrtle) and water (the willow that lives next to rivers and brooks).

Maimonides (GUIDE FOR THE PERPLEXED) saw them as symbols of the change from the Israelites' existence in the wilderness, "a place . . . there was not even water to drink" (NUMBERS 20:5) to their rejoicing in a country full of fruit trees and rivers reflecting God's fulfillment of His promise of "a good land, a land of brooks of water [willow], and fountains issuing from valleys [where etrogim grow] and hills [where myrtles thrive], a land of . . . honey [date palms]" (DEUTERONOMY 8:7–8).

The qualities of the four species are likened to those of four categories of Jews. The etrog, possessing both taste and aroma, stands for Jews who have knowledge of Torah and do good deeds. The palm's fruit (date), with taste but no aroma, represents people with Torah knowledge. The myrtle, with no taste but aroma, represents people who do good, and willow, with neither aroma nor taste, stands for those self-concerned and ignorant of Torah.

We serve God with all four elements held together, the spiritually lofty with the simply mundane, the scholar, aristocrat, merchant and laborer. In society, all elements must likewise hold together, so that the wise and righteous can influence those less so, and because each contributes its part to society's functioning and progress when they unite for common welfare. As our sages put it, "As one does not fulfill his duty on Sukkot unless all four species are bound together, so some will not be redeemed unless all Jews hold together," a strong message about the need for unity among our diverse segments.

Similarly, those that bear fruit (citron and palm), the wise, must be bound closely with those that do not (willow and myrtle), for the prayers of the sages produce mercy for everyone else, and the non-scholars provide physical comfort for the sages and their disciples.

From the body of Israel the rabbis moved to the body of the individual, seeing through their shapes the palm as backbone, the citron as heart, the myrtle as eye and the willow as mouth. Together they express our desire to use all our vital components to worship God, and to atone for transgressions resulting from an envious eye, malicious mouth or lustful heart. In mysticism, each species represents one letter in God's name. The lulav is the vov ("and") uniting them as a conduit for Divine energy into the world.

Myrtle represents beauty and mercy (like the heroine of the Purim story who had the same Hebrew name [*hadas{sah}*].) Since when cut it stays fresh for days, myrtle became an ancient symbol for success and immortality. In contrast, willow leaves droop as soon as the branches are cut. On the one hand representing our exit from the desert to the Land full of water, it also symbolized our exile from the Land and the sadness and longing we have felt at the separation. However, just as the leaves fall and grow again, God continually provides new life and hope for the Jews.

Considered perfect and full and therefore a symbol of purpose in life, the etrog is not bound to the other species, each imperfect through the lack of one quality or another. Because of what it represents, an etrog used in the Sukkot ritual must be flawless. The critical element is the *pittam,* the protuberance at its top. The remaining part of the blossom through which the developing fruit had been nourished, it must be intact in order for the etrog to be kosher (ritually valid).

It is considered desirable to have your own lulav and etrog, for they are used every morning of the holiday, at home and in synagogue. However, the synagogue usually has one set for the use of anyone who needs it.

OBTAINING The concept of *hidur mitzvah,* beautifying the commandment, that all *mitzvot* should be performed with regard to aesthetics, has traditionally been carried to extremes for Sukkot. While we should buy the choicest example of each species, people throughout our history have in particular sought the perfect etrog, often paying excessive prices for the privilege of owning one. The sages advised that we spend up to one-third more than what we would normally expect to pay. To prevent exploitation by the once-a-year opportunity for citron sellers to clean up in the concentrated market, each year a few religious leaders agree on a maximum price.

It is considered an enhancement of the *mitzvah* to choose your own lulav and etrog. If you are in Israel or a religious Jewish enclave, you can go to one of the stores selling them, or to an open Sukkot market, such as the ones in front of Mashbir Department Store in Jerusalem or in Tel Aviv's Yitzhak Rabin Square. There you will see religious Jews choosing each of the four species separately, going from shop to shop or booth to booth with a magnifying glass—literally—to ensure the quality of their selections.

Most of us do not have the opportunity for such choices, but have to order our four species from a Jewish supply store or through a synagogue. Many congregations take orders from members during the Days of Awe and deliver the items in time for Sukkot. The lulav comes with an etrog as a set.

To protect the etrog—though it is hardy, you do not want to chance damaging or losing its *pittam*—most people keep it wrapped in flax in the box in which it is delivered, or transfer it to a special etrog box. That could be something as makeshift as a plain wooden or metal receptacle, or as elegant as a carved olive wood or engraved silver container especially designed for the purpose. They are available at outlets that sell Judaica items.

You can keep the lulav fresh by placing it in the refrigerator wrapped in a damp towel or aluminum foil, enclosed in a plastic bag with a few drops of water, or in a vase with just enough water to keep the bottom moist.

ARAVOT

For Hoshanah Rabbah, branches of willows are needed for the "beating" ceremony symbolic of summoning rain. Worshippers may use the aravot from their lulavim, synagogues often make additional switches available, and some Jewish bookstores sell them. It is traditional to use five twigs bound together with a palm leaf. In addition to inducing rain and obliterating sin, the willow beating is said to represent elimination of a danger to the community: The Jew it symbolizes, ignorant of Torah and negligent in helping others, although acceptable in the mix of all Jews, threatens communal welfare and continuity when acting alone. Thrashing it is also said to express our sadness at still being in exile.

SIMKHAT TORAH FLAGS

Reminiscent of the standards carried by the Twelve Tribes of Israel as they progressed through the desert (NUMBERS 2:2–31, 10:14–28), paper flags are carried by children as they follow the processions on Simkhat Torah. Sometimes provided by the synagogue, the flags can be purchased in Jewish bookstores, or made by the children.

MEMORIAL CANDLE

As for all other holy days on which we recite the memorial service *Yizkor*, it is customary for anyone who has lost a parent to light a yahrtzeit candle the evening before the service takes place. (Some people light for grandparents.) The candles can be purchased at a Jewish supply store, or in supermarkets that carry kosher items. They come in small cans or glasses, and burn for twenty-five hours, long enough to last from candlelighting time through the end of *yom tov.*

How Do We Celebrate? Observance

Think about the anticipation most people experience as Thanksgiving approaches. We look forward to the warm embrace of family and friends and allowing ourselves to splurge on lavish meals. That's the kind of feeling Sukkot, the original thanksgiving, is meant to generate. Happiness pervades this holiday. The Torah commands three observances to foster that emotion: living in the *sukkah,* gathering together the four species, and rejoicing during the holiday. (The liturgy refers to the festival as *Zeman Simkhateinu,* the Season of Our Rejoicing.)

There is the excitement of a new and different living arrangement for a week, out in the autumn air; the anticipation through the party-like atmosphere of erecting and decorating the structure; the novelty of eating and possibly sleeping in a harvest booth scented with palm or pine and fall fruits. Having come through the deprivations of Yom Kippur, we relax in the relief of reaching a milestone of accomplishment and can let ourselves go in the singing and dancing that cannot help but raise our spirits.

Orthodox and Conservative Jews in the Diaspora celebrate in these ways for nine days: the first two as full holidays, days three through seven as *khol* (intermediate) *hamoed* (festival days), and the last two as full holidays, Shemini Atzeret (day eight) and Simkhat Torah (day nine). In Israel and for the Reform, the festival lasts eight days, with the first and last as full holidays, and the last as a somewhat schizophrenic combination of the solemn Shemini Atzeret and the spirited Simkhat Torah.

The intermediate days are alike in character to *khol hamoed* Pesakh, the other extended festival in our year. Comparable to eating matzoh for the former, the commandment for the latter is dwelling in the *sukkah.* While no biblical prohibitions limit work and travel on these days, in traditional circles people sometimes refrain from doing any non-essential work, and do not write.

DWELLING IN THE SUKKAH

For the entire period of Sukkot, we eat our meals and, where weather permits, sleep in the *sukkah*. If you do not have your own *sukkah*, ask a friend who has one to invite you for a least one meal, or make *kiddush* in a synagogue *sukkah* (this is easy as it is generally organized to take place after services).

CANDLELIGHTING As for all Jewish holidays, we usher in Sukkot by blessing and lighting candles and reciting *shehekhiyanu,* if at all possible in the sukkah (SEE "BLESSINGS"). If the candles are in danger of being blown out, they should be moved into the house.

USHPIZIN Maimonides admonished that anyone who sits comfortably with his family within his own walls and does not share with the poor is performing a *mitzvah* not for joy, but for the stomach. In addition to extending personal invitations to the needy (in former times it was customary to have at least one poor person at a Sukkot meal; donation of funds today often substitutes), we open our homes symbolically. With a formula established by the kabbalists in the sixteenth century, based on the earlier Zohar, on each night of Sukkot we invite one of seven exalted men of Israel to take up residence in the *sukkah* with us. "When a man sits in the shadow of faith [*sukkah*] the Shekhinah [Divine Presence] spreads Her wings on him from above and Abraham and five other righteous ones of God (and David with them) make their abode with him. . . . A man should rejoice each day of the festival with these guests."

The inspiration for *hakhnasat orekhim* (hospitality to guests) goes all the way back to our first patriarch, and the first guest honored, Abraham. He would sit outside waiting for the opportunity to invite dusty wayfarers into the shade of his tent, and then run to prepare a meal of the choicest ingredients. (A midrash based on the apocryphal Book of Jubilees claims that the first booth, on which the holiday Sukkot is based, was built by Abraham when he greeted the three Angels who came to tell him his wife Sarah would at last bear a child [GENESIS 18:1–10]. Jubilees [16:21] traces other observances of Sukkot to Abraham's tents in Beersheva, where he erected an altar and circled it while praying.)

We perform a short ceremony to welcome the *ushpizin* (Aramaic for guests). A complete daily/festival *siddur* will contain the full text for the invitation that they join us. Following it and prayers that our fulfillment of the *mitzvah* of *sukkah* will be worthy of Divine favor, on the first day we say: "I invite to my meal the exalted guests, Abraham, Isaac, Jacob, Joseph, Moses, Aaron and David. May it please you, Abraham, my exalted guest, that all the other exalted guests dwell here with me and with you—Isaac, Jacob, Joseph, Moses, Aaron and David." On each day, a different one of the seven is singled out, in order.

The Sephardim, who often set aside a special chair laden with holy books for the *ushpiz,* invite the patriarchs (Abraham, Isaac and Jacob), then the leaders/prophets (Moses and Aaron), then royalty (Joseph and David). They also often send provisions to the poor along with a note saying: "This is the share of the *ushpizin.*" Recently, it has become popular in some circles to invite matriarchs and other important women of Israel—Sarah, Rachel, Rebecca, Leah, Miriam, Abigail and Esther—either paired with the men or on their own.

In addition to serving as a reminder of our duty to the poor (it is said that the *ushpizin* would refuse to enter a *sukkah* where the poor are not welcome), each of these exalted personages represents uprootedness. (Abraham left his father's home for the land God promised to show him [GENESIS 12:1], Isaac went to Gerar during a famine [GENESIS 26:1], Jacob fled from his brother Esau to the habitat of Laban [GENESIS 28:2], Joseph was sold to merchants and taken to Egypt [GENESIS 37:23–36], Moses fled to Midian after inadvertently killing an Egyptian [EXODUS 2:11–15] and he and Aaron wandered the Sinai for forty years [EXODUS 13 AND ON], and David hid from Saul in the wilderness [I SAMUEL 20, 21].)

Each in his wanderings contributed to the world through a respective personal characteristic (a version of those cited in reference to self-improvement on Shavuot): loving-kindness, strength, splendor, glory, holiness, eternity, sovereignty. Reflecting the periods of homelessness and wandering in their lives, our temporary dwellings can inspire us to emulate the benefits they brought to the world. Many people put up plaques or pictures of the *ushpizin,* containing the blessing and scenes from their lives. (Laminated ones are available through Jewish supply sources.)

KIDDUSH AND OTHER BRAKHOT Once our guests—worldly and otherwise—are comfortably established beneath our shelter, we recite a special festival *kiddush* (full text found in a *siddur*), followed by the blessing used every time we take a meal in the *sukkah* (*leisheiv b'sukkah*).

If a person other than the one who did candlelighting makes *kiddush*, *she-hekhiyanu* is then said, and refers to both the first day of the festival, and the first use of the *sukkah*. On the second day, candles are again lit with the *brakhah* and *shehekhiyanu*. This time, *shehekhiyanu* immediately follows *kiddush* (so it refers only to the new holy day) and then *leisheiv b'sukkah* is recited. Traditional Jews follow with the ritual handwashing and blessing over bread.

On intermediate days, we continue to say the blessing for dwelling in the *sukkah*. Since the end of the festival in the Diaspora coincides with Shemini Atzeret, an independent holiday, the rabbis disagreed over whether or not we are still supposed to live in the *sukkah* on that day. By accepted common practice, we eat meals but do not say the blessings. (In Israel, the *sukkah* is not used at all after the seventh day of the festival.)

When we leave the *sukkah* for the last time, we express our hope that we will deserve to sit in the *sukkah* that will be built at the time of the messiah, which we pray will be during our lifetime (FOR ALL, SEE "BLESSINGS").

COMFORT AND JOY Since the *sukkah* is a memorial to God's protection, it is meant to enhance the joy of the festival. If you do not feel joy, you cannot appropriately fulfill the *mitzvah* of dwelling in the *sukkah*. This understanding led to an unusual approach by the rabbis. While they generally encourage us to perform *mitzvot* beyond the requirements stated, in this case they encourage us *not* to stay in the *sukkah* when conditions make it uncomfortable.

Exceptions to the stringent Talmudic laws about sleeping in it developed in Europe where inclement weather made doing so unreasonable. Due to the often-uncomfortable nature of the structures, women and children were generally excused from even having meals in them. (Women were not obligated anyway—under the general principle that they are not bound to *mitzvot* that must be performed at certain times of the day. However, they voluntarily took the *mitzvah* of dwelling in the *sukkah* on themselves, and therefore it is customary for them to fulfill it.) If it rains enough to "spoil the soup," as the rabbis say, you are supposed to leave. (The laws for the first night are somewhat different, as explained in the section on halakhah.) The rabbis had a name for anyone exempted who remains in the *sukkah* despite discomfort: ignoramus!

Those anxious to perform the *mitzvah* of eating in the *sukkah* despite terrible conditions fulfill the obligation by reciting *kiddush* and eating just a small piece of bread or cake in it. The idea is that it is preferable to be comfortable in your house enjoying the holiday than to be miserable in the *sukkah*, cursing the discomfort and worse, the cause of it.

However, do not dismiss the backyard adventure sleeping in the *sukkah* can be for children, especially equipped with toasty sleeping bags. Sometimes a whole family "sleeps out" at least one night during the week.

To enhance the celebration it is customary to sing in the *sukkah*. Some people prepare special readings for each might, such as a relevant eight-part story, text on the *ushpiz* of the day, appropriate sections of Ecclesiastes (the scroll assigned to this festival), or psalms that deal with God's shelter (27, 31, 34, 36, 57, 63, 91).

TAKING UP THE LULAV AND ETROG

In a traditional Jewish home, every member of the family fortunate enough to have its own lulav and etrog recites the benediction over them first thing in the morning, before breakfast, every day throughout the festival. (You can actually bless the four species anytime during the day.) When possible, the b*rakhah* is made in the *sukkah*.

PROCEDURE Technicalities of saying benedictions determine the way we hold the four species prior to and following recitation of the blessing. For all *mitzvot*, we are supposed to first say a blessing, then immediately perform the *mitzvah*. So that there will not be a lapse of time in the case of the lulav and etrog (such as would result if we said the blessing and then first went to pick up the four species), we should have them in hand when we say the blessing. However, since we cannot fulfill the *mitzvah* until after the *brakhah*, they have to be in hand differently beforehand and afterward.

The generally followed custom is to stand, pick up the lulav in your right hand (composed of three of the four species it is considered dominant and therefore held in the usually dominant right hand) with the spine (the long green shaft running its length) toward you, and the etrog, with its *pittam* down (opposite the way it grows), in your left (closer to the heart, whose shape it resembles). On the first day only, *shehekhiyanu* follows the *brakhah* that covers all four species (SEE "BLESSINGS").

Then turn the etrog so the *pittam* faces up, and, keeping your hands close enough together that the lulav and etrog touch, with enough force to slightly rustle the leaves, wave the lulav in six directions: east, south, west, north, above and below. Since we face east, this means in front of us, right, over the right shoulder, left, up and down. (The Sephardim wave right, left, front, back, up and down. The Syrian Jews actually turn to the direction and wave three times in front of themselves and up and down in each position.)

The customary procedure is to hold the lulav and etrog with your hands together, extend your arms out, shake the four species, draw your arms back into you, and repeat twice more. Then go to the next direction. It is a moderately rapid movement; don't labor over it.

Those who do not bless the four species at home do so at synagogue following the *Shakharit Amidah* just before *Hallel,* one of the places in the service where we use the lulav and etrog. The other is during the procession around the altar, called *hoshanah* after the accompanying prayer. On the Sabbath, we do not use the four species, to avoid having anyone carry them from home to synagogue or one home to another, which is prohibited on the day of rest.

MEANING Like the four plant types themselves, the wavings (*na'ahnu'im*) have symbolic significance. They represent Israel's acceptance of God's sovereignty over all of nature (the four directions), heaven (up) and earth (down). Talmud likened the motion to the offering of omer brought on the second day of Passover and waved in four directions to contain ill winds, and to a sacrificial offering on the altar. Lifting the lulav expresses joy (as when you lift a child or a trophy into the air), and victory, publicly proclaiming Israel's successful emergence from the Divine Judgment of Rosh Hashanah and Yom Kippur. (When people used to appear before a judge, the one who exited holding palm branches was recognized as the victor.) According to midrash, the outcome of the Yom Kippur judgment of all nations of the world is not revealed until the first day of Sukkot. The procession of Israelites around the altar (or bimah), their lulavim held aloft, proclaims Israel's victory, and hints at messianic fulfillment as promised in Isaiah (55:12): "You shall leave in joy and be led home secure. Before you mountains and hills shall shout aloud, and all the trees of the field shall clap their hands . . ." When we shake the lulav, the palm leaves hit against each other, as though clapping, bringing to mind God's promise to Israel.

HALLEL We recite the Psalms of Praise (113–118) for the full duration of Sukkot since, with a unique complement of sacrifices, each day is considered a holiday in its own right. The wavings are done four times during the verse of *hodu l'Adonai,* give thanks to God (PSALM 118:1), twice in *ana hoshiah,* we implore you, save us (PSALM 118:25) and twice in the last *hodu l'Adonai* (PSALM 118:29). Hodu contains six words (excluding the name of God); we wave in one direction as each word is slowly enunciated. (Just follow the service leader.) The pattern is followed for the six syllables of the phrase beginning *ana,* and then for the six words in the verse of *hodu* in the concluding paragraph of *Hallel.*

HOSHANOT Immediately after the *khazzan's* repetition of the *Mussaf Amidah,* we recite special prayers, the *hoshanot* (multiple of *hoshanah*). Medieval poems and prayers predominantly composed by the eighth-century Rabbi Elazar Hakallir, they ask God to deliver us. Each consists of twenty-two verses or stanzas in alphabetic order.

For the service, the Ark remains open once Torah scrolls are taken from it and held at the bimah by members of the congregation. After introductory verses, the *khazzan* leads everyone (only men in Orthodox congregations) carrying the lulav and etrog around the bimah as they read the *hoshanah* of the day. (Since the contents are connected with the days of the week, the order changes depending on when the festival begins.) The congregation repeats each line. On the Sabbath, the Ark is opened and verses said, but the *Sifrei Torah* are not removed and no procession takes place (remember—we do not pick up the four species on the Sabbath).

For convenience, since they already have the lulavim and etrogim in hand, the Sephardim conduct hoshanot immediately after *Hallel* as part of *Shakharit.*

Circling, a symbol of perfection and completion and part of Sukkot, Hoshanah Rabbah and Simkhat Torah celebrations, is popular in other Jewish ceremonies (as when the bride circles the groom seven times in a traditional wedding) and art. In folk beliefs, a "magic ring" could keep out bad spirits.

Among the Jews, it was believed that one could gain God's favor by setting an object apart within a circle. The righteous Honi "The Circle Maker" made this concept famous: He would draw a ring around himself and refuse to budge until God had granted his requests (SEE "STORIES TO READ" IN CHAPTER ON TU B'SHEVAT). Ingathering suggests collecting within the protective circle of our arms. We draw the lulav and etrog back to us almost in a circling motion, creating an insular, secure space enveloping God's spirit within it.

READINGS FROM TORAH AND PROPHETS

While the Torah readings consist of the straightforward festival laws, commandments and sacrifices (LEVITICUS 22:26–23:44, NUMBERS 29:12–16), the Haftarot provide colorful glimpses of Sukkot celebration future and past.

Zekhariah 14, read on the first day, describes the festival at the time when all nations of the world will gather in Jerusalem to praise God together. Their acknowledgement that He is the supreme king will indicate acceptance of one moral standard and bring universal peace. On the second day we read I Kings' description of the dedication of Solomon's Temple, which took place during Sukkot (8:1–21). Ezekiel 38, read on the intermediate Sabbath, previews the war of Gog and Magog—by tradition to take place during the season of Sukkot—from which Israel will emerge victorious in the messianic era.

Also on this Shabbat, we read the scroll assigned to the holiday, Kohelet (Ecclesiastes). Popularly known thanks to the Byrd's hit song, "Turn! Turn! Turn!" which uses its verses "For every thing, there is a season . . . ," the book is attributed to King Solomon. He penned it at a different point in this life than when he wrote the sensual Song of Songs we read on Pesakh, much older, toward the end of his days, and philosophical about what life has meant. Having explored every experience open to him, physical and spiritual, uplifting and degrading, having chased gratifying pleasures and maintained a moral highroad, he warns that anything not done in service to God is "vanity of vanities, all is vanity" (1:2).

Contrasting the two continually opposed facets of life, good and evil, material and spiritual, and expressing the range of human mood, Ecclesiastes is a treatise on what brings permanent joy: not the fleeting pleasures of the body, but devotion to something much greater than the self. Solomon concludes with the message "The end of the matter, all having been heard, fear God and keep His commandments; for this applies to all mankind" (12:13).

At the time of our greatest material abundance, when we might mistakenly applaud our self-sufficiency, Solomon reminds us that there is nothing new under the sun, that things of this world are temporary and can be fleeting, that true happiness comes in being content with what we have and recognizing the source of whatever that is. The lesson eloquently complements the meaning of the *sukkah*.

BEATING THE WILLOWS

Although Hoshanah Rabbah, on the seventh day of Sukkot, is part of *khol hamoed,* it seems to have greater status because of the synagogue service. Since the day has been seen from the Middle Ages as a "Yom Kippur Katan" (little), when the annual judgment verdict is delivered, it is approached as the last opportunity for those who have not yet completed their repentance process. (It certainly cannot be said that Judaism does not give us every last chance to fulfill our obligations!) That's why we see and hear similarities to the Day of Atonement: the Torah scrolls wear white vestments, the cantor wears a *kittel,* candles may be lit in the synagogue, the plaintive chants of Yom Kippur embrace our prayers, we say the verses of the Days of Awe—"remember us for life"—and conclude with the same passages used to end Yom Kippur. Some congregations also insert shofar blasts during the service.

Unlike the other days of Sukkot when we remove one scroll from the Ark and make one procession encircling the bimah, on Hoshanah Rabbah all the scrolls are removed from the Ark and seven processions, each one to the recitation of a *hoshanah,* are made. After each *hoshanah* we recite a Scriptural verse related to one of seven *sefirot* (part of the kabbalistic system representing qualities of God): kindness (PSALMS 89:3), strength (PSALMS 89:14), splendor (MICAH 7:20), triumph (PSALMS 16:11), glory (PSALMS 8:2), foundation (PSALMS 145:17) and kingship (ZEKHARIAH 14:9). These correspond to the attributes of the heavenly visitors to the *sukkah,* and the qualities attributed by David to God (I CHRONICLES 29:11), to which our circuits correspond and through which we hope to gain God's favor.

The seven circuits represent the seven heavens, separating God from the earth, which we want to pierce with our supplications. They also stand for the seven times Joshua's army marched around Jericho. I Kings relates that for rebuilding the city against His will and Joshua's decree, God punished Israel with years of drought (17:1). Therefore, on Hoshanah Rabbah when we pray for dew and rain—mentioned seven times in Torah as blessings—we appropriately remember that lack of them and consequent famine resulted from disobeying God's commandments. In addition, the crumbling walls symbolize the collapse of the walls of our transgressions. In one tradition, a scroll is returned to the Ark after each circuit.

It has long been the custom to stay up all night on Hoshanah Rabbah to meditate, study and read holy books. Many congregations go through Deuteronomy in its entirety, as that book summarizes all the laws and warnings found in Torah. (Some read all five books to make up for any failure during the previous year to review the weekly portions and translation [per Talmud's requirement].) Others recite the Thirteen Attributes from the Days of Awe services.

Since King David is the honored *ushpiz* on this day, Psalms, attributed to his authorship, is read (in some places punctuated by shofar blasts at the conclusion of each of its five books). Kabbalists in particular recall David, who is said to have remained awake, except for a short nap, every night. Concentrating on *Tikkun* (improvement) *Leil* (for the night of) *Hoshanah Rabbah,* a compilation of selections from Deuteronomy, Psalms and Zohar, they attempt to "unite" the darkness of night with the light of day.

As on Shavuot, synagogues and Jewish institutions (like Hillels) often arrange special study sessions for this night and serve coffee and cake to participants. Traditional men often follow it by going to the *mikvah* for a ritual bath.

PROCEDURE For the processions, the knotted rings holding the lulav together are usually removed so that the leaves wave more freely in expression of joy. Following the *hoshanah* prayers, we put down the four species, take up willow branches and beat them on the ground or against a chair while reciting a passage asking for forgiveness, dew and rain. According to ritual law, the bundle needs to be beat only five times, but many people continue thrashing away until most of the leaves are gone. Women and children also participate in this

407

ritual. Since it is a custom continued only through the force of folk tradition, and not a biblical commandment or rabbinic ordinance, no blessing accompanies the action.

The same calendar alteration that ensured Yom Kippur will never fall immediately before or after a Shabbat also ensures that Hoshanah Rabbah cannot fall on the Sabbath, when the beating ritual could not take place (since we are not supposed to hurt or destroy plants).

Reform congregations treat the seventh day of Sukkot as no different than any other part of *khol hamoed* and with no special Hoshanah Rabbah services or rituals.

SHEMINI ATZERET

Just as Sukkot gives us a transitional period between the Days of Awe and our normal routines, the last day of the festival, the Eighth Day of Solemn Assembly, or the day we are held back to extend the party with God, eases us out of the transience of the *sukkah.*

As a separate holiday in its own right, referred to as *Shemini Khag* (festival) *Ha'atzeret,* it is honored with the lighting of candles and reciting the festival *kiddush.* Common practice is to do *kiddush* and eat in the *sukkah* in the evening and morning, but not to recite the blessing for dwelling in the *sukkah,* or to take up the four species. (In Israel, where Shemini Atzeret clearly follows Sukkot, the *sukkah* is not used at all.) At the conclusion of the last meal we recite the blessing for leaving the *sukkah* (SEE "DWELLING IN THE SUKKAH" EARLIER IN CHAPTER AND "BLESSINGS "AT END OF BOOK).

PRAYER FOR RAIN The distinct feature of the day is recitation of the prayer for rain so that the earth will be able to produce in the coming year. We do not say it earlier during Sukkot, which marks the beginning of the rainy season in Israel, because we do not want rain to prevent us from dwelling in the *sukkah,* or to interfere with our enjoyment of doing so.

From the beginning of Shemini Atzeret until the first day of Pesakh, we insert a phrase in the second benediction of the *Amidah*: "who causes the wind to blow and the rain to fall" (*mashiv haruakh u'morid hageshem*). However, the full prayer for rain, except for on the holiday itself, is not included in the ninth benediction of the *Amidah* until the seventh day of the month of (Mar)Kheshvan in Israel, and in the Diaspora on December 5, based on the rabbinic calculation on the Gregorian calendar of the start of winter weather (the difference in dates in and outside of Israel has to do with the needs for rain in both places). The start of saying the prayer was delayed beyond Shemini Atzeret in recognition that the pilgrims needed time to return home before the seasonal rains began.

In the synagogue, the prayer for rain (analogous to the prayer for dew recited on the first day of Pesakh) is said during the *khazzan's* repetition of the *Mussaf Amidah*. He wears a *kittel,* the Ark is opened and the congregation stands. In asking God to send rain to the earth, we remind Him of the merits of the patriarchs Moses and Aaron and specific connections they had with water, as well as the Twelve Tribes who crossed the parted waters and for whom God sweetened bitter water in the desert. We ask that the rain be for a blessing, life and plenty.

Saying the prayer outside Israel heightens our awareness of our connection to the Land and the Jews who live there, reminding us that our destiny is joined with that of our homeland.

YIZKOR As on the last day of the other pilgrimage festivals (as well as Yom Kippur), the service in memory of the deceased is part of the day's observance (except among the majority of Reform congregations, which include it only at Pesakh and Yom Kippur [FOR MORE DETAILS, SEE CHAPTER ON PESAKH].

SIMKHAT TORAH

Next to Purim, the Jewish calendar offers no abandon like the Rejoicing in the Torah. If you are going to go to an Orthodox *shul* any day of the year, this is the one. You will be pulled into the uplifting atmosphere and get a glimpse into what religious joy means.

One of the names given to our sacred writings to express the feeling is "Bride" to which Israel is wedded. This is the perfect image for Simkhat Torah, whose celebrations take on the symbolism and rituals of a marriage feast. If you have ever been to a traditional Jewish wedding, you'll understand the comparison. An exuberant expression of the Jewish people's love for our holy book, it is a day full of exceptions, for the sake of celebration, to the usual restrictions such as reading Torah after nightfall and indulging in liquid spirits.

Like all festivals, it begins with candlelighting at home, with *shehekhiyanu;* prior to the evening meal, *kiddush,* the *brakhah* for handwashing and *motzi* are recited (SEE "BLESSINGS"). Since there is no biblical reference for Simkhat Torah, a holiday developed in the Middle Ages, liturgically it is regarded as a second day of Shemini Atzeret—with the addition of special ceremonies surrounding the completion of the annual cycle of Torah readings.

The celebration begins with responsive reading of a set of verses taken from various parts of *Tanakh,* the *Atah Hareita* (You Have Been Shown). Many congregations auction the privilege of reciting verses. The purchaser says the first section, then distributes the honors among other members.

The Ark is opened and all Torah scrolls removed. So that the Ark will not be empty, a *Khumash* or candle, symbolizing the Torah, might be placed inside. The scrolls are distributed to the first group of people to be honored (in traditional synagogues, the Kohanim and Leviim, but any categories can be used: scholars, donors, *shul* volunteers, long-time members, newcomers).

Led by the Torah bearers, congregants parade around the synagogue. In liberal settings, women and girls participate in the processions, called *hakafot* (circuits), adapted from the ancient Temple lulav ritual. In traditional settings the procession passes the women's section to give women the chance to kiss the Torah. (Out of respect, it is customary for both men and women to not touch the Torah directly, but to bring the spine of a *siddur* or *makhzor* or the edge of a tallit or handkerchief to the scroll and then touch it to the lips.) Since the eighteenth century, children have marched along behind the adults, like a little army carrying their paper flags. Today, it is also common for children to carry miniature or stuffed versions of the Torah.

For each *hakafah* short verses are chanted responsively asking God to give us success and save us now. At the completion of a circuit, the leader breaks out in song, and dance circles form around those with the Torah scrolls, whirling, stomping and kicking in spirited Khassidic or folk dances to Yiddish, Hebrew and Israeli songs. Those who do not join the dancing sing and clap.

At some arbitrary time, the scroll bearers pass the *Sifrei Torah* to the next group of people who will carry them, and another *hakafah* around the sanctuary begins.

To give celebrants a chance to rest, some congregations insert a short *devar Torah* (homiletic lesson) about midway through the proceedings. On one or more circuits, or after the Torah reading, it is customary to sing the traditional "*Sisu v'Simkhu*" (Rejoice and be Glad [with the Torah]). During the *hakafot* you might hear scores of the more than eight hundred *piyyutim* written for the holiday, in Ladino, Aramaic, Yiddish, Judeo-Arabic and Hebrew, more than for any other festival. Since the celebration is meant to be participatory, service leaders generally give everyone who wants it the chance to carry a Torah before the end of the evening.

At the conclusion of the *hakafot*, all Torah scrolls but one are returned to the *Aron Kodesh*. Although reading from the Torah in synagogue at night is usually prohibited, the rabbis deemed it improper to have the *Sifrei Torah* out of the Ark without being used for their proper purpose. So on Simkhat Torah night, we read from the final portion of Deuteronomy, containing Moses' farewell, stopping before the end of the book (33:26).

> *It has been told you what is good and what the Lord requires of you: Only to do justly and to love mercy and to walk humbly with your God.*
>
> MICAH

The next day, the *hakafot* again take place. When finished, the needed scrolls are kept out of the Ark for an extended Torah reading ceremony. First, Deuteronomy 33:1–26 is read, with aliyot given to as many men as want them— up to everyone in synagogue. (In very large congregations, the crowd splits into manageable groups, each around its own Torah scroll.)

At the end of each aliyah, the honoree customarily pledges a *tzedakah* contribution, then makes a *kiddush* over wine or liquor that has been set out in the rear of the sanctuary or just outside it, along with cake, fruit, herring and perhaps gefilte fish and taffy apples. The custom of celebrating with joyous feasting at the completion of the cycle of Torah reading (called *siyyum*) is based on King Solomon's experience: When he awoke from the dream in which God endowed him with the wisdom of Torah, in gratitude, he offered sacrifices at the Temple and then prepared a feast for all his servants (I KINGS 3:15).

Since in the joyful abandonment of the day it is not unusual for people to celebrate a little too strenuously, Kohanim are exempt from the service called *Dukhan* (literally platform, the place where the priests stood in the Temple, and where the Kohanim stand in the synagogue to give the priestly blessing, usually part of festival observance), as they might have difficulty concentrating on any duty other than rejoicing of the law. Sometimes they perform the *Dukhan* during the repetition of the *Shakharit Amidah,* instead of that of *Mussaf,* the usual place, before the feasting and celebration have disturbed the solemn atmosphere necessary for the blessing.

Once the adults have been called to Torah, "all the lads" (*kol hanearim*), boys under the age of bar mitzvah, are called up together. In a ritual based on Jacob's blessing of his grandchildren (GENESIS 48:8–20), an esteemed adult spreads a prayer shawl over their heads and pronounces the aliyah blessing, which the boys repeat word for word.

The person honored with reading the blessings for the last verses, Deuteronomy 33:27–34:12, is called *Khattan Torah,* Groom of the Law. (In some places he is actually a newlywed, in others an esteemed member of the congregation or someone who has paid for the honor.) At the conclusion of the reading, the end of the Torah, the congregation calls out *khazak, khazak venitkhazek!* (be strong, be strong and let us be strengthened), the exclamation made whenever a book of *Khumash* has been completed.

Hagbah (raising the scroll before the congregation following a Torah reading) is done in a special way. Instead of lifting with the left roller in the left hand and the right in the right, the person crosses his hands to take the opposite roller in each hand and uncrosses them when he raises the scroll to reverse it, with the writing facing the congregation (instead of facing the *hagbah,* as usual). This symbolizes turning of the Torah back to its beginning, and reminds us of the expression "Turn [the Torah] over and over for everything is in it" (PIRKEI AVOT 5:25). The congregation rises with the scroll and chants the phrase used at every presentation of the Torah following a reading, *"V'zot ha Torah, asher sahm Moshe lifnei b'nai Yisrael al pi Adonai b'yad Moshe"* (This is the Torah Moses placed before the children of Israel by the command of God through Moses' hand.)

As at an *uf-ruf,* the calling of a groom-to-be to Torah on the Shabbat before his wedding, the congregation pelts the *Khattan Torah* with candies (in some places nuts and raisins) representing the sweetness of Scripture.

From the second scroll, the Creation account is read (GENESIS 1:1–2:3) after blessings recited by *Khattan Bereshit,* Groom of the Beginning, another honoree.

The entire congregation recites the verse *"Vay'hi erev, vay'hi voker"* (it was evening, it was morning) for each day, then the reader recites the phrase. At the sixth day, the congregation continues reading through the verses for the seventh day. In some synagogues, a tallit is spread over the bridegrooms. (We read the full Torah portion of Bereshit [in the beginning] on the Shabbat following the festival.)

The Haftarah, Joshua 1, picks up the story of Israel following Moses' death. Just as we turn again to life, immediately starting the Torah reading cycle again with the birth of the world and humanity, the account of our history continues as the mantle of leadership passes to Moses' successor, who leads us to the next stage in our development. Going from the end to the beginning without hesitation shows our on-going devotion to Torah, a sort of annual renewal of vows.

Some congregations take advantage of this time of joyful affirmation of the *mitzvah* of Torah study by holding special consecration ceremonies for children entering religious school for the first time. It is customary to give the children something sweet, so they associate learning with the pleasurable taste (a custom also on Shavuot). Mini Torah scrolls might also be given. (Reform congregations often hold their consecrations on the Sabbath during Sukkot.)

CONCLUSION

As on all festivals, the brief ceremony to mark the transition between sacred and ordinary time, *Havdallah*, is performed, either following the *Ma'ariv* service in synagogue, or at home after nightfall. On a weeknight, only the blessings over wine and separation are made. If the departure of the festival coincides with the close of Shabbat, we recite the full *Havdallah*, including the blessings over spices and fire (SEE "OBSERVANCE" IN CHAPTER ON PESAKH AND "BLESSINGS" AT END OF BOOK).

ISRU KHAG

Although our festival has already been extended for an extra day, the day following the extension, like the day after Pesakh and Shavuot, is another occasion of holding back the holiday so we can sustain its spirit and carry it with us into the workweek. Unmarked in the Diaspora except for the omission of penitential prayers and the prohibition of fasting, in Israel, boisterous celebration marks the occasion (SEE "CUSTOMS").

FOR FURTHER EXPLORATION

FOR CHILDREN

Abrams, Judith Z. *Sukkot: A Family Seder.* Rockville, MD: Kar-Ben Publishing, 1993.
> The ceremony for parents and children includes traditional blessings for candlelighting, wine, khallah, lulav and etrog, four questions on the history and customs of the holiday, songs and music with transliterations. All ages.   ☺✡

Where Do We Begin? Preparation

RITUAL ITEMS

A midrash tells us that God gave Israel the days between Yom Kippur and Sukkot as a special gift, a time when He considers the nation pure, having just emerged from judgment. Presumably, being preoccupied with obtaining a lulav and etrog and building the *sukkah* would keep one out of trouble.

To earn extra "*mitzvah* points" during the Ten Days of Repentance, Jews traditionally prepared the four species then. (Today, synagogues complete orders for them prior to the Day of Atonement). Some people use the time to begin to get their booths ready. Starting construction of the *sukkah* immediately following Yom Kippur services is considered to be particularly meritorious.

Seizing that moment has practical advantage: It is not only in Israel that the holiday coincides with the rainy season. You need good weather to erect the *sukkah*, and you cannot count on having it at the last minute. Obviously, you will want to obtain the supplies needed, or purchase a pre-fab model, well before the construction date. If you want to get branches for s'khakh from your parks department, early inquiries would be prudent.

The same holds true for extending invitations if you plan to host meals in your *sukkah*. Particularly in communities where many families have booths, schedules for sharing meals are established in the weeks prior to the holiday. That is also the time to engage the children in making decorations for the *sukkah*.

SPIRITUAL

A Khassidic anecdote reminds us that not all advance work for Sukkot is material: A member of his sect wanted a special benediction from the Dizekover rabbi that he would obtain a regal palm branch, a flawless citron and a lovely myrtle and willow. The rabbi informed him, "What you require is an honest mind, a generous heart and a meek spirit. Once you have acquired these, then you can seek and find an extraordinary lulav and etrog."

What Are We Supposed to Do? Halakhah

FESTIVAL LAWS

All the laws of festivals that apply to the pilgrimages and to Rosh Hashanah, and the *khol hamoed* laws in effect for Pesakh, govern Sukkot (SEE "HALAKHAH" IN CHAPTER ON PESAKH).

TZEDAKAH

We are obligated to increase charity the day before Sukkot. Providing for the poor and others in need is inherent in celebration of the festival.

CONSTRUCTING THE SUKKAH

WALLS The shelter should have four walls, though theoretically two and part of a third will qualify it. (The regulations about minimum widths and areas of opening of an incomplete wall are technical and should be reviewed with an authority.) If you do not have enough materials for four full walls, it is preferable to make three that are finished. Already existing walls, like sides of a house or fence, may be used. A permanent part of a house—like a porch or attic room—may be used if the roof is removable.

Any material is acceptable, as long as it will withstand a normal wind and prevent candles from being extinguished. If you use cloth for the walls, it must be tied down so it will not flap in the wind.

SIZE The minimum height of walls is approximately three feet (traditionally ten *tefakhim,* which different authorities designated as being between three and three and three-eights inches each. The structure must be at least twenty-six inches long and twenty-six inches wide, an area considered just sufficient to accommodate the head and major portion of one's body, plus a table.

The walls may not be higher than thirty feet (twenty cubits, each about eighteen inches). If taller, when you are inside you tend not to look up, do not see the covering and therefore are not aware that you are in a *sukkah*. In addition the walls rather than the covering, as required, would create the shade inside of the structure.

COVERING The *s'khakh* must be composed of materials that grow from the earth and have been detached from it. Straw, cornstalks, bamboo reeds (as long as they are not in bundles of more than twenty-five pieces), and narrow wood beams are all acceptable. The material should be organic and unprocessed, and not susceptible to ritual impurity (metals, leather, and foodstuffs may not be used). You are not supposed to use boards or beams wider than sixteen inches, even if stood on edge, because they resemble those used for a house roof or ceiling.

More decorative leafy tree branches are used whenever possible. They must last for the duration of the holiday without becoming dried and brown. Branches whose leaves continually drop or that emit an unpleasant odor are not appropriate.

The *s'khakh* should be spaced evenly with no gaping holes or openings wider than eleven and a half inches. It should provide more shade than sun though not be placed so that it prevents rain from falling into the booth, and should allow you to see the stars at night when you look up through it.

Just as a *sukkah* may not be built under a tree whose branches reach over it, it may not be built under a permanent overhang that extends over it more than six feet. An area of a *sukkah* under a shorter overhang does not count as part of the booth, so no one should sit there.

Since the element that makes the booth a *sukkah* is the *s'khakh,* it should be put on last. If you leave a booth standing from one year to another, the *s'khakh* has to be replaced. Check with a local rabbinic authority about the particulars.

DECORATION Any decorative ornaments, like the *sukkah* itself, are considered dedicated for sacred purpose for the duration of the festival, and therefore may not be removed—even if they fall down—or used for any other purpose. Not even a splinter of wood from a wall can be taken for a toothpick. (For the same reason, once the holiday has ended, the *sukkah* is to be treated with respect, carefully stored for the next year, or burned. It should not simply be discarded.)

DWELLING IN THE SUKKAH

FULFILLING THE MITZVAH During the seven days of the festival, you are to regard the *sukkah* as your principal abode and your house as just a temporary residence. Any activity you normally do at home—eat, drink, sleep, spend leisure time—should be done in the *sukkah*. Since it is a sanctified space, time spent in it should be devoted to study of Torah and matters of sanctity, rather than to idle talk. In keeping with honoring the space, the finest tableware should be brought into it, and dirty dishes removed as soon as a meal is finished.

The essential aspects of dwelling—the ones most detailed in the laws—have to do with eating and sleeping. Since there are numerous technicalities regarding what constitutes a snack, a meal and a nap, consult a detailed guide or an authority.

EATING In general, you may not eat a meal outside the *sukkah*. While it is permissible to have any amount of beverages and fruit, vegetables, bread or cake up to the volume equivalent of an egg outside of it, taking all sustenance inside is commendable.

The exemption for weather (see below) does not hold for the first night of the festival, when the obligation to eat in the *sukkah* is more stringent than during the rest of the week. Some authorities say a piece of bread at least the volume of an olive (*k'zayit*) must be eaten in the *sukkah* despite heavy rain. Because of dispute on the matter, no blessing is made.

You should wait an hour or two (some postpone a meal until as late as midnight) in the hope the rain will cease. If it does not, or the presence of guests or young children precludes postponing your dinner, make *kiddush* in the *sukkah*, don't recite the *ushpizin*, eat the minimum amount required, and finish the meal indoors. In case of inclement weather on the second night, you may do *kiddush* and have the meal in the house, then go into the *sukkah* and eat the minimum amount.

If the light goes out in your *sukkah* on Shabbat, when it may not be relit, and one is on in the house, you should eat there (unless you can eat in a neighbor's *sukkah*).

SLEEPING Original law forbade even a nap outside the *sukkah*. It was relaxed in recognition of weather conditions in northern latitudes. If it is too cold to sleep outside, you may sleep in the comfort of your permanent home. (The pious, especially in warmer climates, make every effort to sleep in the *sukkah*.)

EXEMPTIONS In certain conditions or situations, you are excused from the obligation to dwell in the *sukkah*. Except for discomfort, however, it is considered meritorious to transcend the excuse and observe the *mitzvah* (though you do so without saying the blessing). It is also commendable to do something to remind yourself of the holiday if you cannot be in a *sukkah*—such as including Torah discussion at your meals.

If dwelling in the *sukkah* causes physical distress (wind, flies or bees bother you or enough rain falls that it would damage the food) you are excused. Sickness (even a headache) exempts you from the obligation. (A sick person's attendant is also exempted if the patient needs him/her.) If women and young children fulfill the obligation to eat in the *sukkah*, they recite the benedictions. Any other exempt person who remains in the *sukkah* despite discomfort is not to recite a blessing.

If you are away from home during the holiday you do not have to take meals or sleep in a *sukkah*. But if you have the opportunity to have a meal in a *sukkah*, you should take advantage of it.

The bride, groom and wedding party are exempt for the traditional seven days of celebration following the wedding. This is because the *sukkah* is not the most comfortable setting for a couple's wedding night, and because one kind of joy (wedding) should not be mixed with another (festival).

If you are engaged in performing another *mitzvah,* such as Torah study, redeeming captives or visiting your teacher, you are excused from the *mitzvah* of *sukkah.*

BRAKHOT The benediction for sitting in the *sukkah* is recited only if you will perform a function requiring you to be in it—such as eating a meal. It does not have to be said before each meal if you remain in the *sukkah* between one and another, if you leave it for only a short period of time, or if you are just visiting someone. If you forget to say the blessing before you start eating, you may say it anytime during the meal.

SELECTING THE FOUR SPECIES

In order to perform the ritual and say the *brakhot,* you need to have all four species. If some of your four species are invalid, and no kosher set is available on loan in your vicinity, then you should use what you have but not make a *brakhah.* Don't substitute species other than those identified. Details of the validity of the species, and the differences in what is acceptable the first two days and the rest of the week need to be reviewed with an authority.

ETROG The *pittam* (tip) must be intact. The species of etrog that naturally grows without a *pittam* is acceptable, but the result of grafting (lemon and citron) is not. It should be at least the size of an egg (smaller is considered not ripe and therefore not yet a fruit); there is no maximum size, but you need to be able to hold it in your hand. The fruit is valid even if up to half of it is scarred, if it is perforated but no part of it is missing. (Many people prefer etrogim that are totally free of spots of any kind.)

LEAVES The other species should be fresh and green. If you will choose your own, check a detailed guide regarding specific characteristics in terms of shape and composition. The palm should be about fifteen inches long and four inches longer than the other twigs, each of which should be between ten and eleven inches long.

The lulav is to be tied in three places with palm fronds. (Some consider the

419

point where the myrtle and willows are attached as one of the points, and therefore tie it in two more places up the shaft. Others place three rings above the holder.) The top four inches are to be left untied so the leaves rustle when the lulav is shaken.

USING THE FOUR SPECIES

OWNERSHIP On the first day (or first two days in the Diaspora) of the festival, the lulav and etrog you use must belong to you. You may use those of another person if s/he gives them to you as a gift (with the understanding that you will return them). Since a minor is not empowered to transfer ownership, you may not use the four species of a child, and for the same reason if a child will be using another's s/he should be the last to do so. On intermediate days, since *the mitzvah* is performed only in commemoration of the Temple and not by commandment or ordinance, you may borrow the lulav and etrog without acquiring ownership. Synagogue sets bought with public funds are considered jointly owned property.

WOMEN Although women are exempt from the obligation of the four species, they have accepted the *mitzvah* on themselves and therefore may recite the *brakhah*.

TAKING UP There is disagreement as to whether left-handed people reverse the order of picking up the four species (taking the lulav in the left hand, etrog in right); majority holds that they do not. Nothing should create a barrier between the hands and the four species, so it is appropriate to remove tefillin straps and rings.

The *mitzvah* should be fulfilled only during daytime, after sunrise. If you must leave home before that time, you may take up the species as long as it is after dawn (seventy-two minutes before sunrise). It is prohibited to eat before fulfilling the *mitzvah,* but you may have a snack if necessary. Also, if the four species won't be available in the morning (in case you do not have your own), do not defer the meal until noon because it is forbidden to fast on a festival or the intermediate days.

SIMKHAT TORAH

It is a *mitzvah* to participate in the Torah procession honoring completion and beginning of the reading cycle, for it symbolizes the observance of the *mitzvah* of continual Torah study.

What Other Things Do People Do? Customs

OTHER TIMES AND PLACES

FOUR SPECIES From ancient days, Jews have treated the lulav and etrog with reverence. Men sometimes undertook difficult journeys during the Middle Ages to obtain etrogim, and have always been willing to spend beyond their means for the choicest ones. Due to the high cost, several people would often form partnerships in order to merit in ownership, if only partial. This created the necessity of having a messenger ferry it among the co-owners, at home and at different synagogues, so that each could take up the four species. Sometimes one etrog sufficed for an entire community. The Judeo-Spanish auctioned the honor of providing the four species for a congregation; sometimes a set was purchased exclusively for the women to use.

The etrogim of Corfu, renowned for their beauty, were particularly prized (leading to the Eastern European expression "a girl like a Corfu etrog")—until rumors that they were the result of grafting put them out of favor.

The custom of using sugar bowls, candy or soap dishes of silver, wood and glass to protect the etrog and its *pittam* led to the creation of boxes especially for the fruit. Centuries of folk art have left us with incredible versions in wood, pottery and silver, some elaborately shaped or decorated. (One of the earliest surviving is from late seventeenth-century Germany, and other examples are family treasures or parts of museum collections.)

The Moroccans decorated their lulavim with colorful silk ribbons and protected the tips with decorative caps. The Judeo-Spanish placed seven rings along the top third of the lulav so one could be removed on each circuit on Hoshanah Rabbah.

Once the holiday ended, children often turned the lulav leaves into braided rings and bracelets. Members of many communities saved the lulav and/or willows, keeping them upright in flower pots all year as a sign for good health for the family. Sephardim placed them above the door lintel based on the biblical instruction to "take a cluster of hyssop and use it to dip the blood of the Passover sacrifice on the doorpost" (EXODUS 12:22). Many used them before Pesakh to light the fire for baking matzah or burning *khametz*. The lulav leaves sometimes replaced the feather for the *khametz* search.

European Jews treated the *aravot* with dignity and placed them on top of the *Aron Kodesh*. In several Sephardic communities, the *aravot* were beaten lightly on the backs of household members as a good omen for fertility or health (a custom shared by many cultures). Some people marched around with them as they burned. Moroccan Jews used them to fuel a fire for broiling meat that was considered a remedy for barren women.

Most of the superstitious customs regarding conception and childbirth, however, revolved around the etrog. According to tradition, the etrog, not the apple, was the Garden of Eden's "forbidden fruit," and an agent, per folk medicine, for facilitating birth. Talmudic legend asserts that one who eats an etrog will have fragrant children, so it became customary for women to bite the *pittam* off the etrog after Hoshanah Rabbah services (when the etrog no longer holds ritual value). Eastern European Jews believed that a pregnant woman who did so would have a male (fostered by a popular German legend that Princess Louise bit the *pittam,* made the prescribed accompanying supplication and gave birth to the boy who later became Frederick William IV, King of Prussia). The *pittam* was placed under the pillow of a woman in labor in the belief that it would alleviate her pain.

Others used the etrog for *Havdallah* until it dried. Filled with cloves it lasted longer, and provided a sweet way to revive the faint during the next year's Yom Kippur services. Many collected the citrons following the festival, and turned them into jelly eaten on Tu B'Shevat.

BUILDING THE SUKKAH For Eastern European Jews, the *sukkah* became a symbol of the destroyed Temple (based on Amos' promise to "raise up the *sukkah* of David" [9:11], understood as the Temple, at the time of the messiah). Following the biblical commandment to build the altar without using tools of metal—considered instruments of war—they constructed their *sukkot* without the use of nails, emphasizing its representation of peace. The wealthy commissioned folk artists to paint murals on their *sukkah* walls. (The Israel Museum in Jerusalem owns a magnificent example, the Fischach *Sukkah* from nineteenth-century Germany, depicting scenes from the Bible and local culture.)

It was common to convert a room in a house (such as an attic space) or a storage shed into a *sukkah* by having a roof that could be raised and lowered by means of hinges or a pulley. *S'khakh* was placed over the opening for the duration of the festival. Beginning in the Middle Ages, communal *sukkot* were built to accommodate travelers.

DECORATING THE SUKKAH The Jews in Europe and Russia sprinkled fine sand on the ground of the *sukkah*, perhaps in remembrance of the desert journey the festival commemorates. Hollowed out eggs decorated with paper or feathers became birds. Strings of cranberries or plums were used to resemble the grapes gathered in the valley of Eshkol in Canaan when representatives of the Twelve Tribes were sent to explore the Land (NUMBERS 13:23). The Judeo-Spanish decorated with circular or six-pointed baked pastries.

In some communities, a light was kindled each night in honor of the particular *ushpiz* of the day; others lit seven candles every might, for all seven distinguished guests. Jews in Calcutta placed a Bible in the corner of the *sukkah* and each night opened it to a section on the life of the heavenly guest. Moroccans also studied the appropriate sections of Zohar.

In Israel, in order for those in the armed services to be able to observe the holiday, *sukkot* are constructed on navy boats or put on wheels and carried to field units, even during times of combat. The Lubavitch Khassidim do the same with their "Sukkahmobile," visiting schools, hospitals, public institutions and shopping centers, where they distribute literature and invite people to bless the lulav and etrog.

USE OF THE SUKKAH Even before it became popular to include great women of Israel among the honored guests each night, North African Jewish women went into the *sukkah* during the day to welcome the matriarch Rachel.

In Salonika, the first days of the holiday were devoted to family visits. The men and children made the rounds, while the women stayed home to receive guests. They served a "sweet table," a tray containing a jar of preserves with a water chaser, and exotic citrus fruits. Adults were given traditional gifts of eggs made brown by boiling them with onion skins, and children received apples. In addition to inviting friends to join them in them in the *sukkah*, Moroccans also sent gifts of fancy foods from one house to another.

A napkin hung in front of a Jerusalem *sukkah* entrance indicated a meal was in progress and invited guests to come in and partake of it. In predominantly Jewish neighborhoods, it is still customary to "tour" *sukkot*, sometimes on the initial days going to a succession of them to make *kiddush* with wine and cake. In Israel, where you see *sukkot* on balconies, rooftops, squares of land in front of buildings, and municipal settings—creating a scene out of Nehemiah (8:16–18)—the army and individual cities often run contests for the most beautiful.

WORSHIP If a Syrian Jew were prevented from attending synagogue due to illness, and he recited *hoshanot* at home, he placed a *Tanakh* on a table or chair and walked around it with the lulav and etrog to fulfill the *mitzvah* of the *hakafot*.

On the evening of the second day of Sukkot, pious Eastern European Jews performed their version of the *Simkhat Beit Hashoavah*. They lit candles and lamps throughout the synagogue and used the money raised by auctioning honors to pay for apples and brandy consumed by the participants.

Today in religious communities, and throughout the city of Jerusalem, *Simkhat Beit Hashoavah* celebrations are often held on one of the intermediate nights and are more like big parties, with klezmer groups (traditional Eastern European street music), singing, dancing, food and drink. Often the fifteen *Shir Hamalot* (Songs of Ascent, Psalms 120–134) are recited, as was done in the Temple.

HOSHANAH RABBAH SYMBOLS AND SUPERSTITIONS The custom of staying up all night to apply oneself to Torah study developed because of belief that at precisely midnight, the heavens open and a wish uttered at that very moment would be fulfilled. Common folk in the Middle Ages also believed that one's shadow cast by the moon on this night indicated the verdict s/he had received on Yom Kippur: if headless, one would die during the coming year—unless s/he repented, in which case punishment would be reduced to an illness.

Despite the solemnity imposed on the day for inducing rain, it was a time for pranks and frivolity, especially in Oriental Jewish communities (Yemen, Persia, India, Bukhara). Children playfully hit passersby with palm leaves and adults grabbed lulavim and etrogim from children, threw water on each other or tossed one another into lakes or streams.

INTRODUCING A BOY On Simkhat Torah in Cochin (India), the six-year-old boy of a leading family chanted a portion of the prophets to mark his entry into the group of those allowed to read from the holy books for the congregation. All the men of the synagogue then blessed him, and his female cousins gave him gifts. After services, the family hosted a feast for the community. In Yemen, a boy was introduced to the community and blessed by them on the first Simkhat Torah of his life, as he was in Morocco. There the father presented a magnificent candle to the synagogue, which would be lit on each significant occasion in the boy's life.

REJOICING WITH THE TORAH In Babylon during the tenth century and later in Italy, North Africa and Provence, Simkhat Torah observance included the chanting of elegies for Moses, whose death is recorded in the day's Torah portion. These mournful tunes gave way to brighter songs and hymns once the *hakafot* were instituted.

In various Sephardic communities, the honor and celebration afforded the Torah and the Bridgrooms of the Law and the Beginning included textiles, plaques and flowers almost completely covering synagogue walls or the *Sifrei Torah* piled on the bimah, thrones under silk canopies or lavishly decorated *khuppot*, crowns of myrtle (the plant used in ancient Judean bridal processions) and special bell-adorned hats. Beginning in thirteenth-century Spain, the actual crown of the Torah scroll was placed on the honorees' heads. In Vienna—where Simkhat Torah services were so popular people lined up early and often had to be turned away for lack of space—the *khatanim* wore top hats and tails in the regal ceremonial processions led by the beadle wearing a Turkish fez. Children carried flags whose sticks were topped with apples hollowed to hold candles lit to symbolize the Torah's light. This custom may have developed from the abolished practice of burning *sukkot* at the conclusion of their use, which led to carrying torches into the synagogue. When judged too dangerous, small candles replaced the torches.

Eastern European synagogues added the auction of honors for special Torah portions throughout the year to those for Simkhat Torah in order to generate their operating expenses for the coming twelve months.

The congregation showered the "Bridegrooms" honored on the holiday with candy and other sweets (gathered up afterwards by the children) and in Italy, Holland and England, carrying banners and torches, escorted them home to host feasts. Their festivities became so extravagant in the eighteenth-century, community authorities had to issue *takanot* (edicts for communal benefit) to restrict the ostentation and expenditure.

In the area of Medieval Worms, friends and family showered children too young to attend synagogue with fruits and sweets at home. (A non-Jewish woman stipulated in her will that the fruit from her garden be provided for the Jewish children on Simkhat Torah until the messiah arrived.)

Gunpowder salvos and bonfires, which encouraged leaping and dancing, were often part of Ashkenazi celebration in Central and Eastern Europe. Many well-known Khassidic melodies developed from the enthusiastic rejoicing through the streets and courtyards of their villages and cities.

In Israel, congregations join in massive dancing processions to the Western Wall, behind Torah scrolls under canopies, each like a bride being led under her *khuppah* to the marriage ceremony.

POST HOLIDAY In Salonika, public games on *motzei* (the exit of) Simkhat Torah held in the courtyard of the host bridegroom preceded his banquet for the community. In Israel, expanded versions have turned into the institution of *Hakafot Shniyot* (Second Circuits). At Liberty Bell Park, Mea Shearim and other locations in Jerusalem, and in other spots around the country (such as the Florentine quarter in Tel Aviv and on army bases), people come together by the thousands and tens of thousands for a continuation of the joyous frenzy. As the rest of the Jewish world is just getting into Simkhat Torah, the Israelis—secular and religious alike—and joined by tourists, honor different ethnic groups, professions, and communities as each, with its characteristic dress, music and dancing, is called on to lead a procession.

GREETING

The standard *gut yom tov* (Yiddish) and *khag sameiakh* (Hebrew), "happy holiday," are appropriate on Sukkot and Simkhat Torah. During *khol hamoed, a guten yom tov* (Yiddish) or *mo'adim l'simkhah,* a good or joyous holiday, are also exchanged. Some people continue to wish others Yom Kippur's *gemar tov* (be sealed for good) through the seventh day of Sukkot since repentance and therefore the chance to avert a bad verdict are possible until then. On Hoshanah Rabbah, people traditionally have wished each other *pikta tovah,* a good note, referring to the judgment to be issued that day. The Sephardim continue their greetings of the new year, *tizkeh leshanim* (may you merit long life), rejoined with *tizkeh vetikhyeh veta'arikh yomim* (may you merit, live and have length of days).

DRESS

Shabbat clothes are appropriate for the *yom tovim.*

What Is There to Eat? Traditional Foods

No one dish or menu is associated with Sukkot, although foods harvested in the fall, as you would expect, are generally used. In ancient times they included figs, dates, pomegranates, apricots, squash, romaine lettuce, onions, barley and wheat. For Eastern Europeans, seasonally plentiful cabbage, cucumbers, sweet potatoes and apples were turned into stuffed cabbage, pickles, tzimmes and strudel.

Cabbage dishes were particular to Simkhat Torah in some communities, since the Hebrew word for cabbage, *k'ruv,* means "cherub," an illusion to the angels carved onto the Ark of the Covenant (EXODUS 25:18–22). Berliners ate the cabbage dish *vasser kal* on Hoshanah Rabbah because of the hymn *Kol Mevasser* (Announcing Voice) recited as the willows were beaten.

In America, many of the same dishes popular for Thanksgiving appear first on the Sukkot table. Casseroles, which retain their heat from the kitchen to the *sukkah,* are popular, as are stuffed vegetables (perhaps "being stuffed" indicating abundance).

Throughout the holiday, bread is dipped in honey, as we began doing on Rosh Hashanah, for a sweet year. Khallot on Hoshanah Rabbah take on the symbolic shapes of the earlier holiday, like rounds and ladders, as well as keys for opening the heavenly gates, and hands, for receiving the Divine decree. As for other holidays that encompass the practice or theme of beating and concealment, kreplakh (dough pockets filled with meat and completely sealed) are the most traditional menu component on Hoshanah Rabbah. Some make a festive meal after morning services that features kreplakh, nuts, and carrots cut in rounds, representing wealth.

Do You Hear Music? Songs to Sing

The songs associated with this festival for the most part are those traditional for the *hakafot,* particularly of Simkhat Torah. They include folk tunes and numerous Khassidic *nigunim* (melodies), among them *"Yom Tov Lanu"* (Our Holiday), about celebration of Sukkot, *"Sisu V'Simkhu"* (Rejoice and Be Happy) expressing our feeling for Torah; and *"Mipi El"* (From the Mouth of God), appreciation accompanying the Simkhat Torah circuits.

"Lamah Sukkah Zu?" (Why this *Sukkah?*), a folksong, is a child's request for his father to explain the rituals of the holiday. Folksongs and more recently created Israeli tunes are widely used in Simkhat Torah celebrations. One of the most appropriate is the lively *"U'shavtem Mayim"* (You Shall Draw Water), Isaiah's promise of joyful salvation known to thousands of Jewish youth group and summer camp veterans who learned not just the song, but the dance choreographed to it. You'll be able to pick up the simple tune for the refrain of the *Hoshanot* during the services.

FOR FURTHER EXPLORATION

High Holidays and Sukkot Melodies. Cedarhurst, NY: Board of Jewish Education of Greater New York and Tara Publications.

> There is an accompanying cassette tape for the booklet of traditional tunes for the fall holidays, whose words are transliterated into English.

428

What Tales are Told? Stories to Read

A number of poems for this holiday season convey simple ideas and images about the ritual items and observances, making them appropriate for children. Israel Zangwill described a *sukkah* in his poem "A Tabernacle Thought." Hayim Nahman Bialik wondered about the dreams of the moonlit lulav and etrog in "Foreigners," and their fate following the holiday in "Elegy on the Etrog and Lulav." In the equally brief "Beating the Willow" he describes the noise and passion surrounding the Hoshanah Rabbah thrashings. Saul Tchernichovsky's "Sukkah" tells how his father built and his mother decorated the booth, and "Hakkafot" describes the synagogue scene during the processions with the Torah.

The celebration of the last set of fall holidays provided rich material for Sholom Aleichem, and other writers who recreate the scenes and sentiments prevalent in traditional homes.

FOR FURTHER EXPLORATION

FOLKTALES AND STORIES
Refer to anthologies and story collections in "More Good Information."

FOR CHILDREN
Adler, David A. *The House on the Roof.* New York: Bonim Books, 1976.
  Based on an historic occurrence that inspired a folktale, this updated version concerns an old man and crusty landlady who wants the shack he has constructed on top of her building removed. Ages 5–9.

Lebovics, Aydel. *The Wind and the Sukkah.* Brooklyn: Merkos L'Inyonei Chinuch, 1990.
  When a big wind blows the wood, s'khakh and lulav of people building their *sukkot* into the backyard of someone who never had a *sukkah,* the neighbors insist he keep the materials so he can observe the holiday, too. Ages 4–8.

Singer, Isaac Bashevis. *A Tale of Three Wishes.* New York: Farrar Straus Giroux, 1976.
  After staying up to wait for the sky to open on Hoshanah Rabbah, three children think they have wasted their wishes. An old man tells them how to achieve what they really want. Ages 7–11.　　 ☼

Khanukah—

Festival of Religious Freedom

(KHAH' NEW KAH)
KISLEV 25-TEVET 2*
(LATE FALL–EARLY WINTER; NOVEMBER–DECEMBER)

This post-biblical holiday marks an historic victory over enemies — internal as well as external — who tried to obliterate Judaism in the Jewish homeland during the Second Temple era. Rather than commemorating the military triumph that secured Jewish autonomy, the festival instead celebrates the reaffirmation and persistence of our religious heritage. Also known as the "Feast of Lights" for its main ritual, it is a joyous eight-day family event that holds striking messages for the modern age.

---

*Since Kislev can have either twenty-nine or thirty days, the last day of Khanukah can fall on the second or third of Tevet.

Origins—WHY WE CELEBRATE KHANUKAH

Traditions—HOW WE CELEBRATE KHANUKAH

Origins—

WHY WE CELEBRATE KHANUKAH

Where Did It Begin? Historic Foundation

THE EVENTS BEHIND THE HOLIDAY

In 168 BCE, the ruler of the Hellenic Syrian kingdom, Antiochus Epiphanes IV, stepped up his campaign to quash Judaism so that all subjects in his vast empire—which included Eretz Yisrael—would share the same culture and worship the same gods. He marched into Jerusalem, vandalized the Temple, erected an idol on the altar, and desecrated its holiness with the blood of swine. Decreeing that studying Torah, observing the Sabbath and circumcising Jewish boys were punishable by death, he sent Syrian overseers and soldiers to villages throughout Judea to enforce the edicts and force Jews to engage in idol worship.

When they reached Modi'in (about twelve miles northwest of the capital), they demanded that the local leader, Mattathias the Kohein (a member of the priestly class) be an example to his people by sacrificing a pig on a portable pagan altar. The elder refused and killed not only the Jew who stepped forward to do the Syrian's bidding, but also the king's representative. With the rallying cry "Whoever is for God, follow me!" Mattathias and his five sons (Jonathan, Simon, Judah, Eleazar and Yokhanan) fled to the hills and caves of the wooded Judean wilderness.

Joined by a ragtag army of others like them, simple farmers dedicated to the laws of Moses, armed only with spears, bows and arrows and rocks from the terrain, the Maccabees (as Mattathias' sons, particularly Judah, came to be known) fought a guerilla war against the well-trained, well-equipped, seemingly endless forces of the mercenary Syrian army. In three years, the Maccabees cleared the way back to the Temple mount, which they reclaimed. They cleaned it, dismantled the defiled altar and constructed a new one in its place. Three years to the day after Antiochus' mad rampage (Kislev 25, 165 BCE), they held a dedication (*khanukah*) of the Temple with proper sacrifice, rekindling of the golden menorah, and eight days of celebration and praise to God. Legal Jewish worship had been reestablished.

That is the history-based story that has been told—with the addition of one element—in homes and Hebrew schools for generations to explain why we celebrate this holiday.

THE COMPLETE PICTURE

The full story takes a little longer to tell, because it begins more than a century earlier and continues for more than one hundred years after the Maccabees retook the Temple. And it is more complex than the children's version of the good Jews against the bad Syrians. While the Maccabees battled an outside oppressor, they also struggled against enemies among their own people. Syria's turn—from initially granting the Jews favored status to attempting to completely obliterate Torah, Temple worship and all vestiges of Judaism—might never have happened without the complicity of Jews all too eager to become more Greek (the culture of the Syrians) than the Greeks.

By the time of the Maccabees, the Jews had endured foreign rule for hundreds of years, under Babylon, then Persia, then Alexander the Great's Asia-to-Africa empire. As Greece met the East under the Macedonian, a highly accomplished culture encompassing art, literature, science and philosophy developed, a sort of ancient Enlightenment. Called Hellenism, it soon supplanted many traditional ways of life and pagan religions.

When Alexander died after just a decade on the throne, his kingdom was divided into three, each ruled by the head of a Grecian (Hellenic) dynasty. Eretz Yisrael, that tiny diamond of territory between major landmasses and political aspirations, was caught between the Syrian Seleucids (ruling the territory that also included Mesopotamia and Persia) and the Egyptian Ptolemies.

At the end of the third century BCE, Syria won control of the area from Egypt. In 176 BCE, Antiochus IV ascended the throne. Calling himself Epiphanes, god manifest, he claimed to be Zeus' embodiment on earth. (Others at the time called him Epimanes, madman.) The Temple priests and upper class Jews of Jerusalem realized that in his trading empire their power depended on commerce, and wanted their city to enjoy the status and economic benefits of other Hellenistic metropolises throughout the Seleucid domain. To qualify, they had to adopt a Greek constitution.

So began an internal power struggle that ignited the rebellion. By bribing Antiochus, always in need of money to finance his military forays, the Hellenizers were able to buy the position of High Priest—which was supposed to be the paragon of Jewish holiness—for men successively more sympathetic to Greek culture.

The influences and allures of Hellenism were so strong the dedicated priests began to abandon their Temple responsibilities in favor of the gymnasium (symbol of Greek emphasis on physical perfection, the scene of competition between naked athletes). Among the aristocracy, Greek fashion, manners and names proliferated. Jewish men who wanted to hide their distinctness subjected themselves to painful operations to reverse their circumcisions, and self-expression, science and external beauty received preference over morality, spirituality and inner truth.

By their choices, the community's leadership condoned the erosion of Jewish values. They also sent a strong message to Antiochus that the Jews themselves wanted to forsake their ancient heritage for modern Hellenism.

Some did remain faithful to Jewish life, the Pietists (or *Khassidim*, unrelated to the eighteenth-century Eastern European movement). But since they believed that the situation in Judea was God's justified punishment for Israel's transgressions, they counted on their own repentance to spur God to redeem them. For the most part, they remained passive, until Menelaus, someone not even in direct line for the hereditary position (only descendants of Aaron were eligible [NUMBERS 18:1]), became *Kohein Gadol*. When rumor spread of Antiochus' death in his war against Egypt, Menelaus' more moderate predecessor Jason and his followers forced the pretender to flee.

Upon learning what had transpired in Jerusalem, the enraged Antiochus (not deceased after all) invaded the city, ordered a massacre of his enemies, desecrated the Temple and outlawed Judaism outright. In the face of an ascendant Rome, Antiochus had to abandon his aspirations for Egypt and realized the imperative of unifying the diverse peoples under his rule in order to secure his kingdom against the two empires to his west.

435

The attempt to eliminate what distinguished them from others, to get them to forsake the one Ruler they recognized above all others, presented the Jews who cared anything about their tradition with three choices. They could acquiesce and fully become Hellenes, as many preferred to do. They could die for their religious beliefs, as another large number did. Or they could fight back, a choice not presented by any other population, and one that Antiochus, motivated by political expediency rather than anti-Semitism, never anticipated.

From the beginning, the revolt was a minority guerilla campaign. As Mattathias' initial act of resistance demonstrated, the rebels directed their action both at the Syrians *and* at the Hellenists. Going through the countryside destroying pagan altars and circumcising boys who had not ritually been brought into the covenant, Mattathias and his followers were not fighting for each Jew to make his or her own religious choices, but for the nation of Israel to be able to obey God.

On his deathbed, Mattathias designated his son Judah to be in charge of the resistance. He became known as the Maccabee, or Judas Maccabeus, usually translated as "hammer" (*mahkehbet*) and understood as designating the hammer-like blows his attacks inflicted on the enemy. Some historians have suggested it was actually a reflection of Judah's appearance, "hammerhead," since by common practice in Hellenistic circles people received names according to physical characteristics.

More likely, particularly because of the preferred spelling of Maccabee in Hebrew (מכבי), it was an acronym, either for *Mattayahu Kohein Ben Yokhanan* (Mattathias the Priest, son of Yokhanan), by which his sons perpetuated their father's name, or for the phrase *Me Khamokhah B'Elim Adonai* (Who is like You among the Mighty, O Lord [EXODUS 15:11]), the phrase under which Judah went into battle.

THE CONFLICT CONTINUES

A year after the Maccabees' triumph at the Temple, the Hellenists still refused to give up their fight. Displeased that the "old-fashioned" Jews were once again in religious power, and that Torah law had been reinstated, they repeatedly invited the Seleucids to send more troops. Political maneuverings in Syria on more than one occasion saved the Maccabees, by frightening the Syrian commanders home, to protect their personal positions, after hurried peace negotiations. Yet the war dragged on for a generation. First Eleazar, in the battle against Nicanor and his elephants, then three more of Mattathias' sons, including the seemingly invincible Judah, died. In 142 BCE, his own people recognized Simon, the last surviving of the Maccabee brothers, as High Priest and political leader. He severed bonds of allegiance to the Syrian rulers, got the Greek garrison out of Jerusalem, and began to mint his own coins, the first ever by a Jewish state. (The British Museum in London holds the world's largest collection of them.) His son John Hyrcanus, who succeeded him, established the Hasmonean Dynasty. (The term first introduced in Talmud may have been Mattathias' family name, from his grandfather, Simon Hasmonai, or a designation meaning prince, possibly related to the position of priesthood.)

Taking the throne violated the people's trust because it transgressed Torah: The Bible (GENESIS 49:10) stipulates that the kingship should always rest in the tribe of Yehudah (descendents of Jacob's son Judah), as it had since the establishment of David's line. It was to be separated from the priesthood, which comes out of the tribe of Levi (from which Aaron descended [NUMBERS 3:6–9]), to balance the secular and the spiritual. The Hasmoneans, though kohanim of the tribe of Levi, were not direct descendants of Aaron and therefore not in line for the high priesthood they occupied, and certainly not for political leadership, which they usurped.

What began in glory ended in ignominy. The nine Hasmonean rulers to be recognized by the Roman Senate engaged in the same kinds of political intrigues, self-aggrandizement and bloodshed as the previous regime. When two brothers—neither of whom qualified for the throne—both claimed the kingship, they called on a representative of Rome to arbitrate. In a foolish repeat of the mistake of the Hellenized Jews, they opened the door to the Roman conquest that ended their rule (when Herod killed the last of them) after just one hundred and three years—and ended Jewish sovereignty in Israel for close to two thousand years.

The Hasmoneans' corruption soon shadowed their early triumphs. Due to the unpopularity of its founders, Khanukah itself came to be largely ignored within

437

a few decades after its origins. Then when Rome's crushing power began to be felt in the Land, the people recognized in Khanukah a message of hope that new Maccabees would rise and independence would be restored. The holiday came to be seen in an entirely different light.

THE WRITTEN RECORD

Although Khanukah is the only important festival in the Jewish calendar not to be mentioned anywhere in the Hebrew Bible (before its events occurred, the Hebrew canon had been closed to all future texts), it is also the only important pre-modern festival for which definitive historical records exist.

Within twenty years of the reclamation of the Temple, The First Book of Maccabees was written. Possibly based on historic records of the Hellenistic period and with the authority of an eyewitness, it chronicles the events from the rise of Antiochus Epiphanes through Hasmonean rule. Evincing great pride in the Maccabees' accomplishments, it stresses that they fought "for God," so that they could carry out His plan for a just world. The original Hebrew manuscript, later lost, was soon translated into Greek for the large Jewish populations living in Hellenic centers.

In describing the purification of the Temple, which occurs far from the end of the book, I Maccabees calls the occasion the "dedication [*khanukah*] of the altar" (4:59). Judah and his brothers, and the entire congregation of Israel, decreed that these days should be kept with gladness and praise at their due season, year after year, for eight days from the twenty-fifth of the month of Kislev (I MACCABEES 4:52–59).

The Second Book of Maccabees, written decades later, confirms much of the action of the previous book. Based on a Greek volume by a Hellenized Jew, Jason of Cyrene, it opens with letters reminding Jews in Egypt to celebrate "the new festival" (II MACCABEES 10:1–8). This suggests it was written to persuade people who were ignoring the holiday to observe it.

Unrestrained in its support of the by-then unpopular founders, the book reflects Jewish spiritual beliefs current at the time, beliefs that developed out of the concept of choosing death over apostasy. Containing mystical references, it records cases of pious Jews who chose to die rather than submit to the Syrians: Mothers knowing they would be slain and their murdered infants hung around their necks circumcised their sons anyway (II MACCABEES 6:10). The revered ninety-year-old scribe Eleazar chose martyrdom rather than eating, or even pretending to eat, pork (II MACCABEES 6:18–31). A celebrated mother (referred to in Talmud as Miriam, in Josephus by the more commonly accepted identification Hannah) encouraged the expression of unfaltering faith in God by her seven sons as she had to watch them, one by one, barbarically tortured to death for refusing to bow to an idol, after which she killed herself (II MACCABEES 7).

In this version of events, the celebration initiated by Judah is called the purification festival (2:16–18) and is described as a second Sukkot, possibly because the Maccabees had missed the festival earlier that year while fighting in the wilderness. They also modeled their celebration on the previous Temple dedication, which had occurred at the harvest festival (I KINGS 8:2, 65, NEHEMIAH 8:14–18). For that reason, they carried lulavim and recited *Hallel*.

The Roman-Jewish historian Flavius Josephus used I Maccabees as a resource for his first-century account of the period in *Jewish Antiquities* but makes his own contribution to the annual commemoration. Recounting that the dedication was celebrated with feasting, "splendid" sacrifices, songs of praise to God and the playing of harps, he mentions a newly popular form of observance: kindling lights, especially torches. In fact, he introduces a new designation for the holiday, *Khag Haorim* (Festival of Lights), which he tentatively tries to explain as representative of the glow of freedom that lit up Jewish life.

The Books of Maccabees were lost to the Jews until the modern era, when they were translated for Jewish use back into Hebrew, and into other languages, from the versions retained by the Church in its Old Testament. However, the Scroll of Antiochus (also called the Scroll of the Hasmoneans) kept their story, of sorts, alive. Modeling it after the Scroll of Esther (SEE CHAPTER ON PURIM), the rabbis wrote the Aramaic text (later translated into Hebrew) to be read in synagogue during the eight-day celebration. That custom, mostly of the Middle Ages, has long since been discontinued except in some Sephardic communities. (After the Torah on Shabbat during Khanukah, some North African congregations read it in Arabic so everyone would understand and be able to publicize the miracle. The Jews of Kurdistan read it at home during the holiday, sometimes accompanied by the same blessings that accompany reading of the Book of Esther on Purim).

Largely a legendary account incorporating various tales popular among the Jews centuries after the actual events, and inconsistent in sequence and details with the Books of Maccabees, the scroll reflects the political situation, rabbinical anti-military attitude, and spiritual orientation of Judaism expressed at the time of its origin, probably shortly after the destruction of the Second Temple. These currents, and its account of the miracle of oil—that added element in the traditional Khanukah story—were incorporated into the Talmud between two and three hundred years later.

THE TALMUDIC TRADITION

Unlike I and II Maccabees, the Talmud barely touches on the armed struggle, never mentions the word Maccabee, and of the leading rebels, names only Mattathias. The Mishnah (on which Talmud commentary is based) makes no reference whatsoever to Khanukah and the few relevant passages in the commentaries begin "What is Khanukah?" (*Mai Khanukah?*) as though its significance had been forgotten. The response redirected the holiday.

The rabbis said that when they reclaimed the Temple, the Hasmoneans found a single cruse of pure oil still bearing the unbroken seal of the High Priest. Although only enough to last one day, it miraculously burned eight days—the amount of time needed to secure a new supply of oil to keep the menorah lit. In the following year, the holiday, to be observed with songs and praises, was ordained, a distinction that presented Khanukah as a rabbinic, and not Hasmonean, proclamation.

This curious bit of revisionism has logical bases. By the time Judah Hanasi compiled the Mishnah (second century), the Hasmoneans had been discredited. As a descendant of the Davidic dynasty—from which all future rulers of Israel were to come—Hanasi was particularly sensitive to the Hasmoneans having trampled his family's rights.

There was another perhaps more compelling reason for his failure to mention the rebels: Rome already dominated Palestine, and Hanasi was the first sage in decades to maintain a decent relationship with that power. It would have been grossly irresponsible to discuss the Jewish overthrow of any oppressive foreign rule, a red flag of rebelliousness that would have instigated terrible consequences for the Jews.

So because of political considerations, the rabbis limited their discussion of the holiday, which had enjoyed a resurgence for nationalistic reasons, to explaining the relatively new kindling custom. On the most basic level, the commemoration represented the relighting of the menorah in the reclaimed Temple. However, by the time the Talmudic rabbis wrote, the attempts to overthrow Rome's yoke had failed miserably. Sovereignty, the Temple, and altar sacrifice were gone. The story of the miracle of oil—which may have originated as an embellishment on the initial dedication account—helped them shift attention away from the physical world—in which the Jews had lost so much—to the spiritual realm and give the holiday a purely religious interpretation. Rather than being tied to the Temple and its ritual objects, Khanukah came to symbolize the continuity of the distinct Jewish way of life. The lights represented Jewish spirituality.

The form of observance may have actually evolved from the practice of using lighted torches during Sukkot's *Simkhat Beit Hashoavah* celebrations (SEE PREVIOUS CHAPTER), or the popularity of carrying lighted torches in the streets of Jerusalem during the harvest festival after which Khanukah was modeled. (According to midrash, when Judah Maccabee and his men reclaimed the Temple, the menorah was missing. But they found eight iron rods, into which they made grooves to hold oil and wicks, and kindled them.) Later, like much observance, the lighting moved from the public domain into the home. Despite the prominence of lights, the "Festival of Lights" around this time was formally named "Festival of Dedication" (*Khanukah*).

Some secular scholars believe that lighting flames in connection with Khanukah reflected winter solstice festivals, such as the one celebrated in Greek pagan culture, in which ancient people lit bonfires and held torchlight processions to encourage the return of the sun, at its most distant during that time of year. (Khanukah arrives at the end of both lunar and solar cycles, a particularly dark period, as the moon wanes toward the close of the month of Kislev, and Earth is furthest away from the sun.)

However, there is no question that the symbolism of fire and light were well

441

rooted in Judaism, from God's first words in the Torah ("Let there be light" [GEN-ESIS 1:3]), to the comparison of Torah to light (including the Aramaic word for it, *Oraisa,* meaning source of light), to God's manifestation as the Burning Bush, to the Temple menorah. All were indicants of God, a fire that does not consume but provides illumination.

MODERN TIMES

When the Torah academies of Babylon opened in the third century, the lighting practice spread to the Diaspora, but until the end of the nineteenth century, Khanukah remained a secondary festival in much of the world. Then Zionism appeared as a major force. While the notion of the miracle of oil had come into disfavor with the rationalism of the Enlightenment, the Maccabees became models of the heroic Jew willing and able to fight for his rights. The initial miracle, of the few against the many, the weak against the strong, gave the Zionists and early settlers in Palestine hope.

Throughout the Holocaust, the Jews—saving bits of butter to fuel small flames held in hollowed potatoes—continued to thank God for the miracle of Khanukah, believing, as had the Jews under Rome, that another miracle was possible. Even if individuals died, they believed the Jewish people, as always, would survive. In 1948, the chances of the new Israelis were likened to those of the Maccabees at the beginning of their struggle. Today, the Jewish state observes Khanukah as a national patriotic holiday. The term Maccabee has come to mean physical prowess, and serves as the name of several sports endeavors including the popular Maccabi soccer teams based in several Israeli cities, and Israel's Olympics (Maccabiah).

Khanukah also enjoyed a resurgence in America, although more due to this society's attention to temporally close Christmas than appreciation of the holiday's significance. In a spirit of fairness, public schools often added Khanukah to their holiday season celebrations, and that reminded families to kindle lights at home. Popular with assimilated Jews as well as the observant, for many it has come to be seen as "a Jewish Christmas." Consequently, although celebrated out of all proportion to its place on the Jewish calendar (especially when compared to the overshadowed biblically-ordained holidays of Shavuot and Sukkot), it is too often diminished by the very culture-borrowing the holiday's founders fought.

FOR FURTHER EXPLORATION

FOR ADULTS

Fast, Howard. *My Glorious Brothers*. Mattituck, NY: Amereon, 1988.
> This historical novel brings the personalities of the Maccabees and the land of Israel to life. Told by Simon as he tries to understand and explain what drove the Jews, and in a small part by a representative of the Roman Senate, it illustrates what set the Jews apart from all other peoples and is interesting and at times moving reading.

The First Book of Maccabees. Ed. by Solomon Zeitlin. Translated by Sidney Tesche. New York: Harper & Brothers, New York, for Dropsie College for Hebrew and Cognate Learning, 1950.
> Detailed explanations of the ancient world and the situation in Judah sets up the apocryphal book, a translation into English (with facing Greek) made for the Jewish reader. (The Second Book of Maccabees, published in 1954, is also available. Later editions of both have been published, and the text is available online.)

"Megillat Antiochus/Scroll of Hashmoneans." *In Daily Prayer Book*. Ed. by Philip Birnbaum. New York: Hebrew Publishing Company, 1977, pp. 713–724.
> The text of the scroll read in synagogues during the Middle Ages appears in Hebrew and in English.

FOR CHILDREN

Zwerin, Raymond A., and Audrey Friedman Marcus. *Like a Maccabee*. New York: UAHC Press, 1991.
> This simple yet lovely telling of the Khanukah story intersperses definitions of what being a Maccabee means, with questions to let the young reader determine if he or she is like a Maccabee. Vibrant illustrations form stage scenes for the action of the story. Ages 3–6.

What Does It Mean? Religious Importance

Had there not been a Maccabean revolt, there would not be a Jewish religion. That struggle—the first ever in the world fought for the right of a people to follow its spiritual conscience—saved Judaism, and transformed it into a system able to survive through millennia of turmoil.

NATIONAL AND INDIVIDUAL SELF-PRESERVATION

The Maccabean age marks the first time people were willing to sacrifice their lives in support of what they believed. Those who continued to follow God's laws saw *mesirat hanefesh* (self-sacrifice, or literally "handing over the soul"), also called *Kiddush Hashem* (sanctification of God's name), as the highest form of service to God.

Giving some significance to their brutally mean deaths, this new concept in religious commitment became a model for Jews throughout history, particularly the Middle Ages. During the Roman persecutions, Crusades, Inquisition, Pogroms, and the Holocaust, victims died believing they were giving up their lives for a higher purpose.

Unlike the way other religions interpreted the idea, Judaism never considered the death a value in itself. Relinquishing life for religious idealism is not for God's sake—a lesson we learn in the Rosh Hashanah story of the near sacrifice of Isaac by Abraham—but for the sake of continuity and the strength of the community.

While this form of resistance may have been viewed as a laudable alternative to accepting the demands of the Syrians, in the end, it could serve no practical purpose for the Maccabees because it would only lead to extinction. As related in Maccabees (I, 2:32–34, II, 6:11), on the Sabbath, the enemy trapped a group of Pietists—men, women and children—in a cave. Not wanting to fight on a holy day, the victims all perished. On hearing of this tragic encounter, Mattathias declared that from then on, the Jews were to defend themselves, even if it meant violating Sabbath law.

His ruling reflected the position of the Pharisees, one that had positive ramifications for the future of Judaism. They believed that sages had the right and duty to interpret the law. Unlike the Sadducees, who took Torah literally and based Jewish service solely in the Temple sacrificial rites, the Pharisees understood that Torah was meant to be explained on earth, and that the study and prayer enabling humans to do so were also avenues to God. Without their leadership, instead of being a vibrant, creative influence, Judaism would have ended when Rome destroyed the Temple.

With this approach the rabbis later formalized Mattathias' ruling based on the commandment "You shall observe my statutes and laws that a man shall live by them" [DEUTERONOMY 30:16], understood to imply "and not die by them." Protecting one's life was a higher value than keeping the Sabbath—and almost every other commandment. The rabbis limited the circumstances under which one should—and is permitted to—die in sanctification of God's name to three: idolatry, murder, and certain sexual abominations.

MIRACLES AND MAN

Consistent with exercising authority regarding *mitzvot*, the Maccabees rejected the post-prophecy idea that only God could vanquish Israel's enemies and restore the Temple. After they took matters into their own hands, acting on behalf of God and according to His laws, the miracle occurred: Judah's out-numbered, outlawed band of guerillas defeated the professional army of Antiochus.

Though a minority of the Jews, the Maccabees and their followers were able to succeed because they unified not only the extreme right wing, the Pietists who stuck to the laws and wanted to wait for supernatural relief, but the left wing as well, the Hellenists, who saw no harm in updating their lives with the fashionable ways of the Greeks, initially not realizing that they posed any threat to their own culture. Together they achieved something outside all normal expectations by acting under the MaCcaBEe standard, or *nes*, "Who is like You among the mighty, O God?"

The Hebrew word *nes* (sign) also means miracle. The "great miracle happened there" because when we follow common guidelines and pursue common goals, we are given the power to create extraordinary results. (If we could forge a coalition between the most religious and the most religiously lax, between the traditionalists and the liberal interpreters today, wouldn't we consider it a miracle?!)

The Maccabees witnessed the miracle of oil because at the darkest moment of Jewish history, when it looked as though Judaism would be extinguished, they themselves searched and found the fuel necessary to keep the lamp lit. As a rabbinic parable interprets it, the undiminished oil was Mattahias himself. In his home, in his soul, the spirit of Judaism continued to burn. He turned the light on the Jews, he ignited their drive to search their souls, where they found the strength and desire to perpetuate their religious tradition. That provided enough fuel for the flames of the menorah, the presence of God among human beings, to continue.

Judaism emerged strengthened, not by withdrawing from the world, but by joining the religious fervor of the Pietists with the positive elements of the competing culture (like sophisticated patterns of reasoning, science, artistic

445

accomplishment). The integration prepared it to better withstand repeated blows from outside forces, and opened avenues through which we are able to share our vision and work toward fulfilling our mission. (It was during the Hellenistic period that seventy-two Jewish scholars translated the Bible into Greek, giving the world the Septuagint, the basis for Judeo-Christian culture and American democracy.)

AN ETERNAL LIGHT TO THE NATIONS

The strongest image and metaphor of Khanukah, and of Judaism, is light. All of Jewish, and world, history, is the struggle to maintain light against the force of darkness, a struggle between the sparks of creativity and the fires of destruction, between the shadows of evil and the radiance of human goodness, being in the dark of ignorance and seeing the light of truth.

The Torah, which illuminates the path that will allow us to enjoy the most enlightened life, is wisdom's light (PROVERBS 6:23). The soul, which provides the vision to make the right choices, is inner light (PROVERBS 20:27). When we follow them, in fulfillment of our mission, the Jewish people is a "light to the nations" (ISAIAH 49:6).

In the world conquered by Hellenism, only two nations were able to retain their identities. Rome succeeded by its military power, Israel by its spiritual purpose. When they prevailed, the Jews did not commemorate their success in battle—fighting was only a means to the end. Instead, they celebrated the rekindling of the lights of the menorah to express recommitment to their religious ideals.

The term Khanukah had been in use long before the Maccabees. Completion of the First Temple (I KINGS 8:63, PSALMS 30:1) and the wall enclosing the city of Jerusalem (NEHEMIAH 12:27) were both *khanukot*. Based on grammatical structure in Scripture, the sages termed completion of the Tabernacle in the wilderness (EXODUS 39:32) and its erection for the first time (NUMBERS 7:1) as dedications as well.

Since the Tabernacle actually represented the universe, with its roof as heaven and its menorah lights as the fixtures of the firmament, the sages also called the Creation of heaven and earth (GENESIS 2:1) a *khanukah,* as they did the prophet Isaiah's reference to the final redemption, when the sun will shine seven times brighter than usual (30:26). Through those designations, they made the

Maccabean rededication part of that continuum that began on the first day of the world and projected to its last.

Each *khanukah* in its way was aimed at widening the circle of light in the world. Primordial light dispelled the darkness of chaos. The sun, moon and stars illuminated the earth, making human life and history possible. The seven-branched menorah placed outside the entrance to the Shrine where God's presence resided represented spiritual light in the Tabernacle—and the universe.

Made from a single piece of gold, the purest firmest metal, the menorah suggested resoluteness and permanence. Yet created in the form of flowering branches, it implied growth. Within an unyielding framework—the Jewish moral tradition—Judaism was to become a greater influence in lightening the burdens of the world.

Its fire, like Israel's moral example, was to be kept aglow constantly (LEVITICUS 24;1-4). After the Temple (said to give light to the whole world) replaced the Tabernacle, was destroyed, rebuilt and defiled, relighting the menorah each time signified that the Jews wanted to continue carrying the torch. We would be a flame of spirituality, countering the darkness of ignorance and evil, shining the light of Judaism's justice, a vision of the brilliance human existence can achieve.

What Does It Mean to Us? Personal Significance

Our tradition includes several moving stories about men lost in a forest or blinding snowstorm who, because they catch a glimpse of a flickering Khanukah candle in a distant window, are able to find their way home. It is so easy for us, especially in our media-saturated world, to get lost in the images and messages of the society around us and, like the Hellenists in Judah Maccabee's day, to be seduced by their superficial appeal. Khanukah candles can be guiding lights helping us "find our way home," back to our history, our values, our spiritual source.

The same candle that shines like a beacon to someone lost in the dark outside, in the house casts an intimate circle of light that pulls the family around it. You can use this glimmer of spirituality as more than a prelude to presents and potato pancakes. Yes, these are nice ways to enhance enjoyment of the holiday and should certainly be employed to get children's attention and generate some excitement for them.

But, remembering what this holiday is all about, you can light a fire inside your family members. It is no accident that we observe this holiday within the embrace of family, the most important element in the transmission of Jewish values and tradition. Khanukah, from the same root as *khinukh*, education, is all about the perpetuation of that tradition: The Maccabees fought not just for the principle of religious freedom, but to be able to live a full Jewish life unencumbered by the negative influences of an alien culture and the allures of easily assimilating into it.

The Greeks stressed the holiness of beauty; the Jews emphasized the beauty of holiness.

EMIL G. HIRSCH

We follow the declaration "Hear O Israel" (the *Shema*) by reciting the commandment to love God and take His laws to heart. The very next phrase instructs "Teach them diligently to your children" (DEUTERONOMY 6:7). Every Jew, not just our religious leadership, is supposed to share in our heritage and be knowledgeable about it. While we are legendary for our emphasis on education, and vastly over represented (population percentage-wise) among those who hold advanced academic and professional degrees, too many of us are in the dark when it comes to our own religious culture.

If we want our children not to be swallowed up by the values (or lack of them) of our secular society we have to give them a sense of belonging to Judaism and the Jewish people that is positive and relevant. The process has to start with the parent. The best Jewish day school cannot do its job if what the child learns there is not reinforced at home and built on the Jewish identity shaped there.

As we know, sometimes to our chagrin, children learn most readily through example. The Talmud says that one who is careful about lighting Khanukah candles will merit children who are *talmidei khakhumim,* wise students. The sages looked on kindling the Khanukah lights as a model for behavior and also indicative that one was keeping a Jewish home in general, and thereby teaching his/her children about Judaism and Jewish values. Even if lighting is all you do, it is a good first step. The challenge is to prolong the glow of Khanukah light beyond the second or third of Tevet.

If Jewish survival is a priority for you (What are the chances your children or grandchildren will be Jewish, that they will intermarry? How would you feel if they did?), you might start by evaluating what you are doing to keep Judaism alive in your own home. (These are not questions pondered by most Jews in western societies today. But in view of the fact that our numbers are falling, intermarriage rising, identification waning and Jewish education failing, ones that demand consideration.) Do the choices you make support how you feel about Judaism and its continuity? (Is Friday night for family Shabbat dinners or school sports competitions? Is it more important that your children attend band-dance-hockey-cheer-leading-drama practice or lessons than Hebrew school? Is money more readily allocated for a new television or new outfits than materials for con-struction of a *sukkah*? Is it preferable to support the local art museum, symphony or dance company rather than the local agency for Jewish education? Do the stories you share, the songs you sing, the words you use, the videos you watch, the rituals you observe include Jewish ones? When it comes to choices between Jewish and non-Jewish activities or items, are they negotiable?) Do you realize the likely ramifications of those choices, and are those the results you want?

> *As lightning springs out of its concealment in the dark clouds to flash through the world, so the divine light, imbedded in matter, emerges through charitable deeds. . . . thus through charity, a sort of divine revelation occurs in the soul.*
>
> SHNEUR ZALMAN

We cannot expect our children to choose to be Jewish (and later be able to raise Jewish children) if it is not integral in their lives. (Try a little experiment. Ask your children to use five words to describe themselves. See where Jewish shows up on their lists. See if it shows up at all.) They must share enough of our common culture to feel they belong to the Jewish people and know enough about what it means to be able to evaluate their religion against others, or none. Many young people who investigate different faiths and get involved with cults are spiritually hungry. But in most cases it does not even occur to them to check out what Judaism has to say in answer to their questions. Exposed to it only superficially, or as burdensome, they have no idea of its depth, wisdom or joy.

You can give these to yourself and your children by enlightening your lives

449

through education at home (following the holiday cycle goes a long way in establishing a Jewish identity) and in the community, where many programs—for all
ages and for families—are available. There will be more, and better ones, as Jewish
communities throughout the country grapple with the problems created by the
double-edged sword of tolerance in our society: acceptability and assimilation.

One way of making the holiday personal and meaningful is by dedicat-
ing each night to a theme, goal or good work. Hadassah, the Women's
Zionist Organization, for example, chooses a quality and corresponding
Hadassah project (first candle is of peace, for its conflict resolution program at Youth Aliyah Neurim; second for heritage and Young Judaea youth
movement, and so on). For the first post September 11 Khanukah, CLAL
(The National Jewish Center for Learning and Leadership) suggested
remembering heroes (first night, firefighters, police officers and citizens
who gave their lives saving others; second night, doctors, counselors and
volunteers. . . .) This kind of dedication can easily be personalized for your
family, its concerns, interests and involvements, and for local, national and
global developments.

You start Khanukah with one small flame, the observance of one holiday,
doing one mitzvah, imparting one piece of information. It lights only the area
immediately around it. Yet as our rabbis say, and as those men lost in forest or
snow would agree, "a little light dispels much darkness." It is a beginning, like
a penlight or match that allows us to put ourselves on the right country path.
Fire has the incredible quality of being able to give itself away without at all
being diminished (like the *shammash* used to light the Khanukah candles, and
whose flame seems to stretch bigger as it kindles the others). As long as it is
fueled, it continues to grow: it takes only a spark to ignite a million-acre blaze.
All you have to do is light the first match.

FOR FURTHER EXPLORATION

Herzl, Theodor. "The Menorah." In *Hanukkah, The Feast of Lights*. Ed. by Emily Solis-Cohen, Jr.
Philadelphia: The Jewish Publication Society of America, 1947, pp. 279–282.

> After years of allowing Khanukah to pass unobserved, the founder of the Zionist movement came to
> recognize that devotion to ancient Jewish tradition, not assimilation into surrounding cultures, was
> the only route to salvation, and decided to expose his children to the beautiful commemoration. This
> essay is still timely.

Traditions—
HOW WE CELEBRATE KHANUKAH

What Do We Use? Ritual Items

KHANUKIAH

Although commonly referred to as a menorah, the candelabra used to hold the Khanukah lights is properly called a *khanukiah* (menorah refers to the lampstand that stood in the Temple). Anything that will hold the oil and wicks or candles can serve as a *khanukiah*—even a row of small glasses, jars or other receptacles.

Originally, individual oil lamps ordinarily used for illumination sufficed, but gradually creative interpretation led to a limitless variety of *khanukiot*, both for hanging on doorposts or walls (these contained upright hacks), or for sitting on windowsills or tables (equipped with flat bottoms or legs).

Judaica collections in synagogues, museums and private homes feature abundant examples made of clay, porcelain, tin, silver, and brass, embellished with historic and decorative symbols and forms (including images drawn from the Maccabean struggle, Scripture, wildlife, and the crests of nobles under whom European Jews received protection). By the Middle Ages the Talmudic injunction against fashioning *khanukiot* to resemble the original seven-branched Temple menorah (to preserve its sacred status) was ignored, and eight and nine-branched versions developed. Today, Judaica artists continue to create new designs of diverse styles.

A *khanukiah* can be made at home or purchased from a Jewish supplies store or catalogue. Candles—forty-four to a box, the total you need for all eight days—are available in the same place, and often in grocery, stationery and drug stores. Many *khanukiot* that normally take candles can be converted for oil by inserting into the candle wells small glass bulbs available, along with the wicks, where *khanukiot* are sold. Any oil you use for cooking is acceptable, olive oil preferred; stores that sell kosher food and Judaica items often stock less

451

expensive olive oil specifically for lighting purposes. Today it is also possible to find boxes of forty-four glass bulbs pre-filled with oil and wick, and, even easier to use and clean up, small glass *khanukiah* inserts containing solidified olive oil that melts as the imbedded wicks burn.

DREIDEL

Though not necessary for observance of the holiday, the spinning top is a traditional part of its celebration. Used for a game of chance played after the candles are lit, it has a Hebrew letter on each of its four sides representing the phrase *Nes gadol hayah sham*, "A great miracle happened there," "here" (*po*), in Israel. A variation of an ancient gambling toy, the dreidel originated in medieval Germany and used to be carved of wood or made of lead (often by young boys who poured metal, obtained by melting spoons, into homemade molds). Collectable pieces, some fashioned of silver and crystal and just for show, are available today, but for play (described below), inexpensive plastic or wood models in a variety of shapes and sizes are widely displayed in Jewish and general stores during the Khanukah season. (Numerous websites provide instructions, and some offer the opportunity to play the game.)

How Do We Celebrate? Observance

Khanukah belongs to the family. Full of images and activities that particularly appeal to children, the festival is centered around a home ceremony that brings members together eight nights in a row for lightheartedness, warmth, and appreciation of the heritage whose survival is being celebrated.

KINDLING PREPARATION

Since shortly after the destruction of the Temple, the centerpiece of observance of this holiday has been lighting the Khanukah lights. The rabbis determined that we kindle these lights to publicize the miracle (*pirsum ha nes*) that occurred. For that reason, the *khanukiah* is supposed to be seen from the street.

Originally celebrants placed it on the left doorpost outside the home, opposite the mezuzzah on the right, to surround anyone standing in the doorway with spirituality. Today it is more common to place the lampstand in or near a window so that it will be clearly visible from outside (some even say that since the lights are mainly directed to those of the household, the *khanukiah* can be placed anywhere in the home). In Israel and in some Jewish neighborhoods elsewhere, you can still see specially made outdoor lamps. Some reconstructed houses in the old city of Jerusalem have niches for them in the walls next to the doorways.

The candles are placed in the *khanukiah* from right to left, the number corresponding to the night of the holiday, beginning with one and adding a single taper or wick each night through eight. In addition, an extra candle, or *shammash* (servant), which is used to kindle the others, is placed in the *khanukiah* every night.

One *khanukiah* may be, and usually is, lit for the entire family, although it has been the custom—and a good learning experience for children—particularly among the devout, for each member of the family to kindle his or her own. The glow from the extra candles, especially on the last night of the festival, creates a gorgeous sight.

Traditionally, the lighting takes place after nightfall, when stars appear, so that the flames will be most noticeable to people returning home from work and shopping. But you can light any time during the night as long as there are still people awake to see the flames.

KINDLING CEREMONY

BENEDICTIONS On the first night, the person who will light the candles—it can be any member of the household, and it is in fact a good idea to involve children—lights the *shammash*, and, holding it in hand, recites three blessings. (The *shammash* does not count as one of the candles being sanctified. Actually, a match could be used to light all the Khanukah candles, but since the Middle Ages, use of the *shammash* has been customary. Originally it was added as a precaution against violating the law that prohibits using the Khanukah candles for any activity. If one did read, or otherwise utilize the *khanukiah's* illumination, it was considered that the light had come from the *shammash* rather than the sanctified flames. In time, it was put to use in kindling the others, and given the name "servant.") Many families chant the blessings to a special tune, which you can learn from a book or recording of melodies for the holiday.

The second blessing, commemorating great miracles performed for our ancestors, is said at just one other occasion of the year, prior to reading the Purim *Megillah*. The *shehekhiyanu,* used at milestone occasions like arriving at a holiday, is omitted on subsequent days (unless for some reason you don't say it the first night, in which case you may say it on another evening, but only once during the holiday because "arrival at this season" refers to its onset [SEE "BLESSINGS"]).

LIGHTING The candles are lit in reverse order from the way they were placed in the *khanukiah,* left to right, so that the last candle put in, the one representing that particular night, is the first one kindled. The *shammash* is placed into its holder and allowed to burn down with the other candles.

Originally, the sages disagreed about the arrangement of the lights. One of the great schools of learning of Talmudic times, that of Shammai, asserted that on the first night, eight candles should be lit, and be diminished by one each subsequent night. This arrangement reflected the observance of Sukkot, when fewer sacrifices were brought on each succeeding day. It also demonstrated a pessimistic attitude, implying that life in the absence of the Temple was a lesser experience, that the glory of Jewish life was in the past, that holiness among Jews and in the world was fading.

Fortunately, the sages ruled in favor of the suggestion of the School of Hillel, that we start with one, and build up each day. The progression moves us from faint illumination in the darkness to light, from little hope in the present to faith in the future, an expression of expectation that our holiness, the impact we can have in the world, can and will increase.

FOLLOW-UP SONGS While the kindling is being done, it is customary to sing *"Hanerot Hallalu"* (These Lights), to remind us that the lights are sacred, used only to express our thanks for the miracles, and not for any other purpose. Based on a Talmud text, the original passage consisted of thirty-six words (with minor variations between the Ashkenazim, Sephardim, and various Khassidim), reflecting the thirty-six candles we light during the holiday (not including the *shammashim*), and reminiscent of the thirty-six righteous people said to exist in each generation on whose merit the world continues.

The Ashkenazim and some Sephardim follow with *"Maoz Tzur"* (Rock, or literally fortress, of My Salvation), the thirteenth-century liturgical poem sung to a medieval German hymn. Recalling the downfalls and rededications of Israel throughout her history, and expressing hope for the restoration of the Temple, it became Khanukah's theme song.

The Sephardim recite Psalm 30 since it was composed by King David to be used when his son Solomon dedicated the First Temple. The Maccabees used this psalm, now almost universally associated with the Khanukah festival, as part of their dedication. Its imagery of an individual saved from danger alludes to Jewish national life.

FOR FURTHER EXPLORATION

Hanukah Melodies. Cedarhurst, NY: Board of Jewish Education of Greater New York and Tara Publications, 1981.
> The compact booklet contains the candlelighting tunes, traditional follow-up songs and other folksongs standard for the holiday. A companion cassette tape is available.

Chanukah Live: The World Celebrates Chanukah Together.
> Lubavitch Khabad produces round-the-world candlelighting ceremonies in multiple venues (such as Western Wall, Eiffel Tower, Red Square, White House, New York's Ground Zero) that can be watched on the organization's website, www.chabad.org   ☼✡

GAMES

Although *Khanukah* was never considered sacred time when work is forbidden, no work is to be done for a half hour after the *khanukiah* is lit in order that we appreciate the flames and what they represent. It became traditional for people freed from the normal routines of household chores and study to pass the time in a variety of games, particularly playing cards and the Khanukah favorite, dreidel.

ORIGIN Legend has it that the spinning top game (called *sevivon* in Hebrew, for spin) developed at the time of the Maccabees as a cover: The Syrians killed any Jews caught studying Torah. Those who risked their lives to learn kept tops within reach, and would play when soldiers approached so as to appear innocent. The markings we know were added later.

The letters—and likely the game itself—were adapted from those on the dreidel (from the German *dreihen,* to spin) popular in medieval Germany. "N" stood for *nischt* (nothing), "G" for *gantz* (all), "H" *halb* (half) and "S" *shtel* (put), forming instructions for play. Though transformed into Hebrew, the letters retained their meaning.

THE GAME Each player (up to five people is optimum) puts an agreed-upon amount—of pennies, nuts, jellybeans—into the common pot. All take turns spinning. If the dreidel lands on nun (נ), the player takes nothing, gimmel (ג), s/he takes all, hei (ה), s/he takes half, and shin (ש , or pei, פ in Israel), s/he puts a predetermined amount into the pot. When the pot is empty, everyone antes up again. The game ends when one person has everything, or after a set number of rounds or amount of time.

You can also play by awarding points for each letter, according to their values in Hebrew: nun equals fifty, gimmel thirty, hei five and shin three hundred. The first to reach one thousand or some other pre-determined number wins.

PARTIES AND EVENTS

Jewish communal organizations, synagogues and families often host parties with special emphasis on activities for children. Candlelighting, latkes (SEE "TRADITIONAL FOODS"), songfests, sporting events and torch relays modeled after the annual event in Israel often take place during the season.

GIFTS AND GELT

Before the influence of commercialized Christmas made it a widespread custom, particularly in America, to give gifts during Khanukah, sometimes on all eight nights, children received Khanukah gelt ("money," in Yiddish).

Possibly in commemoration of the coins minted by the first Hasmonean ruler (SEE "HISTORIC FOUNDATION"), the practice grew out of the custom of providing gifts to support poor yeshivah students and teachers, an appropriate response to the Hellenists' attempt to obliterate Judaism by destroying Jewish texts and outlawing Jewish learning. It became common to give coins to the children who in seventeenth-century Poland distributed the gift money to teachers. Often it was a way to reward them for past studies and encourage them to learn more.

Today, some grandparents still give money, but more often only symbolic packets of foil-covered chocolate coins are handed out while presents of all sorts are more common. To keep gift-giving within reason, some families exchange gifts only on one night, limit the number of major gifts, or designate different nights for different givers: one for parents to children, one for grandparents to children, one for children to parents, one for siblings to each other, and so on.

The important thing to remember about exchanging gifts is that it be done in the distinct spirit of Khanukah. The holiday originated, after all, as a result of the attempt to eliminate our tradition, when Jewish texts were burned, Jewish learning was a crime, and Jewish people were murdered for showing allegiance to the religion. Therefore, items that promote Jewish learning, such as books, video and audio recordings and games, and excursions to places or events of Jewish interest, are most appropriate. Also, a portion of any money received, either as gelt or from gambling at cards or dreidel, is customarily given as *tzedakah*. (In some families, each child chooses one of his or her toys, new or old, to donate to poor children or to a hospital.)

THE KHANUKAH-CHRISTMAS DISCONNECTION

It has become far too common for Jewish families to bring the trappings of Christmas into their homes, whether in the form of extravagant gift-giving (sometimes even moved from the eight days beginning Kislev 25 to December 25!), decorations, family parties on Christmas Day, or caroling get-togethers.

Such things are usually done under the mistaken impression that Christmas is not a religious holiday. It is not surprising that Jews uneducated in our own rich tradition are misled by the season's commercialization and because our society has so broadly embraced the occasion as to make it a national holiday.

This does nothing to change the fact that Christmas—meaning Christ's Mass—is a celebration of the birth of the man Christians believe to be the messiah. With all due respect to the multitudes of people who accept this theology, the concept is anathema to Judaism. In addition, Jews have suffered horrendously through two thousand years of anti-Semitic persecutions often perpetuated in Jesus' name or beliefs attributed to his inspiration.

So no matter how anyone tries to justify substitutes for or supplements to our own winter holiday, they are totally inappropriate. (A Christmas tree by any other name—like "Khanukah bush"—is still a Christmas tree—and like its ornaments, mistletoe, wreaths and even the exchange of gifts, symbolic of aspects of the man and his life being celebrated [in this case, the cross on which he was crucified and his immortality through resurrection]).

Treating a religious occasion as a secular event does not change its intrinsic identity. And diverting attention from what in Judaism is attractive and valuable robs our children of an opportunity to learn about and be proud of positive aspects of their own religion. It also destroys the message of the festival: The Maccabean Khanukah resulted from the struggle (without which there would never have been a Christianity) against adopting the customs of other people, against the Jews becoming indistinguishable and undistinguished from those around us. When Khanukah is not an isolated incidence of Jewish observance, but kept in the perspective of an incredibly rich schedule of opportunities for celebration throughout the Jewish calendar, it no longer has to be viewed as being in competition with someone else's holiday.

(Maybe if your children have built and decorated a *sukkah,* festooning it with greenery, garlands, fruit and ornaments, or have adorned the house with flowers and branches for Shavuot, they won't feel that they are missing anything. Celebrating Khanukah—as a different holiday—when everyone around them is celebrating Christmas also helps youngsters believe in themselves and their own choices. Seeing that they do not have to follow their peers can give them strength when they face other pressures to conform.)

SYNAGOGUE

While the ritual of Khanukah takes place exclusively at home (except for communal lighting ceremonies), there is some recognition of the holiday in the house of worship.

KHANUKIAH Since the Middle Ages, when transients often slept in the synagogue, communities have kindled lights for the holiday there. Usually placed on the southern wall, the location of the golden menorah in the Temple, the *khanukiah* is lit before *Ma'ariv* to be seen by people coming home from work. For those who attend services, it does not substitute for lighting at home. It has also become customary for the *khanukiah* to be kindled before *Shakharit* in the morning, without the blessings, to remind people how many candles are to be lit at night, when the next Jewish day starts.

PRAYER The services are the same as on ordinary weekdays with two additions. *Hallel* is chanted daily, because each day has a distinct nature as continuance of the miracle of the oil, and Khanukah itself, as an independence celebration of sorts, warrants the thanksgiving. During the *Amidah,* we insert the paragraph *Al Hanisim* (For the Miracles), which summarizes the story of the Maccabees and thanks God for delivering us.

READINGS FROM TORAH AND PROPHETS The portions of the Torah, read on every day of Khanukah, connect this commemoration of dedication with the initial dedication of the Shrine in the wilderness, when the heads of the Twelve Tribes of Israel brought offerings. On the first day of Khanukah we read about the offering of the first tribe, on the second day, the offering of the second, and so on, until the last day, when we read about the offerings of the last five tribes and the verse about lighting the menorah (NUMBERS 7–8:4).

On the Shabbat of Khanukah, in addition to the regular Torah portion and the passage from Numbers, we read a special Haftarah. (Some scholars believe the custom of reading prophetic portions began during the Maccabean era, when Antiochus forbade Torah but not *Neviim*. It was also during this time that the rabbis, to inspire the people and make education accessible to the masses, extended the *Hockheil* custom [SEE "HISTORIC FOUNDATION" IN CHAPTER ON SUKKOT] by dividing the Torah into portions to be read on Shabbat over the course of the year, as well as Mondays and Thursdays when large numbers of people came into town for market.)

Zekhariah presents the image of a menorah kept lit by a flow of unending oil from an unseen source (2:14–4:7). Written three hundred years before the

Maccabean revolt, it supported the rabbis' tradition of stressing the miracle of the oil over the military offensive, particularly with its famous summary phrase, "Not by might, nor by power, but by My spirit—said the Lord of Hosts" (4:6). It clearly places the emphasis on dedication to Jewish ideals, instructing that only through spiritual replenishment will Judaism and the Jewish nation triumph.

When a second Shabbat falls during the week of Khanukah, we read the Haftarah describing the preparation of ornaments and implements for the dedication of Solomon's temple, the second *"khanukah"* (I KINGS 7:40–51).

TEVET 10

If you are keeping track of all special days in the Jewish calendar, the next follows Khanukah by one week. Commemorating the day that Babylonian King Nebukhadnezzar began his siege of Jerusalem, which prepared the way for the destruction of the Temple and the first exile, Tevet 10 is a minor fast day (FOR EXPLANATION, SEE CHAPTER ON TISHA B'AV).

Where Do We Begin? Preparation

Aside from making sure you have the appropriate supplies—*khanukiah* (cleaned of last year's residue wax and carbon!), candles or wicks and oil, potatoes if you will be making the traditional delicacy latkes, dreidels and any gifts or coins you intend to distribute—there is little that must be done in advance.

However, families that enjoy decorating the house for the holiday begin getting ready several weeks early. "Happy Khanukah" signs, paper chains, cut-outs of holiday symbols and so on can be purchased at a Jewish goods or party supplier or made at home or school. (The idea is not to compete with the lawn displays, blinking lights and rooftop ornaments of non-Jewish neighbors, but to create a festive atmosphere that will enhance the Jewish spirit of the holiday.)

Extended families often get together for kindling the lights, a meal, singing, games and gift exchanges one night during the week (the fifth candle was traditional, but today the most convenient night is chosen). Obviously, if you attend or host such a gathering, you will need to allow time to shop and cook.

What Are We Supposed to Do? Halakhah

A number of halakhot pertaining to the main observance of Khanukah have changed over the years because of shifts in patterns of life and living conditions since the original writing and codification of the laws.

SUITABLE KHANUKIOT

The lamp used for Khanukah must be dedicated to the use of kindling lights for this holiday, and must be distinct from any other source of illumination in the house. Although the original vessels were the clay oil lamps in common use, the post-Talmudic sages disapproved of pottery *khanukiot*, unless cleaned every night, in favor of metal or glass, which did not become soiled and unsightly after just one use. In other words, the holiday is to be honored with an attractive lamp.

Anything that holds the flames will do, as long as the lights are all at the same level, the wicks remain separate to make distinct flames, the flame of one candle does not melt the wax of another, and the *shammash* sits at a different height, or off to the side, from the other lights.

Ever since the invention of the incandescent bulb, the question of whether an electric *khanukiah* may be used has generated debate. Their reasons differ, but authorities on halakhah do not sanction their use for other than decorative purposes. Since the *khanukiah* is modeled on the Temple menorah, fuel and wick must be used, according to some. Others explain that at the time it is lit, the lamp is supposed to contain enough fuel to burn for the prescribed amount of time. (If it doesn't, it must be extinguished and relit.) An electric lamp does not store the required amount of current, but continually draws it from an outside source. Also, turning it on may be an indirect, rather than the required direct, action. Merely twisting a bulb in its socket does not fulfill the spirit of kindling lights.

MAKING KINDLING A PRIORITY

Maimonides ruled that even a person supported by charity should borrow, beg or sell a garment in order to purchase oil and a lamp and be able to kindle

Khanukah lights. That is because of each household's contribution to publicizing the miracle.

If you must choose between lights for the holiday or for the Sabbath, provide the latter as a matter of domestic peace and comfort. (At the time this ruling was made, Sabbath lights were often the only illumination in a home.) But between Khanukah lights and wine for Sabbath *kiddush*, the lights take precedence.

POSITIONING THE KHANUKIAH

Maimonides asserted that we be diligent in performing the "exceedingly precious" *mitzvah* of lighting the Khanukah lamp because it promotes recognition of the miracle and provides a means of praising God for it. Originally, the halakhah stipulated that the *khanukiah* be hung on the doorpost—so that anyone passing your home saw it, and it had the added benefit of encouraging observance in Jewish neighborhoods, where everyone would know whether or not a family complied.

When hostility from non-Jewish neighbors made it dangerous for Jews to openly observe the holiday, the rabbis ruled that the *khanukiah* could be lit inside. Today publicizing the miracle is primarily directed at those in the home, who, often more than passers-by, need to be reminded of the Maccabees' achievement. So the lamp may be placed anywhere. Still, when possible it is preferable to kindle the lights near a window facing the street or the entryway, if the flames will not be extinguished when the door is opened.

FUEL

If you use oil, that from olives is preferred. The original Khanukah cruse contained olive oil and it provides a clear light (although not necessary, the clarity enhances the *mitzvah*). A midrash provides an additional basis, comparing Israel to the olive because of its by-product: All liquids mingle with one another, except oil. Likewise, Israel remains separate in following God's laws. Using olive oil for Khanukah reminds us of the distinctness by which Israel has survived and for which the Maccabees fought.

LIGHTING THE LIGHTS

OBLIGATION Both men and women are bound to the *mitzvah* of kindling. A man, woman, or religiously mature youth (a girl twelve years of age, a boy thirteen) can light on behalf of the entire household.

TIME Once the time for lighting has arrived, you may not eat, drink, perform work, or study until the *khanukiah* has been kindled. The rule of lighting at nightfall, when the stars appear, was made so that the last pedestrians coming home from the marketplace would see the flames. Since our routines are less tied to natural light today, the *khanukiah* may be kindled any time people are still outside or awake in the household. If you light after everyone else in your home has gone to sleep, and there is no one on the streets, you do not recite the blessings.

On *Erev Shabbat,* you kindle the Khanukah lights before the Sabbath candles, more than an hour before nightfall. (Once the latter are kindled, no fire can be made.) To comply with the halakhah that at least one of the Khanukah lights burns a minimum of thirty minutes after the sun goes down, you need to use a thinner wick or bigger candle. Following Shabbat, the synagogue *khanukiah* is lit prior to *Havdalah.* At home, it can be kindled either before or after *Havdalah.*

BENEDICTIONS Since tradition requires that performance of a *mitzvah* be preceded by the recitation of a *brakhah,* all three blessings (two on all but the first night) must be recited prior to kindling any lights. The first blessing uses the phrase "Who has commanded us to kindle" even though lighting Khanukah lamps was not directly instructed by God in the Torah. Deuteronomy 17:11 was interpreted to mean that the sages had the authority to make rulings to which we are to adhere. As Maimonides presented it, the implication of the blessing is ". . . Who has sanctified us with His commandments, having commanded us to heed the sages who have instructed us to kindle . . ." (The Khanukah candle-lighting *brakhah* became the format for all subsequent kindling benedictions.)

DURATION Although the lights are supposed to burn for a minimum of thirty minutes, most authorities agree that the *mitzvah* is fulfilled once they are lit. For that reason, you do not have to relight them if they become extinguished or if they do not burn the full half hour (as long as the amount of fuel necessary for thirty minutes of burning is present). If they are relit, the blessings are not repeated.

If the lamp is still burning after people have left the streets, you may extinguish it. Any oil left over can be added to and used the next day. Any oil left on the eighth day should be burned so that it not be used for purposes other than the sacred one for which it was designated.

Once lit, the *khanukiah* is not to be moved until the flames have been extinguished, so as not to appear that the light is serving a purpose other than expressing thanks to God.

TRAVEL When you are away from home, if someone in your household kindles in your behalf, it is not necessary for you to light a *khanukiah* yourself. If one is not being lit for you, and you are unable to light your own, you can be a partner in someone else's home if you share the expense of the oil. Otherwise, if you see the flames of another person's *khanukiah,* you recite the second blessing and the *shehekhiyanu.* (The existence of portable *khanukiot* in Judaica collections, some cleverly installed in cigarette and other travel cases, testifies that wayfarers made provisions to fulfill the *mitzvah* of the occasion.)

WORK

There are no restrictions on work during the week of Khanukah.

MOURNING

Since Khanukah is a festival, fasting and funeral eulogies, except for a scholar, are prohibited. Outward signs of sadness are to be avoided.

TZEDAKAH

Charity should be donated during the holiday, especially to support those who study Torah.

What Other Things Do People Do? Customs

OTHER TIMES AND PLACES

FESTIVITIES Khanukah has been a week punctuated by parties, a feeling of relaxation and optimism even in the most oppressive external circumstances. In the spirit of pride and hope, Eastern European Jews often closed their shops early and devoted their evenings to socializing and annual concerts. The restriction against using the light of the candles for any purpose, and the fact that they are to be enjoyed, provided the luxury of leisure time not often available in prior generations. With this free time, forms of entertainment not generally indulged became popular Khanukah pastimes. The fifth night, when the youngsters received their gelt, was often set aside for family get-togethers.

Although at this time rabbis traditionally visited small villages to teach Torah and inspire people to obey God throughout the year, even study was interrupted once candles were lit. Yeshivah students instead engaged in Talmudic riddles and *gematria* arithmetic puzzles whose answers were numbers totaling forty-four (the count of candles consumed in the *khanukiah*). Prohibitions against gambling were relaxed for dreidel, chess, checkers, dominoes and card games like kvitlakh, played with a set of thirty-one numbered and artfully decorated cards representing the kings the Israelites fought on their entrance to Canaan. (The rabbis usually forbade gambling because they considered the transfer of funds without work robbery. At Khanukah they sanctioned it as being in the spirit of the season—some viewed the games as contests of wit, and often the winnings were donated to *tzedakah*.)

Children in Yemen received coins every day of Khanukah, with which they bought small bags of sugar with a pinch of red coloring used to make a Khanukah "wine." Every night they took their drinks to the home of a different one of their friends, whose mother had cooked up a peas and lentils treat. Eastern Europeans enjoyed kugel, and often roast goose or duck with dumplings, as their holiday treats. The Moroccans served couscous and rooster. Many Sephardim had the custom, on the last night, of roasting nuts and seeds on a large tray for the children, who grabbed handfuls for immediate gratification and to take to school the next day.

HONORING WOMEN Among the Sephardim, the nights toward the end of the festival had special connotations. The Tunisians called Rosh Khodesh Tevet (the sixth or seventh candle, depending on the number of days in Kislev) "New Moon of the Daughters," when parents gave gifts to their girls and grooms gave to their brides. A bride's father then hosted a feast for friends and relatives of both families.

The seventh night was widely dedicated to Jewish women, in commemoration of the contributions they made to the Maccabees' victory (and all of Jewish history). In special gatherings, women recalled that by decree, maidens on their wedding nights first had to surrender to the Syrian governor, and retold the stories of Hannah and Judith (from the apocryphal Book of Judith). The beautiful widow (in Hebrew *Yehudit,* meaning "Jewess") used her physical charms and quick mind to best the captain of the enemy. After convincing Holofernes that she was aligning with his side, she fed him salty cheese to make him drink an excess of wine. Once he fell into intoxicated sleep, she decapitated him and left the headless body to frighten his men, who retreated. (Although set in the Babylonian period, the Book of Judith is thought to have originated at the time of the Maccabees. Medieval Hebrew versions understood the story in the context of the Hasmonean revolt.)

In remembrance, the women ate cheese dishes, sang, danced, received special blessings and sometimes embraced the Torah scrolls in the synagogue. Often they took a vacation from all household chores on that day, and frequently for the entire Khanukah week.

Some European communities dedicated the eighth night to Judith, when her story was read in Yiddish. Called *zot* (literally "this is," but implying this is the essence, the culmination, of) Khanukah, alluding to the day's Scriptural portion dealing with the dedication of the Tabernacle (NUMBERS 7:84), it was a day for giving charity, telling stories of Jewish heroes, and enjoying elaborate meals.

CANDLES AND KINDLING When the Jews of Antioch (Syria) received their candles from Jerusalem, they sang praises to them, then sold them publicly in the synagogue to raise money for their religious school. If a congregation had a beadle (also known as a *shammash*), he would send each member family a decorative taper to use in lighting their *khanukiot,* for which he was financially rewarded. As gifts, children received candles, each in the shape of a hand with the fingers upright, to protect them against the "evil eye."

The ancestors of Aleppo's Jews wandered for months following their expulsion from Spain in 1492 before being allowed to settle in Syria around Khanukah of that year. In thanks, they lit an extra candle for finding a country willing to accept them and began the lasting custom of having two *shammashim*. They also light twelve oil lamps in the synagogue, in memory of the gifts of the heads of Israel's tribes during the Tabernacle dedication in the wilderness.

Yemenite children make their own *khanukiot* of clay; the Tunisian children decorate theirs with flowers and receive coins called flower money.

The Jews of Aden all dressed in blue and attended afternoon services together. Upon returning to their homes, they kindled their doorpost *khanukiot* at the same time, lighting up the entire community. In Venice, Jewish families rode their gondolas through the canals, serenading at every home displaying a *khanukiah*.

Today, *khanukiot* are seen in public squares all over the world, as the Lubavitch Khassidim continue their campaign to keep Khanukah in as much evidence as Christmas, and remind Jews to rededicate themselves to their tradition.

TENDING TO THE NEEDY In many communities, particularly among the Sephardim, providing for those in need took special forms. The Judeo-Spanish called the Sabbath that fell during the festival *Shabbat Khalbasha* (clothing the poor). The rabbi expounded on the importance of providing garments, which were later brought to the synagogue and distributed during Rosh Khodesh Tevet (at the end of Khanukah). Whenever a person in need would approach someone and quote from the Torah portion that usually falls during Khanukah, "*Shuvu shivru lanu mei'aht okhel*" (Go again, buy us a little food [GENESIS 43:2]), s/he would receive food or money.

The children of Damascas, and Sephardic children in Israel sometimes accompanied by teachers, went through their communities reciting the same phrase to collect food or money to buy it. On the eighth day of the festival, with the help of rabbis, they used the donated food to prepare three banquets: one for the poor, one for their teachers, and one for themselves. Leaders of the Jewish community in Turkey visited the affluent to collect money for the poor, distributing latkes from the platters they carried to each contributor. The Bukharans baked coins into cakes for their needy relatives and teachers. Children of the poor Persian Jews went door to door for contributions. In return for a gift, they burned a piece of grass to ward off the "evil eye."

IN THE LAND OF THE MACCABEES In Israel, of course, Khanukah is a national holiday and one with special meaning. Not only did the Maccabean victory and rededication miracle take place there twenty-one hundred years ago, but the conditions of the struggle for survival were repeated as the modern state came into being. During the holiday period, when new buildings (like the Tel Aviv Museum) and settlements (particularly strategic *nakhal* ["take possession," a special army unit] kibbutzim), are traditionally dedicated, *khanukiot* crown public buildings. Prior to the start of school vacation, which coincides with Khanukah, the curriculum is devoted to the holiday and its history. Families, schools, organizations, hotels, and kibbutzim hold gatherings, parties, dances and other special events.

This is also the time in Israel for meetings and conferences, especially on the subject of education—and for touring the country. Sephardim in Jerusalem visit the grave of Simon the Just, the last high priest before Hellenization tainted the position, and children climb the hills to pick a white flower studded with red dots called "Blood of the Maccabees."

On *Khag Hamakkabim* (Festival of the Maccabees, as it is called in Israel), members of the Maccabi sports movement gather at the ancient Maccabee catacombs in Modi'in, the starting point for a reenactment of their triumphant march into Jerusalem. Torches are lit from a bonfire to begin the Freedom Torch Relay. At predetermined positions, runners pass their torches to successors, who carry them to towns and cities throughout the county. On reaching Jerusalem, the torch is used to kindle a *khanukiah* at the president's residence during a public ceremony, and is then carried to Mount Zion, where it kindles another in memory of Holocaust victims. (Torches, extinguished en route and relit in New York, have at times been sent to America to symbolize the Israel-Diaspora connection.)

Other processions, races and outdoor celebrations are held for Israeli teens. By providing meals and gifts at old age homes and hospitals, and sponsoring activities at army posts and absorption centers (where new immigrants are prepared to enter Israeli society), the Israelis continue a Khanukah tradition of community service.

FOR FURTHER EXPLORATION

The Book of Judith. Ed. by Solomon Zeitlin. Trans. by Morton S. Enslin. Philadelphia: E.J. Brill, Leiden, for Dropsie University, 1972.
  The text of the apocryphal book translated into English for Jewish use is supplemented with explanatory material. (Several Internet sites present the full text.)

Sussman, Susan. Hanukkah: *Eight Lights Around the World.* Niles, IL: Albert Whitman & Company, 1988.
  After summarizing the story behind the holiday, the book provides a glimpse into the celebrations of eight contemporary families reflecting the different circumstances and customs of their surroundings. A thread of eternity in the common last word of each section connects the pictures of Israel, Mexico, Argentina, America, France, India, Morocco and the Soviet Union. ◎✡

GREETING

On this holiday, it is appropriate to say either *khag sameiakh* ("happy holiday" in Hebrew) or *gut yom tov* (the Yiddish version).

What Is There to Eat? Traditional Foods

The fact that feasting is not part of ordained Khanukah observance (the Syrians wanted spiritual subordination, not physical annihilation) has never stopped people from indulging in at least one festive meal in honor of the occasion. Those who recite psalms and songs of thanksgiving elevate these repasts to the status of *mitzvah* banquets, but most people are content to concentrate on the special dish that has become intimately associated with the holiday.

It is not unusual to hear people wax ecstatic about latkes, on paper the simple potato pancake, a mix of grated potatoes, onion, egg and a pinch of flour or *matzah* meal. But in the mouth these crispy concoctions provide particular pleasure. (According to a folk proverb, Khanukah's latkes teach us that we cannot live by miracles alone. The fourteenth-century Italian Jewish writer Kalonymous ben Kalonymous wrote a poem extolling them.)

The Khanukah connection has nothing to do with the main ingredient and everything to do with the oil in which they are fried—to commemorate the miraculous oil used to rededicate the Temple. A more complex connection links the Hebrew words for the Hamoneans (*Hashmonayim*), oil (*shemen*), and eight, (*shemoneh*), the number that symbolizes completion of a holy task and elevation above the mundane earth (circumcision of a Jewish boy and sacrifice of firstborn animals in the Temple take place on the eighth day, the dedication of the Temple itself lasted eight days).

Although many families swear by the latkes of their mother or grandmother; recipes found in virtually any Jewish cookbook and typically in Jewish publications in the weeks prior to the holiday are remarkably similar. Perfectly delicious plain, latkes are usually eaten with sour cream, or, preferably, applesauce. Oriental Jews add sugar and sesame seeds to theirs, and a wide variety of vegetables serve as the main ingredient in place of potato alone.

In Israel, latkes, called *levivot* in Hebrew, are supplanted in popularity by *sufganiot,* jelly doughnuts. Other communities developed their own variations of the oil-fried food for Khanukah, such as tempura-style vegetables and fruits, *fritto misto,* in Rome, and deep-fried sweets dipped in honey or sugar in Greece and Iran.

Latkes may have developed from the custom of eating cheese pancakes in honor of Judith when Eastern European Jews had to substitute what was most available to them, potatoes, for the unattainable cottage cheese. Among some people, it is still customary to eat various cheese dishes. In addition to using them to trick the head of the Greek army, Judith had taken dairy food with her to his encampment so that she could continue to scrupulously follow Jewish dietary laws. Eating cheese dishes on Khanukah also commemorates this commitment to our heritage.

FOR FURTHER EXPLORATION

FOR CHILDREN

Drucker, Malka. *Grandma's Latkes.* San Diego: Harcourt Books, 1996.
  Grandma passes on the tradition to the next generation by teaching her granddaughter Molly how to make the potato pancakes, and why we eat them. Her recipe is included at the end of the book illustrated with hand-painted woodcuts. Ages 4–8.

Wikler, Madeline, and Judyth Groner. *Miracle Meals: Eight Nights of Food N' Fun for Chanukah.* Rockville, MD: Kar-Ben Copies, Inc., 1987.
  Recipes for soups, latkes, dairy and meat dishes, desserts, fun foods, and ideas for Khanukah parties and games follow the story of the holiday and information about lighting candles. Ages 3–10.

Do You Hear Music? Songs to Sing

Starting with psalms at the Maccabees' dedication of the Temple, singing has always attended Khanukah festivities. Unfortunately, often the only song anyone knows is the banal "I Have a Little Dreidel" (known to practically everyone, Jewish or not, since it is the one token Khanukah tune included in public school Christmas programs). We have better examples than that, a repertoire of folk songs in Yiddish and Hebrew.

Aside from the musical theme of the holiday, *"Maoz Tzur"* (SEE "OBSERVANCE") the most traditional songs include *"Mi Yimalel?"* (Who Can Retell), a tribute to the brave Maccabees who led Israel to redeem itself; *"Y'me Khanukah"* or *"Oy Khanukah"* or *"Erev Khanukah,"* describing the way the holiday is celebrated; and *"Levivot"* (Latkes), in appreciation of the holiday delicacy. Felix Mendelsohn wrote *"Neirot Dolkim"* (Burning Candles) in honor of the glow on the street created by candles in the windows, and the composer Debbie Friedman, who writes new music for old liturgy and Scriptural passages, created a wonderfully upbeat version of the Zekhariah verse read on Shabbat Khanukah, "Not By Might, Not By Power."

FOR FURTHER EXPLORATION

Friedman, Debbie. *Not By Might, Not By Power.* New York: Transcontinental Music Publications, 1980. Traditional songs for the holiday are given new life with Friedman's wonderful music in this recording, which focuses on renewal and rededication. ☺✡

What Tales Are Told? Stories to Read

Both the history of the holiday, with its drama and heroic themes, and its celebration, reflecting the security of family and the carefreeness of childhood, have been captured in the poems, essays and stories of some of our most beloved writers.

The most eminent modern Hebrew poet, Hayim Nahman Bialik, a leader of the Hebrew literary renaissance, presented the pleasantness of the festival in "For Khanukah" and "My Dreidel." He also used the positive image of the Maccabees to express disgust at the cowardly Jews who hid helplessly during the Kishinev pogrom (in "City of Slaughter"). Another of our esteemed poets, Saul Tchernichovsky, expressed the same sentiments in "A Night in Khanukah." The poem bitterly scorns ghetto residents who had lost the legacy of the Maccabean spirit.

Emma Lazarus (whose "The New Colossus" adorns the base of the Statue of Liberty) celebrates the Maccabean victory in "The Banner of the Jew" and "The Feast of Lights"; the Hebrew poet and Yiddish novelist Zalman Shneour wrote "Khanukah Candles" and the Israeli poet Natan Alterman, "It Happened on Khanukah."

For Theodor Herzl, the image of the Maccabee served as an inspiration and a promise of how the Jews would return to self-determination and strength, as expressed in his essay "The Menorah" (SEE "PERSONAL SIGNIFICANCE"), and writings about his vision of the Jewish state.

Henry Wadsworth Longfellow, the nineteenth-century epic poet, portrayed the conflict between Judaism and Hellenism in his five-act tragedy *Judah Maccabeus*. Others have created fictional accounts of episodes in the Maccabean revolt against the Syrians, such as Howard Fast in his novel *My Glorious Brothers* (SEE "HISTORIC FOUNDATION"). Stories and books for this holiday are full of family togetherness, one generation helping or teaching another, gathering to celebrate and solve problems, reflecting the warmth and values of the occasion and providing models for your own observance.

FOR FURTHER EXPLORATION

FOR ADULTS

Steinberg, Milton. *As A Driven Leaf.* Springfield, NJ: Behrman House, 1996.
> This marvelous novel is based on the life of the second-century sage, Rabbi Elisha ben Abuyah, who renounced Judaism because he thought the logic of the Greek system would answer his doubts— only to find tragedy. Though set later than the time of the Maccabees, it shows how Hellenism invaded the traditional beliefs of the Jews, and is a classic about the conflict between Jewish faith and Greek philosophy.

FOR CHILDREN

Goldin, Barbara Diamond. *A Hanukkah Tale—Just Enough is Plenty.* New York: Puffin, 1990.
> A charming story of a poor family in a small village in Poland who may not have one kopek left after all the preparations for Khanukah, and the peddler who entertains and rewards them, won a National Jewish Book Award. Ages 3–8.

Levine, Arthur A. *All the Lights in the Night.* New York: Tambourine Books, 1991.
> Two boys escaping from their shtetl to join an older brother in Palestine draw strength from the Khanukah candles they light on the run. Beautifully illustrated, the book is based on the true story of the author's grandfather. Ages 6–10.

Singer, Isaac Bashevis. *The Power of Light.* New York: Farrar, Straus, Giroux, 1990.
> The eight moving stories of miracles and visitations support the lessons of the holiday. Ages 8–12.

Wurtzel, Yehuda and Sarah Wurtzel. *Lights: A Fable About Hanukah.* Chappagua, NY: Rossel Books, 1985.
> The full-length story book version of the animated children's program tells of one light—the Jewish spirit—that refused to be extinguished during the Greek oppression. With humor and drama, expressing hope and joy, it shows how the Jews were drawn to the pleasures of the Hellenistic world, and later had to struggle to restore light once it was curtailed. This is a thoughtful and effective telling of the story and what it means. Ages 6 and up.

Lights: A Fable About Hanukah
> The original version of the book described above is deservedly highly acclaimed. In twenty-eight minutes, it presents the message of the holiday beautifully. ✡

Of Added Note

MUSIC

In the 1700s, Frederick, Prince of Wales, commissioned George Frideric Handel to create a composition to commemorate the Duke of Cumberland's triumphant return from battle in Scotland. The result was the oratorio *Judah Maccabeus,* with a libretto by a Greek scholar based on I Maccabees and *Jewish Antiquities,* first performed in 1747. ("See the Conqu'ring Hero Comes" from the oratorio has been adapted into Hebrew as *"Hi'ne Bo."*)

More recently, Boston's Public Radio International (WBGH) Sound & Spirit host Ellen Kushner teamed with Shirim Klezmer Orchestra to create *The Golden Dreydl: A Klezmer Nutcracker*—adapted from Tchaikovsky (with such results as "Kozatsky 'till You Dropsky," "Dance of the Latkes Queens," and "March of the Maccabees").

IN ISRAEL

HAKFAR HAHASHMONA'I, a working village from the Second Temple period reconstructed near Moshav Shilat (about ten miles east of Lod), portrays what everyday life was like for the people who lived in the days of the Maccabees and provides opportunities for visitors to participate in the occupations and activities of the time. The Maccabees' actual birthplace, **MODI'IN,** is nearby. Sites of several key battles offer little to see but the topography—but that remains virtually unchanged and provides insight into Judah's wit and tactics: **BEIT HORON** (en route to Jerusalem), site of an early victory in the war, **EMMAUS** (twenty minutes from Jerusalem in the Jewish National Fund's Park Canada), where Judah outsmarted major generals, **ELASA** (six miles away), where he died in a surprise assault from the Seleucids, and **BEIT ZEKHARIAH** (near Moshav Eleazar), where Judah's brother Eleazar died. Portions of Jerusalem's **OLD CITY WALLS**, north from Mount Zion to Jaffa Gate, date from the Hasmonean era. Ruins of another Hashmonean wall, and of a gate in it can be seen at the north end of **CARDO**, the ancient shopping street in the Jewish Quarter of Jerusalem's Old City. (The text of I Maccabees serves as a valuable guide for a visit.)

Tu B'Shevat—
New Year of the Trees

(TOO' BEH SHVAHT')
SHEVAT 15
(MID-WINTER, JANUARY—FEBRUARY)

Over the centuries, this minor holiday has been transformed probably more than any other occasion on the Jewish calendar—from an agricultural technicality to a celebration of national ideals. For generations it was observed mainly by spiritual Jewish sects and Hebrew school students, but recently adults have recognized the relevance of its messages about Zionism and environmentalism.

Origins—WHY WE CELEBRATE TU B'SHEVAT

Traditions—HOW WE CELEBRATE TU B'SHEVAT

Origins—
WHY WE CELEBRATE TU B'SHEVAT

Where Did It Begin? Historic Foundation

AN AGRICULTURAL NECESSITY

The fifteenth of Shevat became a special day because of a commandment in the Torah. The law (DEUTERONOMY 14:22) instructed Jewish farmers to contribute ten percent of the fruit from their orchards to the Temple to help support the priesthood. The way the commandment is phrased—". . . you must take a tithe . . . year after year"—suggested to the sages that the fruit offered had to have grown in a specific year. The problem was, how were they to determine when the growth started and in that way know which fruit to count?

They decided the cut-off would be the date when fruit began to flower. By then the soil, having soaked up winter rainwater, could nourish new growth.

After some wrangling between the people of the plains and valleys of the geographically diverse Israel (who saw the almond trees blossom around the first of Shevat), and the people of the hills and mountains (where flowers did not appear until the fifteenth), the latter date was accepted. Since then the New Year of the Trees—in Hebrew called *Rosh* (head) *Hashanah* (of the year) *La* (of the) *Ilanot* (trees)—has been celebrated on Shevat 15.

We know the holiday as Tu B'Shevat based on the system in which each letter of the Hebrew alphabet represents a number. Tet (ט) is nine, and vov (ו), which also functions as a vowel that can have an "oh," or, in this case, "oo," sound) is six, together fifteen. *B'Shevat* means of (the month of) Shevat. Outside the Holy Land, the holiday is also called *Khamisha Asar* (the fifteenth) *B'Shevat*.

POST-TEMPLE TU B'SHEVAT

The date started to assume the character of a holiday after the Second Temple was destroyed and the Jews were effectively excluded from Israel for two

477

thousand years (SEE CHAPTER ON TISHA B'AV). From its origins as the simple distinction between one fruit-growing season and the next, Tu B'Shevat became a powerful symbol.

Even though the soil of Israel was no longer under their feet, the Jews considered it central to their national self-image. Their thoughts and prayers throughout the year were full of desire connected with the Land, and Tu B'Shevat gave them a special opportunity to display their longing to return to it and make it productive again. To recognize the day, they indulged in the luxury of eating fruit grown in Israel.

But it was the Kabbalists who originated the celebration of the tree. Centuries after the exile began, these Jewish mystics living in the northern Israeli city of Safed focused on the symbolism of the tree as life, an image as old as the story of Creation (GENESIS 2:9). They understood "the new year of the tree" to be The New Year of THE Tree, the Tree of Life. And the Tree of Life, they said, was actually a symbol of God, whose roots in the heavens carry nourishment, or energy, to the branches extending to earth. So the Kabbalists embraced Tu B'Shevat as rejoicing for renewal and growth not just of trees, but of the entire universe.

With their typical life-affirming exuberance, they designed a special service, modeled somewhat on the Seder for Passover, in honor of the day. It included eating fruits that grow in Eretz Yisrael, drinking four glasses of wine, and reading from *Tanakh*, Talmud, and Zohar.

The original sixteenth-century Tu B'Shevat liturgy, expanded by the addition of poems and rituals, spread from Safed to Sephardic communities in Europe, North Africa and Asia, and was eventually published in 1753 in Salonica, Greece, as *Pri Etz Hadar* (Fruit of the Goodly Tree). It became customary for Jews throughout the world to eat fifteen kinds of fruit from trees, the number corresponding to the date of the observance.

IN MODERN TIMES

When European Jews began to establish agricultural settlements in Eretz Yisrael in the late nineteenth century, they were fulfilling the dream of Jews for

almost two thousand years before them. As they reclaimed the Land long celebrated by Tu B'Shevat, and revived Jewish life on it, the holiday was again transformed.

The Jewish National Fund (*Keren Kayemet Le Yisrael*, established in 1884 to collect money to buy up property in Palestine) arranged highly spirited annual Tu B'Shevat planting ceremonies. Surrounded by marching bands and banners, thousands of people carrying young trees went singing and dancing to the hillsides. (Today, almost one-seventh of the entire population of the State of Israel goes to the countryside to plant saplings.)

Outside pre-state Israel, the day was often devoted to activities centered on the Land, its geography and produce. Palestine Day, as it was known in America, meant parties, songs, games and stories in school, synagogue and home.

Many Sephardim, particularly Turks, Moroccans and Iraqis, continued to conduct Tu B'Shevat sedarim throughout the centuries. During the 1980s, American Jews looking for meaningful rituals discovered the oriental tradition, and have adopted, and adapted, the ceremony for their families and communities.

What Does It Mean? Religious Importance

At first glance, Tu B'Shevat may seem to lack religious underpinnings. It is not an obligation commanded by the Torah. And it does not commemorate an event of national significance demonstrating the involvement of God in human, and particularly Jewish, history. Yet this minor folk festival embraces two ideals central to Judaism: the primacy of the Land of Israel, and the irrevocable partnership between God and the people of Israel.

PRIMACY OF THE LAND

Early in the saga of the Jews, God guaranteed that the descendants of Abraham would inherit a certain piece of Middle Eastern real estate (GENESIS 12:7). This covenant was repeated with the patriarchs Isaac and Jacob, and with Moses (GENESIS 15:7–21; 26:3; 35:12; EXODUS 3:8).

As the property promised to them by God himself, the Land was inherently holy. Eretz Yisrael, as it became known, indicated not just a geographic destination, but also an emotional homeland and a spiritual grounding as well.

Here Jews could express themselves with no restrictions and could openly show their devotion to God. This was the only place in the world where all six hundred and thirteen *mitzvot* apply, and the only place where all could be fulfilled (SEE CHAPTERS ON YOM HA'ATZMAUT AND TISHA B'AV).

The Jews who went into exile felt that along with their political base, they had lost their spiritual center. Israel was not just the place they lived, but where God resided with them. The Holy of Holies, the innermost chamber of the Temple, was God's special abode on earth, the resting place of the Shekhinah, His spirit. When His home was destroyed His people scattered to other nations. The Jews could no longer be as close, physically or otherwise, to Him. Their generations of longing to return was partly a yearning to end the estrangement from God.

PARTNERSHIP WITH THE LAND OWNER

According to the Talmud, "When the Holy One, Blessed by He, created the first man, He took him to all the trees of Paradise, and told him: "See my works, how handsome and fine they are: everything I have created was created for you. Make sure not to spoil and destroy My world, because what you spoil—no one can repair'" (KOHELET RABBAH 7:13).

The practice of tithing, the original reason behind Tu B'Shevat, is supposed to remind us to recognize the real "owner" of the Land: even though we work on it, even though it supports us with food and other products, it does not really belong to us. The Jews were made sovereign in the Land so they could be its caretakers, acting as God's representatives on earth.

This concept, that Jews act in partnership with God, is central to Jewish tradition. All notions of Paradise aside, our earth is deliberately incomplete and imperfect. The purpose of Jewish existence is to perfect the world according to God's commandments.

The process, *tikkun olam*, means bringing the morality of Torah law to others by behaving morally ourselves. Tu B'Shevat draws attention to some of the ways we act in concert with God, the first environmentalist. When we show appreciation for the things the earth produces, we also show our recognition that we are responsible for its well-being. When we plant trees, we express our thanks to those who prepared for us in the past, and our concern for those who will come after us. In however small a way, we are contributing to recreating the world as it existed at the very beginning, as it is supposed to be, with all things living in perfect balance.

What Does It Mean to Us? Personal Significance

Just when the world seems its bleakest, in those dreary days of mid-winter, along comes Tu B'Shevat and reminds us that, even if we cannot yet see it, a change in nature is about to occur. Marking a transition in stages of growth for trees, this holiday can be a turning point for us, too.

Many of us, at some time, experience what might be called "psychological winters." Like hibernating animals, we limit or eliminate our involvement with life. We become complacent, sluggish, pessimistic, ineffectual, maybe even bored or depressed. This internal climate may, but often does not, have anything to do with the weather outside.

Tu B'Shevat does two things. It assures us by example that new possibilities exist even when they seem to be least viable—and may even be invisible. It also tells us it's time to wake up, to throw off the inhibiting blanket and experience psychological and physical renewal. Like the trees beginning to draw on stored energy and nutrients to send out new shoots and fruit, we must summon our inner strengths to emerge from a stagnant period.

A new beginning, which a season change is, holds great potential for growth. Tu B'Shevat is a time for us to take steps that will help us and our families grow toward meeting our potentials—in any and all aspects of our lives, whether through keeping commitments in areas of personal improvement, increasing opportunity for and time spent learning, encouraging the development of natural talent, enhancing skills, or applying energies to address needs in the community and help others.

Traditions—

HOW WE CELEBRATE TU B'SHEVAT

What Do We Use? Ritual Items

HAGGADAH

If you choose to observe the holiday by hosting a Tu B'Shevat seder, you will need a text for the service. The original one developed by the kabbalists of Safed, based on the Passover Haggadah, is an anthology of readings about trees and the Land of Israel from Scripture, commentaries on it and the standard work of Jewish mysticism (Zohar), plus blessings for ritual foods and wine.

Like many people have done in recent decades, you can create your own version—which can include songs, history, stories, questions, activities and other devices incorporated, like at Passover, to engage children and other participants.

FOR FURTHER EXPLORATION

FOR ADULTS

Tu Beshvat: A Mystical Seder for the New Year of the Trees. Trans. by Yehoshua Bergman. Jerusalem: Diaspora Yeshivah.

> Based on the original kabbalists' seder, this haggadah is published both in English and Hebrew versions. (Available from the Yeshivah, PO Box 6426, Jerusalem, Israel, and online at www.shemay israel.co.il/tubishvat/index1.html).

Fisher, Rabbi Adam. *Seder Tu Bishevat—The Festival of Trees.* New York: Central Conference of American Rabbis Press, 1989.

> The haggadah contains two sedarim, one for teens and adults, one for children, full of stories, songs and blessings.

FOR CHILDREN

Appleman, Harlene Winnick, and Jane Sherwin Shapiro. *A Seder for Tu B'Shevat.* Rockville, MD: Kar-Ben Copies, Inc., 1984.

> This charming haggadah for children is easy to use and nicely illustrated.

On the Internet, you can find downloadable Tu B'Shevat haggadot, including versions produced for various communal celebrations, as well as reference to other published versions.   ☺✡

How Do We Celebrate? Observance

EATING FRUIT

Since leaving Palestine, Jews throughout the world have maintained connections with the Land on Tu B'Shevat by eating fruits produced there.

For the kabbalists, this symbolic gesture causes tremendous spiritual ramifications. According to their explanation, every piece of fruit, the parent generation, holds the seed of the next generation; in other words, the potential for new life. If, when we eat the fruit—which releases the seed—we do so in a holy way, with proper blessing and gratitude, then we are helping God to renew nature, and the flow of life continues.

With Israel's agricultural richness and exports, today we have many choices for Tu B'Shevat feasting in addition to the dried figs, dates, raisins and carob of previous generations. Oranges, avocados, bananas, pomegranates, olives, and almonds are wonderful staples for Tu B'Shevat meals, either in their natural forms or as recipe ingredients.

PLANTING TREES

THE MEANING OF TREES In the Jewish scheme of the world, trees have always occupied a key and revered role. According to the Creation story, before any other living thing, seed bearing plants and fruit trees were put on the earth (GENESIS 1:11–12). In other words, the first thing God did once He had firm land was to plant trees!

The Tree of Life, which He placed at the heart of the Garden of Eden, became a symbol of Jewish existence, a core value of individual and communal living: continuity.

The Talmud sages held wonderfully imaginative discussions about trees in life and legend. They believed that mankind, which they often compared to trees, owes its existence to them and should treat them with special recognition. Serious consequences would result from destroying a tree. The Torah (itself called a Tree of Life [PROVERBS 3:18]) prohibits the destruction of fruit trees, even in times of war (DEUTERONOMY 20:19–20), and to prevent the loss of Israel's natural

forests, the sages prohibited the Jews from allowing goats to graze uncontrolled. Today in Israel, anyone who wants to destroy a tree must apply for a license, even if the tree is on his or her own property.

ADDING A TREE TO THE ENVIRONMENT Rabbi Yokhanan ben Zakkai, who lived in Jerusalem as it was being sacked by the Romans, cleverly taught the priority of planting. "If you should be holding a sapling in your hand when they tell you the Messiah has arrived," he advised, "first plant the sapling, then go out and greet him."

> *Trees and plants and flowers have language, feeling and prayer of their own.*
>
> BAAL SHEM TOV

Planting a tree—a concrete, practical act—has represented hope since ancient times. On Tu B'Shevat in Palestine, trees were planted for children born during the previous year: for a boy, a cedar, with the wish that the child would grow to be tall and upright; for a girl, a cypress, which was graceful and fragrant. Later, branches from the cypress and cedar of a bride and groom were used to make the *khuppah* (canopy) for their wedding ceremony. The planting was associated with two of the most important times in an individual's life, birth and marriage, two occasions when we concentrate on the possibilities for the future. So powerful is the symbol of hopefulness and the continuity of life that even in the Theriesenstadt concentration camp children planted a tree.

Planting was also considered a way to create eternity. As the Talmud relates, the righteous man Honi once encountered a man planting a carob tree. "How long will it take to bear fruit?" he inquired. "About seventy years," the man replied. "Do you think you will live long enough to taste its fruits?" The man explained, "I have found ready grown carob trees in the world. As my forefathers planted them for me, so I plant for my children."

As a result of the Jewish National Fund (JNF) reforestation projects in Israel, the land once desert now supports successful farming endeavors, and millions of trees cover the hills. Visitors to Israel, on Tu B'Shevat or other times, can participate in the Plant a Tree with Your Own Hands Program. A popular alternative is to purchase tree certificates, through local and national JNF and Hadassah offices. Each inexpensive certificate represents one tree planted in Israel in

memory or honor of an individual, special occasion, and so on. (Only large plantings, not individual trees, are actually designated on site, as shown in JNF's entertaining and informative videotape, *Grandpa's Tree*. Outside of Israel, symbolic plantings are often done for the holiday, with trees planted in one's yard or community, or houseplants started from seeds, particularly parsley, which will sprout in time for Passover use.

FOR FURTHER EXPLORATION

The JNF Education Department produces copies of a prayer used in Israel when trees are planted there. It can be adapted for other tree planting ceremonies (42 East 69 Street, New York, NY 10021; 800-542-8733, 212-879-9300; www.jnf.org).

The National Arbor Day Foundation sells trees that can be planted in your climate and offers tree planting instructions, suggestions for Arbor Day ceremonies that can be adapted for Tu B'Shevat, other educational and membership information (100 Arbor Avenue, Nebraska City, NE 68410; 402-474-5655, www.arborday.org). ☺✡

READINGS

The Kabbalists introduced the idea of reading relevant texts during their Tu B'Shevat seder. A meaningful Scriptural passage (such as the traditional ones listed below), a poem or commentary recited prior to eating a particular fruit can add new dimension to holiday observance.

FOR FURTHER EXPLORATION

Relevant passages from Torah (full of imagery of, instructions about and identifications with trees and other plant life) include Genesis 1:11–18, Leviticus 26: 3–18, Deuteronomy 8:1–10, Ezekiel 1, Amos 9:13–15, Psalms 104:10–16, Job 14:7–9, and Song of Songs.

Hareuveni, Nogah. *Nature in Our Biblical Heritage*. Lod, Israel: Neot Kedumim.
   Written by the founder of the Biblical Nature Reserve in Israel (SEE "OF ADDED NOTE"), the book highlights the importance of nature in Torah, as evidenced through references to specific natural elements and the interaction of biblical characters with them (available through the Neot Kedumim gift shop, PO Box 1007, Lod, Israel 71110, 972-8-977-0782, giftshop@Neot-Kedumim.org.il).

Trees, Earth & Torah: A Tu B'Shevat Anthology. Ed. by Ari Elon et al. Philadelphia: The Jewish Publication Society, 1999.
   Fifty-eight authors, musicians, artists and cooks contributed to this compendium of biblical and rabbinic text, essays, fiction, crafts, recipes, and songs focused on Tu B'Shevat, trees, Israel, and ecology. The book includes translation of the first haggadah for the holiday, *Pri Etz Hadar*, a model ecological seder for today, examination of the tree planting program in Israel, activities related to trees and the holiday, a list of environmental organizations, publications and videos, and other material to enhance understanding and observance of Tu B'Shevat. ☺✡

TZEDAKAH

During the service for Yom Kippur, we repeatedly say the phrase "but [repentance and prayer and] *tzedakah* annul the evil decree." We mean that through actions we take to help others we can alter for the better the scales of justice being weighed on our behalf.

On Tu B'Shevat, the decree concerns trees: tradition states that as the beginning of their growth cycle, it is a day of judgment for them. Therefore, our efforts for trees are warranted.

As a festival, and particularly one so closely associated with eating, Tu B'Shevat also calls for *tzedakah* for those who cannot afford to purchase fruit. The Sephardim of the sixteenth century, while observing the holiday with their intricate ceremony, also established the *Ma-ot Perot* (Fruit Fund) to provide fruit for the poor. In some places, it became traditional to give ninety-one coins, to correspond to the numerical value of the word *ilan* (אילן), Hebrew for tree: aleph (א) equals one, yud (י) is ten, lamed (ל) thirty, and nun (ן) fifty.

Today it is appropriate to contribute to a local *Ma-ot Perot* or *Ma-ot Khitim* (wheat fund), which provides food for needy Jews for holidays and Sabbath; a synagogue *tzedakah* box, whose contents go to the needy; a food pantry or food drive; or to a national or international organization such as MAZON, A Jewish Response to Hunger (1990 S. Bundy Drive, Suite 260, Los Angeles, CA 90025-5232, 310-442-0020, 310-442-0030 fax, www.mazon.org). The organization, whose name means food in Hebrew, serves as an umbrella organization to collect and distribute money for food to groups throughout the world. It encourages donors to contribute three percent of the amount spent on food for a *simkhah* (joyous event, such as a *brit,* bar mitzvah—or Tu B'Shevat seder).

FOR FURTHER EXPLORATION

The American Society for Protection of Nature in Israel is the domestic support branch of Israel's largest environmental non-governmental organization. Through field study centers and urban branches throughout the State of Israel, SPNI runs nature education programs, hikes and holiday excursions that emphasize the importance of nature, the Land, history and the environment. Funding allows it to help preserve and maintain sites and its activities (28 Arrandale Avenue, Great Neck, NY 11024, 212-398-6750, aspni@aol.com, www.spni.org).

Neot Kedumim, The Biblical Landscape Reserve (SEE "OF ADDED NOTE"), is also aided by an American support branch, American Friends of Neot Kedumim (Steinfeld Road, Halcott Center, NY 12433, 845-245-5031, 845-254-9836 fax, AFNK@catskill.net).   ◉✡

TU B'SHEVAT SEDER

There are probably as many variations of the Tu B'Shevat seder as there are people who conduct them. All, however, share three major themes: appreciation of the Land of Israel as the fruitful Jewish homeland; rejoicing at the continuity of life from generation to generation—for us as individual Jews, as a people, and as a nation restored to our own country; and recognition of our responsibility to provide for others through conservation and contributions.

The seder designed by the Kabbalists was an opportunity to worship and study, with participants sometimes staying up the entire night in celebration. First they created the proper environment, covering tables with white cloths adorned with flowers and fragrant branches. Also on the tables were lit candles and pitchers of red and white wine.

They opened the seder by reading thirteen biblical passages about the produce of the Land of Israel. Then they studied a section of Talmud (such as tractate Zeraim, "seeds," which deals with agriculture), and part of Zohar. Prayers that their eating of fruit would bring strength and abundance for trees followed. This pattern continued, interspersed with drinking wine and eating fruit that had been properly blessed. The wine progressed from pure white (representing dormancy in winter), to pure red (life in bloom), with shades in between (for stages of thaw and new growth).

They ate the fruits in groupings, one following each cup of wine. Some Kabbalists chose thirty different fruits, ten in each of three categories representing different levels of creation and types of personalities: externally protected but internally giving (inedible peels, or thick-skinned, including pomegranate, walnut, almond, pine nut, chestnut, hazelnut, coconut, Brazil nut, pistachio and pecan); superficially sweet but unavailable at the core (inedible pits, or hard-hearted, including olive, date, cherry, jujube, persimmon, apricot, peach, loquat, plum and hackberry), accessible both at the surface and inwardly (totally edible, or full of goodness, including grape, fig, apple, etrog, carob, lemon, pear, raspberry, blueberry and quince). Some also highlighted the seven species that grow in Israel (DEUTERONOMY 8:7–9): wheat, barley, grape/raisin, fig, pomegranate, olive, date.

Using the traditional Tu B'Shevat haggadah as a model, others have altered the service since its origins, and continue to give it new expression today. Four questions (designed, like those in the Passover Haggadah, as devices to draw children and other participants into the explanation of why the commemoration is important), history and customs of the holiday, readings and songs around a theme such as conservation or feeding the hungry, symbolic tree plantings and collecting money or food for *tzedakah* have all been incorporated into modern versions. The seder is done either with tastes of foods from just the seven species, from the three Kabbalistic categories, or from all four groups, or with a full meal of dishes using the traditional fruits and nuts paced throughout the ritual.

FOR FURTHER EXPLORATION

See haggadot suggested under "Ritual Items" earlier in this chapter.

Where Do We Begin? Preparation

The rabbis provided no guidelines about getting ready for Tu B'Shevat on the personal level, in the home or in the community. Taking thirty days to learn the whys and ways of the holiday would certainly be in keeping with the general pattern of holiday preparation throughout our year. Depending on how you choose to celebrate, however, preparing might require no more than adding a few items to your grocery shopping list. Give yourself a few months if you want to write your own haggadah, and at least several weeks to organize a seder.

What Are We Supposed to Do? Halakhah

For the most part, the laws connected with Tu B'Shevat have little impact for the majority of Jews today, particularly outside of Israel. Anyone concerned about following religious law, though, should be aware of a few restrictions.

FASTING

In the tenth century, Rabbeinu Gershom Meir Hagolah designated Tu B'Shevat a festival, and therefore a day of rejoicing. In its honor, no one is to do anything that would be inconsistent with celebration. Consequently, delivering a funeral oration or proclaiming a public fast are prohibited. So is individual fasting: if a wedding takes place on the fifteenth of Shevat, even the bride and groom who would normally not take food from sunrise until after the ceremony do not abstain from eating.

PRAYER

In keeping with the joyous aura of Tu B'Shevat, the daily service is modified to eliminate prayers that would dampen the spirit of the day, which are omitted on all festival days (SEE "HALAKHAH" IN CHAPTER ON PESAKH).

BLESSINGS

A number of *brakhot* (blessings) that we say over food, drink, fragrance and phenomena relate to Tu B'Shevat observances: drinking wine or grape juice, eating tree-grown fruits, eating produce of the earth, eating fruit of the new season for the first time since Rosh Hashanah, smelling fragrant edible fruits or nuts, smelling fragrant shrubs and trees or their flowers, smelling fragrant herbs, grasses or flowers, seeing exceptionally beautiful trees (a *brakhah* that also covers people and fields), seeing fruit trees in bloom during the spring (said once a year), and expressing thanks after eating fruit and grains. You can find the blessings in a standard comprehensive *siddur*.

AGRICULTURE

The remaining halakhot related to Tu B'Shevat concern plants and fruits that grow in Israel and regulations regarding the tithing of them. Even though the Temple and priesthood responsibilities no longer exist, we are still required to set aside portions of Israeli-grown grain, fruits and vegetables we plan to eat. If you are concerned about when and how to do this, consult a rabbinic authority and become familiar with the distinctions before going to Israel or eating produce grown in Israel.

What Other Things Do People Do? Customs

OTHER TIMES AND PLACES

Creativity in connection with Tu B'Shevat did not stop with the kabbalists' seder. Colorful practices for eating, distributing, collecting and even trying to influence fate with fruit developed, largely in Sephardic communities.

FRUITFUL SUPERSTITIONS Hoping to affect nature, the Kurdistani Jews placed sweet fruits such as raisins in rings around trees, then prayed for an abundant fruit season. Some barren women, similarly believing in the power of sympathetic magic, would plant raisins and candy near trees, or embrace trees at night, praying for fertility and many children. Family members brought young girls eligible for marriage to trees for an imitation wedding ceremony. If, shortly after, buds were found on the tree to which one was "married," she knew her turn would soon arrive. (In Salonica, it was believed that the trees themselves embrace on Tu B'Shevat, and anyone seeing them do so would have his/her wish fulfilled.)

FRUIT FEASTS Persian Jews climbed onto their neighbors' roofs and lowered empty baskets into the houses through the chimneys. The baskets would be sent back laden with fruit. Some designed rituals, called *Las Frutas* (The Feast of Fruits) that were even more elaborate than the seder. In one custom of the day, children received bags of fruit (*balsas de frutas*) to be worn as pendants around their necks. Although in Bucharia and Kurdistan the holiday was known as "the day of eating the seven species," the Jews there actually ate thirty different types of fruit. (The Indian Jews counted fifty!)

The wealthy of villages of some countries, like Morocco, hosted lavish feasts for all the residents at which as many as one hundred different kinds of fruit, nuts and vegetables were eaten—or they would invite all the townspeople into their homes and fill their hats with fruit. In Morocco, this home feast was often preceded by a banquet in the synagogue after *Ma'ariv*. During the day on the fifteenth, the children would visit relatives to fill sacks with gifts of fruit.

The Ashkenazim, much less colorful by comparison, recognized the day primarily by eating fruits that gave them a connection with Israel (perhaps from an ornamental dish, such as the nineteenth-century Austrian hand-painted ceramic Tu B'Shevat plate now in the collection of the Israel Museum in Jerusalem). The wealthy would get dates, raisins, figs and, occasionally, a costly orange—a splurge even for them. Others would have *bokser* (Yiddish for carob), which grew in great abundance, and was therefore less expensive. (When fresh, it is chewy and tastes faintly like the date. After it's been off the tree for a while—which is how the Diaspora Jews eat it—it loses much of its appeal.)

After their Hebrew lessons in the *kheder,* the children would give up bags of fruit brought from home, the contents of which would all be mixed and redivided so that rich and poor alike would share the same sweets. American Hebrew schools distributed bags of the same kinds of fruits to their students, an observance which continues today.

According to the tradition of the Khassidim, God decides the fate of trees and their fruits on Tu B'Shevat. Therefore, they pray that God will grant a beautiful etrog for the next Sukkot—and following the fall festival, make preserves of the citrus fruit to eat on Tu B'Shevat.

GREETING

When speaking with or meeting someone on Tu B'Shevat, the appropriate phrase is *khag sameiakh,* meaning "happy holiday" in Hebrew. Many American Jews, descendents of Yiddish-speaking Europeans, use the expression *gut yom tov.*

DRESS

In keeping with the spirit of rejoicing, clothing normally worn for attending synagogue or participating in a special occasion is appropriate. Khassidic rabbis sometimes wore their *yom tov* clothes in honor of the festival.

What Is There to Eat? Traditional Foods

There are no customary dishes for Tu B'Shevat, so any recipes that incorporate the fruits and nuts traditionally eaten on this day are appropriate.

Do You Hear Music? Songs to Sing

Several children's songs written specifically for Tu B'Shevat are popular in Israel and among American Hebrew school students. The most typical is probably *"Hashekeidiya"* (The Almond Tree), since the subject, the first tree to blossom as spring approaches—just in time for the holiday—is the symbol of Tu B'Shevat. Other songs dealing with trees, planting, harvesting and the landscape of Israel, drawn from Scripture and developed by the Israeli pioneers, are also popular for this day. Among those familiar to generations of Israelis and American Jewish youth group and summer camp participants are *"Artzah Aleinu"* (Our Land); *"Eitan Bameedbar"* (A Cedar in the Desert); *"Eitz Khayim"* (Tree of Life), which we sing when the Torah is returned to the *Aron Kodesh* after being read; *"Eitz Rimon"* (Pomegranate Tree); *"Eitzei Zeitim Omdim"* (The Olive Trees Are Standing); *"Nad Ilan"* (The Tree is Swaying); *"Nitzanim Niru"* (Buds Are Seen); *"El Ginot Egoz"* (To The Nut Garden), from Song of Songs; *"Eretz Zavat Khalav"* (Land of Milk and Honey), Torah's description of the Land of Israel; *"Tzaddik Katamar"* (The Righteous Shall Bloom), from Psalms, describing the people of Israel; and *"Veyashav Ish"* (Every Man Shall Sit . . .), the prophetic version of everyone being at peace under his fig tree or vine at the time of the messiah. The Yiddish lullaby *"Rozhinkes Mit Mandlen"* (Raisins and Almonds) was also often sung among the Eastern European Jews.

FOR FURTHER EXPLORATION

Tu B'Shevat and Purim Melodies. Ed. By Velvel Pasternak. Cedarhurst, NY: Board of Jewish Education of Greater New York and Tara Publications.
   Words and music for some holiday songs are included in the booklet, which has a companion cassette tape.

What Tales Are Told? Stories to Read

While the Jewish world's literary luminaries did not choose this holiday as subject matter, there are Tu B'Shevat folktales based on Talmudic references, stories from Eastern Europe collected in Jewish anthologies, and some wonderful books that portray holiday observance in past decades and relate Tu B'Shevat themes appropriate for any day or age.

492

FOR FURTHER EXPLORATION

FOR CHILDREN

Ganz, Yaffa. *The Gift that Grew.* New York: Feldheim Publishers, New York, 1987.
A young boy gets a second chance—and learns how to give one to a tree—after he takes a little too much from it. Ages 4–8.

Gershator, Phillis. *Honi and His Magic Circle.* Philadelphia: The Jewish Publication Society, 1980.
This is a picture book version of the tales about the Jewish Johnny Appleseed based on Talmud. Ages 5–10.

Rosenfeld, Dina Herman. *A Tree Full of Mitzvos.* Brooklyn: Kehot Publication Society, 1998.
A maple tree wants to do *mitzvot* just like the family that lives next to him. Ages 5–8.

Ross, Betty Ann. *Dates as Sweet as Honey.* New York: Board of Jewish Education of Greater New York, 1982.
This picture book tells how American and Israeli children celebrate Tu B'Shevat and includes a refrain that teaches the seven species. Preschoolers.

The Great Kapok Tree: A Tale of the Amazon Rain Forest (by Lynn Cherry, New York: Harcourt Brace Jovanovich, Publishers, 1990), *Johnny Appleseed: A Tall Tale Retold* (by Steven Kellogg, New York: Morrow Junior Books, 1988), *The Lorax* (by Dr. Seuss, New York: Random House, 1976), and *The Giving Tree* (by Shel Silverstein, New York: HarperCollins Junior Books, 1986) share the themes and messages of Tu B'Shevat. ❧

Of Added Note

IN ISRAEL

On six hundred and twenty-five acres in the foothills of the Judean Mountains, **NEOT KEDUMIM—THE BIBLICAL LANDSCAPE RESERVE** recreates biblical landscapes that fostered the values of the Jewish people. In addition to hundreds of plants mentioned in *Tanakh*, the site features wild and domesticated animals and facilities and utensils used by the people of the Land, such as ancient and reconstructed olive and wine presses, threshing floors, cisterns and ritual baths. The site, which strives to bring the Bible to life, won the 1994 Israel Prize for its contribution to the state. Located just ten minutes from Ben Gurion Airport midway between Jerusalem and Tel Aviv, it is easily accessible. In advance of a visit, or for those unable to actually go there, the attractive website provides a list of more than two hundred biblically-mentioned plants, flowers and trees featured in the Reserve, a photo album of flowers named in the Song of Songs, virtual tours of themed areas of the Reserve, and holiday tie-ins (www.Neot-Kedumim.org.il).

493

Purim—

Triumph over Evil

ADAR 14 OR 15
(BETWEEN WINTER AND SPRING, MARCH)

This last festival of the Biblical holiday calendar is the most boisterously observed occasion of the year. Jews throughout history recognized that the Purim saga not only records a near-tragedy in Persia long ago, but tells the story of Jews living in a non-Jewish environment—in any place and time. While not ignoring its religious significance, they chose to celebrate the triumph in fabulous secular style.

Origins—WHY WE CELEBRATE PURIM

Traditions—HOW WE CELEBRATE PURIM

Origins—

WHY WE CELEBRATE PURIM

Where Did It Begin? Historic Foundation

THE RECORDED STORY

Approximately twenty-five hundred years ago, the modest young Esther, who was Jewish, married the Persian King Ahasuerus, who was not. This put her in the position of later being able, with her righteous cousin Mordecai, to avert a plot by the king's Jew-hating advisor Haman to kill all their people. Recorded in the Book of Esther in the *Ketuvim* (Writings) section of the Bible, the events of their struggle include elements of comedy and tragedy, intrigue and seeming coincidences.

The account begins at the time that King Ahasuerus had just consolidated his rule over the Persian empire of one hundred and twenty-seven provinces. He celebrated with almost six months of banquets for the provincial potentates, and then a week of feasting for the residents of the capital, Shushan. The comfortable Jewish community there was well represented and actively participated in the Persian frivolities.

When his Queen Vashti refused to appear during the party at his command— either out of modesty (one explanation is that the king wanted her to dance naked to entertain the guests who had been drinking for a week), vanity (the sanitized Hebrew school version says she did not want to be seen with an unsightly blemish that erupted on her face) or as a political adversary (her supposed lineage as the granddaughter of the Babylonian King Nebukhadnezzar gave her her own power base)—the king heeded his advisors' counsel to do away with her.

This left him without a wife. So, again at the urging of his advisors, he held a beauty contest throughout the land in order to find a new queen. He chose Esther (as she was known in Persian circles, or Hadassah, to her Jewish friends). At the advice of Mordecai, who had raised her, she did not reveal her Jewish identity.

497

Shortly after Esther became queen, Mordecai, sitting as usual at the palace gate so he could keep tabs on his ward, overheard two of the king's servants plotting Ahasuerus' assassination. He reported the scheme to Esther, who told the king on Mordecai's behalf. After the plotters were punished, the incident was recorded in the king's chronicles, then promptly forgotten.

Meanwhile, Ahasuerus elevated one of his advisors, Haman, to the position of chief minister. The egotistical Haman couldn't contain his rage when Mordecai refused to bow down to him, and decided to kill not only that obviously observant Jew, but all the Jews of the empire, even those who considered themselves more Persian than Jewish.

It is for his virtues, not his vices, that the Jew is hated.

THEODOR HERZL

After casting lots (*pur,* from the ancient Akadian word for dice, means "lot" in the Persian language, *purim* is its Hebreicized plural) to determine the most auspicious day for the genocide, he sought the king's approval using an argument typical of anti-Semites: that the Jews were dispersed throughout the realm, followed their own laws rather than the king's, and were not to be tolerated (ESTHER 3:8).

Considered alternately a buffoon, for his drunkenness and easy sway by his advisors, and a closet anti-Semite all too eager to approve Haman's plan, Ahasuerus gave his chief minister the authority to immediately dispatch a letter to all provinces calling on the citizens to arm and prepare to massacre every Jew on the thirteenth day of the twelfth month.

When Mordecai learned what was happening, he donned sackcloth and ashes and began to mourn. Esther, on hearing of the reason for her uncle's behavior, at first denied his urging to plead with the king. He advised her not to expect that she alone would be safe, just because she lived in the king's house. So she rallied to her tradition, prayed and fasted for three days after asking that the Jewish community support her by acting likewise. Then she bolstered her courage and visited the king uninvited—a forwardness punishable by death— won his favor and requested that he and Haman come to a special banquet she was preparing just for the two of them.

At the banquet, she again sidestepped the king's offer to give her practically anything, and requested once more that the two most powerful men in Persia attend another private dinner party. Haman's euphoria at his exalted position and treatment was ruined when he bumped into the unyielding Mordecai outside the palace. Haman couldn't wait for the day of the planned massacre to get rid of his mortal enemy, so at the urging of his wife Zeresh and advisors, he erected a huge gallows in his yard. Then he ran back to the palace with plans to request the king's permission to hang Mordecai the next morning.

That night the king had trouble sleeping: he didn't know why his dear wife was conducting these tête-à-tête-à-têtes as though he and Haman were equals. In his restlessness, the king called for the book of chronicles to be read to him, and discovered that Mordecai never had been rewarded for disclosing the assassination attempt. When the king asked for his input as to how a man should be

The treacherous are trapped by their malice. At death the hopes of a wicked man are doomed, and the ambition of evil men comes to nothing.

PROVERBS 11:3-7

honored, Haman (who had been conveniently hanging around in the courtyard), assuming the king planned to reward him, suggested that the lucky gentleman be adorned in the king's robes and the king's crown, paraded through the streets on the king's horse and proclaimed as the king's honoree.

Haman was understandably reluctant when he learned that he was to do all he had described for the hated Mordecai. And the suspicious king was none too pleased with his own situation either: His supposed right-hand man seemed to be too close to Queen Esther and suggested that someone other than the king wear the royal crown. Also, according to his solution to the Jewish problem, Haman would destroy the very man who had saved the king's life.

At the second banquet, which followed Haman's humiliation at having to lead the elevated Mordecai through the streets, Esther finally revealed herself, identified the evil plotter, and pleaded for her people. Haman was ordered to be hanged. Since by Persian law the king could not simply rescind a decree, a new letter was sent to the provinces to supercede the first. It allowed the Jews to arm and fight back to defend themselves. On the predetermined day, they killed those who tried to destroy them. Mordecai received Haman's position, and he and Esther wrote letters proclaiming the day after the fighting stopped an occasion for celebration by all Jews in every generation to come.

FOR FURTHER EXPLORATION

FOR ALL

Esther in any Jewish Bible
   The Book of Esther also appears in numerous editions of the Five Scrolls (along with Ruth, Lamentations, Song of Songs and Ecclesiastes), and on its own.

FOR CHILDREN

Davis, Linda. *A Purim Story.* New York: Feldheim Publishers, 1988.
   This simple retelling of the story of Purim uses cartoonish illustrations and funny expression effective in making children laugh. Ages 5–8.

Feder, Harriet K. *It Happened in Shushan.* Rockville, MD: Kar-Ben Copies, 1988.
   Using pictographs for key people and places, this is a cute original telling of the Purim story that effectively involves readers with humor. Ages 3–7.

Wolkstein, Diane. *Esther's Story.* New York: William Morrow and Company, 1996.
   Enhanced with magnificent artwork, the picture book for older readers tells the Purim story in the form of a diary written by the heroine. Ages 8–12.

Also see *My Very Own Megillah* (Saypol and Wikler) in "More Good Information".

THE HISTORICAL CONTEXT

No historical evidence has been found to support the details—or even the main events—of Esther's story. Many secular scholars doubt that it did take place, or even could have occurred. They regard it as an adaptation of a nature myth (designed to legitimize the Jewish celebration of their neighbors' pagan festivities); a veiled and re-situated account of the Maccabean defeat of the Syrian General Nicanor (which occurred a good few hundred years later than the backdrop to Purim [SEE CHAPTER ON KHANUKAH]); or as a fancifully exaggerated version of an averted plan to destroy the monotheistic Jews, possibly during the reign of Persia's polytheistic Xerxes II (485–465 BCE) or Ataxerxes II (403–358 BCE), both of whom have been identified as Ahasuerus.

The rabbis, of course, have their own speculations, presented in Talmudic discussion and midrash as fact. They say Ahasuerus' reign coincided with the anticipated fulfillment of a prophecy made by Jeremiah. As all but the weakest Jews were being driven from the kingdom of Judah around the beginning of the sixth century BCE, the prophet foresaw that after seventy years of exile, the soon-to-be destroyed Temple would be rebuilt and the Jews restored to their homeland (JEREMIAH 25:11–12). The prediction worried rulers like Ahasuerus, because they realized a renewed Israel would threaten their own power.

The third year of Ahasuerus' reign, when all those banquets took place, was, according to the rabbis, the date he calculated as the end of the seven-decade expulsion. Since the Jews didn't seem to be going anywhere, the king thought that the prophecy had been wrong, that the threat to him was gone, and that the Jews would remain his loyal subjects. (He had simply miscalculated the beginning and end dates of the seventy-year period.)

When the Jews participated in his royal party, explain the rabbis, they were celebrating their own permanent estrangement from the Land of Israel, and doing it in the style of their hosts. (Tradition holds that goblets used at the banquet were actually the holy vessels stolen from the Temple when it was destroyed by Nebukhadnezzer in 586 BCE, bad enough for the pagans, but unconscionable for the Jews.) Abandoning their belief in redemption, and many of the Torah ways of life, they readily chose assimilation—repeatedly warned against in Torah and by the prophets—and in the process, invited annihilation.

A TRUE AND ETERNAL STORY

HISTORY'S PROOF Whether or not the events leading up to Purim happened just as they are presented in the Book of Esther, whether one reads the book as history, romance, political intrigue, myth, or farce, its story is absolutely true. It presents an account of the enduring experience of the Jew living in others' lands, not the first, nor the last, time enemies have plotted, or will plot, our destruction, either physical or spiritual.

In the days of oppression in later eras and other places—Maccabees against Syria (SEE CHAPTER ON KHANUKAH), the Great Revolt and Bar Kokhba Rebellion against Rome (SEE CHAPTERS ON LAG B'OMER AND TISHA B'AV) and the ensuing wanderings in hostile nations, the messages of Purim provided comfort to the Jews. They supported the idea that God was still with them, and therefore fostered the belief that eventually they would prevail.

The notion of "Purim" became so entwined with the idea of God's role in Jewish destiny that Jews in danger of destruction because of natural disasters, individual or communal persecution marked their escapes by establishing their own Purims. The *Encyclopedia Judaica* lists more than one hundred—with intriguing names like Plum Jam Purim, Curtain Purim and Purim de las Bombas—which the

501

communities or families of those Jews saved from execution, freed from prison, rescued from massacre, and redeemed in numerous other ways celebrated on the anniversaries of their rescues. Often written documents prepared as scrolls, the same format as the Book of Esther, were created to record the events, and later read amidst joyful celebration by the descendants of those who had been saved.

The rabbis' broadened interpretation of Purim as part of Israel's eternal battle against Amalek supported the theme of the Jews' ultimate victory over injustice. Amalek was the tribe that attacked the just-liberated Israelites of the Exodus (SEE CHAPTER ON PESAKH) as they wandered weakly in the desert (DEUTERONOMY 25:17–18). In the Torah, God insists that we be continually vigilant in doing away with Amalek. The struggle started with the tribe's ancestor Esau (also known as Edom), who fought from before birth with his twin brother Jacob (also known as Israel), whose sons became the founders of the Twelve Tribes (GENESIS 25:23–28).

Centuries later, King Saul, a descendent of Jacob's son Benjamin, came up against the Amalekites, descendents of Esau, led by King Agog. (Through the prophet Samuel, Saul was instructed to kill Agog and his family, and not take any spoils [I SAMUEL 15:3]. Saul's failure to obey cost him the kingship.)

The Amalekites showed up again in the form of Haman, identified as an Agagite (descendent of Agog [ESTHER 3:1], and his sons, pitted against Mordecai, identified as a descendant of Benjamin (ESTHER 2:5).

MODERN EVIDENCE Whether or not one accepts the national genealogy by which students of Medieval history claim Germany evolved from Edom, only Holocaust revisionists would argue that the Nazis were not the embodiment of the depraved evil represented by Amalek and Haman. The Nazis themselves recognized the connection. In Poland, Hitler ordered synagogues closed for the entire day of Purim and prohibited the reading of the Book of Esther. Secular journalists wrote that the story of Purim foreshadowed the end of Hitler, who himself said in a 1944 speech that if the Nazis went down in defeat, the Jews would celebrate a second triumphant Purim. Indeed, on October 16, 1946, ten Nazis were hanged at Nuremberg, the fulfillment of Esther's image of the ten sons of Haman hanged again, as she had requested in Persia (ESTHER 9:13). As reported in news publications of that day, on his way to the gallows, Julius Streicher shouted "Purim Fest, 1946!"

The sages declared that even after the messiah arrives, Purim alone would remain a holiday to be observed by the entire world. As long as the Jews remain faithful to our God and our people (and history has proven that even when we try to abandon them we are brought back, brutally, if necessary), we can never be eradicated from the earth, as Torah promises. And there will rise up Hamans who will plot to destroy us, because our beliefs are a denial of and an affront to their claims to absolute power—and history has also proven this. Therefore, we will always have reason to celebrate, not only our temporary victories, but our ultimate indestructability. When Amalek is finally eradicated, in the time of messiah, the Book of Esther will testify to the long and imperative fight.

FOR FURTHER EXPLORATION

See story collections in "More Good Information" for accounts of several "special" Purims and Purim celebrations in special circumstances.

Praeger, Dennis, and Rabbi Joseph Telushkin. *Why the Jews? The Reason for Antisemitism.* New York: Simon and Schuster, 1983.

> The authors explain why, no matter what positions the Jews have held in societies, no matter what they have done throughout history, hatred of them has persisted. The authors suggest practical—if sometimes radical—ways of dealing with this unique prejudice .

ACCEPTANCE INTO CANON

While the Jewish people readily adopted Purim, the sages were more reserved in their recognition of Esther's account. First, they had to contend with the principle that the Law of Moses is complete, that nothing in the way of observance is to be added to or taken from it. Secondly, here was a document to be included in a religious body of text that contained not one mention of God. And on top of that, it ordained a method of celebrating, encouraging drinking and revelry, totally out of keeping with traditional Jewish behavior.

Just after the destruction of the Second Temple, the sages (largely as a result of the persuasiveness of Rabbi Akiva) decided to include Esther as part of the Hebrew Bible. They found support in the book of Deuteronomy (31:18): "*Anokhi haster asteer*—I will utterly hide my face." They understood *asteer* (hidden) as a pun on Esther, and connected it to the fact that God is not revealed in the Book of Esther.

An entire tractate of the Talmud, Megillah, records the arguments for and against accepting the Book of Esther, and elaborates on its events and characters.

It states that the text we know was edited and canonized between the fifth and fourth centuries BCE by the Men of the Great Assembly (the central authority on Jewish matters), of which Mordecai was a member, based on the letters written by him and Esther. They ordained the *mitzvah* of reading it at first as an informal retelling of the story. Prior to the destruction of the Second Temple, even before the Book of Esther had been accepted as a sacred text, selected portions were read on days chosen to coincide with gatherings—such as market days for farmers.

By the end of the second century, the book was being read publicly on Purim morning. The rituals associated with the holiday today (SEE "OBSERVANCE") were formally established during the following century. Throughout the Middle Ages, special foods and entertainments developed to add to the gaiety of the occasion, with masquerades and parodies especially popular to reflect the themes and turnabouts in the Purim story.

Kabbalists of the sixteenth century regarded this holiday so highly, they connected it to the day considered the holiest of the year, Yom Kippur—or, in its formal biblical name, Yom Hakippurim, "a day like Purim." Both holidays share the use of lots (cast to determine the day to kill the Jews, to choose Azazel—Yom Kippur's symbolic scapegoat); the notions of fate and providence; the power of prayer to avert negative outcomes; and the role of self-transformation.

What Does It Mean? Religious Importance

GOD'S ROLE IN HISTORY

The absence of any reference to God is one of the most striking features of the Book of Esther, making it unique among Bible texts. It is also the element that strengthens the book's value, because it helps us recognize and relate to God in a world in which His presence seems to elude us.

This is the opposite of the way things were when the Jewish people was created. At our birth (which we celebrated twelve months ago at the beginning the Jewish holiday cycle, with Pesakh, a commemoration of our redemption *from* exile), the Jews needed constant assurances—signs and wonders—that the God who had led them into the perilous wilderness was still among them. They were like infants who know only what they see before their eyes, but which, when out of sight, might as well not exist. By the time we reach Purim (the end of the festival year, and a commemoration of our redemption *in* exile), there are no more obvious signs, wonders, and prophets showing us God's involvement in our lives.

Having been thrown off the Land as punishment for not following Torah, the Jews who experienced Haman's original oppression would naturally wonder whether the promise of the ultimate redemption remained in effect. Purim resoundingly says: "it does!"—proclaiming the message that although God's presence is not obvious, He has not absented Himself. The fact that He is not recognized at a specific place—like the Tabernacle in the desert or the Temple in Jerusalem—is supposed to reassure us that He is any place, or every place.

The little twists of the Purim story, the seeming coincidences, can be read as God's intervention. In essence, this indirect indication of His lasting protection provided the Jews in all generations with a national will to live.

LIVING AS JEWS IN EXILE

Logic and world history tell us that the conquered Jews should have adopted the customs and standards of those among whom they were forced to live. Instead, as Purim instructs, they saved themselves by *not* "fitting in" with the surrounding populations, but by maintaining their values and way of life. The philosophy they developed to compensate for their generally miserable situation embraced the belief that their difference was positive, that they had a system of life worth protecting, and they had somewhere to go with it.

Their design of the commemoration of Purim for all generations developed out of this attitude. It provides guidelines for how to live as Jews—how to preserve ourselves—in the Diaspora.

The custom of giving gifts to friends, and especially to the poor, along with coming together to pray and fast, teach us the importance of unity and community. We are responsible for each other; working together we can accomplish miracles.

Retelling the story of Purim instructs us to learn, not only the Book of Esther, but all the books of Torah. They tell us who we are, where we came from, where we are going—and, most important, how to get there.

The self-transformation of Esther and the Jewish community of Persia illustrates the importance of recognizing the influences of other cultures, including subtle economic and social pressures, which interfere with our spiritual values and can make us blind to political realities. At the same time, the Book of Esther clearly shows that it is not necessary to abandon Judaism for professional or political advancement, or vice versa. One can be both a loyal citizen *and* a practicing Jew (a fact much ballyhooed when Senator Joseph Lieberman, an openly observant Jew, was chosen as Al Gore's running mate in the 2000 American presidential campaign).

COUNTERING EVIL

One of the hallmarks of Purim is our raging against Amalek/Haman. The original attack by Amalek against the former Egyptian slaves came from behind, when they were starving and exhausted (DEUTERONOMY 25:18). And it came immediately after the Israelites expressed doubts—despite everything He had done for them—as to whether or not God was still providing protection (EXODUS 17:2–7).

This is a paradigm of Jewish history. Amalek—Haman, Antiochus, Hitler, Arafat, Hussein—arises when we are weak, when our defenses are down. When we fight viciously among ourselves, when we are scattered and assimilated, when we stray from the commandments that define and defend us as Jews, when we lose faith in our mission and disavow our relationship with God, we invite Amalek. For what is absolute depravity but godlessness?

We readily recognize the external enemy (perpetrators of pernicious anti-Semitism, attacks on Jews and Jewish interests throughout the world, attempts to delegitimize and annihilate the State of Israel). We must be equally vigilant against Amalek within our own community and potentially within each of us (failure to respect others whose level of observance or political views differ from our own, acquiescence to moral relativism, denial or inertia when confronted by evil, hardheartedness).

What threatens to eliminate us, we who are supposed to be a kingdom of priests, is our own denial of our responsibilities: If we do not live as Jews, upholding the moral standards that are supposed to light the way for all nations, then we cease to exist.

What Does It Mean to Us? Personal Significance

During the last decade of the twentieth century, we thought we would soon enjoy peace between Israel and her Arab neighbors; we thought anti-Semitism the expression of rogue and readily controlled fringe fanatics; we believed the existential danger to us to be sharply diminished. But early in the twenty-first century, it re-erupted with ferocity—proving, once again, the message of the Purim saga.

As real and immediate as the external peril, one of the greatest threats to Jewish survival remains (again as it was in Persia) assimilation. While the Book of Esther warns us about the consequences of abandoning our religion, it also teaches that it is never too late to return to the faith and strength of our heritage. Although the rabbis go to great lengths to explain how Esther continued to live according to Jewish law, it can be argued that she herself was as assimilated as her Persian Jewish friends. Being an orphan indicates that she was cut off from her past. She used her Persian name. And she intermarried—the most visible symbol/symptom of assimilation. Yet she summoned the courage to do something that risked her own comfortable situation because it had the potential to save thousands of fellow Jews.

The actions of one person—in this case Esther interceding with the king—started the ball rolling toward solving a critical problem. The lesson is that each individual, regardless of where s/he might seem to be in terms of commitment to the community, can make a difference in fighting against what could destroy us. And our greatest weapon, one of the ways the Book of Esther instructs us to safeguard our Judaism while living in exile, is education. The dignity and pride in being Jewish that sustained the Jews through decades of oppression and millennia of uprootedness came through their knowledge of who and what they were, their understanding and appreciation of their special way of life. It gave them the tools, with or without God's direct intervention, to take matters of redemption into their own hands.

On Purim we celebrate our ultimate, if seemingly unnatural, invincibility. We are about to start another year marking the progression of the Jewish people through time and space. What better opportunity could there be for you to assess what you are doing to contribute to the survival of the Jewish family, community and people? What each of us does can determine whether or not another Jew, whether or not his/her children or grandchildren, will survive, will be Jewish.

A Talmudic maxim instructs that to save one life is to save the entire world, for who knows where that one saved person and his/her actions will lead (SAN-HEDRIN). Exposing someone to the richness of Judaism could be considered saving a life. (We are instructed to "live" by following Torah.) This doesn't necessitate changing your whole lifestyle. It doesn't mean having to become an Orthodox Jew. It means knowing enough to answer the questions "What does it mean to be Jewish? Why is it important to be Jewish?"

What you learn yourself, what you teach your children—and the *way* you teach them, how you extend yourself to fellow Jews, will determine what they know and how they feel about Judaism and being Jewish. (How about inviting an uninvolved friend to a Purim feast, or making sure that someone who knows nothing about it receives a *mishloakh manot* package [SEE "OBSERVANCE"] just to prompt questions?) This is a great time to plan and implement things you can do, for yourself, for children and others, to give all of you the opportunity to be part of Jewish destiny, part of what the Purim saga demonstrates is an eternal endeavor.

FOR FURTHER EXPLORATION

Gordis, Daniel. *Does the World Need the Jews? Rethinking Chosenness and American Jewish Identity.* New York: Scribner, 1997.
> This is an important, insightful, fascinating discussion of why being Jewish and perpetuating Jewish tradition and values matter to our society and the world. ☜✡

Traditions—

HOW WE CELEBRATE PURIM

What Do We Use? Ritual Items

MEGILLAH

Originally, the story of Esther was written on one long strip of pieced-together animal skins that formed a scroll. Based on the Hebrew word for roll (*galah*), it is called a *megillah*. (The other scrolls of the Bible, Ruth, Lamentations, etc., also took this form and are collectively called *megillot*.) The person who reads the Purim saga aloud publicly on the holiday must do so from a scroll (just as the Torah reading is done from the Torah scrolls, and not from a printed *Khumash*).

Few if any individual members of congregations have their own *Megillot*. Painstakingly written by hand, and often illuminated or housed in decorative holders, they are treasured heirlooms and Judaic collectibles. It is more common for people attending the service to use a book form of *Megillat Esther*. Synagogues generally provide copies.

GROGGER

Formerly made of wood and often intricately designed and carved, the noise-maker used during the synagogue reading of the *Megillah* is an inexpensive metal or plastic toy today. As you grasp the handle and whirl the gadget around, the toothed wheel inside hits against a tongue to make a grating sound. If you have a special noisemaker at home, you can bring it to the service, otherwise, the synagogue usually distributes groggers. They are available in Jewish book-stores and through vendors of Judaica in the weeks prior to the holiday.

How Do We Celebrate? Observance

MEANINGFUL FRIVOLITY

It is no wonder that Purim is the most raucous, fun-filled holiday of the Jewish year: it represents the promise that Jews will always, in the end, triumph over our oppressors. It celebrates the unrestrained joy in survival over death, and in the process, mimics the topsy-turvy nature of the Purim story's events. Just to be sure it would always be distinct from the non-Jewish festivities also celebrated as secular carnivals, study and doing things for others were incorpo-rated into observance to give the holiday a spiritual dimension.

MEGILLAH READING

The synagogue reading of the *Megillah* is like no other service you've ever seen in a house of worship. It begins solemnly enough: Just before the reading begins, a *mahazit hashekel* (half shekel—the biblical and modern unit of currency in the Holy Land) collection is made (SEE "PREPARATION") with the money going to the needy. The *Megillah* is unrolled, each section to be folded as it is read to resemble the letters (*iggerot*) that were sent to the Jews in all of Persia's provinces. The person to read the *Megillah,* hoping he is worthy, blesses God and expresses thanks for the miracles of Purim and says the *shehekhiyanu* in gratitude for being kept alive to reach the occasion.

Then the fun begins. While the content and message are to be taken seriously, the delivery is not. Congregants, especially children, create an electric atmosphere as they anticipate the first of fifty-four mentions of the name of the evil Haman. Because of the Torah's commandment to blot out Amalek (DEUTERONOMY 25:19), it is part of the *Megillah* reading ritual for the name of Haman (and in some congregations the naming of his sons) to be met with all manner of eradication methods—banging on the seats, stomping the floor, twirling deafening groggers, blowing horns. (In some communities, only the six times the text uses the villain's full name, "Haman the son of Hammedatha the Agagite" generates the loud response.)

In keeping with the party atmosphere produced by the noisemaking, the reader may take on different voices for the various characters, or speed through the text trying to trip up the children as they strain to hear *"Haman"* (hah-mahn' in Hebrew). Communities use differing melodies for the *Megillah,* some borrowing sections from other holiday liturgies and even popular tunes of the day, particularly for the four verses chanted by the entire congregation dealing with Mordecai's origins and triumph (2:5, 8:15, 8:16 AND 10:3). Some place special emphasis on verse 6:1, about the king's sleepless night, the beginning of the Jews' salvation, and the trop (cantillation) of Lamentations (SEE CHAPTER ON TISHA B'AV) is used for verse 2:6 because both deal with the destruction of Jerusalem.

The blessing following the *Megillah* reading praises God for having fought for us, avenged us and punished our enemies. A special prayer, *Shoshanat Ya'akov* (Rose of Jacob, understood as the Jewish people) gives the highlights of the

Purim story in terms of curses on the villains and praises for the heroes. A special reference to Kharvonah, the servant who alerted the king that Haman had already erected the gallows—thereby providing a convenient way for him to be immediately executed—reminds us of our debt to righteous gentiles.

While most people today attend readings of the *Megillah* on the evening of Adar 14, it is reading the next morning that is commanded (SEE "HALAKHAH").

THE PURIM SEUDAH

Esther and Mordecai proclaimed Purim a time of feasting and merrymaking (9:17, 22). This ordinance developed into the special Purim meal, or *seudah,* which takes place during daylight hours on the holiday. Giving pleasure to the body, it most appropriately commemorates our success against a decree to physically destroy us.

As a secular meal, it does not include a *kiddush* (blessing over wine), except perhaps for a nonsense parody version (SEE "CUSTOMS") but nonetheless encourages partaking of plenty of wine. In fact, the most notable feature of the Purim *seudah* is the injunction, uncharacteristic among Jews, to drink until you don't know (*ad lo yodah*) the difference between *barukh Mordecai v'arur Haman* (blessed be Mordecai and cursed be Haman).

This is not an invitation to drink uncontrollably, but a way to recognize your limit. Once you reach the point of confusion, stop. (You are responsible for any damage caused by merrymaking and intoxication!) You are not supposed to get rip-roaring drunk on Purim, but happily tipsy. Not only does wine add to frivolity, it highlights the theme of drinking—and how it helped create the miracle—throughout the Purim story. The saga opens with a series of wine-infused banquets (1:1–9), Esther's coronation is celebrated with a banquet (2:18), the Jews' fate is sealed with a banquet between Ahasuerus and Haman (3:15), Esther hosts two banquets for the king and Haman (5:6, 6:7) and the book ends with the Jews celebrating and agreeing to annually celebrate with feasts (9:17–19).

But why imbibe *ad lo yodah*? It seems to be a very strange notion in a tradition that stresses remembering and making choices between different values. The formula may have been derived from a liturgical poem of Talmudic times whose alternate verses ended "cursed . . ." and "blessed . . ." Only one who was sober could keep the rhymes straight. Another possibility is that since the *gematria* (numerical value) of both phrases is five hundred and two, they equal each other, and when you're drunk you can no longer prove the values to be the same.

The "same" means that God is to be praised equally for Haman's downfall (cursed be Haman) and Mordecai's elevation (blessed be Mordecai). Wine, according to Jewish thought, takes us away from petty distractions and gives us greater spiritual awareness. Under its influence, even when we can no longer distinguish the two benefits, we should continue praising God and His protection of us.

PORTIONS TO FRIENDS

The *Megillah* tells us to celebrate Purim by sending gifts to friends—*mishloakh manot* (the sending of portions [9:19, 22]), called *shalakh mannes* in Yiddish. The gift giving serves as an expression of brotherly love and unity, which is our strongest defense against threats to our spiritual and physical survival. The portions (which traditionally were made up of kosher food) also serve as symbolic compensation for the participation of Shushan's Jews in the non-kosher banquet of the king. Since we are commanded to fulfill *mishloakh manot,* it is actually proper not to thank the giver (although one may, and probably should, acknowledge that a package has in fact been received). Providing *mishloakh manot* to people who would otherwise not receive them (for instance, nursing home residents) is a particularly nice gesture. Since the instruction is to "send," traditionally the packages are delivered (in Jewish neighborhoods often by children) and the messengers appropriately tipped.

TZEDAKAH

The same passage of the *Megillah* also expressly states that we are to make presents to the poor (*matanos lo evyonim*). In times past, it was common to give gifts of food, or to directly provide money to those in need. Today the donations are made through contributions to an organization or synagogue.

This cornerstone of Jewish life is one of the critical elements that sets us apart from Amalek, who attacks the weak, while we do whatever we can to help them stand on their own. It also fosters unity, making us worthy of protection and redemption. You can give Purim *tzedakah* any time prior to the holiday.

MERRYMAKING

Purim became a time to make fun of everything, even those things considered most sacred: holy text, religious leaders, prayers. Jesters and musicians, light-hearted songs, dressing in costume and doing pranks enliven the day. Today, costume parties and carnivals, with games like Dunk Haman, Pin the Crown on Esther, Hamantaschen Toss and a variety of other games of skill and chance are popular Hebrew school, youth group, Jewish community center and synagogue events widely held for and by children and teenagers.

FOR FURTHER EXPLORATION

See *Building a Jewish Life/Purim* (Grishaver) in "More Good Information."   ❧

Where Do We Begin? Preparation

A Talmudic saying reminds us "when Adar begins, joy is increased," for in this month Purim, the Hashmonean victory over the Syrian General Nicanor (SEE CHAPTER ON KHANUKAH), the day of the order to rebuild the walls of Jerusalem and a miraculous escape of sages from their enemies all took place. (In Galicia in the eighteenth and nineteenth centuries, Adar wall tablets called *misheniknas,* after the initial word of the saying, were popular.) A positive upbeat month, it leads, immediately after Purim, into readying for Pesakh.

The personal preparations for Purim for the most part center on secular activities, while the religious preparations are communal in nature.

SYNAGOGUE SERVICE

Adar starts a cycle of special Torah selections, *arba* (four) *parshiot* (sections), read in the synagogue on the Sabbaths between the end of winter and the beginning of spring. Two directly relate to Purim.

SHABBAT SKEKALIM The first special Sabbath is named for the Torah commandment requiring each male older than twenty years of age to contribute a half shekel to the Temple before the first day of the month of Nissan (EXODUS 30:13–15). The money was used to pay for sacrifices offered on behalf of the community. Since as of the first of Nissan only new shekalim could be used to buy the animals, reminding people of the obligation on the first Shabbat of Adar gave them a month to fulfill it. The reading, done in addition to the regular Torah portion, consists of the first six verses of Ki Thasa (EXODUS 30:11–16) pertaining to the *mitzvah,* and a special Haftorah (II KINGS 11:17–12:17) on the subject. The collection was set for Purim because of traditionally high attendance at synagogues on that date.

Fulfillment of the *mitzvah* continued even after the Temple no longer stood, the money collected going to support institutions in the Land of Israel. Three mentions of the term *mahazit hashekel* in the commandment inspired the custom of using three coins to fulfil it. It also became commonplace for a silver dollar or packet of coins to be placed on the collection plate so that even the poor could seem to be giving the full amount required: they would put down some coins, "borrow" the silver dollar or packet, and then put it back, as though it were their gift.

This Purim collection of shekelim holds special significance as a reminder of the ten thousand talents of silver Haman offered King Ahasuerus to pay for the destruction of the Jews (ESTHER 3:9). It symbolizes our redeeming ourselves, particularly through the giving of *tzedakah.*

SHABBAT ZAKHOR The Sabbath preceding Purim, "Shabbat of Remembrance," sets the stage for the Purim tale. We must read its particular extra portion (DEUTERONOMY 25:17–19) accompanied by its Haftarah (I SAMUEL 15:1–34) once a year. Twelve months is the period of time after which we generally forget things: it defines the period of mourning for a deceased loved one and when an abandoned object is considered ownerless. Since the *parshah* commands us to remember the deeds of Amalek and erase his memory, the Sabbath preceding Purim is the most appropriate occasion for reading it.

The purpose of the *parshah,* which is to be heard by both men and women, is to warn us of the consequences of not eliminating what threatens to eliminate us. What we must blot out is the vestige of Amalek (evil); what we must not forget is our own Jewishness (moral responsibility). The week before we will hear about how the assimilated Jews of Persia were almost eliminated, we are being warned not to so identify with the society around us that we lose our unique identity and mission.

PERSONAL

COSTUMES You'll want to give yourself ample time to prepare costumes for any children in the family who will be attending Purim parties or carnivals, or want to dress up for the *Megillah* reading.

FAST OF ESTHER A day of fasting (*ta'anit*) from sun up to sun down is supposed to be observed on the day before Purim (Adar 13). It ostensibly commemorates the fast of Mordecai and Esther that Esther instituted among all the Jews, prior to her visit to the king (ESTHER 4:16). In keeping with Judaism's system of measure-for-measure reward and punishment, it is the flip side of feasting in celebration of Purim's outcome: denying pleasure to the body appropriately atones for the transgressions committed by the Jews when they shamelessly indulged their bodies during King Ahasuerus' banquet. Fasting was also commonly practiced among Jews whenever they prepared for battle (as with the Persians who had been instructed to massacre them), in remembrance that their strength and victory would come from God.

Ta'anit Esther became the custom well after other observances were adopted for Purim, possibly as an adaptation of the periodic Monday and Thursday fasts the Jews followed. While it carries less obligation than the fasts ordained in *Tanakh* and others in Talmud (SEE CHAPTERS ON TISHA B'AV AND YOM KIPPUR), some, particularly the Persian (Iranian) Jews, as might be expected, have kept it as faithfully, reciting special *selikhot* (penitential) prayers and selections of Torah recited on all other fast days.

HOME

The number and elaborateness of the *mishloakh manot* you plan to send to friends will determine how much time you need to assemble them. Some people do simple packages—particularly if they send many—that may consist of one or two hamantaschen and a few pieces of candy or a piece of fruit together in a plastic sandwich bag. Others use bakery-type boxes lined with colored tissue paper, wicker baskets, Purim containers available in Judaica stores, decorative gift bags, or baskets made of construction paper to hold small packets of dried fruit, candy, bottles of wine or juice, hardy fresh fruit like oranges and/or a varied assortment of baked goods (the Sephardim include baklava and other pastries made with paper-thin dough, sugar and ground nuts).

Additional time will be needed for cooking, baking and setting up the house if you will be hosting a Purim *seudah*.

What Are We Supposed to Do? Halakhah

WHEN WE CELEBRATE

The date of Purim, Adar 14, commemorates the day after the fighting took place in the Persian Empire. As the *Megillah* tells us, fighting continued in the Fortress Shushan for two days, not ending until the fourteenth of Adar (ESTHER 9:18). Therefore, the rabbis ruled that Shushan Purim was to be celebrated by inhabitants of walled cities on Adar 15. To avoid the disappearance of this recognition were Shushan ever to lose its Jewish population, they decreed that any city that had had walls at the time of Joshua would keep Shushan Purim on Adar 15, as Jerusalem does today. Outside walled cities, Shushan Purim is treated as a half-holiday, marked mainly by the prohibition of fasting and eulogies constant for all festival days.

In cities—like Jaffa, Acco, Safed, Tiberius, and Lod—that may have been walled in Joshua's day but about which we do not know with certainty—the *Megillah* is read on both days, but on the fifteenth only at night and without the blessings.

A slight complication occurs during the Jewish leap year, with its two months of Adar. Since Purim and the special days that come earlier in the month lead to Pesakh, Adar II was designated as Purim's month so that the redemption of Esther and the Jews of Persia would be temporally related to the redemption of

Moses and the Israelites of Egypt, bringing the Jewish festival year full circle. However, so as not to "slight" the days that would have been the holiday, the fourteenth and fifteenth of Adar I are considered minor festivals, called Purim and Shushan Purim Katan (or "little"). They share a joyful mood and prohibition of activities related to mourning.

The day of Purim never falls on Shabbat, but Shushan Purim on occasion does. When that occurs, the *Megillah* is read Thursday night and Friday morning; gifts are sent to the poor on Friday and the Purim *seudah* is held and *mishloakh manot* sent to friends on Sunday.

If Purim begins on Saturday night, the *Megillah* is read after *Havdallah*.

MEGILLAH

Every man, woman and child is commanded to hear the reading of the *Megillah* in its entirety, at night and especially during the day. The evening reading of convenience, which does not fulfill the *mitzvah*, can be done any time between nightfall and sunrise. The obligatory *Megillah* reading, which usually takes place on the morning of Adar 14 (15 for walled cities), can be done anytime between sunrise and sunset.

The Temple priests had to put aside their duties, and even someone engaged in studying Torah must take a break to listen to the reading. Only burying the dead takes precedence. Women, who are generally exempt from the positive duties of Jewish law specified for fixed times, must be present at the *Megillah* reading, since Purim commemorates the salvation of the Jews through the actions of a woman. And since the obligation regarding hearing the *Megillah* is the same for a woman as for a man, some authorities rule she may be the one to read it aloud, even to a congregation of men (as long as she is technically proficient).

If no synagogue *minyan*—preferable for the reading—is present, the *Megillah* must be read individually. Before the reading, you can eat or drink only if you are sick. It is prohibited to recite the *Megillah* by heart. Verses 2:5, 8:15, 8:16 and 10:3 are read aloud by the congregation, then repeated by the reader. At the worlds *"B'leilah hahu"* (that night [6:1]), the reader should raise his voice to emphasize the turning point of the story; at *"ha'iggeret hazot"* (those letters [8:9])

517

he should shake the *Megillah*. The names of the ten sons (9:7–9) should be read in one breath, from *"Khameish meiot ish"* to *"aseret"* (five hundred men . . . the ten [9:6–10]), since they were hanged at the same time. An early ruling allowed for the *Megillah* to be read in any language understood by the community but later it was determined that it must be read in Hebrew.

As you are supposed to hear every single word, which is difficult in the general atmosphere in the synagogue on Purim, you should have your own copy of the *Megillah* and say each word to yourself.

The scroll from which the story is read to the congregation must be created according to rules as stringent as those for preparing a Torah scroll or liturgical work: sewn parchment skins attached with dried sinews, to form one scroll, written in Assyrian (square form) letters with ink, following lined rules incised into the skins.

GIFTS OF FOOD

To fulfill the *mitzvah* of *mishloakh manot,* you must give at least two portions (two different types of food, or one kind of food fixed two different ways) to one friend. The food must be ready to eat without requiring the recipient to do any preparatory work. Even the poor who receive *tzedakah* must send portions: if they cannot afford to do so, they must at least arrange to exchange with a friend.

The person receiving a gift that fulfills the obligation of *mishloakh manot* must be acquainted with you. Though it is traditional to send *manot* through a messenger, it is not required, but the gift is to be given during the day of Purim.

GIFTS TO THE POOR

Every male and female must give food or money to the poor—the equivalent needed for a minimal Purim meal to at least two people. The recipient need not be aware of the identity of the donor, and may use the money for purposes other than paying for a Purim meal. If you cannot give donations directly to those in need, make a contribution to an organization that will appropriately distribute the money. If there is no one to give to immediately, set aside money, clearly designated as Purim *tzedakah,* to be given at a later date. If you do not have the means to present a lavish meal, give more than one *mishloakh manot* package *and* give to the poor, first do the latter.

TORAH READING/PRAYER

During the *Shakharit* synagogue service on Purim, three passages from Exodus 17 recounting the attack of the Amalekites against the Israelites are read. The service also includes Psalm 22 (according to tradition, the prayer offered by Esther after her three-day fast, in preparation for her visit to the king), and some recite Psalm 83 (beseeching God to not be aloof, but to deal with His—Israel's— enemies). The *Amidah* of the three daily services and the *Birkat Hamazon* include *Al Hanissim* (we thank You for the miracles), the prayer that gives a concise account of Purim and the miraculous salvation. *Hallel* is not said, however, since the Jews remained under foreign dominion, and the *Megillah* itself serves as praise of God. Prayers normally omitted on festival days (SEE "HALAKHAH" IN CHAP- TER ON PESAKH) are also omitted on Purim.

PURIM FEAST

Feasting on Purim is obligatory, and encompasses both eating and drinking: the Book of Esther uses the word *mishteh* to describe the celebrations. The term is derived from the root of *shoteh,* meaning drinking, the indulgence that led to all the miracles of the holiday.

Since the *Megillah* refers to future celebration of Purim as days of rejoicing (9:22), the religious obligation of the *seudah* is that it take place during the day after the *Minkhah* service (or before midday on *Erev Shabbat* so as not to interfere with the Shabbat evening meal). Candles should be lit, as light accompanies joy, and Torah, considered light by the Jews, should be studied prior to eating ("The Jews enjoyed light" [ESTHER 8:16]). The festive meal includes bread and meat—but not in the form of a sandwich—and wine to the degree that your thinking becomes clouded and you cannot tell the difference between "blessed be Mordecai" and "cursed be Haman" (SEE "OBSERVANCE"). If imbibing makes you sick, it is permissible to drink just a little more than normal, or to fall asleep, because when asleep you cannot "tell the difference." It is preferable not to eat alone, and only under extenuating circumstances are you permitted to leave your family on Purim.

WORK AND CELEBRATION

While it is permissible to work on Purim, all unnecessary labor—that not related to supporting others or avoiding loss—is prohibited. Creative work is not. Most authorities allow weddings to take place on Purim, but many prefer that they be scheduled for other times according to the idea that no joy should be intermixed with another.

MOURNING

If you are sitting shiva when Purim occurs, you continue to observe the laws of mourning. While you should not partake in festivity, you should also not diminish the joy of the community. For that reason, you are not obligated to display the signs of grief publicly (you may wear leather shoes and sit on a chair). You may either assemble a *minyan* for prayer and the reading of the *Megillah* at home, or pray at home and then attend the synagogue to hear the *Megillah* read. It is appropriate to send modest portions to friends, but unless poor, or one of only two Jews in a community, a mourner should not receive gifts (but his/her spouse may).

It is forbidden to deliver a funeral address on Adar 14 and 15, since they are festival days.

What Other Things Do People Do? Customs

The level of excitement generated by Purim seems more consistent with a just-won victory than the commemoration of an ancient event. And that is how the celebrants often felt: even though the post-Persian Jews had not yet been released from their Hamans, Esther's story provided such a powerful model, they believed in a similar outcome and celebrated as though it already had been accomplished. For one day, they forgot their dreary precarious lives, and in throwing off all discipline—which allowed them great creativity and humorous self-expression—felt that they had some control over their own fates.

OTHER TIMES AND PLACES

REHANGING HAMAN One of the earliest Purim customs developed in Babylonia and Persia during the Talmudic era: beating and burning Haman in effigy. Spirited shrieking, singing and jumping through hoops suspended above the fire accompanied the symbolic destruction of the enemy.

Although fifth-century Christians, likening Haman on the gallows to Jesus on the cross, prohibited such public celebration of Purim as a mockery of their savior, the Jews continued, often inviting violent attacks as a result. The effigies were particularly popular in Italy during the Middle Ages. Elevated to trumpet blasts and shouts of *"Ira!"* (vengeance), prior to being set ablaze on a pyre the effigy was part of a sports tournament between Jewish fathers on horseback and their sons on foot. Using nuts as pellets and wooden sticks as lances, they raced through the streets and attacked the representational puppets.

The Jews of Caucasus threw a blackened piece of wood representing Haman into the fire. Until outlawed by the Christians, Jews in eighteenth-century Frankfurt placed a house of wax containing figures of Haman, his wife Zeresh and two guards on the reader's desk in the synagogue, and lit it as the *Megillah* reading began. (The Yemenite Jews perhaps avoided censure by simply using candles, ten of them, at the evening and morning services.)

MEGILLAH Persian children spent the weeks before Purim writing out the Book of Esther in proper square letters, then took their finished versions of the *Megillah* to the public reading. Instead of going to synagogue, many would gather at the site believed to be the burial place of Mordecai and Esther in Hamadan. The Jews of that city, located in southwest Persia, believed it was the biblical Shushan.

Since the name of God does not appear in the Book of Esther, artists felt free to illustrate it, and it became the only Jewish biblical book whose text is ornamented with gold leaf, miniatures and decorative borders. Customs arose in writing of the text itself: the names of Haman's sons were placed on ten lines, one directly under the one above, and the vov (ו, "and") before the last name was elongated to resemble the gallows on which they were all hanged. Sephardic Jews presented engraved *Megillah* scrolls to bridegrooms (in Yemen it was the grooms who paid for the privilege of reading the story to the congregation). When the Jews moved to Eastern Europe, it became more popular to create elaborate cases to hold the scrolls. Substantial examples of illuminated *Megillot* and of carved wood and silver Purim scroll cases, from the sixteenth century on, are found in Jewish museum and private collections.

When ancient congregations heard "Haman," they whispered "cursed be Haman and cursed be his offspring," a practice continued by the Austrian Jews in the Middle Ages, who whispered *"zekher tzaddik liverahkhah"* (may the memory of the righteous be a blessing) after Mordecai's name, and *"shem rehaim yirkav"* (may the name of the wicked rot [BASED ON PROVERBS 10:7]). The practice may have been related to the *seudah* drinking custom. In some communities, erasing the name of Amalek, written on paper, accompanied the verbal eradication. (In Yemen, where noisemakers were forbidden as inappropriate in a solemn synagogue setting, upon returning from the service the head of a house would write "Haman" on paper with ink, and then wash it off in a cup of water.) Over time, the method of following the commandment became less and less reserved. In Venice, hand clapping drowned out the sound of Haman's name. Others did away with Haman by stomping out his name written on the soles of their shoes. Children in medieval Europe drew pictures of the villain on two stones or pieces of wood and knocked them together.

The grogger we associate with Purim developed in the thirteenth and fourteenth centuries in Germany and France, where people made their own, some of them quite elaborate. The grinding noisemakers spread throughout Europe. In his diary, Samuel Pepys recorded that he was almost deafened when he visited a London synagogue in the 1600s. In the following century, the Board of Trustees of the Spanish Portuguese congregation in that city apparently lost sight of the *Megillah's* warning against the dangers of assimilation, and were so wary of being negatively viewed by their quietly-worshipful non-Jewish neighbors that they promised to evict anyone making a disturbance in the synagogue. The community leaders in Posen, Poland, also prohibited the use of groggers in the synagogue in order to preserve decorum.

SPECIAL FOODS The Italians made a poppy seed-filled pastry known as *orecchie de aman* (Haman's ears), after the former European custom of cutting off the ears of a criminal before he was hanged, and in Western Europe, another kind of poppy seed cookie, *mohn plaetzen,* was popular. Some communities baked special cookies bearing the names of Vashti and Zeresh, which allowed the Jews to "devour" their enemies. Sephardim used a special Purim khallah called *keylitsh,* exceptionally large, braided to represent long ropes used to hang Haman, and sometimes decorated with raisins.

Non-Jews in Middle Eastern countries began to call Purim *id al sukar*—sugar festival—not for the various sweets sold for the holiday, but for all the items fashioned out of sugar by confectioners: *megillot,* inkpots, pens, clocks, cups, the Messiah on a donkey (as illustrated in Bella Chagall's reminiscence, "Purim Gifts"). Sometimes a school principal commissioned a candy piñata-like Haman, paid for with contributions from the students and hung in the doorway of the school for the childen to hit until it fell apart and they could eat the pieces.

For many, it became popular to serve turkey for the *seudah.* In Russian, turkey—considered the most foolish of fowl—translates to "cock of India." The Book of Esther tells us that Ahasuerus reigned from India to Ethiopia; but, even more appropriate, according to some views, he was somewhat of a turkey himself. The Jews of thirteenth-century Provence preferred goose and chicken, and later the Italians ate all kinds of fowl, along with pancakes, macaroni and jellies. (An Italian parody designates twenty-four dishes, all fowl, supposedly set down by Moses at Sinai as the Purim menu.)

MASKS, MASQUES AND MASQUERADES In general, Purim is one holiday where the Ashkenazim celebrated with as much, if not more, color and abandon than their Oriental cousins. This was probably due to their exposure to Carnivale and Mardi Gras, held around the same time of year, in the Catholic countries they inhabited. Just as the church had reworked the pagan new year and Roman bacchanalian feasts widely practiced so that they would be religiously acceptable, the Jews transformed the popular pre-Lenten celebrations to fit their religious values.

Costumes Although masquerading did not become part of Purim until the Middle Ages, the *Megillah* sets the precedent for it. First, there is Esther's name, which lays the foundation of hiddenness, which a costume and mask accomplish for one's identity. Then there's a series of costume changes in her story: the Jewish maiden puts on the robes of a Persian queen, Mordecai and Esther change into sackcloth. Later Mordecai dresses up in the king's garments. And the roles change: Haman goes from elevated minister to servant of Mordecai to hanged traitor, the king from condemner to pardoner of the Jews, and Esther from assimilated Jew (masquerading as a non-Jew) to Persian Queen to heroine of her people.

Originally, the European Jews may have simply donned peasant's clothes to avoid anti-Semitic attacks that occurred periodically over hundreds of years at this season. Masks may have helped them feel uninhibited as they danced around foolishly and engaged in silly pranks like flour throwing, ghetto donkey rides, and street games. Gradually the costumes became more elaborate and focused, portraying biblical characters. The celebrants paraded through the streets, going house to house, performing and demanding wine, sweets or money. Although some rabbis disapproved, men and women were even permitted to wear each other's clothing, a transgression normally strictly prohibited.

Entertainment Sometimes a Purim King, and later the Purim Rabbi, would lead the entertainment and serve refreshments to townspeople. By the 1800s, Purim had become known in Europe as the Day of Students because the yeshivah boys would dress up and go house to house mocking their rabbis, teachers, community leaders and great Jewish personages in the tradition of parodies extending back several hundred years. Kalonymous ben Kalonymous of Rome may have started the grand heritage with the *Masseket Purim* (Tractate of Purim), the oldest and best-known parody. Based on the format and method of Talmudic discussion, it expounds on the nature of this holiday with great wit. Other parodies—some written by such illustrious Jewish poets as Solomon Ibn Gabirol (1021–1069), Abraham ibn Ezra (1092–1187), and Judah Halevi (1080–1142) took off from synagogue liturgy and popular songs of the day.

These humorous works liberally exploited wine and the effects its excesses produce. (Recently, the tradition has continued with college campus debates pitting the contributions to world peace of the hamantasch against those of the latke.

The revelers, accompanied by a klezmer group (traditional Eastern European street musicians whose name is a contraction suggesting both music and musician) would act as troubadours and minstrels, performing their improvisations and set pieces in home after home with good-hearted levity. (In Amsterdam in the early 1800s, prior to Purim the humorous songs composed for the holiday were circulated in a special publication so everyone could become familiar with them.)

The people enthusiastically welcomed these *Purimspiels* (Purim plays), which developed into biting satires on the life of the time. They provided an opportunity for the people to vent their feelings and express control over the outcome of their situations. Spreading throughout Poland, Russia, Lithuania, Galicia, Romania and Western Europe, they became so popular, they were performed in theaters for large audiences. In 1713 Frankfurt, the Jewish leaders thought the humor so shocking and obscene, they prohibited further performances, but in other communities, an entire two-week theater season revolved around Purim. Plays such as *Ahasuerosspiel, David and Goliath,* and *The Sale of Joseph* were so popular, even Christians attended the shows, some of which continued in Eastern Europe until the turn of the twentieth century.

In 1912, the pioneers in Eretz Yisrael organized the first Purim carnival in the first all-Jewish city in the modern world, Tel Aviv. Named *Adloyodah* ("Until you don't know"), it has developed into a two-day festival of float- and band-filled parades, street decorations and theater, a children's pageant, Queen Esther election, sports carnival, masquerade balls, and throngs crowding around the Great Synagogue to hear the reading of the *Megillah*.

Gifts Another kind of performing evolved around the exchanging of *mishloakh manot*—when people had to carefully consider what to send to whom to ensure that friends honored each other with gifts of equal value—as amusingly detailed in Sholom Aleichem's story, "Two Shalachmones, or A Purim Scandal." In the eighteenth and nineteenth centuries special plates, decorated with lines or scenes from the *Megillah,* were used to transport one's food gifts to friends.

Sometimes gifts of coins were given to children. From the habit of sending

Christian servants to solicit donations for those in need, the Jews in France and Provence started the practice of giving gifts to the non-Jews as well.

Providing money for the poor probably reached its Purim height in Western Europe and America in the mid-1800s to early 1900s, with Purim balls held for charity. The Queen Esther Society and the Purim Association of New York, both founded in the latter half of the nineteenth century, sponsored such events for a number of years. (Hadassah, the Women's Zionist Organization named for the heroine of the Purim story, which has done so much to help Israel and Jews in need, was founded on the holiday in 1912.)

Judeo-Spanish communities didn't wait for Purim itself to show their generosity. On Shabbat Zakhor—called Shabbat de Foulares (derived from the Portuguese word for gift), the women created a special pastry representing the hanging of Haman. On this day, also known as Shabbat Hakallot (Sabbath of the Brides), in-laws in particular sent trays of new clothing, to round out the trousseau, to a bride (a woman was considered one for the first year of marriage) in return for the trays of sweets delivered to them.

GREETING

Yiddish-speaking Jews wish each other *"gut Purim,"* the phrase sung by *Purimspielers* when they entered a home to perform or *"freilikhen* (joyous) *Purim."* Another traditional greeting is *"freilikhen Purim un kushern Pesakh"* (happy Purim and kosher Pesakh) in anticipation of the next festival. In Israel, *"khag sameiakh"* or *"Purim sameiakh"* (happy holiday or happy Purim) is said.

DRESS

It is customary to wear Sabbath or holiday clothes for the *Megillah* reading. Many synagogues also encourage children to come dressed in their Purim costumes. It has become commonplace for them to pretend to be all kinds of characters and figures from popular culture (drawn from cartoons, secular books, television programs). But since this is a Jewish holiday (and not merely "our

Halloween") what a great opportunity it provides to draw on our own rich culture and heritage in choosing a character or an object for dress-up. You don't have to be limited to the preponderance of Esthers, Mordecais, Hamans and Ahasueruses. Bible figures, people important in Jewish history, famous Jewish writers, musicians, scientists, rabbis and objects that have significance to us— *tzedakah* box, book, *kiddush* cup, *Megillah,* even a hamantasch, bagel or khallah—can be effective costume subjects. There are plenty of ways to be glamorous, scary, messy or silly—and still be Jewish.

What Is There to Eat? Traditional Foods

Since Rashi (the eleventh-century Torah commentator considered one of Judaism's greatest teachers) said that Haman was hanged on the third day of Passover, on Purim, Eastern European Jews in the Middle Ages ate matzah balls and fritlekh, a small thin cracker resembling matzah. Fortunately, much more appetizing treats were developed for the holiday.

The delicacy most readily identified with Purim is hamantaschen ("Haman's pockets"), a three-cornered pastry traditionally filled with a honey-poppy seed mixture. First mentioned in an eleventh-century poem by Abraham ibn Ezra, it was probably an adaptation of a German dessert called *mohntaschen* (*mohn* means poppy seeds, *taschen,* pockets), whose name with slight alteration yielded Haman, and whose shape was associated with the tri-cornered hat said to have been worn by him. (Others claim the three sides represent the three patriarchs, Abraham, Isaac and Jacob, by whose merit the Jews were able to succeed against their enemy.) Later it became customary to fill the pastry with prune jam, to commemorate the rescue of eighteenth-century Bohemian Jews when a plum merchant was wrongly accused of murder (SEE "HISTORIC FOUNDATION"). Just about any fillings are used today (chocolate, apple-cinnamon, apricot preserves, nuts), but poppy seed and prune jam remain the most traditional.

For some reason, it became a custom to eat kreplakh, dough filled with chopped meat, on days when beating occurs (as on Yom Kippur and Hoshanah Rabbah). On Purim, the kreplakh—and versions of it developed in other countries—carry additional meaning, as the filling is completely concealed within the dough, suggesting the aspects of hiddenness of the Purim story.

Some people eat chickpeas, according to a tradition that says they comprised Esther's sole intake as she maintained kashrut in the palace. (A variation is cooked and salted beans.) In Morocco on Purim morning, the Jews eat a dairy couscous cooked in butter and milk (*berkuls*), and many have a special breakfast, *seudah shel Haman* or *kebura di Haman,* during which everyone mocks the villain.

Do You Hear Music? Songs to Sing

The joyousness expressed during the *Megillah* reading carried over into the home, and along with parodies and *Purimspiels,* songs became part of the celebrations. In the sixteenth and seventeenth centuries, Jews composed folksongs expressing the happiness of the day, describing revenge on Haman, extolling Esther and Mordecai, and focusing on sending gifts and enjoying hamantaschen. Pioneers in the Land of Israel in the late nineteenth century dealt with Purim themes as well as the carnival atmosphere in their folksongs. Some were original, others Yiddish poems translated to fit new melodies, or parodies of Yiddish folksongs. And in America, words were often written to the tunes of folk songs, nursery rhymes or simple popular tunes like "It Ain't Gonna Rain No More," "Polly Wolly Doodle," "Farmer in the Dell," "Bicycle Built for Two," and "Ten Little Indians."

Among the songs most well-known for the holiday are the Khassidic folk tunes *"Shoshanat Yaakov"* (referring the people of Israel) and *"Mishenikhnas Adar"* (about joy increasing during the month); the children's Yiddish celebratory *"Heint Iz Purim"* (Today is Purim) and *"Hop, Mein Hamantaschen!,"* *"A Gitn* (a good) *Purim"* in Yiddish and *"Khag* (holiday of) *Purim"* in Hebrew express the fun of the celebration. *"Utsu Etsa,"* a traditional Hebrew folk tune (Form Your Plot) is a short affirmation that attacks against us will fail because God remains with us.

Among the songs best known to American children are the amusing "In Shu-Shu- Shushan Long Ago" and "Once There Was a Wicked Wicked Man."

FOR FURTHER EXPLORATION

Tu B'Shevat and Purim Melodies. Ed. by Velvel Pasternak. Cedarhurst, NY: Board of Jewish Education of Greater New York and Tara Publications.

Some of the traditional songs, with words transliterated into English, are included in this compact booklet. A companion tape is available.   ☙✡

What Tales Are Told? Stories to Read

Celebrated writers, Jewish and non-Jewish, have been attracted by the color, romance and drama of Esther's story and the customs it inspired. Judah Halevi reveals the plot against the Jews in the conversation presented in his twelfth-century poem "The Banquet of Esther." Perhaps the first drama authored by a Jew—actually, two of them, Solomon Usque and Lazaro Gratiam—deals with the Purim saga: *Esther* was published in Spain in 1567. Jean Baptiste Racine, the well-known dramatist of seventeenth-century France, later wrote a play by the same name.

The revival of the Hebrew language in the 1800s generated numerous poems, short stories and plays to add to the glut of Purim books produced a century earlier, and later, the Nobel-prize-winning Israeli writer Samuel J. Agnon, and the beloved Sholom Aleichem were among those who also wrote about Purim celebration.

FOR FURTHER EXPLORATION

FOLKTALES

See anthologies in "More Good Information" for folktales, Sholom Aleikhem, K'tonton and other stories about Purim celebrations in other times.

FOR CHILDREN

Goldin, Barbara Diamond. *Cakes and Miracles—A Purim Tale*. New York: Viking Press, 1991.

A blind boy wants to help his mother prepare for Purim. A vision he has in a dream provides him guidance, and results in a surprise for his village. Beautifully written, the book includes the history of the holiday and recipes for hamantaschen. Ages 5–10.

Schul, Yuri. *The Purim Goat*. New York: Four Winds Press, 1980.

A ten-year-old boy who lives in a shtetl with his mother finds a way to make their goat worth keeping just in time for Purim. Holiday songs sung at the time are included. Ages 8–10.   ☙✡

Of Added Note

MUSIC

George Frideric Handel wrote two oratorios based on the Purim saga, *Esther,* and *Haman and Mordecai.* Several other versions of the *Megillah's* story have also been set to music: the overture to Franz Grillparzer's *Esther,* the dramatic *Esther Queen of Persia* by A. W. Binder, and Darius Milhaud's opera *Esther de Carpentras,* which moves the story to Provence for the updated context of a threat from the bishop.

ART

The story of Esther has inspired artists for more than seventeen hundred years. Murals in the third-century Dura Europus synagogue show Mordecai's triumphant ride through Shushan on the king's horse and Ahasuerus and Esther on their thrones. (The latter subject may have been chosen for political reasons, as the Romans ruled Dura, once part of Persia, at the time of the synagogue's construction. The Jews, hoping for a return to the previous jurisdiction, presented an idealized Ahasuerus.)

European church leaders later likened Esther's modesty, courage and self-sacrifice to similar qualities of Mary, and the Jewish queen's intercession with Ahasuerus on behalf of the Jews with Mary's intercession with God on behalf of mankind. Consequently, Renaissance artists like Botticelli, Tintorello, Reubens and Rembrandt created scenes from the Book of Esther for churches. Their paintings of climactic points in the story are among the holdings of the Rijksmuseum in Amsterdam and the Hermitage in Leningrad.

At that time, the mother in aristocratic Italian families customarily gave her daughter a bridal chest. Called a *cassone,* it was adorned with an appropriate myth or biblical scene, those from Esther being particularly popular because they glorified feminine virtues. Among extant panels from the *cassoni* are those attributed to the school or workshop of Botticelli; they depict Esther on her way to the palace, Mordecai's triumph, and the elevation of Esther.

Blessings

For explanations of when and how to make the *brakhot,* see the appropriate holiday chapters.

BEDIKAT KHAMETZ Before beginning the search for *khametz* on the night before Pesakh:

בָּרוּךְ אַתָּה, יהוה אֱלֹהֵינוּ, מֶלֶךְ הָעוֹלָם, אֲשֶׁר קִדְּשָׁנוּ בְּמִצְוֹתָיו, וְצִוָּנוּ עַל בִּעוּר חָמֵץ.

Barukh Atah, Adonai Eloheinu, Melekh Haolam, asher kidshanu b'mitzvotav, v'tzivanu al biur khametz.

Blessed are You, Lord our God, King of the Universe, Who has sanctified us with His commandments and commanded us to remove the leaven.

BIUR KHAMETZ The following morning, the morning before the first Seder, to nullify your connection to the *khametz* :

כָּל חֲמִירָא, וַחֲמִיעָא, דְּאִכָּא בִרְשׁוּתִי וְדְלָא חֲמִתֵּה, וּדְלָא בַעֲרִתֵּה, וּדְלָא יָדַעְנָא לֵהּ, לִבָּטֵל וְלֶהֱוֵי הֶפְקֵר כְּעַפְרָא דְאַרְעָא.

Kol khamirah v'khami'ah, d'ikah, virshuti [d'lah khamitei ud'lah vi'ahrtei, ud'lah y'dahnah lei] libahteil v'lehhevei hefkeir, c'ahfrah d'ahr'ah.

Any leaven that may still be in the house, which I have [not seen or have not removed] shall be as if it does not exist, and as the dust of the earth.

While the *khametz* is being destroyed, replace the bracketed section with:

. . .דַּחֲזִיתֵּה וּדְלָא חֲזִיתֵּה, דַּחֲמִיתֵּה וּדְלָא חֲמִיתֵּה, דְּבַעֲרִתֵּה וּדְלָא בַעֲרִתֵּה. . .

. . . dahkhazitei ud'lah khazitei, dahkhamitei ud'lah khamitei, d'viahrtei ud'lah b'ahrtei. . . .

. . . or have not seen, which I have or have not removed. . .

ERUV TAVSHILIN In order to be able to cook on *yom tov* for Shabbat, when the holiday falls immediately preceding the day of rest (SEE EXPLANATION IN CHAPTER ON PESAKH):

בָּרוּךְ אַתָּה, יהוה אֱלֹהֵינוּ, מֶלֶךְ הָעוֹלָם, אֲשֶׁר קִדְּשָׁנוּ בְּמִצְוֹתָיו,
וְצִוָּנוּ עַל מִצְוַת עֵרוּב.

Barukh Atah, Adonai Eloheinu, Melekh Haolam, asher kidshanu b'mitzvotav, v'tzivanu al mitzvat eruv.

Blessed are You, Lord our God, King of the Universe, Who has sanctified us with His commandments and commanded us concerning the *mitzvah* of *eruv*.

בַּהֲדֵין עֵרוּבָא יְהֵא שָׁרֵא לָנָא לְמֵפֵא וּלְבַשָּׁלָא וּלְאַטְמָנָא
וּלְאַדְלָקָא שְׁרָגָא וּלְמֶעְבַּד כָּל צָרְכָנָא, מִיּוֹמָא טָבָא לְשַׁבְּתָא לָנוּ
וּלְכָל יִשְׂרָאֵל הַדָּרִים בָּעִיר הַזֹּאת.

Bahadein eiruvah y'hai shahrei lanu l'meipei, ul'vashalah, ul'ahtmana, ul'adlaka sh'raga, ul'mehbad kol tzarcana, m'yoma tava l'shabata. Lanu ul'khol yisrael, hadarim ba'ir hazot.

With this *eruv* it shall be permissible for us to bake, cook, and to keep the food warm, to light the candles and to prepare all necessary things on the festival for the Sabbath. This shall be permitted to us and to all Jews who live in this city.

CANDLELIGHTING To initiate the first two and last two days of Pesakh, both days of Shavuot, and Rosh Hashanah, Yom Kippur, the first two days of Sukkot, Shemini Atzeret, Simkhat Torah, and all eight nights of Khanukah; note the special wording used on Yom Kippur:

בָּרוּךְ אַתָּה, יהוה אֱלֹהֵינוּ, מֶלֶךְ הָעוֹלָם, אֲשֶׁר קִדְּשָׁנוּ בְּמִצְוֹתָיו,
וְצִוָּנוּ לְהַדְלִיק נֵר שֶׁל *וּשַׁבָּת וְשֶׁל יוֹם טוֹב וְיוֹם הַכִּיפּוּרִים.

Barukh Atah, Adonai Eloheinu, Melekh Haolam, asher kidshanu b'mitzvotav, v'tzivanu l'had-lik ner shel [Shabbat v'shel]* yom tov (on Yom Kippur, replace yom tov with: Yom Hakippurim).

Blessed are You, Lord our God, King of the Universe, Who has sanctified us with His commandments and commanded us to kindle the lights of [Sabbath and of]* the festival (Yom Kippur).

---

*said when Sabbath and *yom tov* or Yom Kippur coincide

KHANUKAH CANDLELIGHTING On all eight nights of Khanukah; on the first night only, follow with *shehekhiyanu*:

בָּרוּךְ אַתָּה, יהוה אֱלֹהֵינוּ, מֶלֶךְ הָעוֹלָם, אֲשֶׁר קִדְּשָׁנוּ בְּמִצְוֹתָיו, וְצִוָּנוּ לְהַדְלִיק נֵר שֶׁל חֲנֻכָּה.

Barukh Atah, Adonai Eloheinu, Melekh Haolam, asher kidshanu b'mitzvotav, v'tzivanu l'had-lik neir shel Khanukah. *

Blessed are You, O Lord Our God, King of the Universe, Who has sanctified us with His commandments, and commanded us to kindle the lights of Khanukah.

בָּרוּךְ אַתָּה, יהוה אֱלֹהֵינוּ, מֶלֶךְ הָעוֹלָם, שֶׁעָשָׂה נִסִּים לַאֲבוֹתֵינוּ, בַּיָּמִים הָהֵם בַּזְּמַן הַזֶּה.

Barukh Atah, Adonai Eloheinu, Melekh Haolam, sheh asah nisim l'avoteinu, b'yamim, hahelm b'azman huzeh.

Blessed are You, Lord our God, King of the Universe, Who made miracles for our fore-fathers in those days at this time.

SHEHEKHIYANU At the start of the first two days of Pesakh, Shavuot, Rosh Hashanah, and Sukkot, the start of Shemini Atzeret and Simkhat Torah following the *brakhah* for candlelighting, and, by someone other than the person who lights candles, following *kiddush*; following the *brakhah* for candlelighting on Yom Kippur; when putting on new non-leather clothes (as for Rosh Hashanah) for the first time; following the *brakhah* for lulav and etrog the first time you take up the four species on Sukkot, and on the first night of Khanukah, after the other two blessings:

בָּרוּךְ אַתָּה, יהוה אֱלֹהֵינוּ, מֶלֶךְ הָעוֹלָם, שֶׁהֶחֱיָנוּ, וְקִיְּמָנוּ, וְהִגִּיעָנוּ לַזְּמַן הַזֶּה.

Barukh Atah, Adonai Eloheinu, Melekh Haolam, shehekhiyanu, v'kiyamanu, v'higgiyanu l'az-man hazeh.

Blessed are You, Lord our God, King of the Universe, Who has kept us alive, sustained us, and brought us to this season.

---

*Some, particularly the Judeo-Spanish, use the wording *ner Khanukah* [Khanukah light], implying that the light is exclusively for the *mitzvah* of kindling, rather than *ner shel Khanukah*, implying the light has other use unrelated to the occasion.

OMER On the second night of Passover, when the Omer count begins:

בָּרוּךְ אַתָּה, יהוה אֱלֹהֵינוּ, מֶלֶךְ הָעוֹלָם, אֲשֶׁר קִדְּשָׁנוּ בְּמִצְוֹתָיו, וְצִוָּנוּ עַל סְפִירַת הָעֹמֶר.

Barukh Atah, Adonai Eloheinu, Melekh Haolam, asher kidshanu b'mitzvotav v'tzivanu al sefirat haomer.

Blessed are You, Lord our God, King of the Universe, Who has sanctified us with His commandments and commanded us concerning counting the Omer.

הַיּוֹם יוֹם וְאֶחָד] לָעֹמֶר.

Ha yom yom [ehkhad] l'Omer.

Today is the (first, second, etc.) day of the Omer.

BLESSING OF CHILDREN On Rosh Hashanah, the same *brakhot* used on *Erev Shabbat* (see a Yom Kippur *makhzor* for the longer version used on that holiday):

(For a son):

יְשִׂמְךָ אֱלֹהִים כְּאֶפְרַיִם וְכִמְנַשֶּׁה.

Y'simkhah Elohim k'Efraim v'k'Menasheh.

May God make you like Efraim and Menasseh.

(For a daughter):

יְשִׂמֵךְ אֱלֹהִים כְּשָׂרָה רִבְקָה רָחֵל וְלֵאָה.

Y'simaikh Elohim k'Sarah, Rivka, Rakhel v'Layah.

May God make you like Sarah, Rebecca, Rachel and Leah.

(Continue for both):

יְבָרֶכְךָ יהוה וְיִשְׁמְרֶךָ. יָאֵר יהוה פָּנָיו אֵלֶיךָ וִיחֻנֶּךָ. יִשָּׂא יהוה פָּנָיו אֵלֶיךָ, וְיָשֵׂם לְךָ שָׁלוֹם.

Y'v'rekhekha Adonai v'yishmarekhah. Ya'air Adonai pahnahv eilekha v'khunekhah. Yisah Adonai pahnahv eilekhah v'yahseim l'khah shalom.

May the Lord bless you and watch over you. May the Lord shine His face towards you and show you favor. May the Lord be favorably disposed towards you and may He grant you peace.

KIDDUSH, YADAYIM, MOTZI To initiate holiday meals on the last two days of Pesakh, both days of Shavuot and Rosh Hashanah, the first two days of Sukkot, on Shemini Atzeret and Simkhat Torah:

בָּרוּךְ אַתָּה, יהוה אֱלֹהֵינוּ, מֶלֶךְ הָעוֹלָם, בּוֹרֵא פְּרִי הַגָּפֶן.

Barukh Atah, Adonai Eloheinu, Melekh Haolam, borei pri hagaffen.

Blessed are You, Lord our God, King of the Universe, Who creates the fruit of the vine.

(Except for the last two days of Pesakh, follow with *shehekhiyanu,* see above.)

בָּרוּךְ אַתָּה, יהוה אֱלֹהֵינוּ, מֶלֶךְ הָעוֹלָם, אֲשֶׁר קִדְּשָׁנוּ בְּמִצְוֹתָיו, וְצִוָּנוּ עַל נְטִילַת יָדָיִם.

Barukh Atah, Adonai Eloheinu, Melekh Haolam, asher kidshanu b'mitzvotav, v'tzivanu al netilat yadayim.

Blessed are You, Lord our God, King of the Universe, Who has sanctified us with His commandments and commanded us regarding washing the hands.

בָּרוּךְ אַתָּה, יהוה אֱלֹהֵינוּ, מֶלֶךְ הָעוֹלָם, הַמּוֹצִיא לֶחֶם מִן הָאָרֶץ.

Barukh Atah, Adonai Eloheinu, Melekh Haolam, hamotzei lekhem min ha'aretz.

Blessed are You, Lord our God, King of the Universe, Who brings forth bread from the earth.

APPLE AND HONEY On Rosh Hashanah, when eating apple dipped in honey follows the khallah (and on all subsequent occasions when the fruit and honey are eaten):

בָּרוּךְ אַתָּה, יהוה אֱלֹהֵינוּ, מֶלֶךְ הָעוֹלָם, בּוֹרֵא פְּרִי הָעֵץ.

Barukh Atah, Adonai Eloheinu, Melekh Haolam, borei pri ha'eitz.

Blessed are You, Lord our God, King of the Universe, Who creates the fruit of the tree.

NEW CLOTHING When putting on new non-leather clothing for the first time, as on a second day of *yom tov* to give us a reason to say the *shehekhiyanu* at candlelighting or *kiddush*:

בָּרוּךְ אַתָּה, יהוה אֱלֹהֵינוּ, מֶלֶךְ הָעוֹלָם, מַלְבִּישׁ עֲרֻמִּים.

Barukh Atah, Adonai Eloheinu, Melekh Haolam, malbish arumim.

Blessed are You, Lord our God, King of the Universe, Who clothes the naked.

SMELLING SPICES On sniffing spices, as for a lift during Yom Kippur services:

בָּרוּךְ אַתָּה, יהוה אֱלֹהֵינוּ, מֶלֶךְ הָעוֹלָם, בּוֹרֵא מִינֵי בְשָׂמִים.

Barukh Atah, Adonai Eloheinu, Melekh Haolam, borei minei v'samim.

Blessed are You, Lord our God, King of the Universe, Who creates species of fragrance.

DWELLING IN THE SUKKAH Before partaking of every meal eaten in the *sukkah* (said after *kiddush*):

בָּרוּךְ אַתָּה, יהוה אֱלֹהֵינוּ, מֶלֶךְ הָעוֹלָם, אֲשֶׁר קִדְּשָׁנוּ בְּמִצְוֹתָיו, וְצִוָּנוּ לֵישֵׁב בַּסֻּכָּה.

Barukh Atah, Adonai Eloheinu, Melekh Haolam, asher kidishanu b'mitzvotav, v'tzivanu leisheiv b'sukkah.

Blessed are You, Lord our God, King of the Universe, Who has sanctified us with His commandments and commanded us to dwell in the *sukkah*.

TAKING UP THE FOUR SPECIES The first time of using the lulav and etrog, followed by *shehekhiyanu* (above) :

בָּרוּךְ אַתָּה, יהוה אֱלֹהֵינוּ, מֶלֶךְ הָעוֹלָם, אֲשֶׁר קִדְּשָׁנוּ בְּמִצְוֹתָיו, וְצִוָּנוּ עַל נְטִילַת לוּלָב.

Barukh Atah, Adonai Eloheinu, Melekh Haolam, asher kidishanu b'mitzvotav, v'tzivanu al netilat lulav.

Blessed are You, Lord our God, King of the Universe, Who has sanctified us with His commandments and commanded us concerning the taking of a palm branch.*

LEAVING THE SUKKAH After the last meal in the *sukkah* (lunch on Shemini Atzeret):

יְהִי רָצוֹן מִלְפָנֶיךָ, יהוה אֱלֹהֵינוּ, וֵאלֹהֵי אֲבוֹתֵינוּ, כְּשֵׁם שֶׁקִּיַּמְתִּי וְיָשַׁבְתִּי בַּסֻּכָּה זוֹ, כֵּן אֶזְכֶּה לְשָׁנָה הַבָּאָה לֵישֵׁב בְּסֻכַּת עוֹרוֹ שֶׁל לִוְיָתָן. לְשָׁנָה הַבָּאָה בִּירוּשָׁלָיִם.

Y'hi rahtzon milfanekhah, Adonai Eloheinu, veilohei avoteinu, k'sheim shehkiyamti v'yahshavti bah'sukkah zu, kein ezkeh l'shanah ha'bu'uh letshev b'sukkaht o'ro shel livyatan. L'shanah ha'ba'ah b'Yerushalayim.

May it be Your will, Lord our God and God of our fathers, just as I merited and sat in this *sukkah*, so may I merit the coming year to sit in the *sukkah* of the skin of Leviathan. Next year in Jerusalem.

HAVDALLAH At the close of Pesakh, Shavuot, Rosh Hashanah, and Simkhat Torah that fall on weekdays. (Note: At close of these *yom tovim* and Yom Kippur that coincide with Shabbat, full Sabbath *Havdallah* [found in *siddur*] used; for weekday Yom Kippur, add blessing over fire *if candle is lit from pre-existing flame*):

בָּרוּךְ אַתָּה, יהוה אֱלֹהֵינוּ, מֶלֶךְ הָעוֹלָם, בּוֹרֵא פְּרִי הַגָּפֶן.

Barukh Atah, Adonai Eloheinu, Melekh Haolam, borei pri hagaffen.

Blessed are You, Lord our God, King of the Universe, Who creates fruit of the vine. Only for weekday Yom Kippur and candle lit from pre-existing flame:

בָּרוּךְ אַתָּה, יהוה אֱלֹהֵינוּ, מֶלֶךְ הָעוֹלָם, בּוֹרֵא מְאוֹרֵי הָאֵשׁ.

Barukh Atah, Adonai Eloheinu, Melekh Haolam, borei m'orei ha'aish.

Blessed are You, Lord our God, King of the Universe, Who creates the illuminations of fire.

---

*Only one of the species is mentioned since the tallest element covers all.

בָּרוּךְ אַתָּה, יהוה אֱלֹהֵינוּ, מֶלֶךְ הָעוֹלָם, הַמַּבְדִיל בֵּן קֹדֶשׁ לְחֹל, בֵּן אוֹר לְחֹשֶׁךְ, בֵּן יִשְׂרָאֵל לָעַמִּים, בֵּן יוֹם הַשְּׁבִיעִי לְשֵׁשֶׁת יְמֵי הַמַּעֲשֶׂה. בָּרוּךְ אַתָּה, יהוה, הַמַּבְדִיל בֵּן קֹדֶשׁ לְחֹל.

Barukh Atah, Adonai Elokeinu, Melekh Haolam, hamavdil bein kodesh l'khol, bein oer l'khoshehk, bein Yisrael la'amim, bein yom hash'vi'i l'sheshet y'mei ha'ma'aseh. Barukh Atah, Adonai, hamavdil bein kodesh l'khol.

Blessed are You, Lord our God, King of the Universe, Who makes a distinction between sacred and secular, between Israel and the other nations, between the seventh day and the six working days. You are blessed, Lord, Who makes a distinction between the sacred and the secular.

More Good Information

The annotated bibliographies given throughout the book are for materials that deal with individual holidays or specific aspects of them. In this section you'll find references for comprehensive anthologies, series or collections (some classics) covering multiple holidays that may also be helpful, as well as resources to help you find them, and more. You will discover new books, audio and video recordings and other materials to help you keep the holidays fresh every year by visiting a library, bookstore or the Internet.

GENERAL HOLIDAY INFORMATION

FOR ADULTS

ArtScroll. Brooklyn: Mesorah Publications.
> Highly respected and widely used, the books in the far-ranging ArtScroll library include separate volumes on the holidays (covering history, laws, liturgy, and observance for each, based on Talmudic and traditional sources), special texts used for them (such as *Akdamus, Aseres Hadibros* and *Pirkei Avos* for Shavuot), the five *megillot,* festival halakhah, and much more.

Basic Principles of Chabad Chassidic Philosophy: Holiday Series. Brooklyn: Sichos in English.
> These four sets of cassettes cover the spiritual dimensions of the holidays (Rosh Hashanah, Yom Kippur and Sukkot; Sukkot, Simkhat Torah, Khanukah and Purim; Passover and Days of the Omer; and Shavuot, Tisha B'Av and the month of Elul) Presented on a beginning level, they relate the messages of each to everyday situations through intellectual study of Torah (788 Eastern Parkway, Brooklyn, NY 11213; 718-778-5436, www.sichos inenglish.org, sie100@aol.com).

The Hanukkah Anthology; The Passover Anthology; The Purim Anthology; The Rosh Hashanah Anthology; The Shavuot Anthology; The Sukkot and Simhat Torah Anthology; The Yom Kippur Anthology. Ed. by Philip Goodman. Philadelphia: The Jewish Publication Society, 1949–1992.
> Each of these volumes is a wonderful resource presenting a broad array of material—biblical and historical narratives, Talmudic references, essays on liturgy, law, music, art, culinary traditions, worldwide customs, reminiscences of celebrations in foreign lands and trying times, explanations of a holiday's themes and literary selections for children and adults. This is where you will find many of the legends and folktales that convey values and illustrate Jewish life in others times and places.

Greenberg, Irving. *The Jewish Way: Living the Holidays.* New York: Touchstone Books, 1993.
> This warm, insightful, inspiring book is not only about living the holidays, but about Judaism as a living evolving religion. Greenberg demonstrates the interrelatedness of holidays, their recurring themes and our destiny, and gives the special days in our year renewed relevance for today and tomorrow.

Schauss, Hayyim. *The Jewish Festivals: History and Observance.* New York: Schocken Books, 1996.
> Among various aspects of the holidays through history are fabulous descriptions of the activities in Jerusalem during the pilgrimage festivals, drawn from midrash, that conjure up the sights, sounds, smells and sensations of the occasions.

FOR CHILDREN

Fisher, Adam. *My Jewish Year—Celebrating Our Holidays*. West Orange, NJ: Behrman House, 1993.
This beautiful and exciting introduction to holidays combines the emotions surrounding their celebration with the traditions of observance. Engagingly illustrated, ritual, history, legend and activities make the holidays integral to the young readers' lives. Ages 7–9.

Grishaver, Joel Lurie. *Building a Jewish Life/Haggadah; Hanukkah; Passover; Purim; Purim Megillah; Rosh Hashanah and Yom Kippur; Rosh Hashanah Mahzor; Sukkot and Simhat Torah*. Los Angeles: Torah Aura Publications, 1987–1998.
Directed at children, written for parents and teachers to provide a bridge between classroom learning and home observance, the books explain the concepts of a holiday in terms children can relate to based on their lives. Each volume is somewhat different in format, and may include history, a story—perhaps in the form of a modern midrash, and learning activities. The texts are based on tradition and traditional sources so closely, the only clue to the fact that they were produced with a "liberal" orientation is the explanation of *mitzvah* provided for parents in the supplementary material. Ages 7–8. (A series of activity books for the same holidays is available for younger children, ages 5–6.)

Rouss, Sylvia. *Fun with Jewish Holiday Rhymes*. New York: UAHC Press, 1992.
Rhymes and movement activities, some with places to insert a child's name, teach Judaic symbols and concepts with fun. Ages 3–6.

Saypol, Judyth and Madeline Wikler. *All About Hanukkah; My Very Own Haggadah; Megillah; Rosh Hashanah; Shavuot; Simchat Torah, Sukkot; Yom Kippur*. Rockville, MD: Kar-Ben Copies, Inc., 1974–1988.
Each of the slim books in this popular series is full of lovingly presented information adapted for the young child: stories, prayers, projects, themes, objects used, activities. Contents vary by holiday to reflect its main and most relevant aspects for the audience. Ages 5–10.

HOLIDAY INSIGHTS AND INSPIRATION

Blech, Rabbi Benjamin. *More Secrets of Hebrew Words: Holy Days and Happy Days*. Northvale, NJ: Jason Aronson Inc., 1993.
Looking at *gematria,* acronyms, roots and words within words provides insights into terms and concepts connected with holidays to give new layers of meaning to observance and themes. This is a fascinating educational and entertaining supplement to an understanding of the holidays.

CLAL Holiday Resource Cards
The National Jewish Center for Learning and Leadership publishes a series of elegant brochures, each focused on a holiday, to help celebrants approach and observe them with meaning. With a few brief questions and a few practical steps, the text helps the reader experience the occasion in a personally relevant way (available for a contribution; 440 Park Avenue South, New York, NY 10016-8012; 212-779-3300; 212-779-1009 fax; www.clal.org).

BOOKS OF FOLKTALES, LEGENDS AND STORIES

Aleichem, Sholom. *The Best of Sholom Aleichem*. Northvale, NJ: Jason Aronson, 1989; *Happy New Year! and Other Stories*. New York: Dover Publications, 2000; *Favorite Tales of Sholom Aleichem*. New York: Avenel Books, 1991; *A Treasury of Sholom Aleichem Children's Stories*. Northvale, NJ: Jason Aronson, 1996.
These are just a few of the collections of stories by the beloved writer who captured the essence of Eastern European Jewish character, life and celebrations with his amusing tales.

540

The Best of Olomeinu. Comp. by Rabbi Yaakov Fruchter. Ed. by Rabbi Nosson Scherman. Brooklyn: Mesorah Publications, Ltd.,1986.

Stories that appeared in the popular magazine for Orthodox children over a forty-year period have been compiled into seven volumes, each grouped around a season, holiday or Shabbat. The stories treat Jewish subjects in the context of mystery, history or fantasy and reflect the experiences of Jews in all times and places. Ages 10–14.

Chagall, Bella. *Burning Lights.* New York: Biblio Press, 1998.

The charming reminiscences of holiday celebrations in pre-Revolution Vitebsk, Russia, in this book are told from the point of view of the child. They lovingly express all the wonder, magic and excitement home observance can hold. The author's husband, artist Marc Chagall, provided pen and ink illustrations.

Weilerstein, Sadie Rose. *The Best of K'tonton: The Greatest Adventures in the Life of the Jewish Thumbling, K'Tonton Ben Baruch Reuben.* Philadelphia: The Jewish Publication Society, 1988.

K'tonton is a little Jewish boy, no bigger than a thumb. His amusing and heart-warming adventures— almost all of which take place on holidays—teach holiday themes and traditions, and Jewish values. This had been a classic for more than half a century. Ages 3–8

The following four volumes contain a wealth of stories that exemplify holiday values. (See also Holiday Anthology series under General Holiday Information.):

Frankel, Ellen. *The Classic Tales—4,000 Years of Jewish Lore.* Northvale, NJ: Jason Aronson Inc., 1989.

Labovitz, Annette, and Eugene Labovitz. *Time for My Soul—A Treasury of Jewish Stories for Our Holy Days.* Northvale, NJ: Jason Aronson Inc., 1987.

Nissan, Mindel. *The Complete Story of Tishrei.* Brooklyn: Kehot Publication Society, 1998.

Sadeh, Pinhas. *Jewish Folktales.* Trans. by Hillel Halkin. New York: Doubleday, 1989. ☙

HALAKHAH

In addition to the following, see also ArtScroll (under General Holiday Information).

Grunfeld, Dr. Dayan I. *The Sabbath: A Guide to Its Understanding and Observance.* New York: Feldheim Publishers, 1981.

This compact, easy-to-read book is a good introduction to the practical observance of the day of rest. It presents the meaning of Sabbath, concept of *melakhah* (the prohibited work), classification of the thirty-nine categories, and a rundown of which activities fall into each.

Nadoff, Rabbi Yisroel. *Yom Tov in Halachah: A Comprehensive Guide to the Halochos of Yom Tov and Their Application to Everyday Life.* Jerusalem/New York: Feldheim Publishers, 1997.

Concise in explanation but broad in scope, this volume presents modern halakhic solutions to potential commonplace holiday problems—from carrying a key ring to writing on a cake. It is readable and practical.

Zucker, Rabbi Dovid, and Francis, Rabbi Moshe. *Chol HaMoed: Comprehensive Review of the Laws of the Intermediate Days of the Festivals.* Lakewood, NJ: Halakhah Publications, 1981.

Well-organized and lucidly written, this book takes the complication out of the intricacies of *khol hamoed* observance. Conditions under which activity is allowed or prohibited are simply and clearly differentiated. ☙

PRAYER BOOKS

Each of the movements (Orthodox, Conservative, Reform, Reconstructionist) has its own *siddurim,* which you can find at any Jewish library or bookstore. Several include special readings on key themes in Judaism, or services for the modern commemorative days. These selections reflect the Orthodox tradition and were selected because they are widely used and comprehensive in scope.

The Complete ArtScroll Siddur. Trans. and Commentary by Rabbi Nosson Scherman. Brooklyn: Mesorah Publications, Ltd., 1989.

> For weekday, Sabbath and festival use at home and in synagogue, it includes the full text of daily and special services, blessings for a wide variety of situations, the holiday rituals, texts of the prophetic readings for special Sabbaths, Torah readings for the holidays, halakhot of prayers, the Book of Psalms and prayer said for a sick person. What makes the volume so useful is its explanation of the development and significance of the prayers and rituals, and instructions (when to stand, sit, read silently, and so on). Ashkenazi and Sephardic versions are available, as is a linear version, with transliteration of the Hebrew and line-by-line translation especially helpful for beginners.

The NCSY Bencher—A Book of Prayer and Song. Ed. and Trans. by David M. L. Olivestone. New York: National Conference of Synagogue Youth/Union of Jewish Congregations of America, 1983.

> If you have ever been to a traditional wedding or bar mitzvah, you may have seen copies of this book on the tables (with the names of the celebrants and the date of occasion on the cover). Provided so that guests can participate in the grace after meals, it is a handy little book to have at home for ushering in holidays. Candle lighting, *kiddush, Birkat Hamazon, Havdallah* as well as blessings for numerous occasions and a selection of songs are included. Everything is transliterated.   ☞✡

COOKBOOKS

Next to books, food is possibly the one item for which the Jews are known. (You can tell an occasion is a Jewish one by the type and amount of food served.) There seems to be a recent proliferation of Jewish holiday and kosher cookbooks, some of them aimed at adapting traditional recipes for health consciousness. Part of the fun of using them is reading the customs, history, personal anecdotes and reminiscences that often accompany the recipes.

FOR ADULTS

Angel, Gilda. *Sephardic Holiday Cooking: Recipes and Traditions.* Mt. Vernon: Decalogue Books, 1986.

> This is a great introduction to authentic Sephardic cooking, full of vignettes about the holiday customs and how they differ from those of the Ashkenazim, commentary on dishes and seasonal ingredients, full menus, and more than two hundred recipes, in English and Ladino.

The Kosher Palette. Livingston, NJ: Joseph Kushner Hebrew Academy/Kushner Yeshiva High School, 2000.

> This could be the most attractive, most reliable and most creative fundraising cookbook ever produced, full of great recipes and ideas for entertaining.

Locke, Norton. *The Land of Milk and Honey, A Cooking Book/An Epicurean Tour of Israel with a History of Foods in the Holy Land.* Fort Lauderdale: Ashley Publishing Co., Inc., 1992.

> With this fun and fascinating book you can serve what Abraham did for Rosh Hashanah and what Saul did for Sukkot. Liberally peppered with quotes from Scripture, the text covers the culinary tradition of Jews in Israel, based on Torah and historical records going back as far as 2500 BCE. You'll find recipes for every holiday (measurements, utensils and so on are adapted for the modern cook). One note: The book refers to the New Testament, but from the standpoint of history, not religion. It takes a decidedly Jewish view. If in doubt, check out the epilogue.

Machlin, Edda Servi. *The Classic Cuisine of the Italian Jews, Traditional Recipes and Menus and a Memoir of a Vanished Way of Life*. New York: Everest House Publishers, 1981.
> The reminiscences of the author about her medieval Tuscan hometown Pitigliano include the preparations and celebrations surrounding the holidays. Descriptions of each festival and suggested menus introduce the recipes, arranged by course and annotated with anecdotes and vignettes. (More menus, recipes and recollections fill *The Classic Cuisine of the Italian Jews II* [Giro Press, 1992].)

Nathan, Joan. *The Jewish Holiday Kitchen*. New York: Schocken Books, 1998.
> Easy to follow, the book is enhanced with short explanations of Jewish holidays, the life cycle, kashrut and the development of Jewish food customs, with Scriptural and literary quotes.

Roden, Claudia. *The Book of Jewish Food, An Odyssey from Samarkand to New York*. New York: Alfred A. Knopf, 1997.
> In addition to more than eight hundred recipes from the variety of nationalities within both Ashkenazi and Sephardic traditions, this beautifully designed book contains a wealth of information about the history and customs of Jewish communities throughout the world. This is a fabulous volume.

Zeidler, Judy. *The Gourmet Jewish Cook*. New York: William Morrow and Company, 1988.
> Here are updated and elegant versions of old standards and new ideas based on traditional food customs. Sections defined by holiday include suggested menus and reflect a range of ethnic and modern international cuisines. There are some fabulous recipes here.

FOR CHILDREN

The Animated Children's Kosher Holiday Cookbook. Ed. by Yaacov Peterseil and Rivka Demsky. New York: Jonathan David, 1991.
> With an introduction by Rabbi Shlomo Riskin that beautifully explains kashrut and its value in Jewish life, the chapters begin with the basic *mitzvot* of a holiday, its customs and symbols. Riddles, gems of history, comments by great rabbis related to food stories and drawn versions of the Claymation figures that illustrate the "Animated" series are sprinkled throughout the book.

Nathan, Joan. *The Children's Jewish Holiday Kitchen—70 Fun Recipes for You and Your Kids*. New York: Schocken Books, 2000.
> The explanations and vignettes provide information to be relayed to children, but are not for them to read themselves. Each recipe gives the list of ingredients and list of equipment, and then steps are identified as to whether they are to be done by the child alone, adult alone, or both.

SONGBOOKS

Like folktales, traditional Jewish and Israeli songs appear in a multitude of collections.

Friedman, Debbie. *The Best of Debbie Friedman*. Cedarhurst, NY: Tara Publications, 1987.
> Known for her work with children and concerts, contemporary musician Debbie Friedman has brought bright, soul-touching new melodies to traditional liturgy, Scripture, folksongs and blessings. Complementary recordings and additional Debbie Friedman songbooks and recordings, plus CDs, cassettes, videos and sheet music by more than one hundred and eighty North American contemporary Jewish recording artists are available through Sounds Write Productions, Inc., 800-9-SOUND-9; www.soundswrite. com.)

Jewish Holidays in Song. Comp., Arr. and Ed. by Velvel Pasternak. Milwaukee: Hal Leonard Publishing Company, 1998.
> Organized by holiday, the book includes traditional folk tunes, well-known parts of liturgy, and melodies for blessings. All Hebrew is transliterated, and English translation is provided.

Siddur in Song. 100 Prayerbook Melodies. Compiled, Ed. and Arr. by Velvel Pasternak. Cedarhurst, NY: Tara Publications, 1986.

> Tunes for weekday, Sabbath, Rosh Khodesh, Torah reading, *Hallel,* and *Mussaf* services, and some special tunes for holidays, are included. The companion tape and CD are available.

The Songs We Sing. Selected and Ed. by Harry Coopersmith. New York: The United Synagogue Commission on Jewish Education, 1950.

> This book is valuable for its sheer comprehensiveness. There are liturgical selections from all the major holidays, folksongs, Israeli work, folk and dance songs, Yiddish classics, cantillations for reading Scripture, prayer motifs, and the tunes for the major blessings.   ☞✡

SOURCES OF PRODUCTS AND INFORMATION

For people who do not have access to Jewish books and ritual items locally, catalogues and websites provide easy solutions and help keep you apprised of new products. Reviews and advertisements in Jewish periodicals resources.

AllJudaica.com (Rosenblums World of Judaia, Inc., 2906 West Devon Avenue, Chicago, IL 60659; 800-626-6536).

> The oldest and largest Jewish bookstore in the Midwest, and its website, offer a vast selection of printed materials, ritual items, games, toys, audio and video recordings.

Hamakor Judaica, Inc.—The Source for Everything Jewish (www.jewishsource.com; PO Box 48836, Niles, IL 60714-0836; 800-476-2388; 847-966-4033 fax).

> Books, videos, musical recordings and ritual items—holiday and otherwise—in a variety of styles and price ranges can be ordered. Full color catalogues are distributed several times a year.

Jewishmusic.com/Tara Publications (www.jewishmusic.com; PO Box 707, Owing Mills, MD 21117; 800-827-2400, 410-654-0880; 800-827-2403 and 410-654-0881 fax; info@jewishmusic.com)

> Books, cassettes and CDs in English, Yiddish and Hebrew, covering classics, contemporary music, and holiday themes include a selection of Sephardic/Ladino recordings.

Shamash, The Jewish Network (www.shamash.org)

> This is a web directory of and links to a multitude of all sorts of Jewish information: products, services, Israel, Jewish studies, media, Jewish communities of the world, Yiddish and Hebrew resources, translation, arts, museums, publishers, travel, kashrut and more.

ShopInIsrael.com

> A few American volunteers concerned about the economic impact suffered by Israelis due to the second Palestinian intifada established this site to give friends of Israel worldwide the opportunity to buy directly from Israeli merchants. The site links shoppers to Israeli suppliers, manufacturers and distributors for every type of item for any occasion.

www.askmoses.com

> At this Khabad-affiliated site, you can direct questions—in English, Hebrew, Russian, Spanish or French—to a member of the staff of male and female scholars, many of them world-class authors, lecturers and practicing rabbis. The site operates 24/6.

www.leslikoppelmanross.com

> For more holiday ideas and insights, check the author's website, which is updated in advance of each holiday.   ☞✡

GLOSSARY

The pronunciations given are for the Hebrew rendition of words or phrases. Where the Yiddish (and Americanized version) is significantly different, it is also provided. Explanations of holiday names are covered in the appropriate chapters.

aggadah (ah'-gah-dah'): "legend" or folklore; from the *aggadata*, the non-legal discussions of Talmud

ahavat Yisrael (ah hah-vaht' yis-roh-eil'): "love of Israel," denoting the feeling of one Jew toward all others and unity within the nation

Akeidah (ah-kay-dah'; Yiddish: uh-kay'-duh): "binding;" the biblical account of Abraham's test of loyalty when God asked him to sacrifice his son Isaac (GENESIS 22), during the preparation for which Isaac was bound with rope

aliyah (ah-lee-ah'; Yiddish: ah-lee'-yuh): "ascent;" the honor given to one called to "go up" to recite the blessings before and after a section of Torah verses is read; also immigration to Israel, since moving to the Holy Land is considered an elevation; plural: *aliyot*

Amidah (ah mee'-dah): the central prayer of all services, recited while standing (amad, to stand); also referred to as the Silent Devotion, since it is said to oneself, and as *Shemonah Esrei* (Eighteen), for the number of benedictions it originally contained (now nineteen)

arba kanfote (ahr-bah' kahn-fote'; Yiddish: ahr'-buh kahn'-fus): "four corners;" the undergarment worn by religious Jewish men that has ritual fringes (tzitzit) at each of its corners, (PER NUMBERS 15:39), as a reminder of the commandments; also called *tallit* (garment) *katan* (small)

Aron Kodesh (ah-rone' koe'-desh): "Holy Ark;" the enclosure on the eastern wall of a synagogue in which the Torah scrolls are housed

Ashkenazi (ash-ken-ah-zee'; Yiddish: ahsh-ken-ahz'-ee): a Jew from West, Central or Eastern Europe or one descended from Jews of this region, and the customs and liturgy of Jews from this region; from the Hebrew word for Germany (*Ashkenaz*), which was the center of European Jewish life; plural: Ashkenazim

atzeret (aht-tzer'-rette; Yiddish: aht-seh'-ress): solemn assembly; the last day of Pesakh and Sukkot as designated in Torah, and the Talmudic designation for Shavuot as the conclusion of Pesakh

bar mitzvah (bahr mitz'-vah): "son of commandment;" a Jewish male of thirteen years or older, and the coming of age ceremony in which he participates signifying that he is taking on the responsibilities of living by Torah; for females, called bat (daughter [of]) mitzvah and held at age twelve among the Orthodox

bimah (bee'-muh): "platform;" raised place in the synagogue from where the service is conducted and the Torah read

birkat hamazon (beer-kaht' hah-mah-zone'; Yiddish: beer'-kus hah-mah'-zun): "blessing for the food;" grace said after any meal at which bread has been blessed and eaten

blood libel: malicious lies fabricated since the twelfth century claiming that Jews kill Christians and use their blood for making *matzah* for Passover; used to incite deadly riots and pogroms against Jews

brakhah (brah-khah'; Yiddish: bruh'-khuh): "blessing;" prayer of praise or gratitude, from *barukh*, praised or blessed; plural: *brakhot*

brit (breet; Yiddish: bris): "covenant;" circumcision of a Jewish male at the age of eight days to bring him into the covenant of the Jewish people; formally *brit milah* (covenant of circumcision)

Diaspora: Greek for "dispersion," indicating the place outside the Land of Israel where Jews live and their situation there

etrog (et'-roag; Yiddish: es'-rug): "citron;" lemon-like fruit considered a symbol of beauty and perfection used as a ritual item on Sukkot; plural: etrogim

Eretz Yisrael (eh'-rehtz yis-roe-ail'): "the Land of Israel"

erev (eh'-rehv): "evening;" the start of the Jewish day, and therefore the beginning of every Jewish holiday; used to designate the daytime prior to the start of a holiday or Shabbat (for instance, all of Friday is called *Erev Shabbat*)

eruv tavshilin (eh'-roov tahv-she'-lin): Aramaic for "mixture of cooked foods;" a ritual to allow us to cook for the Sabbath on a holiday when the Sabbath immediately follows the holiday

Five Scrolls: Song of Songs (Shir Hashirim), Ruth (Rut), Lamentations (Eikhah), Ecclesiastes (Kohelet) and Esther (Esteir); part of the Writings section of the Hebrew Bible and each assigned for reading on a festival with which it has some thematic or historic connection

gabbai (gah'-bie): the synagogue treasurer or caretaker; one who keeps order during services

galut (gah-loot'; Yiddish: gul'lus): "exile;" the situation of the Jewish people outside of the Jewish homeland and before the final redemption; related to geulah (redemption) and *Go'al Yisrael* (Redeemer of Israel)

Gaon (gah-ohn'; Yiddish: g-own or goon): "eminence, excellence, genius;" the title of the heads of the Babylonian Talmudic academies between the sixth and eleventh centuries and title of respect for select other exceptional leader/scholars (such as the Vilna Gaon); plural: *gaonim*

Gemara (gah-mah'-rah; Yiddish: guh-moor'-uh): collected commentaries and elaborations on the Mishnah

gematria (geh-mah'-tree-ah): system of deriving deeper meaning from Jewish text through the numerical values assigned to letters and words

gemillut khassadim (guh-mee'-loot khah-sah-dim'; Yiddish: g-mee'-loose khah-suh'-dim): "acts of loving kindness;" one of the pillars, according to Jewish tradition, on which the world stands, along with Torah and Divine service

genizah (geh-nee'-zuh): storage place for damaged or unused Scripture and other Jewish holy texts, which may not be discarded or destroyed

Golem (goe'-lum): legendary clay automaton created by Rabbi Judah Loew of Prague in the mid-seventeenth century to protect the community against attacks instigated by blood libels

Haftarah (hahf-toh-rah'; Yiddish: hahf-taw'-ruh): "conclusion;" selection from the prophets read after the Torah portion on Sabbath, holidays and fast days; plural: haftarot

Haggadah (hah-gah-dah'; Yiddish: huh-guh'-duh): "narration, telling;" printed version of the Passover Seder service, a collection of Scripture, literary selections and songs; from the verb *l'haggid*, to tell; plural: *haggadot*

hakafot (hah-kah-fote'; Yiddish: hah-kaw'-fes): "circuits;" the circlings around the inside of the sanctuary or outdoors made by congregants carrying the Torah and dancing behind it on Simkhat Torah; singular: *hakafah*

halakhah (hah-lah-khah'; Yiddish: huh-luh'-khuh): body of Jewish law according to which a Jew is supposed to live; a combination of Torah commandments and the rabbinic interpretation of them; from the same root as "to go" and "ways"; plural: halakhot

Hallel (hah'-lail): "praise;" Psalms 113–118 chanted on festivals

hatarat nedarim (hah-tah'raht neh-dah-rim'): "annulment of vows," customarily done on *Erev Rosh Hashanah*

Havdallah (hahv-dah-lah'; Yiddish: hahv-duh'-luh): "separation," the prayer and ritual recited at the close of every Shabbat and festival day to make a distinction between sacred and ordinary time

hillula (hih-loo'-lah); Aramaic for "celebration," originally used to designate wedding festivities, later applied to the yahrtzeit of a famous rabbi or scholar, whose soul wed with God; used among Sephardim for pilgrimages to the burial sites of great scholars

hoshanah (hoe-shah'-nah): "please save us," a contraction of *hoshiah nah* series of supplications made during processions around the synagogue on Sukkot and Hoshanah Rabbah; plural: *hoshanot*

Isru Khag (iss'-roo khahg'). "to bind the festival;" the day following the pilgrimage festivals specially designated so that we will carry the mood of the holiday into our everyday lives

Kabbalah (kah-bah-lah', Yiddish: k-buh'-luh): Jewish mysticism, from the Hebrew verb *likabeil*, to receive (as in receiving understanding); system designed to uncover the secrets of the universe and God dating back to the earliest studies of Torah; see also Zohar

kaddish (kah-deesh'; Yiddish: kah'-dish): "sanctification;" prayer marking the end of a section of a service; one version is recited by mourners during the eleven months following the death of a parent (thirty days for a child, spouse or sibling)

karet (kah'-rette; Yiddish: kohr'-ess): "excision" from the community; biblically ordained punishment for refusing to identify with the Jewish people, specifically by purposely not participating in the Passover sacrifice and not undergoing circumcision

kasher/kashrut (kah-shair', kash-root'; Yiddish: kah'-sher; kash'-ruse): ritually fit for use (from the same root as the words for honest and wholesome); kosher; the system of Jewish dietary laws

ketubah (keh-too'-bah; Yiddish: k-soo'-buh): marriage contract

Khabad (khah-bahd'): a sect of Khassidim originally from the town of Lubavitch who use the acronym standing for the levels of intellectual approach to Torah study: *Khokhma* (wisdom), *Binah* (understanding) and *Das* (knowledge); the Khassidim most active in educational outreach among Jews

khag (khahg): "festival;" descriptive word and in biblical terms often part of the name of holidays (*Khag Hamatzot, Khag Hakatsir,* etc.)

khallah (khah-lah'; Yiddish: khal'-luh): the loaf of bread, usually in braided form, used for Shabbat and festivals; plural: khallot

khametz (khah-maitz'; Yiddish: khuh'-mitz): "leaven;" substances that are leavened or could become leavened and are totally prohibited to Jews during Passover

Khassidim (khah-see-deem'; Yiddish: khah-see'-dum): "the pious"; adherents of the religious revolutionaries of the early 1700s who, under the leadership of Baal Shem Tov (Master of the Good Name) reacted against a Judaism that had become stale and formal through emphasis on Talmud scholarship and emphasized instead meditation, communion with God and spiritual joy to bring the religion back to the masses; gradually put more stress back on learning and today are on the conservative end of Judaism

khazzan (khah-zahn'; Yiddish: khah'-zun): "cantor;" synagogue prayer leader.

kheder (khay'-dehr): "room;" the traditional Jewish school for young boys in Europe and later America

khesbone hanefesh (khesh'-bone hah-neh'-fesh): "accounting of the soul;" the personal evaluation done around Rosh Hashanah

khet (khait): error or wrongdoing, from the archery term meaning to miss the mark; used to designate our shortcomings during the Days of Awe

khol hamoed (khole' hah-moe'-aid): intermediate festival days, those between the first two and last two days of Pesakh and Sukkot

Khumash (khuh-mahsh'; Yiddish: khuh'-mush): the printed version of the Torah, from the word *khameish,* five, for the Five Books of Moses

khuppah (khuh-pah'; Yiddish: khuh'-puh): wedding canopy

khurban (khur-bahn'; Yiddish: khor'-bun): "destruction by fire;" refers to the destruction of Jerusalem in 586 bce and 70 ce and sometimes to the Holocaust

kibbutz (kee-bootz'): communal farm in Israel

kiddush (kee-doosh'; Yiddish: kid'-dish): "sanctification;" prayer sanctifying Sabbath and festivals, usually chanted over a cup of wine

kinot (kee-note'; Yiddish: kee'-nus): "elegies" the poems recited on Tisha B'Av; sometimes used to refer to the book of Lamentations in rabbinic literature; singular: kinah

kippah (kee-pah'; Yiddish: kee'-puh): "skullcap," worn by men when praying, or by traditional men as a sign of commitment to Jewish law; called yarmulke in Yiddish

kitniyot (kit'-nee-yote'; Yiddish: kit'-nee-us): "legumes," specifically rice, millet, peas, beans, peanuts, corn and buckwheat, which Ashkenazim are prohibited from using on Pesakh but are permissible for Sephardim

kittel (kit'l): white robe reminiscent of the Temple priests' vestments worn over regular garments by men for the Passover seder, on Rosh Hashanah and Yom Kippur, by the groom on his wedding day and a father at his son's *brit*, to represent mercy, purity and mortality

Klal Yisrael (klal' yis-roe-ail'): "all of Israel;" an expression of the unity and indivisibility of the Jewish people

Kohein (koe'-hein): priest of the Temple; descendant of the tribe of Levi who served in the Temple; *Kohein Gadol* was the high priest, a descendant of Aaron (the first high priest) and member of one of the three categories of Jews, along with Levi, a descendant of the tribe of Levi who served as priests in the Temple; and Yisraeli, an ordinary Israelite; plural: kohanim (Leviim, Yisraelim)

lukhot habrit (loo-khote' hah-breet'; Yiddish: lukh'-os hah-brees'): "tablets of the covenant;" the stones on which the Ten Commandments were engraved

lulav (loo'-lahv): "palm leaf;" the ritual item used for Sukkot consisting of palm, myrtle and willow leaves

Ma'ariv (mah'-reev): "from erev;" evening prayer service

Maftir (mahf'-teer): concluding Torah verses, the last verses (or *parshah*) of any weekly or holiday Torah reading; also used to designate the person called to the Torah for that *parshah*, "one who concludes," because he generally reads the haftarah ("conclusion")

Mah Nishtanah (mah' nish-tah-nah'; Yiddish: mah nish-tah'-nuh): "why is this different?" the first phrase of and designation for the "Four Questions" recited at the Passover Seder

makhzor (mahkh-zur', Yiddish: makh'-zoor): "cycle," the prayer book for the holy days and festivals throughout the year; also applied to the festival liturgies in which poems specific to each holiday are included

Ma-ot Khitim/Perot (mah'-ote khee'-tim/pay-rote'; Yiddish: mah'-os khee'-tim/pay' ros): "fund for wheat/fruit;" community collections to provide food for the poor on the holidays, respectively, of Passover and Tu B'Shevat

Marranos: hidden Jews of Spanish-Portuguese descent who renounced Judaism during the fifteenth-century Inquisition to save themselves, but continued to observe Jewish practices in secret

Matan Torah (mah-tan' toe-rah'; Yiddish: mah'-ten toe'-ruh): "giving of the Torah" during the Revelation at Mount Sinai

matzah (maht-zah'; Yiddish: maht'-zuh): unleavened bread eaten during Passover made from water and flour in less than eighteen minutes; referred to as *shmurah* (guarded) if every step of the process from the time the wheat was reaped has been supervised; *ashirah* (rich) if made with other ingredients such as fruit juice or eggs; plural: *matzot*

megillah (meh-gee-lah'; Yiddish: meh-gill'-uh): "scroll;" from the word for "to roll;" the parchment strips on which certain books of the Bible were recorded; especially used to designate the Book of Esther; plural: *megillot*

menorah (meh-noh-rah'; Yiddish: meh-noh'-ruh): "candelabra;" the seven-branched lamp used in the Temple and—popularly but incorrectly—the eight-branched lamp used for the lighting of Khanukah candles (properly called a *khanukiyah*); plural: menorot

mezzuzah (meh-zoo-zah'; Yiddish: meh-zuz'-uh): "doorpost;" a piece of parchment containing parts of the *Shema* (DEUTERONOMY 6:4-9; 11:13-21) encased and affixed to the doorpost of a Jewish home

Midrash (mih'-drash): the part of Talmud that consists of rabbinic interpretation of the Torah in the form of homilies, parables and allegories that derive ethical and spiritual lessons from Scripture; related to the word *d'rash*, for "to investigate" or "to lecture"

mikvah (mick-vah'; Yiddish: mick'-veh): ritual bath

Minkhah (min-khah'; Yiddish: min'-khuh): afternoon prayer service

minyan (min-yahn'; Yiddish: min'-yun): group of ten people (by tradition men) needed in order to conduct a public prayer service

Mishnah (mish-nah'; Yiddish: mish'-nuh): Code of Oral Law, the official recorded version of the laws, decisions, opinions and ethical teachings transmitted orally by religious authorities for generations after the giving of the Torah and compiled in written form in the third century

mitzvah (mitz-vah', Yiddish: mitz'-vuh): "commandment," any of the six hundred and thirteen given in Torah governing virtually every aspect of a Jew's life; often popularly mistranslated as "good deed"; plural: *mitzvot*

moshiakh (mah-shee'-akh): "anointed one" derived from *mashakh*, to anoint, as a king; the term used for messiah

motzi (moe'-tzi): "bringing out;" the blessing said over bread at the beginning of the meal (bread which is brought forth—or taken out of—the earth); also used to designate the end of the Sabbath (*motzei Shabbat*) or festivals

Mussaf (moo'-sahf): "addition;" the extra prayer service read on Sabbaths, festivals and new moons

Neviim (nehv-ee-eem'; Yiddish: n'-vee'-im): "prophets;" the section of the Hebrew Bible containing the prophetic writings

omer (oh'-mehr): measure of grain, usually identified as a sheaf; the period of time marking the progress of the barley harvest from the second day of Pesakh through Shavuot during which every day is counted (Omer)

Oriental: Jews from Middle Eastern and Asian communities such as Yemen, Ethiopia, Soviet Georgia, Bukhara, Cochin (India), and Persia, often grouped with Sephardim

parshah (par'-shah): "section;" a grouping of verses from a Torah reading, a set part of the sidrah; plural: parshiot

pesakh (peh'-sahkh): "paschal," referring to the lamb offered on the night of the Exodus and its commemoration, the holiday of Passover

Pharisees: fathers of rabbinic Judaism who believed in extrapolating from Torah according to Oral Law and that study and proper behavior was just as valid in serving God as Temple sacrifice

Pidyon Haben (pid-yahn' hah-ben'; Yiddish: pid'-dyun huh-ben'): "redemption of the (firstborn) son;" a ceremony on the thirty-first day after the birth when the first child born to a mother is a male, in which the father pays a kohein five shekalim (today, five dollars in coins), as was done in Temple times, to release the child from the obligation of being dedicated to God and of serving the priests (EXODUS 13:1-2, NUMBERS 18:16)

piyyut (pee-yoot'): Greek for liturgical poem; major part of liturgies for festivals; plural: *piyyutim*

Rosh Khodesh (roesh' khoe'-desh): "head of the month;" the one or two days that mark the beginning of each new month

sabra: term for a native-born Israeli, from the fruit of the cactus plant of the same name, which has a hard prickly outside, but is sweet inside

Sadducee: member of the aristocracy connected with the priesthood in Second Temple days who believed in a literal interpretation of Torah and in the supremacy of sacrifice as the way to serve God

Seder (say'-dir): "order;" refers to the order of service and in particular to the home ceremony conducted on the first two evenings of Pesakh; plural: *sedarim*

sefer (say'-fehr): "book;" plural: *sifrei* (used when referring to multiple Torah scrolls, Sifrei Torah)

Sefirah (s-fee-rah'; Yiddish: s-fee'-ruh): counting; the forty-nine days between Pesakh and Shavuot during which the omer is counted, a period for self-improvement and spiritual elevation; also, one of the ten spheres that make up the world in kabbalah's view; plural: *sefirot*

Selikhot (s-lee-khote'; Yiddish: slikh'-us): "forgiveness," series of penitential prayers recited in the week prior to Rosh Hashanah and at other times when repentance is made

Sephardi (s-phahr-dee'; Yiddish: s-phahr'-dee): a Jew descended from those expelled from Spain or Portugal in 1492, predominantly those who settled in Arab countries, and their customs and liturgy; from the Hebrew word for Spain (*Sepharad*); often used to refer to all non-Ashknazi Jews (also see Oriental); plural: Sephardim

Seudah (soo-dah'; Yiddish: soo'-duh): "festive meal," required as part of holiday or Shabbat observance, especially the meal eaten as part of Purim celebration; seudah mafseket, the meal that "interrupts," immediately precedes a fast; *seudat mitzvah* refers to the special meal following fulfillment of a commandment at a joyous occasion (brit, bar mitzvah, wedding, siyyum); *shalosh seudot* (often garbled as "*shallushudus*") is the third meal of Shabbat, served on Saturday afternoon/evening

Shabbat (shah-baht'; Yiddish: shah'-bus): Sabbath; to stop work, rest

Shakharit (shah-khah-reet'; Yiddish: shakh'-ris): morning prayer service, from one of the words for morning, *shakhar*

shalosh regalim (shah-loesh' reh-gah-leem'): "three pilgrimages," the festivals when all Israelite men were required to go to the Temple in Jerusalem with seasonal offerings, Pesakh, Shavuot and Sukkot

shammash (shah-mahsh'; Yiddish: shahm'-us): "servant;" the auxiliary candle used to light the flames of the Khanukah menorah; in European synagogues, the sexton

shehekhiyanu (sheh-heh-khee-yah'-noo): "Who has kept us alive;" prayer of gratitude and celebration, recited at the arrival of a holiday, or when something is experienced for the first time during a Jewish year (eg: new fruit eaten, new garment worn, major accomplishment made)

Shekhinah (sheh-khee'-nah): Divine Presence in the world; God's feminine nature

Shem Hameforash (shem' hah-meh-foh'-rash): "Explicit Name;" the ineffable Name of God, said only by the High Priest during the Temple *Avodah* service on Yom Kippur

Shema (sheh-mah'): "hear," from "Hear O Israel, the Lord our God the Lord is One;" central creed of Judaism, the declaration of faith in One God, said in daily prayers, prior to retiring for the night and, if possible, just before death; the biblical passages Deuteronomy 6:4-9, 11:13-21 and Numbers 15:37-41

shmittah (shmee'-tah): sabbatical; the seventh year in which the land in Israel is given complete rest, debts are forgiven and slaves released, per Leviticus 25:2-4 and Deuteronomy 15:1

Shira (sheer'-ah): "song;" Exodus 15:1-18, the song sung by the Israelites after they left Egypt, "Song of the Sea;" part of daily services, read on the Sabbath when we reach that section of Torah, on the seventh day of Passover commemorating the crossing of the Reed Sea, and special Sabbaths

shiva (shiv'-uh): weeklong mourning observed by the deceased's immediate family; from same root as seven (*sheva*), for the seven days of the period

Shoah (show'-ah): modern Hebrew word for the Holocaust, meaning devastation, ruin; often Hashoah (The Holocaust)

shofar (show-fahr'; Yiddish: show'-fer): ram's horn instrument used to call the nation together since earliest times and a main ritual item of Rosh Hashanah

shul (Yiddish: shool): modest place of worship, a small synagogue

siddur (see-duhr'; Yiddish: sid'-der): prayer book; indicating the order (seder) of service, plural: *siddurim*

sidrah (sid'-ruh): portion of Torah read on Sabbath or a festival; plural: sidrot

simkhah (sim-khah'; Yiddish: sim'-khuh): "joy," feeling generated by a holiday; also, a happy occasion, such as a *brit*, bar mitzvah, or wedding

siyyum (see'-yoom): "conclusion;" celebration marking the conclusion of study of a tractate of Talmud, three tractates of mishnayot (sections of Mishnah) with commentary, or a book of *Tanakh* with commentary

streimel (strie'-mul): fur-trimmed hat worn by certain sects of Khassidim for Shabbat, festivals and other joyous occasions

sukkah (soo-kah'; Yiddish: sook'-uh): "booth;" structure in which a Jew lives during the holiday of Sukkot; plural: *sukkot*

ta'anit (tah-ah-neet'): "fast;" as in Fast of Esther or Fast of the Firstborn

tallit (tah-leet'; Yiddish: tahl'-lis): "garment;" prayer shawl with ritual fringes (tzitzit) on each corner as a reminder of the commandments; plural: talleisim; see also Arba Kanfote

Talmud (tahl'-mood): collection of books embodying collected Jewish wisdom: Mishnah, Gemara and Midrash (see all above), developed in two versions, the Babylonian and Jerusalem, by the sages of the academies in each of those places

Tanakh (tah-nahkh'): acronym for the entire Hebrew Bible, made up of the initials of each part, *Torah* (Five Books of Moses), *Neviim* (Prophets) and *Ketuvim* (Writings)

tefillah (teh-fee'-lah): prayer (from the reflexive verb *"l'hitpaleil"* meaning self-examination)

tefillin (teh-fih'-lin): "phylacteries," or prayer accessories, two small leather boxes containing parchments on which the text of Exodus 13:1-10, 11-16, Deuteronomy 6:4-9 and 11:13-21 (*Shema*) has been written, attached with leather strips—one on the left arm and one on the forehead during morning prayer (PER DEUTERONOMY 11:18)

tehillim (teh-hih'-lim): "psalms" (when capitalized, the *Tanakh* Book of Psalms)

teshuvah (t-shoo'-vah): "turn, return;" make repentance by turning away from bad and turning toward good and God's commandments; also indicates one who has come back to a Jewish way of life, *ba'al*, or for a female *ba'alat* (master [of]) teshuvah

tikkun (tee-koon'): "repair or improvement;" the study session on the night of Pesakh, Shavuot or Hoshanah Rabbah or the collection of Scriptural, Talmudic and literary passages used for it

tikkun olam (tee-koon' oh-lahm'): "perfection of the world;" the Jewish mission on earth and basis for social action agendas

Torah (toe-rah'; Yiddish: toe'-ruh): "teaching," the Five Books of Moses; also referred to as *Torah Sheh Bikhtav* (Written Torah) and by non-Jews as Old Testament; any insight or instruction derived from the study of classic Jewish text; the scroll containing the Hebrew text of the five books, also referred to as *Sefer Torah*

Torah Sheh B'al Peh (toe-rah' sheh b'ahl peh'): Oral Law or Oral Tradition, the body of explanations believed by Orthodox Jews to have been given at Mount Sinai along with the written law that allowed for understanding of Torah's intent, and for interpretation in accordance with changing conditions in the world

Twelve Tribes: The descendants of the sons of Jacob who became the Jewish people: Reuben, Simeon, Levi, Judah, Issachar, Zevulun, Dan, Gad, Naftali, Asher, Joseph (represented by his sons, Ephraim and Menassah) and Benjamin

tzaddik (tzah-deek'; Yiddish: tzah'-dik): "a righteous person;" plural: *tzaddikim*

tzedakah (tzeh-dah'-kah; Yiddish: tzu-duh'-kuh): "justice;" from the same root as *tzaddik*, just or virtuous; contribution to help those less fortunate (commonly called charity), and in that way create a just balance in the world

yahrtzeit (yahr'-tzite; Yiddish: yor'-tzite): memorial; anniversary of death; describes the memorial candles burned on occasions when the deceased are recalled

Yamim Nora'im: (yah-meem' noh-rah'-yim): "Days of Awe": Rosh Hashanah, Yom Kippur and the days in between

yeshivah (yeh-shee-vah'; Yiddish: yeh-shee'-vuh): academy devoted mainly to the study of Talmud and rabbinic commentary; plural: yeshivot

yetzer harah (yay'-tzir hah-rah'): "evil inclination" in human nature

yetzer hatov (yay'-tzir hah-tove'): "good inclination" in human nature

Yetziat Mitzrayim (yeh-tzi'-yaht mitz-rah'-yim): "departure from Egypt;" the Exodus

yishuv (yee-shoov'): "settlement;" the Jewish colony in pre-State Palestine

yizkor (yiz-kohr'; Yiddish: yis'-kir): "May [God] remember;" memorial service held on the last day of pilgrimage festivals and Yom Kippur

Yom Tov (yome' tove; Yiddish: yum' tof and often mispronounced as yun'-tif): "good day;" holiday

yovel (yoe'-vell): jubilee; the fiftieth year, when all land is returned to its original owners; a precept of the social justice system ordained by Judaism

zeman (z-mahn'): "time or season;" used for pilgrimage festivals as *Zeman Kheruteinu* (Season of Our Freedom, Pesakh), *Zeman Matan Torateinu* (Season of Giving of Our Torah, Shavuot) and *Zeman Simkhateinu* (Season of Our Rejoicing, Sukkot)

Zohar (zoe'-hahr): "brilliant, splendid light;" the central work of kabbalah

INDEX

HOLIDAY DEVELOPMENT TIMELINE

HISTORY	DATE	HOLIDAY
Exodus from Egypt	Nissan 15, 1300* BCE	**Pesakh**
Revelation at Mount Sinai	Sivan 6, 1300* BCE	**Shavuot;** establishment of **Rosh Hashanah** *(Yom Zikhron Teruah)* **Yom Kippur** **Sukkot**
Beginning of conquest of Canaan	Nissan, 1260* BCE	
David's conquest of Jerusalem	1096 BCE	
Dedication of Solomon's (the First) Temple	Tishrei 8-22, 955 BCE	
Split of Eretz Yisrael into rival Kingdom of Israel and Kingdom of Judah	932 BCE	
Assyrian conquest of Israel, loss of Ten Tribes	722 BCE	
Babylonia Conquest, Destruction of First Temple	Av 7-10, 586 BCE	**Tisha B'Av** **Fasts of** **Tevet 10** **Tammuz 9** **Gedalia**
Return of Babylonian captives, rebuilding of Temple	518 BCE	possible suspension of Tisha B'Av and Fasts
Planned annihilation of Jews of Persian empire	Adar 13, 450* BCE	**Purim,** **Shushan Purim**
Syrian-Greek domination of Holy Land	from 300 BCE	

---

*Approximately